The
Theatre
Guide

there was bitterness and regret at the contrast between 'what life could be and what life was'.

Anouilh's early plays, however, show the bitterness leavened by laughter and strongly influenced by the form and gloss of ★MARIVAUX (for example, the Pirandellian play-within-a-play *The Rehearsal*, where behind brilliant comic dialogue you can detect a typical confrontation between purity and the artifice of the aristocratic world). In *Ring Round the Moon* the crippled old lady exploiting her power by rearranging the lives of those around her is another veneer for the playing out of a deeper battle between power and money on the one hand, and poverty and purity on the other.

Anouilh's heroines or heroes frequently sacrifice themselves for a nobler cause. Becket and Joan in *The Lark* are both martyrs to their faith and purity, a theme re-enacted in *Antigone* and by Orpheus and Eurydice, Romeo and Jeanette, and even Medea. *Poor Bitos*, about the humiliation of a smug communist deputy at a party where the guests are dressed in Revolutionary costume, is also seen by some as Anouilh's self-portrait etched in self-disgust. Currently Anouilh appears to be making something of a minor come-back in the growing re-evaluation of works of the 1950s, but he has not had a recent major revival with one of the national companies or in the West End.

Antigone

Antigone was written against a background of the German occupation: some saw it as an apologia for the Nazis, others as a statement against them. The play follows ★SOPHOCLES but is typical Anouilh in its heroine's option for the purity of death rather than the muckiness and compromise of life. Sophocles' version dices with the conflict between secular and divine law (another, more modern and interesting reading could see it as a reassertion of the female and instinctual over man-made law), but Anouilh's Antigone is not so much the victim of an unjust law as a martyr to purity. Creon argues with her and, unlike Sophocles' Creon who is thoroughly guilt-stricken for the trail of tragedies his decisions have provoked, Anouilh's Creon is a thoroughly modern pragmatist who puts duty – upholding the security of the state – above personal emotion. To what extent Anouilh sympathises with Creon's response remains a question for conjecture.

TRY THESE:

★PIRANDELLO; ★SARTRE's *Les Mouches* for another wartime play subversively attacking the Vichy regime; ★SHAW for another treatment of St Joan; ★RATTIGAN for other personal pains treated with similar skill.

ARBUZOV, Aleksei Nicolaevich   [1908 – 86]

Russian dramatist, actor and director

PLAYS INCLUDE:

Tanya (1939), *It Happened in Irkutsk* (1959), *The Promise* (1965, also known as *My Poor Marat*), *Tales of Old Arbat* (1970), *An Old Fashioned Comedy* (1978, also known as *Do You Turn Somersaults?*)

A prolific dramatist who ranges from 'Brechtian' techniques to the sentimental, melodramatic and near vaudeville, Arbuzov's first big success was *Tanya*. His most popular play in the USSR was probably *It Happened in Irkutsk*, a personal drama set against the construction of a power station in Siberia, using a Brechtian chorus, but in the West he is best known for *The Promise*, which was last revived in London in 2002. Like many of his plays it spans a long period, presenting the interaction of a woman and two men – would-be doctor, poet and bridge-builder – in Leningrad in 1942, at the time of post-war reconstruction (1946) and post-Stalin (1959) in the same Leningrad flat. Though the development of their romantic relationships is somewhat predictable, it is the most tightly written of his plays.

TRY THESE:

★WHITEMORE's *The Best of Friends* for an affectionate look at English friendships over a long time span; ★ROBERT HOLMAN's *Today* for contrasting views of English idealism pre- and post-war; ★COLLINS' *The Strongest Man in the World* for a personal drama set ostensibly in the Soviet community; Peter Arnott's *White Rose*, an elegant, somewhat Brechtian play about a female Russian fighter pilot; ★BRECHT and ★CHEKHOV for contrast.

ARDEN, John   [1930–   ]
English dramatist and collaborator with
Margaretta D'Arcy

PLAYS INCLUDE:
All Fall Down (1955), *The Waters of Babylon*
(1957), *Live Like Pigs* (1958), *Serjeant
Musgrave's Dance* (1959), *The Happy Haven*
(1960, with D'Arcy), *The Business of Good
Government* (1960), *Ironhand* (1963), *The
Workhouse Donkey* (1964), *Armstrong's Last
Goodnight* (1964), *Ars Longa, Vita Brevis*
(1965, with D'Arcy), *Left Handed Liberty*
(1965), *The Royal Pardon* or, *The Soldier Who
Became an Actor* (1966, with D'Arcy), *The
True History of Squire Jonathan and His
Unfortunate Treasure* (1968), *The Hero Rises
Up* (1968, with D'Arcy), *Harold Muggins is a
Martyr* (1968, with D'Arcy), *200 Years of
Labour History* (1971, with D'Arcy) *The
Ballygombeen Bequest* (1972, with D'Arcy),
The Island of the Mighty (1972, with D'Arcy),
The Non-Stop Connolly Show (1975, with
D'Arcy), *The Little Gray Home in the West*
(1978, with D'Arcy), *Vandaleur's Folly* (1978,
with D'Arcy)

Barnsley born, a student of architecture and, in
his own words, 'a product of English public
schools and three years as a conscript in
Scotland', Arden began writing plays at university Considered one of the most influential
political dramatists of his generation, Arden's
output has been indelibly influenced by his
meeting with Margaretta D'Arcy in 1955.
D'Arcy started her career in Dublin in small
experimental theatres, after which. she went to
London where she acted in club theatres and at
the Hornchurch Rep, one of the first regional
companies to be local-authority funded. Her
involvement with community theatre stems
from these early experiences, and much of her
writing has been community-orientated.

Most of Arden's major stage plays
appeared in a ten-year period from the late
1950s to the late 1960s, ceasing abruptly after
a famous if painful controversy over the RSC's
handling of *The Island of the Mighty*. Arden
and D'Arcy's work was developing an increasingly anti-English, pro-Irish and community
stance: *The Hero Rises Up* is an anti-heroic
view of Nelson; *The Ballygombeen Bequest* is
an attack on absentee landlordism in Ireland;

The Non-Stop Connolly Show is a pro-Irish
Republican epic which, according to Arden's
biographer, Albert Hunt, should be regarded
as a masterpiece. Unsurprisingly this political
emphasis led to legal difficulties, accusations
of censorship and their effective withdrawal
from the British theatre. Instead Arden's and,
to some extent, D'Arcy's recent work has been
in the novel and radio, culminating in *Whose
is the Kingdom?*, a 1988 nine-part BBC radio
series on early Christianity, a theme which has
run through several of Arden's plays.

Always a moralist, Arden's dissenting voice
has increasingly swung away from the earlier
anarchic detachment where there are no heroes
(even the so-called pacifism of *Serjeant
Musgrave's Dance* is hotly disputed by some
commentators, who feel it is difficult to decide
which side Arden's sympathies are on), through
political activism to revolutionary socialism by
the late 1970s. Others, however, argue that the
seeds of Arden the revolutionary were implicit
from the beginning, particularly in the fact that
the plays were usually sparked off by historical
and contemporary political events. *Armstrong's
Last Goodnight*, for example, though set in
sixteenth-century Scotland, was inspired by the
Congo War and intended as an analogous,
moral parable on the subject of violence.
Written in Lowland verse, it emerged as a
rumbustious, sardonic study in realpolitik,
opposing the urbane politician (Lindsay) with
the highland rebel, Johnny Armstrong.

Arden, from the beginning, rejected
naturalism and though his plays were about
social, political and economic issues – small-
town corruption (*The Workhouse Donkey*),
the welfare state (*Live Like Pigs*), violence and
militarism (*Serjeant Musgrave's Dance*) – his
use of bold, imagistic techniques – epics,
parables, sometimes grotesque comedy – and
the fact that they have an obvious polemical
intent, inevitably led to Arden being
compared with ★BRECHT, an influence he has
always denied. Yet other observers, playing the
influence game, detect a kinship with ★BEN
JONSON and ★ARISTOPHANES in such plays as
The Workhouse Donkey.

Serjeant Musgrave's Dance
A small group of soldiers invade a bleak
mining town in northern England in the

1880s, ostensibly on a recruiting drive. But the men are deserters, and their leader, Serjeant Musgrave, who has become fanatically anti-war, is as terrifying in his religious zeal as the evil against which he inveighs: he demands the death of twenty-five townspeople to match the death of a local boy who died in a colonial war and who was the trigger, in reprisal, for the death of five men. A male-oriented play, where women are seen either as whores (sexual and dangerous) or mothers (asexual and comforting), it seems hard in retrospect to see it as anything other than a passionately pacifist, anti-imperialist play.

TRY THESE:
★ BARNES for similar epic treatments of historical subjects; ★ OSBORNE's *A Patriot for Me* for another army play with echoes of male sexual fear of women (also *Look Back in Anger*); for contrasting treatment of Nelson to *The Hero Rises Up*, ★ RATTIGAN's *Bequest to the Nation*; for scrutiny of American national figures, ★ KOPIT's *Indians*; for small-town corruption, ★ AYCKBOURN, ★ BRENTON and ★ HARE's *Brassneck*, ★ FLANNERY's *Our Friends in the North*, ★ GOGOL's *The Government Inspector*; ★ JOHN MCGRATH adapted *Serjeant Musgrave's Dance*.

ARDREY, Robert   [1908 – 80]
American scientist and dramatist

PLAYS INCLUDE:
Thunder Rock (1939), *Jeb* (1946), *Shadow of Heroes* (1958)

Probably best known today for his scientific theory of 'the territorial imperative', Ardrey worked for most of his career as a dramatist and screenwriter. *Thunder Rock*, first staged at the beginning of World War II, receives very occasional starry revivals. It is an atmospheric allegorical piece in which a lighthouse keeper's encounters with the spirits of ship-wrecked travellers rekindle his fighting spirit. *Jeb*, an investigation of racism in the American South, was uncomfortably enough in advance of its time to be commercially unsuccessful.

TRY THESE:
★ PIRANDELLO's *Six Characters in Search of an Author* for its use of 'unfinished' characters; ★ EDGAR's *Maydays* deals with the Hungarian uprising which is the subject of *Shadow of Heroes*; ★ BARRIE's *Mary Rose* for ghosts; ★ BARAKA, ★ BULLINS, ★ HANSBERRY's *A Raisin in the Sun*, ★ AUGUST WILSON for racism.

ARISTOPHANES   [c. 450 – 385 BC]
Greek comic dramatist

SURVIVING PLAYS:
The Acharnians (425 BC), *The Knights* (424 BC), *The Clouds* (423 BC), *The Wasps* (422 BC), *Peace* (421 BC), *The Birds* (414 BC), *Lysistrata* (411 BC), *The Thesmophoriazousae* (410 BC, sometimes called *Women at the Festival* or *The Poet and the Women* or *Women at the Thesmophoria*), *The Frogs* (405 BC), *Ecclesiazousae* (392 BC, sometimes called *Women in Parliament*), *Wealth* (388 BC, sometimes called *Plutus*)

Aristophanes' plays, the only surviving representatives of Greek Old Comedy, used to be infrequently performed in the contemporary professional theatre. Although it is far from a feminist play, *Lysistrata* has continued to be staged fairly regularly both because of its concentration on sexual politics and because of its anti-war message. However, the growing willingness to stage adaptations and translations and the increasing emphasis on physical theatre in Britain has begun to re-establish Aristophanes' work in the current repertory, with recent productions of *The Frogs* and, less successfully, *The Birds* (National Theatre, 2002). In Stephen Sondheim and Burt Shevelove's 1974 musical version of *The Frogs*, staged originally in a swimming pool at Yale University with a cast including ★ CHRISTOPHER DURANG, Meryl Streep and Sigourney Weaver, ★ SHAW and ★ SHAKESPEARE replace ★ AESCHYLUS and ★ EURIPIDES as the dramatists who might be restored to life.

TRY THESE:
★ AESCHYLUS, ★ EURIPIDES, ★ SOPHOCLES for Greek tragic drama; Menander for later Greek comedy; Plautus and Terence for Roman comedy; ★ LITTLEWOOD and THEATRE WORKSHOP's *Oh What a Lovely War* for blending popular forms.

The Birds by Aristophanes in a version by Sean O'Brien directed by Kathryn Hunter, National Theatre and Mamaloucos Circus, 2002. Franky Mwangi as Sparrow, Josette Bushell-Mingo as Hoopoe. (Stephen Vaughan/ArenaPAL)

ARRABAL, Fernando   [1932 –   ]

Spanish dramatist born in Spanish Morocco, who writes in French

PLAYS INCLUDE:

Les Deux Bourreaux (1958, *The Two Executioners*), *Le Cimetière des Voitures* (1964, *The Vehicle Graveyard*), *Fando et Lis* (1964, *Fando and Lis*), *L'Architecte et l'Empereur d'Assyrie* (1967, *The Architect and the Emperor of Assyria*), *Et ils Passerent des Menottes aux Fleurs* (1969, *And They Put Handcuffs on the Flowers*)

Arrabal's voluminous output of plays reflects his nightmarish childhood, during which his father mysteriously disappeared from prison at the beginning of the Spanish Civil War and his mother tried to behave as though his father had never existed. Unresolved difficulties over this, plus a strict Spanish Catholic upbringing, have led to a number of sado-masochistic plays filled with disturbing images of torture, suffering, blasphemy and eroticism, often involving members of the same family, at which one is horrified to find oneself laughing. In *The Architect and the Emperor of Assyria*, two men stranded on a desert island play a series of games, exchanging roles of master and slave, mother and child, victim and executioner, until finally one eats the other. The play owes something to ★ARTAUD and ★BECKETT, but also to Lewis Carroll, whom Arrabal greatly admires. Arrabal has never been particularly popular in the British professional theatre,

TRY THESE:

★PIRANDELLO for role-swapping; ★GENET for role-playing; ★WALCOTT's *Pantomime* is a variation on the master–slave theme.

ARTAUD, Antonin   [1896 – 1948]

French actor, director, theorist

WORKS INCLUDE:

Jet de Sang (1925, *Jet of Blood*), *La Coquille et le Clergyman* (1927, *The Seashell and Clergyman*, film script), *Les Cenci* (1935, *The Cenci*), *Le Théâtre et son Double* (1938, *The Theatre and its Double*; incorporating his First and Second Manifestos of the Theatre of Cruelty, 1931–5)

It is possible, but misleading, to regard Artaud as the archetypal mad genius. Badly affected by meningitis when young, he spent much of his life struggling against an addiction to drugs, and much of the rest in lunatic asylums. He is also one of the most important and seminal theatrical thinkers of the twentieth century, with a considerable (but disputed) influence on a wide variety of authors and especially directors. His principal theoretical work, *Le Théâtre et son Double*, influenced by his partial understanding of performances of Cambodian and Balinese dance, recommended a 'total theatre' that would use sound, light, gesture and visual image rather than relying on the written or even the spoken word, to disturb fundamentally the imagination and subconscious of audience and actors alike; it has in different ways influenced Barrault, Peter Brook, ★MAROWITZ, Grotowski, ★ADAMOV, ★ARRABAL, ★GENET, Pip Simmons, Julian Beck, and the Open Theatre – partly because it is full of memorable but somewhat gnomic pronouncements which one can interpret to suit one's own inclinations (e.g. 'We are not free, and the sky can still fall on our heads; and the theatre exists to remind us of this fact').

Artaud's life is sometimes treated as myth (as with ★DYLAN THOMAS and Marie Lloyd) and used as matter for plays, such as ★MAROWITZ's *Artaud at Rodez*.

Jet of Blood is less than four pages long, but manages to touch on many obsessions – Artaud's and our own. It would be very un-Artaudian to describe the plot, but the following stage directions give the flavour: 'The Whore bites God's wrist. An immense jet of blood shoots across the stage, and we can see the Priest making the sign of the cross during a flash of lightning that lasts longer than the others.' 'An army of scorpions comes out from under the Nurse's dress and swarms over her sex, which swells up and bursts, becoming glassy and shining like the sun. The Young Man and the Whore flee.' It was included in the Peter Brook, ★CHARLES MAROWITZ Theatre of Cruelty season at LAMDA in 1964, and student groups attempt it from time to time.

TRY THESE:

★WEISS for a dramatist and La Mama for a group influenced by Artaud's ideas; Claudel for impossible stage directions (*The Satin Slipper*, etc.); Expressionism for a non-illusionistic approach to theatre.

AUDEN, W. H.
(Wystan Hugh)   [1907 – 72]
British poet, dramatist and critic

ISHERWOOD, Christopher
(William Bradshaw)   [1904 – 86]
British novelist, dramatist and screenwriter

JOINT PLAYS INCLUDE:
The Dog Beneath the Skin; or, Where is Francis? (1936), *The Ascent of F6* (1937), *On the Frontier* (1938)

Although both produced theatre work independently, their best-known plays are the jointly written verse dramas of the 1930s. *I Am a Camera* and the musical *Cabaret* are based on Isherwood's Berlin stories but are not his dramatisations.

Left-wing intellectuals from elitist Oxbridge backgrounds, Auden and Isherwood were politicised by the Depression, by the Spanish Civil War and by living in Germany. All their joint work, and Auden's *Dance of Death* (1934), set out to attack capitalist power and bourgeois values; *Ascent of F6*, with its protagonist clearly modelled on T. E. Lawrence, added elements of mysticism as well. Their style is not naturalistic and suggests strong Brechtian influence. Despite the evident homosexual content in some of both men's other work, these verse dramas do not explore such themes. *The Dog Beneath the Skin* is a morality play in verse which makes use of a chorus, song and dance, masks, cabaret, and a Master of Ceremonies to present the life of a man-sized dog as it passes from owner to owner through a society peopled with caricatures – a general, financier, churchman, etc. Savagely satirical in its time, it may seem naive when set against contemporary polemics.

TRY THESE:
★BRECHT, who compared these plays with ★ARISTOPHANES; for other modern verse drama, Ronald Duncan, ★ELIOT, ★FRY; for socialist plays in the epic tradition, ★BOND, ★BRENTON,

★CHURCHILL, ★EDGAR, Henry Livings; ★TERRY JOHNSON's underrated *Cries from the Mammal House* for a disenchanted view of the contemporary male using an animal metaphor; ★JARRY for a similarly eclectic dramaturgy.

AYCKBOURN, Alan   [1939 –   ]
British dramatist and director

PLAYS INCLUDE:
Mr Whatnot (1963), *Relatively Speaking* (1967), *How the Other Half Loves* (1969), *Time and Time Again* (1971), *Ernie's Incredible Illucinations* (1971), *Absurd Person Singular* (1972), *The Norman Conquests* (1973, comprising *Table Manners, Round and Round the Garden, Living Together*), *Absent Friends* (1974), *Confusions* (1974), *Jeeves* (1975, adapted from P. G. Wodehouse, with music by Andrew Lloyd Webber; revised as *By Jeeves*, 1996), *Bedroom Farce* (1975), *Just Between Ourselves* (1976), *Ten Times Table* (1977), *Joking Apart* (1978), *Sisterly Feelings* (1979), *Taking Steps* (1979), *Suburban Strains* (1980, with music by Paul Todd), *Season's Greetings* (1980), *Way Upstream* (1981), *It Could Be Any of Us* (1983), *A Chorus of Disapproval* (1984), *Woman in Mind* (1985), *A Small Family Business* (1987), *Henceforward . . .* (1987), *Man of the Moment* (1988), *The Revengers' Comedies* (1989), *Callisto 5* (1990), *Body Language,* (1990), *This is Where We Came In* (1990), *Invisible Friends* (1991), *Wildest Dreams* (1991), *Time of My Life* (1992), *Dreams from a Summer House* (1992, with music by John Pattison), *Mr A's Amazing Maze Plays* (1993), *Communicating Doors* (1994), *Haunting Julia* (1994), *The Champion of Paribanou* (1996), *Things We Do for Love* (1997), *Comic Potential* (1998), *The Boy Who Fell into a Book* (1998), *House and Garden* (1999), *Damsels in Distress* (2001), *Role Play* (2001), *Snake in the Grass* (2002), *The Jollies* (2002)

Ayckbourn is one of Britain's most important and commercially successful dramatists, a staple of the West End and regional repertory, who was critically undervalued for many years because of his predilection for popular forms and theatrical ingenuity. Because his plays have their roots in more traditional theatrical forms, rather than in a self-consciously avant-garde experimental theatre, they were sometimes dismissed as no more than a 'good night out' by critics unable to see beyond the surface to the murky secrets of domestic life beneath.

After starting his theatrical career as an actor and stage manager with Donald Wolfit's company, he moved to Stephen Joseph's Studio Theatre Company in the early 1960s, where he began directing and writing with Joseph's encouragement. Most of his plays begin at Scarborough where, as artistic director of the Stephen Joseph Theatre, he usually writes at least one new play annually for their repertory season. Many of these have transferred to London, but he continues to base his work in Scarborough.

A superb theatrical craftsman, his plays are often constructed around a tour de force of staging. For example, *The Norman Conquests* is a trilogy of plays, each of which stands on its own, and presents the same events from the garden, sitting room and dining room; in *House and Garden* Ayckbourn took this further with two plays involving the same cast playing simultaneously in two theatres; more than one household is on stage simultaneously in *How the Other Half Loves*, *Absurd Person Singular* and *Bedroom Farce* (where the shifts in occupancy of three onstage bedrooms suggest farce, but the absence of the bedroom of the couple whose relationship is on the verge of collapse manifests concretely the bleak absence at the heart of the relationship); in *A Small Family Business* and *Things We Do for Love* (written, unusually for Ayckbourn, for proscenium-arch theatres) we are presented with cross-sections of houses; the riverboat in *Way Upstream* floated on real water (problematically at the National Theatre, but not elsewhere); *Sisterly Feelings* and *Intimate Exchanges* exist in multiple versions determined by chance. Ayckbourn's assault on the traditional boundaries of theatrical space and time is part of a sustained interrogation of the ways that society constructs its realities, and his deconstruction of traditional genres and theatrical conventions matches his analytical deconstruction of the pieties of social organisation.

Increasingly, the comings and goings of married couples are injected with a note of black comedy, and the social groups are fraught with suggestions of the darker arenas of human interchange. The social niceties of the tea party in *Absent Friends* are disrupted by the inability of the participants to cope with the idea of death, and in *Just Between Ourselves* and *Woman in Mind*, what begins as the familiar comic theme of a sterile marriage transforms into tragedy as the wife descends into catatonia and breakdown. Michael Billington hailed Ayckbourn as the best contemporary feminist dramatist for *Woman in Mind*, but while this is clearly arguable Ayckbourn is one of the theatre's sharpest observers of contemporary suburban values. He has blossomed into a major writer of children's plays, experimented with science-fiction theatre, created music theatre with Paul Todd and John Pattison, encouraged new writers and directed award-winning revivals. True, his playing with the conventions of the thriller has been less successful than his reworking of the structures of comedy (perhaps because the thriller itself has become a less familiar theatrical form), but his work constantly challenges audiences to engage critically with the ways in which we structure our lives (and the ways in which our lives are structured for us), while never forgetting the importance of engaging them in the actual event of theatre.

TRY THESE:

★COONEY is the most celebrated contemporary exponent of traditional farce, the conventions of which Ayckbourn liberally exploits; ★FRAYN's *Noises Off* is one of the funniest and cleverest examples of theatrical sleight-of-hand; ★DE FILIPPO, ★FEYDEAU, ★LABICHE and ★SIMON for contrasting approaches to farce and the family; ★STOPPARD as another juggler of theatrical conventions; Ayckbourn has adapted ★OSTROVSKY's *The Forest* and ★SHERIDAN's *A Trip to Scarborough*, itself based on ★VANBRUGH's *The Relapse*; ★TERRY JOHNSON adapted the television version of *Way Upstream*; Simon Burt's *Got to be Happy* for the nuances of non-communication.

BABE, Thomas [1941 – 2000]
American dramatist

PLAYS INCLUDE:
Kid Champion (1974), *Mojo Candy* (1975), *Rebel Women* (1976), *Billy Irish* (1977), *Great Solo Town* (1977), *A Prayer for My Daughter* (1977), *Fathers and Sons* (1978), *Taken in Marriage* (1979), *Salt Lake City Skyline* (1980), *Kathleen* (1980), *Buried Inside Extra* (1983), *Planet Fires* (1984), *Demon Wine* (1987), *A Hero of Our Time* (1988), *Great Day in the Morning* (1993)

Buffalo-born and Harvard-educated, and one of America's toughest, most independent dramatists, Babe has yet to achieve the recognition he deserves. Associated with Joe Papp's off-Broadway Public Theatre, where many of his plays began, he is interested both in revisionist treatments of history (*Fathers and Sons* and *Salt Lake City Skyline* are about Wild Bill Hickok and union organiser Joe Hill, respectively) and in closer-to-home, more domestic themes. In *A Prayer for My Daughter*, arguably his best-known work, a Sergeant Kelly ignores the suicidal telephone calls of his own daughter to concentrate on the young murder suspect, Jimmy, whom he starts treating as a kind of aberrant 'daughter'. *Taken in Marriage*, which brings a quintet of women together in a New Hampshire church hall to attend a marriage rehearsal fraught with domestic volatility, and *Buried Inside Extra*, a play about journalists which inaugurated the Royal Court's exchange with the Public, are best seen as vehicles for actors, who tend to rip into Babe's roles with abandon.

TRY THESE:
★KOPIT's *Indians* and much of ★LINNEY and ★SHEPARD for iconoclastic views both of history and of the American West; ★BRENTON and ★HARE's *Pravda*, ★HECHT and MACARTHUR's *The Front Page*, Stephen Wakelam's *Deadlines* for alternative dramatic treatments of journalism.

BAGNOLD, Enid (Lady Roderick Jones) [1884 – 1981]
British novelist and dramatist

PLAYS INCLUDE:
The Chalk Garden (1955)

Bagnold was the author of *National Velvet* (filmed in 1944 with Elizabeth Taylor) and numerous other successful novels. *The Chalk Garden*, the most successful of her original plays, was described by Kenneth Tynan as probably 'the finest artificial comedy to have flowed from an English (as opposed to an Irish) pen since the death of Congreve'. *The Chalk Garden* is an apparently typical 'Haymarket play' of the 1950s, when the Theatre Royal was the showcase for star-studded (in this case Edith Evans and Peggy Ashcroft) middle-class theatre with its heart in the right place. However, as Lib Taylor has shown, underneath the conventional narrative that reveals Miss Madrigal, the governess who brings life to the household and garden of the eccentric Mrs St Maugham, as a convicted murderer, is a challenge to patriarchal assumptions about the family and the nature of motherhood. It still surfaces from time to time.

TRY THESE:
★HUNTER, ★DODIE SMITH, ★HOME for plays of the period; ★HELLMAN's *The Children's Hour* and ★IBSEN for plays of domestic revelation.

BAINS, Harwant [1963 –]
British dramatist

PLAYS INCLUDE:
The Fighting Kite (1987), *Blood* (1989)

Bains was hailed as a possible successor to ★HANIF KUREISHI, much to his irritation ('just because I've got a brown face and write plays'). Southall-based, and the son of Indian parents, Bains takes up some of the same issues the young Kureishi and, to some extent, ★KARIM ALRAWI explored in the early 1980s: racial violence and cultural identity. Bains' first play, *The Fighting Kite*, a sprawling, episodic account of a racial attack in Southall, had its share of stereotyped cut-outs of National Front skinheads, but handled the emotional response of its young, second-generation British Asians to their sense of alienation (neither 'English' nor accepted back on the Indian subcontinent) with subtlety and sensitivity. His second play, *Blood*, a violent political thriller, received harsh treatment at the hands of some critics who found the language and plot bordering on the crudely sensational. But others applauded the ambitious scope of the play, which tried to chart the legacy of India's bloody Partition of 1947 through the fate of two contrasting young Punjabi Sikh brothers who settle in Britain. His later work for television includes *Two Oranges and a Mango* and the series *Grease Monkeys*, about an Asian family running a garage, based on his radio series of the same name.

TRY THESE:

★EDGAR's *Destiny* for a bold attempt to pinpoint the rise of post World War II British fascism; Farrukh Dhondy's *Vigilantes* explored the problems of cultural identity within the first generation of the British Bangladeshi community; for Afro-Caribbean equivalents, ★PHILLIPS' *Strange Fruit*, ★WHITE's *The Nine Night*; for a female view of being young, black and British, ★RUDET's *Money to Live*; for a view of linkage between violence, history and dehumanisation, ★FLANNERY's Jewish equivalent in *Singer*; ★BEHAN's *The Hostage* and many plays on prison have made similar observations; for a contrasting view, ★SHERMAN's *Bent*.

BALDWIN, James   [1924 – 87]
American dramatist

PLAYS INCLUDE:

Blues for Mr Charlie (1964), *The Amen Corner* (1965), *A Deed from the King of Spain* (1974)

Baldwin's theatrical reputation rests on his two early plays, both of which struck a lasting chord on their New York debuts, and one of which (*The Amen Corner*) made London history in 1987 as the first-ever all-black nonmusical British production to open in the West End (where, sadly, it lost its £150,000 investment). In *Blues for Mr Charlie*, Baldwin told an unforgettable tale of racial poison based on a true story – a white jury's acquittal, in 1955, of two white men who murdered black Chicagoan Emmett Till in Mississippi. In *The Amen Corner*, which was performed briefly at Howard University in 1955, and opened on Broadway in 1965, Baldwin drew on his own background as the son of a Harlem minister to depict the crumbling domestic life and fading religiosity of Sister Margaret Alexander, the censorious pastor of a 'storefront' Harlem church. An avowed homosexual, perhaps best known for his novels, the expatriate Baldwin, who spent much of his later life in France, was a vociferous champion of civil liberties and of both sexual and racial equality. Interestingly, however, in an interview before his death, he played down the importance of race in his plays, saying with customary wryness: '*The Amen Corner* is not about black people or white people. It's about the people in the play.'

TRY THESE:

★BARAKA, ★BULLINS, ★HANSBERRY's *A Raisin in the Sun*, ★AUGUST WILSON for detonating treatments of racism; ★WOLFE's *The Colored Museum* takes satiric aim at Baldwin's dramatic style; ★ABBENSETTS, ★BAINS, ★KUREISHI, ★MATURA for British parallels.

BANCIL, Parv
British dramatist

PLAYS INCLUDE:

Made in England (1998), *Crazy Horse* (1998)

Bancil began writing with the Hounslow Arts Co-op in 1986. He has been particularly concerned with the experience of second-generation British Asians and how they negotiate their identities in the country they were born into or brought up in but which still appears to regard them as 'immigrants'. *Made in England* tackles this theme through an examination of Asian underground music and its relationship to the record companies. *Crazy Horse* examines father–son relationships.

TRY THESE:
★BAINS, ★KUREISHI for earlier takes on British Asian experience; ★EDGAR's *Destiny* for some of the forces that inform that experience historically; ★BUTTERWORTH's *Mojo* for record-company exploitation; ★GUPTA for a contemporary female British Asian voice.

BANDELE, Biyi   [1967 –   ]
Nigerian-born dramatist

PLAYS INCLUDE:
Death Catches the Hunter (1993), *Marching for Fausa* (1993), *Two Horseman* (1994), *Things Fall Apart* (1997, from Chinua Achebe); *Oroonoko* (1999, from ★APHRA BEHN); *Brixton Stories* (2001)

Bandele has what has been described as a 'magic realist' approach to theatre that may owe something to the rich variety of traditions both European and African that he draws on in his writing. *Brixton Stories*, which he has described as 'an instinctive celebration of Brixton', uses only two actors to convey something of the teeming multiculturalism of the area. Bandele based the play on his own novel *The Street*, having already successfully adapted both Achebe for LIFT and *Oroonoko*, ★APHRA BEHN's novel of slavery, for the RSC.

TRY THESE:
★IKOLI for similar portraits of Peckham; ★ABBENSETTS, ★ALRAWI, ★BAINS, ★KUREISHI, ★MATURA for ethnic minority experiences in Britain; ★SOYINKA is the pre-eminent Nigerian dramatist.

BARAKA, Amiri (Leroi Jones) [1934 –   ]
American dramatist

PLAYS INCLUDE:
A Good Girl is Hard to Find (1958), *Dante* (1961), *Dutchman* (1964), *The Baptism* (1964), *The Slave* (1964), *The Toilet* (1964), *J-E-L-L-0* (1965), *Experimental Death Unit No. 1* (1965), *A Black Mass* (1966), *Slave Ship: A Historical Pageant* (1967), *Madheart* (1967), *Arm Yrself or Harm Yrself!* (1967), *Great Goodness of Life (A Coon Show)* (1967), *Home on the Range* (1968), *Resurrection in Life* (1969), *Junkies Are Full of (SHH . . .)* (1970), *Bloodrites* (1970), *A Recent Killing* (1973), *The New Ark's a Moverin'* (1974), *Sidnee Poet Heroical* or *If in Danger of Sun, the Kid Poet Heroical* (1975), *S-I* (1976), *The Motion of History* (1977), *What Was the Relationship of the Lone Ranger to the Means of Production?* (1979), *At the Dim' Cracker Party Convention* (1980), *Boy & Tarzan Meet in a Clearing* (1982), *Money* (1982), *Primitive World* (1984), *The Life and Life of Bumpy Johnson* (book for the musical, 1990), *General Hag's Skeezag* (1991), *The Election Machine Warehouse* (1996), *Skin Trouble* (1999)

Baraka's plays seek to engage the black community by confronting it with an image of its own acquiescence or by elaborating myths of a heroic past or a revolutionary future. In his manifesto, *The Revolutionary Theatre*, Baraka proclaimed that theatre 'should force change; it should be change'. *The Dutchman*, *The Slave* and *The Toilet* (set in a high-school toilet, a tapestry of festering bigotry brought to the boil) mark the beginning of the black revolutionary theatre of the 1960s. *Slave Ship* traces the black experience from Africa to America. Using a series of vignettes, the play shows the murderous conditions of the Middle Passage, the brutalisation of blacks by both blacks and whites, and attempts to organise black revolts. Baraka has since moved away from an exclusively black nationalist position to embrace a form of Marxism and he remains an active campaigner on political, social and cultural issues as well as performing in jazz/poetry events. Appointed as Poet Laureate of New Jersey, his response to the attack on the World Trade Center in September 2001 ignited fierce controversy over freedom of expression.

Dutchman
Dutchman is the best received of Baraka's works. Clay, a well-dressed, black intellectual is accosted on a subway train by Lulu, a white bitch goddess. When her advances are politely rebuffed, she verbally emasculates her victim and ridicules his white middle-class dress and demeanour. Clay articulately counters her racial stereotyping. He describes the music of a Bessie Smith or a Charlie Parker as the expressions of neurotics who suppress their rage 'to keep from being sane'. In a sense Clay

in his three-button suit proclaims his own spiritual death, a fact that does not escape Lulu, who moves rapidly in for the kill with a drawn switchblade. She quickly disposes of Clay's dead body before approaching another young black man boarding the train.

TRY THESE:
★LORCA and ★STRINDBERG (especially *Miss Julie*) for often explosive theatrical rituals; ★PINERO's *Short Eyes* and ★RABE's *Streamers* as 1970s equivalents to *The Toilet*, in which constricted environments heighten racial tension; for chronicles of racism and the black experience, ★BULLINS, ★KENNEDY, ★SHANGE, ★WESLEY, ★SAMM-ART WILLIAMS, ★AUGUST WILSON; ★WOLFE's *The Colored Museum* for the myths and stereotypes of the African-American experience; for British parallels and contrasts, ★MATURA, ★PHILLIPS, ★RECKORD; Gabriel Gbadamosi's *No Blacks, No Irish* shows racism and prejudice in 1950s England.

BARKER, Howard   [1946 –   ]
British dramatist

PLAYS INCLUDE:
Chook (1970), *No One Was Saved* (1970), *Alpha Alpha* (1972), *Claw* (1975), *Stripwell* (1975), *That Good Between Us* (1977), *Fair Slaughter* (1977), *The Hang of the Gaol* (1978), *The Love of a Good Man* (1979), *The Loud Boy's Life* (1980), *No End of Blame* (1981), *The Poor Man's Friend* (1981), *Victory* (1983), *A Passion in Six Days* (1983), *Crimes in Hot Countries* (1983), *The Power of the Dog* (1984), *Scenes from an Execution* (radio, 1984; staged, 1989), *The Castle* (1985), *Downchild* (1985), *Women Beware Women* (1986, reworking of ★MIDDLETON's play), *Pity in History* (1986), *The Possibilities* (1988), *The Last Supper* (1988), *The Bite of the Night* (1988), *Seven Lears* (1988), *Golgo* (1989), *A Hard Heart* (1992), *The Europeans* (1993), *Hated Nightfall* (1994), *Judith* (1995), *(Uncle) Vanya* (1996), *The Gaoler's Ache for the Nearly Dead* (1996), *Wounds to the Face* (1997), *Ursula* (1998), *A House Of Correction* (1998), *He Stumbled* (2000)

One of a generation of British dramatists deeply concerned with political and social issues, Barker has never received the degree of critical acclaim given to some of his contemporaries, probably because his interest in the psychopathology of capitalism and patriarchy leads him to deal in much of his work with the grotesque and the distorted, often in highly scatological language. At his best Barker is a brilliant and provocative writer; at his worst he can be numbingly verbose. Some of his earlier work, such *The Loud Boy's Life*, *Downchild* and *A Passion in Six Days* (a dramatic cantata about a Labour Party conference), was concerned with specifically Labour party themes.

His plays firmly eschew naturalism in favour of an incisive and theatrically inventive cartoon-like style that juxtaposes private desires with public postures and aims for psychological and socio-political truth rather than the texture of everyday life. He shares with ★GAY and ★BRECHT a crucial perception of the apparent identity of interest between criminal and politician and the inherent corruptions of capitalism. The 'criminal' strand in his work is well represented by, for example, *Alpha Alpha* (a study of two brothers patterned on the Kray twins), *Claw* (in which the hero acts as procurer for the Home Secretary) and *Stripwell*, where a judge is faced with both the criminal activities of his son and a man he sentenced returning for revenge.

Barker is a history graduate and many of his plays also pursue an interest in historical moments and their lessons for the present. *Victory*, subtitled punningly 'Choices in Reaction', a fine example of this second strand, deals with the aftermath of the Restoration of Charles II, mixing historical and stereotypical characters in an extraordinary evocation of the collapse of the ideals of the Commonwealth. The play is notable for a brilliant explanation of the nature and contradictions of capitalism involving Charles himself, a banker called Hambro, Nell Gwyn, the skull of the parliamentarian Bradshaw, and a large store of gold.

The Castle
The Castle is an extraordinary meditation on issues of gender, power, rational and emotional knowledge, war and peace, in which a returning Crusader confronts the peaceful female community established by his wife in his absence. The battle lines, both medieval and

contemporary, are drawn between creativity and destruction in confrontations and dialogue that are brilliantly imagined and draw to the full on Barker's ability to write with a poetic density of language, comic as well as tragic, which uses everyday idiom as much as architectural imagery to create an extraordinarily flexible language. In Nick Hamm's original RSC production there were superb performances from Penny Downie as the fecund matriarch, Harriet Walter as her lesbian lover, Ian McDiarmid as the returning Crusader and Paul Freeman as his castle-building architect.

TRY THESE:

★ BRENTON shares many of Barker's preoccupations and much of his approach to writing for the theatre; ★ EDGAR has also tackled similar issues, particularly in *Destiny* (fascism and Labour reactions to it) and *Maydays* (opposition to totalitarian impulses); ★ FLANNERY looked at corruption and the Labour party in *Our Friends in the North*; ★ IBSEN's *The Master Builder* also uses architecture metaphorically; ★ BARNES uses an inventive rhetorical style reminiscent of Barker, particularly in *Leonardo's Last Supper*; ★ WERTENBAKER's *The Grace of Mary Traverse* explores capitalism and the present through the past; ★ BEHN, ★ CHURCHILL, ★ GEMS and ★ LEVY have all explored the relationships of gender and power to capitalism; ★ DE ANGELIS's *Playhouse Creatures* for Restoration actresses.

BARNES, Peter   [1931 –   ]
British dramatist

PLAYS INCLUDE:

Time of the Barracudas (1963), *Sclerosis* (1965), *The Ruling Class* (1968), *Leonardo's Last Supper* (1969), *Noonday Demons* (1969), *Lulu* (1970, from ★ WEDEKIND), *The Bewitched* (1974), *Frontiers of Farce* (1976, adapted from ★ FEYDEAU and ★ WEDEKIND), *Laughter* (1978, from ★ FEYDEAU), *Red Noses* (1985), *Scenes from a Marriage* (1986, from ★ FEYDEAU), *Sunsets and Glories* (1990), *Corpsing* (1996), *Dreaming* (1999)

Much of Barnes' theatre work achieves the aim he stated in a published text of *The Ruling Class*, 'to create by means of soliloquy, rhetoric, formalised ritual, slapstick, song and dances, a comic theatre of contrasting moods and opposites, where everything is simultaneously tragic and ridiculous'. Barnes generally confronts wider political issues, emulating the broad scale, richness of character and theatricality of ★ BEN JONSON, though eschewing his values. He has also 'adapted' a number of Jacobean plays, including Jonson's *The Alchemist*, *The Silent Woman*, *Bartholomew Fair*, *Eastward Ho* and *The Devil is an Ass* (in which nearly half of the material is new) and ★ MARSTON's *Antonio* plays. Other adaptations include ★ FEYDEAU farces. *Laughter* opens with a custard pie slammed in the face of an author, and the vitality of music-hall humour jostles, sometimes uncomfortably, with the harsh cruelties which Barnes uses to make emotive attacks on the use of power by the State, the Church and big business. For example, *Leonardo's Last Supper* is an imaginative debate about the value of art, set in a charnel house where da Vinci's corpse revives. A passionate attack on Toryism, class and privilege, *The Ruling Class* presents a rampaging madman who inherits an earldom and believes he is God. It shows his return to 'sanity', confirmed when he makes a pro-hanging and pro-flogging speech to his cobwebbed fellow peers in the House of Lords. On its first production Ronald Bryden hailed *The Ruling Class* as 'a pivotal play', and Harold Hobson placed it on a level with *Waiting for Godot*, *Look Back in Anger* and *The Birthday Party*, but Barnes' later work has been less rapturously received. His characteristic mixture of ironic juxtaposition, metatheatrical comment, popular forms and political themes, death and humour has always required a management prepared to take a risk, and the RSC's seven-year delay in producing *Red Noses* is evidence of how uncomfortable some can feel about his work. *Red Noses* was his first play in London for seventeen years. Set in France at the time of the Black Death, it is populated by roaming bands of guilt-ridden flagellants, red-nosed comics who confront disease with laughter and are tolerated by the Church because they keep the people cheerful. When the plague abates and their performances begin to become subversive they are ruthlessly squashed. Barnes is not a polemicist and, though the bold and epic scale of the play gives marvellous opportunities to performers, its characters' hope that 'every jest should be a small revolution' is not answered.

Most of Barnes' recent work has been for radio and television and it took a further fourteen years before he had another London production. Critics liked the Manchester production of *Dreaming* (1999), another historical play that demonstrated that Barnes still had the same capacity for effectively ironic juxtaposition that characterised his earlier successes, but it fared less well in London.

TRY THESE:
★ BOND (especially *We Come to the River*);
★ BERKOFF for outrage; ★ BENNETT for satire;
★ BRENTON and ★ HARE's *Pravda*, ★ NICHOLS' *The National Health*, and *Privates on Parade* for contemporary satires on an epic scale; ★ DEAR,
★ KOPIT, ★ WOLFE for historical debunking;
★ BOLT's *A Man for All Seasons* and ★ WHITING's *The Devils* for more straightforward treatments of history.

BARRIE, (Sir) James Matthew   [1860 – 1937]
British dramatist and novelist

PLAYS INCLUDE:
Ibsen's Ghost (1891), *Walker, London* (1892), *The Professor's Love Story* (1894), *The Little Minister* (1897), *Quality Street* (1902), *The Admirable Crichton* (1902), *Peter Pan* (1904), *What Every Woman Knows* (1908), *The Twelve Pound Look* (1910), *Dear Brutus* (1917), *The Truth About the Russian Dancers* (1920), *Mary Rose* (1920), *Shall We Join the Ladies?* (1922), *The Boy David* (1936)

Barrie, born of a poor Scottish family, went South after leaving Edinburgh University. He started his career as a journalist, then struck gold with the novel of *The Little Minister* in 1891 and wrote prolifically and very successfully through the Edwardian era and beyond. Although *What Every Woman Knows*, *Mary Rose*, with its odd mixture of innocence, fantasy and slightly sinister unquiet spirit, and the equally whimsical toing and froing of the classes in *The Admirable Crichton* surface from time to time, in recent years *Peter Pan*

has been the only one of Barrie's many plays to be revived regularly. His one act plays, such as *Ibsen's Ghost*, *The Twelve Pound Look*, and the tantalising first act of the thriller *Shall We Join the Ladies?*, are often more effective than the full-length ones and well worth reviving.

Peter Pan
The plot centres on Peter Pan (the Boy Who Never Grew Up), who flies off to the Never Never Land with the Darling children (Wendy, John and Michael), leaving their father to take refuge in the dog kennel. After defeating the Pirates, they return to Bloomsbury with the Lost Boys, leaving Peter to forget all that has happened and wait for the next generation of Darlings. Usually revived as a Christmas entertainment, the play is a Freudian's delight and must have bewildered a great many children over the years. Captain Hook, however, remains one of the great bravura parts.

TRY THESE:
⋆ SHAW for class issues in *The Admirable Crichton*;
★ CORRIE offers a rather different Scottish sensibility; the use of a ghostly spirit in *Mary Rose* has parallels, from ★ ELIOT in *The Family Reunion* to
★ PAGE's *Salonika*, though none treat it with the almost touching feyness of Barrie.

BARRY, Philip   [1896 – 1949]
American dramatist

PLAYS INCLUDE:
A Punch for Judy (1921), *You and I* (1923), *The Youngest* (1924), *In a Garden* (1925), *White Wings* (1925), *John* (1927), *Paris Bound* (1927), *Cock Robin* (1928, with ★ ELMER RICE), *Holiday* (1928), *Hotel Universe* (1930), *Tomorrow and Tomorrow* (1931), *The Animal Kingdom* (1932), *The Joyous Season* (1934), *Bright Star* (1935), *Spring Dance* (1936), *Here Come the Clowns* (1938), *The Philadelphia Story* (1939), *Liberty Jones* (1941), *Without Love* (1942), *Foolish Notion* (1945), *My Name is Aquilon* (1949), *Second Threshold* (completed posthumously by Robert Sherwood, 1951)

Educated at Yale and Harvard, Barry wrote American comedy of manners about the sophisticated set of which he was a part, but not without healthy criticism of upper-class complacency and snobbery. His two best-known plays make his bemused contempt clear, even as they introduce the so-called 'Barry girl', a clear-headed, no-nonsense rich kid who is more on the ball than her posh surroundings might suggest. In *Holiday*, the self-made Johnny Case becomes engaged to the heiress Julia Seton only to find he has more in common with her younger sister Linda, who shares his desire for a 'holiday' from rampant materialistic pursuits. In *The Philadelphia Story*, later made into the stage and screen musical *High Society*, the moneyed divorcée Tracy Lord forsakes the dour stiff she's supposed to marry for a man defined more by his personality than his social position. Not all Barry's plays treat the mores of the well-heeled: *John* is a Biblical tragedy, *Cock Robin*, written with ★ELMER RICE, a comic mystery; and *Liberty Jones*, an allegory. But he remains best known for his social satire on the swells among whom he moved so easily.

TRY THESE:
★AYCKBOURN and ★COWARD for British equivalents to Barry's deceptive dark domestic frivolity, specifically *Private Lives*, a play about divorcés getting back together; ★KAUFMAN for comparable sophistication; ★GURNEY, ★HOWE, ★DENNIS MCINTYRE, ★GREENBERG, ★SIMON for modern chroniclers of American class.

BARRY, Sebastian   [1955 –   ]
Irish novelist, poet and dramatist

PLAYS INCLUDE:
The Pentagonal Dreamer (1986), *Boss Grady's Boys* (1988), *Prayers of Sherkin* (1990), *White Woman Street* (1992), *The Only True History of Lizzie Finn* (1995), *The Steward of Christendom* (1995), *Our Lady of Sligo* (1998), *Hinterland* (2002)

The vast majority of Barry's plays draw on aspects of his family history to create compelling narratives of the intersections between the personal and the political. Traditional Irish themes such as emigration fuel *Boss Grady's Boys* and *White Woman Street*; threats to communities, economic troubles and the

failure of aspiration underpin *Prayers of Sherkin* and *The Only True History of Lizzie Finn*, which is based on the life of Barry's grandmother. In *Our Lady of Sligo* a woman in hospital relives her painful family relationships and her dashed hopes. The intersection between family and history emerges most clearly in *The Steward of Christendom*, where Barry explores the ramifications of the career of his great-grandfather, Thomas Dunne, who served in the Dublin police and handed over Dublin Castle to Michael Collins when home rule was achieved. As a catholic policeman he occupied an ambiguous position in the complex interplay of forces in the struggle for independence. Like much of Barry's work the play explores events from the perspective of a more recent time. The play is set in the 1930s when Dunne, who is in his seventies and is mad, looks back both on the struggles of his career and the difficulties of bringing up his daughters alone in Dublin. The contrasts between his private and official selves are reinforced by the sense of the differences between rural and urban Ireland, and another level of complexity is added by the fact that we are looking back on the 1930s while the protagonist looks back to the early 1900s. The cool reception of *Hinterland* in London ended Barry's run of successes, although the resemblances between its protagonist and the former Taoiseach Charles Haughey had guaranteed it more success in Ireland.

TRY THESE:
★O'CASEY for the struggle for Irish independence; ★SYNGE for communities under threat and Irish rural life; ★BOLGER, ★FRIEL, ★MURPHY for similar issues; ★HUTCHINSON for contemporary Irish police issues; ★DECLAN HUGHES for contemporary Irish themes; ★GARY MITCHELL for Ulster.

BARTLETT, Neil   [1959 –   ]
British performer, director and dramatist

PLAYS INCLUDE:
Antibody (1983), *Dressing Up* (1983), *Pornography* (1985), *A Vision of Love Revealed in Sleep* (1986), *Sarrasine* (1990), *Night After Night* (1994, with Nicholas Bloomfield), *The Seven Sacraments of Nicolas Poussin* (1997)

A determinedly anti-establishment figure, despite his first in English from Magdalen College, Oxford, and a director's traineeship at the Bristol Old Vic, Bartlett set up his own company, Gloria, in 1987. *Antibody* was one of the first plays to deal with AIDS in Britain, but *Dressing Up* began his highly flamboyant explorations into drag, followed, by *A Vision of Love Revealed in Sleep* and *Sarrasine* – two of the most extraordinary theatrical spectacles to have burst on the British public since Lindsay Kemp first came to prominence. As Carl Miller has written: 'Bartlett drags high and low culture into creative collusion', an entirely suitable pun on a process that has relocated drag from the small gay cognoscenti fraternity into a broader dramatic arena. Both spectacles featured performer Bette Bourne in ways which fused high art with low camp, and made points about the importance of the living presence of the performer, the nature of artifice and reality and the politics of gay persecution.

Jim Hiley described Bartlett as 'the most tumultuous, the least categorisable talent to emerge in the 80s'. His multiple careers as director, translator, adapter, dramatist and novelist are ample testimony to the accuracy of that judgement. He became artistic director of the Lyric, Hammersmith, in 1994, where he has pursued an innovative policy with a strong European element. As a director, he was responsible for Complicité's *More Bigger Snacks Now*, and Annie Griffin's equally mould-breaking solo shows *Blackbeard the Pirate* and *Almost Persuaded*, her country-and-western music satire. He adapted ★WILDE's *The Portrait of Dorian Gray* (1994) and has translated ★GENET (*Splendids*), ★KLEIST (*The Prince of Homburg*, 2002) ★LABICHE (*The Threesome*, 2000), ★MARIVAUX (*The Dispute*, *The Island of Slaves* and *The Game of Love and Chance*), ★MOLIÈRE (*The Misanthrope* and *School for Wives*), and ★RACINE (*Bérénice*),

Bartlett's visual theatre uses text, image and music in contrapuntal abundance – satirising itself even at its most outrageous, and delighting in the contradiction. He is, nonetheless, equally at home in the quieter waters (structurally speaking) of the novel; his homage to Oscar Wilde, *Who Was That Man?*, and his contemporary account of gay life, *Ready to Catch Him Should He Fall*, have both been warmly received.

A Vision of Love Revealed in Sleep

Sleep was originally performed by Bartlett, onstage throughout and naked, as a solo show in a disused warehouse. This studied and luxurious tribute to an all but forgotten Jewish Victorian painter and poet, Simeon Solomon, a friend of Rossetti, Swinburne and Pater, who was disgraced and reduced to poverty after being caught in a public toilet with a labourer, was actually taken from Solomon's own erotic prose poem. Reflecting the imagery of the poem through Bartlett's own nakedness, and merging his own circumstances with those of Solomon, it became a witty and moving 'hymn' to art, homosexual love and defiance. Solomon's own refusal to apologise was apparently one of the reasons Bartlett was attracted to his subject. In later incarnations Bartlett was joined by three drag queens – heightening the production's wonderful mix of 'high art' with 'low culture'. The sight and sound of Bette Bourne singing Cole Porter's 'In the Still of the Night' remains an indelible memory and comment on the emotional repercussions of AIDS.

TRY THESE:
Lindsay Kemp for theatre of divine outrage, ★GENET, ★TREMBLAY for mixing the sacred and profane; Robert Lepage and Peter Brook for director-auteurs who also favour an ongoing work-in-progress approach; ★NOËL GREIG and ★OSMENT for contrasting gay sensibility.

BEATON, Alistair
British writer

PLAYS INCLUDE:
Feelgood (2001)

Beaton's television credits include contributions to such series as *Spitting Image* and *Not the Nine O'Clock News* so it was no surprise that his play about the trials and tribulations of a prime minister at his party conference was welcomed as the return of theatrical political satire. Updated during its run to maintain its topicality, it seems likely to have been an interesting one-off, and it was noteworthy that its attacks on Tony Blair, while particularly welcomed by right-wing newspapers, appear to have done nothing to dent his General Election majority.

TRY THESE:
★ BRENTON for a long-standing commitment to political satire; ★ GAY for eighteenth-century satire; ★ BARKER, ★ GRANVILLE-BARKER's *Waste* and ★ HARE for party politics; ★ ELDRIDGE's *A Week with Tony* for contemporary Conservative politics; David Lindsay's late medieval *Satire of the Three Estates* for an early Scottish satire; Justin Butcher's *The Madness of George Dubya* for Gulf War II satire.

BEAUMARCHAIS, Pierre Augustin Caron de   [1732 – 99]
French dramatist

PLAYS INCLUDE:
Eugénie (1767), *Les Deux Amis* (1770, *The Two Friends*), *Le Barbier de Séville* (1775, *The Barber of Seville*), *Le Mariage de Figaro* (1784, *The Marriage of Figaro*), *Tarare* (1787), *La Mère Coupable* (1792, *The Guilty Mother*)

As well as being a dramatist, Beaumarchais was a watchmaker, musician, financier, courtier, pamphleteer, gunrunner and secret agent, in all of which he achieved some distinction but no lasting success. He wrote two very good plays (*The Barber of Seville* and its sequel *The Marriage of Figaro*) which might be more often performed in English had they not also been the bases of two superlative operas. The first has a plot that can be described in a few lines – old guardian, young ward, young nobleman in disguise, clever servant to help him; the second would need several pages to describe, and combines non-stop comic invention with sharp social satire. *The Marriage of Figaro* is possibly unique in being a successful sequel. There is a third in the series, *The Guilty Mother*, which has a strange combination of elevated moral tone and prurient plot: the Almavivas have come to live in France because of the Revolution, and like to be known as Citoyen and Citoyenne. The hero finds that he is the illegitimate son of the Countess and Chérubin, the latter having been killed in the wars, and so he can marry the Count's illegitimate daughter

by the gardener's daughter. There was going to be a fourth episode of this increasingly depressing story, but Beaumarchais died first. *The Marriage of Figaro* was revived at the Manchester Royal Exchange in 2002.

TRY THESE:
★ MARIVAUX for eighteenth-century French comedy (though their language and approach are very different, Marivaux being a natural miniaturist and Beaumarchais a poster artist); ★ FEYDEAU for plot complications; ★ HORVÁTH for updating and development in *Figaro Gets a Divorce*.

BEAUMONT, Francis   [1584/5 – 1616]
English Renaissance dramatist, collaborator with ★ JOHN FLETCHER

PLAYS INCLUDE:
The Knight of the Burning Pestle (1607), *Philaster* (pre-1610, with ★ FLETCHER), *The Maid's Tragedy* (pre-1611, with ★ FLETCHER)

Although Beaumont is traditionally associated with Fletcher, his place in the contemporary repertory rests largely on his own *The Knight of the Burning Pestle*. A lively blend of satire at the expense of middlebrow taste, this uses plays within plays, popular songs, apparent interruptions from the audience, romance and melodrama in a heady mixture that has maintained its appeal because the tastes and attitudes it confronts are easily recognisable today. Michael Bogdanov staged the last major British revival, for the RSC in 1981. There was something of a Beaumont and ★ FLETCHER revival at that time with successful productions of *The Maid's Tragedy*, a love, honour and duty tragedy, by both the Glasgow Citizens' and the RSC, but there has been little recent interest in Beaumont.

TRY THESE:
★ DEKKER's *Shoemaker's Holiday*, ★ HEYWOOD's *Fair Maid of the West* and *Four Prentices of London* (the prime object of Beaumont's parody) are more complimentary to citizen taste than ★ MIDDLETON's *A Chaste Maid*, which shares more of Beaumont's standpoint; ★ JONSON's *Bartholomew Fair* and ★ SHAKESPEARE's *The Merry Wives of Windsor* also offer portraits of the middle

classes from this period; there are many plays about theatre companies and interrupted performances, including ★ SHERIDAN's *The Critic*, ★PIRANDELLO's *Six Characters in Search of an Author* and ★ STOPPARD's *The Real Inspector Hound*.

BECKETT, Samuel   [1906 – 89]
Irish/French dramatist and novelist

PLAYS INCLUDE:
En Attendant Godot (1953, as *Waiting for Godot*, 1955), *Endgame* (1957), *All That Fall* (1957), *Act Without Words I* (1957), *Krapp's Last Tape* (1958), *Embers* (1959), *Act Without Words II* (1959), *Happy Days* (1961), *Words and Music* (1962), *Cascando* (1963), *Play* (1963), *Eh Joe* (1966), *Come and Go* (1966), *Breath* (1969), *Not I* (1972), *That Time* (1976), *Footfalls* (1976), *Ghost Trio* (1976), *. . . But the Clouds . . .* (1977), *A Piece of Monologue* (1980), *Rockaby* (1980), *Ohio Impromptu* (1981), *Quad* (1982), *Catastrophe* (1982), *Nacht und Träume* (1983), *What Where* (1983)

Born in Ireland of Anglo-Irish parents, Beckett went to Paris in the late 1920s where he worked for a while with James Joyce and later as a lecturer in English. In 1938 he settled in Paris, where he lived until his death, writing in both French and English and translating his own work into English. He was active in the French Resistance during World War II, and was awarded the Nobel Prize for Literature in 1969.

Beckett began writing as a critic; his first published work was a piece on *Finnegan's Wake*, written at Joyce's request. In 1931 he produced a study of Proust; he then wrote verse, short fiction and novels and turned to drama, he said, for 'relaxation'. *Waiting for Godot* arrived in England at a period in which there was a growing interest and awareness of non-realist forms of drama and of the innovations of European theatre. A play in which two tramp-clown figures wait for Godot, who never arrives, it was greeted with both mystification and acclaim. It is, famously, a play in which nothing happens, twice, and its minimalism encouraged both audiences and other writers to reassess what drama actually needed if it was to entertain and stimulate them.

Martin Esslin claimed Beckett as the figure who brought Absurdism to public attention, but Beckett himself did not accept that characterisation, nor can his considerable output and the range of his experiments in drama be neatly categorised. Beckett himself consistently refused to explain his work, continuing to direct and to produce drama that defies easy definition. Existentialism, Christian allegory and nihilism have all been employed as theoretical accounts of Beckett's work, but he has said only 'I meant what I said'. To reduce the stark and complex imagery and language of Beckett's oeuvre to a single 'meaning' would be to diminish its power.

Beckett's work is full of powerful images which are not referred to or explained, often images of human immobility: in *Play*, the three voices are trapped in jars; Winnie of *Happy Days* is gradually buried up to her neck in sand; in *Endgame*, one of the characters cannot walk, another cannot sit. These images can be seen as metaphors for inescapable traps; in Beckett's plays, as in ★SARTRE's *Huis Clos*, there is literally no way out.

Beckett's plays became increasingly minimalist in their exploration of the limits of the dramatic form. In *Acts Without Words* he produced the works with no verbal language, only sounds, and in a television piece in which actors silently moved around a floor diagram, he raised the question of what a 'play' is; at what point does drama cease to be drama and become dance or mime? He also wrote a number of monologues, most memorably for women: *Not I*, *Rockaby* and *Footfalls*. *Not I* is a stunning visual theatrical effect, performed on a darkened stage on which only a shadowy draped figure and a spotlit mouth are visible. The draped figure moves slightly during the course of the play, while the mouth babbles a fragmented and pain-filled discourse. Billie Whitelaw has described the experience as 'falling backwards into Hell, emitting cries'. When Whitelaw was confronted with the script she told Beckett: 'You've finally done it, you've written the unlearnable and you've written the unplayable'. When she asked Beckett if the character was dead he responded 'Let's just say you're not quite there'.

Waiting for Godot by Samuel Beckett, directed by Peter Hall, Old Vic Theatre, 1997. Ben Kingsley as Estragon, Greg Hicks as Lucky, Alan Howard as Vladimir and Denis Quilley as Pozzo. (Billie Rafaeli/ArenaPAL)

The setting, timing and direction of a Beckett play are as integral as the text; his stage directions are extremely precise. In *Footfalls* the character is described as 'compulsively pacing', but the footfalls are not arbitrary, they are minutely scripted: 'starting with right foot (r) from right (R) to left (L) . . .'. Beckett places enormous demands upon the performer, but Whitelaw says: 'I think if that is what he's written, that is what he wants. And I think it's up to anyone who's actually doing his work to follow that as faithfully as they can'.

Despite the difficulty of much of Beckett's work, he is not as obscure as is often thought; his plays are full of comic invention and punning. He had a fascination with clowning (his one film, *Film*, 1965, was made with Buster Keaton): *Waiting for Godot* employs comic routines that are worthy of Laurel and Hardy.

Endgame

The four characters of *Endgame* exist in a bare set, with only two small windows. Two of them are locked in a symbiotic relationship: Clov cannot sit, Hamm, blind and impotent, cannot stand. They hate, but need, each other, in a pairing that echoes the master – servant relationship of Pozzo and Lucky in *Waiting for Godot*. The senile Nell and Nagg are encased in dustbins, their concerns only the immediately physical. In a bitter image of a marriage, unable to reach one another except to scratch, Nagg wistfully reminisces about the erotic (a theme also explored in *Krapp's Last Tape*). The claustrophobic world of the play is never specified, the world outside the room only available through the telescope through which Clov sees a barren landscape. Written in a period when nuclear war seemed a very real threat, one possibility is that this is a post-holocaust world. The only clue Beckett offered is his reply to an actor that 'the play doesn't happen only in one person's mind'. The play is full of theatrical references: Clov and Hamm evoke Caliban and Prospero in ★SHAKESPEARE's *Tempest*; Hamm (who often sounds Shakespearean) is a reference to 'ham' acting (and to Hamlet?); at one point Clov turns his telescope directly onto the audience and reports: 'I see a multitude in transports of joy.'

TRY THESE:
★IONESCO and ★GENET were seen with Beckett to represent a European 'Theatre of the Absurd'; ★STOPPARD's *Rosencrantz and Guildenstern Are Dead* clearly owes a great deal to *Waiting for Godot*; ★KANE and ★PINTER have obviously been influenced by Beckett; for a contrasting master–servant relationship, see ★WALCOTT's *Pantomime*.

BEHAN, Brendan   [1923 – 64]
Irish dramatist, journalist, house painter and alcoholic

PLAYS INCLUDE:
The Quare Fellow (1954), *An Gaill* (1958, reworked as *The Hostage*), *Richard's Cork Leg* (completed posthumously by Alan Simpson, 1972)

A member of the IRA at fourteen, sent to Borstal for three years, sentenced at nineteen to fourteen years in jail for political offences and attempted murder, Behan drew on his own life for his autobiographical books *Borstal Boy* (1958) and *Confessions of an Irish Rebel* (1965) and early radio plays which Alan Simpson adapted for the Pike Theatre Club, Dublin. His first stage play, *The Quare Fellow*, set in a prison on the eve of an execution, was 'developed' by ★JOAN LITTLEWOOD for a new version presented by Theatre Workshop (1956) and in the West End, and had an important effect on attitudes to imprisonment and capital punishment. *An Gaill*, commissioned by the Irish language society Gael Linn, and reworked by Theatre Workshop as *The Hostage*, presents a picaresque set of characters in a brothel used as an IRA safe house where a British soldier is held prisoner. Much of its success was due to the Workshop's style of songs, repartee and audience confrontation. *Richard's Cork Leg*, a political comedy about fascism, was left unfinished and completed by Alan Simpson in 1972.

Behan's own curtain speeches, colourful behaviour and alcoholic interviews attracted as much media attention as his plays. Although Behan claimed 'I'm not a postman . . . I don't deliver messages', both plays have a great deal to say to their audiences and the Theatre Workshop productions affected attitudes both to the topics discussed and to ways of presenting theatre.

TRY THESE:
For plays on Irish politics, ★FINNEGAN, ★FRIEL, ★MCGUINNESS, ★O'CASEY; ★GENET's *The Balcony* and ★SHAKESPEARE's *Pericles* for rather different uses of brothel settings; for plays on prison brutality, Jack Henry Abbott's *In the Belly of the Beast*, John Herbert's *Fortune and Men's Eyes* and ★PINERO's *Short Eyes*.

BEHN, Aphra   [1640 – 89]
English dramatist and novelist

PLAYS INCLUDE:
The Forced Marriage (1670), *The Rover* (1677), *The Feigned Courtesans; or A Night's Intrigue* (1678), *The Roundheads; or The Good Old Cause* (1681), *The City-Heiress; or Sir Timothy Treat-All* (1682), *The Lucky Chance* (1686), *The Emperor of the Moon* (1687)

The first woman to earn her living by the pen, Behn was renowned both for her wit and for her prolific output. In her lifetime she was one of the most frequently performed dramatists, and actually left behind eighteen plays, as well as novels and poetry. An early champion of a woman's right to free expression – Virginia Woolf suggested that 'all women together ought to let flowers fall upon the tomb of Aphra Behn . . . for it was she who earned them the right to speak their minds' – she was consistently vilified by male critics for daring to write as bawdily as they did. After the opening of *The Lucky Chance* an accusation of indecency brought from her a typically robust plea to be accorded the same freedom to write that men enjoyed. Her plays deal with subjects familiar to Restoration audiences fattened on a diet of elegant debauchery, double standards in high places, sexual intrigue and cuckoldry. She wrote tragicomedies, historical comedies, political lampoons and, with the *commedia dell'arte*-based *The Emperor of the Moon*, is credited with a forerunner to the English pantomime.

After two-and-a-half centuries of neglect, Behn is enjoying a small renaissance: *The Lucky Chance* was revived by the Women's Playhouse Trust (1981) and *The Rover* by the RSC (1986) and the Goodman Theatre in Chicago (1988–9). Modern audiences enjoy her plays particularly for their good humour and energy, whilst recognising her early feminist claims for equality in relationships between the sexes. A night with Behn is still a good night out and her plays have as much to offer as those of her better-known male contemporaries. Her novel *Oronooko* was adapted for the RSC in 1999 by ★BIYI BANDELE, there was a fringe production of *The Feigned Courtesans* (Old Red Lion) in 2002 and the Wales Actors' Company are staging *The Rover* in 2003.

TRY THESE:
Other Restoration dramatists such as ★CONGREVE, ★DRYDEN, ★ETHEREGE, ★FARQUHAR, ★WYCHERLEY, ★VANBURGH; ★BOND's *Restoration* and ★CHURCHILL's *Serious Money* for modern similarities; ★WERTENBAKER's *The Grace of Mary Traverse* for a similar concern for women in their social context, using a historical setting; ★DE ANGELIS for women in Restoration theatre.

BENNETT, Alan   [1934 –   ]
British dramatist and actor

PLAYS INCLUDE:
Forty Years On (1968), *Getting On* (1971), *Habeas Corpus* (1973), *The Old Country* (1977), *Enjoy* (1980), *Kafka's Dick* (1986), *Single Spies* (1988, *An Englishman Abroad*, televised 1983, and *A Question of Attribution*), *The Madness of George III* (1991), *Talking Heads* (1992), *The Wind in the Willows* (1996), *The Lady in the Van* (1999)

Bennett first attracted attention as a writer and performer in revue on the Edinburgh Fringe, especially with *Beyond the Fringe* with Jonathan Miller, Dudley Moore and Peter Cook, which had long runs in London and New York. Bennett is a very funny writer, adept at using the techniques of farce and music hall, but, while he will find humour in the predicament of cancer patients, geriatrics, Jewish mothers, social workers' cases or homosexual spies, his characters are not butts for laughter. He has a telling ear for the nuances of everyday speech and an eye for the clinching detail but he explores a wide variety of dramatic forms from monologue to biography to history play so that there is no typical Bennett format.

Forty Years On seemed to please everyone, 'a good night out' and a clever satire with songs which analyses Britain in the twentieth century via a revue put on by a boarding school (much of it began life as pastiches of literary and other styles). *The Old Country*, a cerebral discussion of national identity through the image of a British defector living in the USSR, made more demands on audiences. *Enjoy* manages to be illuminating about class values, town planners, the generation gap, sexual politics and fashionable sociology in a play that continually surprises. An ageing working-class couple in the north of England, living in a house due for demolition, and due for removal to a new estate, are visited by an apparently female social worker who, the audience does not realise, is actually their son in drag. Proud of their children, they try to play it his way, and they also boast of their prostitute daughter: 'She's exceptional. You won't find girls like her on every street corner.' *Kafka's Dick*, in which Kafka, his parents and his publisher materialise in the suburban home of a would-be biographer, found appreciative audiences at the Royal Court, but the first production failed to transfer to the West End. It fared better in a 1998 revival at a time when public opinion had become more concerned about the negative aspects of 'celebrity'. Bennett's exploration of the king's madness and its implications in *The Madness of George III* is a typical example of his ability to combine comic and tragic impulses in a single structure.

His television monologue series, *Talking Heads*, and *Single Spies* (a double bill about two English spies, Guy Burgess and Anthony Blunt, which includes an appearance by Elizabeth II), both transferred successfully to the stage, and *The Old Crowd* (1979) and *The Insurance Man* (1986) explored techniques outside the apparent naturalism of most of his other television plays. His screenplays include *A Private Function* (1984), the ★ORTON biography *Prick Up Your Ears* (1986), and *The*

Madness of King George (1994), retitled so the American audience would not think it was the third film in a series.

TRY THESE:
Denise Deegan's *Daisy Pulls It Off* and John Dighton's *The Happiest Days of Our Lives* for satire on the English public school system; ★SIMON GRAY's *Butley*, ★HAMPTON's *The Philanthropist*, ★NICHOLS and ★ORTON for satire of social mores; ★WILCOX's *Lent* for linking the school play with homosexuality; ★JULIAN MITCHELL's *Another Country* for homosexuality and spies; ★STAFFORD for dynastic politics.

BENT, Simon
British dramatist

PLAYS INCLUDE:
Bad Company (1991), *Wasted* (1993) *Goldhawk Road* (1996), *Shelter* (1997) *Sugar Sugar* (1998), *A Prayer for Owen Meany* (2002, from John Irving), *The Associate* (2002), *Accomplices* (2002)

Bent has carved himself out a comic niche that marks him as the inheritor of the mantle of ★JOE ORTON and ★HAROLD PINTER. His characteristic approach is to bring together an unlikely group of characters in a microcosmic environment and then explore the ensuing tensions. In *Bad Company* it's the end of the season at a seaside resort and some bored young adults find things to keep themselves occupied including, inevitably, sex and violence. In *Wasted* a similar group try to run a communal house with all the usual difficulties. *Goldhawk Road* owes something to ★JONSON's *Volpone* with its tale of potential beneficiaries jockeying for position at a deathbed. *Sugar Sugar* is set in a seaside guesthouse where the arrival of a new guest awakens dangerous forces. In *The Associate* two workmen about to redecorate a pensioner's council flat share a roast breakfast with him as he regales them with Pinteresque tales of how the world has maltreated him. Although Bent has demonstrated a great talent for creating situations and writing biting comedy, Paul Taylor has suggested he is 'less adept at creating plots with enough narrative dynamism to propel his oddballs through a sustained drama'.

TRY THESE:
★ PINTER's *The Birthday Party* and ★ ORTON's *Entertaining Mr Sloane* for comparisons; ★ BOND's *Saved*, ★ CORTHRON, ★ PRICHARD, ★ UPTON for rootless young people finding ways to occupy their time.

BERKOFF, Steven   [1937 –   ]
British actor and dramatist

PLAYS AND ADAPTATIONS INCLUDE:
The Penal Colony (1968), *Metamorphosis* (1969), *The Trial* (1970), *Agamemnon* (1973), *The Fall of the House of Usher* (1974), *East* (1975), *Greek* (1979), *The Murder of Jesus Christ* (1980), *Decadence* (1981), *One Man* (1982), *West* (1983), *Harry's Christmas* (1985), *Sink the Belgrano!* (1986), *Kvetch* (1987), *Brighton Beach Scumbags* (1991), *Sturm und Drang* (1994), *Massage* (1997), *Messiah* (2000)

Berkoff is as widely known as a performer as he is a writer. He studied mime in Paris with the École Jacques Le Coq, an emphasis very evident in his performances and plays, which rely as much for their impact on movement as on language. After working in repertory theatre Berkoff went on to found the London Theatre Group, where he began to direct and to develop adaptations from literature into theatre. Kafka and Edgar Allan Poe were favoured authors for this treatment, which often involved expressionistic sets and acting style. The London Theatre Group also developed a version of ★ AESCHYLUS' *Agamemnon*, and Greek tragedy became an informing principle of Berkoff's own writing. His first original play was *East*, which used a juxtaposition of street language with high tragedy and blank verse to produce a vitriolic and abrasive account of East End life. *Greek* employed the Oedipus myth to polemicise about mothers, marriage and women. *West* rewrote the Beowulf legend into a scabrous attack on the British upper classes and was (ironically) a great success in the West End, as was his National Theatre revival of his adaptation of *The Trial* in which he starred with Anthony Sher. *Messiah*, his most recent work, treats Christ as a guerrilla waging a campaign against the Romans.

Metamorphosis
Metamorphosis was the most successful of the London Theatre Group's productions. In Berkoff's hands Kafka's tale of a young man who wakes up to discover he has been transformed into a beetle becomes a sustained scream of rage against the constraints of conventional society. First performed with Berkoff at the Round House in 1969, *Metamorphosis*, which is highly stylised using acrobatics and mime to powerful effect, has toured extensively in Britain and overseas and is now, as a spectacular showcase for an actor, a regular feature of the Edinburgh Festival.

TRY THESE:
★ BENNETT's *Kafka's Dick* is a wildly imaginative but very Bennett-like play on fame and literature, in which Kafka is omnipresent; Lindsay Kemp is as idiosyncratic and unique in his performance style; ★ CARTWRIGHT's *Road* uses language explosively; the ★ CAPEK brothers' *Insect Play* is another insect-infected metaphor for society.

BERNARD, Jean-Jacques   [1888 – 1972]
French dramatist

PLAYS INCLUDE:
Martine (1922), *L'Invitation au Voyage* (1924, *Invitation to the Journey*), *Le Printemps des Autres* (1924, *Other People's Springtime*), *Le Roy de Malousie* (1928, *The King of Malousie*), *La Louise* (1930, *Our Louise*), *A La Recherche des Coeurs* (1931, *Searching for Hearts*), *Les Soeurs Guedonec* (1931, *The Guedonec Sisters*), *Jeanne de Pantin* (1933), *Nationale 6* (1935, *Highway No 6*), *Deux Hommes* (1937, *Two Men*), *Le Jardinier d'Ispahan* (1939, *The Gardener of Ispahan*)

Writing just prior to the generation of ★ COCTEAU, ★ GENET and ★ GIRAUDOUX, Bernard is the best-known exemplar of the 'theatre of the inexpressible', a French school of writers including Denys Amiel and Charles Vildrac in which it's our unspoken dialogue that resonates, not the words themselves ('subtext', as acting teachers might put it). *Martine*, the story of a peasant girl's misplaced attraction for Julien, a callow upper-class journalist, proceeds inevitably to its sad ending, as Martine's passivity hardens into a tacit acknowledgement of perpetual rejection (see Claude Goretta's film *The Lacemaker* for a contemporary update on this theme). *Nationale 6* tells a similar story of an ordinary provincial girl done in by an overactive imagination, and in *Les Soeurs Guedonec* two spinsters pass a miserable holiday in complete silence, accompanied by three loud orphan children. The National Theatre once tried its hand with *Martine* but there has been no significant recent interest.

TRY THESE:

★CHEKHOV, ★PINTER, ★BECKETT for transmuting the 'inexpressible' into art rather than just an end in itself; equally, ★ROBERT HOLMAN and ★DURAS for the 'inexpressible' recall of past emotions; for treatments of class clashing, ★CHEKHOV's *Three Sisters*.

BETTI, Ugo   [1892 – 1953]
Italian dramatist and judge

PLAYS INCLUDE:

Il Paese delle Vacanze (1942, *Summertime*), *L'Aurola Bruciata* (1942, *The Burnt Flowerbed*), *Curruzione al Palasso di Giustizia* (1949, *Corruption in the Palace of Justice*, also translated for radio as *The Sacred Seals*), *La Regina e gli Insorti* (1951, *The Queen and the Rebels*)

Some Italian critics considered Betti's later plays even better than those of ★PIRANDELLO, whose influence is evident in his work. Betti's themes are moral and in the wider sense religious: his translator Henry Reed suggested that his major theme was 'man's fatal disregard of God'. Carefully plotted and well constructed in a conventional way, his plays tend to be set in rather unlocalised symbolic settings, though the dialogue is naturalistic. His interest is in the personal and ethical problems of his protagonists rather than any political dialectic: the rebels in *The Queen and the Rebels* or the contending powers in *The Burnt Flowerbed*, for instance, are abstractions without identifiable ideologies. His concerns in these plays are the sacrifice by which a prostitute saves the life of a worthless queen and so herself gains 'queenly' virtues, and a similar self-sacrifice intended to destroy the cynicism of a former politician. With the general reassessment of mid-twentieth-century drama, a fringe production of *The Queen and the Rebels* in 2002 might presage a Betti revival, though the odds remain against it.

TRY THESE:

★GENET's *The Balcony*, ★PIRANDELLO; ★COLLINS' *Judgement* for moral enquiry; ★ANOUILH, ★GIRAUDOUX for ethical discussions.

BETTS, Torben   [1968 –   ]
British dramatist

PLAYS INCLUDE.

Spurning Comfort (1998), *A Listening Heaven* (1999), *Mummies and Daddies* (1999), *Incarcerator* (1999), *Five Visions of the Faithful* (2000), *Clockwatching* (2001), *The Biggleswades* (2001), *Silence and Violence* (2002)

A Liverpool graduate who subsequently trained as an actor, Betts earned rave reviews for a burst of plays at the turn of the century. He has been hailed as an outstanding new voice without the benefit of a production by one of the national companies or in the West End. His stint as writer in residence at Scarborough inevitably brought comparisons with ★AYCKBOURN. Certainly there are similarities to the master in the excruciating tragic-comic domestic situations captured in acutely observed dialogue in *Clockwatching* or *A Listening Heaven* but *Incinerator* is a verse drama of 'cartoon savagery' (Michael Billington). Connal Orton, the literary manager at Scarborough who opened Betts' unsolicited script for *A Listening Heaven*, has suggested that he has now moved beyond his 'social realist phase' and that 'his more overtly poetic plays' are, in Betts' words, 'about characters who can use language and so create tragedy, rather than characters who cannot (thus creating comedy)'.

TRY THESE:

★CHURCHILL's *Serious Money* for modern verse drama; Betts has already been compared by reviewers to ★ALBEE, ★BARKER, ★BERKOFF, ★O'NEILL and ★PINTER.

BILL, Stephen   [1948 –   ]
British dramatist

PLAYS INCLUDE:
Girl Talk (1977), *The Old Order* (1979), *The Final Wave* (1979), *Piggy Back Riders* (1981), *The Bottom Drawer* (1982), *Naked in the Bull Ring* (1985), *Over the Bar* (1985), *Crossing the Line* (1987), *Curtains* (1987), *Heart-landers* (1989, with ★ANNE DEVLIN and ★DAVID EDGAR), *Over a Barrel* (1990), *Stitched Up* (1990), *The Antigone Project* (1992), *What the Heart Feels* (1996)

Relatively unrecognised nationally until the success of *Curtains*, which won three awards when it was produced at the Hampstead Theatre in 1987, Bill has a solid record of regional successes in the UK, including *The Old Order*, for which he won the 1979 John Whiting Award. Set in Birmingham, *Curtains*, an acutely observed savage comedy about a family birthday celebration which turns into a wake, presents an everyday situation of a family's attitudes to the problems of ageing and to euthanasia in terms which are memorably comic as well as horrific. It is a well-crafted, almost old-fashioned play, which uses the familiar devices of the family gathering and the unexpected return of the prodigal to unlock themes and to analyse the roots of situations. However, as the shortness of its West End run sadly indicates, its sombre material did not make it a popular favourite.

TRY THESE:
★BLEASDALE and ★RUSSELL use Liverpudlian settings and ★BYRNE uses Glaswegian settings in similar ways to Bill's use of Birmingham; ★SOPHOCLES' *Oedipus* for family reunions that go wrong; ★SHEPARD's *Buried Child* for calamitous consequences of a prodigal's return; contemporary dramatists who share some of Bill's preoccupations are ★AYCKBOURN, ★ORTON and ★NORMAN (*Night Mother*); contemporary dramatists from Birmingham include Alan Drury, ★ELYOT, ★RUDKIN and ★ZEPHANIAH.

BLEASDALE, Alan   [1946 –   ]
British dramatist

PLAYS INCLUDE:
The Party's Over (1975), *Down the Dock Road* (1976), *It's a Madhouse* (1976), *Should Auld Acquaintance . . .* (1976), *No More Sitting on the Old School Bench* (1977), *Pimples* (1978), *Crackers* (1978), *Love is a Many-Splendoured Thing* (1979), *Having a Ball* (1981), *Are You Lonesome Tonight?* (1985), *On the Ledge* (1993)

A Merseyside writer who until 1985 had developed a strong reputation without ever having been seen in the West End, Bleasdale is a gritty comic satirist who has reached his widest theatre audience with what is, paradoxically, his most earnest work, *Are You Lonesome Tonight?* This overtly hagiographic musical about Elvis Presley aims to set the record straight about a musical legend Bleasdale thinks has been vilified. Set on the last day of the King's life, before drugs and booze killed him at forty-two in 1977, the musical is an unabashedly sentimental picture of a bloated talent looking back sardonically on his younger self, before he allowed himself to be mercilessly corrupted by managers, promoters and the press. Earlier stage plays of note include *It's a Madhouse*, set in a psychiatric hospital in the north-west of England, and *Having a Ball*, about four men awaiting surgery in a vasectomy clinic. *On the Ledge* is a very dark tale of urban blight that shares the social pessimism of Bleasdale's television series *Boys From the Blackstuff*, a 1983 howl of rage against unemployment, set in Liverpool, that tapped the psychic pulse of Britain. Peter Smith's 1985 film *No Surrender* had a strong Bleasdale script about rival factions in a Liverpool nightclub where the tensions mirror those in Northern Ireland. The powerful television series *The Monocled Mutineer*, a 1986 World War I parable of powerlessness in Thatcher's Britain, and *GBH* (1991), which wickedly satirised the battle for ascendancy in Liverpool between the Labour Party and the Trotskyite Militant Tendency, stirred up major controversies. His later television work *Jake's Progress* (1995) is a bleak study of a dysfunctional family but *Melissa* (1997) is based on one of Francis Durbridge's murder mysteries from 1962. His television adaptation of *Oliver Twist* was screened in 1999 and his *Henry VIII* is scheduled for 2003.

TRY THESE:

★RUSSELL as the other pre-eminent Liverpudlian writer; ★KUREISHI as an urban realist with a comparable sense of humour; ★ORTON for black comedy.

BLESSING, Lee   [1949 –   ]
American dramatist

PLAYS INCLUDE:

The Authentic Life of Billy the Kid (1979), *Oldtimers Game* (1982), *Nice People Dancing to Good Country Music* (1982), *Independence* (1983), *Riches* (1984, formerly *War of the Roses*), *Eleemosynary* (1985), *A Walk in the Woods* (1987), *Two Rooms* (1988), *Down the Road* (1989), *Cobb* (1989), *Fortinbras* (1991), *Lake St Extension* (1992), *Patient A* (1993), *Chesapeake* (1999), *Going to St Ives* (2000), *Rewrites* (2001)

Minnesota dramatist Blessing's best-known play, *A Walk in the Woods* (winner of the Best Play award from the American Theatre Critics Association), presents two statesmen negotiating in uncharacteristic poses of casualness and friendliness: we find them human. As potential annihilation hovers over the world, talks of disarmament are set in the context of hope – in the woods. Placed in the harmonious milieu of the natural, we are reminded of the dangers of the artificial. A peculiar tension of pessimism and possibility dissolves into a nihilism that is inherent in survival games. The two rooms of *Two Rooms* are the windowless cubicle where a hostage is held in Beirut and the room, stripped of furniture, where the prisoner's wife hopes to share psychically her husband's ordeal. Some critics pointed to the obvious similarities to ★SARTRE's *No Exit*, but the play's lack of action or point of view distressed others. *Cobb* explores the myth surrounding Ty Cobb, baseball star, portrayed at three stages of his life by three actors. Blessing sees Cobb as a symbol of American greed (the player was an early investor in General Motors and Coca Cola), power (he frequently had violent encounters with strangers), and racism

(the strangers were often black). *Patient A* is based on the true story of Kimberley Bergalis, the first known case of a patient becoming HIV positive as a result of contact with a dentist. It is a three-hander with Blessing himself appearing as a character. His early *Independence* and *Eleemosynary* feature all-female casts and concern relationships between mothers and daughters, strained by the mother's mental breakdown in the former, and a grandmother's stroke in the latter. He brought his interests in politics and the maternal together in *Going to St Ives*.

TRY THESE:

★BECKETT's *Endgame* is perhaps the most memorable of all survival games; for diplomacy see ★EDGAR's *The Shape of the Table* and ★LITTLEWOOD's *Oh What a Lovely War*; ★HENLEY's *Crimes of the Heart* features three sisters dealing with the legacy of a mentally ill mother; ★NELSON's *Principia Scriptoriae* and ★HAVIS's *Morocco* for Americans held prisoner in foreign lands; ★STOPPARD's *Rosencrantz and Guildenstern* for new takes on Hamlet; ★FIERSTEIN and ★KRAMER for HIV/AIDS.

BLOCK, Simon
British dramatist Plays include:

PLAYS INCLUDE:

Not a Game for Boys (1995), *Chimps* (1997), *A Place at the Table* (2000), *Hand in Hand* (2002)

Block is a witty writer whose plays cover a wide range of topics with astringently accurate character observation. In *Not a Game for Boys* he takes three cab drivers playing a crucial table tennis match as the starting point for an exploration of issues in friendship and masculinity. *Chimps* takes the comic situation of the door-to-door salesman from hell and extends it into a ★PINTERESQUE nightmare. In his recent plays Block has demonstrated a willingness to tackle subjects that others might find too taxing: *A Place at the Table* has a television company commissioning a wheelchair-using writer to create a disability sitcom; in *Hand in Hand* he deals with some of the ways in which British Jews react to the Palestinian situation.

TRY THESE:
Block has been compared to ★SIMON GRAY and
★MAMET; ★GODBER, ★IKOLI's *Pot the Black*,
★PAGE's *Golden Girls*, ★STOREY for sports and
games; ★AYCKBOURN's *Man of the Moment* for
bad television; Graeae and ★KEMPINSKI for disability; the male protagonist in *Hand in Hand* is
called Ronnie, a name redolent of ★WESKER's
trilogy; for other responses to Palestine, ★HARE's
Via Dolorosa and ★PASCAL's *Crossing Jerusalem*.

BOGART, Anne   [1951 –   ]
American writer and director

PRODUCTIONS INCLUDE:
Hauptstadt (1979), *Inhabitat* (1979), *Out of
Sync* (1980), *Women and Men: A Big Dance*
(1982), *History, An American Dream* (1983);
The Making of Americans (1985, adapted
from Gertrude Stein), *'1951'* (1986, with
★MAC WELLMAN), *No Plays No Poetry But
Philosophical Reflections Practical Instructions
Provocative Prescriptions Opinions and
Pointers from a Noted Critic and Dramatist*
(1988), *The Medium* (1993), *Culture of Desire*
(1998), *Bob* (1998), *Room* (2000)

Bogart is one of the USA's most innovative
and creative directors/writers. Although she
creates theatre pieces that most would term
'experimental', she told Catherine Sheehy in a
Theatre interview that 'I usually personally
resent being called avant-garde because I
spend most of my time thinking about history, tradition and culture'. Her most widely
acclaimed piece may be *No Plays No Poetry*,
described by a *New York Times* critic as 'an
avant-garde carnival that carries the audience
from scene to scene in a choreographed comic
pageant that sends up the theoretical writings
of Bertolt Brecht'. According to Bogart, 97 per
cent of the text came directly from ★BRECHT's
critical writing. As a sideshow Barker spouted
the history of the theatre according to Brecht,
a tent opened and the audience could wander
to any of nine scenes, including one where
nine actors playing Brecht argued about acting or another where Tina Shepard played
Brecht playing Charlie Chaplin playing Hitler.
Much of her work depends on 'sampling'
other writers and cultural figures. For example, *The Medium* drew on Marshall McLuhan

and *Culture of Desire* uses Dante's journey and
Warhol's career as a framework, *Bob* (seen in
London in 2001) is created from the words of
Robert Wilson and scripted by Jocelyn Clarke
who did the same for Virginia Woolf in *Room*.

TRY THESE:
★MUSSMANN's *Civil War Chronicles* for questions
as to how history is often perceived and conceived; ★FOREMAN, Nancy Reilly, Richard
Schechner, Peter Sellars, the Wooster Group
for other Americans engaged in the rearrange-
ment of theatrical forms; ★BARTLETT and Ariane
Mnouchkine for European parallels.

BOGOSIAN, Eric   [1953 –   ]
American actor, dramatist and screenwriter

PLAYS/MONOLOGUES INCLUDE:
Men Inside (1981), *Voices of America* (1982),
FunHouse (1983), *Talk Radio* (1984),
Drinking in America (1986), *Sex, Drugs, Rock
& Roll* (1990), *SubUrbia* (1994), *Pounding
Nails in the Floor with my Forehead* (1994),
31 Ejaculations (1996), *Griller* (1998), *Wake
Up and Smell the Coffee* (2000), *Humpty
Dumpty* (2002)

In *Talk Radio*, the late-night talk jockey Barry
Champlain (Bogosian) asserts, 'This decadent
country needs a loud voice – and that's me'.
This voice, one that characterises much of
Bogosian's work, offers various versions of the
macho male in a political comedy context that
exploits their stereotypical fictions and makes
them real. The characters embrace attributes
of greed and fear that encumber America's ego
– the boastful, the phoney, the hypocritical. As
philistines of a decaying culture, Bogosian's
characters are caught in addiction and victimisation. At the same time as monologist
Bogosian enacts the compulsive behaviour of
the white American male, he strips bare his
psyche. Bogosian has appeared in many films
including Oliver Stone's version of *Talk Radio*.

TRY THESE:
★SPALDING GRAY, and ★HOLLY HUGHES for
trenchant use of the monologue; see also
★GODBER for the British macho male and
★POLIAKOFF's *City Sugar* for a decadent DJ.

BOLGER, Dermot   [1959 –   ]
Irish poet, novelist and dramatist

PLAYS INCLUDE:

The Lament for Arthur Cleary (1989), *Blinded by the Light* (1990), *In High Germany* (1990), *The Holy Ground* (1990), *One Last White Horse* (1991), *A Dublin Bloom* (1994, from James Joyce's *Ulysses*), *April Bright* (1996), *The Passion of Jerome* (1999), *Consenting Adults* (2000)

Bolger's initial success came as a novelist, his second book, *The Woman's Daughter* (1987) bringing him the AE Memorial Award, the Macaulay Fellowship and the Sunday Tribune Arts Award. His first stage play, *The Lament for Arthur Cleary* – based on his poem of the same name – was premiered to widespread critical acclaim at the Dublin Theatre Festival of 1989, picked up a Fringe First the following summer in Edinburgh and subsequently won the Samuel Beckett Award for Best First Play of that year.

After fifteen years away – bumming round Europe, putting down no roots Arthur Cleary comes home. He feels the need to belong again, but the Dublin he has carried in his head and his heart is long gone. Not just the streets of his boyhood, but the neighbourhood ways and hierarchies have been swept aside by a new set of circumstances: drug trafficking on the pavements where Cleary was once cock o' the walk. Nowhere in his inner being, not even in the soft corners of his heart where he holds the love of a young girl he's just met, can Cleary accommodate that change. He meets his death – Celtic inevitability. Was that not, after all, the reason for his homecoming?

Bolger pinpoints the eternal baggage of the migrant and the exile – a fixed vision of a time and place when they themselves had rooted identity. It's common to all races, but with the Celts it's a particular shackle. At home or abroad they cannot let go of the past, centuries of it, albatross-like around their psyche. Hence *The Lament* – wild with heady, poetic imagery and yet tough with its spare, rapidly shifting scenario, fond with its regard for Arthur and sorrowing at the needless waste of a bright spirit.

Bolger's subsequent theatre work has continued to tackle many of the themes he raises elsewhere in his writing. *April Bright* explores family life through juxtaposing the experiences of two families living in the same house half a century apart, and the ghostly theme is carried through in *The Passion of Jerome* where sexual shenanigans are interrupted by a poltergeist. *Consenting Adults* is a two-hander with a man and a woman role-playing in a hotel room, touching on themes of desire and identity.

TRY THESE:

★O'CASEY, ★SYNGE, for earlier issues within tightly knit communities; ★FRIEL, ★MURPHY, Graham Reid (with his Billy plays, set in modern Belfast) for modern parallels; ★O'NEILL'S *Anna Christie* has a nostalgia for the exiled Irishman; ★BRYDEN for Scottish parallels and contrasts; ★DYER, ★HORSFIELD for contrast to the football fans of In High Germany; ★COWARD's *Blithe Spirit* for another unfortunate ghostly manifestation; ★KANE, ★PINTER, ★SHEPARD, ★SIMON for hotel encounters; ★MARIE JONES' *Stones in His Pockets* and ★MCCAFFERTY's *Mojo Mickybo* for recent Irish two-handers.

BOLT, Robert   [1924 – 95]
British dramatist and screenwriter

PLAYS INCLUDE:

The Critic and the Heart (1957), *Flowering Cherry* (1957), *A Man for All Seasons* (radio version 1954; staged 1960), *The Tiger and the Horse* (1960), *Gentle Jack* (1963), *The Thwarting of Baron Bolligrew* (1965, for children), *Vivat! Vivat Regina!* (1970), *State of Revolution* (1977)

A schoolteacher who began writing plays for children and then for radio, Bolt modelled *The Critic and the Heart* on ★MAUGHAM's *The Circle*, while contemporary critics greeted *Flowering Cherry*, his first popular success, as Chekhovian. Its picture of an insurance salesman living among his own illusions has an edge of non-naturalism that contrasts with its largely conventional structure. Bolt continued to try out different theatrical forms, describing *A Man for All Seasons* as 'bastardised' ★BRECHT. *A Man for All Seasons* presents the conflict between Sir Thomas More and Henry VIII, and the title role gave Paul Scofield a triumph in both play and film. Here most clearly is the thread that runs right through Bolt's work, of personal integrity, responsibility and the use of power. Actors and director are offered chances to create striking theatre and the play has proved a durable favourite

Bolt's involvement in the Campaign for Nuclear Disarmament is reflected in *The Tiger and the Horse*, in which an academic wife has to decide whether to sign an anti-bomb petition although doing so will jeopardise her husband's elevation to Vice Chancellor of his university.

Bolt originally proposed that *Vivat! Vivat Regina!* should be given an *Oh What a Lovely War* pier-end-style presentation. It was intended to provide a meaty role for his wife, Sarah Miles, as Mary Queen of Scots, but he overwrote the part and the more sparsely written Elizabeth I is dominant in performance. *State of Revolution* attempts to present a political dialectic rather than a personal story but its hagiographic portrayal of Lenin against a complex revolutionary background does not come off as well as his Tudor portraits. His films have been more successful in handling epic themes. It would be good to see if *Gentle Jack*, drawing parallels between pagan folklore and capitalist mores with its onstage presentation of the god Pan and mixture of folk elements, theatrical effects and direct address to the audience could be made to work today.

TRY THESE:

★BRECHT, ★BRENTON, ★EDGAR, ★HARE, ★LITTLEWOOD, ★PETER SHAFFER for historical epics; ★BARNES for debunking history; for plays on anti-nuclear issues, ★BLESSING's *A Walk in the Woods*, ★BRENTON's *The Genius*, ★CLARK's *The Petition*, ★DARKE's *The Body*, Steven Dietz's *Fooling Around with Infinity*, ★FORNES' *The Danube*, ★FRAYN's *Copenhagen* and ★LANFORD WILSON's *Angels Fall*; ★LOWE for plays with an anti-war theme; ★EURIPIDES' *The Bacchae* for Dionysiac experiences and ★RUDKIN's *Afore Night Come* for countryside rituals to parallel *Gentle Jack*.

BOND, Edward   [1934 –   ]
British dramatist

PLAYS INCLUDE:
The Pope's Wedding (1962), *Saved* (1965), *Narrow Road to the Deep North* (1968), *Early Morning* (1968), *Black Mass* (1970), *Passion* (1971), *Lear* (1972), *The Sea* (1973), *Bingo: Scenes of Money and Death* (1973), *The Fool: Scenes of Bread and Love* (1975), *Stone* (1976), *A-A-America* (1976, *Grandma Faust* and *The Swing*), *The Bundle* (1978), *The Woman* (1978), *The Worlds* (1979), *Restoration* (1981), *Summer* (1982), *Derek* (1983), *Choruses from after the Assassination* (1983), *Human Cannon* (1985), *The War Plays: A Trilogy* (1985, *Red, Black and Ignorant, Tin Can People, Great Peace*), *Burns* (1986), *September* (1989), *In the Company of Men* (1989), *Jackets* (1989), *Olly's Prison* (1993), *Tuesday* (1993), *Coffee: A Tragedy* (1995), *At the Inland Sea: A Play for Young People* (1997), *Eleven Vests* (1997), *Crime in the Twenty-First Century* (1999)

Bond, one of the most radical of dramatists, was once called 'the most important and controversial dramatist writing in Britain today'. Notorious for a scene in *Saved* in which a baby is stoned to death, he has consistently written from a Marxist perspective, and argues that the shock of such violent images is necessary to represent the violence that is done to people by capitalism.

Born in London, Bond left school at fourteen, worked in factories and offices, writing plays in his spare time, and sending them to the Royal Court. *Saved*, developed with the Writers' Group at the Court, was instrumental in ridding British theatre of the censorship of the Lord Chamberlain. The theatre's attempt to stage the play under club conditions led to a prosecution, which showed that such conditions did not offer any protection from censorship. In 1968, The Theatres Act abolished the powers of the Lord Chamberlain, and *Saved* and *Narrow Road to the Deep North* were toured throughout Europe under the auspices of the British Council. *Black Mass* was written for the anti-apartheid movement; *Stone* for Gay Sweatshop; *Passion* was commissioned by the Campaign for Nuclear Disarmament. Many of Bond's plays offer

Saved by Edward Bond, directed by Bi l Gaskill, Royal Court Theatre, 1968. (Morris Newcombe/ArenaPAL)

radical re-readings of historical events, texts and figures that are commonly held as a source of national pride: *Bingo* confronts the dying and unheroic ★SHAKESPEARE and ★BEN JONSON; *The Fool* is about the 'peasant poet' John Clare. Bond has described his reworking of *King Lear* in *Lear* as 'an attack on Stalinism, as seen as a danger to Western revolution, and on bourgeois culture as expressed in Shakespeare's *Lear*'. Bond's desire to contest the usual connotations of specific genres and assumptions about classics also led him to write opera libretti (*We Come to the River* and *The English Cat*) and to adapt works by ★CHEKHOV, ★WEBSTER and ★WEDEKIND.

Much of his most recent work is aimed at young actors and audiences: in 1979 he had cast his play *The Worlds* with a non-professional cast of young people from the Court's Young People's Theatre Scheme in an early demonstration of his commitment to his principle that 'New writing needs new acting, new directing and new audiences.' Never a popular dramatist, his voice has been less widely heard in recent years as his type of political drama has become increasingly unfashionable and as a generation of 'In Yer Face' dramatists has extended his violent metaphors into new territory.

Saved

Saved is a difficult play to watch; dealing with a community of young people in south London it charts their desperate and violent lives. Its first performance at the Royal Court provoked extreme, and extremely polarised, reactions. The *Daily Telegraph* critic reported 'cold disgust' and horror at the scene in which a group of young men stone a baby to death (and was not alone in his reaction), while other critics and writers greeted the power of Bond's writing and imagery with acclaim. It is not only that scene which makes the play so harrowing; in one section, the baby wails unrelentingly while no one on stage responds to its cries, and the audience is made to physically experience the frustration and apathy of the play's characters.

TRY THESE:

★KANE's *Blasted* excited as much controversy as *Saved*; *The Pope's Wedding* was first staged on the set of ★BECKETT's *Happy Days*, and the pile of sand became a contributory factor to the final image of Scobey; ★ARDEN, ★DUFFY, ★JELLICOE, ★SOYINKA and ★WESKER were also members of the Writer's Group; ★BRECHT is a strong influence and *The Narrow Road to the Deep North* and its companion play *The Bundle* use an oriental setting in ways reminiscent of *The Caucasian Chalk Circle* and *The Good Person of Sezchuan*; *The Woman* is a rereading of the Trojan wars more familiar in ★EURIPIDES' *The Trojan Women*, ★SHAKESPEARE's *Troilus and Cressida* or ★GIRAUDOUX's *The Trojan War Will Not Take Place*; *Restoration* is a rereading of issues dealt with in Restoration comedy by such writers as ★BEHN, ★CONGREVE, ★ETHEREGE, ★FARQUHAR, ★WYCHERLEY, ★VANBURGH; Bond himself has drawn attention to the Oedipal elements in *Saved* (see ★SOPHOCLES); ★SAUNDERS for a parallel with *The Pope's Wedding*; ★BLOCK, ★PRICHARD, ★UPTON for disaffected youth to parallel *Saved*.

BOUCICAULT, Dion(ysus Larner)   [1820 – 96]
Irish actor and dramatist

PLAYS INCLUDE:
London Assurance (1841), *Love in a Maze* (1851), *The Vampire* (1852), *The Corsican Brothers* (1852), *The Poor of New York* (1857), *The Octoroon* (1859), *The Colleen Bawn* (1860), *Arrah-na-Pogue* (1864), *The Shaughraun* (1874)

Greatly admired as an actor in Britain and the USA, Boucicault was a wide-ranging and prolific dramatist who wrote nearly 150 original plays and adaptations, operettas, pantomimes and melodramas (including sixteen plays in one year). *London Assurance* (restored to the modern repertory by a 1975 RSC production) presents the courtship by a young gentleman, who is heavily in debt, of a cynical country beauty. She is at first happy at the idea of marriage to an old man who will provide her with a secure income, until she falls in love with his son. A witty piece which owes a great debt to earlier comedies of manners, its characters are sharply drawn, and a plot which turns upon a father not recognising his disguised son is acceptable within a structure that includes some farce-like devices. Boucicault rewrote for local audiences: *The Streets of London* and *The Poor of Liverpool* (1864) are almost identical to *The Poor of New York*, itself a version of a French play about the poor of Paris. Many of his plays offer opportunities for spectacle: the burning of a Mississippi steamer in *The Octoroon*, or, in *Arrah-na-Pogue*, the whole scene sinking slowly as the hero climbs an ivy-clad turret to seize the villain and hurl him to his death. Though melodramas like *The Vampire* follow the pattern for the genre, his work shows careful construction and keen observation. *The Octoroon* was one of the first plays in which an American black slave was treated seriously, and the social themes which often attracted him prefigured later dramas about the common people. His Irish plays, such as *The Shaughraun*, provided fine vehicles for himself but, though he fought to establish copyright for dramatists in the USA and was the first to receive a royalty instead of a flat fee, he died an impoverished teacher of acting in New York.

His plays continue to be revived fairly regularly in Ireland and more occasionally elsewhere: the Abbey's *Colleen Bawn* played successfully at the National Theatre in 1999 and the Watermill, Newbury, ventured far from the beaten track with *Love in a Maze* in 2002: apparently unperformed since 1851, the play was welcomed as 'a light and deliciously frothy summer entertainment. Particularly in the final half hour when, weather permitting, the action moves . . . into the Watermill's enchanting garden where a towering maze, designed to look like a pink and white tiered wedding cake, provides the setting for the resolution of true love' (*Guardian*).

TRY THESE:

The various versions of *The Phantom of the Opera* offer many of the attractions that delighted Boucicault's nineteenth-century audiences; *London Assurance* shows resemblances to the plays of ★GOLDSMITH and ★SHERIDAN (as well as another RSC revival, John O'Keefe's *Wild Oats*), and through them to ★CONGREVE and other Restoration comic dramatists; Donald Sinden, who played in the RSC revival of *London Assurance*, considered it the equal of ★WILDE's *The Importance of Being Earnest*; Boucicault's con-

cern with Irish politics marks him out as an ancestor of ★O'CASEY and ★FRIEL.

BRECHT, Bertolt   [1898 – 1956]
German dramatist, poet, theatrical innovator and theoretician

PLAYS INCLUDE:

Baal (1918), *Drums in the Night* (1922), *In the Jungle of Cities* (1923), *Edward II* (1924, with Lion Feuchtwanger, after ★MARLOWE), *The Elephant Calf* (c. 1924–5), *Man is Man* (1926), *The Threepenny Opera* (1928, with music by Kurt Weill, after ★GAY's *The Beggar's Opera*), *Happy End* (1929, with Elisabeth Hauptmann and music by Weill), *He Who Says Yes* and *He Who Says No* (1930), *The Measures Taken* (1930), *The Exception and the Rule* (1930), *The Rise and Fall of the City of Mahagonny* (1930; with music by Weill), *The Mother* (1932, from ★GORKY), *St Joan of the Stockyards* (1932), *The Seven Deadly Sins* (1933, with Weill, also known as *Anna Anna*), *Senora Carrar's Rifles* (1937, after ★SYNGE's *Riders to the Sea*), *Fear and Misery of the Third Reich* (1938, also known as *The Private Life of the Master Race*), *Mother Courage and Her Children* (1941), *The Resistible Rise of Arturo Ui* (1941), *The Life of Galileo* (1943), *The Good Person of Szechwan* (1943), *Schweik in the Second World War* (1943), *The Caucasian Chalk Circle* (1945), *Mr Puntila and His Servant Matti* (1948), *The Days of the Commune* (1949), *The Tutor* (1950, after Jacob Lenz)

Brecht is one of the most influential (if often unacknowledged) figures in contemporary culture. His example has changed theatrical practice and affected a generation of socialist dramatists, his principles have informed contemporary film theory and a whole genre of 'agit-prop' theatre productions and companies, and his 'distancing effects' are now ingrained practice on stage and in much television and film.

Brecht's history is bound up in the rise of fascism in Germany. Working in 1918 at Augsburg military hospital gave him a lifelong commitment to pacifism. He became involved in the theatre through drama criticism and his first plays were very much influenced by Expressionism. *Baal*, the life of a poet, prefigures his later work in its deliberately shocking effects. Brecht went on to become part of a group of radical intellectuals in the theatre and cultural life of Berlin, becoming increasingly involved with Marxist theory, and beginning to develop an aesthetic practice that integrated with his politics, and which was bound up with the social and economic conditions of the period. He became very much part of the European avant-garde, exchanging ideas with the Formalist group in Russia.

During the 1920s Brecht's collaboration with Kurt Weill gave rise to the musical productions *The Threepenny Opera*, *The Seven Deadly Sins* and *The Rise and Fall of the City of Mahagonny* (produced in the year of the German economic crash), which presents a society in which *anything* can be had for money. These plays were much influenced by the Berlin cabaret of the 1920s and early 1930s, and Brecht argued that the theatre should be a place in which audiences could relax, smoke and drink, the better to take up the points of the play for discussion.

Brecht was on the Nazis' list of banned writers, and fled to Denmark the day after the Reichstag fire. The Danes refused to hand Brecht over to the German authorities, but when Germany invaded Denmark, Brecht escaped to Finland. The events of the rise of fascism are charted in the ironically allegorical *The Rise and Fall of Arturo Ui*, in which Brecht made an analogy between the rise of Nazism and Chicago gangsters. He spent the years of the war in exile in Hollywood, where he wrote the script for the film *Hangmen Also Die*. In 1947, after an appearance before the House of Representatives' Un-American Activities Committee, Brecht moved to Switzerland, and in 1949 he returned to East Germany, to take up an offer of his own theatre and extensive subsidy, founding the Berliner Ensemble on his own principles of political theatre. On his death it was taken over by his widow, Helene Weigel.

Brecht wrote some forty plays altogether, which can roughly be divided into three groups (although there are elements of each phase in most of his plays): the early expressionist plays and the musical pieces he devised

with Weill; the *Lehrstücke* (or 'learning pieces') and parable plays and his 'epic theatre'. In his plays, Brecht often turned to fable and to history, to construct 'Parables' for the theatre, offering radical re-readings of familiar texts. When this led to accusations of plagiarism, Brecht's reply was ★'SHAKESPEARE was a thief', not an unreasonable analogy.

In *The Messingkauf Dialogues* (one of his many writings on theatre) Brecht sets out his principles for a 'Theatre of Reason' (also known as epic theatre), in which acting, direction, set design and all aspects of theatrical production were organised to produce a dramatic effect which challenged the audience and which implicated them in the dramatic events. Central to Brechtian theory is the '*Verfremdung*' effect (often mistakenly translated as 'alienation effect'; 'distancing' is closer), which refers to devices in staging, acting, music and direction that encourage the spectator to avoid cathartic identification. Songs that comment on the action of the play, placards to describe the context, direct address to the audience, open set changes all demonstrate the theatre as a place of work. Acting, too, becomes a means of distancing. Brecht was thoroughly opposed to Stanislavsky's method of acting the psychological 'truth' of a character.

Brecht's achievement was to demonstrate his principles in the theatricality of his plays: their politics become something which the audience experiences and is given space to think about and to debate. Few have achieved such a stimulating and actively engaging political theatrical practice since it is hard to produce work which combines dialectical toughness, humour and theatricality in the way that Brecht usually did. Brecht's politics are integral to the structure and form of his drama; his plays are structured around a dialectical principle, between scene and scene, between audience and stage, and between theatrical event and political practice. A Brechtian theatre practice should never be static, but should respond to contemporary political events, and engage the audience in a challenge to 'common sense' modes of perception. For example, in *The Good Person of Szechwan* and *The Caucasian Chalk Circle* the difficulties of behaving humanely are dramatised in, respectively, a woman who has to invent a male protector (actually herself in disguise) to fend off claims on her, and a woman who asserts the claims of nurture over biological motherhood in a child custody case.

Mother Courage and Her Children

This play belongs to the 'epic' period of Brecht's work. Although it is often taken as a study of the struggle of a resilient woman and her family and her doughty survival in a period of war (the Thirty Years' War), the play is structured specifically not to be seen as the study of a single individual, but as parable and metaphor. Mother Courage is a small business woman, who struggles with her cart to scrimp a living for her daughter, the dumb Kattrin, and her sons. Over the course of the play she is confronted with decisions that become increasingly complex, and more overtly political. Mother Courage resolutely asserts that she is not interested in politics, only the survival and care of her family, but the consequence is that she loses them all. Her fate is not a simple one: the play makes it quite clear that other decisions could have averted the events of Mother Courage's tragedy. Brecht once said: 'We must be able to lose ourselves in the agony and at the same time not to. Our actual emotion will come from recognising and feeling the double process'. This double process is at work in Mother Courage: while her situation is undoubtedly moving, the play constantly points to the events and system which have placed her there, and to her own collusion in that system. The play is intercut with songs at the moments at which Mother Courage is required to take action, which point to the far-reaching implications of individual acts. The play has a stunning distancing effect at the moment when Kattrin, silent for the entire play, creates its most violent and loudest noise. In a moment in which she has to make a political choice between saving other lives or her own, by banging on a drum she alerts the villagers who are about to be destroyed.

TRY THESE:
★BOND called his own theatrical project 'Rational Theatre', in homage to BRECHT's 'Theatre of Reason'; Nigel Gearing's *Berlin Days, Hollywood Nights*, ★HAMPTON's *Tales from Hollywood*;

★GRASS's *The Plebeians Rehearse the Uprising* include Brecht among their characters; ★BOGART's *No Plays, No Poetry* is a staging of Brecht's theoretical work; ★GALSWORTHY, ★O'NEILL, ★PIRANDELLO, ★SHAW and ★STRINDBERG were among the dramatists banned by the Nazis; ★BARKER, ★BRENTON (whose *The Genius* is a response to *Galileo*, which he adapted for the National Theatre), ★EDGAR, ★TREVOR GRIFFITHS and ★JOHN MCGRATH are dramatists who have inherited Brechtian principles of theatre; for child custody, ★DANIELS' *Neaptide* and ★RAVENHILL's *Handbag*; ★CHURCHILL's *Serious Money* has similarities to the analyses of capitalism in *Mahagonny* and *The Threepenny Opera*; *St Joan of the Stockyards* and *Simone Marchard* are treatments of a St Joan figure to be contrasted with ★SHAW's *Saint Joan* and ★ANOUILH's *The Lark*; *Happy End* has remarkable similarities to the much later musical *Guys and Dolls*; Manfred Karge, author of *Man to Man*, worked with Brecht at the Berliner Ensemble; Georg Kaiser, Ernst Toller for Expressionism.

BRENTON, Howard   [1942 –   ]
British dramatist

PLAYS INCLUDE:
Gum and Goo (1969), *Heads* (1969), *The Education of Skinny Spew* (1969), *Revenge* (1969), *Christie in Love* (1969), *Wesley* (1970), *Fruit* (1970), *Lay By* (1971, with ★BRIAN CLARK, ★TREVOR GRIFFITHS, ★DAVID HARE, ★STEPHEN POLIAKOFF, Hugh Stoddart, ★SNOO WILSON), *Scott of the Antarctic* (1971), *Hitler Dances* (1972), *England's Ireland* (1972, with TONY BICÂT, ★BRIAN CLARK, ★DAVID EDGAR, Francis Fuchs, ★DAVID HARE, ★SNOO WILSON), *A Fart for Europe* (1973, with ★DAVID EDGAR), *Magnificence* (1973), *Brassneck* (1973, with ★DAVID HARE), *The Churchill Play* (1974), *Weapons of Happiness* (1976), *Epsom Downs* (1977), *Deeds* (1978, with ★KEN CAMPBELL, ★TREVOR GRIFFITHS, ★DAVID HARE), *Sore Throats* (1979), *A Short Sharp Shock* (1980, with Tony Howard), *The Romans in Britain* (1980), *Thirteenth Night* (1981), *The Genius* (1983), *Sleeping Policemen* (1983, with ★TUNDE IKOLI), *Bloody Poetry* (1984), *Pravda* (1985, with ★DAVID HARE), *Greenland* (1988), *Iranian Nights*

(1989, with Tariq Ali), *Moscow Gold* (1990, with Tariq Ali), *Berlin Bertie* (1992), *Ugly Rumours* (1998 with Tariq Ali), *Collateral Damage* (1999, with Tariq Ali and Andy de la Tour), *Snogging Ken* (2000, with Tariq Ali and Andy de la Tour)

Although he has achieved recognition as one of Britain's leading dramatists, with plays produced by the National Theatre, RSC and even a Royal Court season in 1988 which included revivals of *Bloody Poetry* and *Sore Throats* as well as the premiere of *Greenland*, Brenton remains an independent figure committed to contemporary political satire as well as to writing for television (characteristically witty contributions to *Spooks*) and working with students. A committed socialist, Brenton tackles his themes with a cartoon-like ferocity and humour that has not diminished since his early fringe days with the Combination and Portable Theatre. Brenton's work is consistently engaged with topical issues and immediate concerns, as in *Wesley*, written to be performed in a Methodist chapel, or *Scott of the Antarctic*, performed on an ice rink. But even in his most topical plays there is an abiding concern with making people aware of the underlying nature of their situation, what represses them and what sustains them, and encouraging them to change things for the better. In *Epsom Downs* Brenton and the Joint Stock Theatre Group take the temperature of Britain on Derby Day 1977 in a kaleidoscopically inventive re-creation and interrogation of the contradictions of that event as the ghost of the suffragette Emily Davison attempts to persuade a modern woman to try to slash the picture as she did when she ran out in front of the king's horse in the 1913 Derby. The play is comically incisive in its presentation of contradictions and in its interweaving of threads within the apparently haphazard events of Derby Day. Brenton has written on the criminalisation and corruption of society, from his early *Revenge* through to *Pravda*, and on the difficulties of effecting change, from the gesture politics of *Magnificence* to the nuclear politics of *The Genius*, in which two mathematicians try to evade the forces that would turn their discoveries to destructive use. His *One Once* (1999),

workshopped with students at what is now London Metropolitan University, is an exciting exploration of the construction of identity in the context of modern ideas about cloning.

His is an uncomfortable talent, with a particular capacity for anatomising the unhealthy state of Britain today and exhuming the uncomfortable truths about the past that people would rather forget in ways that antagonise the Establishment. There was a major row over The *Romans in Britain* when moral uproar over the simulated anal rape of a Druid led to a prosecution that was ultimately abandoned. It was probably more than coincidental that *Romans* says some rather uncomfortable things about imperialism, including the current situation in Northern Ireland, since there was considerable resistance throughout the 1970s to theatrical treatments of the Irish question. From his anti-Enoch Powell version of *Measure for Measure* at Exeter in 1972, through the presentation of the ghost of Airey Neave in *A Short Sharp Shock*, to his work with Tariq Ali (*Iranian Nights* arises from the Salman Rushdie affair, and *Moscow Gold* offers a carnivalesque Meyerholdian picture of Gorbachev's rise to power and his attempts to hold together the Soviet Union against the forces of reaction and disintegration) and their topical satires with Andy de la Tour, he has been an astringent unsettler of the cosy and the complacent.

Bloody Poetry

Bloody Poetry, commissioned by the touring company Foco Novo of which Brenton was a board member, grapples with sexual and other politics, the role of the artist and the need to make revolutions in the heart and mind as much as in the body politic. Byron, ★SHELLEY, Mary Shelley and Claire Clairemont reach out for a model of existence which is beyond their grasp, at great cost to themselves and to their families. Brenton has described this as a utopian play, which has led some critics to castigate him for his male characters' sexism, but he is actually concerned with the forces, sexism included, which militate against the creation of utopia. Other forces also stand in the way: some people refused to see the play because it had 'bloody' in the title, others because of the presence of 'poetry'!

TRY THESE:
Brenton has adapted ★BRECHT, ★BÜCHNER,
★GOETHE and Manfred Karge's *The Wall Dog;*
★JONSON's *Bartholomew Fair* also takes the
nation's temperature on a holiday; ★NICHOLS' *The
National Health* does the same through an institu-
tion; ★JELLICOE's *Shelley* and ★LOCHHEAD's *Blood
and Ice* tackle the Shelleys, ★LUCIE's *Progress* for
an attempt to build a new society, flawed by old
sexisms; ★BARKER's *Scenes from an Execution,*
★DEAR's *The Art of Success* for the role of the artist
and their relationship to the body politic;
★BEATON for contemporary satire; Justin
Butcher's *The Madness of George Dubya* for Gulf
War II satire.

BREUER, Lee   [1937 –   ]
American avant-garde writer and director

PRODUCTIONS INCLUDE:
Red Horse Animation (1970), *The B-Beaver
Animation* (1974), *The Lost Ones* (1977), *The
Shaggy Dog Animation* (1977), *Prelude to
Death in Venice* (1980), *Sister Suzie Cinema*
(1980), *Red Beads* (1982). *Hajj* (1983); *The
Warrior Ant* (1988), *Lear* (1990), *An Epidog*
(1995), *Ecce Porco* (2002), *Red Beads* (2002)

In 1970 Breuer was a co-founder of Mabou
Mines with David Warrilow, JoAnne Akalaitis,
Philip Glass and Breuer's sometime wife,
actress Ruth Maleczech. Long acclaimed as a
leading experimental theatre group, the company's work is intellectual in conception,
drawing inspiration from various sources and
often blending multimedia staging with heavy
use of linguistic play.

Breuer travelled through Europe during
the 1960s, and much of his early work reflects
the alienating effects of the European avant-
garde. In recent years, Breuer's work has
drawn heavily upon the intermingling of
diverse cultures to shed new light on both traditional and innovative material. His multicultural stagings have achieved mixed results
ranging from spectacular fusing of disparate
elements to what one critic has labelled
'grotesque hybrids'. His 1982 collaboration
with composer Bob Telson, *Gospel at Colonus,*
a sung gospel version of Greek tragedy, was a
stunning illumination of the deepest spiritual
elements in ★SOPHOCLES. His *Lear,* with all

the sexual roles reversed, featured Ruth
Maleczech as Queen Lear with her three sons.
Frank Episale's review of *Ecce Porco* gives
some idea of Breuer's work: 'Over the course
of four hours, the audience is treated to a
Bunraku-style puppet named John who mas-
turbates while having phone sex with a dog, a
flying tantric sex therapist, a heartfelt monologue from Marge Simpson, and a piggish
man named Porco who re-enacts scenes from
the lives of Meyerhold and Orson Welles.'

TRY THESE:
★GENET for early inspiration; ★BECKETT,
★HANDKE and ★IONESCO for redefining the
range of theatrical possibility; ★BOGART,
★FOREMAN, San Francisco Mime Troupe, Peter
Sellars Robert Wilson, The Wooster Group,
Meredith Monk for other pre-eminent figures in
the American avant-garde; Laurie Anderson for
multimedia performance.

BRIDIE, James (Osborne Henry
Mavor)   [1888 – 1951]
Scottish doctor and dramatist

PLAYS INCLUDE:
The Sunlight Sonata (1928, as Mary
Henderson), *The Anatomist* (1930), *Tobias
and the Angel* (1930), *Jonah and the Whale*
(1932), *A Sleeping Clergyman* (1933), *Colonel
Wotherspoon* (1934), *Mary Read* (1934), *The
Black Eye* (1935), *Storm in a Teacup* (1936,
adapted from Bruno Frank), *Susannah and
the Elders* (1937), *The King of Nowhere*
(1938), *What They Say* (1941), *Mr Bolfry*
(1943), *It Depends What You Mean* (1944),
The Forrigan Reel (1944), *Dr Angelus* (1947),
Daphne Laureola (1949), *Mr Gillie* (1950),
The Baikie Charivari (1952), *Meeting at
Night* (1954)

Bridie's plays range from biblical and hagiographic tales to a play based on the Edinburgh
body-snatchers Burke and Hare (*The
Anatomist*), to the episodic history of an eighteenth-century woman pirate (*Mary Read*).
Mr Bolfry, one of his most successful plays,
tells how the Devil visits a Scots minister in
the shape of another clergyman. Together
they form an alliance against non-believers,
but when they meet later as antagonists the

issue is undecided. The minister returns home thinking himself triumphant, only to see the Devil's umbrella rise and stalk slowly from his house. *A Sleeping Clergyman* is a study of heredity through three generations, which shows that though 'evil' may persist through seduction, blackmail and murder, 'good' can reappear just when the world most needs it – in this case medical genius. Although it tends to be individual perform-ances in Bridie's plays that people remember, rather than the plays themselves, they are still occasionally revived, particularly in Scotland, where Bridie was a co-founder of the Glasgow Citizens' Theatre, and instrumental in estab-lishing the Royal Scottish Academy of Music (now the Academy of Music and Drama).

TRY THESE:
★FRY for religious themes; ★CHEKHOV as another dramatist who brought his doctor's observation of character to his work; ★GOOCH's *The Women-Pirates Ann Bonney and Mary Read*; ★BARRIE, as a Scottish contemporary; ★HELLMAN for discus-sions of moral values; ★O'MALLEY's *Talk of The Devil*, ★DEKKER, ★FORD and ★ROWLEY's *The Witch of Edmonton*, ★HAVEL's *Temptation* for dev-ilish visitations.

BRIGHOUSE, Harold   [1882 – 1958]
British dramatist

PLAYS INCLUDE:
Dealing in Futures (1910), *Lonesome Like* (1911), *Graft* (1912, originally entitled *The Polygon*), *Garside's Career* (1914), *Hobson's Choice* (1915), *Zack* (1916)

Part of the 'Manchester School' of dramatists, Brighouse wrote and produced some seventy plays, mostly realistic and set in Lancashire. The most well known of these is *Hobson's Choice*, a play 'built like an iron girder' (Michael Billington), whose heroine, the strong-minded and down-to-earth Maggie Hobson, thirty years old and thought 'past the marrying age', marries the shy but talented boot-maker Willie Mossop out of hand (he not having much say in the matter), and with him takes over the town's boot-making busi-ness from her heavy father. The play is still revived in Britain, most recently in 2002, and

the comedy *Zack* played at the Royal Exchange, Manchester in 1976 and 1986 with some success. Several of his one-act plays, such as *Lonesome Like*, would easily bear revival if anyone did one-act plays any more.

TRY THESE:
★HOUGHTON for another 'Manchester School' dramatist; Elizabeth Baker's *Chains* and Githa Sowerby's *Rutherford and Son* for contemporary women dramatists' views of similar issues; ★DE ANGELIS's *Iron Mistress* for a modern angle; ★GUPTA for a contemporary version of *Hobson's Choice*.

BRYDEN, Bill   [1942 –   ]
Scottish dramatist, director and filmmaker

PLAYS INCLUDE:
Willie Rough (1972), *Benny Lynch* (1974), *Old Movies* (1977), *Civilians* (1981), *The Ship* (1990), *The Big Picnic* (1994).

Bryden's plays are only a small part of his work in theatre, television and film. As Associate Director at Edinburgh's Lyceum (1971–4), Bryden staged *Willie Rough*, deriving from his grandfather's experience, an examination of working-class life against the backdrop of ship-yard politics between the wars. *Benny Lynch* was again about the aspirations and daily drudge-and-grudge of the working classes, represented by this 'bonniest o' fechters' who rose to world status only to end, exploited and discarded, in the gutter. In 1981 he wrote and directed *Civilians*, a fond, anecdotal glimpse of 1940s Greenock life, for the (short-lived) Scottish Theatre Company. As Head of Drama Television with BBC Scotland he encouraged writers such as Peter MacDougall, ★IAN HEGGIE and ★JOHN BYRNE and at the National Theatre he directed an enormously successful promenade version of the medieval *Mysteries*. Conceived as part of Glasgow's year-long thrash as European City of Culture in 1990, *The Ship* was a spectacularly staged celebration of Clyde shipbuilding in its last years of great-ness. A disused riverside engine shed became an ad hoc theatre and, thanks to designer William Dudley, the inner decks and shell of a liner-in-progress encompassed the performing space. The action, such as it was (mostly short scenes of anecdotal exchange between workers interspersed with jock-rock music), culminated in a cunning *coup de théâtre*, the apparent launching of the boat. The sheer persuasive showmanship of all this did much to offset the banalities of the script, which reduced the hard men and hard times of post-war Clydeside to a series of ciphers and clichés. Critical reaction was mixed, but *The Ship* proved one of the most popular events of Glasgow's 1990 programme and confirmed Bryden's charismatic image as a shaker and mover within theatre.

TRY THESE:
★ CORRIE's *In Time o' Strife* (1927) portrays a Fife mining community during the last days of the General Strike; Ena Lamont Stewart's *Men Should Weep* and Benedict Scott's *Lambs of God* both show darker sides to tenement life in the 1930s and 1940s; Roddy McMillan's *The Bevellers* is a lively, shrewd depiction of men at work – the 'bevelling' is the finishing edge on mirrors;
★ BOLGER's *The Lament for Arthur Cleary* as an Irish equivalent of the exile's nostalgia for home;
★ HARRISON adapted the *Mysteries* for Bryden's production; Keith Dewhurst's adaptation of *Lark Rise to Candleford* for promenade performance.

BÜCHNER, Georg   [1813 – 37]
German dramatist

PLAYS INCLUDE:
Danton's Death (1835), *Leonce and Lena* (1836), *Woyzeck* (1836)

Although his plays were not performed until many years after his death, Büchner is one of the major influences in contemporary world drama. Somehow he managed to foreshadow many of the great theatrical movements of the twentieth century: Epic theatre, Surrealism, Expressionism, and the Theatre of the Absurd. The sense of history as a major force dominates his work, as does society as the destroyer of the individual. His principal characters struggle unsuccessfully to communicate their feelings until they recognise their helplessness and incomprehension in the face of the forces that destroy them.

The son of a doctor, Büchner studied medicine at the Universities of Strasburg and Giessen. Strongly influenced by the revolu-

tionary 'Young Germany' movement, he developed his own political philosophy, which turned its back on the educated classes, placing its hopes instead with the peasantry. After his involvement with an abortive attempt to overthrow the government of the state of Hesse in 1834, he withdrew from revolutionary politics. He wrote *Danton's Death* in 1835 and the following year became a lecturer in anatomy at the University of Zurich. He worked on *Woyzeck* that year, drawing on the details of a controversial court case, but died of typhoid fever in 1837 with *Woyzeck* still not complete. In *Woyzeck* the central character, Woyzeck, is a repressed and oppressed soldier, crushed by his social superiors, goaded by his mistress, tormented by his own sense of guilt. Although Büchner never put the play into a final form, each of its scenes is remarkably powerful, and cumulatively they create an overpowering atmosphere of alienation and bleakness. Woyzeck ultimately perishes, but in highly ambiguous circumstances which deliberately confuse suicide and accident. Berg's operatic treatment, *Wozzeck*, owes its title to a misreading of the manuscript.

TRY THESE:
Kafka's *Metamorphosis* and *The Trial* for a sense of the individual being crushed; ★ ABBOTT's *Three Men on a Horse* for a more light-hearted treatment of the little man at the mercy of external forces; ★ MILLER's *Death of a Salesman*, ★ O'NEILL for individuals crushed by social forces; Büchner was much influenced by ★ SHAKESPEARE; his plays in turn influenced such apparently opposed figures as ★ ARTAUD and ★ BRECHT; Ariane Mnouchkine's *1789* is the French Revolution play; see also ★ GEMS' adaptation of Stanislawa Przybsiewska's *The Danton Affair*, which itself was highly influenced by *Danton's Death*; ★ WEISS's *Marat/Sade* for other aspects of the French Revolution; Linda Mussmann for an extended engagement with *Danton's Death*.

BUFFINI, Moira   [1967 –   ]
British dramatist

PLAYS INCLUDE:
Jordan (1992, with Anna Reynolds), *Blavatsky's Tower* (1997), *Gabriel* (1997), *Doomsday Girl* (1998), *Silence* (1999), *The*

Games Room (2000), *Loveplay* (2001), *Dinner* (2002)

After studying drama and English at university, Buffini trained as an actor, winning a *Time Out* award for her performance in *Jordan*, a monologue based on the true story of a woman who killed her infant son after being abused by her husband. *Gabriel* centres on reactions to the mysterious eponymous character, washed up naked on a beach in wartime Guernsey with no memory and no identity. *Silence* is a first-millennium comedy about non-stereotypical knights and maidens, while *Loveplay* is a satirical history of two thousand years of sex in the same place. *Dinner* is a darkly comic account of the dinner party from hell complete with the stranger who has crashed his van just outside the house and a Pinteresquely menacing waiter. Buffini appears to be developing a strong comic voice but as yet the jury is out on whether she can sustain fully worked-out dramatic structures to deliver her perceptions.

TRY THESE:

★ AYCKBOURN's *Communicating Doors*, ★ SCHNITZLER's *La Ronde*, ★ SIMON for variations on sex over the years/with different partners; ★ BARKER's *The Castle* for a different take on the medieval period; ★ ISITT, ★ SENECA, ★ SHAKESPEARE's *Titus Andronicus*, ★ WHITEHEAD for bad culinary experiences; ★ CHRISTIE's *The Mousetrap* for a stranger with a broken-down car.

BULGAKOV, Mikhail Afanasievich   [1891 – 1940]
Russian novelist, journalist and dramatist

PLAYS INCLUDE:
The Days of the Turbins (1926, a dramatisation of his novel *The White Guard*), *The Crimson Island* (1927), *Flight* (1928), *Zoyka's Apartment* (1928), *Dead Souls* (1928, from ★ GOGOL), *Molière* (1936), *Don Quixote* (1940), *The Last Days of Pushkin* (published 1943)

Born in Kiev, Bulgakov qualified as a doctor, and became a professional writer in 1919. Pavel Markov, the Moscow Arts Theatre's dramaturg, asked him to turn his novel *The White Guard* (about the horrors of the civil war in Kiev, and unusually sympathetic to the White side) into a play. At first delighted, Bulgakov was soon disconcerted by the cutting and reshaping required to suit the company and the changing of the title and the ending to suit the censor (the Bolsheviks are welcomed to the strains of *The Internationale*). He went on to write thirteen more plays and to become arguably the most important Soviet dramatist of the period. His theatrical career was blighted by *Molière*, in which the contemporary relevance of references to the frustrations of the artist controlled by the State were only too obvious. After four years in rehearsal, it was taken off after less than a week. But Bulgakov had his revenge in the very thinly disguised, very unkind and very funny accounts of the Moscow Arts Theatre and of Stanislavsky's system, in his novel *Black Snow* (written 1936–7, published 1965). The best section of the book is perhaps the instruction to the author to write in older roles (his play has no character over twenty-eight, but the company includes nobody under fifty). *The White Guard* is perhaps his best-known play in Britain; but adaptations of his novels *The Master and Margarita* and *The Heart of a Dog* have been successful. The National Theatre staged Keith Dewhurst's adaptation of *Black Snow* in 1991 and *Flight* in a version by ★ RON HUTCHINSON in 1998. The Old Red Lion staged the British premiere of *Zoyka's Apartment* in 1999.

TRY THESE:
★ ARBUZOV, ★ GORKY, ★ MAYAKOVSKY for other well-known Soviet dramatists; ★ MOLIÈRE for his own plays; on the theme of state control and artistic freedom, musical variations in ★ STOPPARD's *Every Good Boy Deserves Favour* and ★ POWNALL's *Master Class*, with Shostakovich and Prokofiev as characters.

BULLINS, Ed   [1935 –   ]
American dramatist

PLAYS INCLUDE:
The Theme of Blackness (1966), *The Electronic Nigger* (1968), *The Gentleman Caller* (1969), *The Duplex* (1970), *The Fabulous Miss Marie* (1970), *The Taking of Miss Janie* (1975), *Leavings* (1980), *American Griot* (1990),

Salaam, Huey Newton, Salaam (1991), *City Preacher* (2001)

Continual torment surrounds Bullins' drama as he presents a sceptical, and even cynical, view of the dichotomy of black participation in a white, intellectual, middle-class community, and the exclusion from that life of the majority of blacks whose life in the inner-city slum plays out its own self-awareness. *The Electronic Nigger* dramatises the collective recognition of black artists and intellectuals of the 1960s – a rebellious voice that refuses the stamp of approval by the white literary establishment. *The Duplex* accomplishes Bullins' intent to write for a black audience, to expose the tragedy of the ghetto with a dramatic structure that is more about life than theatre. Scenes assault, conflicts abide, resolutions are sparse. As with the black ghetto, the play's end provokes frustration with no relief in sight. Bullins exposes the corruption of white values that represses and denies any respectability to being black in America. Bullins' idiom clearly articulates the voice of black power that is resolute with future confrontation and promised change.

TRY THESE:
★BARAKA traces a similar evolutionary black awareness; ★KENNEDY's *Funnyhouse of a Negro* struggles with black identity. ★HANSBERRY's *A Raisin in the Sun* places her black family in a middle-class district, struggling for acceptance; ★WOLFE also shows the dichotomy of black participation in white society through astringent satire.

BURKE, Gregory   [1968 –   ]
Scottish dramatist

PLAYS INCLUDE:
Gagarin Way (2001), *The Straits* (2003)

Burke, a Dunfermline-born dropout from Stirling University, is proof that occasionally showbiz clichés can come true. His is the one about the writer who sends in the unsolicited script that goes all the way to the National Theatre. Burke sent *Gagarin Way* to the Traverse Theatre Edinburgh in 1998; John Tiffany, the literary director, liked it and it

won a Fringe first at the 2001 Edinburgh Festival before a run at the National Theatre and in the West End. Finally, Burke was declared to be the 'Most Promising Dramatist' of 2001. *Gagarin Way* takes its title from a street named after the first man in space in a Fife mining village that was a communist stronghold. The play deals with two disillusioned workers in an electronics factory who decide to kidnap a visiting manager as a protest against the way globalised business treats its workers as expendable commodities. However, he turns out not to be the faceless international capitalist they are expecting but a local man who has become a successful player in the global market. As the *Daily Telegraph* put it: 'It's slick, funny, original and violent (both in language and in deed), and above all it is grippingly theatrical . . . Great jokes collide with Marxist dialectic, brutal violence is combined with hilarious cock-ups, while the dialogue has a foul-mouthed vigour that puts one in mind of ★DAVID MAMET'.

As Burke said: 'I wanted to write something about the twentieth century and I wanted to write something about economics and I wanted to write about men . . . I didn't expect it to be a comedy but when you consider the themes which emerged while I wrote it – Marxist and Hegelian theories of history, anarchism, psychopathology, existentialism, mental illness, political terrorism, nihilism, construct theory, globalisation and the crisis in masculinity – then it couldn't really be anything else'.

TRY THESE:
★CORRIE for Scottish mining communities; ★EDGAR's *That Summer* for the 1984 miners' strike; ★FO's *Trumpets and Raspberries* for political kidnapping; ★PINTER's *The Dumb Waiter* for hit men; ★SARTRE and ★GENET are discussed in the play; reviewers compared Burke to ★BUTTERWORTH and ★MCDONAGH.

BUSCH, Charles   [1955 –   ]
American writer and performer

PLAYS INCLUDE:
Theodora, She-Bitch of Byzantium (1984), *Times Square Angel* (1984), *Vampire Lesbians of Sodom* (1984), *Gidget Goes Psychotic*

(1986, later changed to *Psycho Beach Party*), *Pardon My Inquisition*, or *Kiss the Blood Off My Castenets* (1986), *The Lady in Question* (1988), *Red Scare on Sunset* (1991), *You Should Be So Lucky* (1994), *Queen Amarantha* (1997), *Shanghai Moon* (1999), *Die, Mommy, Die!* (1999), *The Tale of the Allergist's Wife* (2000)

All of Busch's camp comedies are filled with suspense, transformations and redemptions. The heroines, played by Busch in drag, range from vampire show-business queens, to the multiple personalities of Chicklet (a stand-in for Gidget), to Gertrude Garnet a concert pianist. Hollywood provides endless fascination for Busch. *Times Square Angel* sends up film noir as he plays Irish O'Flanagan, a 1940s torch singer. *The Lady in Question* spoofs World War II anti-Nazi films and enjoyed a lengthy off-Broadway run. In *Red Scare on Sunset*, the audience finds itself in the strange position of cheering on a heroine whose politics are repulsive (she is a right-wing McCarthyite who rats on her husband), and critics largely seemed to feel this ambiguity gave the play a depth his previous work may have lacked. *Shanghai Moon* and *Die, Mommy, Die!* target exotic eastern melodrama and the Grand Guignol films of the 1960s respectively. All Busch's characters satirise Hollywood stereotypes; his dialogue is filled with the pungent humour of psychosexual clichés and the occasional hype of comic-book smut. Busch's women avoid the punch of cynicism and animosity that often accompany the convention of the drag show. Rather he allows the presentation of the woman as glamorous and heroic to be the liberation of a whole vocabulary of expression that is less political and more aesthetic.

TRY THESE:

★LUDLAM's *Theater of the Ridiculous* for camp that explores sexual ambiguity: the drag queen with pathos can be found in *La Cage aux Folles* and ★FIERSTEIN's *Torch Song Trilogy*; ★EICHELBERGER for a unique blend of camp with high art; ★BARTLETT's *Sarrasine* and *A Vision of Love Revealed in Sleep*; ★O'BRIEN's *The Rocky Horror Picture Show* for another version of camp.

BUTLER, Leo
British dramatist

PLAYS INCLUDE:
Made of Stone (2000), *Redundant* (2001), *Devotion* (2002)

Sheffield-born Butler won the George Devine award for *Redundant*, his second play. It is a familiar Royal Court portrait of life in the grim estates of the inner city with teenage pregnancy, drugs and social security payments providing the context for an astutely observed complex central character.

TRY THESE:

★BOND, ★CARTWRIGHT, ★DUNBAR, ★WYNNE are among the dramatists who have covered similar territory on the Royal Court stage.

BUTTERWORTH, Jez   [1969 –   ]
British dramatist

PLAYS INCLUDE:
Mojo (1995), *The Night Heron* (2002)

Butterworth's first play, *Mojo*, was a huge success, winning Olivier, George Devine and *Evening Standard* awards for its author with its bleakly savage account of Soho low life in the 1950s. Critics praised Butterworth for creating 'a pulsating, rhythmic sort of diction' (*Evening Standard*) and for his skill in imagining a Tarantino-like world of skulduggery in the music business as vested interests clash over the fate of a pop singer. The subsequent film was less successful but Butterworth's second play, *The Night Heron*, suggested that he was more than a creator of superior gangster pastiche. Set in the Fens, it blends a raft of narrative threads into a complex weave of resonances. Two former gardeners at a Cambridge college and their lodger, a former inmate of Holloway prison, try to make ends meet by winning a poetry competition but as they can't actually write a good poem they kidnap a student to write one for them. Like the eponymous bird, the characters are in the wrong place at the wrong time: the college was Corpus Christi, Andrew Marvell's *The Garden* makes an appearance and there is a strong sense that these are characters expelled from Eden and searching for redemption.

TRY THESE:

Critics compared *Mojo* to ★BECKETT on speed (*Observer*) and ★TOURNEUR's *The Revenger's Tragedy*; ★ACKLAND for *Soho*; ★PINTER for parallels; ★RUDKIN's *Afore Night Come* for rural menace; ★BOND's *The Pope's Wedding* and ★CHURCHILL's *Fen* for other views of East Anglian rural isolation.

BYRNE, John   [1940 –   ]
Scottish artist, designer and dramatist

PLAYS INCLUDE:

Writer's Cramp (1977), *The Slab Boys* (1978. also known as *Paisley Patterns*), *Cuttin' a Rug* (1979; originally *The Loveliest Night of the Year*, also performed on radio as *The Staffie* and as *Threads*), *Normal Service* (1979), *Still Life* (1982), *Candy Kisses* (1984), *Colquhoun and Macbryde* (1988), *The Government Inspector* (adapted from ★GOGOL, 1997)

Widely known to British television audiences in the 1980s after the success of his series *Tutti Frutti* and *Your Cheatin' Heart*, Byrne has been delighting theatre audiences in Scotland, England and the USA for years with his ironic observations on literary pretension (in *Writer's Cramp*) and everyday working life in *The Slab Boys* trilogy, which starts with adolescence in *The Slab Boys* itself, takes us through the staff dance in *Cuttin' a Rug*, and ends in the cemetery in *Still Life*. Byrne trained at the Glasgow School of Art and his work reveals in its different moods both a painter's eye for detailed observation and a cartoonist's gift for caricature. The interest tends to be less in plot and more in the presentation of memorable characters. In recent years he has concentrated on his work as a visual artist, although the *Slab Boys* trilogy is still produced in Scotland.

TRY THESE.

★HASTINGS' *Tom and Viv* and ★PINTER's *No Man's Land* offer contrasting views of the literary world; ★LUCIE's view of an advertising agency in *Fashion* makes an interesting comparison with the television station of *Normal Service*; ★WESKER's *Trilogy* is one of the best known modern set of linked plays, ▲HEGGIE for robust Glaswegian dialect.

C

CALDERÓN DE LA BARCA, Pedro [1600 – 81]
Spanish dramatist

PLAYS INCLUDE:
The Phantom Lady (1629), *The Constant Prince* (1629), *Life is a Dream* (1635), *The Physician of His Honour* (1635), *Three Judgements in One* (1636?), *The Mayor of Zalamea* (1643), *The Great Theatre of the World* (1645), *The Painter of his own Dishonour* (1650)

Calderón is the most polished Spanish dramatist of the Golden Age – less prolific than ★LOPE DE VEGA, he borrowed freely from his predecessors, tightened up plots and characterisation, and added a peculiarly intense line in passionate conflicts with often shocking outcomes. He studied for the priesthood, but soon took up duelling, women and poetry. His first known play was staged at the Spanish court when he was twenty-three, and he claimed to have written about 120 secular plays, eighty *autos sacramentales* (the Spanish form of morality play, performed on great church occasions) in his later and more pious years, and twenty minor pieces. He is also credited with the invention of the *zarzuela*, the classic Spanish musical form. His range covers comedies of manners, cloak-and-sword plays, historical plays and honour-and-jealousy plays such as *The Physician of His Honour*, his most notorious 'honour' play, in which a husband has his wife's blood drained on the mere suspicion of adultery, and the King not merely commends his action but offers our hero another bride. *The Mayor of Zalamea*, based on an earlier work attributed to ★LOPE DE VEGA, is the story of a Spanish peasant whose daughter is raped by an aristocratic captain, and who then becomes the Mayor and sentences the captain to garrotting – all are agreed that the captain deserved it and that justice was done, but of course the girl still ends up in a nunnery. *Life is a Dream*, commonly thought his masterpiece, is a complex and unusual play about the Polish Crown Prince Sigismondo, hidden away in a tower in a wood by his father because of a prophecy that he would grow up as a monster of cruelty, and his gradual education and emergence as a wise ruler. The plot incorporates philosophical discussion of reason versus natural impulses and free will defeating superstitious prophecy.

TRY THESE:
Von Hofmannsthal and Max Reinhardt for an updating of *The Great Theatre of the World*, Grotowski for his version of *The Constant Prince*; ★HANDKE's *Kaspar* for mysterious upbringing; ★CAMERON's *Strugglers*, Eve Lewis's *Ficky Stingers*, ★MASTROSIMONE's *Extremities* for very different handlings of rape; ★LORCA for later Spanish drama.

CAMERON, Richard [1948 –]
British dramatist and director

PLAYS INCLUDE:
Handle with Care (1985), *Strugglers* (1988), *The Moon's The Madonna* (1989), *Can't Stand Up for Falling Down* (1990), *Pond Life* (1992), *Not Fade Away* (1993), *Almost Grown* (1994), *The Mortal Ash* (1994), *All of You Mine* (1997) *The Glee Club* (2002)

A sensitive chronicler of the joys and sorrows of adolescent experience with a sophisticated eye for structure, Cameron won the *Sunday Times* Playwriting Award three times, but his concern for childish things and the unabashed kindness of spirit of his plays did not attract professional directors or adult audiences until *Can't Stand Up for Falling Down*. This is the story of the damage wrought on three women by one boorish, unthinking man, who never actually appears in the play. The women tell their tales in interweaving monologues: Jodie watches as the man bullies to death her simple-minded childhood friend. Ruby becomes pregnant and then is deserted by him, and Lynette is trapped in a violent marriage with him. A loose narrative that ranges widely over place and time dovetails to a thriller-like conclusion that is devastating and yet poignantly optimistic as the three women come together for mutual support. His writing has a lightness and sureness of touch, an emotional honesty that is tender and lyrical but also encompasses cruelty and suffering, and does not shy away from difficult subjects. For the National Student Drama Company he wrote and directed *The Moon's the Madonna*, about child abuse, which was short-listed for the Independent Theatre Award, and *Strugglers*, set in a special school, which won the *Sunday Times* Award. In *Strugglers*, a seemingly meandering plot portraying the day-to-day concerns of a group of teenagers just about to leave school builds in complexity and momentum as the Real World encroaches bringing with it heartbreak, disillusionment, failure and even rape. *The Glee Club*, set in 1962 Doncaster, charts the challenges posed to an older generation of the working class by a new generation, new music, homosexuality, and the breakdown of the old mining communities in the face of new economic realities.

TRY THESE:
★ DUNN's *Steaming*, ★ GEMS' *Dusa, Fish, Stas and Vi*, Tony Roper's *The Steamie* shows women supporting each other under crisis; for offstage presences ★ BECKETT's *Waiting for Godot*; Helen Cooper's *Mrs Vershinin* gave flesh to the offstage wife of ★ CHEKHOV's *Three Sisters*; for groups of young people, ★ BENT's *Bad Company* ★ BOND's *Saved*; ★ POWNALL for plays centred on music.

CAMPBELL, Ken   [1941 –   ]
British director, dramatist and actor

PLAYS INCLUDE:
Old King Cole (1969), *Jack Shepherd* (1969, also known as *Anything You Say Will Be Twisted*), *Bendigo* (1974, with Dave Hill and Andy Andrews), *The Great Caper* (1974), *Walking Like Geoffrey* (1975; with Dave Hill and Andy Andrews), *Skungpoonery* (1975), *School For Clowns* (1975), *Illuminatus* (1977), *Deeds* (1978, with ★ HOWARD BRENTON, ★ DAVID HARE, ★ TREVOR GRIFFITHS), *The Hitch-hikers Guide to the Galaxy* (1979), *The Third Policeman* (1980), *War with the Newts* (1981), *Recollections of a Furtive Nudist* (1988), *Pigspurt* (1992), *Jamais Vu* (1993), *Mystery Bruises* (1994), *Choice Chunks* (1996), *Theatre Stories* (1997), *Violin Time* (1997), *Makbed* (1998), *History of Comedy Part One* (2000), *If I Ruled the National Theatre* (2001), *Children of Bisu* (2002)

Campbell's directorial debut – organising the shallow end for the Summer Water Show at Bournemouth Baths – heralded a brilliant career as Britain's champion of anarchic fun. Ken Campbell's Roadshow toured to bars and theatres throughout Britain with a uniquely eccentric entertainment of staggering inventiveness coupled with red-noses and ferret-down-the-trousers interludes. Gleefully iconoclastic, Campbell recognised no boundaries, taking on the challenge of the *Illuminatus* books, triumphantly portraying Howard the talking dolphin as an operatic tenor, and adapting Flann O'Brien and Douglas Adams for the stage. In *War with the Newts* the hilarity included a newt family called Olivia Newt, and John. In Michael Coveney's words, Campbell is 'a master of the ebulliently childish caper' who reaches for any and every theatrical device without regard to consistency or convention, demanding that the audience keep up with the crazed inventiveness on the stage. His one-man shows continued to enliven the theatrical scene throughout the 1990s and he even appeared in ★ YASMINA REZA's *Art*. *Makbed* is a pidgin version of ★ SHAKESPEARE's *Macbeth*.

TRY THESE:
Rose English, ★ IONESCO, ★ JARRY, ★ SIMPSON and ★ SNOO WILSON share something of Campbell's anarchic surreal inventiveness; ★ STOPPARD for another version of *Macbeth*; ★ CASDAGLI, ★ DAVID HOLMAN ★ LAVERY, ★ SHEPPHARD, ★ DAVID WOOD, Stephen Wyatt are other British dramatists who have written for children.

CAPEK, Karel   [1890 – 1938]
Czech novelist and dramatist

PLAYS INCLUDE:
The Robber (1920), *R.U.R.* (1921), *The White Plague* (1937), *The Power and the Glory* (1937), *The Mother* (1938); and with his brother Josef, *The Insect Play* (1922), *The Makropoulos Secret* (1922), *Adam with Creator* (1927)

A socialist and pacifist, Capek's second play *R.U.R.* (Rossum's Universal Robots) gave the world the word 'robot' and offered a protest against the dehumanising elements of mechanisation and industrial capitalism. Its final moments, when two advanced robots (androids as we would now call them) have emotions of love and sacrifice, with the suggestion that humans have a second chance in this new Adam and Eve, have been frequently copied, although Czechs consider Capek's last antifascist plays his best. *The Mother*, produced only months before Hitler marched into Czechoslovakia, shows a small nation invaded by a fascist state, provoking civil war. The mother, already a soldier's widow, has a pilot son killed in an air crash, two other sons – one fascist, one communist – die in a feud, and she sees her last son, an anti-violence poet, go off to fight. Capek's love of freedom was in the end stronger than his pacifism but he died soon after, three months before his brother was taken off to Belsen by the Nazis. *The White Plague* has been staged in the USA as a response to the AIDS epidemic.

The Insect Play
John Gielgud, who played the Chief Butterfly in the British premiere, declared this was a part almost certain to ruin the reputation of an actor, but Capek's expressionist vision of human greed, violence and self-interest presented through parallel behaviour in the insect world can still be disturbingly effective. When the insects' physical characteristics are used to highlight their human counterparts, the play has the harsh reality of a Steve Bell cartoon. The presentation of this parallel world and its tramp observer – the only human character – has precursors in fabulists from Aesop to Swift but its bite is closer to that of ★BRECHT and less easy to sweeten.

TRY THESE:
★EDGAR, ★GALSWORTHY and ★SHAW for presentations of industrial relations; for animal fables, ★AUDEN's *On the Frontier*, ★BERKOFF's adaptation of Kafka's *Metamorphosis*, ★TERRY JOHNSON's *Cries from the Mammal House*, ★TOM MCGRATH's *Animal*, adaptations of George Orwell's *Animal Farm*; ★BENNETT's *Kafka's Dick* for a similar use of disturbing and fabulous metaphor.

CARR, Marina   [1946 –   ]
Irish dramatist

PLAYS INCLUDE:
Low in the Dark (1989), *Deer's Surrender* (1990), *Ullaloo* (1991), *This Love Thing* (1991), *The Mai* (1994), *Portia Coughlan* (1995), *By the Bog of Cats* (1998), *On Rafferty's Hill* (2000), *Ariel* (2002)

Carr has established herself as major voice in both Irish and British theatre with a sequence of very dark plays in which there are recurring themes of families trapped in self-destructive patterns of behaviour across the generations, absent family members casting shadows over the present, the revelation of past horrors, incest, deaths foreshadowed or enacted out of narrative sequence. The Irish Midlands cast a bleak shadow over plays that are haunted, sometimes literally so, by the ghosts of the dead but also by myths both familial and drawn from classical, Christian and Irish legend. For example, *The Merchant of Venice* provides Portia Coughlan with her first name, the river she lives by and her suitors, but part of her husband Raphael's attraction is that like her dead twin Gabriel he has the name of an archangel, while Carr herself has said that the plot of *By the Bog of Cats* is 'completely Medea'.

Although Carr has had some difficulties with naturalistic reservations, particularly in respect of *On Rafferty's Hill* and *Ariel*, and there has been some unease, given historical representations of the Irish on stage, about the grotesque picture she paints of an introverted rural society, for most audiences and critics there is a mythic power in her work that outweighs its tendency to melodramatic theatricality.

TRY THESE:

Carr has expressed her admiration for
★CHEKHOV, ★IBSEN, ★O'NEILL and ★TENNESSEE
WILLIAMS; ★EURIPIDES for *Medea*; incest links
Portia Coughlan to the *Oedipus* story, as treated
by ★SOPHOCLES (Portia's husband's limp relates
him to other Oedipal figures like Stanley in
★PINTER's *Birthday Party*; ★SYNGE (particularly
Riders to the Sea for tales of the death of fisher-
men to compare with *The Mai*); ★YEATS for
dramas of Irish myth.

CARTWRIGHT, Jim   [1958 –   ]
British dramatist

PLAYS INCLUDE:

Road (1986), *Bed* (1989), *Two* (1990), *The
Rise and Fall of Little Voice* (1992), *I Licked a
Slag's Deodorant* (1996), *Hard Fruit* (2000)

Bolton-born Cartwright's first play, *Road*,
called the most exciting play of the decade in
Britain, owed much to Simon Curtis's clever
promenade production at the Royal Court
Upstairs in 1986. Constructed round a series
of vignettes, Cartwright's raw, grim account
of unemployment in Thatcher's Britain, seen
through the eyes of its narrator Scully and the
inhabitants of a Lancashire street, certainly
signalled the arrival of an angry new voice,
albeit one capable of capturing great tender-
ness. The play became a multiple award
winner, although its exuberant use of
language masked what some felt was its formlessness. Jim Hiley in the *Listener* worried that
there was barely a hint of dignity or sense of
resistance in the characters, and Ros Asquith
in the *Observer* noted that in this 'Under Milk
Wood for the Great Unemployed, men talk
ideas, women only sex'. Recent revivals have
tended to confirm their judgements.

If echoes of Dylan Thomas ran through
his first play, his second, *Bed*, with its stream-
of consciousness monologues about sleep
and dreams and its surrealistic talking head,
found itself likened to ★BECKETT (such references would presumably be denied by
Cartwright who claimed at the time he'd only
ever read four books in his life). In *Two*
Cartwright reverts to a series of working-class
cameos enacted by a pub owner and his wife
in marital difficulties. *The Rise and Fall of*

Little Voice (filmed as *Little Voice*, 1998) centres on the shy teenager with a superb singing
voice (played by Jane Horrocks), her relationship with her mother and the exploitative theatrical agent who sees her as a meal ticket. *I
Licked a Slag's Deodorant* returns to the
underclass with its addict-prostitute and her
client adrift in an uncaring world, while *Hard
Fruit* explores male bodybuilding.

TRY THESE:

★HEGGIE's *A Wholly Healthy Glasgow* and
★SYNGE's *Playboy of the Western World* for bold-
ness of dialect; ★DYLAN THOMAS's *Under Milk
Wood*, ★MCCAFFERTY's *Scenes from the Big Picture*,
★WILDER's *Our Town* for a specific sense of place;
★OSBORNE's *Look Back in Anger* and *The
Entertainer* for 1950s national vitriol; for more
views of Thatcher's Britain, ★ALRAWI,
★CHURCHILL, ★HARE, ★HOLBOROUGH, ★LUCIE;
★GEMS' *Piaf* for exploited singers; Manfred
Karge's *The Conquest of the South Pole* for
unemployment.

CASDAGLI, Penny   [1948 –   ]
British dramatist (also known as Maro Green)

PLAYS INCLUDE:

Wolfchildren (1980), *This Way or That?* (1982),
The Green Ginger Smuggler (1984), *Thumbs
Up!* (1985), *More* (1985, with Caroline
Griffin), *The Memorial Gardens* (1987, with
Caroline Griffin), *Pardon, Mr Punch!* (1987),
The Beggar in the Palace (1988, with Caroline
Griffin). *Mortal* (1990, with Caroline Griffin),
Aesop's the Fable Man (1994)

Casdagli's pioneering work has demonstrated
– sometimes to an initially sceptical world –
ways both of increasing access to young
people's theatre and of gaining from the
diversity that entails. While at the Unicorn
Theatre she first addressed the question of
drama that could cater for deaf as well as
hearing children, developing work that introduced sign language in a way that made it
integral rather than a distracting extra. Her
Pardon, Mr Punch!, applauded by the *Times
Educational Supplement* as 'a marvellously
jolly play', won the British Theatre
Association's *Drama* Magazine award for
young people's theatre in 1988. Subsequently

Casdagli drew multilingualism into her plays, particularly those done under the aegis of the Neti-Neti Theatre Company, started by her and Caroline Griffin in 1987. At its best, the richly layered effect of this acts as a strong symbol for the imaginative potential of a multicultural society.

Her plays with Caroline Griffin have proved equally innovative – *More*, a highly physical piece of theatre, looked at the hidden disabilities of agoraphobia and anorexia, *The Memorial Gardens* at child abuse. *The Beggar in the Palace* rewrote the *Odyssey* from a feminist viewpoint.

TRY THESE:
Graeae as a company concerned with disabilities; ★CAMPBELL, ★DAVID HOLMAN ★LAVERY, ★ADRIAN MITCHELL, ★SHEPPHARD, ★DAVID WOOD, Stephen Wyatt are other British dramatists who have written for children.

CHAMBERS, Jane [1937 – 83]
American playwright

PLAYS INCLUDE:
The Marvelous Metropolis (1957), *Christ in a Treehouse* (1971), *Random Violence* (1973), *A Late Snow* (1974), *Common Garden Variety* (1976), *Late Summer at Bluefish Cove* (1980), *Kudzu* (1981), *My Blue Heaven* (1982), *The Quintessential Image* (1983)

Chambers broke new ground in her frank writing about homosexual life. Nine months before her untimely death, she received the Fifth Annual Award of the Fund for Human Dignity, given as an acknowledgement of those who have made a major contribution to public understanding and acceptance of lesbians and gays. Chambers never concealed her homosexuality and created characters who dealt openly with the issues surrounding a gay lifestyle. Chambers will be best remembered, however, for *A Late Snow* and *Bluefish Cove* among the many plays she wrote on homosexual themes.

TRY THESE:
For pioneering work on gay themes, Mart Crowley, *The Boys in the Band*; for women's relationships, ★CHURCHILL, *Top Girls*; for homosexual lifestyles,

★FIERSTEIN, ★LANFORD WILSON's *Burn This*; Jill Posener's *Any Woman Can* for lesbian coming out; Split Britches for lesbian performance.

CHAPMAN, George [c. 1560 – 1634]
English dramatist and poet

PLAYS INCLUDE:
Monsieur D'Olive (1604), *Bussy D'Ambois* (1604), *Eastward Ho!* (1605, with ★JONSON and ★MARSTON), *The Widow's Tears* (pre-1609), *The Revenge of Bussy D'Ambois* (c. 1610), *The Wars of Caesar and Pompey* (c. 1613)

Chapman's densely philosophical and erudite approach to writing may go some way to explain the discrepancy between his academic (traditionally high) and theatrical (virtually non-existent) reputations. A friend of and collaborator with ★BEN JONSON, Chapman pursued the career of a professional writer with sufficient assiduity to serve a prison term for overstepping the mark in his criticism of the Scots and James VI and I in *Eastward Ho!*, which the RSC revived in 2002. The revival was greeted with some enthusiasm for its lively satirical presentation of London life in the early seventeenth century. *Bussy D'Ambois*, a revenge tragedy in the familiar Renaissance mode, and its sequel *The Revenge of Bussy D'Ambois* are proof that the Renaissance theatre knew how to cash in on success as much as Hollywood does!

TRY THESE:
Most Renaissance dramatists used revenge plots and malcontent figures; ★SHAKESPEARE's *Hamlet* is the most famous example of both, but ★KYD's *The Spanish Tragedy* started the vogue for revenge and there are notable examples in ★FORD, ★MIDDLETON, ★TOURNEUR and ★WEBSTER.

CHEKHOV, Anton [1860 – 1904]
Russian dramatist

PLAYS INCLUDE:
On the High Road (1884), *Ivanov* (1887), *The Bear* (1888), *The Wood Demon* (1889), *The Wedding* (1890), *Platonov* (c. 1890, not produced until the 1920s), *The Seagull* (1896), *Uncle Vanya* (1899), *The Proposal* (1899),

Three Sisters (1901), *The Cherry Orchard* (1904)

Chekhov is a master at depicting groups, charting the nuances of dialogue and character with extraordinary sensitivity and subtlety. Many of his plays deal with temporary communities that are coming to an end; their elegiac qualities seem to foreshadow events in Russia with remarkable prescience.

Born the son of a grocer and the grandson of a serf, and brought up in a small port town on the Sea of Azov, he went to the University of Moscow to train as a doctor in 1879. On graduation, he practised medicine in Moscow and wrote for the *St Petersburg Gazette*. His first full-length plays, *Ivanov* and *The Wood Demon*, were unsuccessful. In 1890 Chekhov travelled through Russia and Siberia as a medical practitioner, the first of many such journeys, in order to assist peasants. He then settled on a small estate outside Moscow, where he attempted to be an enlightened landlord and provided medical care and schooling for the peasants in the area, experience that is central to *Uncle Vanya* and *The Cherry Orchard*.

After the failure of the first production of *The Seagull*, Chekhov swore that he would never have another play produced. However, Stanislavsky persuaded him to revive *The Seagull*. Stanislavsky gave it a very careful production at the Moscow Arts Theatre, employing his methods of acting and direction, and the play was recognised as an important new drama. *Uncle Vanya*, a reworking of *The Wood Demon*, followed *The Seagull* quite successfully, although *Three Sisters* was not well received. In 1904, just as he was beginning to be recognised internationally as a major dramatist after the first production of *The Cherry Orchard*, Chekhov suffered two heart attacks and died in the German spa town of Badenweiler. In notebooks of the period of *Three Sisters* Chekhov wrote: 'We struggle to change life so that those who come after us might be happy, but those who come after us will say as usual, it was better before, life now is worse than it used to be'. Chekhov's plays stand as powerful statements that attest to the fact that things were never better, and that hope for the future matters more than anything.

Chekhov's plays appear regularly in the repertory, though an over-reliance on Stanislavskian naturalism and the misguided perception of Chekhov as a uniformly melancholy writer unfortunately persist.

Three Sisters

This is a study of three sisters, locked in a small military town, watching their lives drift past. The constant refrain of the play is the cry of the youngest sister Irina, 'Let us go to Moscow', but as the play progresses, even she, the youngest and therefore most hopeful, comes to realise that they will never leave, and that even if they did reach Moscow, they would take themselves and all their frustrations with them. Each of the sisters suffers the frustration of her hopes: Olga, the eldest, has given up all hope of children; the most sensual of the sisters, Masha, is trapped in a sterile marriage and loses the lover who promises her romance; Irina never achieves her ambition to see Moscow. The men who come within the orbit of the sisters also suffer from unfulfilled hopes and ambitions: the sisters' brother Andrei ends the play married to the vulgar Natasha; the Doctor has not sustained the commitment and conviction with which he entered medicine; Vershinin, the glamorous commander, has hopes for a 'beautiful life' in another two centuries. None of the characters can achieve contentment, with the exception of Andrei's wife, Natasha, whose dreams are only of material comforts. The play ends with the three sisters standing alone, their youth and romance leaving with the soldiers. Olga reaffirms the importance of their lives in a final and wistful speech: 'We shall be forgotten – our faces, our voices, even how many of us there were. But our sufferings will turn to joy for those who live after us.' The experience of the audience watching the play is such as to reaffirm its slender hopes, the act of watching *Three Sisters* confirms that they have indeed not been forgotten.

TRY THESE:

Chekhov said '★IBSEN is my favourite author' and claimed *The Wild Duck* as his favourite play;

★FRAYN's *Wild Honey* is a version of *Platonov*;

★FRIEL has adapted *The Cherry Orchard* to an Irish setting and his *Afterplay* brings together Sonia from *Uncle Vanya* and Andrei from *Three Sisters* after the Revolution; Michael Picardie's *The Cape Orchard* applied it to South Africa, and ★TREVOR GRIFFITHS' version stressed its politics; his *Piano* is partly a reworking of *Platonov*; ★MATURA transferred *Three Sisters* to Trinidad in his *Trinidad Sisters*; ★SHAW claimed *Heartbreak House* was Chekhovian; ★HUNTER was routinely compared to Chekhov; Helen Cooper's *Mrs Vershinin* tells the story of how she came to be the offstage neurotic in *Three Sisters*; ★FRAYN, ★MAMET and ★LANFORD WILSON have translated/adapted Chekhov's major plays; ★BECKETT's *Waiting for Godot* for a play about longed-for transcendence; ★SHAKESPEARE's *King Lear* offers a rather different group of three sisters; Michael Pennington for a Chekhov one-person show; the Manchester Royal Exchange paired *The Seagull* with Brad Fraser's *Cold Meat Party*.

CHILDRESS, Alice   [1920 – 94]
American dramatist and novelist

PLAYS INCLUDE:
Florence (1949), *Just a Little Simple* (1950, from ★LANGSTON HUGHES), *Gold Through the Trees* (1952), *Trouble in Mind* (1955), *Wedding Band* (1966), *The World on a Hill* (1968), *Young Martin Luther King* (1969), *String* (1969, from Maupassant), *Wine in the Wilderness* (1969), *Mojo* (1970), *When the Rattlesnake Sounds* (1975), *Let's Hear it for the Queen* (1976), *Sea Island Song* (1977, reworked as *Gullah*, 1984), *Moms* (1987)

Childress joined the (amateur) American Negro Theatre in 1940, and was its director from 1941 to 1952, while earning her living in a variety of menial jobs. The ANT staged her first play, *Florence*, in which a black mother is reconciled to her daughter's desire to be an actress after a bruising encounter with a white actress, and she played a significant part in the fight for black writers and performers to be taken seriously in the USA. For example, *Gold Through the Trees* is believed to have been the first play by a black woman to have a professional production in the USA (Rosemary Curb) and *Trouble in Mind* earned her the first OBIE for a black woman. It deals with an issue that still remains only too relevant today: the stereotyping of black characters by white writers and the difficulties of black actors faced with either playing stereotypes or not working. *Wedding Band* tackles an equally hot potato with its story of an interracial marriage in the Deep South in 1915.

Childress's current reputation in Britain depends on Nick Kent's 2000 revival of *Wine in the Wilderness* at the Tricycle. Michael Billington described the play as a variation of the Pygmalion story in which a painter who is creating a triptych of black womanhood is persuaded that 'real beauty is to be found not in dead myths but in the rich variety of 1960s black America'.

TRY THESE:
★PINNOCK's *Water* was commissioned as a response to *Wine in the Wilderness*; ★BALDWIN, ★BARAKA, ★BULLINS, ★HANSBERRY's *A Raisin in the Sun*, for American black experience in the 1950s and 1960s; ★WOLFE's *The Colored Museum* for a satirical history of the attempts to dramatise the black experience; ★KHAN-DIN's *East is East* for a British interracial marriage.

CHONG, Ping   [1946 –   ]
American writer, director and performer

WORKS INCLUDE:
Fear and Loathing in Gotham (1975), *Humboldt's Current* (1977), *Nuit Blanche* (1981), *A.M./A.M. – The Articulated Man* (1982), *Anna into Nightlight* (1982), *The Games* (1983, with Meredith Monk), *A Race* (1984), *The Angels of Swedenborg* (1985), *Nosferatu* (1985), *Kindness* (1986), *Noiresque: The Fallen Angel* (1989), *Maraya – Acts of Nature in Geological Time* (1989), *Skin – A State of Being* (1989), *4 a.m. America* (1990), *Deshima* (1990), *Elephant Memories* (1990), *American Gothic* (1992), *Undesirable Elements* (1993-), *Edda: Viking Tales of Lust and Revenge* (2001), *Children of War* (2002)

Chong, a one-time performer with Meredith Monk, formed his own Fiji Company in 1975 'to question the syntax of theatre'. His highly visual theatre mixes media and metaphor, while cultural traditions and paradigmatic experiences permeate the works. His characters, all explorers of one kind or another, grapple with geography, history and memory in the context of imperialism and the violence of the Western world. Human experience is played out in haunting images composed of verbal, visual, gestural and sound texts that expose the oppression of 'the other'. Chong's work is not for all audiences; theatregoers have been known to stomp out of his performances infuriated by the ambiguities. While Chong's work is undeniably attractive in physical production, as critic Michael Feingold once observed 'you never know what he might achieve if he put his mind to creating a work that communicated more than mere effects'.

TRY THESE:

★ BOGART, ★ FOREMAN, San Francisco Mime Troupe, Peter Sellars, Robert Wilson, The Wooster Group, for other figures in the American avant-garde; Laurie Anderson for multimedia performance; Pina Bausch, Martha Clarke as dancers whose work crosses boundaries.

CHRISTIE, Agatha
(Mary Clarissa)   [1890 – 1976]
British author of detective stories and dramatist

PLAYS INCLUDE:

Black Coffee (1930), *Ten Little Niggers* (also known as *Ten Little Indians*, 1943), *Appointment with Death* (1945), *Murder on the Nile* (1945), *The Hollow* (1951), *The Mousetrap* (1952), *Witness for the Prosecution* (1953), *The Spider's Web* (1954), *Towards Zero* (with Gerald Verner; 1956), *Verdict* (1958), *The Unexpected Guest* (1958), *Go Back for Murder* (1960), *The Rule of Three* (1962), *Fiddlers Three* (1971), *Akhnaton* (published 1973)

One of the most successful thriller writers of all time and the author of the longest-running play ever, *The Mousetrap* (now past its fiftieth anniversary), Christie excels at telling a story. Though her characters verge upon the stereotypical, they have firm roots in the backgrounds of the middle-class audiences that have flocked to see her plays, giving them opportunities to identify with the characters and vicariously enjoy the excitement of involvement with murder and mayhem. However, her characters are not mere ciphers

and she sometimes uses them to voice ideas that reveal a strong concern for the problems in relationships. As in many of her novels, the revelation of 'who-done-it' is often not signalled in the plot and comes as a surprise.

Christie's detective stories have also been adapted for the stage by other writers and been made into a number of feature films and adapted for television. Those featuring her detectives Miss Marple and the Belgian Hercule Poirot have been hugely successful.

The Mousetrap
Christie herself thought that 'It is the sort of play you can take anyone to. It is not really frightening. It is not really horrible. It is not really a farce but it has a little bit of all these things and perhaps that satisfies a lot of different people.' The play enlists many of the clichés of its genre: a manor house cut off by snow drifts but only an hour from London, a solidly realist set with a suspiciously large number of levels and doors appropriate to the demands of murder or farce, expository telephone calls and radio broadcasts, and atmospheric music anticipating the deaths within the play. A cast of stereotypes to be murdered or suspected of murder includes the déclassé young couple attempting to cope with opening the manor as a guesthouse, an effete young man, a mannish woman, a funny-sinister foreigner and the detective whose heroic cross-country skiing enables him alone to reach the isolated house. Harold Hobson described the play as 'a parable of the social outlook of our times', but it never quite manages to bring to the surface the maelstrom of confused sexual identities, child abuse and debates about the influence of environment and heredity on the formation of character that lurk beneath the generic commonplaces of resolution and disclosure

TRY THESE:

★ BRECHT's *Caucasian Chalk Circle* for the nature/nurture debate; ★ AYCKBOURN for enterprising plot manipulations; ★ PRIESTLEY's *An Inspector Calls* for the use of a detective plot to make a moral point; ★ STOPPARD's *The Real Inspector Hound* for a parody of the genre; ★ ANTHONY SHAFFER's *Sleuth* is more psychologically oriented; Ira Levin's *Deathtrap*; ★ DORFMAN's

Death and the Maiden for a superb psychological thriller concerned with the abuse of human rights; Stephen Mallatratt's *The Woman in Black*, adapted from Susan Hill's novel, a spine-tingling ghost story.

CHURCHILL, Caryl   [1938 –   ]
British dramatist

PLAYS INCLUDE:

Owners (1972), *Objections to Sex and Violence* (1975), *Light Shining in Buckinghamshire* (1976), *Vinegar Tom* (1976), *Cloud Nine* (1979), *Three More Sleepless Nights* (1980), *Top Girls* (1982), *Fen* (1983), *Softcops* (1984), *A Mouthful of Birds* (1986, with ★DAVID LAN) *Serious Money* (1987), *Icecream* (1989), *Hot Fudge* (1990), *Mad Forest* (1990), *Lives of the Great Poisoners* (1991, with Orlando Gough and Ian Spink), *The Skriker* (1994), *Thyestes* (1994, from ★SENECA), *Hotel* (1997), *This is a Chair* (1997), *Far Away* (2000), *A Number* (2002)

Churchill is one of Britain's outstanding dramatists, with a series of vibrant and inventive plays over thirty years. Her recent work has explored issues of the collapse of traditional structures and ecological meltdown (*The Skriker* and *Far Away*) and human cloning (*A Number*), characterised by a haunting, elliptical allusive poetic language that suggest a writer at the height of her powers.

After writing extensively for radio, which is traditionally more accommodating to female writers, and juggling the demands of her husband's career and of childcare, Churchill moved into theatre in the early 1970s, learning different ways of working collectively as a result of her ventures with Monstrous Regiment and particularly Joint Stock. Inevitably, Churchill tackled many of the fashionable themes of British political and feminist theatre in the 1970s, including witches (*Vinegar Tom*), terrorism (*Objections to Sex and Violence*), and seventeenth-century revolutionary sects (*Light Shining in Buckinghamshire*), as well as more unusual topics such as the nature of ideology and repression in the all-male *Softcops*, inspired by a reading of the French theorist Michel Foucault. Her work was particularly associated with treatments of sexual politics, especially in *Cloud Nine* (in which the links between patriarchy and colonisation are mercilessly and wittily exposed) and *Top Girls*, a study of a 'successful' career woman. She has always been keenly aware of the socio-political dimension of oppression, which affects men as well as women, as in *Fen*, her study of the quiet horrors of rural life (notable for a stunning central performance from Jennie Stoller), and in the earlier urban landscape of *Owners*. Churchill uses time shifts, uneven ageing (the characters in *Cloud Nine* are twenty-five years older in part two than they were in part one, but a hundred years have passed), cross-race and cross-gender casting, doubling, pastiche Victorian light verse and also rhyming couplets, as part of a strategy of upsetting and destabilising conventional assumptions about both drama and life itself. Some people interpreted *Top Girls* as a hymn in praise of its central character, and the runaway success in Britain of her exposé of the financial markets, *Serious Money*, owed much to its popularity with the very people it satirised, who flocked to see it both at the Royal Court and in the West End. *Mad Forest* is a fine treatment of Romania after the overthrow of Ceausescu, researched in Romania with a group of students from the Central School of Speech and Drama.

Top Girls
The play begins with a gathering of women from different periods and cultures to celebrate the promotion of Marlene, the central character, within the Top Girls employment agency. The choice of relatively unfamiliar historical characters reminds us of the way that women's histories have been submerged by traditional male-dominated approaches to history. It also brings us into a critical relationship with Marlene's story from the very beginning, forcing us to supply many of the connections between the first scene and the more 'normal' narrative that follows in which the women who played party guests reappear as contemporary women. In the first scene Marlene is apparently emancipated from the traps and entanglements of family and children that have constrained the others, but

Far Away by Caryl Churchill, directed by Stephen Daldry, Royal Court Theatre, 2000 (Cclir Willoughby/A'enaPAL)

much of the rest of the play is concerned with destabilising this privileged position by trapping audiences into semi-agreement with her and then encouraging them to see her putative success in a far wider context in which she is just as much a victim of the system. The play is both enormously funny and chilling in its brilliantly observed presentations of the everyday contradictions of life. Churchill, like ★ BRECHT, suggests that what we need is a new way of seeing if we are to understand and confront the pressures the characters in *Top Girls* fail to grasp. Although it can be seen as a surgically precise anatomy of the Thatcher years, the Background/Oxford Stage Company production seen in the West End in 2002 revealed it had lost none of its power.

TRY THESE:
★ DANIELS' *Byrthrite* is another play about seventeenth-century women; ★ BOND's mixture of 'historical' and invented characters in *Early Morning* ran into some of the same problems with critics as *Top Girls*; among other contemporary women dramatists are ★ DANIELS, ★ GEMS, ★ HORSFIELD, ★ KEATLEY, ★ LAVERY, ★ LOCHHEAD, ★ MACDONALD, ★ MCINTYRE, ★ PINNOCK, ★ RAIF, ★ WERTENBAKER; one of the great poisoners is Medea, also the subject of plays by ★ EURIPIDES and ★ SENECA.

CIXOUS, Hélène   [1937 –   ]
French feminist, novelist and dramatist

PLAYS INCLUDE:
Portrait de Dora (1976, *Portrait of Dora*), *La Prise de l'École de Madhubaï* (1983, *The Capture of the Madhubaï School*), *L'Histoire Terrible Mais Inachevée de Norodom Sihanouk, Roi du Cambodge* (1985, *The Terrible But Unfinished Story of Norodom Sihanouk, King of Cambodia*), *L'Indiade* (1987, *The Indiad*), *La Nuit Miraculeuse* (1989, with Ariane Mnouchkine), *On ne part pas, on ne revient pas* (1991), *L'Histoire (qu'on ne connaîtra jamais)* (1994), *Voile Noire Voile Blanche* (1994, *Black Sail White Sail*), *La Ville parjure ou le réédes Erinyes* (1994)

Born in Algeria, Cixous is one of the most important French feminist theorists. Since 1967 she has also published novels, short stories and essays, and she made a tentative entry into playwriting in 1976, when Simone Benmussa produced her *Portrait de Dora* at the Théâtre d'Orsay. After an experiment with an opera libretto (*Le Nom d'Édipe*, Avignon Festival 1978) she had some success with *La Prise de l'École de Madhubaï* at the Petit Odéon in 1983, where most of the set in the tiny theatre was taken up with a banyan tree; most of the play was a discussion on social responsibility and individual rights between a female bandit and a friendly prime minister with an umbrella. Since then, Cixous has been engaged in a rewarding partnership with Ariane Mnouchkine and the Théâtre du Soleil, for whom and with whom she has researched and written two substantial and successful historical plays, one on the history of Cambodia and one on the partition of British India.

TRY THESE:
★ DURAS, with whom she seems to have very little in common, but they were both born in French colonies and they have both written about what was formerly French Indo-China; ★ SPALDING GRAY's *Swimming to Cambodia* and ★ EDGAR's *Destiny* for Cambodia and India; ★ TERRY JOHNSON's *Hysteria* for another sceptical look at Freud; ★ HAMPTON's *The Talking Cure* for Freud and Jung, ★ WRIGHT's *Mrs Klein* for Melanie Klein.

CLARK, Brian   [1932 –   ]
British dramatist

PLAYS INCLUDE:
Lay By (1971, with ★ TREVOR GRIFFITHS, ★ DAVID HARE, ★ STEPHEN POLIAKOFF, Hugh Stoddart, ★ SNOO WILSON), *England's Ireland* (1972, with Tony Bicât, ★ DAVID EDGAR, Francis Fuchs, ★ DAVID HARE, ★ SNOO WILSON), *Truth or Dare* (1972), *Campion's Interview* (1976), *Whose Life Is It Anyway* (1978), *Post Mortem* (1978), *Can You Hear Me at the Back* (1979), *Switching in the Afternoon; or, As the Screw Turns* (1980), *The Petition* (1986)

Originally a collaborator with younger left-wing dramatists such as ★DAVID HARE on plays for the anti-establishment Portable Theatre Company, Clark did not pursue consciously political theatre. The 1972 television version of his best-known play, *Whose Life Is It Anyway*, was written in the same period and is more typical. In it an accident victim, paralysed from the neck down, fights for the right to die. It provides the opportunity for a virtuoso central performance, but little opportunity for non-verbal theatre. Clark not only argues his case but also writes elegantly and entertainingly, with an excellent feel for the mores and preoccupations of the English middle class. The professional and domestic problems of the mid-life male are explored in *Can You Hear Me at the Back* and in the 1979 British television series *Telford's* Change, both of which provide sensitive portraits that will assure the troubled professional that he (rather than she, although Mary Tyler Moore took the lead in *Whose Life* on Broadway) is not alone – but do not look to Clark for the political critique his earliest work might seem to promise. In *The Petition* Clark is persuasive if predictable in his mainstream treatment of the anti-nuclear issue through discussions between a general and his quintessentially 'decent' middle-class wife, but the impact is fatally undermined by the melodramatic device of her political consciousness being made coincidental with the revelation that she is dying of cancer.

TRY THESE:

For hospital, illness, and disability plays of various kinds see ★KEMPINSKI's *Duel for One*, ★MEDOFF's *Children of a Lesser God*, ★NICHOLS' *The National Health*, ★PAGE's *Tissue*, ★POMERANCE's *The Elephant Man*, ★YOUNG's *Crystal Clear*, Graeae Theatre Company; ★VAN ITALLIE's *The Traveller* creates a language to describe aphasia; ★BECKETT's *Happy Days* offers another version of immobility; for anti-nuclear issues see ★BARKER's *The Passion*, ★BOLT's *The Tiger and the Horse*, ★BOND's *War Plays*, ★BRENTON's *The Genius*, ★DANIELS' *The Devil's Gateway*, ★DARKE's *The Body*, ★EDGAR's *Maydays*.

CLIFFORD, John   [1950 –   ]
English-born dramatist now working in Scotland

PLAYS INCLUDE:

How Like an Angel (1983), *Losing Venice* (1985), *Lucy's Play* (1986), *Playing with Fire* (1987), *Ines de Castro* (1989), *The Girl Who Fell to Earth* (1991), *Light in the Village* (1991), *What's in a Name* (1992), *Dreaming* (1994), *War in America* (1996)

Clifford has a sophisticated academic background, a degree in Arabic and Spanish affording him the cadences and philosophies of two cultures strikingly different from our own. His stylish, vigorous translations of ★CALDERÓN, ★LORCA and Tirso de Molina match the Hispanic influences, both thematic and stylistic, in his original plays. For instance, the events used in *Ines de Castro* derive from Portuguese legends about the doomed love affair between Pedro, heir to the throne, and a woman, Ines, who is from an enemy land. The plot is reminiscent of a Jacobean revenge tragedy. The writing melds the stateliness of Calderón, the poetic escape of Lorca, the gusto of medieval morality, and something which is Clifford's own, the heartfelt anger of the very gentle.

Losing Venice

Since winning a Fringe First award in 1985, *Losing Venice* has been performed worldwide. It travels well because it depends on one simple, inspired notion: encourage adults to use their imagination with the same limitless scope enjoyed in childhood. And at one level, the games set in motion are not dissimilar – a Duke decides to go to war because that is what Dukes do, just as he gets married because that is also what Dukes do. And Dukes do these things because they are mimicking other Dukes, just like children mimic grown-ups. So off they go, the Duke, his Poet, his Servant, to retrieve Venice (which wasn't actually theirs, but shouldn't be taken over by anyone else) and they have adventures and catastrophes – without benefit of props, or fancy locations, but all through conjuring with words and by acting as if such things are so – and eventually they come home, heroes – by their own account anyway. Meanwhile, home has crumbled away, poverty and disorder reign.

And the women who've struggled through these domestic battles aren't all that impressed with this macho bluster and hollow victory. It is a delicious, sly, droll play which astutely deflates national and male chauvinism, warmongering (an exercise in cosmetic politicking usually), scrutinises the actual usefulness of the poet within society, celebrates female common sense and loving, and does so with wit and panache.

TRY THESE:
Mario Vargas Llosa's *Kathy and the Hippopotamus* for an exploration of escapism/imagination and human relationships; ★DE VEGA, ★CORNEILLE's *Le Cid* for the corrosive effects of honour and familial duty; honour and compromise are poignantly depicted in ★C. P. TAYLOR's *Good*; ★BARKER is adept at using history to point up cogent moral and social issues of our time.

CLEUGH, Grae   [1968 –   ]
British dramatist

PLAYS INCLUDE:
Fucking Games (2001)

Cleugh won the Olivier Award for Most Promising Playwright on the strength of his debut full-length play presented at the Royal Court Theatre Upstairs. Terrence treats his long-term partner Jonah with disdain and has a secret lover who arrives with his boyfriend who is actually more interested in a traditional monogamous relationship. As the play's title suggests, it follows in the ★MARK RAVENHILL tradition of explicit homosexual sex but it concentrates more on the domestic power games of a long-established couple than on wider issues.

TRY THESE:
★ALBEE's *Who's Afraid of Virginia Woolf?*, ★ELYOT's *My Night with Reg,* ★LEIGH's *Abigail's Party* for domestic power struggles.

COCTEAU, Jean   [1889 – 1963]
French avant-garde poet, filmmaker and dramatist

PLAYS INCLUDE:
Les Mariés de la Tour Eiffel (1924, *The Wedding on the Eiffel Tower*), *Orphée* (1927), *Antigone* (1928), *La Voix Humaine* (1930, *The Human Voice*), *La Machine Infernale* (1934, *The Infernal Machine*), *Les Chevaliers de la Table Ronde* (1937, *The Knights of the Round Table*), *Les Parents Terribles* (1938, *The Terrible Parents*), *L'Aigle a Deux Têtes* (1946, *The Eagle Has Two Heads*)

Cocteau was a permanent avant-gardist in the 1920s and 1930s (or, as his enemies put it, the ultimate in trendy chic); his talents included poetry, drawing, film- and playmaking, and he had a considerable vogue in England after World War II, but his reputation dipped before reviving in the 1980s with London productions of *Orphée, The Infernal Machine* (Cocteau's variations on the Oedipus story), and the short, bravura piece for solo actress and telephone, *The Human Voice*.

TRY THESE:
★ANOUILH, ★GIRAUDOUX and ★SARTRE for using modernised Greek plays and legends to comment on contemporary French affairs; ★BERKOFF, ★DUFFY, ★WERTENBAKER for some British parallels.

COLLINS, Barry   [1941 –   ]
British dramatist

PLAYS INCLUDE:
And Was Jerusalem Builded Here (1972), *Beauty and the Beast* (1973), *Judgement* (1974), *The Strongest Man in the World* (1978), *Toads* (1979), *The Ice Chimney* (1980), *Atonement* (1987)

Collins is best known for his dramatic monologue *Judgement* – a horrific tale of cannibalism based on a real wartime incident when seven Russian soldiers were left for sixty days without food, recounted by one of the two survivors. Described by Steve Grant as having the 'hypnotic rhetoric of a John Donne sermon, the moral intensity of a Conrad novel and finely observed lyric detail of a

Louis MacNeice poem', Collins' two-and-a-half-hour tour de force has provoked magnificent performances from such interpreters as Peter O'Toole, Colin Blakely and Ben Kingsley. A much-travelled piece, this cool, clinical investigation into the moral and philosophical laws of human degradation, survival and the nature of guilt and sanity conjures with themes Collins has continued to readdress, though perhaps nowhere else with so much control.

TRY THESE:

★ WERTENBAKER's *The Grace of Mary Traverse* for eighteenth-century riots to compare with the Luddite riots in *And Was Jerusalem Builded Here*; compare images of destructive love in *Atonement* with ★ STRINDBERG's *Creditors*, ★ SHEPARD's *Fool for Love*, ★ STRAUSS's *The Tourist Guide* and the sterility of a marriage in ★ RUDKIN's *Ashes*; for mountain-climbing plays to compare with *The Ice Chimney*, *K2* by Patrick Meyers and ★ AUDEN and ISHERWOOD's *The Ascent of F6*; for sporting champions ★ GODBER, ★ PAGE's *Golden Girls*, ★ STOREY; for cannibalism, ★ SHAKESPEARE's *Titus Andronicus*.

CONGREVE, William   [1670 – 1729]
English dramatist

PLAYS INCLUDE:
The Old Bachelor (1693), *The Double-Dealer* (1693), *Love for Love* (1695), *The Mourning Bride* (1697), *The Way of the World* (1700)

English-born and Irish-educated, Congreve lived a fashionable life (his mistresses included the actress Anne Bracegirdle and the Duchess of Marlborough), indulged in some unsuccessful theatrical management, and wrote three comedies that are still staged. Although the satirical edge of Congreve's work is less sharp than ★ WYCHERLEY's, public taste had changed sufficiently to make both *The Double-Dealer* and *The Way of the World* more successful with their later audiences than they originally were. *The Mourning Bride* is a tragedy but the other plays deal with the usual characters and issues of the period's comedy: arranged marriages and pretended marriages; the conflict between country and town values; lust and romance; rakes and fops

and heiresses and mistresses; comic intrigues and revenges; age and youth and money and lack of it. Yet within this conventional material, which is beautifully organised and wittily presented, the most interesting feature is Congreve's treatment of the romantic figures: in *The Double-Dealer*, *Love for Love*, and *The Way of the World* there are men and women who move towards a marriage based on mutual respect rather than money. The attitude to marriage is wary but ultimately positive, as in the so-called 'proviso scene' in *The Way of the World* where Millamant and Mirabell lay down the ground rules of their marriage even as far as discussing how to bring up their children!

TRY THESE:

Other Restoration comic writers, such as ★ BEHN, ★ ETHEREGE and ★ WYCHERLEY; other writers of comedy of manners, such as ★ PHILIP BARRY, ★ COWARD, ★ GOLDSMITH, ★ LUCIE, ★ MOLIÈRE, ★ SHERIDAN, ★ WILDE; ★ BOND's *Restoration* uses conventions and themes derived from the practice of Restoration writers to make modern points.

COOKE, Trish   [1963 –   ]
British dramatist

PLAYS INCLUDE:
Shoppin People (1989), *Running Dream* (1989), *Back Street Mammy* (1989)

Cooke was born in Bradford of Dominican parents. She later became an actress, television presenter, prize-winning children's book writer and an *EastEnders* script writer. *Running Dream* is about the interaction between three sisters after their mother leaves to go to England. *Back Street Mammy* audaciously weaves poetic and naturalistic forms in its exploration of the consequences of a young woman's finding herself pregnant after a one-night stand. Some reviewers dismissed her experimentation with nightmarish nursery rhymes, wordplay and dialogue as 'pretentious', but others found the play perceptive, warm-hearted and joyous. Juggling with ideas about choices, independence, and generational conflicts, what could have been a routine drama of adolescence became in Cooke's hands a vigorous and imaginative expression of hope profoundly on the side of life, if sceptical of marriage.

TRY THESE:
★ PINNOCK has written about young black women and their experiences; ★ LOCHHEAD for a woman-centred Scottish writer; ★ ELLIS, ★ MOFFATT, ★ ZEPHANIAH for contemporary black male writers; ★ MACDONALD for adolescent stirrings.

COONEY, Ray   [1932 –   ]
British dramatist

PLAYS INCLUDE:
One for the Pot (1961, with Tony Hilton), *Chase Me Comrade* (1964), *Charlie Girl* (1965, with Hugh and Margaret Williams), *My Giddy Aunt* (1967, with John Chapman), *Bang Bang Beirut, or, Stand by Your Bedouin* (1966, with Tony Hilton) *Not Now, Darling* (1967, with John Chapman), *Move Over, Mrs Markham* (1968, with John Chapman), *Why Not Stay for Breakfast* (1970, with Gene Stone), *Come Back to My Place* (1973, with John Chapman), *There Goes the Bride* (1974, with John Chapman), *Two Into One* (1981), *Run for Your Wife* (1983), *Wife Begins at Forty* (1985, with Arne Sultan and Earl Barrett), *It Runs in the Family* (1987), *Out of Order* (1990), *Funny Money* (1995), *Caught in the Net* (2001)

Cooney appeared in the farces *Dry Rot* and *Simple Spymen*, (both written by John Chapman) for Brian Rix's Whitehall Theatre Company. He then wrote for them his first play, *One for the Pot* (1961, with Tony Hilton), a classic farce with Brian Rix playing four brothers, and later *Chase Me, Comrade* (1964). After other successful farces (all in the British line of cheerful suggestive sex rather than the manic and more explicit style of ★ FEYDEAU or ★ ORTON,) he formed the Theatre of Comedy Company in 1983 and put on his own *Run For Your Wife*.

Cooney takes a perfectly mundane situation and swiftly transforms it by a series of misunderstandings into a collision of circumstances and the threat of ultimate disaster for our hero. In *Run for Your Wife*, for instance, a bigamous husband does his frantic best to keep his two wives from a catastrophic meet-

ing. The improbabilities in Cooney's plots are made up for by a repeated, accelerating flurry of old jokes, and trousers choreographed to drop at just the right time. Cooney is a master of Brian Rix/Whitehall theatre farce, a genre abhorred by theatre sophisticates but ever popular with audiences who want nothing more than to be entertained, their prejudices firmly intact. He is adept at catching contemporary issues, from defecting Russian ballet dancers (*Chase Me Comrade*) and James Bond-style Arab villainy (*Bang Bang Beirut*), to political sleaze (*Out of Order*) and internet dating (*Caught in the Net*, a sequel to *Run for Your Wife*) but his characters' attitudes to homosexuality could scarcely be described as progressive.

TRY THESE:
★ AYCKBOURN, ★ DE FILIPPO, ★ FRAYN'S *Noises Off*, ★ TRAVERS, ★ CHURCHILL's *Cloud Nine* for different approaches to farce; ★ STOPPARD's *Dirty Linen* for political sleaze; the eighteenth-century Irish playwright Arthur Murphy's *All in the Wrong* is a classic example of misunderstandings carried to the limit.

CORNEILLE, Pierre   [1606 – 84]
French dramatist

PLAYS INCLUDE:
Mélite (1629), *Clitandre* (1631), *L'Illusion Comique* (1636, *The Illusion* or *The Comic Illusion*), *Le Cid* (1636 – 7, *The Cid*), *Horace* (1640), *Cinna* (1640), *Polyeucte* (1641), *Rodugune* (1644 – 5), *Oedipe* (*Oedipus*, 1659), *Tite et Bérénice* (1670, *Titus and Berenice*), *Suréna* (1674)

Corneille was a lawyer from Rouen; his early plays were comedies or tragicomedies, but after the success of *The Cid* he settled down to write heroic tragedies, somewhat in the Spanish manner, with strong-willed heroes and heroines in impossible situations that they cope with whatever the cost. He suffered from being the first major French dramatist to try to keep the neo-Aristotelian rules, the three unities of time, place and action. Unlike Racine, he usually had too much plot for the requisite twenty-four hours, and was much discouraged by the resulting criticism.

The Illusion has a magician, a play within a play within a play, and characters who appear to die, and are then revealed as a company of actors sharing out the takings, but *The Cid* is more typical. It is the archetypal 'Love against Honour' play. Rodrigue (the Cid) loves Chimène, but has to kill her father in a duel because the latter has insulted his (Rodrigue's) father; Chimène loves Rodrigue, but has to demand his life from the King because he has killed her father. Happily, the King needs to keep Rodrigue alive to beat the Moors, and persuades Chimène to declare her love by telling her Rodrigue is dead. The play is called a tragicomedy, but no one seems quite sure whether this is a happy ending or not. The language is elevated and the sentiments of all concerned excessively noble, but the effect can be very powerful. Corneille's plays are not often produced in Britain.

TRY THESE:

★RACINE for seventeenth-century French drama and for keeping to the neo-Aristotelian rules better; ★CALDERÓN for the influence of Spanish ideas of family honour.

CORRIE, Joe   [1894 – 1968]
British dramatist

PLAYS INCLUDE:
In Time o' Strife (1927), *Martha* (1935), *Hewers of Coal* (1937)

Corrie, an admirer of ★SEAN O'CASEY, wrote most successfully about Scottish mining – mainly one-act plays for groups in the Scottish Community Drama Association. Amongst his best plays are *Hewers of Coal*, the archetypal pit-disaster play, and *Martha*, which occupies similar territory to ★J. M. BARRIE's *Mary Rose*, in this case the ghostly return of a mother's lost son from World War I. Corrie's greatest play, *In Time o' Strife*, chronicles the last days of the post-General Strike miners' lockout in a small Scottish village. Although Corrie is sometimes sentimental, his sentiment is grounded in a genuine understanding and compassion for his characters and their predicaments, and it goes along with an unsentimental analysis of the responsibilities for those predicaments.

TRY THESE:
★BURKE's *Gagarin Way* and Ena Lamont Stewart's *Men Should Weep* for other examples of Scottish communities under strain; ★SYNGE's *Riders to the Sea* for the impact of sons' deaths on a mother in a peasant community; ★GALSWORTHY's *Strife* for a presentation of strikes from within a more established theatre; ★EDGAR's *That Summer* and Peter Cox's *The Garden of England*, for the 1984 miners' strike.

CORTHRON, Kia
American dramatist

PLAYS INCLUDE:
Wake Up Lou Riser (1992), *Come Down Burning* (1993), *Cage Rhythm* (1993), *Life by Asphyxiation* (1995), *Seeking the Genesis* (1996), *Splash Hatch on the E Going Down* (1997), *Digging Eleven* (1999), *Force Continuum* (2000), *Breath, Boom* (2000), *The Venus de Milo is Armed* (2003, workshopped 2001)

Corthron has tackled a whole range of socio-political issues ranging from the Ku Klux Klan in modern America (*Wake Up Lou Riser*) to prison (*Cage Rhythm*) to police brutality (*Force Continuum*). *The Venus de Milo is Armed* has many resonances for a post-September 11 America with its tale of land-mines and limblessness in Africa and the USA. Two of her works have had London productions: *Splash Hatch on the E Going Down* (Donmar Warehouse, 1999) contrasts its pre-cocious protagonist's academic understanding of environmental pollution with her inability to cope with the personal realities of her husband suffering from lead poisoning; *Breath, Boom*, commissioned by the Royal Court, explores the lives of female gang members in Harlem. Based, like *Seeking the Genesis*, on research into the lives of inner-city black gangs, it eschews political moralising for clear-sighted presentation of characters and issues.

TRY THESE:
★BEHAN's *The Quare Fellow* and ★PUIG's *Kiss of the Spider Woman* for alternative treatments of prison life; ★CHURCHILL's *Far Away* for environmental issues; for gangs, ★BENT, ★BOND's *Saved*, ★UPTON.

COWARD, Noël   [1899 – 1973]
British dramatist, actor, singer and screenwriter

PLAYS INCLUDE:
The Young Idea (1921), *The Vortex* (1924), *Fallen Angels* (1925), *Hay Fever* (1925), *Easy Virtue* (1926), *Semi-Monde* (written 1926, performed 1977), *Bitter Sweet* (1929), *Private Lives* (1930), *Cavalcade* (1931), *Design for Living* (1933), *Tonight at 8.30* (1936), *Operette* (1938), *Blithe Spirit* (1941), *Present Laughter* (1943), *This Happy Breed* (1943), *Relative Values* (1951), *Quadrille* (1952), *Nude with Violin* (1956), *Waiting in the Wings* (1960), *Sail Away* (1961), *Suite in Three Keys* (1965)

Whether you see him as the doyen of bitchery or the ultimate connoisseur of camp, Coward was more than an accomplished lyricist, actor and cabaret performer. He was a great wit in a direct line from ★CONGREVE to ★SHERIDAN, ★OSCAR WILDE and ★JOE ORTON (Millamant's 'I Love To Give Pain', from *The Way of the World*, could serve as the subtext for Coward's creations). The consummate man of the theatre himself, theatrical folk figure heavily in Coward's plays, whether it's the matriarchal actress, Judith Bliss, in *Hay Fever* or the preening comedian Garry Essendine in *Present Laughter*, who admits 'I'm always acting'. Non-actors in his plays act, too: the hyper-theatrical Madam Arcati in *Blithe Spirit*, the polyglot houseboy Sebastien in *Nude with Violin*. For Coward, as for ★WILDE, acting equals artifice equals disguise, and the tension in his work often comes from the effort required to sustain a pose without which characters, and their egos, dry up. Coward's plays may come adorned with comic frills that continue to entice, but at his best he is as serious and penetrating a dramatist as Britain has known. Michael Grandage's 2002 production of *The Vortex* reminded audiences that Coward's original reputation was made by a melodramatic exposé of fashionable vices such as promiscuity, women taking young lovers, and cocaine addiction.

Hay Fever
Hay Fever is an anarchic precursor of 'get the guest' in ★EDWARD ALBEE's *Who's Afraid of Virginia Woolf*. Coward's eccentric Bliss family invites guests to their home in Cookham only to drive them away again through their own accumulated eccentricities. The play both revels in, and comments on, the English fondness for ill-mannered artifice, and at its best – the visiting 'drearies' skulk away as the family carries obliviously on over breakfast – it can be a deliriously funny experience. As usual with Coward, a critique is implied: the Blisses may be lethally exciting with their fondness for games and poses, but his characters' poor and pricelessly funny manners also serve to isolate them; they are fundamentally alone.

Private Lives
Written by Coward for himself and Gertrude Lawrence to act, *Private Lives* is one of the simplest yet most subtle of comedies, and one can take pleasure in the perfect rhythms of its language: 'Don't quibble, Sybil' and 'very flat, Norfolk' have both entered the language. A divorced husband and wife, Amanda and Elyot, bump into one another on their second honeymoons only to end up ditching their new spouses, Victor and Sibyl, and absconding to Paris. Typically for Coward, elegant repartee hides hideous manners, and the characters are both aware of – and blind to – their own ruthlessness. Underneath the comic surface is a very serious, almost existential, point, about the bleakness of living.

TRY THESE:
★PHILIP BARRY and ★ORTON for epigrammatic similarities in tone; ★SIMON for variants on similar ideas; ★HELLMAN's *Little Foxes* for another ruthless family; ★SIMPSON's *One Way Pendulum* and ★AYCKBOURN for more middle-class versions of the comic cruelties of English eccentrics; ★LUDLAM and ★BUSCH for campier wit; ★IBSEN for less comic dysfunctional families; Peter Hall for linked productions of *Design for Living* and ★PINTER's *Betrayal*.

CRAZE, Tony   [1944 –   ]
British dramatist

PLAYS INCLUDE:
The Love You Take (1981), *Kaleidoscope* (1981), *Confrontations* (1981), *Shona* (1983), *Living with Your Enemies* (1985), *Angelus*

Private Lives by Noël Coward, directed by Howard Davies, Albery Theatre, 2001. Alan Rickman as Elyot, Lindsay Duncan as Amanda. (Pete Jones/ArenaPAL)

(1987) *Going West* (1988), *Megabodies* (1989), *Flying Ashes,* (1990, based on *Letters of Love* by Julia Voznesenskaya), *Passion* (2002)

Craze, a former journalist and screenwriter (he trained at the London Film School), was artistic director of the Soho Poly, which staged three of his major plays. Craze's plays pack a powerful, emotional punch (though his dialogue can be irritatingly cryptic), showing individuals not only at loggerheads within the family but also victims of blighted dreams which reflect the way society has failed them. *Living with Your Enemies* relates a mother's lost opportunities, sacrificed in bringing up her children, back to her post-war youth and the promises offered by the creation of the Welfare State. The flawed but explosive *Angelus* is a three-hander in which the spectre of a Jimmy Porter figure is resurrected for the 1980s in Mick, bully-boy, drugs dealer and sinner seeking redemption. With its desperate spiritual yearnings, *Angelus* indicates that Craze is more than simply an adherent of the raw 'slice of life' school of drama. Both *Shona* (the first winner of the Verity Bargate Award), which is a terse, painful blast against modern psychiatric practices, and *Going West* (about a couple of hobos on the road from New York to LA) show that Craze is a champion of the underdog – his is a voice of compassion, chronicling the area where frustrated dreams turn into anger and despair. *Passion* is a brave exploration of the vexed issues of the Palestinian situation.

TRY THESE:
★MARCHANT's *The Lucky Ones* for angst in the working class; for images of insanity,
★AYCKBOURN's *Woman in Mind*, ★DURANG's *Beyond Therapy*, ★EDGAR's *Mary Barnes*,
★MERCER's *In Two Minds*, ★MURRAY's *The Admission* and *Bodycell*, ★ORTON's *What the Butler Saw*, ★WEISS's *Marat/Sade*; for generational conflict between mothers and offspring, ★KEARSLEY, ★PAGE, ★RAIF; ★PHILLIPS' *Strange Fruit*, for generational differences in terms of the black community; for other responses to Palestine see ★BLOCK's *Hand in Hand*, ★HARE's *Via Dolorosa*, ★PASCAL's *Crossing Jerusalem*.

CRIMP, Martin   [1956 –   ]
British dramatist

PLAYS INCLUDE:
Living Remains (1981), *Three Attempted Acts* (1985, radio), *A Variety of Death Defying Acts* (1985), *Definitely the Bahamas* (1986), *Dealing with Clair* (1988), *Play with Repeats* (1989), *No One Sees the Video* (1991), *Getting Attention* (1991), *The Treatment* (1993) *Attempts on Her Life* (1997), *The Country* (2000)

Crimp can rightly be claimed as a product of the Orange Tree Theatre at Richmond. As the *Daily Telegraph*'s Charles Spencer has noted, 'he appears to deal with humdrum people in humdrum situations but nothing is as it seems'. Beneath the surface, Crimp implies worlds of darker meaning, thereby creating growing atmospheres of tension, even of menace. When you add to this his spiky, spare, apparently naturalistic but actually rigorously controlled and often very funny dialogue, it's little wonder he has been hailed, in some quarters, as a new ★PINTER. Crimp's plays are certainly very much products of today, thinly disguised comedies of manners, expertly reproducing recognisable types and surface tics. Crimp likes to peel back the layers of social behaviour to reveal the horrors and void beneath the veneer of contemporary life. *No One Sees the Video*, a scathing attack on market research (based on his own experience), ended up as a series of short albeit brilliant sketches, ultimately lacking depth in characterisation, burdened with a heavy-handed plot development and an inconclusive ending. More successful, perhaps, was *Dealing with Clair*. A story set in very typical late 1980s territory, yuppie-land, it brought together Clair, a young female estate agent, a sleekly upwardly mobile couple anxious to get the best possible price for their home, and a somewhat mysterious cash buyer. Clair's possible murder at the end only coincidentally paralleled the mystery surrounding the real-life disappearance of Suzy Lamplugh, a young London estate agent. As in *No One Sees the Video*, Crimp's line is one of moral scruple highlighting the greed and avarice behind smooth yuppie smiles, the emptiness and moral bankruptcy behind sleek market researchers, rather than just denouncing unethical real-estate practices or consumerism. In *Getting Attention* a sense of tension around the possibility of knowing – and doing nothing – is perhaps really at issue, not just the child abuse that is the ostensible subject. *Attempts on Her Life* was a radical experiment, with speeches unassigned to characters, and in *The Country* Crimp's characteristic sense of immanent danger is transplanted from the city in what Michael Billington described as 'an assault on the pastoral myth' (*Guardian*).

TRY THESE:
Crimp has translated plays by ★GENET, ★IONESCO, Bernard-Marie Koltès, ★MARIVAUX and ★MOLIÈRE; ★BRENTON and ★HARE's *Pravda* and ★HARE's *Secret Rapture*, ★JEFFREYS' *Valued Friends*, ★LUCIE's *Fashion*, for other critiques of contemporary moral values; ★ANOUILH for another example of social satire digging away at the heart of moral darkness; ★MILLER's *The Price* for linking consumer spending and the nation's emotional state; ★AYCKBOURN for another British playwright fond of peeling away social exteriors to reveal the ooze beneath; ★MEYER's *Etta Jenks* for an American equivalent of Liz in *No One Sees the Video*, a reluctant beginner who takes on the traits of her original oppressors, with a vengeance; ★ROBERT HOLMAN's *Rafts and Dreams* also deals with child abuse, though in a somewhat surreal manner.

CROSS, Felix   [1953   ]
Trinidad-born performer, writer and composer

MUSICAL PLAYS INCLUDE:
Blues for Railton (1985), *Mass Carib* (1987), *Glory* (1988), *Passports to the Promised Land* (2001)

Cross's major contribution to black theatre lies in his cross-cultural pieces of musical theatre and his artistic directorship of Nitro (formerly Black Theatre Co-op). *Blues for Railton* signalled the creation of a new form of black theatre in Britain. Adapted with David Simon from Simon's original novel, it is a tragicomedy about the experiences in Britain of a black immigrant family whose sense of identity was underlined through musical leitmotifs and rituals recalling Afro-Caribbean rituals and rhythms. In *Mass Carib* his achievement of fusing Western and Afro-Caribbean musical idioms developed into a full-blown synthesis of the Roman Catholic mass absorbed into Afro-Caribbean musical forms. Incorporating elements of carnival, masks, and drumming, it also told the story of the enforced conversion to Christianity of the slaves taken to the Caribbean, bringing them up to date as immigrants arriving in Britain brandishing British passports. *Mass Carib* was, by any standards, a tremendously impressive theatrical and musical achievement as well as a celebration of Afro-Caribbean cultural survival-by-adaptation (African Shango gods, for instance, being given Christian names). *Glory*, following a similar theme, but with a more complex, anti-imperialist text by Cross, combined a strong storyline with magnificent musicianship and theatrical spectacle, this time using calypso alongside African Shango rituals and aspects of carnival. Cross's text ambitiously tries to interweave personal tragedy (a young woman abused by her father), with the story of Trinidad and Tobago's struggle for political independence from the British – a heavy mixture to sustain. Some critics carped about its over-simplicities (mostly in the white characters). Others accepted its shortcomings and still marvelled at its scope. *Passports* deals with the experiences of two families arriving in Britain in the 1950s, using a similar fusion of musical influences, but some felt that the quality of the music was carrying a rather less well-achieved drama.

TRY THESE:
★BREUER's *The Warrior Ant* for a full-scale West Indian carnival; Stephen Sondheim for the musical writer-composer par excellence; ★MATURA's *The Coup* for a contrasting and almost farce-like view of post-colonial Trinidad.

DANIELS, Sarah   [1957 –]
British dramatist

PLAYS INCLUDE:
Ripen Our Darkness (1981), *Masterpieces* (1983), *The Devil's Gateway* (1983), *Neaptide* (1984), *Byrthrite* (1987), *The Gut Girls* (1988), *Beside Herself* (1990), *Head-Rot Holiday* (1992), *The Madness of Esme and Shaz* (1994), *Blow Your House Down* (1995), *Dust* (2003)

Daniels first came to prominence with *Ripen Our Darkness* – a play famous for the line 'Dear David, your dinner and my head are in the oven' – premiered, like *Byrthrite*, at the Royal Court Upstairs. Her attacks on patriarchy involve the rebellion of mothers (*Ripen Our Darkness* and *The Devil's Gateway*) and the discussion of lesbian custody of children in *Neaptide*. *Byrthrite* is a warning for women about the possible consequences of modern genetic engineering and reproductive techniques and is linked to a familiar theme of the persecution of the old 'wise women' of the seventeenth century (though by no means treated in familiar fashion, and, in its high-camp, historical setting, a breakaway from Daniels' usual quasi-naturalism). *The Gut Girls* continues the historical theme with its celebration of Victorian working-class women, and *Beside Herself* tackles childhood abuse in a mythological frame.

Needless to say, Daniels' plays and her expression of unpalatable truths (especially if you are a man) provoked, in their turn, vitriolically hostile reviews from critics (mostly but not exclusively male), particularly over *Masterpieces* and *Byrthrite*. But Daniels' early protagonists are recognisable suburban wives and mothers rebelling – wittily – against their roles as general moppers-up after men and the male value system that has put them there. In Daniels' world, the personal becomes graphically political. Despite the outcries,

Daniels won the George Devine Award in 1982 for *Neaptide*. Daniels' concern with the ways in which society labels 'difficult' women as mad continued in *Head-Rot Holiday*, written for the Clean Break company, which is set in a mental hospital, and in *The Madness of Esme and Shaz*. Daniels has written extensively for television, particularly *EastEnders* and *Grange Hill*.

Masterpieces

This uncompromisingly didactic play makes a direct link between the seemingly innocuous dinner-table misogynist joke and male violence against women. It is a tale of growing awareness, focused on Rowena, a social worker (the archetypal Daniels heroine), who gradually moves from naivety to anger, from passivity to action and wholesale rejection of the manmade world in which she lives and to which she has, in the past, given tacit acceptance. The play has an irrefutable emotional force about it and has deservedly come to be regarded as a feminist classic, even if some find its philosophical links and dramatic structure questionable.

TRY THESE:
For a contrasting male treatment of pornography, ★LUCIE's *Progress*; ★RAVENHILL's *Handbag* for Wildean custody issues; ★WANDOR scripted Gay Sweatshop's *Care and Control*, an earlier treatment of lesbian custody; ★CHURCHILL's *Vinegar Tom* and ★DEKKER, ★FORD and ★ROWLEY's *The Witch of Edmonton* for witches; ★LAVERY for an adventurer using wit to attack the bastions of patriarchy; ★SHAKESPEARE's *The Winter's Tale* uses the same Demeter myth as *Neaptide*; ★CHAMBERS as an American pioneer of lesbian drama; the use of mythological figures in the first scene of *Beside Herself* parallels some of ★CHURCHILL's stylistic devices in *Top Girls*.

D'ARCY, Margaretta

See ★ ARDEN, John

DARKE, Nick   [1949 –   ]
British dramatist

PLAYS INCLUDE:
Never Say Rabbit in a Boat (1978), *Landmarks* (1979), *A Tickle on the River's Back* (1979), *Say Your Prayers* (1980), *The Catch* (1980), *High Water* (1980), *The Body* (1983), *The Oven Glove Murders* (1986), *The Dead Monkey* (1986), *Ting Tang Mine* (1987), *Kissing the Pope* (1987), *The King of Prussia* (1999), *The Riot* (1999)

An erstwhile actor, Cornish-born Darke remains an enigmatic dramatist who has yet to achieve an unchallenged success. Many of his plays draw on the terrain of his upbringing, but his psychological grasp often falls short of his geographical one, and his writing becomes more earnest and pedantic the further it strays from his own roots. In *The Body*, an eccentric West Country community must contend with the presence of an American airforce base in one of those plays about the bomb that shows what poor art can come out of good politics. In *Ting Tang Mine*, originally staged as a Cornish community play in 1984 under the title *The Earth Turned Inside Out*, the fate of two rival mining communities becomes an unconvincing parable of Thatcherite avarice. Greed's relationship to the screen gets the treatment in *The Oven Glove Murders* and Californian morality comes under the cudgel in *The Dead Monkey*, about a childless West Coast couple whose relationship has been kept alive for fifteen years by the now-dead simian of the title. Like many of Darke's plays, the topic is interesting but the style derivative. David Soul and Alexa Hamilton revived it in 1998 but without reversing earlier judgements. *Kissing the Pope*, inspired by a visit to Nicaragua, an earnest attempt to confront that area's tragic ironies, failed to find general favour, being labelled as simplistic agit-prop and propaganda. However, Darke's sensitive examination of the relationship between a young Contra and a young Sandinista 'growing up to be a man in a violent world, having to decide why to kill

before you know why to live' was generally praised. *The King of Prussia* and *The Riot*, both on Cornish historical themes with resonances for the new century, failed to achieve a long-looked-for breakthrough.

TRY THESE:
★ KAUFMAN and HART's *Once in a Lifetime*, ★ KOPIT's *Road to Nirvana*, ★ MAMET's *Speed-the-Plow*, ★ SHEPARD's *Angel City*, ★ CHARLES WOOD (especially *Has 'Washington' Legs?* and *Veterans*) for theatrical looks at the machinations of the movie industry; *Ting Tang Mine* is reminiscent of ★ SYNGE's *Playboy of the Western World*; ★ ALBEE and ★ RABE for a kind of American Absurdism which Darke seems to want to emulate; ★ CLARK's *The Petition*, ★ DANIELS' *The Devil's Gateway*, ★ EDGAR's *Maydays* for other plays about American airforce bases; ★ ARDEN's *Serjeant Musgrave's Dance* for small-town disturbances.

DAVIES, Andrew   [1936 –   ]
British dramatist

PLAYS INCLUDE:
Filthy Fryer and the Woman of Maturer Years (1974), *Rose* (1980), *Prin* (1990)

Now firmly established as Britain's leading adapter of classic novels for television, Davies, a former teacher and lecturer, has written successfully for many media (his children's book *Conrad's War* won the 1978 Guardian Award and Boston Globe Horn Award). *Prin*, a sourly funny 'well made' comedy, focuses on that familiar breed the English eccentric, in the form of the principal of a teacher's training college for physical education fighting a rearguard action against the grey drabness of modern educational policies. Prin is at once a symbol of the enlightened progressive in all its dangerous, thrilling glory (shades of Jean Brodie), and at the same time more than faintly ludicrous in her refusal to move with the times. A bullying tyrant to friend, foe and young female lover alike, she is given all the best lines, but finally deprived of happiness.

TRY THESE:
Muriel Spark's *The Prime of Miss Jean Brodie* and ★ SIMON GRAY's *Butley* for other articulate but fairly bilious educationalists; ★ MARCUS's *The*

Killing of Sister George has obvious affinities with *Prin* in its depiction of lesbian life and loves; ★WILDE for paradoxes in dialogue and character; ★PETER SHAFFER's *Equus* and *Amadeus* for flawed genius and mundane mediocrity.

DE ANGELIS, April   [1960 –   ]
British dramatist

PLAYS INCLUDE:
Breathless (1986), *Wanderlust* (1988), *Women in Law* (1988), *Frankenstein* (1989), *Iron Mistress* (1989), *Crux* (1990), *Fanny Hill* (1991, from John Cleland), *Hush* (1992) *Playhouse Creatures* (1993), *Soft Vengeance* (1993, adapted from Albie Sachs), *The Positive Hour* (1997), *A Warwickshire Testimony* (1999), *A Laughing Matter* (2002)

De Angelis worked as an actress with Monstrous Regiment, ReSisters and Lumiere and Son before embarking on an increasingly distinguished writing career. *Breathless*, an award winner in the 1987 Second Wave Young Women's writing festival at the Albany, propelled her into prominence. A short, gothically atmospheric drama written with verve, wit and very contemporary consciousness about women and science, it rehashed the old Frankenstein myth and the stereotypical helpless Victorian heroine, with a contrasting pair of drooping mistress and obsessive maid, working away in the dungeons amongst the test tubes, frustrated at not being taken seriously as scientists. *Women in Law* carries on in something of the same vein. It uses a gothic setting, a thriller convention, and another, even more extravagant variant of *la châtelaine enchainée* (this one owes more than a little to a demented kind of Bette Davis/Miss Favisham) who is, again, a scientist manqué pining for a lost career as a marine biologist. Commissioned by the ReSisters theatre company, the play was ostensibly written to back up ideas about women and violence and the way they are treated in law, and though the polemic was laudable, the play suffered from its obvious brief. In *Wanderlust*, de Angelis's wilder shores and tongue-in-cheek imagination takes on the Great Man myth of David Livingstone, to make some serious points about colonialism in Africa. *Iron Mistress*

continues to investigate the historical configurations of psychological confrontations between mothers and daughters. *Crux* uses the suppression of a medieval women's community's attempts to explore issues of power and desire. *Hush*, unusually for de Angelis, is set in modern times and caused Irving Wardle to declare that 'after this well-plotted moral thriller . . . the obsequies for the State-of-England Play have been premature'. *The Positive Hour* similarly deals with contemporary crises in the family as a social worker finds herself at the centre of a nexus of personal and professional crises. *A Warwickshire Testimony*, for the RSC, examines the realities of rural life through an initial focus on the village post office that is about to be sold off to incomers. As the couple who had run the office try to come to terms with their displacement, de Angelis opens the play up to explore the realities of a past that was never the bucolic idyll that nostalgia offers as a substitute for actual experience.

Her interest in women in history turned in a new direction with *Playhouse Creatures*, an exploration of the first generation of English actresses as they attempt to negotiate the public and private perils of establishing their new profession in Restoration London, which she followed with *A Laughing Matter*, in which she tackled the theatre of the late eighteenth century and the reasons for ★DAVID GARRICK's reluctance to stage ★GOLDSMITH's *She Stoops to Conquer*.

TRY THESE:
★LEVY for a similar kind of verve and imaginative drive; ★BRENTON's *Bloody Poetry* for the Shelleys; Graeae for a version of Frankenstein; ★BARKER's *The Castle* for medieval communes of women and *Victory* for another version of Nell Gwyn; ★JEFFREYS' *The Libertine* for another version of the period of *Playhouse Creatures*; Restoration writers, such as ★BEHN, ★CONGREVE, ★ETHEREGE and ★WYCHERLEY; ★SHERIDAN for eighteenth-century comedy; ★BOND's *Restoration* uses conventions and themes derived from the practice of Restoration writers to make modern points; ★DANIELS' *Masterpieces* for a social worker in crisis.

A Laughing Matter by April de Angelis, directed by Max Stafford-Clark, National Theatre and Out of Joint, 2002. Christopher Staines, Jason Watkins as David Garrick, Monica Dolan as Peg Woffington. (Pete Jones/ArenaPAL)

DEAR, Nick   [1955 –   ]
British dramatist

PLAYS INCLUDE:
The Perfect Alibi (1980), *Temptation* (1984), *The Bed* (1986), *Pure Science* (1986), *The Art of Success* (1986), *Food of Love* (1988), *In the Ruins* (1990), *Zenobia* (1995), *The Villain's Opera* (2000), *Power* (2003)

Portsmouth-born Dear came to attention with *The Art of Success*, an RSC production that earned him an Olivier Award nomination for the Most Promising Newcomer in Theatre. Set in the eighteenth century, the play is purposefully revisionist and anachronistic in order to make a retroactive point about opportunism and lust, with the Prime Minister Walpole as the Mrs Thatcher of his time facing off against the similarly Thatcherite entrepreneurial satirical artist William Hogarth. The play compresses ten years into one night and takes various liberties with personal and political history, but there's no denying the vigour of Dear's scatology-laden language. His follow-up play *A Family Affair* (1988) (an ★OSTROVSKY adaptation for Cheek by Jowl) has a similarly contemporary bent in its depiction of a society both goaded on, and paralysed, by matters financial. *In the Ruins* is a bravura, virtual monologue by King George III, which contrasts the image of the monarchy with the reality of the monarch. Dear's adaptation of Tirso de Molina's *The Last Days of Don Juan* was very successful for the RSC in 1990/1. *Zenobia* is a retelling of the story of the third-century AD warrior queen who challenged Roman rule, and *The Villain's Opera* an updating of ★GAY and ★BRECHT that won few plaudits. His other work includes the films of Jane Austen's *Persuasion*, which won a BAFTA award in 1996, and *The Gambler*.

TRY THESE:
★BOND's *Bingo* and ★PETER SHAFFER's *Amadeus* for analogous debunkings of historical greats; ★BARKER and ★JONSON for a similar robustness of language; ★HORVÁTH and ★SHAW for Don Juans; Dear's other adaptations include ★ARBUZOV's *The Promise* for the Tricycle in 2002, ★GORKY's *Summerfolk* and ★MOLIÈRE's *Le Bourgeois Gentilhomme*.

DE FILIPPO, Eduardo   [1900 – 85]
Italian actor, poet and dramatist

PLAYS INCLUDE:
Oh These Ghosts! (1946), *Filumena* (1946), *Inner Voices* (1948, translated by ★N.F. SIMPSON), *Fear Number One* (1950), *My Darling and My Love* (1955), *Saturday, Sunday, Monday* (1959, translated by ★KEITH WATERHOUSE and ★WILLIS HALL), *Ducking Out* (1982, translated by Mike Stott), *Napoli Milionaria* (English version by Peter Tinniswood, 1991)

De Filippo wrote more than fifty plays. Born into a family of actors (one of three illegitimate children), he began his career by touring with the famous Scarpetta acting company before founding a company with his brother Peppino and sister Titina.

Based on his experience as an actor, and his early days writing comedy and musical sketches, his later Neapolitan comedies are nothing if not supremely actable, distinguished by their craftsmanship and a Pirandellian involvement with the fine line between illusion and reality. As in ★AYCKBOURN's plays the comic impetus comes from the recognisable ordinariness of domestic life crashing up against the unexpected, the surreal, or the inappropriate emotional over-reaction. In *Saturday, Sunday, Monday*, the quintessential de Filippo, the inevitable matriarch presides over the warring factions of an extended family – squabbling offspring, eccentric relatives, a paranoid husband, opportunistic friends and lumbering maid – as they somehow live, love, fight, survive the heightened emotions of the rituals of Sunday lunch and become reconciled. Paternity and female subterfuge form the lynchpins of *Filumena* in which, when a wealthy businessman threatens to marry a younger woman, his long-standing mistress hoodwinks him into marriage by refusing to disclose which of her three illegitimate sons is his. *Filumena* tells us as much about male pride as it does about female deviousness.

TRY THESE:
★BILL's *Curtains* for the joys (or otherwise) of families; ★PIRANDELLO, ★FO and ★RAME are other regularly performed twentieth-century Italian dramatists.

DEKKER, Thomas   [c. 1572 – 1632]
English dramatist and pamphleteer

PLAYS INCLUDE:
The Shoemaker's Holiday (1599), *The Honest Whore* (1604, with ★THOMAS MIDDLETON), *Sir Thomas Wyatt* (pre-1607, with ★THOMAS HEYWOOD (?) and ★JOHN WEBSTER), *The Roaring Girl* (1610, with ★THOMAS MIDDLETON), *The Virgin Martyr* (1624, with ★PHILIP MASSINGER), *The Witch of Edmonton* (1621, with ★JOHN FORD and ★WILLIAM ROWLEY)

A rather shadowy figure who seems to have earned his living as a kind of house dramatist cum play doctor and pamphleteer, Dekker was imprisoned on more than one occasion for the debt that dogged him throughout his life. He seems to have spent much of his life producing collaborative work in whatever style was needed by the theatre manager Philip Henslowe. Dekker's own dramatic work is generally genial, compassionate, London-centred and populist as in *The Shoemaker's Holiday* with its Dick Whittington-like tale of a cobbler who rises to become Lord Mayor of London while a disguised young nobleman woos and wins the daughter of the current Lord Mayor and receives the King's pardon for doing so. *The Roaring Girl* is particularly interesting since its portrait of a woman who scandalises contemporary society by wearing men's clothing and indulging in typical male pursuits like smoking and brawling is based on a real person, Mary Frith, who herself sat on stage to watch an early performance of the play. Dekker is also credited with the sympathetic portrayal of the witch in *The Witch of Edmonton*.

TRY THESE:
★JONSON satirised him in *The Poetaster*; ★AUDEN and Isherwood, ★BRENTON and ★HARE, ★HECHT and MacArthur are examples of successful twentieth-century partnerships; among other contemporary writers who have also collaborated successfully are ★IKOLI and Tariq Ali (with ★BRENTON), ★CHURCHILL (with ★LAN), ★EDGAR (with Susan Todd), ★TREVOR GRIFFITHS (with ★BRENTON, ★CLARK, ★HARE, ★POLIAKOFF, Hugh Stoddart and ★SNOO WILSON on *Lay By* and with ★BRENTON, ★CAMPBELL and ★HARE on *Deeds*); for another real-life portrait of a woman stepping outside traditional roles, ★WERTENBAKER's account of intrepid traveller Isabelle Ebhardt in *New Anatomies*; ★BEHN for other prototype feminists.

DELANEY, Shelagh   [1939 –   ]
British dramatist

PLAYS INCLUDE:
A Taste of Honey (1958), *The Lion in Love* (1960), *The House That Jack Built* (1978)

Delaney's main stage claim to fame is based on *A Taste of Honey*, the play she wrote at nineteen. Born in Salford, this one-time salesgirl, cinema usherette and photographer's lab assistant who left school at sixteen, wrote what has come to be regarded as one of the definitive plays of the 1950s. *A Taste of Honey*, her first play, was accepted by ★JOAN LITTLEWOOD's Theatre Workshop, was filmed (with Rita Tushingham as Jo) and is regularly revived in Britain. *The Lion in Love*, about a disturbed and unhappy family, again took a mother and daughter as its focal point, but its more symbolic treatment found less favour, and some thought it was swamped by Littlewood's production. The play is seldom revived, although its style, themes, and sensitivities prefigure the work of such contemporary British dramatists as ★AYSHE RAIF and ★JULIA KEARSLEY. A revival giving us a chance to 'compare and contrast' would be fascinating. Delaney has written many screenplays, notably *Charley Bubbles* (1968, starring Albert Finney) and the highly acclaimed *Dance with a Stranger* (1985) about the last woman to be hanged in Britain, Ruth Ellis.

A Taste of Honey
This play breaks many of its time's conventions about motherhood and female sexuality in its portrait of Jo, the young working-class, reluctant mother-to-be and anti-heroine. In another sense it is very much of its time in celebrating a working-class approach, at once unsentimental and free of moral judgements, to illegitimacy, racial intermarriage, or homosexuality. With its female-centred focus, and final opting for a life without men, it is a play

that predates the concerns of later feminist writers – the optimism and the vulnerabilities, as well as the strengths of women – by well over a decade. However, despite its apparent affiliation to the realistic school of 'kitchen sink' drama, its original production by Littlewood made sure that audiences were not let off the hook as she confronted them with the challenges and the responsibilities raised by the play's sexual politics.

TRY THESE:
★ JELLICOE's *The Sport of My Mad Mother* for a bold, non-realistic treatment of the mother image; ★ WATERHOUSE and Willis Hall's *Billy Liar* for the theme of transposing grim reality into dreams; ★ MACDONALD and ★ PAGE for more recent images of mother–daughter conflict; ★ OSBORNE's *Look Back* in *Anger* for a contrasting treatment and male view of pregnancy; ★ IBSEN's *Hedda Gabler* for another image of reluctant pregnancy; for more warring families, ★ DE FILIPPO's *Ducking Out*.

DE VEGA CARPIO, Lope Félix   [1562 – 1635]
Spanish dramatist

PLAYS INCLUDE:
Fuenteovejuna (1612, *The Sheep Well*), *The Simple Lady* (1613), *Peribanez* (1614), *The King is the Best Judge* (c. 1620), *Punishment without Revenge* (1631)

De Vega claimed to have written an amazing total of 1,500 plays, of which about 480 survive (mostly in manuscript). He also wrote three novels and 3,000 sonnets, married twice, had some seven major love affairs, and sailed with the Spanish Armada. He fixed and developed the form of the Spanish *comedia*, attacking the pseudo-Aristotelian unities and freely mixing comedy and tragedy (and indeed pastoral and historical as well). His plays are well constructed, more inclined to entertaining action than subtle characterisation (most of his work was done at speed to satisfy the demands of theatre directors), and often deal with questions of family honour and paternal authority (of which he is in favour). As suggested by the Young Vic's 2003 staging of *Peribanez*, the rest of his plays could

well yield something revivable, though perhaps not many of the plays where private executions are condoned in the cause of restoring a wife's honour. The best of these is probably *The King is the Best Judge*, in which the king, disguised as a mayor, obliges a nobleman to marry a village girl he has abducted, has him beheaded and then grants her half of his estate and gives her back to her young lover – a satisfying solution on both a personal and a civic level. ★ JOHN OSBORNE adapted *La Fianza Satisfecha* as *A Bond Honoured* for the National Theatre in 1966, but the play one is most likely to see at present is a version of *Fuenteovejuna*. This play is unusual in that the people of the village become a collective protagonist. The overlord snatches the mayor's daughter Laurencia from her wedding and imprisons the groom, but she escapes and incites the townspeople to behead him. The whole village, even under torture, declare that 'Fuenteovejuna did it', and finally King Ferdinand collectively pardons them for the justice of the act and reunites the lovers. The play is popular with progressive political groups, but some of the honour-and-revenge plays would give them more trouble.

TRY THESE:
★ CALDERÓN, who borrowed plots from de Vega and refined his plays; ★ AESCHYLUS' *The Persians* for another collective protagonist; ★ GOOCH for an adaptation of *Fuenteovejuna*; ★ ADRIAN MITCHELL's adaptation of Robert Browning's *The Pied Piper* presents a town the children want to escape from; for a different view of communities see ★ CARTWRIGHT's *Road*.

DEVLIN, Ann   [1951 –   ]
Northern Irish dramatist

PLAYS INCLUDE:
Ourselves Alone (1985), *Heartlanders* (1989, with ★ STEPHEN BILL and ★ DAVID EDGAR), *After Easter* (1994)

Devlin has written extensively for television (she won the Samuel Beckett Award for her television plays *A Woman Calling* and *The Long March* in 1984), radio and film. Her solo stage plays both centre on the Northern Irish situation. *Ourselves Alone*, which won both the George Devine and Susan Smith Blackburn Awards, is a warm, toughly plotted political thriller, set in the aftermath of the 1981 hunger strikes of Northern Ireland. Something of a trailblazer, it was an early attempt to show the tragic consequences of entrenched views, from a female perspective. As such, its central focus was less concerned with the pros and cons of Republicanism than with showing the struggle of three sisters to escape stifling familial and political bonds. Argument has raged about whether the play reinforced certain stereotypes (chauvinism of Irish men), and whether the portrait of women was unduly pessimistic (one responds by escaping to England, another, a former IRA supporter, settles down to blissful maternity, the third waits for a prisoner to be released but finds he wasn't worth the wait). In *After Easter* the story is again of three sisters: one, living in England, is mentally disturbed, a second tries to pass for an American, and the third is settled close to the family home. They are brought together by their father's heart attack in a forced family reunion that results in domestic confrontations and revisiting of past conflicts.

TRY THESE:

★REID's *Tea in a China Cup* and ★MARIE JONES for Belfast plays with a specifically women-centred focus; ★MORNIN's *Kate* and *Built on Sand* for the effects of the Troubles on women; ★FINNEGAN for a more stylised, many-faceted exploration of Northern Ireland's religious and political loyalties; ★HUTCHINSON's *Rat in the Skull* for a different variant; ★O'CASEY for similar concerns; ★CARR for sisters suffering and ★CHEKHOV for the *Three Sisters*; ★AYCKBOURN, and ★ELIOT's *The Family Reunion* for other versions of unhappy families.

DE WET, Reza
South African dramatist

PLAYS INCLUDE

Crossing (1994), *Three Sisters Two* (1997), *Yelena* (1998), *On the Lake* (2001)

A leading South African dramatist who writes in both Afrikaans and English, de Wet's major impact in Britain so far came from the 2002 premiere of *Three Sisters Two*, presented at the Orange Tree in tandem with ★CHEKHOV's original. De Wet sees parallels between her own situation as an Afrikaner in South Africa and the situation underlying *Three Sisters*. The play is set in the aftermath of the Revolution: Andrei, Olga and Irina are still where they were but Vershinin, now a general in the White army, has returned. De Wet attempts something similar with *Uncle Vanya* in *Yelena*, and *The Seagull* in *On the Lake*. Her *Crossing*, seen at Riverside Studios in 2000, is set in South Africa in 1930 and tells the story of how two sisters who live by a river are haunted by the spirit of a woman who ignored their warning not to try to cross the river.

TRY THESE:

Helen Cooper's *Mrs Vershinin* tells the story of how she came to be the offstage neurotic in *Three Sisters*; ★FRIEL has adapted *The Cherry Orchard* to an Irish setting and his *Afterplay* brings together Sonia from *Uncle Vanya* and Andrei from *Three Sisters* after the Revolution; Michael Picardie's *The Cape Orchard* applied it to South Africa; ★MATURA transferred *Three Sisters* to Trinidad in his *Trinidad Sisters*; ★FUGARD for other South African plays.

DORFMAN, Ariel   [1942 –   ]
Argentinean-born dramatist, now a Chilean citizen

PLAYS INCLUDE:

Death and the Maiden (1991), *Reader* (1995), *Widows* (1997), *Purgatory* (2000)

Under threat from the Peron regime because they were Jews and his father was politically active, Dorfman's family left Argentina for the USA in 1945. They fled the USA because of McCarthyism and settled in Chile, where Dorfman established himself as a novelist, poet and critic. As an adviser to the government of Salvador Allende, he was persona non grata after the Pinochet coup and once more went into exile in Europe and the USA. He campaigned against the human rights abuses of the Chilean dictatorship, returned there in 1983 but left again when political repression increased in 1986 after Pinochet survived an assassination attempt. After the restoration of democracy in Chile in 1990 he was able to return again but he also works at Duke University in the USA.

Dorfman's most famous play is *Death and the Maiden*, a worldwide success, which was filmed in 1994. A woman who was repeatedly tortured and raped to the sound of Schubert believes that she has one of her tormentors at her mercy in an isolated beach house. The play draws very directly on first-hand knowledge of exile and torture to explore complex issues of morality, revenge, justice and forgiveness. In *Widows* Dorfman again uses a setting in an unnamed South American country to purse his concern for the victims of state violence: here the inspiration is the relatives of the 'Disappeared' who wait for a river to wash up the dead. The women become a modern-day Greek chorus united by their shared grief. *Reader* is about an efficient censor in the future who finds himself attempting to censor what turns out to be the story of his life.

TRY THESE:

★HAVEL, ★PINTER's *One for the Road* and *Mountain Language*, ★STOPPARD's *Every Good Boy Deserves Favour* for political repression;
★PIRANDELLO for parallels with *Reader*;
★EURIPIDES' *Women of Troy*, ★SYNGE's *Riders to the Sea* for parallels with *Widows*; for music and repression, ★C. P. TAYLOR's *Good*.

DOWIE, Claire   [1956 –   ]
British dramatist and performer

PLAYS INCLUDE:

Cat and Mouse (1986), *Adult Child/Dead Child* (1988), *Why is John Lennon Wearing a Skirt?* (1990), *Leaking from Every Orifice* (1993), *Death and Dancing* (1993), *All Over Lovely* (1998), *The Year of the Monkey* (2000, originally radio), *Designs for Living* (2001)

Birmingham-born Dowie was once a stand-up comic and performer of her own poems on the alternative cabaret circuit before developing what she describes as 'stand-up theatre'. Her monologues, often interlaced with poetry, are nerveless exposures of the individual rebelling against social conformity. *Cat and Mouse* and *Adult Child/Dead Child* set a sombre, indeed devastating tone, the first being 'about' child abuse, and the second

'about' an unloved child teetering on the edge of schizophrenia. She doesn't so much portray her roles as inhabit them, dragging the audience along with her on a journey that, in *Adult Child*, takes her from unwanted home environment to lonely bedsit and psychiatric treatment as she tries to come to terms with the rules of an adult world pressing her to conform. *Why Is John Lennon Wearing a Skirt?* is a two-hour tour de force, part hilarious satire, part invective, against wearing a skirt and the whole teenage peer-pressure of becoming a woman (she just wants to be herself; the Beatles are her gang and John Lennon her model). Dowie is the quintessential outsider, never half so funny as when she is puncturing sacred cows, the women's movement included. *Leaking from Every Orifice* deals with a lesbian woman who gets pregnant by a gay man while *Designs for Living*, commissioned by Ruby Tuesday, a group created 'to present the very best of lesbian theatre', has three characters locked in a complex dance of sexual attraction, complicated by difficulties with gender stereotyping.

TRY THESE:

★CRAZE, ★EDGAR, ★MURRAY, for other British playwrights who have tackled the subject of schizophrenia; ★BOGOSIAN and ★SPALDING GRAY for American monologues; ★CRIMP's *Getting Attention*, ★CROSS's *Glory!*, ★ROBERT HOLMAN's *Rafts and Dreams* all touch on the issue of child abuse; ★COOKE, ★MACDONALD, ★PINNOCK for contrasting examples of young women and teenage development: ★COWARD's *Design for Living* for a parallel with *Designs for Living*; ★RAVENHILL's *Handbag* for the complexities of homosexual pregnancy.

DREXLER, Rosalyn   [1926 –   ]
American dramatist, novelist and painter

PLAYS INCLUDE:

Home Movies (1964), *Hot Buttered Roll* (1966), *The Line of Least Resistance* (1968), *Skywriting* (1968), *Softly, and Consider the Nearness* (1973), *The Writer's Opera* (1979), *Graven Image* (1980), *Delicate Feelings* (1984), *Green River Murders* (1986), *The Heart That Eats Itself* (1988), *Dear* (1996), *Occupational Hazard* (1996)

Drexler has distinguished herself as a playwright, novelist, screenwriter, painter and sculptor. A strong visual sense pervades her work, although she is as apt to get a laugh with elaborate puns as with sight gags. Absurdist situations and wordplay pervade her writing.

Her semi-autobiographical novel *To Smithereens* (1972) recounts the story of a woman turned wrestler to please her art-critic lover who found female wrestlers a turn-on. This experience clearly inspired the peculiar angle on traditional male–female relationships evidenced in Drexler's early work, long before the women's movement got off the ground. In *Home Movies,* a resurrected husband challenges his wife to a wrestling match as sexual foreplay; in *Hot Buttered Roll,* a billionaire engages a crew of burly-girls to give him a kick that will break his sex-o-meter. *Delicate Feelings* is about two lady mud wrestlers. In 1979, Drexler won her second OBIE for *The Writer's Opera,* a comedy examining the role of women as artists and mothers inspired by the life of Suzanne Valadon and her son Maurice Utrillo.

TRY THESE:
★ CHURCHILL's *Cloud Nine* for sexual role reversal; ★ IONESCO for Absurdism; ★ FEIFFER for comic-book sketches, ★ HOWE for comic conceits; ★ TERRY for early feminist playwriting; ★ LUCKHAM for wrestling as a metaphor; ★ SACKLER, ★ STOREY for other sporting metaphors.

DRYDEN, John   [1631 – 1700]
English dramatist, poet and critic

PLAYS INCLUDE:
The Indian Queen (1664, with Sir Robert Howard), *The Indian Emperor* (1665), *The Tempest* (1667, with Sir William Davenant), *Tyrannic Love* (1669), *The Conquest of Granada* (in two parts, 1670 and 1671), *Marriage à la Mode* (1672), *Aureng-Zebe* (1675), *All for Love* (1677), *Oedipus* (1678, with Nathaniel Lee), *Troilus and Cressida* (1678)

Dryden, one of the great literary figures of his age, wrote singly or in collaboration, nearly thirty plays but the only one of his plays to be staged regularly is *All for Love.* It is a treatment of the Antony and Cleopatra story, which is usually compared unfavourably with ★ SHAKESPEARE's play by those who assume, wrongly, that because Dryden adapted *The Tempest* he did the same to *Antony and Cleopatra.* The fact that the very occasional productions of Dryden's *Tempest* demonstrate that it is a good acting play tend to be forgotten in routine denunciations of the depravity of even daring to adapt the Bard. Something similar happens with *All for Love,* which tends to get castigated for not achieving the epic grandeur and flexibility of ★ SHAKESPEARE's play; in fact it is a far more concentrated and domestic work dealing with the theme in terms of a love/honour conflict of the kind beloved of Restoration tragedy.

TRY THESE:
★ SHAW's *Caesar and Cleopatra* is another treatment of the Cleopatra story which, like *All for Love,* is sometimes staged in repertory with ★ SHAKESPEARE's *Antony and Cleopatra;* ★ OTWAY's *Venice Preserv'd* is the only other tragedy from the period still staged regularly; Dryden's comedies are seldom revived but those of his contemporaries ★ BEHN, ★ CONGREVE, ★ ETHEREGE and ★ WYCHERLEY make more frequent appearances in the current repertory.

DUFFY, Maureen   [1933 –   ]
British novelist, poet and dramatist

PLAYS INCLUDE:
The Lay Off (1962), *The Silk Room* (1966), *Rites* (1969), *Solo* (1970), *Old Tyme* (1970), *A Nightingale in Bloomsbury Square* (1973)

Novelist, lesbian and feminist, whose dramatic output has been small but significant, Duffy is a writer of rich imagination and plunderer of classical mythologies, 'pitched between fantasy and realism' (Frank Marcus). *Rites,* her main claim to dramatic fame, is set in a ladies' public lavatory and loosely based on ★ EURIPIDES' *The Bacchae.* Its emphasis on a group of women can be seen as a precursor to ★ NELL DUNN's *Steaming.* But it is considerably more audacious in its mix of classical and modern ritual (a latter-day chorus inveighing against daily frustrations) and violence (the murder of a transvestite lesbian). It is a brave and questioning play that prefigures many of the concerns of later female playwrights about language, territory, gender and making the personal public and political. *Solo* and *Old Tyme* are other studies based on the mythological characters of Narcissus and Uranus respectively. *A Nightingale in Bloomsbury Square* is more of a biodrama-cum-monologue around the figure of Virginia Woolf, nudged on by Vita Sackville-West and Freud.

TRY THESE:
★CHURCHILL and ★LAN's *A Mouthful of Birds* and ★LAVERY's *Kitchen Matters* are also based on *The Bacchae*; ★MACDONALD's *When I Was a Girl I Used to Scream and Shout* for another example of female privacy made public.

DUMAS, Alexandre (fils)   [1824 – 95]
French dramatist and novelist

PLAYS INCLUDE:
La Dame aux Camélias (1851, variously translated as *The Lady of the Camellias*, but most often as *Camille*), *Le Demi-Monde* (1855), *Le Fils Naturel* (1858, *The Natural Son*), *Francillon* (1857)

In general, Dumas fils' worthy studies of contemporary problems of the bourgeois family have survived much less well on stage than have adaptations of the yarns of his reprobate father (*The Three Musketeers*, *The Count of Monte Cristo*, etc.). However, his first play, *La Dame aux Camélias*, remains one of the most potent myths of the present day, and there is often a version running somewhere (even though it is generally the opera version *La Traviata*). Modern permutations include ★TERENCE RATTIGAN's *Variation on a Theme*, and echoes of the theme in ★TENNESSEE WILLIAMS' *A Streetcar Named Desire* and *Camino Real*. Recent versions by women writers have reassessed Camille in terms of her relationship to society and the values of the times. ★PAM GEMS' *Camille* made most of the characters a good deal less high-minded (especially Alfred's father, who becomes improbably wicked instead of improbably noble) and stressed the power of money as the driving force in society.

TRY THESE:
Zola's *Nana* rings the changes on the courtesan theme; ★PINERO for the 'woman with a past' in *The Second Mrs Tanqueray*; ★Shaw for an attack on this kind of play in *Mrs Warren's Profession*; ★LUDLAM's *Camille* for a comic take on this character; ★GEMS for feminist reassessments of other mythical/legendary figures such as Piaf and Queen Christina.

DUNBAR, Andrea   [1965 – 90]
British dramatist

PLAYS INCLUDE:
The Arbor (1980), *Rita Sue and Bob Too* (1981), *Shirley* (1986)

Dunbar was brought up on a council estate on the outskirts of Bradford, and sent *The Arbor*, her first play, written at the age of fifteen, to the Royal Court Young Writer's Festival. Produced at the Theatre Upstairs and transferred to the main stage in an expanded version, it is a bleak study of life on a council estate in Bradford, of the violence and deprivation of family life in the midst of urban decay. Sex offers the only pleasure, and that is seen to lead to abuse and pregnancy. Dunbar was regarded as a return to the Royal Court's heyday of finding and championing work by working-class writers.

The film *Rita Sue and Bob Too* was developed from the play of the same name and incorporated sections from *The Arbor*. It was filmed on the council estate where Dunbar lived, and provoked the same kind of critical controversy as her plays: does Dunbar offer a patronising and unnecessarily bleak account of working-class life, or is that how it is? Dunbar remained unimpressed and continued to live in Bradford with her children until her tragically early death. Her plays present a stark account of the frustrations and impoverishment of economic deprivation, and she wrote with a remarkable ear for nuances of language.

TRY THESE:
★DELANEY's *A Taste of Honey* for obvious echoes (*Shirley* is like *A Taste of Honey* for the 1980s); ★WESKER for affinities with the gritty social realism of family life; ★CARTWRIGHT's *Road*, ★REID's

Joyriders; ★KEARSLEY and ★RAIF for likeminded contemporaries.

DUNN, Nell   [1936 –   ]
British novelist and dramatist

PLAYS INCLUDE:

I Want (1972, with Adrian Henri; staged 1982), *Steaming* (1981), *The Little Heroine* (1988), *Cancer Tales* (2001)

London-born Dunn made her name in 1963 with the award-winning television play *Up the Junction*, a gritty tale of down-and-out urban life that summed up a whole era. Her most famous stage play, *Steaming*, started out at the Theatre Royal, Stratford East, before transferring with great success to the West End, and to Broadway and being filmed. Hailed on both sides of the sexual politics divide, this apparent celebration of female solidarity, set in a public Turkish bath threatened with closure, posed more problems about voyeurism and the male gaze than it answered, and could be seen as a more populist successor to ★MAUREEN DUFFY's *Rites* without the moral clout. *The Little Heroine*, staged by the Nuffield Theatre Southampton, is another variation on exploring the vulnerabilities – and strengths – of women, this time through the example of a young heroin junkie and her successful kicking of the habit.

TRY THESE:

★FORNES' *Fefu and Her Friends* and ★MACDONALD's *When I Was a Girl I Used to Scream and Shout* for other female intimacies unveiled; ★GEMS' *Dusa, Fish, Stas and Vi*, ★WASSERSTEIN's *Uncommon Women* for women under pressure finding support in each other; ★C. P. TAYLOR's *Withdrawal Symptoms* takes withdrawal from heroin and from Empire together, in a fine study of the personal and the political.

DURANG, Christopher   [1949 –   ]
American dramatist and actor

PLAYS INCLUDE:

I Don't Generally Like Poetry But Have You Read 'Trees' (1972, with ★ALBERT INNAURATO), *The Mitzi Gaynor Story, or Gyp* (1973, with ★ALBERT INNAURATO), *The Idiots Karamazov* (1974, with ★ALBERT INNAURATO), *Titanic* (1974), *Death Comes to Us All, Mary Agnes* (1975), *When Dinah Shore Ruled the Earth* (1975, with ★WENDY WASSERSTEIN), *Das Lusitania Songspiel* (1976, with Sigourney Weaver), *A History of the American Film* (1976, with music by Mel Marvin), *The Vietnamization of New Jersey* (1977), *'Dentity Crisis* (1978), *The Nature and Purpose of the Universe* (1979), *Sister Mary Ignatius Explains It All for You* (1979), *Beyond Therapy* (1981), *The Actor's Nightmare* (1981), *Baby with the Bathwater* (1983), *The Marriage of Bette and Boo* (1985), *Laughing Wild* (1987), *Seeking Wild* (1992), *Sex and Longing* (1996), *Betty's Summer Vacation* (1998), *Mrs Bob Cratchit's Wild Xmas Binge* (2002)

Durang's early works were primarily parodies and often written in collaboration with fellow Yale Drama School graduates ★ALBERT INNAURATO, ★WENDY WASSERSTEIN and Sigourney Weaver. On his own, he wrote the zany comic circus, *A History of the American Film*, in which a variety of actors play screen icons from Cagney to Bogie to – most memorably – Anthony Perkins in *Psycho*. Latterly the tone has darkened. In *Sister Mary Ignatius Explains It All for You*, four former students of an authoritarian nun return to her classroom to exact revenge for her wrongheaded instruction. *The Nature and Purpose of the Universe*, *Baby with the Bathwater* and *The Marriage of Bette and Boo* are blackly and anarchically funny depictions of households in crisis. *Bette and Boo* in particular wreaks wonderful havoc with traditional ideas of 'family drama'. Whether you regard him as the quintessential American 'diaper dramatist' – Benedict Nightingale's term for what he sees as the terminal self-absorption of Durang and his literary peers – or as a tough-minded satirist lashing out at his Catholic upbringing, Durang is an idiosyncratic absurdist who writes with bracing irreverence about such dark subjects as the destructive pieties of Catholicism, the ideals of family life and seductive cultural fashions. In Britain recent revivals of *Beyond Therapy*, a wry depiction of two men and a woman attempting to negotiate their sexual identities in the face of their therapists, have drawn attention to a neglected voice

TRY THESE:

★O'MALLEY's *Once a Catholic* for contrasting take-offs of Catholic dogma; ★TALLY for another Playwrights' Horizons-schooled author fuelled by familial disorder; ★AYCKBOURN, ★CRAZE's *Atonement*, ★DE FILIPPO's *Ducking Out*, ★FEIFFER's *Grown Ups* for those domestic intersections where home and hatred meet; ★GUARE's *House of Blue Leaves* for antic comedy featuring nuns and an impending visit from the Pope; Durang has written a number of short plays drawing on, amongst others, ★O'NEILL, ★TENNESSEE WILLIAMS, *Medea*, ★SHAWN's *Aunt Dan and Lemon* and ★GIRADOUX's *The Madwoman of Chaillot*.

DURAS, Marguerite   [1904 – 96]

French novelist, dramatist and writer of screen-plays

PLAYS INCLUDE:

Le Square (1965, *The Square*), *La Musica* (1965), *Les Eaux et les Forêts* (1965, *The Waters and the Forests*), *Le Shaga* (1967), *L'Amante anglaise* (1968, *A Place Without Doors* or *The Lovers of Viorne*), *Suzanna Adler* (1971), *India Song* (1973), *L'Éden-Cinéma* (1977, *Eden Cinema*), *Savannah Bay* (1984)

Duras, born near Saigon in what was then French Indo-China, used her recollections of these childhood years for her novel *Le Barrage Contre le Pacifique* (*The Sea Wall*, 1950), her play *Eden Cinema*, and her autobiographical novel *L'Amant* (*The Lover*, 1984). It is characteristic of her methods to rework material into different forms and to try to break down the boundaries between media. Her first play, *The Square*, was taken from her novel of the same name; *A Place Without Doors* is the second version of a play about a horrifying real-life murder, and she turned it into a novel as well, treating the story from a different point of view each time. Most of her characters are women, and they suffer; they are often in love, about to take leave of their lovers, or abandoned by them. The plays are not linear, but unfold gradually like petals and the dialogue is full of hesitations, pauses, fragments of memory, ellipses, and the sudden recollection of violent or painful events. The story is not explained; sometimes there is only a stream of discourse, with questions left about motives or ideas or even identity. Duras is concerned with the processes of the artist's own mind rather than those of society, and with problems of language, rather than ideas or a story line.

Savannah Bay

This ninety-minute two-handed Proustian play was written for Madeleine Renaud, who played an ageing actress visited each day by a girl who may be her grandchild, and with whom she reconstructs the story of her daughter Savannah, who met a lover, gave birth, and later drowned in Savannah Bay in Siam. Both characters obsessively relive this story and gradually unfold it in a dream-like and elliptical text, with recurring images of two lovers on a white rock; it has strong resemblances to *Eden Cinema*, where again there is a piecing together of memories by an old and a young woman.

TRY THESE:

★CIXOUS, who was also born in a French colony, and who writes about what was formerly French Indo-China, but with quite different intent; ★BECKETT for the nature of memory; ★COWARD's *Private Lives* for an aftermath to divorce to contrast with *La Musica*.

DÜRRENMATT, Friedrich   [1921 – 90]

Swiss dramatist

PLAYS INCLUDE:

It Is Written (1947), *The Blind Man* (1948), *Romulus the Great* (1949), *The Marriage of Mr Mississippi* (1952), *An Angel Comes to Babylon* (1953), *The Visit* (1956), *The Physicists* (1962), *The Meteor* (1966), *King John* (1968), *Play Strindberg* (1969)

After studying at the Universities of Bern and Zurich, Dürrenmatt decided to commit himself full-time to writing, becoming one of the leading dramatists in the German language and achieving worldwide fame as a dramatic theorist. Clearly influenced by the pre-war German Expressionists and by ★BRECHT, Dürrenmatt's sense of theatricality is allied to an acute perception of the moral dilemmas of the contemporary world. But unlike Brecht,

Dürrenmatt's ability to chill in the midst of grotesque comedy, the clarity with which he raises great issues of personal and public morality, lead not towards an argument for political change, but towards despair. And although his characters frequently achieve a transcending dignity and even heroism, they do so in a world that renders individual action and sacrifice irrelevant. Although much of his work is built on the form of classical Greek tragedy, this sense of individual irrelevance denies the possibility of catharsis. To Dürrenmatt, the human condition is unchangeable and meaningless, and best examined through sardonic humour.

The Visit

A bitter fable of greed and human weakness, its highly convoluted plot revolves round the return of an ageing millionaire Claire Zachanassian to her economically depressed hometown, raising local expectations of a substantial act of charity. However, the millionaire is bent on vengeance on the town's most honoured citizen, Alfred III, who wronged her many years before. He denied that her unborn child was his and bribed two men to assert that she was no better than a prostitute, with the result that she left the town destitute and in disgrace. Since then, she has diligently whored and married her way to a fortune, and the price she demands for the town to share her wealth is the death of Alfred. At first the townspeople refuse, but money eventually talks and they strangle him during a celebration of the town's new wealth. The old woman gives her money to the town, and is cheered on her departure.

TRY THESE:
For expressionist influences on Dürrenmatt's style, Georg Kaiser, Ernst Toller and ★WEDEKIND; for comparisons with modern German writing, ★FRISCH, Manfred Karge, ★KROETZ; ★MÜLLER, ★SCHIMMELPFENNIG; ★IBSEN's An Enemy of the People for the dubious motivations of townspeople; ★MEYER's Etta Jenks also features a heroine who wreaks a terrible revenge on her original oppressors; ★SHAW's Mrs Warren's Profession for another successful prostitute.

DYER, Charles (Raymond)   [1928 –   ]
British dramatist, actor and director

PLAYS INCLUDE:
Clubs Are Sometimes Trumps (1948), Rattle of a Simple Man (1962), Staircase (1966), Mother Adam (1971)

Now virtually forgotten, Dyer's major plays, Rattle of a Simple Man (about a prostitute and a football fan) and Staircase, handled subjects and characters then rarely treated in theatre – Staircase was extensively cut by the censor – and centre on dependence and our attempt to escape loneliness. This is not a theatre of action but of need. In his characters Dyer shows the audience their own inadequacies and fears; but while stripping away self-illusion he also offers hope and a lot of laughs.

Staircase

This two-hander set in a Brixton barber's shop presents the mutual dependence of two middle-aged homosexuals: Harry, a totally bald barber, and Charlie Dyer, the ex actor he picked up in a teashop years before, who faces a summons after being caught cross-dressing by police raiding a club. Charlie has created a more successful fantasy life, peopled by characters who are all anagrams of his own name, to cover a period he spent in jail on a sex charge, and clings to the fact that he was once married and fathered a child. Harry is self-disgusted by his baldness and the physical side of life. The characters fascinate and repel at the same time, totally convincing yet offering a parallel of the struggle in any relationship. Dyer's work is totally unsentimental. At the end of the published text Dyer suggests that Harry, perhaps even the summons, perhaps all we have seen, exist only in Charlie's imagination. The play was filmed in 1969 with Richard Burton and Rex Harrison.

TRY THESE:
★FIERSTEIN, ★GENET, ★KRAMER and ★SHERMAN for treatments of male homosexual relationships; for two-handed relationships, ★PUIG and ★KEMPINSKI; ★GEMS' transvestite farce Aunt Mary and the work of ★BUSCH and ★LUDLAM for images of the seemingly outrageous, expressing questions about society's conventional images of gender.

E

EDGAR, David   [1948 –   ]
British dramatist

PLAYS INCLUDE:
A Fart for Europe (1973, with ✶HOWARD BRENTON), *Excuses, Excuses* (1973), *Dick Deterred* (1974), *Saigon Rose* (1976), *Blood Sports* (1976), *Destiny* (1976), *Wreckers* (1977), *Our Own People* (1977), *Mary Barnes* (1979), *The Jail Diary of Albie Sachs* (1979), *Teendreams* (1979, with Susan Todd), *The Life and Adventures of Nicholas Nickleby* (1980, adapted from Dickens), *Maydays* (1983), *Entertaining Strangers* (1985, revised version 1987), *That Summer* (1987), *Heartlanders* 1989, with ✶STEPHEN BILL and ✶ANNE DEVLIN), *The Shape of the Table* (1990), *The Strange Case of Dr Jekyll and Mr Hyde* (1991, from Stevenson), *Pentecost* (1994), *Albert Speer* (2000), *The Prisoner's Dilemma* (2001)

One of Britain's major dramatists, Edgar has written over fifty plays for both radical touring companies and the National Theatre and the RSC. He is active in socialist debates on theatre and culture, and established the highly successful MA in playwriting at Birmingham University. Edgar was born in Birmingham, of a theatrical family, and much of his early work was written for political theatre groups (*Wreckers* was written for 7:84, *Teendreams* for Monstrous Regiment) or in response to political events (*Dick Deterred* followed Nixon's part in Watergate, *A Fart for Europe* was written as an anti-EEC polemic at the time of Britain's entry into the EEC). As a socialist dramatist Edgar has chosen to base his intervention in the theatre, believing that television is an isolating experience, while theatre has to be experienced in a collective audience.

Destiny established Edgar as a major dramatist. An analysis of fascism and racism in British culture through its links with the imperialist past, and the wave of immigration in the 1970s, it juxtaposes a politician at the moment of a by-election with soldiers of 1947 discussing the independence of India. In the contemporary scenes, *Destiny* explores the relation of parliamentary politics to fascist groups, and also the way in which immigration becomes a scapegoat for the problems of British society. Written as a response to the rise in National Front activity in the mid-1970s, a period in which the Anti-Nazi League (which Edgar was involved with) was a central campaign for the Left, the play acts as a warning about the conditions that give rise to totalitarianism, and draws an analogy with the position of the Jews in Germany. *The Life and Adventures of Nicholas Nickleby*, Edgar's greatest success, was developed over a long period with the cast, who thoroughly researched and devised the play with Edgar. The result was a collaborative project and a conviction in the performances and production that is rarely seen in mainstream theatre. *Maydays*, an epic account of dissent in Britain and Europe from 1945 to the 1980s, was the first new play the RSC produced on the main stage at the Barbican, and established an important precedent. Edgar has said that the complicated set, which includes a moving train and a gate at Greenham Common, was written in as a strategy, so that the play technically had to be put on at the main stage at the Barbican and could not be relegated to the small Pit Theatre, where new writing invariably ended up.

✶ANN JELLICOE invited Edgar to collaborate in a theatre community project in Dorset that became *Entertaining Strangers*. Based on research into the history of Dorchester, and devised by and for the local community, it was given a production in revised form by the National Theatre. *The Shape of the Table*, although considered a static, talking-head piece by some (most of the action takes place around a large conference table), is a fascinating attempt to analyse the realpolitik behind momentous changes in eastern Europe at the end of 1989, in an imagined capital not a million miles away from Prague. Edgar followed this with two more plays directly concerned with the remaking of Europe after the collapse of communism: *Pentecost* takes the discovery of a mural in a church in an anarchic eastern European country as the staring point for an exploration of the ethical, moral, aesthetic and political questions associated with the making and remaking of countries; in *The Prisoner's Dilemma*, he is concerned with ethnic cleansing and the search for a political settlement. In the gap between *Pentecost* and *The Prisoner's Dilemma*, Edgar returned to history and the story of Hitler's architect and industrial organiser Albert Speer to examine some of the roots of the contemporary events and their ramifications.

TRY THESE:
✱ CHURCHILL employs a similar juxtaposition of past and present to that of *Destiny* in *Cloud Nine*; ✱ BRECHT is the effective originator of the dialectical theatre practised by ✱ BRENTON, Edgar, ✱ BOND, ✱ TREVOR GRIFFITHS and ✱ JOHN MCGRATH; *Saigon Rose's* treatment of venereal disease anticipates AIDS plays such as ✱ KRAMER's *The Normal Heart*; Mary Barnes' treatment of schizophrenia links it with ✱ CRAZE's *Shona*, ✱ STOPPARD's *Every Good Boy Deserves Favour*, and ✱ HEATHCOTE WILLIAMS' *AC/DC* though their approaches are very different; ✱ MERCER's *In Two Minds* for women and madness; ✱ ALRAWI's *A Child in the Heart* is an exploration of British racism and National Front allegiances in London's East End; ✱ BRENTON and Tariq Ali's *Moscow Gold* and ✱ CHURCHILL's *Mad Forest* for plays emerging from *glasnost*; ✱ DANIELS' *The Devil's Gateway* and ✱ REID's *My Name Shall I Tell You My Name* both use Greenham Common; ✱ DE ANGELIS's *Soft Vengeance* for a hero of the anti-apartheid struggle also featured in *The Jail Diary of Albie Sachs*.

EDMUNDSON, Helen   [1964 –   ]
British dramatist

PLAYS INCLUDE:
Ladies in the Lift (1988), *Flying* (1990), *Anna Karenina* (1992, from Tolstoy), *The Clearing* (1993), *The Mill on the Floss* (1994, from George Eliot), *War and Peace* (1996, from Tolstoy), *Mother Teresa is Dead* (2002)

Edmundson, a Manchester drama graduate, is best known for her imaginative adaptations of nineteenth-century blockbuster novels for Shared Experience. Apart from the sheer pragmatic difficulties she surmounts in filleting the novels to playable size, Edmundson's ability to discover dramatic devices to express key issues, such as having three Maggies in *Mill on the Floss*, marks her out as one of the major adapters of her time. In her original play *The Clearing* Edmundson tackles modern-day issues of ethnic cleansing through the Irish situation in the 1650s: an Anglo-Irish marriage collapses in the face of the brutalities of Cromwell's troops. *Mother Teresa is Dead* tackles another issue of the colonial legacy. Jane has left her husband and son in England and gone to help in a children's refuge in India. Her husband's arrival crystallises important debates about the limits of charity, how privileged Westerners can transcend the domestic and engage with a wider world and the extent to which the woman remains the victim of patriarchy even as she tries to fight the worst effects of global capitalism.

TRY THESE:
✱ KUSHNER's *Homebody/Kabul* for an American take on the situation in *Mother Teresa is Dead*; ✱ HARE's *A Map of the World* for an earlier view; ✱ BRENTON's *The Romans in Britain*, ✱ MCGUINNESS's *Mutabilitie* for parallels to *The Clearing*; for divided families, ✱ SHAKESPEARE's *Romeo and Juliet*; ✱ ENSLER and ✱ KANE for responses to the Balkans; for other Shared Experience adaptations Mike Alfreds' *Bleak House* and *A Handful of Dust*, Giles Havergal's *The Heat of the Day* (with Felicity Browne) and *Pamela* (with Fidelis Morgan), Polly Teale's *Jane Eyre* and *After Mrs Rochester*.

EICHELBERGER, Ethyl   [1945 – 90]
American actor, dramatist and director

PLAYS/PERFORMANCES INCLUDE:
Phèdre (1977), *Neferti-ti* (1978), *Medea* (1980), *Minne the Maid* (1981), *Elizabeth I and Mary Stuart* (1982), *Marie Antoinette*

(1982), *Hamlette* (1984), *Medusa* (1985), *Leer* (1985), *Casanova* (1985), *Rip Van Winkle (1986)*, *The Lincolns* (1988), *Ariadne Obnoxious* (1988), *Herd of Buffalo* (1989), *Das Vedanya Mama* (1990)

Ethyl Eichelberger (born James Roy Eichelberger in Pekin, Illinois) became convinced of the power of cross-dressing on stage to make a political statement, to force audiences to re-examine their notions of sexual stereotypes. His plays are dense, filled with obscure facts, puns, double entendres, and flexibility for ad-libs; the pace was dizzying, displaying a frenetic style with echoes of vaudeville, burlesque and the Yiddish stage. He juxtaposed dancing on pointe with acrobatics and cartwheels, added accordion-accompanied songs to nearly all performances, and incorporated fire-eating into his last plays. His plays remain unpublished, as it is widely felt that their impact on the printed page could not approach the dynamic and uniqueness of their onstage incarnations.

TRY THESE:
✱BUSCH for cross-dressing; ✱BOGOSIAN for monologue in the camp tradition; ✱BARTLETT for a British comparison; ✱LUDLAM for influence; *Leer* and *Hamlette* are adaptations of ✱SHAKESPEARE.

ELDER, Lonne   [1931 – 96]
American dramatist

PLAYS INCLUDE:
A Hysterical Turtle in a Rabbit Race (1961), *Kissing Rattlesnakes Can Be Fun* (1966), *Seven Comes Up, Seven Comes Down* (1966), *Charades on East Fourth Street* (1967), *Ceremonies in Dark Old Men* (1969), *Splendid Mummer* (1988), *King* (1990, book of the musical, lyrics by Maya Angelou and Alistair Beaton, music by Richard Blackford)

An African-American dramatist who refused 'to bend from the truth' in his plays, Elder achieved celebrity in the 1960s when black playwrights were finally making their voices heard. Through his political activities for the NAACP (National Association for the Advancement of Colored People), Elder met such notables as ✱LANGSTON HUGHES, ✱LORRAINE HANSBERRY, and Douglas Turner Ward, whose poetic realism was to shape his work. Elder worked as an actor before making his mark as a writer, performing as Bobo in the landmark 1959 Broadway production of ✱HANSBERRY's *A Raisin in the Sun*, and as Clem in Ward's *Day of Absence*. From 1965 to 1967, Elder attended the Yale School of Drama on a scholarship for filmmaking and playwriting. He joined the Negro Ensemble Company in 1967, as head of the Playwrights Unit. Shortly after his successful play *Ceremonies in Dark Old Men*, Elder moved to California to forge a career as a screenwriter. With several Hollywood films to his credit, Elder organised a symposium, in 1972, to address his concerns over the portrayal of African-Americans on film and television.

Although Elder returned to writing for the theatre, his reputation as a dramatist is largely based on the award-winning *Ceremonies in Dark Old Men*. Set in a Harlem barbershop, the play chronicles the struggles of the Parker family in their efforts to overcome the debilitating effects of ghetto life. The family patriarch, who let his wife work herself to death to support the family, must now face the legacy he has left to his children, as his unemployed sons and bread-winning daughter choose divergent, and sometimes fatal, paths to their dreams.

TRY THESE:
✱FULLER's *Zooman and the Sign* for an examination of the brutalisation of the ghetto;
✱BALDWIN's *The Amen Corner* has a Harlem setting, as does *Story in Harlem Slang*, one of three Zora Neale Hurston short stories adapted by ✱WOLFE in *Spunk*.

ELDRIDGE, David   [1973 –   ]
British dramatist

PLAYS INCLUDE:
Serving It Up (1996), *A Week with Tony* (1996), *Summer Begins* (1997), *Falling* (1999), *Under the Blue Sky* (2000)

Eldridge wrote his first play, *Serving It Up*, as a student at Exeter University. He has described it as 'a pretty angry play' that grew out of his fury with 'the Tory government, with the Sloane rangers and PC types I was studying alongside and with myself'. His major success so far has been *Under the Blue Sky*, in which three pairs of teachers at different stages of their lives confront individual moments of choice. The format is similar to ✱SCHNITZLER's *La Ronde*, in that each pair is linked to the others, though not in this case by moving on from one partner to another, but by shared acquaintanceship. Eldridge's great skill lies in creating an entirely believable world out of these three couples and their attempts to establish their relationships through thematic interlinking to wider issues, effectively blending modern-day terrorism, fantasies of wartime heroism and the realities of World War I in an apparently slight edifice, which is actually as tightly structured as ✱CHEKHOV.

TRY THESE:

For teachers, ✱GODBER, ✱RATTIGAN, ✱RECKORD, ✱NIGEL WILLIAMS; ✱TREVOR GRIFFITHS' *Country* was the inspiration for *A Week with Tony*.

ELIOT, T. S.
(Thomas Stearns)   [1888 – 1965]
Anglo-American poet and dramatist

PLAYS INCLUDE:

Sweeney Agonistes (1926), *The Rock* (1934), *Murder in the Cathedral* (1935), *The Family Reunion* (1939), *The Cocktail Party* (1949), *The Confidential Clerk* (1953), *The Elder Statesman* (1958)

One of the great poets of the twentieth century (he won the 1948 Nobel Prize for Literature), Eliot led a mid-century revival of verse drama, which ultimately failed because it assumed that the 'poetic' in the theatre was a function of the text rather than the whole theatrical process. The most innovative of his plays is *Sweeney Agonistes*, an unfinished piece which has proved very effective in performance, with its jazz rhythms and dialogue that anticipates the early ✱PINTER. *Murder in the Cathedral* is probably the most successful of the plays because the historical subject sanctions the use of non-naturalistic dialogue, but the verse of *The Family Reunion* is probably the most flexible. *The Cocktail Party* tends to

be given star productions from time to time but it already shows the pernicious effect on his work of Eliot's decision to adapt contemporary theatrical forms: there is an uneasy match between the poetic impulse and the drawing-room form which becomes more pronounced in his last two plays, and these are (justly) seldom revived. The success of the musical *Cats*, based on his *Old Possum's Book of Practical Cats*, indicates another route that might have led Eliot, an admirer of the music hall, to find the popular audience he craved.

TRY THESE:

✱AESCHYLUS, ✱EURIPIDES, ✱SOPHOCLES, who provided models for Eliot's plays, generally in terms of the use of the chorus, and specifically in respect of particular plots; medieval drama, particularly *Everyman*, for the inspiration for *Murder in the Cathedral*, ✱FRY for contemporary verse dramas; Paul Webb's *Four Knights in Knaresborough* for the later life of the knights from *Murder in the Cathedral*; Tom Courtenay's *Pretending To Be Me* for the poet Philip Larkin; ✱HARRISON and Ted Hughes, particularly Peter Brook's production of *Orghast*, for contemporary poets in the theatre.

ELLIS, Michael J.   [mid-1950s –   ]
British dramatist

PLAYS INCLUDE:

A Temporary Rupture (1983), *Starliner 2001*, *A Soap Odyssey* (1984), *Chameleon* (1985), *Sticky Fingers* (1989)

An East Ender of Jamaican parents, Ellis picked up various writing awards whilst still at school. Temba toured *Chameleon* for a year to enthusiastic houses, despite a lukewarm reception from reviewers. It is easy to see why there was this discrepancy, however: Ellis's office-bound two-hander is not especially sophisticated, but it is unusually satirical about its leading character, the awful, social-climbing Benjamin, and it is a brave and cautionary tale against buying into the system and against ignorance. *A Temporary Rupture* carries on in like vein as a sprightly dig at the macho insensitivity of young black males, with a jilted girlfriend getting her own back on the returning former lover and father of her child. Both plays would certainly repay further viewing.

TRY THESE:
✷MARCHANT's *The Lucky Ones* is also an office-based saga of contrasting attitudes to 'making it'; for other dramatists writing about being black in Britain, ✷COOKE, ✷IKOLI, ✷KAY, ✷MATURA, ✷MOFFATT, ✷PHILLIPS, ✷PINNOCK, ✷RECKORD, ✷RUDET, ✷ZEPHANIAH; for contrasting styles, ✷WALCOTT and ✷WHITE.

ELTON, Ben   [1959 –   ]
British dramatist, scriptwriter and comedian

PLAYS INCLUDE:
Gasping (1990), *Silly Cow* (1991), *Popcorn* (1996), *The Beautiful Game* (2000, with music by Andrew Lloyd Webber), *We Will Rock You* (2002, script of the Queen musical)

Born in Catford, Elton studied drama at Manchester University, where he wrote and directed several plays, some of which were taken to the Edinburgh Festival. On leaving university, he quickly carved out a successful career as a comedy scriptwriter and stand-up comedian, co-writing the hugely successful television series *The Young Ones* (with Rik Mayall and Lise Mayer) and three series of *Blackadder* (with Richard Curtis). The blend of social comment and prurient humour both in his routines, which he performed live and on television, and in his scripts brought him a huge, young audience. Elton's commitment to social and environmental issues – explored in his first novel, *Stark* – were evident in his first West End play, *Gasping*. This was a sharp, bitterly funny comedy about a vast multinational company introducing the concept of purified 'designer air', and ending up privatising oxygen. Despite a tendency to indulge himself with gags at the expense of plot, Elton acquitted himself well in his debut, although some critics thought it would work better on television. The savaging meted out to *Silly Cow*, which followed *Gasping*, was altogether easier to justify. Depicting the deserved downfall of a gutter-tabloid critic, *Silly Cow* was overwritten, full of improbable holes, and suffered from the dilution of its main theme with some indulgent, affectionate broadsides at the pretensions of actors. Nevertheless, Elton remains a sharp, popular writer who is able to command large audiences for overtly, if not subtly, political, comic plays, as he demonstrated with the success of *Popcorn*, based on his own novel. It is an examination of the glamorisation of gore that pitches a Tarantino-like film director into a truly murderous situation. The play explores the complex issues around why violence is popular entertainment, how far the media actually influence what people do and the social responsibilities of the entertainment industry. His musical *The Beautiful Game*, focusing on a football team, deals with young people growing up in Northern Ireland at the beginning of the troubles and how sectarianism impacts on ordinary adolescent lives.

TRY THESE:
✷CHURCHILL's *Not …Not …Not …Not …Not Enough Oxygen* anticipates *Gasping* by nearly twenty years; ✷BRENTON and ✷HARE's *Pravda* (which is also a fairly vitriolic swipe at tabloid journalism), ✷CHURCHILL's *Serious Money*, ✷LUCIE's *Fashion*, ✷JEFFREYS' *Valued Friends* for other political satires of 1980s values; ✷REID's *Tea in a China Cup* and ✷MARIE JONES for Belfast plays with a specifically women-centred focus; ✷FINNEGAN for a more stylised, many-faceted exploration of Northern Ireland's religious and political loyalties.

ELYOT, Kevin
British dramatist

PLAYS INCLUDE:
Coming Clean (1982), *Consent* (1989), *The Moonstone* (1990, from Wilkie Collins), *Artists and Admirers* (1992 from ✷OSTROVSKY), *My Night with Reg* (1994), *The Day I Stood Still* (1998), *Mouth to Mouth* (2001)

Birmingham-born Elyot's main claim to fame is the multiple award winning *My Night with Reg*, a brilliantly economical account of the devastation AIDS inflicts on a small group of gay friends. At first we believe that the action is continuous between scenes but gradually we realise that the seasons have changed and the major events have occurred offstage: characters come and go, relationships are formed and decay and are replaced by others. Gradually it emerges that the offstage Reg has infected virtually all the characters with HIV/AIDS. Unrequited love blights the protagonist's life but his routine sexual conservatism cannot save him. All this may suggest an evening of unrelieved gloom but Elyot has a sure grasp of narrative and his story emerges out of the everyday minutiae of domestic comedy. His characters are not supermen, nor are they gay stereotypes, just people trying to live their lives and coming to terms with some unpalatable facts. In *The Day I Stood Still*, the arrival of an unexpected visitor acts as a catalyst for revelations about how a group of lives have intertwined, nearly connected and gone off at a variety of tangents. *Mouth to Mouth* has a central character who has to hear about everyone else's problems but is never allowed to voice his own. Elyot makes the dramatist character in *Mouth to Mouth* declare that he is 'always being accused of writing the same thing'. However, Elyot's craftsmanship and control of his medium is more than adequate compensation for the family resemblances between the plays with their deceptive chronologies, revelations about the past and unfulfilled central characters.

TRY THESE:
✳FIERSTEIN, ✳NOËL GREIG, ✳HARVEY, ✳KONDOLEON, ✳KRAMER, ✳KUSHNER, ✳RAVENHILL, ✳SHERMAN for varieties of gay experience and some responses to AIDS; ✳CHEKHOV (particularly *Three Sisters*) for structure; ✳IBSEN for the explosive return of the outsider; ✳BECKETT's *Waiting for Godot* and ✳ODETS' *Waiting for Lefty* for absent title characters.

ENSLER, Eve   [1953 –   ]
American dramatist and feminist campaigner

PLAYS INCLUDE:
Scooncat (1987), *Floating Rhoda and the Glue Man* (1993), *Extraordinary Measures* (1995), *Vagina Monologues* (1996), *Conviction* (1999), *Lemonade* (1999), *Necessary Targets* (2001)

Ensler's plays are concerned with social and political issues, from the early *Scooncat*, about a man dominated by technology, to *Extraordinary Measures*, about the ways in which a man's family and friends react to him

as he lies unconscious in hospital dying of AIDS, and *Necessary Targets*, about two American women in Bosnia. Ensler's most famous play, the *Vagina Monologues*, started as an off-off-Broadway one-person show and has mutated into an extraordinary worldwide success, usually played by a three-woman cast, often including theatre or film stars or non-theatrical celebrities. Based on Ensler's interviews with many women, it is a powerful and often funny staging of feminist concerns about the position of women in the contemporary world. Inevitably much of the material deals with the abuse of women in wars and in domestic violence but it is not an anti-male polemic, rather a powerful reminder that despite the advances of feminism in some areas of some societies, there is still a massive need for action against the systematic abuse of women. The play's success has enabled Ensler to fund-raise for women's charities, to publicise human rights abuses and to create her own campaigning body, V-Day.

TRY THESE:
✳ELYOT, ✳FIERSTEIN, ✳KRAMER, ✳KUSHNER, ✳RAVENHILL for some responses to AIDS; ✳ADSHEAD's *Bogus Women*, ✳EDGAR, and ✳KANE's *Blasted* for responses to the Balkans; ✳CLARK's *Whose Life Is It Anyway* for hospital drama; ✳CHURCHILL, ✳DANIELS, ✳DE ANGELIS, ✳GEMS, ✳WANDOR for versions of feminism; *Mum's the Word* by Linda A. Carson. Jill Daum, Alison Kelly, Robin Nicol, Barbara Pollard and Deborah Williams for a softer version of contemporary women's experience.

ETHEREGE, George   [1634 – 91]
English dramatist

PLAYS INCLUDE:
The Comical Revenge: or, Love in a Tub (1664), *She Would If She Could* (1668), *The Man of Mode* (1676)

Etherege has some claims to have invented what we now call Restoration comedy in his plays, which present fashionable, witty, amoral characters engaged in a round of sexual intrigues in a recognisable version of contemporary London society. His own life could have been a model for one of his characters:

his actress mistress, Elizabeth Barry, also had a liaison with the Earl of Rochester (identified as the original of Dorimant in *The Man of Mode*); his outrageous behaviour as ambassador in Regensburg scandalised the inhabitants and he ended his career by joining James II in exile in Paris where he died.

The contemporary canvas is broadest in *The Comical Revenge*, where the humiliation of a venereally diseased French valet at the hands of English female servants gives the play its title, and contrasts with three other plots, including a rather more 'heroic' one largely conducted in rhyming couplets. Etherege, like other Restoration dramatists, is much more open about women's sexuality than dramatists of many other periods, though his view can be inferred, not unfairly, from the title of his second play, *She Would If She Could*. As with ✱WILLIAM WYCHERLEY, the difficulty is knowing where celebration of a society ends and criticism of it begins. Particularly in *The Man of Mode*, the only one of his plays to appear regularly in the modern repertory, the absence of an obvious authorial point of view and explicit moral judgements leads to contradictory evaluations of the characters and of the play. Clearly Sir Fopling Flutter, the man of mode of the title, is a comic butt because of his ridiculous pretensions to be fashionable, but the energetic protagonist Dorimant's dealings with various potential and actual mistresses and wives are much more open to scrutiny. This can be regarded either as masterly ambiguity or as poor dramatic technique.

TRY THESE:
Other Restoration comic writers, such as ✱BEHN, ✱CONGREVE and ✱WYCHERLEY; other writers of comedy of manners, such as ✱COWARD, ✱GOLDSMITH, ✱SHERIDAN, ✱WILDE; ✱BOND's *Restoration* uses conventions and themes derived from the practice of Restoration writers to make modern points.

EURIPIDES   [484 – 406/7 BC]
Greek dramatist

SURVIVING PLAYS INCLUDE:
Alcestis (438 BC), *Medea* (431 BC), *The Children of Heracles* (c. 429 BC), *Hippolytus* (428 BC), *Hecuba* (c. 425 BC), *The Suppliant Women* (c. 420 BC), *Andromache* (c. 419 BC), *Heracles* (c. 416 BC), *The Women of Troy* (415 BC), *Electra* (413 BC), *Helen* (412 BC), *Iphigenia in Tauris* (c. 411 BC), *Ion* (c. 411 BC), *Orestes* (408 BC), *The Phoenician Women* (c. 408 BC), *The Bacchae* (produced c. 405 BC), *Iphigenia in Aulis* (405 BC), *Cyclops* (date unknown); *Rhesus* is also attributed to Euripides

Euripides wrote over ninety plays during a long career but was less immediately popular than his contemporary, ✱SOPHOCLES. His subjects are those of the other Athenian tragic dramatists – stories of the gods and heroes, particularly those relating to the Trojan wars, but his treatment of them is more domestic and more sceptical, almost realistic and sociological rather than religious and philosophical. It was probably this aspect of his work, together with his penchant for experiments in form, that made him a controversial figure. *The Bacchae*, a very powerful treatment of the relationship between the Apollonian and the Dionysiac impulses, was influential on various experimental theatres in the twentieth century (e.g. the Performance Group's *Dionysus* in 1969) and continues to inspire dramatists with its theme of the difficulty of balancing the impulse to ecstasy with the need for restraint. The National Theatre staged a version by Colin Teevan in 2002. In the last decade London has seen productions of more than half of his extant plays with excellent versions of *Medea* and *Women of Troy* by Kenneth McLeish and of *Alcestis* by Ted Hughes.

TRY THESE:
✱AESCHYLUS and ✱SOPHOCLES wrote the other surviving Greek tragedies; see ✱ARTAUD for a theory of theatre with close connections to *The Bacchae*; ✱CHURCHILL and ✱LAN (*Mouthful of Birds*), ✱ELIOT, ✱GIRAUDOUX, ✱HARRISON, ✱O'NEILL and ✱SOYINKA are among modern playwrights who have tackled themes drawn from Greek drama; ✱DUFFY and ✱LAVERY have both adapted *The Bacchae* from a lesbian feminist perspective; *The Greeks*, John Barton and Kenneth Cavander's 1980 RSC production, used seven of Euripides' plays in its marathon cycle of the Trojan wars, but Barton's Greek cycle *Tantalus* did not draw directly on Euripides.

FAGON, Alfred [1937 – 86]
Jamaican-born British dramatist

PLAYS INCLUDE:
11 Josephine House (1972), *Death of a Black Man* (1975), *Four Hundred Pounds* (1983), *Lonely Cowboy* (1985)

Fagon emigrated to Britain in 1955, worked on the railways and served in the army before emerging as a professional actor and dramatist in the 1970s. He died while out jogging and, before any of his friends found out, was buried anonymously because the police believed he was a vagrant. As his subsequent *Times* obituary put it, 'his plays take as their theme the relationship between the cultures of the English and Caribbean peoples, their friendships and conflicts'. This theme is characteristically treated in the form of a comedy of manners with an underlying seriousness, as in *11 Josephine House* with its black family trying to adjust to the temptations of English life, particularly as manifested in the white woman who causes the black preacher's fall from grace. In *Four Hundred Pounds* TeeCee's sudden refusal to pot the black in a snooker game on ideological grounds loses him and his more pragmatic gambling partner that sum of money, and in *Lonely Cowboy* a couple's attempt to start a café leads first to comedy and then tragedy as the values of a world they try to ban from their café reassert themselves.

TRY THESE:
11 Josephine House has affinities with ✱MOLIÈRE's *Tartuffe* and ✱BALDWIN's The *Amen Corner*; Fagon's work offers interesting points of comparison with other British black writers such as ✱ABBENSETTS, ✱ELLIS, ✱IKOLI, ✱MATURA, ✱PHILLIPS and ✱RHONE.

FANNIN, Hilary [1962 –   ]
Irish actor and dramatist

PLAYS INCLUDE:
Mackerel Sky (1997), *Sleeping Around* (1998, with Stephen Greenhorn, ✱ABI MORGAN and ✱MARK RAVENHILL)

Fannin appeared in a successful RTE comedy series, *Upwardly Mobile*, and has written several works for radio. Her *Mackerel Sky* is a semi-autobiographical study of a comically dysfunctional Dublin family in the 1970s. *Sleeping Around* is a modern version of ✱SCHNITZLER's *La Ronde*.

TRY THESE:
✱HARE's *The Blue Room* for another modern version of *La Ronde*; ✱O'CASEY's *Juno and the Paycock* for the dysfunctional Dublin family; ✱IBSEN, ✱O'NEILL, ✱STRINDBERG for less comic dysfunctional families.

FARQUHAR, George [1678 – 1707]
Irish dramatist

PLAYS INCLUDE:
Love and a Bottle (1698), *The Constant Couple, or A Trip to the Jubilee* (1699), *Sir Harry Wildair, being a sequel to The Constant Couple* (1701), *The Inconstant, or The Way to Win Him* (1702), *The Twin Rivals* (1702), *The Stage Coach* (1704), *The Recruiting Officer* (1706), *The Beaux' Stratagem* (1707)

Farquhar left Trinity College, Dublin, to become an actor but took to writing after he injured his opponent in the duel at the end of ✱DRYDEN's *The Indian Emperor*. He married a woman he mistakenly believed to be an heiress and died in poverty aged only 29.

His writing is witty and stylish, and rather warmer than that of ✱CONGREVE and ✱WYCHERLEY. The later plays are more closely drawn from life with a very positive attitude to the situation of women in his society. In *The Constant Couple* he created the role of Harry Wildair, a kind-hearted rake, which became a celebrated breeches part for many years, but he is now best known for his two last plays. *The Recruiting Officer* is, unusually, set in Shropshire, where Sgt Kite is recruiting. Silvia, the daughter of a local justice, enlists, disguised as a man, so that she can be near her lover. Bill Gaskill's National Theatre's production at the Old Vic in 1963 (partly influenced by ✴BRECHT's adaptation *Trumpets and Drums*) emphasised the clarity of Farquhar's presentation of his divided society and its power structures so that the affected mannerisms which had previously tended to suffice for 'Restoration style' began to lose their foothold in contemporary productions. Set in Lichfield, another provincial location, *The Beaux' Stratagem* shows two London beaux seeking country marriages to restore their fortunes, one posing as his own elder brother, the other as his servant. It makes a case for divorce on the grounds of incompatibility and, in introducing Lady Bountiful, added an expression to the English language.

TRY THESE:
✴BEHN, ✴CONGREVE, ✴ETHEREGE, ✴VANBURGH, ✴WYCHERLEY for other 'Restoration' dramatists; ✴GOLDSMITH (who refers to *Beaux' Stratagem* in *She Stoops to Conquer*) and ✴SHERIDAN wrote within broadly similar conventions; ✴AYCKBOURN, ✴PHILIP BARRY, ✴COWARD, ✴LEIGH, ✴LUCIE, ✴SIMON, ✴WILDE for later comedies of manners; ✴WERTENBAKER's *Our Country's Good* centres on the staging of *The Recruiting Officer* as the first production in Australia, performed by convicts.

FARR, David   [1969 –   ]
British dramatist and director

PLAYS INCLUDE:
Max Klapper – A Life in Pictures (1995), *Elton John's Glasses* (1997), *Dark Night of the Soul* (1999), *The Nativity* (1999), *The Danny Crowe Show* (2001), *Joan of Arc's Thoughts on the English as She Burns at the Stake* (2001), *Crime and Punishment in Dalston* (2002), *Night of the Soul* (2002), *The Queen Must Die* (2003), *Great Expectations* (2003, from Dickens)

Former artistic director of London's Gate Theatre, Farr is now the joint artistic director of the Bristol Old Vic and has directed for the RSC, Nottingham Playhouse, the Young Vic and in Zagreb. He achieved considerable success with his version of Dostoevsky at the new Arcola theatre in Dalston but his own plays range across genres: *Max Klapper* is a mixed-media piece for the centenary of cinema, *Elton John's Glasses* is rather more than a study of a football supporter's decline after his team fail to win the FA Cup, *The Nativity* is a reworking of the story of the birth of Christ, *Joan of Arc's Thoughts* is what you might expect from the title, *The Danny Crowe Show* is a satire on the Gerry Springer-type of television show, *Night of the Soul* is a modern ghost story and *The Queen Must Die* is about the 2002 Jubilee.

TRY THESE:
✴HARRISON for a reworking of the medieval mysteries; ✴ANOUILH, ✴BRECHT and ✴SHAW for St Joans; ✴AYCKBOURN's *Man of the Moment* for television; ✴CHURCHILL's *Fen* for ghosts.

FEIFFER, Jules   [1929 –   ]
American dramatist and cartoonist

PLAYS INCLUDE:
The Explainers (1961), *Crawling Arnold* (1961), *The World of Jules Feiffer* (1962), *Little Murders* (1967), *The Unexpurgated Memories of Bernard Mergendelier* (1968), *God Bless* (1968), *Feiffer's People* (1968), *The White House Murder Case* (1970), *Munro* (1971), *Watergate Classics* (1973), *Knock, Knock* (1976), *Hold Me* (1977), *Grown-Ups* (1981), *A Think Piece* (1982), *Jules Feiffer's America* (1987, adapted by Russell Vandenbroucke), *Anthony Rose* (1989), *Eliot's Love* (1990) *A Bad Friend* (2003)

Most prolific as a dramatist in the 1960s, Feiffer was an important figure in the off-, off-off-Broadway and regional theatre movements. Feiffer's is a psychic landscape full of domestic and social violence. *Little Murders*, in which a family shoots at passers-by through their nice, middle-class windows, may best illustrate the author's vision of intermarried urban and domestic blight. Feiffer's plays, like the cartoons for which he is famous, are typified by mordant, often self-mocking, existential humour. But Feiffer is adept at farce too, as evidenced by *Watergate Classics*, a spoof of the Nixon presidency. *Feiffer's People* and *Hold Me*, which the author has dubbed 'sketch plays', have the quick, direct punch of a good drawing. *Grown-Ups*, about an affluent New York family spiralling into emotional chaos, invites comparisons with no less a dramatist than ✱ STRINDBERG. Feiffer's best plays capture the confused searching, the crises of courage and failed political vision of a particular segment of the middle and upper-middle class during the turbulent 1960s, mixed-up 1970s and ruthless 1980s.

Feiffer is an accomplished screenwriter whose credits include *Carnal Knowledge*, *Little Murders* (adapted from his *play*), *Popeye* and *I Want to Go Home*.

TRY THESE:

✱ ALBEE for households in dire distress; ✱ SCHISGAL's *An American Millionaire* for a Feifferesque black farce about violence and affluence; ✱ GUARE's *House of Blue Leaves* and *Six Degrees of Separation* for incisively comic views of two very different New York families; ✱ MAMET's *Edmond* for perhaps the darkest look at urban life; ✱ SIMON for a more sanitised version of New York angst; ✱ DURANG and ✱ KOPIT (especially *Oh Dad Poor Dad*) for comparably deranged families.

FEYDEAU, Georges   [1862 – 1921]
French dramatist

PLAYS INCLUDE:
Tailleur pour Dames (1886, *The Ladies' Tailor*), *Champignol Malgré Lui* (1892, *Champignol in Spite of Himself*), *Le Mariage de Barillon* (1890, *Horse and Carriage*), *M. Chasse* (1892, *Game Pie* or *Monsieur Goes Hunting*), *L'Hôtel du Libre-Échange* (1894, *Hotel Paradiso* or *A Little Hotel on the Side*), *Un Fil à la Patte* (1894, *Cat Among the Pigeons* or *Get Out of My Hair*), *Le Dindon* (1896, *Ruling the Roost* or *Sauce for the Goose* or *An Absolute Turkey*), *La Dame de chez Maxim* (1899, *The Lady from Maxim's*), *La Puce à l'Oreille* (1907, *A Flea in Her Ear*), *Occupe-toi d'Amélie* (1908, *Look After Lulu* or *Mind Millie for Me*), *Feu la Mère de Madame*

(1908, *My Late Mother-in-law*), *Léonie est en Avance* (1911, *Any Minute Now*), *Hortense a dit: 'Je m'en fous'* (1916, *Hortense Said 'Stuff It'*), *A Journey to London* (completed by James Saunders, 1985)

Feydeau's middle-period plays are the archetype of French farce. The principal characters are Parisian bourgeois, their major driving force is extra-connubial lust, and the basic source of the humour is their ever more desperate attempts to avoid being found out. Although no respectable married woman is ever seduced by her husband's best friend, it is not for want of trying on either side. The plots seem to have been constructed by a mad watchmaker, but the status quo is always restored at the end. His later one-act plays (after he left his wife) are more misanthropic, more loosely constructed, and need more careful production; but the full-length plays come up as fresh as ever. Peter Hall's productions of *An Absolute Turkey* (1994) and *Mind Millie for Me* (1996) kept Feydeau in the West End, but *Horse and Carriage*, adapted by Graham Garden in 2001, even with Griff Rhys-Jones and Alison Steadman, did not get to London

TRY THESE:

✱ LABICHE for nineteenth-century French farce; ✱ ORTON for the occasional casual cruelty of the humour (e.g. the man with no roof to his mouth, the character with bad breath, the comic foreigners); perhaps the contemporary English equivalent is ✱ COONEY's farces, also invariably focused on extra-marital lust.

FIERSTEIN, Harvey   [1954 –   ]
American actor and dramatist

PLAYS INCLUDE:
In Search of the Cobra Jewels (1973), *Forget Him* (1982), *Freaky Pussy* (1982), *Flatbush Tosca* (1982), *Torch Song Trilogy* (1982), *La Cage aux Folles* (1983, libretto), *Spookhouse* (1984), *Safe Sex* (1987), *Legs Diamond* (1988, libretto)

Fierstein, who made his acting debut in 1971 with Andy Warhol, now works mainly as an actor, with many credits including *Independence Day*, *Mrs Doubtfire*, *Mulan*, *Cheers* and

The Simpsons. Torch Song Trilogy was a landmark in gay theatre, winning two Tony and Drama Desk Awards (Best Play and Best Actor) and catapulting the author to mainstream fame. The plays that constitute the trilogy (*The International Stud*, *Fugue in a Nursery* and *Widows and Children First*) had been staged independently before Fierstein brought them together. They deal with the life of the hero as he negotiates the intricacies of everyday life and love, his relationship with his mother and his career as a drag queen. As Fierstein said, 'The worth of these plays lies ultimately in the tiny mirrors woven into the fabric wherein we catch our reflections . . . Any little thing that makes you feel less alone is what and why these plays are.' The author's comment may explain the enduring appeal of the trilogy to straight as well as gay audiences. None of Fierstein's subsequent plays matched the success of the trilogy. *Spookhouse*, a Paul Zindel-like tale of a harridan mother living in Coney Island, was not totally convincing, although Fierstein again showed his talent for creating sensitive, intimate scenes. *Safe Sex*, also a trilogy, was one of the first overtly post-AIDS dramas. Though extremely important in terms of its subject matter, it closed after only two weeks.

TRY THESE:

✱KRAMER and ✱SHERMAN as contemporary gay writers whose works have reached a broad audience; ✱ELYOT, ✱LUCAS, ✱MCNALLY, ✱RAVENHILL as dramatists who have written about AIDS and gay life.

FINNEGAN, Seamus   [1949 –   ]
Northern Irish dramatist

PLAYS INCLUDE:
Laws of God (1978), *Paddy and Britannia* (1979), *I Am a Bomb* (1979), *Victims* (1979), *Act of Union* (1980), *Herself Alone* (1981), *Soldiers* (1981), *James Joyce and the Israelites* (1982), *Loyal Willy* (1982), *The Little People* (1982), *Tout* (1984), *North* (1984), *Beyond a Joke* (1984), *Mary's Men* (1984), *Bringing It Home* (1984), *Gombeen* (1985), *The Spanish Play* (1986), *The German Connection* (1986), *Ghetto* (1987), *The Murphy Girls* (1988), *1916* (1989), *Mary Maginn* (1990), *Life after Life* (2000), *Diaspora Jigs* (2001), *Murder in*

Bridgport (2002), *Waiting for the Angels* (2002)

Belfast-born, Catholic-bred former teacher (at the Jewish Free School in London) and onetime political activist, Finnegan has become one of the most prolific commentators on Northern Ireland. Ambitiously wide-ranging in his themes, Finnegan has moved from the early monologues of outrage through the complexities of the situation (*Act of Union*, *Soldiers* and *North*) to exploration of loyalties and principles on a wider scale in *The War Trilogy*, which spans the Spanish Civil War (*The Spanish Play*), the Holocaust in Europe (*The German Connection*) and Israel (the radio play *The Cemetery of Europe*). Eschewing nationalism, Finnegan's plays have been notable for their non-sectarian, even ironical detachment, and for their concern, like James Joyce, with exploring Jewish links Finnegan is equally capable of providing dramatic cameos on a smaller, more domestic canvas such as in *Mary's Men*, a poignant portrait of lost dreams among Belfast's down-and-outers or the two-hander *Diaspora Jigs*, a tale of homelessness. *Murder in Bridgport*, set in Chicago, tackles the paradox that the Irish who have fled from repression turn into oppressors in the USA in a remix of the traditional ingredients of hatred, religion and violence. History, language and the ironies of fate continue to be at the centre of his work.

TRY THESE:
For other contemporary views of Ireland and the Irish, ✱CARR, ✱DEVLIN, ✱FRIEL, ✱HUTCHINSON, ✱MARIE JONES, ✱KILROY, ✱MCGUINNESS, ✱MORNIN, ✱PARKER, ✱REID.

FIRTH, Tim   [1964 –   ]
British dramatist

PLAYS INCLUDE:
A Man of Letters (1991), *Neville's Island* (1992), *A Bigger Slice of the Pie* (1993), *The End of the Food Chain* (1993), *Love Songs for Shopkeepers* (1998), *The Safari Party* (2002), *Our House* (2002)

Perhaps best known for his television work (*Preston Front*) and more recently for the script for the Madness musical *Our House*, Firth has a long-standing relationship with ✱ALAN AYCKBOURN's Stephen Joseph theatre in Scarborough and there are certainly many similarities between his work and the master's. For example, Firth's award-winning *Neville's Island*, a nightmarish comedy in which a group of middle-aged office workers find themselves marooned on an island in a lake when a 'team-building' exercise goes wrong, is reminiscent of *Way Upstream*. Similarly, as couples move round from house to house to eat the separate courses of a meal, *The Safari Party*, which deals with a culture clash between impoverished landowners and rich incomers, centred on the value (or otherwise) of an 'antique' table, recalls many of Ayckbourn's plays.

TRY THESE:

✱DE ANGELIS's *Warwickshire Testimony* for incomers and country-dwellers; ✱BARRIE's *The Admirable Crichton* and ✱SHAKESPEARE's *The Tempest* for men behaving badly after a shipwreck; ✱BUFFINI, ✱ISITT, ✱WHITEHEAD for meals that go badly.

FLANNERY, Peter   [1951 –   ]
British dramatist

PLAYS INCLUDE:
Heartbreak Hotel (1975), *Last Resort* (1976), *Savage Amusement* (1978), *The Boy's Own Story* (1978), *The Adventures of Awful Knawful* (1979), *Jungle Music* (1979), *Our Friends in the North* (1982), *Heavy Days* (1982), *Silence on My Radio* (1983), *Singer* (1989)

Flannery, a Manchester University drama graduate, had most of his work staged by the Manchester-based Contact Theatre Company or the RSC, for whom he was resident dramatist in 1979–80. Much of his work includes songs, often by fellow Manchester student Mick Ford, and he has been particularly concerned with problems of despair and urban decay in *Savage Amusement* and *Jungle Music*. *Our Friends in the North* won the John Whiting Award for its vivid and trenchant re-creation of some of the interlocking strands of corruption in British life between 1964 and

1979, from faulty high-rise blocks and corrupt policemen to Rhodesian sanctions-busting. It has all the virtues of a thriller and reserves its anger for the Labour politicians who wasted their golden opportunity. Perhaps it seemed a little long in performance, but then there was a lot of material to be considered; an updated version would be far more chilling and would presumably be even longer. *Singer* is another epic re-creation of corruption in Britain, centring on concentration-camp survivors who react in chillingly different ways to their experiences. It's partly a panoramic history of post-war Britain, partly a meditation on the meaning of the Holocaust, partly a modern version of Renaissance tragicomedy, complete with chorus out of *Henry V*. A revised version of *The Boy's Own Story*, a monologue for a goalkeeper, toured in 1992–3 but since then Flannery has worked in film and television, achieving a notable success with his television adaptation of *Our Friends in the North*.

TRY THESE:

✱BARKER's *A Passion in Six Days* and *Stripwell*, ✱BARNES' *The Ruling Class*, ✱BRENTON and ✱HARE's *Brassneck* and *Pravda* are among recent British plays that deal with politics, corruption and the establishment; ✱OTWAY's *Venice Preserv'd*, ✱GAY's *The Beggar's Opera*, ✱SHAW's *Widower's Houses*, ✱GRANVILLE-BARKER's *Waste* are examples from the seventeenth, eighteenth, nineteenth and early twentieth centuries; for 'bent' policeman, G. F. Newman's *Operation Bad Apple*, ✱ORTON's *Loot*, ✱NIGEL WILLIAMS' *WCPC*; ✱CHURCHILL's *Serious Money* offers a satirical view of some aspects of City scandals; ✱SHERMAN's *Bent* and ✱C. P. TAYLOR's *Good* for concentration-camp experiences; ✱BAINS' *Blood* for the brutalisation process in terms of the partition of India in 1947.

FLETCHER, John   [1579 – 1625]
English dramatist

PLAYS INCLUDE:
The Woman's Prize; or, The Tamer Tamed (after 1604, with ✱FRANCIS BEAUMONT), *Philaster* (pre-1610, with ✱FRANCIS BEAUMONT), *The Maid's Tragedy* (pre-1611,

with ✱FRANCIS BEAUMONT), *A King and No King* (1611, with ✱FRANCIS BEAUMONT), *Henry VIII* (1613, with ✱SHAKESPEARE), *The Two Noble Kinsmen* (1613, with ✱SHAKESPEARE), *The Custom of the Country* (*c.* 1619, with ✱PHILIP MASSINGER), *The Island Princess* (*c.* 1619)

The son of a clergyman who eventually died in poverty despite having been Bishop of London, Fletcher was a prolific and popular dramatist who succeeded ✱SHAKESPEARE as resident dramatist with the King's Men. His current theatrical reputation rests mainly on his collaborations with Shakespeare and *The Maid's Tragedy*, though he wrote many comedies of manners that might repay attention as precursors of Restoration comedy. He also wrote *The Woman's Prize; or, The Tamer Tamed*, a sequel to *The Taming of the Shrew*, in which Petruchio gets his just deserts at the hands of his second wife. Whether the RSC's 2003 staging of both plays in tandem will restore Fletcher's to the repertory remains an open question. Certainly their revival of *The Island Princess* in 2002 was greeted respectfully rather than as the reclamation of a lost masterpiece. *Henry VIII* is a celebratory epic of the birth of Protestant England in which Henry is presented rather more favourably and seriously than he tends to be in our contemporary picture of him. It uses non-naturalistic dramatic devices in a way that ✱BRECHT would have admired. The two gentlemen who meet at major events throughout the play and remind each other and the audience of the historical context are particularly endearing if you like that kind of approach to dramatic writing (and particularly irritating if you like tightly controlled causality and plausibility).

The Two Noble Kinsmen

The Two Noble Kinsmen is a fascinating study of conflict between honour and love, derived from Chaucer, in which Palamon and Arcite, the kinsmen of the title, imprisoned by Theseus, vie for the love of Hippolyta's sister Emilia. In the subplot the gaoler's daughter, who loves Palamon, goes mad for love and is subsequently cured by the attentions of her former suitor disguised as Palamon. The whole effect is truly tragicomic, with many possibilities of death and disaster, but virtually everything turns out well for everybody in the end, except for Arcite who wins the contest for Emilia but is killed accidentally, thus leaving the way clear for Palamon to marry Emilia. Quite what Emilia makes of this last-minute substitution is not clear. The 1986 RSC revival showed that the play can hold its own; what it needs now is regular revivals so that we can gauge its true strengths.

TRY THESE:
Theseus figures in ✱EURIPIDES' *The Suppliant Women* and *Hippolytus* (which deals with the Phaedra story later dramatised by ✱RACINE, in which Hippolytus dies in a similar way to Arcite); ✱SHAKESPEARE uses Theseus and Hippolyta in *A Midsummer Night's Dream*; the substitution of one beloved for another which figures in *The Two Noble Kinsmen*, ✱SHAKESPEARE's *Two Gentlemen of Verona, Measure for Measure* and *All's Well That Ends Well* has sinister parallels in the substitution of one woman for another in a man's bed in ✱MIDDLETON and ✱ROWLEY's *The Changeling*; ✱BOLT's *A Man for All Seasons* offers a different interpretation of Henry VIII from that of ✱FLETCHER and ✱SHAKESPEARE; ✱SHAKESPEARE's other history plays cover the period from *King John* to *Richard III*.

FO, Dario   [1926 –   ]
Italian performer, dramatist and manager

PLAYS INCLUDE:
Stealing a Foot Makes You Lucky in Love (1961), *Mistero Buffo* (1969), *Accidental Death of an Anarchist* (1970), *Can't Pay? Won't Pay!* (1974), *Female Parts* (1977, with ✱FRANCA RAME), *Trumpets and Raspberries* (1981), *The Opera of Guffaws* (1981 with ✱FRANCA RAME, from ✱JOHN GAY's *The Beggar's Opera*), *The Mother* (1982), *The Open Couple* (1983, with ✱FRANCA RAME), *Elizabeth* (1984), *One Was Nude and One Wore Tails* (1985), *The First Miracle of the Boy Jesus* (1986), *The Pope and the Witch* (1989), *Zitti! Stiamo Precipitando* (1990), *Johan Padan and the Discovery of the Americas* (1991), *The Devil in Drag* (1997)

Accidental Death of an Anarchist by Dario Fo, directed by Michael Grandage, Donmar Warehouse, 2003. Desmond Barrit, Emma Amos, Rhys Ifans, Adrian Scarborough, Paul Ritter, Cornelius Booth. (Marilyn Kingwill/ArenaPAL)

Fo, one of the great comic performers, especially in his solo piece *Mistero Buffo*, which he has performed all over the world, has written many plays, often to the severe embarrassment of the Italian government of the day. His combination of popular farce and savage political comment is unique and very effective. It earned him the 1997 Nobel Prize for Literature, to the discomfort of the Vatican, which finds his irreverence about religion difficult to deal with. Fo's father was a socialist railway worker and amateur actor. He started in the Italian theatre in Milan in the 1950s, with revue sketches, radio comedy and songs, and some early farces with the Fo-Rame Company (founded with his wife ✱FRANCA RAME) from 1959 to 1968, when they established a cooperative group called the Compagnia Nuova Scena, where he first performed his bravura solo act *Mistero Buffo*. A free-wheeling act, developed over the years in response to changing times, it is partly written in *grammelot*, an invented language which he declares was made up by medieval strolling players to avoid political censorship, and in which he satirises the Catholic Church, politicians, big business, repressive laws, and generally presents the irrepressible underdog.

In 1970 he founded a new company, La Comune, a theatrical collective, which worked as a community theatre in a working-class suburb of Milan where his work became overtly political and revolutionary. In December of the same year the company put on 'a grotesque farce about a tragic farce', *Accidental Death of an Anarchist*. This play was based on the death of Giuseppe Pinelli, an anarchist railway worker who had 'accidentally' fallen from a Milan police station window during interrogation about planting bombs. Fo himself played the part of the 'Maniac' who infiltrates police headquarters and shows the implausibility of the police story; the mode is farcical, but the content profoundly disturbing. The show was changed nightly through its run, as more facts about the Pinelli affair emerged. It was revived in London at the Donmar Warehouse in 2003.

Other Fo plays to have received high-profile British productions include *Can't Pay? Won't Pay!*, a well-structured farce about civil disobedience in the face of high prices, and *Trumpets and Raspberries*, which makes hilarious use of the 'double' joke, as the Fiat boss, Agnelli, is saved in an attempted assassination by a Fiat worker, but is given the worker's features by mistake in plastic surgery. Many of Fo's and Rame's works have also become staples of fringe theatre.

TRY THESE:
✱ARDEN and D'Arcy's *Non-Stop Connolly Show*, ✱JOHN MCGRATH for British parallels and contrasts; ✱GOLDONI, Plautus, ✱SHAKESPEARE for plays about doubles; ✱BRECHT for another response to ✱GAY; ✱EDGAR for British agitprop; *Zitti! Stiamo Precipitando* is about AIDS; ✱ELYOT, ✱FIERSTEIN, ✱LUCAS, ✱MCNALLY, ✱RAVENHILL as dramatists who have written about AIDS and gay life.

FOOTE, Horton   [1916 –]
American dramatist, screenwriter and actor

PLAYS INCLUDE:
Wharton Dance (1940), *Texas Town* (1941), *Only the Heart* (1942), *Celebration* (1948), *The Chase* (1952), *The Trip to Bountiful* (1953), *The Traveling Lady* (1954), *A Young Lady of Property* (1955), *Gone with the Wind* (1972, musical), *The Roads to Home* (1982), *Courtship* (1984), *The Road to the Graveyard* (1985), *Blind Date* (1986), *Lily Dale* (1986), *The Widow Claire* (1986), *Talking Pictures* (1990), *The Young Man from Atlanta* (1997)

Veteran dramatist and screenwriter Foote writes in a style that is starkly realistic and marks the slow passage of time in the heat-baked South. Chekhovian in tone and Faulkneresque in sensibility, his work centres on family relationships and characters in search of the roots that give meaning to their lives. A stoic acceptance of life's travails is seen as passive heroism. Foote won Academy Awards for the screenplays for *To Kill a Mockingbird* in 1962 and *Tender Mercies* in 1984. In *The Trip to Bountiful*, probably his best-known play, an elderly woman leaves the cramped Houston apartment she shares with her son and his wife to return to her country home but the journey turns into one of self-discovery. The screen adaptation of *The Trip to Bountiful* earned him an Academy Award nomination and an Oscar for its star, Geraldine Page in 1985.

TRY THESE:

✱ CHEKHOV for realistic writing and passive characters; ✱ MILLER, ✱ SIMON for plays of family relationships, ✱ HENLEY, ✱ TENNESSEE WILLIAMS for plays that reflect the values of the American South; ✱ BOND's *Narrow Road to the Deep North* for a journey of self-discovery.

FORD, John   [1586 – c. 1640]
English dramatist

PLAYS INCLUDE:

The Witch of Edmonton (1621, with ✱ THOMAS DEKKER and ✱ WILLIAM ROWLEY), *Perkin Warbeck* (c. 1622–32), *The Broken Heart* (c. 1629), *'Tis Pity She's a Whore* (c. 1632)

Ford had a legal training at the Middle Temple but may not have practised law. He made his theatrical debut with *The Witch of Edmonton*, collaborated in five plays and wrote another eight by himself. Because *'Tis Pity She's a Whore* deals sensitively and not unsympathetically with incest, Ford has been subject to high moral condemnation and treated as the prime representative of the alleged decadence of the drama during the reign of Charles I. He, ✱ MIDDLETON and ✱ MASSINGER are, in fact, the latest of the pre-Civil War dramatists to be staged on anything like a regular basis in the contemporary theatre, and there can be no denying the sensational quality of *'Tis Pity* in view of such moments as Giovanni's entrance with the heart of his sister Annabella on the point of his dagger. Nevertheless, it is a play well within the Renaissance tradition of scrutinising limits and defying convention that still attracts modern audiences. *Perkin Warbeck*, a very late example of the chronicle play fashionable in the Elizabethan period, is a fascinating study of role-playing with its protagonist, who claims to be the son of Edward IV, choosing to be executed rather than admit his imposture.

TRY THESE:

Ford was clearly heavily influenced by ✱ SHAKESPEARE in both *'Tis Pity She's a Whore* (aspects of *Romeo and Juliet*) and *Perkin Warbeck* (particularly the *Henry VI* plays and *Richard III*, which deal with the historical events preceding the action of Ford's play); ✱ MIDDLETON's *Women Beware Women* has an incest plot which is thought to have influenced Ford's treatment; incest is also a main theme in ✱ SHELLEY's, and ✱ ARTAUD's, *The Cenci* and ✱ RECKORD's *X*; ✱ STOPPARD's *The Real Thing* uses *'Tis Pity* as one of its intertexts; ✱ PIRANDELLO's *Henry IV* (which is not about the English king) is a significant modern play about the construction of identity.

FOREMAN, Richard   [1937 –   ]
American dramatist, director and scene designer

PLAYS INCLUDE:

Angelface (1968), *Elephant Steps* (1970, music by Stanley Silverman), *Total Recall* (1971), *Sophia: The Cliffs* (1972), *Classical Therapy* (1973), *Vertical Mobility* (1974), *Sophia = Wisdom* (1974), *Rhoda in Potatoland* (1975), *Book of Splendors (Part 1)* (1976), *Book of Splendors (Part 2)* (1977), *Blvd. de Paris* (1977), *Madame Adare* (1980, music by Stanley Silverman), *George Bataille's Bathrobe* (1983), *Egyptology* (1983), *Miss Universal Happiness* (1985), *The Cure* (1986), *Africanus Instructus* (1986, music by Stanley Silverman), *Love and Science* (1987), *Film is Evil: Radio is Good* (1987), *Symphony of Rats* (1988), *Eddie Goes to Poetry City (Part 1)* (1990), *Eddie Goes to Poetry City (Part 2)* (1991), *The Mind King* (1992), *Samuel's Major Problems* (1993), *My Head Was a Sledgehammer* (1994), *Permanent Brain Damage* (1996), *Pearls for Pigs* (1997), *Benita Canova* (1997), *Paradise Hotel* (1998), *Bad Boy Nietzsche* (2000), *Now That Communism is Dead, My Life Feels Empty* (2001), *Maria Del Bosco* (2002)

Foreman has established himself in the forefront of the American avant-garde as both a dramatist and director. His plays relegate linear plot, emotion, character development and narrative to the expression of the workings of the human consciousness. The overall design resulting from a series of often incomprehensible incidents aspires not to logic, but to psychological truth. As a director, Foreman has developed techniques that allow him to supplement the effects sought by his plays. He sometimes uses untrained actors who speak flatly and without emotion; backdrops, small stages, strings, ropes and other props divide the stage instantaneously, isolating specific words or incidents; sounds, lights, and other effects serve as similar framing devices; he has served as the designer for all of his own plays. Foreman stresses the importance of the visual unity in his productions, asserting that a particular strength of his work 'is the spatial manipulation of actors, scenery, and decor, and all the elements of the theatre choreographed in a given space'. Although he has toured his work all over the world, it has seldom been seen in Britain.

TRY THESE:

*BECKETT, *HANDKE, *MÜLLER, *SIMPSON, *HEATHCOTE WILLIAMS, *SNOO WILSON for other versions of fragmented consciousness; Laurie Anderson, *BOGART, Meredith Monk, Nancy Reilly, San Francisco Mime Troupe, Richard Schechner, Peter Sellars, Robert Wilson, the Wooster Group for the American avant-garde; *BARTLETT and Ariane Mnouchkine for European parallels; Peter Brook and Peter Stein for other singular, spatially oriented directors.

FORNES, Maria Irene   [1930 –   ]
American dramatist and director

PLAYS INCLUDE:

The Widow (1961), *Tango Palace* (1963), *The Successful Life of Three* (1965), *Promenade* (1965), *A Vietnamese Wedding* (1967), *Dr Kheal* (1968), *Molly's Dream* (1968), *Aurora* (1974), *Fefu and Her Friends* (1979), *Blood Wedding* (1980, from *LORCA), *The Danube* (1983), *Mud* (1984), *Sayita* (1984), *The Conduct of Life* (1985), *Cold Air* (1985, adapted from Virgilio Pinera), *The Trial of Joan of Arc on a Matter of Faith* (1986), *The Mothers* (1987), *Abingdon Square* (1987), *Oscar and Berta* (1987), *And What of the Night* (1990), *Enter the Night* (1993), *The Summer in Gossonsass* (1998), *Letters from Cuba* (2000), *The Autobiography of Alice B. Toklas* (2001, from Gertrude Stein)

Fornes was born in Havana, Cuba, then emigrated to the United States and became an American citizen. An artist by training, she has become one of the most consistently innovative American dramatists, eager to work in a range of styles. During the 1970s, Fornes moved away from pieces in the absurdist tradition of *IONESCO and *MROZEK that expressed an ironic attitude about such American myths as economic success and true love, and began to write plays that were often minimalist in their language and conveyed the isolation and anguish experienced by women through the centuries. Fornes actively seeks to inject the spontaneous into her creative process: her first play was composed of scenes each of whose first line came from a different page of a cookbook. The idea for *The Danube*, a romance between an English-language teacher and his pupil that takes place, in post-World War II Hungary before moving into an unnamed post-apocalyptic future came from Fornes' discovery of a recording of Hungarian language lessons in a second-hand record store. *Mud*, a dark, domestic triangle at whose centre is an entrapped and abused woman whose quest for freedom and escape is met with a bullet from her lover/husband, was completed after she came across a broom in a rummage store, and proceeded to make it a. central prop. One of Fornes' most terrifying plays, *The Conduct of Life*, is a brutal look at the moral, spiritual and physical corruption attending the lives of a Latin American colonel (whose job is torturing prisoners) and his wife, who at first wilfully ignores her husband's occupation – as well as the young woman he's brought home as a concubine – although by the end of the play she knows enough to kill him. Fornes has won many OBIE Awards for her work, including one for sustained achievement.

Fefu and Her Friends

Fefu and Her Friends is a mood play that captures both the insecurities and the aggressions of a group of eight women, Set in America during the 1930s, it is nonetheless rooted emotionally in the 1970s, for it explores the position of women on the edge of self-definition. The economy of the language lends the script both a lyricism and a sense of mystery. The women in the play seem to communicate with each other through nuance and implication, as though operating in a private world that only they comprehend. Fornes tries to bring the audience into that world by requiring spectators to walk into the spaces that the characters inhabit, while scenes are being performed (the audience is to be divided into groups, and scenes are to be repeated until each group has participated).

TRY THESE:

✶CHURCHILL, ✶GLASPELL, ✶LEVY for innovative work centred on women; ✶KROETZ for dark, sombre plays written in similar style; ✶MILLER for questioning the American dream; *The Summer in Gossonsass* responds to ✶IBSEN and specifically *Hedda Gabler*; ✶DURAS shares something of Fornes' concerns.

FOSSE, Jon   [1959 –   ]
Norwegian novelist, poet and dramatist

PLAYS INCLUDE:
The Name (1995), *Nightsongs* (1997), *Summer's Day* (1999), *The Girl on the Sofa* (UK première 2002), *Purple* (UK première 2003)

Fosse's plays have been widely staged across Europe but little seen in Britain as yet. His work is generally spare and uncompromising in its presentation of the indignities of daily life collapsing into quiet despair and the violence beyond despair. In *Nightsongs* a couple with a young baby are at the end of their tether, humanity is in short supply, and her attempt at escape will be catastrophic for her as well as him. In *The Girl on the Sofa* Fosse paints a detailed but slow-paced picture of despair, and *Purple*, according to the Edinburgh Royal Lyceum publicity, is 'deep, dark and highly oppressive . . . a subtle but revealing journey of unspoken tension, hidden emotion and adolescent rivalry' as a band rehearses in a deserted factory.

TRY THESE:

✶HARROWER adapted *The Girl on the Sofa* and *Purple*; ✶MOTTON translated *Nightsongs*; Fosse has been compared to early ✶BOND and ✶KROETZ; Fosse's *The Name* won the ✶IBSEN Prize.

FRAYN, Michael   [1933 –   ]
British dramatist, novelist, journalist and translator

PLAYS INCLUDE:
The Two of Us (1970, comprising *Black and Silver, The New Quixote, Mr Foot, Chinamen*), *The Sandboy* (1971), *Alphabetical Order* (1975), *Donkey's Years* (1976), *Clouds* (1976), *Balmoral* (1978, retitled *Liberty Hall*), *Make and Break* (1980), *Noises Off* (1982), *Benefactors* (1984), *Look Look* (1990), *Now You Know* (1995, from his own novel), *Copenhagen* (1998), *Alarms and Excursions* (1998)

Born in Mill Hill, Frayn co-scripted the 1957 Cambridge University Footlights revue 'Zounds', then worked for the *Guardian*, and the *Observer* until 1968, a period during which he wrote four of his novels. He also wrote award-winning articles on Cuba (*Clouds* is about the experience of journalists in Cuba).

Frayn's plays are often comic, but the comedy is very edgy and sometimes even, as in *Noises Off*, manic. Many of them explore behaviour within the constraints and frames of institutions; *Alphabetical Order* is set in the library of a provincial newspaper, *Donkey's Years* at an Oxford college reunion; *Make and Break* is about a businessman's experience of an international trade fair. His film script for *Clockwise* (1986) is about the host of trials and tribulations that thwart the journey of a headmaster (played by John Cleese) to a conference. In a television interview, Frayn acknowledged that the tragicomedy of his plays was something that he associated with ✶CHEKHOV, and in recent years, he has proved himself a sensitive and intelligent translator of Chekhov. Of *Three Sisters* he has said: 'It is about the irony of hopes . . . the way life mocks them', a sentiment that applies to his own work too, particularly perhaps to *Look Look*, an attempt to revisit the territory of *Noises Off* which simply didn't work. *Copenhagen*, a major hit, is about the meeting between the physicists Werner Heisenberg and Niels Bohr in Copenhagen in 1942. Heisenberg is indelibly associated with the uncertainty principle, which runs through the play as it explores what actually occurred at the meeting and how it affected the future

Noises Off by Michael Frayn, directed by Jeremy Sams, National Theatre at the Piccadilly Theatre, 2001. Stephen Mangan, Selina Griffiths. (Pete Jones/ArenaPAL)

development of World War II as well as the relationships between the two men.

Noises Off

Of all Frayn's work, *Noises Off* has been the most successful. It is at one level an extraordinarily well-crafted farce, at another, a play about the hopes and frustrations of a group of actors as they tour the provinces with the farce, 'Nothing On'. 'Nothing On' is a play-within-a-play, complete with a programme that lists the cast biographies of the characters. The first act opens on a traditional farce set, inhabited by the stock character of a cleaning woman, although this is soon interrupted by the interventions of a director, and the cleaning lady emerges as an actress rehearsing for the first night of the farce. The second act turns the set around, and the audience is confronted with the backstage events during a performance of 'Nothing On'. In the third act, the backstage relationships between the actors, stage management and director, after long months of touring, invade the performance of the play to chaotic effect. *Noises Off* is a brilliant parody of a particular kind of farce, of certain kinds of actors, and of theatrical conventions.

TRY THESE:

✳COONEY and Brian Rix, whose farces provide the bones of the play-within-the-play of *Noises Off*; ✳CHEKHOV and ✳ANOUILH, whom Frayn has adapted and translated, and with whom he clearly feels an affinity; ✳FEYDEAU is *the* classic French farceur; ✳AYCKBOURN, like Frayn, uses the conventions of farce innovatively; ✳STOPPARD does the same in *The Real Inspector Hound*, but also tackles uncertainty and physics in *Hapgood* and *Arcadia*; ✳BRECHT (*Galileo*) and ✳BRENTON (*The Genius*) for scientists and moral dilemmas.

FREISTADT, Berta   [1942 –   ]
British poet and dramatist

PLAYS INCLUDE:

Chicken Licken (1981), *Keely's Mother* (1981), *Poor Silly Bad* (1982), *The Burning Time* (1983), *Woman with a Shovel* (1983), *A Fine Undertaking* (1984), *The Life and Death of Laura Normill* (1986)

Freistadt's plays challenge the most comfortable and established ideas from a feminist, often lesbian feminist, perspective, with a dark, surreal sense of humour that frequently mixes Absurdism with realism. Her targets have ranged from the domestic to the grave: chauvinist fathers who stick their daughters into hen coops because they want sons (*Chicken Licken*); possessive mothers who brandish six-foot knives and forks over their daughters because they want to eat them (*Keely's Mother*); echoes of Evelyn Waugh's *The Loved One* in a lesbian farce set in a funeral parlour in *A Fine Undertaking*. *Woman with a Shovel* is a highly dramatic monologue that culminates in a woman turning her pent-up wrath on men with unusual violence. *Poor Silly Bad* is a funny, sensitive portrayal of three women, and particularly of an old woman, Dot, living alone and trying to preserve some degree of dignity and choice in her own death. In the post-Holocaust *The Burning Time*, Freistadt renews the domestic theme (quoting Engels about the modern family being based on slavery) and makes a plea to change the old systems of domination, a stance given a rather more humorous twist in *The Life and Death of Laura Normill*, where a lesbian is waiting at the Pearly Gates to see whether Himself or Satan (a woman of course) will claim her for their own!

TRY THESE:

✳RAME for female domestic and sexual oppressions; Tasha Fairbanks' *Curfew*, like *The Burning Time*, engages with a separatist culture; ✳DREXLER, ✳KENNEDY and ✳YANKOWITZ have also used grotesque and sometimes violent images to put over feminist ideas; ✳ORTON for similar humour; ✳DÜRRENMATT's *The Visit*, ✳MEYER's *Etta Jenks* for contrasting images of a woman wreaking revenge; ✳KEATLEY's *My Mother Said I Never Should*, ✳KESSELMAN's *I Love You, I Love You Not*, ✳MACDONALD's *All Things Nice* explore young and old through a grandmother–granddaughter relationship; ✳KEEFFE's *Not Fade Away* has an independent-minded old pensioner at its centre.

FRIEL, Brian
[1929 –   ]

Northern Irish dramatist

PLAYS INCLUDE:
This Doubtful Paradise (1959), *The Enemy Within* (1962), *Philadelphia, Here I Come!* (1965), *The Loves of Cass McGuire* (1967), *Lovers* (1968), *Crystal and Fox* (1970), *The Gentle Island* (1971), *The Freedom of the City* (1973), *The Volunteers* (1975), *Living Quarters* (1977), *Aristocrats* (1979), *The Faith Healer* (1979), *Translations* (1981), *Three Sisters* (1981, from *CHEKHOV), *The Communication Cord* (1982), *Fathers and Sons* (1987, from *TURGENEV), *Making History* (1988), *Dancing at Lughnasa* (1990), *A Month in the Country* (1992, from *TURGENEV), *The London Vertigo* (1992), *Wonderful Tennessee* (1992), *Molly Sweeney* (1994), *Give Me Your Answer, Do!* (1997), *Uncle Vanya* (1998, from *CHEKHOV), *The Yalta Game* (2001, from *CHEKHOV's *Lady with a Little Dog*), *Afterplay* (2002)

Friel, born in Derry, is probably both the best known and the best contemporary Irish dramatist. His work has been much preoccupied with the current political situation in Ireland in the broadest terms, particularly with the pressures that contribute to the intractability of that situation, the difficulty of rational responses to the legacy of hundreds of years of hostility and mistrust, communities divided by religion and language, and the search for a way out of the impasse. There is a strong emphasis on the theme of exile that reflects one traditional escape route from the economic and political ills of Ireland; in *Philadelphia, Here I Come!* the escape is to America, in *The Gentle Island* it is to Glasgow.

The renewed violence and gradual breakdown of the political situation after 1968 is reflected in such plays as *The Freedom of the City* and *The Volunteers*, which deal directly with aspects of 'the Troubles', but Friel is also concerned with the wider problems of communication and identity. He may not be a particularly daring dramatist in terms of formal experimentation but he makes effective use of splitting a character into public and private selves in *Philadelphia* and of the contrast between the judicial inquiry which 'establishes' that the civil rights marchers were terrorists in *The Freedom of the City* and their innocent behaviour in the flashbacks that show what actually led up to their deaths. In *The Faith Healer* three characters speak four forty-minute monologues in a hauntingly written multi-viewpoint drama that again draws on the themes of exile and return and the pains of both. In *Molly Sweeney*, again based on three characters' monologues, the title character regains sight but loses insight. The play tackles familiar Friel themes of loss and exile and the end of things through the fact and metaphor of blindness. In *Dancing at Lughnasa*, set in 1936, the rural community is placed once again on the edge of time and of place. Pagan rituals locate the events but the son is about to go off to fight against Franco. Friel has adapted several works by Chekhov and the same sense of some imminent cataclysm pervades this play. In *Afterplay* Friel brings together Sonya from *Uncle Vanya* and Andrei from *Three Sisters* in a Moscow café some time after the Revolution.

Translations
Translations, the first play staged by the Field Day company Friel co-founded with the actor Stephen Rea, is a very fine parable of the situation in Northern Ireland that also teases out some of its cultural roots. The play is set in 1830s Donegal, in a world where tramps can read Homer in the original but not *SHAKESPEARE, a world doomed to vanish under the assault of state education (in English) and the Royal Engineers' Survey of Ireland. Earnest English subalterns and unhappy Irishmen try to produce English equivalents of Irish place names in an act of cultural appropriation which remakes Ireland in the image of England. The English Lieutenant Yolland and the Irish woman Maire (who have no common language at all) fall in love, but the barriers of others' suspicion are too great for them to surmount and the play ends in muddle, confusion and destruction. Although the issues are serious and the allegorical applications clear, Friel handles events with a light touch and there is much gentle comedy at the expense of the two lovers failing to communicate – they both actually speak English in the play but neither

Dancing at Lughnasa by Brian Friel, directed by Jonathan Munby, Watermill, Newbury, 2002. Mary Conlon, Aoife Mcmahon, Dido Miles, Carline Lennon, Patricia Gannon. (Colin Willoughby/ArenaPAL)

understands the other – and at the expense of linguistic failures in general.

TRY THESE:
For Irish rural life, ✱SYNGE, particularly *Playboy of the Western World* for parallels with *The Gentle Island*, and *The Well of the Saints* for *Molly Sweeney*; ✱O'CASEY is the great dramatist of an earlier period of political strife in Ireland; contemporary dramatists writing about Ireland include ✱FINNEGAN, ✱MARIE JONES, ✱MCGUINNESS (who wrote the screenplay of *Dancing at Lughnasa*, ✱MORRISON, ✱PARKER, ✱REID, ✱DECLAN HUGHES, ✱MCCAFFERTY, Jimmy Murphy, ✱MURPHY, ✱WALSH; other notable plays with tribunal settings are ✱BRECHT's *The Measures Taken*, ✱EDGAR's *Our Own People*, ✱OSBORNE's *Inadmissible Evidence*; Robert Patrick's *Kennedy's Children* intercuts monologues in a powerful re-creation of the mood of 1960s USA; ✱PINTER's *Old Times* deals with differing recollections of events in ways reminiscent of *The Faith Healer*; ✱NICHOLS' *Passion Play* is a memorable example of the use of two actors to play the public and personal faces of one character; Helen Cooper's *Mrs Vershinin* tells the story of how she came to be the offstage neurotic in *Three Sisters*; ✱DE WET and Michael Picardie's *The Cape Orchard* for South African responses to ✱CHEKHOV; ✱MATURA transferred *Three Sisters* to Trinidad in his *Trinidad Sisters*.

FRISCH, Max   [1911 – 91]
Swiss dramatist and novelist

PLAYS INCLUDE:
Now You Can Sing (1946), *Santa Cruz* (1947), *The Great Wall of China* (1947, revised 1955), *When the War Was Over* (1949), *Oederland* (1951, revised 1961), *The Fire Raisers* (1958, US title *The Firebugs*), *The Fury of Philip Hotz* (1958), *Andorra* (1961), *Don Juan, or The Love of Geometry* (1962)

Born in Zurich, Frisch did not complete his doctoral studies in philosophy because of lack of money, and took up journalism. He went back to university to study as an architect, and produced his first building and his first novel in 1943. He worked simultaneously as a writer and an architect for ten years but then went to live in Rome as a full-time writer. Frisch was an influential figure in bringing new European drama and its ideas to a British theatre that was dominated by the social realism of 'The Angry Young Men'. Edna O'Brien has described him as a 'European brain that is as witty as it is adult'.

The Fire Raisers
This is a key text for the Theatre of the Absurd, and the most 'absurdist' of Frisch's plays. A dark comedy and a cautionary tale, the play is subtitled (with a nod at ✱BRECHT) 'A didactic play without a moral'. Throughout the play a chorus of fire-fighters acts to extend the individual history of Biedermann to a wider political allegory. Biedermann, the central figure of the play, is a Bourgeois (the translation of his German name), who constantly protests his status as 'a good citizen'. Two strangers appear in his house and lodge in the attic, without any protest from Biedermann, where they prepare to raise a fire. The play has an afterpiece in which the devil appears: Biedermann is still protesting his innocence and good citizenship in the face of hell fire. It becomes clear that the fire, and Biedermann's lack of resistance, is a parable for the way in which 'good citizens' can collude with the forces of tyranny. It thus refers to the position of those intellectuals in Germany who did nothing to resist the rise of fascism, but also to any political context in which 'good citizens' refuse to question.

TRY THESE:
✱GENET's *The Blacks*, ✱SARTRE's *The Condemned of Altona*, and *The Fire Raisers* all had their first London productions in 1961, and were significant in bringing an awareness of European theatre to Britain; ✱BECKETT and ✱IONESCO were the other main figures in the so-called 'Theatre of the Absurd'; ✱C. P. TAYLOR's *Good* is another treatment of the contribution of 'good citizens' to the rise of fascism; ✱ADRIAN MITCHELL's deservedly much acclaimed adaptation of *The Pied Piper*, a highly effective utopian allegory, poses more fascinating questions about 'good citizenry'.

FRY, Christopher   [1907 –   ]
British dramatist

PLAYS INCLUDE:

The Boy with a Cart: Cushman, Saint of Sussex (1938), *A Phoenix Too Frequent* (1946), *The Firstborn* (1948), *The Lady's Not for Burning* (1948), *Thor, with Angels* (1948), *Venus Observed* (1950), *A Sleep of Prisoners* (1951), *The Dark Is Light Enough: A Winter Comedy* (1954), *Curtmantle* (1961), *A Yard of Sun: A Summer Comedy* (1970)

Fry's early writing included revue material, lyrics and pageants. He is a Quaker, whose compassion is reflected in all his work – several plays use biblical material or religious and ethical conflicts and he wrote the screenplays for a number of movie bible-epics. He uses words like a skater giving dazzling displays of speed and balance, and his witty verbal dexterity is something you either love or loathe. His plotting is not very strong, but neither is it important. He has written that 'progress is the growth of vision: the increased perception of what makes for life and what makes for death. I have tried, not always successfully, to find a way for comedy to say something of this since comedy is an essential part of man's understanding.'

A Phoenix Too Frequent, Fry's first success, retells Petronius' story of the widow of Ephesus with the addition of the idea that being useful after death is itself a kind of resurrection. Fame came with *The Lady's Not for Burning*, especially its second production with John Gielgud (1949), although few people, including the director, seemed to respond to the dark undercurrent of bitterness and war-weary disenchantment that permeates the play below its springtime charm. The later seasonal pieces more clearly show their sombre colours through the surface glitter. His most direct statement is *A Sleep of Prisoners* in which four soldiers, prisoners in a church, each dream the others into enactments of Old Testament conflicts.

TRY THESE:

✷WHITING for the same combination of verbal skill and comedy with a deep undercurrent; ✷ANOUILH and ✷ELIOT are among other dramatists handling the Becket/Henry II theme of *Curtmantle*; Maxwell Anderson, ✷AUDEN, ✷CHURCHILL's *Serious Money* for other twentieth-century verse drama; ✷BRIDIE for religious drama; ✷COLLINS' *Judgement* for contrasting prison setting with soldiers.

FUGARD, Athol   [1932 –   ]
South African dramatist

PLAYS INCLUDE:

Nongogo (1957), *No-Good Friday* (1958), *The Blood Knot* (1961, revised as *Blood Knot*, 1985), *Hello and Goodbye* (1965), *People Are Living There* (1968), *Boesman and Lena* (1969), *Statements After an Arrest Under the Immorality Act* (1972), *Sizwe Bansi is Dead* (1972, with John Kani and Winston Ntshona), *The Island* (1973, with John Kani and Winston Ntshona), *Dimetos* (1975), *A Lesson from Aloes* (1978), *'Master Harold' . . . and the Boys* (1982), *The Road to Mecca* (1984), *A Place with the Pigs* (1987), *My Children! My Africa* (1989), *Playland* (1993), *A Valley Song* (1996), *The Captain's Tiger* (1999), *Sorrows and Rejoicings* (2001)

The leading South African dramatist of his generation, Fugard has been a major influence in creating an understanding of the black and the 'coloured' person's situations in South Africa. He is to drama what writers like Nadine Gordimer are to fiction – clear-eyed white chroniclers of apartheid and its ills, who remain bound in what is, to co-opt the title of a Fugard play, a tortured and complex 'blood knot' with a homeland they both love and hate. After the collapse of Apartheid, Fugard continued to cast an astringent eye on the strengths and weaknesses of the new dispensation.

Born to an Irish father and a Dutch mother, Fugard established his reputation with *Blood Knot*, which was first performed secretly in a Johannesburg attic because of its mixed-race cast. Interested in dramatically distilled situations, often with very few characters, Fugard has been linked with a writer he expressly admires – ✷SAMUEL BECKETT – particularly because of *Boesman and Lena*, a play about two coloured outcasts inhabiting a plaintive Beckettian void. After collaborations with the black actors John Kani and Winston

Ntshona, Fugard reached into his childhood to write the piercingly autobiographical 'Master Harold'... and the Boys, and into real-life situations, either experienced first hand or read about in the newspapers, to write The Road to Mecca and A Place with the Pigs (suggested by a report of a Red Army deserter who hid in a pigsty for over forty years). If his writing is marred by anything it is an excessive fondness for metaphors which are sometimes used gracefully – the ballroom dancing in 'Master Harold', the detritus in Hello and Goodbye – and often over-emphatically – the resilient aloes plant in A Lesson from Aloes, the 'pigsty' of Pavel's soul in A Place with the Pigs. Still, at his best, Fugard's overwhelming humanity redeems everything. You may quarrel with individual moments from his plays, indeed with individual plays, but the strength of the dramatist's searching and generous vision ultimately silences all argument.

Boesman and Lena

The most Beckettian of Fugard's plays and like most of his works, few of which have more than three characters – an intimate, small-scale piece on vast themes. Two abject castaway 'coloureds' make their way across the mud flats of South Africa's River Swartkops, in what the dramatist calls in his notebooks 'a poem of destruction'. They are a comical and pitiable pair – the talkative fidget, Lena, chattering into the void in an effort to stave off madness, and her brutalising Boesman. An elderly, near-mute black, Outa, appears at the campsite, but the emphasis is on the title characters – two living embodiments of 'white man's rubbish', who like ✱BECKETT's tramps, are bound ever more closely through their mutual teasing and torment.

'Master Harold' ... and the Boys

In a Port Elizabeth tearoom one rainy afternoon, a young boy commits a reprehensible act that will haunt him the rest of his life. Such is the bare-bones background to Fugard's most intensely autobiographical play. Fugard wrote the play to honour his childhood servant, Sam Semela, whom the young Fugard once cruelly humiliated as Hally does in the play. As an act of atonement, it's a piercingly magnanimous gesture. As an

act of playwriting, the work has a devastating simplicity and force that pulls you through its ninety minutes (without interval) from a beginning steeped in good cheer and high spirits to a conclusion that leaves you stunned. As Hally turns on the two black servants, Sam and Willie, whom he has loved as surrogates for the alcoholic father he loathes, Fugard shows the sources of racism in self-loathing, in an inward despair so profound it can only lash out and wound. A shapely and graceful piece of writing, the play makes a restorative theatrical experience out of spiritual depletion.

TRY THESE:
Market Theatre of Johannesburg and Barney Simon as initiators of multiracial and anti-apartheid plays, particularly Woza Albert by Percy Ntwa, Mbongeni Ngema and Simon; for other treatments of apartheid by South Africans, ✱HARWOOD, ✱LAN, ✱WRIGHT; ✱DE ANGELIS's Soft Vengeance and ✱EDGAR's The Jail Diary of Albie Sachs for one of the heroes of the anti-apartheid struggle; ✱ABBENSETTS, ✱MATURA, ✱WHITE for treatments of racism in Britain; ✱HOWE, ✱LEONARD, ✱SIMON for the formation of the artist; ✱TENNESSEE WILLIAMS for a similar use of metaphor; ✱AUGUST WILSON's Joe Turner's Come and Gone for forging a link between black America and black South Africa.

FULLER, Charles   [1939 –   ]
American dramatist

PLAYS INCLUDE:
The Village: A Party (1968, as The Perfect Party, 1969), In My Many Names and Days (1972), Candidate (1974), In the Deepest Part of Sleep (1974), The Lay Out Letter (1975), The Brownsville Raid (1976), Sparrow in Flight (1978), Zooman and the Sign (1980), A Soldier's Play (1981), Sally (1988), Prince (1989), Jonquil (1990), Burner's Frolic (1990)

Fuller confronts the nature of a society that he perceives as basically racist, and he explores the experience of black people struggling to survive in that climate. The world of Fuller's plays is inevitably violent, since its figures often gravitate toward destructiveness in order to claim their rightful place in America.

Frequently, as in *Zooman and the Sign* and *A Soldier's Play*, this racist-engendered violence ends up pitting black people against each other, in what Fuller dramatises as the tragic outcome of a morally chaotic world. *Sally, Prince, Jonquil* and *Burner's Frolic* are a sequence dealing with the aftermath of the Civil War, confronting some of the myths of Reconstruction most familiar from treatments such as *Gone with the Wind*.

A Soldier's Play

A Soldier's Play is a forceful indictment of America's racist attitudes and social structures. As in many of Fuller's dramas, white America is the fundamental cause of this racism, but it is the black's self-hatred, learned at the hands of whites, that ultimately poisons the black person's existence. One of the more complex of Fuller's scripts structurally, it is also one of his most sophisticated in terms of the many points of view that he dramatises. His central character, the black sergeant Waters who heads one of the few all-black units waiting to ship out during World War II, is both hateful and pitiable. Filled with contempt for his own blackness, he loses any sense of moral balance, and in the process destroys what he set out to preserve. *A Soldier's Play* won the 1982 Pulitzer Prize for Drama and was filmed in 1984.

TRY THESE:
✱ WOLFE's *The Colored Museum* for the myths and stereotypes of the African-American experience; ✱ BARAKA ✱ BULLINS, ✱ ELDER, ✱ HANSBERRY's *A Raisin in the Sun*, ✱ AUGUST WILSON for the American black experience.

G

GALATI, Frank [1943 –]
American director and adapter

PLAYS INCLUDE:
Winnebago (1974), *Heart of a Dog* (1985,
from ✱BULGAKOV), *She Always Said No, Pablo*
(1987, conceived by Galati, with words by
Gertrude Stein), *A Flea in Her Ear* (1988,
from ✱FEYDEAU), *The Grapes of Wrath* (1988,
from Steinbeck), *A Long Gay Book* (2003,
from Gertrude Stein)

Galati has combined an academic career with
a career as director and dramatist in the
professional theatre. He is particularly adept
at shaping novels into performable scripts, as
with *Heart of a Dog* and the Tony Award
winning *The Grapes of Wrath*, both of which
retain the philosophical and emotional
essences of the original. Galati preserves
Steinbeck's episodic structure, his many characters and incidents, making Ma Joad the
emotional centre of the story, a choice that
not only lends unity to Galati's play but also
communicates Steinbeck's vision of her as a
symbol of never-ending struggle for existence. Practically all the lines in *The Grapes of
Wrath* are taken from the novel, although
Galati incorporates songs in ✱BRECHTIAN
fashion. The original production was
designed for a large proscenium stage with
the Joads' overburdened truck, as a prop that
gradually took on an emotional resonance of
its own, much like Courage's wagon in
✱BRECHT's *Mother Courage and Her Children*.

TRY THESE:
✱EDGAR's *Nicholas Nickleby* and *Entertaining
Strangers* for creation of a sense of community.

GALLAGHER, Mary [1947 –]
American dramatist

PLAYS INCLUDE:
Little Bird (1977), *Father Dreams* (1978),
Chocolate Cake (1980, with Ara Watson), *Dog
Eat Dog* (1983), *How To Say Goodbye* (1986),
Love Minus (1988), *De Donde?* (1990)

Gallagher chronicles the intimate relationships of unhappy people who see themselves
as outcasts from society. Her characters are
usually middle class and well educated, yet for
reasons they cannot understand they are
unable to acquire even the basic accoutre-
ments of the 'good life': a lover, marriage, a
job, children. In the end, however, the characters usually attain some degree of knowledge
about themselves and often find a measure of
happiness. Although Gallagher often adopts
an episodic structure in her plays, her style
tends to be realistic, her characters recognisable, and their conversation that of day-to-
day living. On occasion, she has diverged
from this style to write plays such as *Dog Eat
Dog*, a satire in which the American capitalist
system disintegrates, or *De Donde?*, an agit-
prop dramatisation of illegal Mexican immigration into the United States. *How To Say
Goodbye*, a carefully detailed picture of a
marriage that falls apart when the couple's
only child becomes terminally ill, was co-
winner of the 1987 Susan Smith Blackburn
Prize.

TRY THESE:
✱KEMPINSKI's *Duet for One* for the impact of
illness; ✱HARE for anatomies of discontent;
✱GANNON's *Keeping Tom Nice* and ✱NICHOLS'*A
Day in the Death of Joe Egg* for families with
children with disabilities.

GALSWORTHY, John   [1867 – 1933]
British novelist and dramatist

PLAYS INCLUDE:
The Silver Box (1906), *Strife* (1909), *Justice* (1910), *The Skin Game* (1920), *Loyalties* (1922), *Escape* (1926), *Exiled* (1929)

Galsworthy practised for a time as a barrister, but then set out methodically to learn to write fiction; after ten years' hard work he hit the jackpot with *A Man of Property* (1906). By contrast his first play, *The Silver Box*, was an immediate success, though it now seems an over-schematic treatment of the theme of 'one law for the rich and another for the poor'. He wrote twenty-six more plays, many of which did well. They tend to be well-made sub-Ibsen problem plays, with mild social criticism, not-too stereotypical characters, a strong narrative line, a touch of melodrama, and upper-middle class settings; but few now appear with any kind of regularity. *Justice*, which Galsworthy meant as a demonstration that society tends to destroy its weaker members, is unusual in having had a direct effect on the law – the silent scene with the prisoner in solitary confinement seems to have persuaded Winston Churchill that the practice should be reformed forthwith. *Strife* is an over-symmetrical but well-crafted strike play that carries a powerful punch on stage. The old Chairman of the Board and the strike leader both suffer from the long strike, and are both repudiated when agreement is reached on the same terms as were offered at the start. Galsworthy meant the play not to take sides, and the cases for capital and labour are both strongly made, but his anti-extremist conclusions are too obviously underlined. He won the Nobel Prize for Literature in 1932.

TRY THESE:
✱ IBSEN for well-crafted plays with a 'social message'; ✱ GRANVILLE-BARKER and ✱ SHAW for similar concerns, but more experimental approaches to character drawing; for other plays about strikes, ✱ EDGAR's *That Summer*, ✱ ODETS' *Waiting for Lefty*.

GANNON, Lucy   [1948 –   ]
British screenwriter and dramatist

PLAYS INCLUDE:
Keeping Tom Nice (1987), *Wicked Old Nellie* (1987), *Janet and John* (1988), *Raping the Gold* (1988), *A Dog Barking* (1988), *Dancing Attendance* (1990)

Gannon only began to write seriously in her late thirties, having worked as a residential social worker. Her plays often reflect her former occupation, concerned as they are with the elderly, the handicapped and the socially disadvantaged. *Keeping Tom Nice*, her first play, about a family's attitude towards their severely handicapped son, won the Richard Burton Award, the Susan Smith Blackburn Prize and the John Whiting Award. She was sometimes accused of being simplistic in her attitudes and wearing her left-wing, anti-Thatcherite politics on her sleeve. However, her plays were popular with audiences and prize-giving bodies alike and represent a powerful voice of the late 1980s. Her television play *Soldier, Soldier* inaugurated an enormously successful television career with such series as *Bramwell*, *Peak Practice* and *Soldier Soldier*.

TRY THESE:
✱ NICHOLS' *A Day in the life of Joe Egg* for an earlier play about bringing up a handicapped child, also ✱ KEARSLEY's *Wednesday*; ✱ KEARSLEY's *Under the Web* dealt like Gannon's *Raping the Gold* with the strains of looking after an aged parent; ✱ MARIE JONES' *The Hamster Wheel* and ✱ VAN ITALLIE's *The Traveller* deal with post-stroke traumas; ✱ MOTTON, ✱ SPENCER for contemporary chronicles of the disadvantaged; ✱ GLENDINNING's *Danny Boy* also deals with the relationship between a mother and her brain-damaged son, in the context of Northern Ireland.

GARDNER, Herb   [1934 –   ]
American dramatist

PLAYS INCLUDE:
A Thousand Clowns (1962), *The Goodbye People* (1968), *Thieves* (1974), *Love and/or Death* (1979), *I'm Not Rappaport* (1984), *Conversations with My Father* (1991)

Gardner has acquired a reputation for writing commercially successful comedies that at the same time reveal the potential for sadness in contemporary life. Gardner's characters are usually social misfits, rejected by the mainstream either because they rebel against middle-class conventions or because, as in the case of the elderly men in *The Goodbye People* and *I'm Not Rappaport*, the world appears to have no use for them anymore. Inevitably, however, these characters overcome the disapproval of the world around them, usually by finding other nonconformists with whom they can share a belief in the joy of living. Stylistically, Gardner employs both the long monologue and the one-liner, and his plays are flavoured with a particularly New York brand of humour. *I'm Not Rappaport* is a moving, if sometimes sentimental, comedy that depicts both the desperation and the feistiness of two elderly men, one black and one white, who become friends after meeting on a park bench. It won the 1986 Tony Award for Best Play. *Conversations with My Father* traces a New York Jewish immigrant family from the 1930s to the 1970s, exploring the tensions caused by the father's desire to be assimilated into American society.

TRY THESE:
✴SIMON for New York humour; ✴UHRY's *Driving Miss Daisy* for ageing across the racial divide; ✴ALBEE's *Zoo Story* for a different use of a park bench.

GARRICK, David   [1717 – 79]
British actor-manager and dramatist

PLAYS INCLUDE:
Miss in Her Teens (1747), *The Clandestine Marriage* (1766, with George Colman the elder), *The Irish Widow* (1772), *Bon Ton; or, High Lift Above Stairs* (1775)

Garrick may have been the greatest actor-manager in the history of the British stage, but as a dramatist he was no more than a very competent hack. Beside a number of farces, he collaborated with George Colman the elder on *The Clandestine Marriage*, which is revived from time to time and was, rather surprisingly, filmed in 1999. It is an amiable farcical comedy

with a reliably well-worn plot, involving a new-rich bourgeois trying to buy his two daughters into marriages with the minor aristocracy. The fun arises because the younger daughter is already secretly married to her father's clerk and is also fancied by both the aged and lecherous Lord Ogleby (the best part in the play) and his son; the satirical possibilities of this marriage market are on the whole fudged, and of course all are reconciled at the end.

TRY THESE:
✴SHERIDAN, ✴GOLDSMITH for more original eighteenth-century comedies; ✴BEHN, ✴CONGREVE, ✴ETHEREGE, ✴JONSON, ✴WYCHERLEY for earlier treatments of similar themes; Garrick is a character in ✴DE ANGELIS's *A Laughing Matter*.

GATTI, Armand   [1924 –   ]
French director, dramatist and filmmaker

PLAYS INCLUDE:
La Deuxième Existence du Camp de Tatenberg (1962, *The Second Existence of the Tatenberg Camp*), *La Vie Imaginaire de l'Éboueur Auguste Geai* (1962, *The Imaginary Life of the Streetsweeper August Geai*), *Chant Public Devant Deux Chaises Électriques* (1966, *Public Song in Front of Two Electric Chairs*), *V as in Vietnam* (1967), *La Journée d'une infirmière* (1970, *The Day of a Nurse*), *La Cigogne* (1971, *The Stork*), *La Passion du Général Franco* (*The Passion of General Franco*; banned until 1976), *Les Sept Possibilités du Train 713 en partance d'Auschwitz* (1987)

Gatti was born into a poor immigrant family in Monaco, and spent part of World War II in a German labour camp. The concentration camp theme recurs in several of his plays. He is an engagingly optimistic and energetic character, who believes that theatre can truly change the world. He wrote a number of plays on political themes during the l960s, influenced by ✴ADAMOV and Planchon (and of course ✴BRECHT), but often showing a fragmentation of character and of reality. For example, his semi-autobiographical play, *La Vie Imaginaire de l'Éboueur Auguste Geai*, shows his father at five different ages, played by five different actors (sometimes all on stage at once), and in seven possible different spaces on stage. These 1960s plays, on subjects such as the Chinese Civil War, the execution of Sacco and Vanzetti, and the Vietnam War, had considerable success all over France. However, Gatti gradually came to believe that the audience should participate in the production rather than merely consume it, devoted himself to the production of community plays and films on politically sensitive themes and often in politically sensitive areas. He was invited to Londonderry by *JOHN ARDEN in 1984, and his film *The Writing On the Wall* (1985) used Catholic teenagers to play Protestant characters and vice versa. Unlike *ANN JELLICOE, he deals with contemporary events, and aims to stir up the community rather than to reconcile it. His results are less artistically finished than hers, and he provokes more local hostility, but his activities seem to have no less of a liberating effect on the participants.

TRY THESE:
*EDGAR's *Entertaining Strangers*, *ELIOT's *The Rock* for community plays; *SHERMAN's *Bent*, *C. P. TAYLOR's *Good* for other versions of concentration camps.

GAY, John   [1685 – 1732]
English poet and dramatist

PLAYS INCLUDE:
The Beggar's Opera (1728), *Polly* (1729)

A friend of Jonathan Swift and Alexander Pope, Gay wrote a number of comedies and the libretto to Handel's *Acis and Galatea* but is remembered largely for *The Beggar's Opera*, a send up of the eighteenth-century fashion for Italian opera and a satire on the Prime Minister Sir Robert Walpole and his administration. It takes a great number of popular songs and folk tunes, provides them with new words and sets them in a tale of thieves, whores and highwaymen, which, in turn, mirrors the corruption of contemporary society. Its first production achieved the then longest run on the London stage. The play's popularity continues but its satire is less personal now and it survives more for its lively action and memorable tunes. *Polly*, a

sequel that carries heroine Polly Peachum to the West Indies, failed to pass the censorship imposed by Walpole and it was seven years before it could be staged. Gay lost most of his profits in South Sea Bubble speculation and died only four years after his great success.

TRY THESE:
*BRECHT's *Threepenny Opera* reworked the story of *The Beggar's Opera*, adding a more consciously political polemic and replacing the songs with new biting lyrics to music by Kurt Weill; Sue Frumin's *Beggar's Opry* (1990) is a lesbian revision of Gay's play; *DEAR's *The Art of Success* for Walpole's Licensing Act as an allegory for modern censorship and his *The Villain's Opera* a further updating of Gay/Brecht; *SOYINKA for another adaptation; Frank Loesser's *Guys and Dolls* for a more sentimental musical approach to thieves and rascals; for satires on political corruption, see *KEEFFE and *MROZEK.

GELBART, Larry   [1928 –   ]
American dramatist, lyricist and screenwriter

PLAYS INCLUDE:
The Conquering Hero (1961), *A Funny Thing Happened on the Way to the Forum* (1962, book with Burt Shevelove), *The Frogs* (1974, book of musical adapted from *ARISTOPHANES), *Sly Fox* (1976, adapted from *BEN JONSON), *Mastergate* (1989), *City of Angels* (1989, book of the musical), *Power Failure* (1991)

Gelbart is one of the most consistently clever writers of comedy in theatre, film (including *Tootsie* and *Bedazzled*) and television (notably as the originator, chief writer and co-producer of the award-winning series *M.A.S.H.*). His plays reveal a comic imagination that is at ease with a range of forms, from the satire of *Sly Fox*, an adaptation of *BEN JONSON's *Volpone* set in San Francisco during the 1800s, to the farce of *A Funny Thing Happened on the Way to the Forum*. The musical *City of Angels* functions on several levels, as a parody of the contemporary Hollywood film industry, a love letter to the Philip Marlowe/Sam Spade style of movie in the 1940s, and a writer's examination of his commitment to art. *Mastergate* sends up the 'investigation' into the Iran

Contra Affair, while *Power Failure*, structured similarly to *SCHNITZLER's *La Ronde*, satirises the abuse of power in the USA. Gelbart brings to his comedies both a realistic appreciation for the dark side of human nature and an ever-hopeful expectation that situations will resolve themselves happily.

TRY THESE:

*HAMPTON's *Tales From Hollywood*, *KAUFMAN's and Hart's *Once in a Lifetime*, *CHARLES WOOD's *Veterans*, for plays about filmmaking; *HARE's *Blue Room* for a version of *La Ronde*.

GELBER, Jack   [1932 – 2003]
American dramatist

PLAYS INCLUDE:
The Connection (1959), *The Apple* (1961), *Square in the Eye* (1965), *The Cuban Thing* (1968), *Sleep* (1972), *Barbary Shore* (1974, from Norman Mailer), *Farmyard* (1975, from *KROETZ), *Rehearsal* (1976), *Starters* (1980), *Big Shot* (1988), *Magic Valley* (1990)

'I have no theory of the theatre to proclaim', Gelber once announced, but the Chicago-born dramatist nonetheless remains associated with the breakdown of the fourth wall and a freer, looser theatrical style in keeping with the improvisatory off-Broadway climate in which he was spawned. Gelber got his start with New York's Living Theatre, who performed what remains his best-known work, *The Connection*, a piece about drug addiction featuring its own play-within-a-play. Celebrated both for its bold realism and its seeming formlessness, *The Connection* opened to general pans ('oh man! what junk!' cried one critic), but time has bolstered its reputation as a frontrunner of the drama of the dispossessed typified by Miguel Pinero, *SAM SHEPARD and *LANFORD WILSON. None of his later plays has garnered equal attention, although their subjects range from scientists in a sleep lab (*Sleep*) to an overtly theatrical piece about the nature of the theatre (*Rehearsal*) in which a play is cast, developed, and then cancelled. Since 1972, Gelber has been devoting the bulk of his energies to teaching as a Professor of English at Brooklyn College in New York City.

TRY THESE:
*PIRANDELLO, *SHEPARD for theatrical games-manship and plays about theatricality; *DUNN's *The Little Heroine* for addicts, *SACKLER's *Goodbye, Fidel*, *TRIANA for Cuba-related works.

GEMS, Pam   [1925 –   ]
British dramatist

PLAYS INCLUDE:
Betty's Wonderful Christmas (1972), *My Warren & After Birthday* (1973), *The Amiable Courtship of Miz Venus & Wild Bill* (1973), *Sarah B Divine* (1973), *Piaf* (1973, produced 1978), *Go West Young Woman* (1974), *Dusa, Fish, Stas and Vi* (1975, originally called *Dead Fish*), *The Project* (1976, expanded and retitled *Loving Women*, 1984), *Guinevere* (1976), *The Rivers and Forests* (1976, from *MARGUERITE DURAS), *My Name is Rosa Luxemburg* (1976), *Franz in April* (1977), *Queen Christina* (1977), *Ladybird, Ladybird* (1979), *Sandra* (1979), *The Treat* (1982), *Aunt Mary* (1982), *Camille* (1984), *The Danton Affair* (1986, from Stanislawa Przybyszewska), *The Blue Angel* (1991, from Heinrich Mann), *Deborah's Daughter* (1994), *Marlene* (1996), *Stanley* (1996), *The Snow Palace* (1998), *Mrs Pat* (2003)

Socialist realist, mother of four, Gems is one of the few women dramatists to span two generations. Rooted in a working-class consciousness with a racy, pungent turn of phrase, she did not, in fact, take up writing full time till after forty, though she had written scripts for radio and television whilst also bringing up her children and had been involved with the early feminism of the 1970s. More than any other writer, she consistently explores the dilemmas and specificity of what it is to be female in a world still largely dominated by men. Her best-known play, *Piaf*, which started out at the RSC's studio theatre and ended up triumphant on Broadway, was a typically earthy – some called it rude – debunking of the myth surrounding the Little Sparrow. Piaf's battle to overcome the pressures of fame, alcohol and drugs is also the story, warts and all, of a gritty, working-class woman searching for economic and sexual independence – a treatment Gems served up

also in *Camille*, which stripped Dumas'
original of its sentimentality to show the high
price of love in a money-regulated market.
Dusa, Fish, Stas and Vi, the play that put Gems
on the map, is a reiteration of these pressures,
worked out through four young women of
the 'post-pill' generation, a theme which
consistently intrigued Gems, a pre-war and
wartime young mother. It is a pioneering
work in its depiction of women struggling
towards self-fulfilment, confronted with
problems of sexuality (anorexia, rejected
love), child-rearing (the children have been
taken by a former husband) and survival (one
character, a physiotherapist by day, is a high-
earning prostitute by night), yet still support-
ive of each other.

Gender is also at the heart of the epic
Queen Christina, which juggles with the
contradictions of gender stereotyping and
choices (Queen Christina was brought up as a
man but longs in the end to give birth; Gems
calls it her 'uterine' play), and the less successful transvestite farce, *Aunt Mary*. The *Danton
Affair*, another epic, but based on the manuscript of Stanislawa Przybyszewska, unusually
for Gems centres on two male protagonists,
and stands rather as an implicit homage by
Gems to the almost forgotten creativity of the
young Polish woman writer whom she also
featured in *The Snow Palace*. She has adapted
works by ✳CHEKHOV, ✳IBSEN and ✳LORCA as
part of what now looks like a career-long
engagement with the creation and maintenance of images of women, both in the plays
of key male dramatists and in fictional and
stage and screen stars from Piaf to Mrs Patrick
Campbell via Marlene Dietrich and one of
her most famous roles in *The Blue Angel*. If
Stanley stands out for having a male title, her
treatment of the artist Stanley Spencer
concentrates on his relations with women.

TRY THESE:

For female stereotypes ✳CHURCHILL's *Top Girls*,
✳DANIELS, ✳DE ANGELIS, ✳HOLBOROUGH's
Dreams of San Francisco; Clare Booth Luce's *The
Women*; for bitchy and unsupportive males,
✳ELYOT, ✳PINTER's *No Man's Land*; ✳LUDLAM's
Camille for a quite different debunking of Dumas;
Gems has described her dramatist son Jonathan
as encapsulating 'the nihilism, the anarchic

humour of his group; ✳HAMPTON's *Tales from
Hollywood* includes ✳BRECHT, ✳HORVATH,
Thomas and Heinrich Mann as characters; ✳TERRY
JOHNSON's *Insignificance* and *Hitchcock Blonde* for
dumb blonde stereotypes.

GENET, Jean   [1910 – 86]
French novelist, poet and dramatist

PLAYS INCLUDE:

Les Bonnes (1946, *The Maids*), *Splendid's*
(1948), *Haute Surveillance* (1949,
Deathwatch), *Le Balcon* (1956, *The Balcony*),
Les Nègres (1959, *The Blacks*), *Les Paravents*
(1961, *The Screens*)

A delinquent and thief who spent much of his
first thirty years in reformatory or jail, where
he began to write, Genet was released from a
life-sentence on the plea of ✳JEAN-PAUL SARTRE
and other French existentialist luminaries who
recognised his prodigious talent. Even those
repelled by the subject matter of his books, in
which he presents the violence and vice of
criminals and prostitutes as a mixture of luminous beauty and masturbatory fantasy, can be
reached by his plays, which act as a mirror to
the 'normal' world in which he sees true vice
and corruption. The tough dream objects and
fantasising homosexuals of his novels and his
romantic obsession with homosexuality give
place to more accessible portraits of men
outside society in the prisoner relationships of
Deathwatch and to more abstract studies of
private and public exploitation and interdependence in *The Balcony* and *The Blacks*. His
theatre is often ritualistic and abstract, its form
sometimes echoing Catholic liturgy. Cross-
casting, both sexual and racial, is intended in
The Maids and *The Blacks*. *The Screens* echoes
the Algerian struggle for independence but the
other plays offer a more general criticism of
society, playing on the prejudices of the audience to intensify their effect. As well as fiction
and autobiographical works, Genet wrote three
screenplays and a ballet scenario.

The Balcony
Set in a brothel where representatives of
establishment power groups – church, police,
etc. – act out their fantasies while a revolution
brews outside, *The Balcony* turns a mirror on

a society that it sees as a whorehouse. Its images, drawn from the conventional repertoire of the pornographer, are not used to titillate but to show how people wilfully preserve the sham of conventional society and power structures. It offers a challenge to directors and to audiences to convey and comprehend the twists and turns of its ideas and provides an opportunity for an Artaudian theatricality.

TRY THESE:

✱WEISS, whose *Marat/Sade* uses a madhouse for its charades and demands similar virtuoso staging; John Herbert's *Fortune and Men's Eyes* and ✱PUIG's *Kiss of the Spider Woman* for homosexuals in prison; Lindsay Kemp for his work based on Genet; ✱CHURCHILL's *Cloud Nine* for the use of cross-casting; ✱BEHAN for alternative treatments of prison life and the brothel setting; ✱KESSELMAN's *My Sister in This House* for feminist treatment of the real-life incident at Le Mans that gave rise to *The Maids*; ✱BARTLETT for the British premiere of *Splendid's*.

GILBERT, (Sir) W(illiam) S(chwenck)   [1836 – 1911]
English librettist, dramatist and director

PLAYS INCLUDE:
The Palace of Truth (1870), *Pygmalion and Galatea* (1871), *Dan'l Druce, Blacksmith* (1876), *Engaged* (1877), *Rosencrantz and Guildenstern* (1891)

Savoy Operas
(with music by Sir Arthur Sullivan) include:
Thespis (1871), *Trial by Jury* (1875), *HMS Pinafore* (1878), *The Pirates of Penzance* (1879), *Patience* (1881), *Iolanthe* (1882), *Princess Ida* (1884), *The Mikado* (1885), *Ruddigore* (1887), *The Yeoman of the Guard* (1888), *The Gondoliers* (1889), *Utopia Limited* (1893), *The Grand Duke* (1896)

Although Gilbert's real claim to fame must be as the librettist half of Gilbert and Sullivan, he was also a considerable (and at times rather sour) dramatist in his own right, ranging from burlesque-extravaganza to comedy to straight melodrama. *Engaged* shows to a high degree the fundamental Gilbertian discrepancy between the characters' noble speeches and their actual intentions; the humble but warm-hearted Scottish peasants whom we find exchanging highly moral platitudes as the curtain rises rapidly prove to be an updated version of Cornish wreckers – they derail trains so that they can rob the passengers; and under the many romantic protestations of true love (Cheviot Hill, the hero, manages to become engaged to three women at once) lies simple fiscal arithmetic. It was revived at the Orange Tree, Richmond, as a Christmas entertainment in 2002 where its satire on cupidity still seemed fresh, even if the wordplay did not appeal to all tastes.

In the operas, too, things are seldom what they seem; the highest principles are applied in a way which somehow produces the most material benefit, as with Pooh-Bah's readiness to humble his family pride for the smallest of bribes; this combines happily with the Carrollian logic of a world in which (for example) all problems are resolved by the mere insertion of a 'not' in a royal decree (*Iolanthe*).

TRY THESE:
Edward Bulwer Lytton's recently revived *Money* for an earlier Victorian account of the corrosive effects of (lack of) money; ✱WILDE for similarities to *Engaged* in *The Importance of Being Earnest*; ✱STOPPARD for variations on the adventures of Rosencrantz and Guildenstern; ✱ORTON for the deadpan delivery of preposterous sentiments.

GILL, Peter   [1939 –   ]
British actor, director and dramatist

PLAYS INCLUDE:
The Sleeper's Den (1966), *A Provincial Life* (1966, from ✱CHEKHOV), *Over Gardens Out* (1969), *Small Change* (1976), *Kick for Touch* (1983), *As I Lay Dying* (1985, from William Faulkner) *In the Blue* (1985), *Mean Tears* (1987), *Cardiff East* (1997), *Certain Young Men* (1999), *Friendly Fire* (1999), *The York Realist* (2001), *Original Sin* (2002)

Welshman Gill began his theatrical career as an actor, but has been largely known as a director since he attracted attention with a sensitive and very naturalistic production of

✷ D. H. LAWRENCE's *A Collier's Saturday Night* at the Royal Court (1965). An associate director at the Royal Court (1970–2) and Director of Riverside Studios (1976–80), he joined the National Theatre where, from 1984 to 1990, he was director of the Studio, running experimental workshops for performers and developing new work with writers, as well as directing for the main auditoria. In 2002 the Sheffield Crucible organised a festival of his work that included his own staging of his new work *Original Sin.*

Of his own plays, *The Sleeper's Den* is a naturalistic study of a poverty-stricken housewife pressured into breakdown by the indifference and demands of her family. Later plays have been more abstract – indeed often highly elliptical – but focus as relentlessly on what would seem to be semi-autobiographical memories taken from Gill's Welsh background. *Over Gardens Out* with its two misunderstood boys driven by violence is also an impressionistic emotional battle in both past and present. Obsessive rugby-playing male bonding plays a damaging role in both *Small Change* (the scars left by an adolescent sexual relationship) and *Kick for Touch* (the triangular relationship of two brothers and a wife). *Mean Tears* is an episodic emotionally compelling presentation of a hopelessly ill-balanced affair between a vaguely academic or literary figure and his younger bisexual love object. *Cardiff East* returns to the community issues of *The Sleeper's Den. Certain Young Men* is about contemporary homosexual life, while a play for young people, *Friendly Fire*, explores a typical Gill theme of people being in love with the wrong people. In *The York Realist* Gill returns to 1962 and stages a cross-class homosexual love across the North–South divide in the context of a production of the York mystery plays. *Original Sin* is a gender-reversed version of ✷ WEDEKIND's *Lulu.*

TRY THESE:

✷ CHURCHILL's *Fen*, ✷ WARD's *Apart from George* for imprisoned emotions (in rural East Anglian communities); for the painful distance between speech and silence in personal relationships, see ✷ BECKETT, ✷ CHEKHOV, ✷ DURAS, ✷ MAMET, ✷ PINTER, ✷ SHEPARD; other contemporaries

charting the parameters of personal pain in relationships are ✷ AYCKBOURN, ✷ GODBER, ✷ RAIF, ✷ SPENCER, ✷ KEARSLEY, ✷ STOREY, ✷ WILCOX's *Accounts* for rugby (league and union). ✷ GODFREY for a National Theatre protégé, under Gill; ✷ HARRISON for the *Mysteries*; ✷ RAVENHILL's *Mother Clapp's Molly House* for gay communities.

GILMAN, Rebecca   [1965 –   ]
American dramatist

PLAYS INCLUDE:
The Glory of Living (1997), *Spinning into Butter* (1999), *Crime of the Century* (2000), *Boy Gets Girl* (2000), *Blue Surge* (2001)

Gilman has been championed by the Goodman Theatre, Chicago, and by the Royal Court, winning awards on both sides of the Atlantic for *The Glory of Living*, a depiction of Southern trailer trash that successfully skirted the potential for caricature to create a portrait of an abusive way of life that explored morality and violence in a way that reminded some critics of ✷ EDWARD BOND. In *Spinning into Butter* Gilman dared to unpick some of the complex issues around racist attitudes and how they get dealt with in a university; unsurprisingly, it has become very popular on American campuses. Gilman dramatises a real-life Chicago mass murder from the 1960s in *Crime of the Century*, focusing on the victims rather than the murderer whose face is never seen. This is something of a Gilman trademark since the original complainant never appears in *Spinning into Butter*, and in *Boy Gets Girl*, an exploration of some of the murky territory of harassment and how it can destabilise the person who is being harassed, the harasser himself vanishes from the action. *Blue Surge* deals with the developing relationships between two policemen and two prostitutes.

TRY THESE:

✷ MAMET generally for parallels, and *Oleanna* specifically, for political correctness in an academic environment; ✷ SIMON GRAY for politically incorrect academics; ✷ CLARE MCINTYRE's *Low Level Panic* for stalking; ✷ BECKETT's *Waiting for Godot* and ✷ ODETS' *Waiting for Lefty* for absent characters.

GIRAUDOUX, Jean   [1882 – 1944]
French dramatist

PLAYS INCLUDE:
Siegfried (1928), *Amphitryon 38* (1929),
Intermezzo (1933), *La Guerre de Troie N'aura
Pas Lieu* (1935, *Tiger at the Gates* or *The
Trojan War Will Not Take Place*), *Électre*
(1937, *Electra*), *Ondine* (1939), *Sodome et
Gomorrhe* (1943, *Sodom and Gomorrah*), *La
Folle de Chaillot* (1945, *The Madwoman of
Chaillot*), *Pour Lucrèce* (1953, *Duel of Angels*)

Giraudoux, a diplomat until 1940, was forty-six when the actor/director Louis Jouvet urged him to try adapting his novel *Siegfried et le Limousin*, the story of a Frenchman brought up as a German who has to choose between his nationalities. The great success of his plays in the 1930s was largely due to the continued partnership with Jouvet, whose inventive staging and superb acting combined with Giraudoux's verbal glitter to cover any deficiencies in the dramatic action. Several of the plays show the fashionable 1930s French interest in updating Greek myth. The most successful of these was *La Guerre de Troie N'aura Pas Lieu*, into which he put all his strong conviction that the French and the Germans were not natural enemies. World War II, therefore, came as a particular catastrophe for Giraudoux, who on the outbreak of war was set to run French propaganda, as an unlikely rival to Dr Goebbels.

In 1955 Kenneth Tynan called *The Trojan War Will Not Take Place* the 'highest peak in the mountain-range of modern French theatre', but fashion has moved against Giraudoux (as against ✶CHRISTOPHER FRY, who translated it as *Tiger at the Gates*), whose work is now seldom seen in Britain.

TRY THESE:
Claudel for poetic rhetoric; ✶ANOUILH,
✶COCTEAU, Gide, ✶SARTRE for relating classical
legends or Greek play themes to contemporary
French concerns; ✶CHURCHILL and ✶LAN's *A
Mouthful of Birds* is based on ✶EURIPIDES' *The
Bacchae*, as is ✶DUFFY's *Rites*; ✶WERTENBAKER's
Love of the Nightingale for another reworking of
Greek legend.

GLASPELL, Susan   [1882 – 1948]
American dramatist

PLAYS INCLUDE:
Suppressed Desires (1915, with George Cram
Cook), *Trifles* (1916), *The Outside* (1917),
Bernice (1919), *Inheritors* (1921), *The Verge*
(1921), *Alison's House* (1930)

With the exception of productions of *The Verge* and *Inheritors* at the Orange Tree, Richmond, Glaspell has been virtually neglected by the British theatre. A founder of the influential Provincetown Players with her husband George Cram Cook and ✶EUGENE O'NEILL, she played an important part in establishing the serious American theatre but the majority of her plays are now neglected. *Trifles*, a murder mystery which presents an acute account of different understandings of the nature of events and motivations on the basis of gender, is finely observed but too short to be frequently revived professionally. *Inheritors*, a well-crafted longer play, which examines the corruption of the pioneering spirit and the American dream, sheds light on the historic roots of many contemporary American attitudes. *The Verge*, with its heroine on the point of a breakthrough into either madness or understanding, anticipates the hothouse atmosphere of ✶TENNESSEE WILLIAMS. *Bernice* and *Alison's House* (based on Emily Dickinson's life) share the device of an offstage female protagonist with *Trifles*; an economical way of suggesting the absences that can constitute the notion of 'woman'.

TRY THESE:
There is a ✶STRINDBERGIAN quality in Glaspell's
analysis of the ways marriage can work, although
her conclusions unsurprisingly differ from his; for
another view of women from the same period try
Sophie Treadwell's *Machinal*; the contrast
between a desire for immolation and a desire for
life in *The Outside* anticipates ✶BECKETT; ✶NOEL
GREIG takes up similar themes in *Poppies*, as does
✶TERRY in *Approaching Simone*.

GLENDINNING, Robin   [1938 –   ]
Northern Irish dramatist

PLAYS INCLUDE:
Jennifer's Vacation (1982, also known as *Stuffing It*), *Mumbo Jumbo* (1986), *Culture Vultures* (1988), *Donny Boy* (1990)

Glendinning was raised on a farm in County Armagh and educated at Trinity College Dublin where he read modern history and political science. He taught for eleven years before co-founding the moderate Alliance Party of Northern Ireland in 1970. He worked as its full-time organiser for five years and stood unsuccessfully for election on two occasions. He combined a return to teaching with a new career as a radio dramatist and quickly established a firm reputation. The Northern Irish troubles form an inevitable backdrop to Glendinning's work, which is concerned more broadly with questions of community and individual identity. His first work for the stage was *Jennifer's Vacation*, an adaptation of one of his own radio plays, produced at the Dublin Festival. He was joint winner of the Manchester Royal Exchange's 1986 Mobil Playwriting Competition for *Mumbo Jumbo*. In *Donny Boy*, Donny, who is mentally impaired, is left holding the gun that killed an RUC officer, and his Catholic mother has to cope with her own complex and wildly confused loyalties. In this harrowing thriller, set in the Belfast battlefield, the terror of everyday life is tempered by much laughter.

TRY THESE:
✴MARIE JONES, ✴MORNIN, ✴REID for writers whose plays, rooted in Belfast, are also concerned with community and the effects of violence; ✴HEGGIE and ✴WALL for other Mobil Award winners; ✴GANNON's *Keeping Tom Nice* and ✴NICHOLS' *A Day in the Death of Joe Egg* for caring for children with disabilities; ✴O'CASEY for earlier Irish troubles.

GLOWACKI, Janusz   [1938 –   ]
Polish-born dramatist

PLAYS INCLUDE:
Cinders (1981), *Hunting Cockroaches* (1985), *Fortinbras Gets Drunk* (1990), *Antigone in New York* (1993), *The Fourth Sister* (2000)

Glowacki was in London in December 1981 when martial law was declared in Poland; he chose not to return to his country and emigrated with his family to New York City. His plays generally focus on the experience of political repression that his characters live with, even in the most supposedly free society, America. The mood of his plays tends to be tragicomic, for the world that Glowacki depicts mingles horror with irony, the potential for imminent death with man's apparently uncontrollable urge to persist. Like other post-World War II Polish dramatists, such as Tadeusz Rozewicz and ✴MROZEK, Glowacki's style is grounded in absurdist theatre, yet he also brings to his writing a humanism and compassion that make his plays particularly accessible to western audiences. *Hunting Cockroaches* presents as its central metaphor the image of two émigrés, a married couple, isolated and in effect imprisoned in their roach-infested Manhattan tenement. Like the two men in ✴BECKETT's *Waiting for Godot*, the man and woman, 'He' and 'She', talk with each other obsessively in order to keep their desperation at bay. The habit of living with political repression has made them fearful even in their new environment, and they experience the economic and social pressures of their new country as yet another form of tyranny, which renders them impotent.

TRY THESE:
✴KUREISHI (who adapted *Cinders*), ✴PINTER for obsessive talking on the edge of disaster; *The Fourth Sister* draws on ✴CHEKHOV; ✴STOPPARD for another take on minor characters from *Hamlet*, ✴SHAKESPEARE for the play Fortinbras comes from; ✴SOPHOCLES for Antigone.

GODBER, John   [1956 –   ]
British dramatist and director

PLAYS INCLUDE:
Up 'n' Under (1984), *Bouncers* (1985), *Shakers* (1986, with Jane Thornton) *Blood Sweat and Tears* (1986), *Cramp* (1986), *Putting on the Ritz* (1987), *Teechers* (1987), *Salt of the Earth* (1988), *On the Piste* (1990), *Shakers Re-stirred* (1991, with Jane Thornton), *Bouncers – 1990's Remix* (1991), *Happy Families* (1991), *April in Paris* (1992),

Up 'n' Under II (1993), *Passion Killers* (1994), *Dracula* (1995, with Jane Thornton), *Lucky Sods* (1995), *Gym and Tonic* (1996), *Weekend Breaks* (1997), *It Started with a Kiss* (1997), *Hooray for Hollywood* (1998), *The Weed* (1998), *Perfect Pitch* (1998), *Unleashed* (1998), *Thick as a Brick* (1999), *Big Trouble in the Little Bedroom* (1999), *Seasons in the Sun* (2000), *On a Night Like This* (2000), *Our House* (2001), *Departures* (2001)

The son of a miner, Godber began writing short stories for Radio Sheffield at the age of sixteen, trained as a teacher and taught for five years, while doing postgraduate work in drama at the University of Leeds. He has worked for television and scripted the film of *Up 'n' Under* but he is most closely associated with the Hull Truck Theatre Co, of which he has been artistic director since 1984. Godber has said: 'I think the theatre should be exciting. It should involve action.' His involvement with Hull Truck is an expression of his commitment to a genuinely serious popular theatre, and also to a theatre outside London, as opposition to the enshrining of 'theatre' at the National Theatre and the RSC. Most of his plays are social comedies that take place in public arenas and are generally concerned with what Godber has called 'working class leisure activities'; *Up 'n' Under* and *Cramp* (which is about a body-builder, and has music by Tom Robinson) both take a sport as their central device. Intensely physical pieces of theatre, they draw heavily on caricature for effect, as do *Bouncers* and *Putting on the Ritz*, both of which are set in discos. *Up 'n' Under*, which won the Laurence Olivier Comedy of the Year Award for 1984, is about rugby league (Godber is himself a rugby player), which becomes a means of exploring the contradictions of machismo and the energy and resources devoted to the game, and also becomes a powerful image of resources that have gone to waste in contemporary Britain (body building is used similarly in *Cramp*). *Bouncers*, similarly, adopts a fairly ambivalent stance towards its macho, working-class characters – celebratory, but there's also something distinctly distasteful about this lot.

TRY THESE:

✱ AYCKBOURN for similar productivity and long-term commitment to theatre outside London; ✱ LUCKHAM's *Trafford Tanzi*, ✱ PAGE's *Golden Girls*, ✱ SACKLER's *The Great White Hope*, ✱ STOREY's *The Changing Room*, ✱ WILLIAMSON's *The Club*, for plays with sport as a central element; ✱ RUSSELL's *Stags and Hens* is the disco play; ✱ BERKOFF for physical theatre; ✱ NIGEL WILLIAMS' *Class Enemy* for a classroom play; ✱ LEIGH for questions of caricature.

GODFREY, Paul   [1960 –   ]
British dramatist

PLAYS INCLUDE:
Inventing a New Colour (1986), *Once in a While the Odd Thing Happens* (1990), *A Bucket of Eels* (1994), *The Blue Ball* (1995), *The Modern Husband* (1995, from Henry Fielding), *The Invisible Woman* (1996, from Terence), *The Candidate* (1997, from Gustave Flaubert)

Godfrey trained and worked as a director in Scotland before turning to writing. As a product of the National's studio wing (which, under ✱ PETER GILL, gave both *Inventing a Colour* and *Once in a While* workshop productions) Godfrey's style – spare, elliptical, fragmented – bears a certain comparison with Gill's own work. *Inventing a New Colour* even has similar protagonists to those in Gill's *Small Change*. However, whereas Gill's youngsters and mothers reflected the pain of growing up in rugby-dominated Wales, Godfrey, who comes from Exeter, locates his lads in Devon during World War II. And his tale of Peter, the London evacuee, billeted on a middle-class couple and their own son, Francis, suggested – though perhaps not as clearly as some would have liked – a sense of lives destroyed beyond repair, 'a poetic elegy for the world before the war' as one critic put it.

Godfrey's concern with mood and atmosphere seemed further distilled in the tone poem-like *Once in a While*. Intending to mount a production of Benjamin Britten's *Noyes Fludde* in Scotland, Godfrey had met Peter Pears just before he died, an event that clearly inspired further enquiry into the nature of artistic creativity and resulted eventually in *Once in a While*.

Far from sensationalising the possible intimacies of the ✶AUDEN–Britten, Britten–Pears relationships, Godfrey opted instead for an understatement of expression that drew harsh criticism from some as 'precious' and 'lean, bloodless realism' but moved Helen Rose of *Time Out* to describe the play's images as lingering 'in the mind with the pleasing insistence of a beautiful melody'.

TRY THESE:

✶MACDONALD for Britain in the Blitz; ✶HARE and ✶LOWE for wartime Britain; ✶CRIMP for a British contemporary with a tendency to write scenes in a short, televisual mode; ✶POWNALL's *Master Class* for a contrasting treatment of musical composition.

GOETHE, Johann Wolfgang von [1749 – 1832]
German dramatist and poet

PLAYS INCLUDE:

Götz von Berlichingen (1773), *Clavigo* (1774), *Stella* (1775), *Egmont* (1788, produced 1796), *Iphigenia in Tauris* (1779, second (verse) version 1787), *Torquato Tasso* (1789, produced 1807), *Faust* Part I (published 1808), *Faust* Part II (published posthumously 1833)

Goethe studied in Leipzig, like the young Faust, and like him studied alchemy and forbidden subjects. *Götz von Berlichingen* was written in what he hoped was a ✶SHAKESPEAREAN manner, under the eager influence of Herder; the result is a story of an honourable robber knight in revolt against tyrannical rulers, and a very untidy construction. *Clavigo* is a curiosity, presenting a heightened version of ✶BEAUMARCHAIS's real-life journey to Spain to avenge his sister's seduction and abandonment by a Spaniard. In *Egmont* the hero is again shown as a noble and honourable humanist who goes to his death as a fighter against tyranny in the revolt of the Netherlands against Spain. Goethe began the play just before accepting an invitation to Weimar, where he inadvertently stayed for the rest of his life, becoming Finance Minister and Lord High everything else. He managed the Court Theatre from 1791 until 1817, when he was displaced by an actress who had the advantage of being the Grand Duke's mistress. From a literary point of view, his reign was a golden age – besides his own plays, he put on most of ✶SCHILLER's – but as a director he was less successful, finding it difficult to get on with the less intelligent actors, and tending to drill them. In a two-year absence in Italy he wrote *Iphigenia in Tauris* (from ✶EURIPIDES) and *Torquato Tasso*, a study of a poetic hero with emotional difficulties that were not unlike his own.

Faust
Goethe's last play, the two parts of *Faust*, was written over a long period, and is usually regarded as unactable, though from time to time somebody is rash enough to try to scale its dizzying heights. The story of the scholar tempted by the devil to barter his soul for the things of this world was already well known, but Goethe turned it into a vast poem on the destiny of man, and his Faust is redeemed at the end (which led George Steiner to call it 'sublime melodrama'). The style of the play shifts from broad farce to high tragedy and most stages in between without warning, changing verse forms as it goes. There have been many attempts to put it on in English, usually making much of the Gretchen episode. ✶HOWARD BRENTON produced a 'vigorous, colloquial and often very funny' (*Guardian*) version for the RSC in 1995.

TRY THESE:

✶MARLOWE for *Dr Faustus*, ✶HAVEL for *Temptation*, ✶WERTENBAKER for Faustian bargains; ✶IBSEN's *Peer Gynt* has Faustian redemptive overtones; ✶EDGAR's *Nicholas Nickleby*, ✶BRENTON and ✶HARE's *Pravda* and *Brassneck* for epic scale; Helen of Troy, who figures in both Goethe's and ✶MARLOWE's treatments of the Faust story also figures in ✶SHAKESPEARE's *Troilus and Cressida*, ✶EURIPIDES' *Trojan Women, Helen, Orestes* and ✶GIRAUDOUX's *The Trojan War Will Not Take Place*; *Iphigenia in Tauris* is a reworking of ✶EURIPIDES' play of the same name; ✶BOND's *The Fool* (about John Clare) and ✶BRENTON's *Bloody Poetry* (about the Shelleys and Byron) are other plays about poets to contrast with Goethe's treatment of Tasso; Robert David Macdonald for another translation of *Faust*.

GOGOL, Nikolai Vasilevich [1809 – 52]

Russian novelist and dramatist

PLAYS INCLUDE:

The Government Inspector (1836), *Marriage* (1842), *The Gamblers* (1842)

Gogol worked as a civil servant, took a course in painting, tried to become an actor and lectured on medieval history – failing at them all – before he achieved success with two volumes of Ukrainian tales in 1831–2. He is best known for his novel *Dead Souls* (of which he destroyed a second volume shortly before his death) and the comedy *The Government Inspector*, of which he wrote: 'I decided to collect everything that was evil in Russia, all the injustices committed in places where justice is most of all expected of man – and laugh it off.' The play is a satire on official corruption in a small provincial town where an impecunious impostor is mistaken for a government official making an inspection. *The Government Inspector* introduced a grotesque farcical realism to the Russian theatre. Its humour found an instant response and aroused considerable official anger that for a time drove Gogol from Russia. Its frequent revivals show how little the basic satire dates and the name part has provided a vehicle for some outstanding interpretations. In Britain Jatinder Verma's 1988 transposition of the play to post-colonial, small-town India was particularly successful. ✶JOHN BYRNE and ✶MARIE JONES have also done recent versions.

TRY THESE:

✶FO and ✶GELBART for similar broad satire of petty officials; ✶BRENTON and ✶HARE's *Brassneck*, ✶FLANNERY's *Our Friends in the North* for local government corruption; ✶COLLINS' *The Strongest Man in the World* as a modern equivalent; ✶KEEFFE's many social satires; ✶IBSEN's *Pillars of Society* for Norwegian hypocrisy and corruption in high places; ✶BULGAKOV dramatised *Dead Souls*.

GOLDONI, Carlo [1707 – 93]

Italian dramatist

PLAYS INCLUDE:

Belisario (1734), *The Servant of Two Masters* (1746), *The Venetian Twins* (1748), *Mine Hostess* (1753, also known as *Mirandolina*), *Il Campiello* (1756), *The Mania for the Country*, *The Adventure in the Country* and *The Return from the Country* (1761, a trilogy), *Le Baruffe chiozzotte* (1762, *The Chioggian Quarrels*), *The Fan* (1763)

Goldoni wrote his first play at eleven and ran away with some travelling players at fourteen. He practised law for a short time before a tragicomedy, *Belisario*, was accepted for performance in 1734 and he became the dramatist of the Teatro San Samuele in Venice. For thirty years he tried to change the pattern of Venetian theatre before accepting the post of Director of the Comédie Italienne in Paris. He remained in Paris until his death.

He wrote about 200 plays in Italian or French, the majority of them comedies. Very few of them have been seen in Britain in recent years and productions have too often been conceived in *commedia dell'arte* style when, in fact, Goldoni's intention was to replace the improvised and now debased *commedia* with scripted plays which would reflect and comment on contemporary society. But he did not want to lose his audience – he had to wean them gradually. He considered that, 'the secret of the art of writing comedy is to cling to nature and never leave her' and, because his comedy is rooted in the way people behave rather than topical political satire, much of it remains relevant today. His comedies are mainly of middle-class life and they become increasingly sharp and critical. There is no 'typical' Goldoni play. *The Servant of Two Masters* comes early in his campaign of reform and still retains much of the structure of *commedia* with its fast-moving farce. *The Venetian Twins* looks like a classic mistaken identity comedy until one of the twins is killed mid-play never to return.

TRY THESE:

✶BEAUMARCHAIS's *Marriage of Figaro* for its treatment of servant and master relationships; ✶MOLIÈRE, writing in a more formal style, is more savage in exposing bourgeois and aristocratic hypocrisies; for dramatists in the Goldoni tradition, ✶DE FILIPPO and ✶FO; ✶SHAKESPEARE's *Twelfth Night* and *Comedy of Errors* for the expected version of separated twins;

★BOUCICAULT's *The Corsican Twins* and ★RUSSELL's *Blood Brothers* for other variations on a theme.

GOLDSMITH, Oliver   [1730 – 74]
Irish dramatist and man of letters

PLAYS INCLUDE:
The Good-Natured Man (1768), *She Stoops to Conquer* (1773)

Goldsmith appears to have been an attractively indigent figure in fashionable London society who, as well as earning the friendship of Dr Johnson, amongst other notables, wrote one play, one poem and one novel that have stood the test of time (*She Stoops to Conquer*, 'The Deserted Village' and *The Vicar Of Wakefield*). Few eighteenth-century dramatists find a regular place in the current repertory but *She Stoops to Conquer*, a genial comedy of manners, owes much of its continuing popularity to its combination of the sentimental and the satirical. The central character, Kate Hardcastle, uses great skill to expose the contemporary double standard of sexual morality and force the otherwise eligible Charles Marlow to come to terms with his own sexism. These characters are surrounded by foils, each with a prevailing character trait that allows actors considerable scope for comic invention. A National Theatre revival in 2002 paired it with *A Laughing Matter* by ★APRIL DE ANGELIS, a new play examining the circumstances that made ★DAVID GARRICK turn it down as too risky.

TRY THESE:
★SHERIDAN is the only other late eighteenth-century British dramatist whose work is regularly performed; the 'Restoration' dramatists ★BEHN, ★CONGREVE, ★ETHEREGE, ★WYCHERLEY offer more robust treatments of similar themes; Goldsmith's Kate herself refers to similarities between ★FARQUHAR's *Beaux' Stratagem* and her play, while her name points to ★SHAKESPEARE's *The Taming of the Shrew*, in which the situation is reversed.

GOOCH, Steve   [1945 –   ]
British dramatist and translator

PLAYS INCLUDE:
Will Wat, If Not, Wat Will? (1972), *Female Transport* (1973), *The Motor Show* (1974, with Paul Thompson), *Strike '26* (1975, with Frank McDermott), *Made in Britain* (1976, with Paul Thompson), *Back-Street Romeo* (1977), *The Woman Pirates Ann Bonney and Mary Read* (1978), *Future Perfect* (1980, with ★MICHELENE WANDOR and Paul Thompson), *Landmark* (1980, revised version of *Our Land, Our Lives,* 1976), *Fast One* (1982), *What Brothers Are For* (1983, from Terence's *The Brothers*), *Taking Liberties* (1984), *Star Turns* (1987)

Keenly interested in community theatre, Gooch has pursued an interest in the labour movement, class and gender issues that has not brought him great recognition, although *The Motor Show* is an important example of the 1970s desire to create theatre for workers at their workplaces. He has found genuinely interesting subjects such as the Peasants' Revolt of 1381 in *Will Wat*, nineteenth-century transportation of women convicts from Britain to Australia in *Female Transport* or late eighteenth-century mock elections involving Samuel Foote and John Wilkes in *Taking Liberties*, but even his treatment of the potentially fascinating story of Ann Bonney and Mary Read in *The Woman Pirates* failed to convince in an ill-received and short-lived RSC production. His translations include ★BRECHT's *The Mother* and *Man is Man*, Harald Mueller's *Delinquent, Big Wolf, Rosie* and *Flotsam*, Fassbinder's *Cock-Artist*, Martin Walser's *Säntis*, and ★KROETZ's *Home Work*. His 1982 version of ★LOPE DE VEGA's *Fuenteovejuna*, in which a village defeats a local tyrant through collective action, was an apt combination of Gooch's own political interests and his talent for adaptation. His other adaptations include works by Dickens, Tankred Dorst and Voltaire as well as ★WEDEKIND's Lulu plays and *The Marquis of Keith*.

TRY THESE:
★WESKER's *Caritas* is also set at the time of the Peasants' Revolt; ★BRIDIE also wrote on Bonney

She Stoops to Conquer by Oliver Goldsmith, directed by Max Stafford-Clark, National Theatre and Out of Joint, 2002. Owen Sharpe as Tony Lumpkin, Jane Wood as Mrs Hardcastle. (Colin Willoughby/ArenaPAL)

and Read: ✱JELLICOE for community theatre; ✱BARKER, ✱BRENTON, ✱EDGAR, ✱TREVOR GRIFFITHS for other, more successful, contemporary British socialist dramatists; ✱CHURCHILL, ✱GEMS, ✱WERTENBAKER for women's treatments of gender issues in both contemporary and historical contexts, particularly Wertenbaker's *Our Country's Good*, which, like *Female Transport*, deals with convicts and Australia.

GORKY, Maxim (Alexei Maximovitch Peshkov)   [1868 – 1936]
Russian dramatist

PLAYS INCLUDE:

The Philistines (1901), *The Lower Depths* (1902), *Summer Folk* (1904), *Children of the Sun* (1905), *Barbarians* (1906), *Enemies* (1906), *Vassa Shelesnova* (1910)

One of the great Russian dramatists, Gorky's importance stems from his success as a dramatist both under the Czar and after the Revolution. His obvious feeling for the downtrodden underclass of Czarist Russia and his enormous status after the Revolution – he was the first president of the Soviet Writers' Union – won him at least the outward approval of Stalin, and he used his position to champion literary culture and to protect other writers from the censor and the secret police.

An orphan at the age of eleven, he worked through his adolescence and youth at every kind of ill-paid, temporary work. He learned to read while employed on a river steamer, turned to writing, and found literary success in 1895 with his story *Chalkash*. He became active in politics, befriended Tolstoy, was befriended by ✱CHEKHOV, and left the country after the failure of the 1905 Revolution. He returned to Russia in 1913, and became a champion of the Bolshevik Revolution. He developed the theory of 'Socialist Realism', which was soon distorted by Stalin's requirement for exclusively positive images of Soviet life. He died of TB in 1936, a death later laid at the door of a supposed Trotskyist plot 'uncovered' during the show-trials of Stalin's enemies.

An implacable enemy of the wealthy and the intellectual in pre-revolutionary society, his sympathy for the poor and the oppressed is powerful and sincere and found its most powerful expression in *The Lower Depths*, probably his best known and most often performed play. Set in a squalid slum in Moscow, the play portrays with unflinching candour the miserable lives of the misfits and failures who live there. Although in his time the realism of his portrayals of poverty was unprecedented – and even today the unremitting pessimism and gloom of his vision is hard to take – it is transcended by Gorky's obvious compassion for suffering and by his anger at its causes. The plays are weakened sometimes by his tendency to moralise and preach – a flaw of which he himself despaired. But Gorky's panoramic view of a society tottering before the fall can still make a powerful impact. Although Gorky has been consistently compared, with ✱CHEKHOV, usually negatively, his political grasp and rigorous examination of bourgeois values can be regarded as a complement to the Chekhovian canvas, not inferior to it. Where *Summer Folk*, for example, focuses on the idle, nouveau riche *dacha* class, *Barbarians*, set in a small provincial town, pits the old peasant and petit-bourgeois Russia of crude greed and corruption against the emotional violence of the new in the shape of two visiting railway engineers. *Enemies* tells us in no uncertain terms about class conflict and why the overthrow of the old order in 1917 was so inevitable; the same goes for *Vassa Shelesnova*, Gorky's last play, which, set ten years before the Revolution, ends on a note of plangent despair.

TRY THESE:

Gorky is a character in ✱DUSTY HUGHES' *Futurists*; ✱IKOLI produced a memorable adaptation of *The Lower Depths*; ✱POWNALL's *Master Class* investigates the whole issue of socialist realism in the context of music; ✱MAYAKOVSKY as a Russian contemporary of Gorky; the visionary who briefly transforms lives is a notable figure in ✱IBSEN's *The Wild Duck* and ✱O'NEILL's *The Iceman Cometh*; ✱MOTTON for his compassion for down-and-outers in the 1980s; ✱TREVOR GRIFFITHS' *Piano* recalls Gorky as well as ✱CHEKHOV.

GOTANDA, Philip Kan   [1949 –   ]
American dramatist

PLAYS INCLUDE:
The Avocado Kid or Zen in the Art of Guacamole (1979), *A Song for a Nisei Fisherman* (1981), *The Dream of Kitamura* (1982), *The Wash* (1985), *Fish Head Soup* (1987), *Yankee Dawg You Die* (1987), *Day Standing on Its Head* (1994) *Ballad of Yachiyo* (1995), *The Sisters Matsumoto* (1998), *Yohen* (1999), *Floating Weeds* (2001), *The Wind Cries Mary* (2002)

Gotanda is one of the foremost Asian-American dramatists in the United States. A Sansei, or third-generation Japanese American, Gotanda is particularly concerned about the place of Japanese Americans in American society and his scripts often encompass two worlds. *The Dream of Kitamura*, for instance, is a stylised tale of murder in the time of the Samurai, while *The Wash* is a realistic drama about two elderly second-generation Japanese Americans on the verge of divorce. *Yankee Dawg You Die* is a more polemical view of the Japanese American situation. *The Wind Cries Mary*, a response to *IBSEN's *Hedda Gabler*, updates the story to 1968 and the dilemma of a Japanese-American woman torn between the demands of tradition and her own feelings. Gotanda has seldom been staged in Britain but *Ballad of Yachiyo* was staged at London's Gate Theatre and *Floating Weeds* had an afternoon reading at the Royal Court.

TRY THESE:
*ABBENSETTS, *FAGON, *HWANG, *KUREISHI, *WESKER for questions of assimilation and marginality.

GRANVILLE-BARKER, Harley   [1877 – 1946]
British director, dramatist, actor and theorist

PLAYS INCLUDE:
The Marrying of Anne Leete (written 1899, produced 1902), *The Voysey Inheritance* (1905), *Waste* (1907), *The Madras House* (1910), *The Secret Life* (written 1919–22, published 1923, produced 1988), *His Majesty* (written 1928, not produced)

After *SHAW, Granville-Barker is perhaps the most important figure in the renaissance of English drama in the early 1900s. He was also an excellent actor who played *IBSEN and *SHAW parts for the Stage Society. Sometimes regarded as the father of Britain's National Theatre movement, from 1904 to 1907 he directed and managed the Court Theatre (now the Royal Court) with John E. Vedrenne. With an ensemble company he produced contemporary European drama, translations of *EURIPIDES, and new British plays, above all those of *SHAW. They lost money, but their influence was seminal.

As a dramatist, he is most often bracketed with *GALSWORTHY (and both are generally cross-referenced to Shaw), but his plays are livelier and less well made than Galsworthy's, and he is better at putting argument on stage than Shaw. Granville-Barker's reputation has been eclipsed by Shaw's but he is a considerable dramatist whose status has been confirmed by major revivals of his plays in Britain over the last thirty years. Even one of his final unperformed plays, *The Secret Life*, dealing with the perhaps autobiographical theme of public versus private life, was resurrected at the Orange Tree, Richmond, in 1988. His early play *The Marrying of Anne Leete* was found unconventional, elliptical and somewhat ambiguous in 1902, and the RSC production in 1975 produced much the same reactions. *The Madras House* (Royal National Theatre, 1977) was revealed as a very rich play: its structure seems loose at first (Granville-Barker is capable of creating the six carefully differentiated unmarried Huxtable girls in Act 2 and then abandoning them altogether) but the theme of the role of women in society holds it together. *The Voysey Inheritance* is a good, well-crafted play, which generates considerable suspense, and the dreadful Voysey family are a fine collection of well-rounded upper-middle-class characters, all visibly related. *Waste*, about the ruin of a politician through a casual affair which leads to abortion and death, was written in 1907, banned by the censor, rewritten in 1926, and then almost unperformed until its quality was shown by the RSC revival in 1985. It is very well constructed, with a modern resonance to the abortion arguments and some fine long suspenseful scenes of political and personal argument.

TRY THESE:
✻IBSEN for problem plays and ✻SHAW for argument plays – Granville-Barker often seems a cross between the two; ✻GORKY was an equally strong examiner of bourgeois values; ✻CHEKHOV too, though in a different vein; for more well-crafted, family dramas with moral intent; ✻HELLMAN, much of ✻RATTIGAN and, perhaps surprisingly, some of ✻COWARD; Elizabeth Robins' *Votes for Women* for its handling of sexual politics.

GRASS, Günter   [1927 –   ]
German novelist, poet and dramatist

PLAYS INCLUDE:
Onkel, Onkel (1958, *Mister, Mister*), *Die Bösen Köche* (1961, *The Wicked Cooks*), *Die Plebejer proben den Aufstand* (1965, *The Plebeians Rehearse the Uprising*), *Davor* (1969, *Beforehand*)

Socialist writer Grass was born in Danzig, which provides the setting for his early novels. He experimented with short absurdist plays, stage design, poetry and sculpture before making a hit with in 1959 with his novel *Die Blechtrommel* (*The Tin Drum*). A committed polemicist, he has been active in German politics as well as in literature. He won the 1999 Nobel Prize for Literature.

His most successful play internationally has been *The Plebeians Rehearse the Uprising*, an interesting metatheatrical piece. It is set in the Berliner Ensemble on 17 June 1953, when the East German workers demonstrated against demands for higher productivity; the boss is (unhistorically) rehearsing the plebeians' uprising against Coriolanus, when a group of construction workers breaks in to ask for a statement of his support. He refuses to give it, seeing the senselessness of this unplanned action, but he also refuses to denounce the uprising when asked by the authorities; and he continues the rehearsal, making the real workers participate, recording their voices and studying their reactions to improve his play. The situation is not treated naturalistically – parts are in verse –

and there are touches of Expressionism; and it is far from being a simple attack on ✻BRECHT.

TRY THESE:
✻HOCHHÜTH for German 1960s 'documentary' drama, but Grass has fewer pretensions and a sense of humour; ✻TREVOR GRIFFITHS' *The Party* for the relationship between rhetoric and political involvement, similarly ✻BULGAKOV's *Molière*.

GRAY, Amlin   [1946 –   ]
American dramatist and adapter

PLAYS INCLUDE:
Villainous Company (1978, adapted from *Henry IV* and other plays of ✻SHAKESPEARE), *How I Got That Story* (1979), *The Fantod* (1979), *Kingdom Come* (1983, from O. E. Rolvaag), *Zones of the Spirit* (1984, includes *Outlanders* and *Wormwood*, suggested by material from ✻STRINDBERG), *A Christmas Carol* (1984, adapted from Dickens)

Gray first received significant recognition with his surreal, hard-hitting satire about the Vietnam War, *How I Got That Story*. North and South Vietnamese and Americans come under Gray's fire, as he demonstrates all factions to be both dishonest and unintelligent. The imaginative script requires that a character called 'The Historical Event' transform into twenty other characters who make up parts of the Event. Since then, Gray's work has tended to be more realistic in style, and he has frequently chosen to write or adapt plays that are set in historical periods. Much of his work has been done with the Milwaukee Repertory Theatre.

TRY THESE:
✻SPALDING GRAY, ✻RABE, ✻CHARLES WOOD, ✻WRIGHT for images of war; ✻BRENTON's *Epsom Downs* for imaginative transformations of actors.

GRAY, Simon   [1936 –   ]
British dramatist and novelist

PLAYS INCLUDE:
Wise Child (1967), *Dutch Uncle* (1969), *Butley* (1971), *Spoiled* (1971), *Otherwise Engaged* (1975), *The Rear Column* (1978), *Close of Play* (1979), *Stagestruck* (1979),

Quartermaine's Terms (1981), *The Common Pursuit* (1984; revised version 1988), *Melon* (1987), *Hidden Laughter* (1990), *Cell Mates* (1995), *Life Support* (1997), *Just the Three of Us* (1997), *The Late Middle Classes* (1999), *Japes* (2001)

Gray is a former university lecturer, a prolific writer (for stage, television and film, as well as of adaptations, novels and even autobiography) whose plays have often involved the affairs of academics and people in publishing. His usually articulate characters are witty and often outrageous, so that audiences react to even his more macabre themes as comedies and have given him greater popular success than his rough handling by critics would suggest. Leading characters are often egocentric, sharp-tongued misfits, badly in need of a psychiatrist (*Melon* is a study of one such character's breakdown). Most of his plays present at least one homosexual character, and a homosexual relationship is central to *Butley* and *Spoiled* (in which a schoolteacher with a pregnant wife teaches a pupil at home and becomes increasingly involved with him). Many of Gray's plays deal with sexual fetishism or sadomasochistic games: *Wise Child* features transvestism, though the crossdresser in fact turns out to be a crook in disguise; *Dutch Uncle* has a masochist seeking the attentions of a policeman by trying to murder his own wife; in *Just the Three of Us* a wronged wife chains up her husband's mistress. Such situations are usually exploited for laughs, though in *The Rear Column*, set in the Victorian Congo, sadism and cannibalism are used more seriously to show the degradation of the whites.

Several of Gray's plays have become award-winning adaptations on television, including *Quartermaine's Terms*, *Butley* and *The Common Pursuit*. His screenplays for television include *After Pilkington* (1987) and *Old Flames* (1990), and for the cinema, *A Month in the Country* (1987), which won the Grand Prix award at the Brussels Film Fair. He has written trenchant accounts of the joys (or otherwise) of theatrical life, including *Fat Chance*, about the *Cell Mates* debacle when Stephen Fry unexpectedly left the cast.

Butley

Butley has a typical Gray protagonist, a bitchy university lecturer with a marriage in collapse, who drives away not only his wife but her replacement, the ex-student, now colleague, with whom he shares office and home. The savage tongue that makes him so offensive is also what provides much of the audience's fun. But if they enjoy seeing his selfishness get its comeuppance, there is also a release for some of their own frustrations in seeing the characters find such vitriolic language for all those rows that happen in any highly stressed relationship. Gray is often too busy scoring points for the serious content of his plays to show, but his exposure of our own selfishness and failure can be caustic and accessible to those prepared to think while they laugh.

TRY THESE:
✱ BENNETT for wit with more compassion, and also for spies to compare with *Cell Mates*; ✱ STOPPARD for wordplay with more intellect (and spies in *Hapgood*); ✱ HAMPTON's *Philanthropist* and ✱ MAMET's *Oleanna* for different views of an academic; ✱ AYCKBOURN and ✱ LEIGH can be as vituperative about middle-class mores, ✱ LUCIE can be as vicious about contemporary media men; ✱ CRIMP's *No-one Sees the Video* is an equally jaundiced swipe at women, work and contemporary mores to compare with *Hidden Laughter*; ✱ PINTER has directed several of Gray's plays; Gray has spoken of his admiration for ✱ AESCHYLUS and ✱ SHAKESPEARE; ✱ PETER SHAFFER's *Five Finger Exercise* for a comparison with the 1950s setting of *The Late Middle Classes*.

GRAY, Spalding   [1941 –   ]
American dramatist, monologist and actor

PLAYS AND MONOLOGUES INCLUDE:
Three Places in Rhode Island (1977), *Sex and Death to the Age 14* (1979), *Booze, Cars, and College Girls* (1979), *A Personal History of the American Theatre* (1980), *Points of Interest* (1980), *In Search of the Monkey Girl* (1981), *India and After* (1982), *Interviewing the Audience* (1982), *Swimming to Cambodia* (1984), *Terrors of Pleasure* (1986), *Rivkala's Ring* (adaptation of ✱ CHEKHOV's *The Witch*, 1986), *Monster in a Box* (1990), *Gray's*

Anatomy (1993), *It's a Slippery Slope* (1997), *Morning, Noon and Night* (1999)

An integral part of the off-off-Broadway theatre since the 1960s, Gray launched his career with the Performance Group's production of ✱SAM SHEPARD's *Tooth of Crime*. He later co-founded the Wooster Group with Elizabeth LeCompte, where he launched his successful solo career as a monologist. A self-described 'poetic journalist', Gray transmutes his daily life into theatrical pieces in which any event – from his nervous breakdown in India to his purchase of a country house in upstate New York – is material for comic, often acidic investigation. Gray has elevated narcissistic storytelling to high art with his amazingly compelling low-key delivery. Some see Gray as a self-obsessed exhibitionist, while others claim he is a profound commentator on our age. In either case, his work reflects the obsession with self-analysis that pervades American life. Worth catching on one of his infrequent visits to Britain or on film.

Swimming to Cambodia

Gray's monologue (filmed by Jonathan Demme in 1987) was inspired by his experience playing the aide to the American ambassador in *The Killing Fields*. With no props except a microphone, a glass of water and several maps of Cambodia behind him, Gray charts a terrifyingly funny journey to the human heart of darkness in which the making of a film about genocide acts as a catalyst for ruminations on sex, death, human compassion and destruction. One remarkable section recounts that LA extras had to be flown to Asia to play Cambodia refugees, since Pol Pot had killed off all the real ones. In a voice capable of sustaining hypnotic waves of discourse, Gray's monologue combines keen-eyed analysis with irony.

TRY THESE:

Laurie Anderson, ✱BOGOSIAN, Karen Finley for use of Self as central performance subject; ✱AMLIN GRAY, ✱RABE, ✱CHARLES WOOD, ✱WRIGHT for images of war; ✱ATHOL FUGARD is a character in *Swimming to Cambodia*.

GREEN, Paul   [1894 – 1981]
American dramatist, screenwriter and novelist

PLAYS INCLUDE:

The Last of the Lowries (1920), *White Dresses* (1923), *The No 'Count Boy* (1924), *In Abraham's Bosom* (1926), *The Field God* (1927), *The House of Connelly* (1928), *Tread the Green Grass* (1932), *Roll, Sweet Chariot* (1934), *Shroud My Body Down* (1934), *Johnny Johnson* (1936), *Native Son* (1941, from Richard Wright)

SYMPHONIC DRAMAS INCLUDE:

The Lost Colony (1937), *The Nighland Call* (1939), *The Common Glory* (1947), *Wilderness Road* (1955), *The Confederacy* (1958), *The Stephen Foster Story* (1959), *Cross and Sword* (1965), *Texas* (1966), *Trumpet in the Land* (1970), *The Lone Star* (1977)

Green was the son of a North Carolina farmer; a poet, novelist and screenwriter as well as dramatist, he filled his plays with all the South's dramatic riches, including tragedy, comedy, burlesque, poetry, music, songs, processionals and mass chants. In his work as in his region, bitter realities often confront the most soaring imagination. His first plays were one-act dramas concerning strained race relations, conflicting religious values and the disintegration of old, wealthy families. Despite uneven reviews, Green was awarded the Pulitzer Prize for *In Abraham's Bosom*, a tragedy of an educated mulatto killed by a white mob when he attempts to open a school for black children.

In 1931 *The House of Connelly*, a drama of the decay of an old southern family, was the Group Theatre's first major production. It was very successful, though Green later complained that the Group convinced him to change the original tragic ending to a happy one for reasons of left-wing political correctness. The Group also produced the satire *Johnny Johnson*, with music by Kurt Weill: the plot revolves round an anti-war folk hero who ends up in an insane asylum.

In the late 1930s, after a decade of favourable critical notices but mixed box-office success, Green turned away from Broadway and put his energies into what he called 'symphonic dramas'. These monumental outdoor historical spectacles – modern secular equivalents of medieval religious pageants – depicted various episodes of exploration, settlement, government and culture in specific southern localities. The best-known symphonic drama was the first, *The Lost Colony*, which has been performed at Roanoke, Virginia, every summer (except during World War II) since 1937.

TRY THESE:

✱LANGSTON HUGHES' *Mulatto*, a black perspective on interracial families; ✱BRECHT for epic theatre and political drama; ✱O'CASEY's *The Silver Tassie* as an anti-war play; ✱Jellicoe for British equivalents of 'symphonic dramas'; ✱FUGARD's *My Children! My Africa!* for a tragic meditation on education and race; ✱HELLMAN for families in decay; ✱HARRISON for a modern version of the medieval *Mysteries*.

GREENBERG, Richard   [1958 –   ]
American dramatist

PLAYS INCLUDE:
The Bloodletters (1984), *Life Under Water* (1985), *Vanishing Act* (1986), *The Author's Voice* (1987), *The Maderati* (1987), *Eastern Standard* (1988), *The American Plan* (1990), *Night and Her Stars* (1994), *Three Days of Rain* (1997), *Hurrah at Last* (1998), *Everett Beekin* (2000), *Take Me Out* (2002), *The Violet Hour* (2002), *The Dazzle* (2002)

Greenberg made his reputation by capturing the manners of the selfish, urban, American middle class. His canvas is small, yet he paints the world of his characters with a fine eye for the isolation that lies beneath the clever surfaces, whether he is dramatising a young man's adolescent troubles, as in the one-act *Life Under Water*, or taking aim at upwardly mobile New Yorkers, as in *Eastern Standard*, a witty and uncompromising portrayal of the carelessness and self-absorption of the yuppies of the 1980s. The characters are well educated, sexually sophisticated and generally successful in their careers, yet they have little ability to sustain intimate relationships. Their one act of social consciousness, which involves 'adopting' a homeless woman for the

summer, is self-congratulatory, and they cannot understand why the woman turns on them when they abandon her at the summer's end. In *Three Days of Rain* Greenberg employs a time shift to unravel the past so that the characters in the first act become their parent in Act 2, whereas in *Everett Beekin* the time slip is from 1947 to the 1990s. *Take Me Out*, given its world premiere at London's Donmar Warehouse, is about a baseball star who outs himself unexpectedly.

TRY THESE:

✱COWARD, ✱LUCIE and ✱ORTON for witty amorality; ✱CRIMP for a newer British voice peeling away the layers of casual selfishness; ✱DURANG for another American dramatist presenting a full-frontal assault on the middle classes; ✱CHEKHOV's *The Seagull* for an older example of casual selfishness; ✱AYCKBOURN, ✱FIRTH for trenchant social observation; Greenberg's version of ✱STRINDBERG's *Dance of Death* enjoyed a Broadway run with Ian McKellen and Helen Mirren (who was replaced by Frances de la Tour for the London run).

GREGORY, (Lady Isabella) Augusta   [1852 – 1932]
Irish theatre manager and dramatist

PLAYS INCLUDE:
Twenty-Five (1903), *Spreading the News* (1904), *The White Cockade* (1905), *The Rising of the Moon* (1907), *The Workhouse Ward* (1908)

Lady Gregory was an energetic Protestant landowner from Galway, who took to the theatre in middle age. After three years of experiment in Dublin with the Irish Literary Theatre (1899–1901), in the company of ✱W. B. YEATS, Edward Martyn and George Moore, and then with the Fay brothers' company, she helped to found the Abbey Theatre in 1904, and was involved in its management almost until her death in 1932. She did not start writing plays until she was fifty, but thereafter wrote around forty, mostly one-act farces, but also more pretentious (and thus less revivable) plays about Irish history, and such ventures as translations of ✱MOLIÈRE into the Galway dialect. She is

probably more important for her management role than for her workmanlike plays;
however, her farcical comedies, such as
Spreading the News, make a lively attempt to
render Irish peasant speech patterns, and the
plots crack along.

TRY THESE:
✱CARR, ✱SYNGE and ✱YEATS for serious
attempts to use Irish speech patterns in the
theatre; ✱FRIEL's *Translations* bemoans the
destruction of native Gaelic by imposed English.

GREIG, David   [1969 –   ]
Scottish dramatist

PLAYS INCLUDE:
A Savage Reminiscence (1991), *And the Opera
House Remained Unbuilt* (1991), *Petra's
Explanation* (1992), *Stalinland* (1992),
Consider the Dish (1993), *Europe* (1994), *One
Way Street* (1995), *The Architect* (1996),
Airport (1996), *Caledonia Dreaming* (1997),
Timeless (1997) *The Speculator* (1999),
Mainstream (1999), *The Cosmonaut's Last
Message to the Woman He Once Loved in the
Former Soviet Union* (1999), *Victoria* (2000),
Casanova (2001), *Lament* (2002), *Not About
Pomegranates* (2002), *Outlying Islands* (2002)

Greig was born in Edinburgh and studied
drama and English at Bristol University. He
has been a playwright in residence at the RSC
and has written several of his plays for
Suspect Culture, the theatre company he
founded with Graham Eatough in 1990. In
The Speculator Greig invents an eighteenth-
century Paris in which financial speculation
(partly personified through the historical
figure of John Law) and erotic speculation
march hand in hand. Greig won a John
Whiting Award for *The Cosmonaut's Last
Message*, with its heady international mixture
of characters from two cosmonauts forgotten
in space, a UFO researcher, a civil servant and
a speech therapist to a peace negotiator. Vicky
Featherstone of Paine's Plough described its
as 'a story about communicating the incom-
municable'. *Victoria*, focused through three
women all called Victoria and all played by
the same actress, tries to encapsulate Scottish
history in the twentieth century, concentrat-

ing on the immediate pre-war period, the
1970s and the 1990s. Greig's *Not About
Pomegranates*, developed with Rufus Norris
and actors from Al-Kasaba Theatre in
Ramallah, was given a rehearsed reading at
the Royal Court in 2002. *Outlying Islands*, set
on a remote Scottish island in 1939, is about a
survey of bird life that turns out to be about
something altogether more sinister.

TRY THESE:
Greig is often compared to ✱PINTER; ✱MARIVAUX
is a character in *The Speculator*; ✱CHURCHILL's
Serious Money for the excitement of speculation;
✱HARE for another British view of the Palestinian
situation; ✱STOPPARD's *Jumpers* for British astro-
nauts; ✱BUTTERWORTH's *The Night Heron* for rare
birds and violent outcomes; Greig adapted Albert
Camus' *Caligula* for the 2003 Donmar Warehouse
production.

GREIG, Noël   [1944 –   ]
British dramatist

PLAYS INCLUDE:
Men (1976), *As Time Goes By* (1977 with
✱DREW GRIFFITHS), *The Dear Love of
Comrades* (1979), *Angels Descend on Paris*,
(1980), *Poppies* (1983), *Rainbow's Ending*
(1984), *Spinning a Yarn* (1984), *Do We Ever
See Grace?* (1985), *Best of Friends* (1985),
Working Hearts (1986), *Laughter from the
Other Side* (1986), *Whispers in the Dark*
(1987), *Plague of Innocence* (1988), *Familiar
Feelings* (1989), *The Death of Christopher
Marlowe* (1989), *Paradise Now and Then*
(1990), *The Good Sisters* (1991, from
✱MICHEL TREMBLAY); *Final Cargo* (1994), *Alice*
(1998, after Lewis Carroll)

A prolific dramatist whose work has covered
an amazingly wide range, Greig's associations
as writer/director with various groups reflect
many of the major theatrical trends of the
past two decades. He was co-founder of The
Combination, one of the first fringe groups to
emphasise group work, improvisation and
flexible working spaces; director at the Almost
Free, scene of the first season of gay plays put
on by Ed Berman; writer/director with the
Bradford community-based company The
General Will; director with Gay Sweatshop

from 1977–87; and writer-in-residence with Theatre Centre, the theatre-in-education group. Greig has written for Graeae, the company of performers with disabilities, and much of his recent work has been community-based and aimed specifically at young people.

A writer who consistently explores the points at which sexuality and social and political forces touch, his early work shows an interest in historical roots, making connections with the present, and linking the personal with the public. *Men*, for example, deals with socialism's inability to extend its ideology into personal, gay politics. *As Time Goes By*, tracing gay repression through three different times, and *The Dear Love of Comrades*, about the personal and the political life of the nineteenth-century socialist Edward Carpenter, have been highly influential. Another important, highly complex exploration of repression and its responses was *Angels Descend on Paris*. Presented in the form of an operetta, this six-character epic, threading its way from Nazi Berlin to Paris, drew on Jacobean tragedy and the story of Bluebeard to explore the responses of people under pressure, sexual identity, role-playing and opportunism. *Poppies*, perhaps his best-known play, is an anti-militaristic and anti-nuclear play. Set on Hampstead's Parliament Hill, where two middle-aged men, Sammy and Snow, are having a picnic, it utilises a favourite Greig technique, mixing past with present and poetry with polemics. A symbolic piece, it was inspired by images of mothers sticking photos of their own children on the wire fencing at Greenham Common air force base.

TRY THESE:

Mart Crowley's *The Boys in the Band* for an earlier example of writing about gays; Jill Posener's *Any Woman Can* for lesbian coming out; *DREW GRIFFITHS for *As Time Goes By*, which deals with the Nazi persecution of homosexuals, treated memorably in *SHERMAN's *Bent*; *SHAPIRO's *Winter in the Morning* shows the responses of a group of young Jews to Nazism and the Warsaw Ghetto; *BARTLETT, *ELYOT, *RAVENHILL for a newer generation of gay writing.

GRIFFITHS, Drew   [1947 – 84]
British dramatist

PLAYS INCLUDE:

Mister X (1975, with Roger Baker), *Indiscreet* (1976, with Roger Baker), *The Jingle Ball* (1976), *As Time Goes By* (1977, with *NOËL GREIG)

Director, dramatist and founder member with Gerald Chapman of Gay Sweatshop in 1975, Griffiths is a seminal figure in the history of gay political theatre in Britain. *Mister X*, the first British gay play to challenge internalised self-oppression and assert gay pride, was hugely influential. Equally significant was *As Time Goes By*, an exploration of gay repression, that drew on three periods in history: Victorian England (*OSCAR WILDE's trial and after), Nazi Germany in the 1930s and America 1969 with the beginning of the Gay Liberation movement in the Stonewall Riots of that year. Again a pivotal piece because of the way it draws together personal and political strands, it subsequently spawned a number of plays, including *MARTIN SHERMAN's *Bent*. *The Jingle Ball* was a spoof pantomime on Cinderella, with the usual male Ugly Sisters, but a female Principal Boy whose love for Cinders was unequivocally lesbian.

Griffiths went on to write further plays for television and radio about gay relationships: *The Only One South of the River* is a comedy set in a gay disco over a straight pub. What they all had in common was a basic love and concern to show gay people with dignity and not a little humour.

Mister X
Based on a pamphlet, *With Downcast Gays* by David Hutter and Andrew Hodges, *Mister X* is a cathartic 'coming out' play that made an enormous impact on audiences, gay and straight, wherever it went. Written in revue form – as though a personalised biography of the cast, with six sections telling different experiences and a gradually changing consciousness about being gay – the production used minimal props (chairs, a table and a tape recorder) in order to tour anywhere. Times may have changed and so too some of the targets of homophobia, but its radical use

of laughter in breaking down stereotypes and overriding humanitarianism make it a seminal work.

TRY THESE:

*NOEL GREIG; *OSMENT, Gay Sweatshop's other 'coming out' play, Jill Posener's *Any Woman Can*; *KAY's *Twice Over* as another gay play dealing with honesty in all relationships; for laughter with a sting in the tail, see *AYCKBOURN, particularly *Absent Friends*, *TREVOR GRIFFITHS' *Comedians*, *LEIGH's *Abigail's Party*, *ORTON, *OSBORNE's *The Entertainer*; *BARTLETT's *Sarrasine* and *A Vision of Love Revealed in Sleep* for a later generation of gay theatre.

GRIFFITHS, Trevor   [1935 –]
British dramatist

PLAYS INCLUDE:
The Wages of Thin (1969), *Occupations* (1970), *Apricots* (1971), *Thermidor* (1971), *Lay By* (1971, with *HOWARD BRENTON, *BRIAN CLARK, *DAVID HARE, *STEPHEN POLIAKOFF, Hugh Stoddart, *SNOO WILSON), *Sam, Sam* (1972), *The Party* (1973), *Comedians* (1975), *Deeds* (1978; with *HOWARD BRENTON, *KEN CAMPBELL, *DAVID HARE), *Oi for England* (1982), *Real Dreams* (1986), *Piano* (1990), *The Gulf Between Us* (1992), *Thatcher's Children* (1993), *Who Shall Be Happy* (1995)

Griffiths is among the most important of contemporary socialist writers, and a central figure in the debate about the role of the dramatist in a capitalist culture. An unequivocal revolutionary Marxist, his work constantly questions which forms and which media are most appropriate to a socialist theatre practice. Because of this, as theatrical and television fashions have changed under the pressure of 'market forces' his work has become increasingly marginalised to regional instead of national platforms.

Born in Manchester, Trevor Griffiths was of the first generation to reap the consequences of the 1944 Education Act and was the first of his family to go to university. His first play, *Sam, Sam*, is a semi-autobiographical tale about two brothers, one of whom moves socially upward while the other is trapped by the class position of the family. Griffiths' first full-length play, *Occupations* (a study of Gramsci), was taken up by the RSC, while his one-act plays *Apricots and Thermidor* were produced by the socialist company 7:84. *The Party* takes the form of a political debate among representatives from left-wing groups at the moment of May 1968.

The productions of *Occupations* and *The Party* on the stages of such Establishment bastions as the National Theatre and the RSC were very much part of Griffiths' desire to make socialist ideas accessible, and to make cultural forms part of a broader political struggle.

Griffiths has often chosen to work in television rather than the theatre in order to achieve the widest possible audience; he has adapted many of his plays for television, has contributed episodes to popular series, and adapted novels for television. His television series *Bill Brand* took the form of a socialist soap opera, in its account of a Labour MP whose career encompassed a range of socialist debates. His film work includes major contributions to the script of Warren Beatty's *Reds*, and *Fatherland* (1986). Griffiths has said: 'I chose to work in those modes because I have to work with the popular imagination ... I am not interested in talking to thirty-eight university graduates in a cellar in Soho'.

Comedians
A study of the nature of comedy, it works both as a scabrous attack on the racist and sexist humour which passes for comedy in British popular culture, and as an exploration of the radical potential of comedy. The play begins in the classroom where an old comedian (originally, and appropriately, played by Jimmy Jewel) is training a group of stand-up comics. The group is made up of a docker, a milkman, an insurance agent, a labourer, a night club owner and a van driver. For them all, success as a comedian is an escape route from the tediousness of their work; in the second act they perform for an agent who may supply the means. While desperate ambition fires most of the group to come out with a spate of cracks against blacks, Pakistanis, Jews and women, the youngest member dumps his prepared act and, in a

stunning alienation effect, turns directly to the audience with a coruscating speech of class hatred. The final act of the play returns to the classroom, where pupil and teacher debate the private and public possibilities of comedy. The play's theatrical practice of challenging the basis of what it is possible to laugh at can be very unsettling for an audience.

TRY THESE:
*BARKER, *BRENTON, *HARE are among the 'political' dramatists of Griffiths' generation; *IKOLI's *Scrape Off the Black*, *MARCHANT's *Lazy Days Ltd*, *PHILLIPS' *Strange Fruit* all contrast brothers' opposing attitudes to life; *DREW GRIFFITHS and Roger Baker's *Mister X* uses comedy to subvert homophobic attitudes and was directly influenced by *Comedians*; *EDGAR, like Griffiths, engaged in the debate about the best form for socialist drama throughout his writing career; D'Arcy and *ARDEN have also engaged in the debate but have turned instead to community-based theatre; *JOHN MCGRATH and 7:84 for a different strand of the argument; *Piano* draws on *CHEKHOVIAN themes and *Platonov* in particular; *ELDRIDGE's *A Week with Tony*, inspired by Griffiths' *Country*, for contemporary Conservative politics.

GROSSO, Nick   [1968 –   ]
British dramatist

PLAYS INCLUDE:
Peaches (1994), *Sweetheart* (1996), *Real Classy Affair* (1998), *Kosher Harry* (2002)

Grosso has been described by the In Yer Face Theatre website as a 'laddish playwright' who 'writes superb dialogue and is master of the subtext'. In his early plays the emphasis is on closely observed subtle power struggles between youngish people in the typical pubs and clubs environments of an urban nowhere. As he says himself, 'if you want a plot, don't come to my plays'. The *Observer* thought that *Kosher Harry*, a study of different varieties of racism, marked his metamorphosis from laddishness into the *PIRANDELLO of North London.

TRY THESE:
Grosso has been compared to *BECKETT, *BERKOFF and *PINTER as well as *PIRANDELLO; *BOND's *Saved* for another comparison.

GUARE, John   [1938 –   ]
American dramatist

PLAYS INCLUDE:
The Loveliest Afternoon of the Year (1966), *Something I'll Tell You Tuesday* (1966), *Muzeeka* (1967), *Cop-Out* (1968), *Kissing Sweet* (1969), *A Day of Surprises* (1970), *The House of Blue Leaves* (1971), *Two Gentlemen of Verona* (1971, from *SHAKESPEARE, musical adaptation and lyrics), *Rich and Famous* (1974), *Marco Polo Sings a Solo* (1976), *Landscape of the Body* (1977), *Bosoms and Neglect* (1979), *Lydie Breeze* (1982), *Gardenia* (1982), *Women and Water* (1984), *The Talking Dog* (1985), *Six Degrees of Separation* (1990), *Four Baboons Adoring the Sun* (1992), *Moon Under Miami* (1995, previously *Moon Over Miami*), *The General of Hot Desire* (1998), *Sweet Smell of Success* (2002, book of the musical)

Guare's work brims with inventiveness: bizarre situations, eccentric characters and unimaginable plots haunt his plays. Although his conceits seem implausible, his writing touches the heart with an inner truth that surpasses surface realism. It is the truth of human aspiration and disillusionment.

After completing an MFA in Playwriting at Yale School of Drama in 1963, Guare achieved immediate success off-off-Broadway with his early one-act plays. *The House of Blue Leaves* earned Guare his second OBIE and a New York Drama Critics' Circle Award for best American play of the season. A scathing farce set in the Queens apartment of an Irish Catholic family on the day of the Pope's visit to New York, the play is rooted in Guare's own Queens childhood. The central character, a zookeeper with aspirations of 'making it' as a songwriter, longs to commit his mentally ill wife Bananas so he can pursue fame and fortune in Hollywood with his ambitious girlfriend. Plot complications abound, including a scheme hatched by his son to blow up the

Pope. Each character pursues his own empty dreams until they explode in their faces literally and figuratively. While uproariously funny, the play ends in the despair and anguish of broken dreams.

Guare's next few plays, although intriguing and imaginative, received little critical acclaim. Reviewers seemed uncomfortable with his neurotically obsessive characters, disorganised plots and quick shifts from farce to tragedy. His poetic language failed to assuage the unease his writing provoked. However, his haunting and touching screenplay for *Atlantic City* (1981) was universally acclaimed, and nominated for an Academy Award for best original screenplay. Guare then turned his hand to a series of historical plays exploring the collapse of the American dream. Set in the nineteenth century, and written in a more serene and subdued style that highlighted his poetic prowess, the plays failed to please the critics.

Six Degrees of Separation has been his major success to date. Here his old themes of unfulfilled dreams, emotional alienation and escape from introspection converge in a whirligig plot. 'Successful' Manhattanites are duped by a con man posing as the son of Sidney Poitier. He works his way into their homes, claiming to be a friend of their children (all away at Ivy League colleges). These sophisticated urbanites are one step removed from Guare's working-class characters in Queens who dreamed of getting to Manhattan. Even on Park Avenue, empty lives illuminate empty dreams. 'Imagination', Guare tells us, 'is God's gift to make the act of self-examination bearable.' Without self-knowledge one can't know anyone else, and the result is the isolation of contemporary life.

TRY THESE:

✳IONESCO for Absurdism; ✳FEYDEAU and ✳ORTON for farce; ✳CHEKHOV for the theme of unfulfilled dreams; ✳STRINDBERG for characters with internal angst; ✳KAUFMAN and Hart for the American dream as farce; ✳SHAWN for a bitter edge; ✳DURANG for farcical treatment of troubled families; ✳GENET for plays revolving around the nature of authentic identity; *The General of Hot Desire* is a response to ✳SHAKESPEARE's sonnets;

✳ODETS wrote the screenplay for the film *Sweet Smell of Success*; Guare adapted *His Girl Friday* from Howard Hawks' film and ✳HECHT and MacArthur's *The Front Page*.

GUPTA, Tanika   [1964 –   ]
British dramatist

PLAYS INCLUDE:

Voices in the Wind (1995), *Skeleton* (1997), *A River Sutra* (1997, from Gita Mehta), *On the Couch with Enoch* (1998), *The Waiting Room* (2000), *Sanctuary* (2002), *Inside Out* (2002), *Fragile Land* (2003), *Hobson's Choice* (2003, after ✳BRIGHOUSE)

London-born Gupta has written extensively for television and radio, emerging as a writer for the theatre with *Voices in the Wind*. She has been a writer in residence at the National Theatre, which staged the John Whiting Award winner *The Waiting Room*. In it a dead woman has to make her journey to the Waiting Room for the dead, guided by a spirit in the guise of Bollywood star Dilip Kumar, but not before she sorts out some family issues. In *Sanctuary* she brings together an assorted group of characters including a Kashmiri refugee, an Afro-Caribbean journalist, a Rwandan massacre survivor and a female vicar in a churchyard that acts as a refuge from the troubles of the world. The play explores the ramifications of colonialism and its legacies in ways that give the lie to any suggestion that Gupta is a parochial 'Asian writer'. After working with Clean Break on *Inside Out* in 2002, Gupta is scheduled to present her updating of *Hobson's Choice* to a modern-day Salford Asian setting at the Young Vic in 2003.

TRY THESE:

The National Theatre presented Gupta's version of ✳BRECHT's *The Good Person of Szechwan* in 2001; ✳BRIGHOUSE for the original *Hobson's Choice*; ✳BUTTERWORTH's *Night Heron* and ✳STOPPARD's *Arcadia* for garden imagery; ✳KHAN-DIN and ✳KUREISHI for British Asian experience; ✳HARE's *Map of the World* for colonial legacies; Peter Brook and Jean-Claude Carrière's version of *The Mahabharata* for a European version of an Indian classic; Jatinder Verma for a different approach to

Asian and European classics; Ray Grewal's *My Dad's Corner Shop* for a heady mix of alien abduction and British Asian experience.

GURNEY, A. R. (Albert Ramsdell), Jr   [1930 –]
American dramatist and novelist

PLAYS INCLUDE:
Three People (1956), *Turn of the Century* (1958), *The Golden Fleece* (1968), *The Open Meeting* (1969), *The Love Course* (1970), *Scenes from American Life* (1970), *The Old One-Two* (1973), *Children* (1974, from John Cheever), *Who Killed Richard Cory?* (1976), *The Golden Age* (1981, from Henry James), *What I Did Last Summer* (1981), *The Dining Room* (1982), *Another Antigone* (1986), *The Perfect Party* (1986), *Sweet Sue* (1987), *The Cocktail Hour* (1988), *Love Letters* (1988), *The Snow Ball* (1991), *The Old Boy* (1991), *The Fourth Wall* (1992), *Later Life* (1993), *A Cheever Evening* (1994), *Overture* (1995), *Sylvia* (1996), *Labor Day* (1998), *The Far East* (1998), *Darlene and the Guest Lecturer* (1998), *Ancestral Voices* (1999), *Human Events* (2001), *A Wayside Motor Inn* (2003)

A. R. ('Pete') Gurney's main subject is the decline of White Anglo-Saxon Protestant (WASP) mores in contemporary America. To him, WASP culture – by turns sincere and pretentious, principled and inflexible – is built upon rituals that have lost much of their meaning. His plays show a society in flux, torn between old and new, age and youth, wisdom and naivety, tradition and rebellion.

Gurney, born to an established Buffalo, New York, family, and educated at the Yale School of Drama, started writing plays in the late 1950s, and quickly decided to concentrate on his own WASP community. In the 1960s and 1970s, when WASP culture was out of fashion, his work was rarely produced except in New England. Then, in the 1980s, the return to more traditional values suddenly gave Gurney an audience, and *The Dining Room*, *The Cocktail Hour* and *Love Letters* all had good runs on and off Broadway.

Although he lists as his influences ✶ARTHUR MILLER, ✶TENNESSEE WILLIAMS, Rogers and Hammerstein, and Cole Porter, Gurney often draws his characters from academia, and his subjects from the classics. *Another Antigone* depicts a young woman's Antigone-like stand against a male professor when she tries to update ✶SOPHOCLES' play; *The Old One-Two* is a Plautine farce on university life; and *The Golden Fleece* and *Children* are dominated, as were many classical plays, by god-like offstage characters. Gurney has also written several chronicles covering the period from the 1930s to the present. *Scenes from American Life* and *The Dining Room* are montages influenced by ✶THORNTON WILDER, and *Love Letters* is the story of a long romance carried on by mail.

TRY THESE:
For classical influences, Plautus' *The Captives*, ✶SENECA's *Medea*, ✶SOPHOCLES' *Antigone*; ✶ALBEE's *Who's Afraid of Virginia Woolf?*, ✶MAMET's *Oleanna*, ✶NELSON's *Some Americans Abroad* for American academics; ✶SIMON GRAY for an English parallel; ✶WATERHOUSE and ✶WHITEMORE for epistolary drama.

HALL, Lee [1966 –]
British dramatist

PLAYS INCLUDE:
Spoonface Steinberg (radio 1997, stage 1999), *Cooking with Elvis* (2000)

Hall is a multitalented writer who has been equally successful in film (*Billy Elliott*, 1999) and radio (*Spoonface Steinberg*), as a stage dramatist (*Cooking with Elvis*) and as an adapter (✱BRECHT, Carlo Collodi's *Pinocchio*, ✱GOLDONI, and Ernst Toller's *Hinkemann*, as *Bollocks*). His reworking of *The Good Hope* by Herman Heijermands, given the ✱BILL BRYDEN/John Tams treatment, received mixed notices and not everyone was convinced by the way *Billy Elliott* treated its socio-political context, but *Spoonface*, a monologue by an autistic child who is terminally ill with cancer, managed to defy expectation by being both comic and life affirming as well as moving. In *Cooking with Elvis* (adapted from a radio play), a former Elvis impersonator, now confined to a wheelchair after a stroke, exists in uneasy limbo, unable to speak or move, while around him his wife and daughter negotiate an uneasy existence. The arrival of the wife's new young lover is the catalyst for explosive developments, and all this is laced with occasional eruptions of Elvis impersonations from the otherwise immobile father.

TRY THESE:
✱NICHOLS' *Day in the Death of Joe Egg* and *The National Health* for 'bad taste' plays about illness and disability; ✱ORTON and ✱PINTER for disruptive strangers; ✱VAN ITALLIE for a post-stroke play; ✱BECKETT's *Endgame* for creative use of a wheelchair.

HALL, Willis
See WATERHOUSE, Keith

HALLIWELL, David [1936 –]
British dramatist

PLAYS INCLUDE:
Little Malcolm and His Struggle Against the Eunuchs (1965), *A Who's Who of Flapland* (staged 1969), *K. D. Dufford Hears K. D. Dufford Ask K. D. Dufford How K. D. Dufford'll Make K. D. Dufford* (1969)

Although he has written extensively for stage, radio and television, David Halliwell appears doomed to be remembered for one play, *Little Malcolm*, which was originally directed by ✱MIKE LEIGH and revived in 1998 at Hampstead with Ewan McGregor in the title role. An expelled art college student tries to change the world but his revolutionary cell falls apart as they decide one of their members is a traitor. The play is an interesting comic study of frustration that taps into the sixties mood of rebellion, while also showing how high moral ideals can be the cover for less worthy motivations.

TRY THESE:
Halliwell's contemporaries ✱JELLICOE, ✱ORTON, ✱PINTER for parallels and contrasts; ✱TREVOR GRIFFITHS' *The Party* for the difficulties of political organisation; ✱BECKETT, ✱IONESCO, ✱SIMPSON for the absurdist qualities of *Little Malcolm*.

HAMPTON, Christopher [1946 –]
British dramatist

PLAYS INCLUDE:
When Did You Last See My Mother? (1964), *Total Eclipse* (1968), *The Philanthropist* (1970), *Savages* (1973), *Treats* (1976), *After Mercer* (1980), *Tales from Hollywood* (1982), *The Portage to San Cristobal of A. H.* (1982, from George Steiner), *Les Liaisons Dangereuses* (1985, from Choderlos de Laclos), *White Chameleon* (1991), *Sunset Boulevard* (1993, book of the musical), *The Talking Cure* (2002)

Oxford University Dramatic Society put on Hampton's first play (written when he was eighteen) *When Did You Last See My Mother?* Taken up by the Royal Court while Hampton was still an undergraduate, it transferred to the West End, despite its then controversial homosexual themes, making Hampton the youngest dramatist in living memory to have a West End production.

On leaving Oxford, Hampton became the first resident dramatist at the Court, which produced *Total Eclipse*, a play about Verlaine that Hampton had written as a student, and then *The Philanthropist*, written while Hampton was resident dramatist. This became, as Hampton puts it, 'disgracefully successful, so much so that I've always felt I left under something of a cloud'.

In the early 1970s Hampton translated and adapted a number of ✻IBSEN's most important plays. He was much affected by *The Doll's House*, and became preoccupied with questions of feminism and gender which he explored in *Treats*, and which have continued to inform his writing. His adaptation of *Les Liaisons Dangereuses* is not only a skilled dramatisation of a great French novel, but also a very contemporary study of sexual power struggles and exploitation, written with a controlled and witty elegance which made it a great success in London and, as *Dangerous Liaisons*, as a film. Although much of his work is focused on witty, literate individuals in crisis, in *Savages* Hampton tackled the issue of the slaughter of Brazilian Indians to facilitate the exploitation of their territory at a time when such issues were not yet fashionable and in *White Chameleon*, an autobiographical piece, he tackled the Suez crisis (he was living in Egypt at the time).

He has translated/adapted works by many writers including Isaac Babel, Lewis Carroll, ✻CHEKHOV, Joseph Conrad, ✻FEYDEAU, Ariane Mnouchkine, ✻MOLIÈRE, ✻YASMINA REZA and ✻ÖDÖN VON HORVÁTH, who also features in *Tales from Hollywood*, a tale of émigré life in which Hampton resurrected him (he died in Paris in 1938) to spar with ✻BRECHT and with Heinrich and Thomas Mann. His latest work, *The Talking Cure*, is about Freud and Jung but its first production suffered from the death of James Hazeldine before the official opening.

The Philanthropist

The Philanthropist was the play that made Hampton a truly 'commercial' playwright. Subtitled 'a bourgeois comedy' the play focuses on the ironically named philanthropist, an academic, whose most apt line is: 'I'm a man of conviction – I think.' The title is a sideways nod at ✻MOLIÈRE's *Le Misanthrope*, of which it is something of an inversion. The play initially appears as an apparently conventional comedy, with wit and wisecracks flying in a bourgeois intellectual setting. But, in the first scene, an undergraduate (playwright) shoots himself, and introduces a dark edge to the comedy. The literary jokes and wit transmute into a bleak desperation. Over the course of the play, Philip, the philanthropist, demonstrates his ineffectuality, and thereby the sterility of the conventions by which he (and, by implication, the conventional form of this kind of play) work. In attempting not to do any harm, he actually wreaks havoc.

TRY THESE:

The treatment of sexual politics in *Les Liaisons Dangereuses* and *Treats* makes an interesting comparison to ✻STRINDBERG and ✻WHITEHEAD; the eighteenth-century setting of *Liaisons* is reminiscent of the world of ✻CONGREVE and ✻SHERIDAN; ✻TERRY JOHNSON (*Hysteria*), ✻PETER SHAFFER (*Equus*) and ✻WRIGHT (*Mrs Klein*) for psychiatrists; ✻HARE's *Plenty* for Suez; ✻DYER for a treatment of homosexuality from the same period as *When Did You Last See My Mother?*

HANDKE, Peter   [1942 –   ]
Austrian dramatist and novelist

PLAYS INCLUDE:

Offending the Audience (1966), *Prophecy and Self-Accusation* (1966), *Cries for Help* (1967), *Kaspar* (1969), *My Foot My Tutor* (1969), *Quodlibet* (1970), *The Ride Across Lake Constance* (1971), *They Are Dying Out* (1974), *A Sorrow Beyond Dreams* (1977), *The Long Way Round* (1989), *The Hour We Knew Nothing of Each Other* (1994), *Zurüstungen für die Unsterblichkeit* (1997, *Constructions for Immortality*), *Die Fahrt im Einbaum oder Das Stück zum Film vom Krieg* (1999, *The Journey in a Canoe, or the Play about the Film of the War*), *La Cuisine* (2002)

Obsessed with the problems of language and communication, Handke constantly challenges preconceptions of theatrical form, style and content. *Offending the Audience* – the title seems all too accurate a description – conspicuously lacks conventional plot or character. This 'Sprechstück' or 'speech piece' presents four speakers of any age or sex who take an hour to work up to a climax of insults to the audience, deploying elaborate, structured sequences, often contradicting themselves, subverting all possible responses. In *Kaspar* Handke takes the story of Kaspar Hauser, who lived without speech in total isolation until he was a full-grown adult, to illustrate his thesis that language defines personality and locks each of us within its patterns of cliché and custom. His later work continues to explore this theme of the 'crisis of language' but *Die Fahrt in Einbaum* caused controversy because of his attitudes to the crisis in Yugoslavia.

TRY THESE:

✶IONESCO, ✶OVERMYER and ✶WELLMAN for word games and the attempt to construct the world by the use of language; ✶BECKETT for a similar theatrical nihilism; ✶STOPPARD for different kinds of word games; ✶KROETZ for a similar obsession with speech and communication; ✶FRIEL's *Translations* for language as the symbol of cultural freedom.

HANNAN, Chris   [1958 –   ]
Scottish dramatist

PLAYS INCLUDE:

Klimkov (1984), *Elizabeth Gordon Quinn* (1985), *Orphan's Comedy* (1986), *Gamblers* (1987, from ✶GOGOL), *The Evil Doers* (1990), *The Baby* (1990), *Shining Souls* (1996, revised 2003)

The individual's right to be just that – individual, non-conformist, apparently wayward and even destructive of self, is a recurring theme in Hannan's work. Even when the play deals with social issues of class, power, the abuse of privilege and the exploitation of the poor and weak, at or near the centre of the action is an individual likely to go against the accepted or expected grain. Such characters are perforce often a blight on the lives of others, who carry the can for their ideals. One such vehement individual is Elizabeth Gordon Quinn, the full-blooded main character in one of Hannan's earliest and strongest plays. Though circumstance has firmly rooted her and her family in a poor Glasgow tenement, Elizabeth believes she is better than her hand-to-mouth, working-class neighbours. And the visible symbol of this superiority is her piano, which she can't play . . . The year is 1919, there is a rent strike. Women are banding together, defying the authorities, refusing to pay. But even though it causes schism within her own family, Elizabeth will not be one of the herd if it doesn't suit her. Hannan treats the ensuing scenes of domestic conflict with touches of wise humour that have elicited comparisons with ✶O'CASEY, and with a fine understanding of the mixed emotions – from admiration to resentment – such free spirits can unleash in us.

Another headstrong woman, Macu, is at the centre of *The Baby*. Set in ancient Rome, this sprawling play deals with the different faces of love and the different forms of tyranny. Macu, in challenging political forces she doesn't agree with, precipitates a new form of personal oppression, an all-consuming grief that taints not only her own life but that of her friends, her enemies and especially her gentle, devoted lover. Hannan attempts a broad canvas – historical fact extended by his complex fiction – and the essential drama of Macu's journey through loss, self-loathing and madness to her inevitable death is jeopardised as a result. *Shining Souls*, his greatest success, is set in Glasgow's Barrowland market as various dispossessed souls try to establish who they are. As Neil Cooper put it in the (Glasgow) *Herald*, reviewing the 2003 Tron production: 'As it gives a metaphysical voice to everyday lives desperately seeking something in the theatre's own backyard, its ambition is as much philosophical as dramatic, fusing biblically epigrammatic homespun wisdom with a deep-rooted music hall intelligence that gift-wraps killer punchlines with a gut-wrenching venom born of tragedy and truth'.

TRY THESE:

✶CARTWRIGHT's *Road* for similarities and contrasts; another Scottish-based playwright concerned with individuals and their rights within society is Peter Arnott – his plays include *White Rose* (1986), *Thomas Muir* (1986) and *Salvation* (1990); ✱CLIFFORD for plays that make cogent points about modern society through a historical perspective; for tub-thumping politics of a Socialist persuasion see ✱JOHN MCGRATH; Hannan adapted ✱IBSEN's *The Pretenders* for the RSC; ✱JONSON's *Bartholomew Fair* for a parallel to *Shining Souls*.

HANSBERRY, Lorraine   [1930 – 65]
American dramatist

PLAYS INCLUDE:
A Raisin in the Sun (1959), *The Sign in Sidney Brustein's Window* (1964), *To Be Young, Gifted and Black* (1969, completed posthumously by her former husband, Robert Nemiroff), *Les Blancs* (1970, completed posthumously by Robert Nemiroff)

Like ✱O'CASEY and ✱DELANEY, Hansberry transformed the grim world around her into something touched with gold dust. Both *The Sign in Sidney Brustein's Window* and *A Raisin in the Sun* are idealistic works, in which the protagonists manage to rise above adversity. The latter play is considered a cornerstone in the development of black theatre – a powerful, poignant protest against racial injustice and white bigotry still valid today despite its solid naturalism and contradictory values (a black family striving for white middle-class values). The warm-hearted characterisations of the downside Chicago family – chauffeur Walter Lee and his dreams of a liquor store and his battle for self-respect, his put-upon wife Ruth, young son, sister-in-law and above all the dominating figure of Momma – still draw audiences into their world. *A Raisin in the Sun* remains inspirational theatre, focusing as it does on a family struggling to maintain their dignity in the face of racism, sexism and a culture whose ethos increasingly is tied to the fast buck. In many ways ahead of its time, the play ran for two years on Broadway (winning the coveted New York Critics' Circle Award for 1959). Hansberry died of cancer at the age of 34. It was she who inspired the song Nina Simone took from the posthumously completed *To Be Young, Gifted and Black*. Robert Nemiroff, her former husband, who completed her last two plays, also co-adapted *Raisin*, a musical version of *A Raisin in the Sun*.

TRY THESE:
✱BALDWIN's *Amen Corner* for comparable style but more bitter analysis of his black community; ✱ARDREY's *Jeb* for a white liberal approach to American racism; ✱TENNESSEE WILLIAMS and ✱MILLER for contemporary white American treatments of the family; Zora Neale Hurston's and ✱LANGSTON HUGHES' *Mule Bone* for contrasting representation of black life and language; ✱PHILLIPS' *Strange Fruit* for a more pessimistic black British view; ✱SHANGE for contrast with black women's writing, thirty years later; ✱KENNEDY, whose surreal, even grotesque, imagery contrasts with that of Hansberry.

HARE, David   [1947 –   ]
British dramatist and director

PLAYS INCLUDE:
Slag (1970), *Lay By* (1971, with ✱HOWARD BRENTON, ✱BRIAN CLARK, ✱TREVOR GRIFFITHS, ✱STEPHEN POLIAKOFF, Hugh Stoddart, ✱SNOO WILSON), *England's Ireland* (1972, with Tony Bicât, ✱HOWARD BRENTON, ✱BRIAN CLARK, ✱DAVID EDGAR, Francis Fuchs, ✱SNOO WILSON), *The Great Exhibition* (1972), *Brassneck* (1973, with ✱HOWARD BRENTON), *Knuckle* (1974), *Teeth 'n' Smiles* (1975), *Fanshen* (1975), *Plenty* (1978), *A Map of the World* (1982), *Pravda* (1985, with ✱HOWARD BRENTON) *The Bay at Nice* (1986), *Wrecked Eggs* (1986), *The Secret Rapture* (1988), *Racing Demon* (1989), *Murmuring Judges* (1991), *The Absence of War* (1993), *Skylight* (1995), *Amy's View* (1997), *The Judas Kiss* (1998), *Via Dolorosa* (1998), *The Blue Room* (1998, from ✱SCHNITZLER's *La Ronde*), *My Zinc Bed* (2000), *The Breath of Life* (2002)

Hare came to prominence in the 1970s as one of a breed of committed socialist writers, many of whom he collaborated with on *Lay By* and *England's Ireland*. He founded Portable Theatre with the dramatist Tony Bicât in 1968 and the Joint Stock company with William Gaskill and Max Stafford-Clark

A Raisin in the Sun by Lorraine Hansberry, directed by David Lan, Young Vic and Salisbury Playhouse production, 2001. Cecilia Noble as Ruth, Lennie James as Walter Lee Younger. (Pete Jones/ArenaPAL)

The Breath of Life by David Hare, directed by Howard Davies, Theatre Royal Haymarket, 2002. Judi Dench as Francis Beale, Maggie Smith as Madeleine Palmer. (Pete Jones/ArenaPAL)

in 1974. He has also been literary manager and resident dramatist at the Royal Court and ran one of the companies at the National Theatre. Hare also carved out a singular niche in television with *Licking Hitler* (1978) and *Dreams of Leaving* (1980).

Fanshen, a documentary drama about the Chinese revolution, was a seminal play of the 1970s, popularising the Joint Stock rehearsal method. Unusually for Hare, the play concentrates on the processes of revolution rather than individual character. His plays are predominantly concerned with the topography of personal relationships and he has cornered a market in 'serious' debate plays, often centred round women. This has attracted star actresses to his work but there are still those who are suspicious of the regularity with which the women are the sacrificial victims of his dramaturgy. *Plenty* attempts to use the story of the mental disintegration of its heroine, a former World War II Resistance worker, to reflect the collapse of British postwar ideals, part of Hare's continuing preoccupation with wartime and immediate post-war England. Audiences have tended to focus on the heroine's neuroticism but Hare insists on the importance of the social context to which she responds. *Pravda* is an exuberantly comic political satire of the newspaper business on an epic scale, featuring an energetically ruthless, reptilian newspaper magnate. As in *Plenty*, the leading female character carries the play's moral force, but remains an unreal, one-dimensional figure, on the periphery of the main action. *The Secret Rapture* concentrates on the contrasting attitudes of two sisters to questions of morality and caring. *Racing Demon* pursues similar spiritual themes in the context of modern attitudes to religious faith and became the first in a trilogy of plays examining the moribund elements of modern British institutions: *Murmuring Judges* tackled the judiciary and *The Absence of War* political parties (facilitated by access to Neil Kinnock's election campaign).

Recent exceptions to Hare's usual interests (which are pursued in *Amy's View* and *The Breath of Life*) are *Via Dolorosa*, a monologue reflecting his experiences on a visit to Israel and Palestine, and *The Judas Kiss*, which is about ∗OSCAR WILDE and Lord Alfred Douglas. The huge success of *The Blue Room*, Hare's version of ∗SCHNITZLER's *La Ronde*, owed a great deal to Nicole Kidman's nudity. A national tour in 2003 starred Tracy Shaw, formerly of *Coronation Street*, and Jason Connery. Hare is scheduled to tackle the 1991 Conservative decision to privatise the railways in a play for Out of Joint and the National Theatre in late 2003.

TRY THESE:

∗BOND and ∗BRECHT, like *Fanshen*, use epic style and geographical or spatially distanced settings; for World War II see ∗RATTIGAN's *The Deep Blue Sea*, Ian McEwan's *The Imitation Game*, ∗LOWE's *Touched*; ∗JONSON, particularly *Bartholomew Fair* and *The Devil is an Ass*, for violently entertaining attacks on capitalism; ∗MARLOWE's *Dr Faustus* for the interplay between a dupe and a satanic figure which parallels the relationship between the ineffectual editor and the magnate in *Pravda*; ∗FRAYN and ∗HECHT and MacArthur for newspapers; ∗BRENTON's *Epsom Downs*, ∗TREVOR GRIFFITHS' *Comedians*, ∗NICHOLS' *The National Health* for plays that examine the state of Britain; for rock musicals taking the temperature of a nation in similar fashion to *Teeth 'n' Smiles*, ∗KEEFFE's *Bastard Angel*; Hare has adapted ∗BRECHT, ∗CHEKHOV and ∗PIRANDELLO; he is increasingly seen as a modern ∗SHAW; ∗PASCAL's *Crossing Jerusalem* for Palestine.

HARRIS, Richard   [1934 –   ]
British dramatist

PLAYS INCLUDE:
Albert and Virginia (1972), *Two and Two Make Sex* (1973, with Leslie Darbon), *Who Goes Bare* (1974 with Leslie Darbon), *Outside Edge* (1979), *The Business of Murder* (1981), *Stepping Out* (1984), *The Maintenance Man* (1986), *Visiting Hour* (1990), *Party Piece* (1991, originally *Local Affairs*, 1982), *Mixed Blessings* (1991, with Keith Strachan), *Dead Guilty* (1995, as *Murder Once Done*, 1994), *Stepping Out the Musical* (1997) *In Two Minds* (2001)

Now probably best-known for his television work, over the years Harris has achieved great commercial success with his stage plays and they remain extremely popular with amateur companies. *The Business of Murder* played for over seven years in the West End before touring for well over a year. *Outside Edge*, an ✱ AYCKBOURNESQUE farce set in a cricket pavilion, won the Evening Standard Comedy Award for 1979 and has been a stalwart of the circuit ever since, as well as spawning a television series. *Stepping Out*, a comedy set in an adult education tap-dancing class, follows the fortunes of nine women and one man as they transform from awkward dancers to a final *Chorus Line* troupe. A gentle, unchallenging play, it was successful in the West End, on Broadway, as a film and eventually as a musical.

TRY THESE:
For women together: ✱ DUNN's *Steaming*, set in a Turkish bath, Tony Roper's *The Steamie*, set in a Scottish bath-house; ✱ AYCKBOURN, ✱ BENNETT, ✱ COONEY, ✱ FRAYN for other forms of English comedy; ✱ ANTHONY SHAFFER for thrillers; Bonnie Greer's *Jitterbug* for the importance of dance in people's lives.

HARRIS, Zinnie   [1973 –   ]
British dramatist and director

PLAYS INCLUDE:
By Many Wounds (1999), *Further Than the Furthest Thing* (2000), *Nightingale and Chase* (2001)

Harris won the John Whiting Award for *Further Than the Furthest Thing*, an extraordinary response to the evacuation of the island of Tristan da Cunha in 1961 when its volcano erupted. Although based on factual events and indebted to family memories of the island, the play moves beyond re-creation of and lament for a way of life into an exploration of the meaning of exile and community that transcends its origins. Similarly, although *Nightingale and Chase* owes something to the time Harris spent as a creative writing teacher in a prison, it transcends the immediate situation of how people react to one another when one returns home after leaving prison into a study of the difficulties of negotiating any kind of liminal moment and the ways in which contradictory expectations can wreck a reunion.

TRY THESE:
✱ CHEKHOV's *Three Sisters* for a sense of exile; ✱ IBSEN for problematic returns; ✱ BEHAN, ✱ GENET, ✱ HOLBOROUGH, ✱ PUIG for prisons.

HARRISON, Tony   [1937 –   ]
British poet and dramatist

PLAYS (ORIGINALS AND TRANSLATIONS) INCLUDE:
Aikin Mata (1965, from ✱ ARISTOPHANES' *Lysistrata*, with James Simmons), *The Misanthrope* (1973, from ✱ MOLIÈRE), *Phaedra Britannica* (1975, from ✱ RACINE), *The Mysteries* (1977 onwards, comprising *The Nativity*, *The Passion*, *Doomsday*), *The Oresteia* (1981, from ✱ AESCHYLUS), *Medea: Sex War* (1985), *The Trackers of Oxyrhynchus* (1988, revised 1990, from ✱ SOPHOCLES), *The Common Chorus* (1992, from ✱ ARISTOPHANES' *Lysistrata*), *Square Rounds* (1992), *The Kaisers of Karnuntum* (1995), *The Labours of Herakles* (1995), *The Prince's Play* (1996, from Victor Hugo)

A poet and translator, Harrison made his theatre debut in 1965, collaborating with James Simmons on an adaptation of Aristophanes in a Nigerian setting. Harrison had spent four years in Nigeria after reading classics at the University of Leeds. His reputation as a poet of international standing was secured by the time he turned his attention to the theatre again in the mid-1970s with much-praised translations of ✱ MOLIÈRE and ✱ RACINE. He has also collaborated with the composer Harrison Birtwistle on an opera, *Yan Tan Tethera*, and has translated Smetana's *The Bartered Bride*. His version of *The Oresteia* was great theatre and marvellous writing. The complete cycle of his medieval mystery plays was presented at the National Theatre's Cottesloe auditorium and subsequently at the Lyceum in 1986. The juxtaposition of an austere classical tradition and proletarian irreverence is sometimes startling, often entertaining and controversial, as in the extended poem *V*. Much of his later work has been staged outside conventional theatres, often in ancient venues, and much of it has been concerned with a dialogue between classical myths and modern experience.

The Trackers of Oxyrhynchus

Two Oxford dons travel to Egypt in 1907 on the trail of a lost manuscript. The rediscovery of a fragment of a satyr play by *SOPHOCLES and the situation of the homeless in present-day 'cardboard city' are used to demonstrate comically the spurious divisions between high and low culture. The effect is brilliantly enhanced by Harrison's imaginative use of language and physical action, and his playing with convention – you don't often find yourself singing along in ancient Greek at the National (and enjoying it!).

TRY THESE:
*BARTLETT, who also translated The Misanthrope, is also an exponent of mixing high and low culture; *AESCHYLUS and *EURIPIDES for ancient Greek drama; *BREUER, *CHURCHILL, *DUFFY, *WERTENBAKER for other modern responses to it; *ELIOT for a major contrast to Harrison's response to the classics; Harrison's second version of Lysistrata updates the story to Greenham Common; for other Greenham plays see *DANIELS' The Devil's Gateway, *EDGAR's Maydays, *NOEL GREIG's Poppies and *REID's My Name Shall I Tell You My Name; John Barton's The Greeks (with Kenneth Cavander) and Tantalus for other approaches to ancient Greek material.

HARROWER, David [1966 –]
Scottish dramatist

PLAYS INCLUDE:
Knives and Hens (1995), The Chrysalids (1996, from John Wyndham), Kill the Old, Torture Their Young (1998), Begin Again (1999), Presence (2001)

Harrower established himself with Knives and Hens, a three-hander set in medieval times in which a young woman learns how to express herself and as result begins to exert control over her life. In Kill the Old, a filmmaker returns to a city not a million miles from Glasgow to make a documentary and the play follows the intercutting lives of his subjects as it exposes their different forms of alienation. Begin Again is a noirish treatment of post-war spiv culture and Presence explores the rites of passage of a young group of Liverpudlian musicians in Hamburg in the early 1960s.

TRY THESE:
Harrower has adapted work by *CHEKHOV, *FOSSE, *IBSEN, *PIRANDELLO; *BARKER's The Castle for medieval women; *FRIEL's Translations for language and love; *CARTWRIGHT and *LUCIE for varieties of alienation; *RUSSELL for the Beatles; *HARE's Teeth 'n' Smiles, *KEEFFE's Bastard Angel for rock bands.

HART, Moss
See KAUFMAN, George S.

HARVEY, Jonathan [1967 –]
British dramatist

PLAYS INCLUDE:
The Cherry Blossom Tree (1987), Mohair (1988), Beautiful Thing (1993), Babies (1994), Boom Bang-a-Bang (1995), The Rupert Street Lonely Hearts Club (1995), Guiding Star (1998), Hushabye Mountain (1999), Out in the Open (2001), Closer to Heaven (2001, musical)

Liverpool-born Harvey established himself with Beautiful Thing, a play about young gay men living in an urban housing estate that challenged all manner of stereotypes by showing true love winning through in the face of initial prejudice. Remarkable for its scenes of burgeoning attraction, it appealed to both gay and straight audiences with its almost fairy-tale quality of love conquering all. Babies is apparently semi-autobiographical in its tale of a young teacher going to a pupil's party, while Boom Bang-a-Bang is about another party, this one involving a group of friends meeting to watch the Eurovision Song Contest. Unsurprisingly neither party goes smoothly. In The Rupert Street Lonely Hearts Club there is a trail of misdirected and unrequited loves, Hushabye Mountain tackles the repercussions for the family and friend after the death of a young man from AIDS and Out in the Open follows a similar path with the survivor of a gay relationship trying to end his period of mourning but beset by secrets and lies on all sides. Closer to Heaven (created with the Pet Shop Boys) uses the gay club scene as its setting. Rather different from these is Guiding Star, which deals with the phenomenon of 'survivor's guilt' as it affects a family whose male members survived the Hillsborough disaster.

TRY THESE:

✱ELYOT, ✱RAVENHILL for different contemporary gay sensibilities; ✱ALBEE's *Who's Afraid of Virginia Woolf?*, ✱ELYOT's *My Night with Reg*, ✱TREVOR GRIFFITHS' *The Party*, ✱LEIGH's *Abigail's Party* for unhappy social gatherings; ✱AYCKBOURN for general social unease and *Absent Friends* for post-mortem social solecisms.

HARWOOD, Ronald   [1934 –   ]
South African-born novelist and dramatist

PLAYS INCLUDE:

Country Matters (1969), *A Family* (1978), *The Dresser* (1980), *After the Lions* (1982), *Tramway Road* (1984), *Interpreters* (1985), *The Deliberate Death of a Polish Priest* (1985), *J. J. Farr* (1987), *Another Time* (1989), *Reflected Glory* (1991), *Taking Sides* (1995), *Mahler's Conversion* (2001)

Born in South Africa, Harwood joined Sir Donald Wolfit's Shakespeare Company as actor and dresser to this last of the old-style actor-managers (an experience which later spawned a biography and the play *The Dresser*). He continued as an actor until 1959, but in 1960 he had a play produced on television and he published his first novel in 1961. His subjects have been varied and his work is difficult to categorise in any medium, though you can expect well-characterised parts for actors and a strong sense of theatre. He won an Oscar for his script for *The Pianist* in 2003.

The Dresser remains probably his most successful play. Inspired by, though not a portrait of, Wolfit and his company, it is set on tour in the provinces in the middle of World War II, as the actor-manager gets through his last performance of *King Lear*. Anyone with memories of that kind of theatre will recognise the authenticity with which Harwood has captured it. *Another Time*, also drawing on Harwood's own experience – this time, a South African childhood (the setting, too, of *Tramway Road*) – was a theatrical tour de force. Ostensibly dealing with the nature of musical genius, the heart and soul of the play

lay in Harwood's uncovering of the sinews of an embattled lower-middle-class Jewish marriage and the process of ageing. *Taking Sides* and *Mahler's Conversion* also tackle musical subjects with Jewish contexts: *Taking Sides* deals with the post-war interrogation of the conductor Wilhelm Fürtwängler, who chose to stay in Nazi Germany, while *Mahler's Conversion* examines why Mahler chose to convert from Judaism to Christianity.

TRY THESE:

For the performer's life, see the very different views of ✱COWARD's *Hay Fever*, ✱TREVOR GRIFFITHS' *Comedians*, ✱HAYES' *Not Waving*, ✱NELSON's *Two Shakespearean Actors*, ✱OSBORNE's *The Entertainer*, ✱PRIESTLEY's *The Good Companions*; Graham Greene for plays about loss of faith; ✱PETER SHAFFER's *Amadeus* for musical genius; ✱POWNALL and ✱C. P. TAYLOR's *Good* for music and totalitarianism; ✱SAUNDERS adapted his novel *The Girl in Melanie Klein*; Harwood adapted Francis Veber's *Le Dîner de Cons* as *See You Next Tuesday*.

HASTINGS, Michael   [1938 –   ]
British dramatist

PLAYS INCLUDE:

Don't Destroy Me (1956), *Yes – and After* (1957), *The World's Baby* (1964), *Lee Harvey Oswald* (1966), *The Cutting of the Cloth* (1973), *For the West* (1977), *Gloo Joo* (1978), *Full Frontal* (1979), *Carnival War a Go Hot* (1979), *Midnite at the Starlite* (1980), *Tom and Viv* (1984), *The Emperor* (1986), *A Dream of People* (1990), *Unfinished Business* (1994)

Hastings has produced memorable plays in a wide range of genres over many years from his debut with *Don't Destroy Me*, an exploration of a Jewish household in Brixton, which was produced when he was only eighteen and working as a tailor's apprentice. *The World's Baby*, a Sunday-night Royal Court performance with Vanessa Redgrave as the central character, a woman whom the play follows over twenty years, was never given a full-scale production.

Lee Harvey Oswald is an example of what was known at the time as 'Theatre of Fact', a sort of documentary account of Oswald's life up to the point of Kennedy's assassination. *Gloo Joo*, a study of a West Indian's experience of London, was produced at the Hampstead Theatre Club and transferred to the West End. *The Emperor*, a controversial account of Emperor Haile Selassie (there were protests outside from Ethiopians and Rastafarians), was a subtle if quirky study of power and its acolyte tendencies. *A Dream of People* is a complex and compelling examination of the resonant relationships between past, present and future, personal and public morality, morality and expediency, all focused through the issue of pensions.

Tom and Viv

Probably Hastings' most successful play, *Tom and Viv* pursues his concern with the theatrical possibilities of biography in a study of the fraught marriage between ✳T. S. ELIOT and his first wife, Vivienne Haigh-Wood. Vivienne ended her life in a mental hospital, and the play explores her mental fragility, her tortuous relationship with Eliot, and the contemporary British upper-class culture that produced Vivienne. The play is ultimately quite unsympathetic to Eliot and his role in their relationship.

TRY THESE:

✳WALCOTT's *O Babylon* for other views of Haile Selassie; ✳MANN for 'Theater of Testimony' documentary style; ✳ABBENSETTS, ✳KEEFFE's *King of England*, ✳MATURA, ✳PHILLIPS, ✳WHITE for contrasting views of West Indians in London; for other plays about poets and their domestic lives, ✳BRENTON's *Bloody Poetry* (Byron and the Shelleys), ✳BOND's *Bingo*, ✳GLASPELL's *Alison's House* (based on Emily Dickinson), ✳LOCHHEAD's *Blood and Ice* (the Shelleys), ✳WHITEMORE's *Stevie* (Stevie Smith).

HAVEL, Vaclav   [1936 –   ]
Czech dramatist, dissident and latterly President

PLAYS INCLUDE:
The Memorandum (1967), *The Garden Party* (1969), *The Increased Difficulty of Concentration* (1972), *Audience, Private View* and *Protest* (three short plays, 1978), *Mistake* (1983), *Largo Desolato* (1987), *Temptation* (1989), *Redevelopment* (1990)

Havel did not like the term 'dissident', but from 1969 until the extraordinary run of events in November 1989 that brought down the Czech communist government and soon after installed him as his country's President, he was known in the West as Czechoslovakia's leading dissident playwright. Havel preferred to see it in terms of 'living in truth'; his plays from that period (notably the three that are known as the Vanek plays, *Audience, Private View* and *Protest*) bear witness to that 'living in truth' as a stubborn, unflinching morality. The plays themselves are far from perfect dramatic models, being short on conflict and little more than talking-head pieces. But the delineations of the characters and their relationship to society are fascinatingly created, and what they have to say about personal integrity, individual responsibility and 'accommodation' to the system have as much resonance for audiences in the West as for those for whom the plays were then intended. In fact, Havel had not been able to see any of his own plays after 1969 (except for a video of *Temptation* smuggled in by the RSC). They were not published openly in Czechoslovakia, though they had been widely performed in the West.

Havel had wanted to study drama at university, but because of his 'bourgeois' family background he was forced to start as a stagehand; he then worked as a lighting technician and later became dramaturg at the avant-garde Prague Theatre on the Balustrade, for which he began to write plays in the 1960s. *The Memorandum* showed one of his recurring themes: life in an organisation where mechanical clichés and deformation of language conceal the fact that nothing actually gets done, and employees are always watching their backs. In 1968 he left the Theatre on the Balustrade, and he was effectively excluded from live theatre after the Soviet invasion of that year, although there were various clandestine stagings including his version of ✳GAY's *Beggar's Opera* in 1975. (It was given its British premiere in 2003 at the Orange Tree). He continued to work for human rights and in 1977 was a founder member of Charter 77. He was imprisoned in 1979 for his involvement in VONS (the Committee for the Defence of the Unjustly Prosecuted). ✳SAMUEL BECKETT dedicated *Catastrophe*, possibly the nearest he ever went to making a political statement, to him during this imprisonment. *Largo Desolato* shows a dissident scholar reduced to near-nervous breakdown by the impossibility of living up to his reputation as a symbol of resistance and is an allegory of the artist's relationship to society. *Temptation* is another satire on organisational hierarchies and yes men. Based on the Faust story, it has a broader satirical sweep than his earlier plays, showing multiple layers of fear, disloyalty and double-cross. Dr Foustka, who wishes to study forbidden knowledge, is tempted to ever-meaner betrayals by a Mephistophelean figure with smelly feet, who turns out to be a spy for the director of his Institute. All is revealed at a wild Walpurgisnacht fancy dress party.

TRY THESE:
✱ MROZEK, for eastern European plays using absurdist techniques to show political desperation; Soviet playwright Alexsandr Gelman's *We, the Undersigned* and *A Man with Connections* for more barbed revelations of bureaucratic bungling under communism; ✱ EDGAR's *The Shape of the Table* features Havel in its fictionalised account of events in Prague in November 1989; ✱ STOPPARD (Kenneth Tynan was the first to link these two Czechs and to see Stoppard's potential political streak); ✱ MILLER's *The Archbishop's Ceiling* for east European dissidents; ✱ GOETHE and ✱ MARLOWE for the Faust story; ✱ WERTENBAKER's *The Grace of Mary Traverse* has Faustian resonances; ✱ BRECHT and ✱ DEAR for responses to ✱ GAY; ✱ SAUNDERS adapted *Redevelopment*.

HAVIS, Allan   [1951 –   ]
American dramatist

PLAYS INCLUDE:
Mink Sonata (1986), *Haul Gout* (1987), *Hospitality* (1988), *Morocco* (1988), *A Daring Bride* (1990), *Lilith* (1990), *Ladies of Fisher Cove* (1991), *Albert the Astronomer* (1991)

A native New Yorker, Havis received graduate degrees in drama from Hunter College and Yale. Though he started writing in the mid-1970s, his work began to be performed only in the late 1980s, largely at off-off-Broadway and regional theatres.

Many of Havis' plays are intrigues dealing with political and metaphysical evil. In *Haut Gout*, an American doctor is caught up in the Haitian revolution; *Hospitality* covers two political detainees in an American immigration service detention centre; and in *Morocco*, an American architect tries to free his wife from a Moroccan prison where she is held on charges of prostitution. *Lilith*, based on Jewish folklore, tells of Adam's divorce from his first wife, and of her ensuing competition with Eve.

TRY THESE:
For a late nineteenth-century look at sex roles, ✱ STRINDBERG's *Miss Julie*; for dark perspectives on modern family life, ✱ ALBEE's *Who's Afraid of Virginia Woolf?*, ✱ FEIFFER's *Little Murders* and ✱ SHEPARD's *True West*; for politics, ✱ EDGAR, ✱ KOPIT's *Indians*, ✱ NELSON's *Principia Scriptoriae*, ✱ RABE's *Streamers*, ✱ WEISS's *The Investigation*; ✱ DANIELS' *Beside Herself* also features Lilith.

HAYES, Catherine   [1949 –   ]
British dramatist

PLAYS INCLUDE:
Little Sandra (1976), *Not Waving* (1983), *Skirmishes* (1982), *Long Time Gone* (1986)

When she was younger, Hayes wanted to be a detective. Instead she became a French teacher, and it was only when she saw ✱ ALAN BLEASDALE's advertisement for new writers for the Liverpool Playhouse that she decided to turn her hand to plays. *Skirmishes*, the play that brought her to public attention, has been performed all over the world. It casts an unsentimental eye on the subject of mother–daughter and sibling relationships. Round a dying mother's bed, a bitter, if witty, war of verbal and emotional attrition is let loose as two sisters give vent to long-stored-up resentments and misunderstandings. Hayes' drama is a searing yet compassionate analysis, confronting painful truths about death, love and the awful taboos to do with duty. Further revelations of female self-doubt and vulnerability were also behind *Not Waving*, about the crumbling fortunes of a female cabaret comic, brought on by ill health, failing confidence (she can't get the audience to laugh any more) and a break-up with her manager. Variations on both subjects turned up again in *Long Time Gone* – another delve into sibling rivalries, and love/hate relationships, this time around the Cain and Abel myth of brothers. Hayes took the 1960s pop stars the Everley Brothers as her model but freely embroidered it in facts and chronology – an approach which some reviewers accepted, but to which others, surprisingly, took a certain exception. She has since written extensively for television, contributing many episodes to the soap opera *Coronation Street*.

TRY THESE:

✱ NORMAN's *'Night Mother* takes an equally painful view of the symbiotic mother–daughter relationship; ✱ KEARSLEY, ✱ MACDONALD, ✱ PAGE and ✱ RAIF have all dealt with mothers and daughters; ✱ DELANEY's *A Taste of Honey* and ✱ JELLICOE's *The Sport of My Mad Mother* for more extended treatments, one realistic, the other surreal; ✱ BILL's *Curtains* also deals with family pressures around a dying mother; ✱ TREMBLAY's *Johnny Mangano and His Astonishing Dogs* has a cabaret club setting for its two downward spiralling performers, ✱ TREVOR GRIFFITHS' *Comedians* and ✱ OSBORNE's *The Entertainer* are more extended explorations of comedy as prop and social weapon; ✱ NICHOLS' *A Day in the Death of Joe Egg* for comparable humour; ✱ BLEASDALE's *Are You Lonesome Tonight?* plays freely with the Presley legend.

HECHT, Ben   [1894 – 1964]
American dramatist

MacARTHUR, Charles   [1895 – 1956]
American dramatist

JOINT PLAYS INCLUDE:

The Front Page (1928), *Twentieth Century* (1932), *Jumbo* (1935, book of the musical), *Ladies and Gentlemen* (1939), *Swan Song* (1946)

A team who found success together writing screenplays, and also on their own, Hecht and MacArthur helped define a style of boisterous, cheerfully anarchic comedy which is definably American in its determined avoidance of anything genteel or refined. The duo

are best known for two plays, *The Front Page* and *Twentieth Century*, both of which became films – or, in the case of the former, several films. Each is a kind of courtship comedy. In *Front Page*, an editor tries to lure his star reporter away from his fiancée by extolling the passion of journalism over that of romance. In *Twentieth Century*, which became a hit Broadway and West End musical in the late 1970s, an egomaniacal Broadway producer makes a young shop girl a star, and when she makes moves to leave him, he spends a lengthy train journey trying to win her back. *Ladies and Gentlemen*, a romantic thriller set during a trial, was MacArthur's attempt to concoct a vehicle for his wife, Helen Hayes.

The Front Page
A perennial favourite for revivals (most recently at Chichester in 2002 and in London at the Donmar Warehouse), this gregarious tale of Chicago newspapermen in the 1920s has spawned three films, one musical (the 1982 *Windy City*) and any number of spiritual children, including the film *Chicago*. Politics were not upmost in Hecht and MacArthur's minds as they spun a rapid-fire yarn about a scheming editor's attempts to keep his star reporter, Hildy Johnson, from succumbing to the enticements of love; but in its subplots about corruption in the sheriff's office and its often blistering portrait of male camaraderie, the play can seem surprisingly biting and contemporary.

TRY THESE:

The Front Page and *Chicago* share a background in Chicago journalism of the 1920s. former *Chicago Tribune* writer Maurine Watkins wrote a play called *Chicago* that eventually (via a silent film and the film *Roxie Hart*) became the 1970s musical and recent film; ✱ BABE's *Buried Inside Extra*, ✱ BRENTON and ✱ HARE's *Pravda*, Stephen Wakelam's *Deadlines* for other newspaper plays; ✱ ABBOTT's *Broadway* and ✱ KAUFMAN and Hart for similarly large-scale, rumbustious American works; ✱ MAMET (especially *Glengarry Glen Ross*) for capturing both the brio and the venality that go with careerism.

HEDDEN, Roger   [1960 –   ]
American dramatist and screenwriter/director

PLAYS INCLUDE:
Been Taken (1985), *Terry Neal's Future*
(1986), *Bodies, Rest and Motion* (1986), *The
Artistic Direction* (1990), *As Sure as You Live*
(1991)

A 1984 graduate of Columbia University,
Hedden observes a society on the run, searching for some greater meaning in life, and yet
never standing still long enough to find it.
'People don't take the time to see what's
around them or inside of them', comments
Hedden. He finds his message best expressed
in comedy, and his deft language explores the
power of dramatic irony In *Bodies, Rest and
Motion* we follow the desperate wanderings of
the principal character who along the way
loses his parents (who moved without leaving
a forwarding address), his girlfriend (whom
he abandons), and the job he thought he
wanted in the 'city of the future' – Canton,
Ohio. *Been Taken* traces the changing expectations of young college students over a five-
year period from their campus antics through
life in the workaday world. He wrote the
screenplay for the film of *Bodies, Rest and
Motion* and produced and wrote the film
Sleep With Me before turning to direction
with *Hi-Life* for which he also wrote the
screenplay.

TRY THESE:
For characters who develop from their college
days, ✱WASSERSTEIN's *Uncommon Women and
Others;* for characters in search of meaning,
✱CHEKHOV's *The Seagull,* ✱GUARE's *House of Blue
Leaves,* ✱WELLER's *Moonchildren,* and
✱TENNESSEE WILLIAMS' *Camino Real.*

HEGGIE, Iain   [1953 –   ]
Scottish dramatist

PLAYS INCLUDE:
Politics in the Park (1986), *A Wholly Healthy
Glasgow* (1987), *American Bagpipes* (1988),
Clyde Nouveau (1990), *Lust* (1992), *Tourist
Variations* (1993, book for musical), *An
Experienced Woman Gives Advice* (1995),
Wiping My Mother's Arse (2001), *Love Freaks*
(2002)

One-time PT instructor, drama teacher and
member of the Royal Court's writing group,
Glasgow-born Heggie took the theatre world
by storm with *A Wholly Healthy Glasgow*.
Awarded a special prize in the first Mobil
Playwriting competition in 1985, it was taken
up by Manchester's Royal Exchange, toured
the Edinburgh Festival and came to the Royal
Court in February 1988 (being televised at
about the same time). Hailed as Glasgow's
answer to ✱DAVID MAMET, Heggie's dialogue,
steeped in Glaswegian, is the driving force of
his work, with its febrile energy and oddball
syntax. Set in a health club, the play has been
seen by some as a metaphor of modern-day
survival; nearly all agreed that, in the words of
the *Observer's* critic, Michael Ratcliffe, it is
'one of the funniest plays of the last few years'.
However, in a post-AIDS climate, it is also fair
to say that its libidinous gay character, with
eyes set on 'a bit of nookie every fifteen
seconds', now seems like a limp-wristed
throwback to another era. *American Bagpipes*,
a suburban comedy about family disintegration, was commissioned and produced whilst
he was writer-in-residence at the Royal
Exchange. *Clyde Nouveau* examines the world
of small-time thieves and big-time property
speculators. *An Experienced Woman Gives
Advice* takes the situation of an older woman
who starts off relaxed about her younger
lover's adventure until more truths are
revealed. *Wiping My Mother's Arse* has some
similarities as a situation gradually unravels
to the discomfort of the characters through
the catalyst of a camp care assistant. In *Love
Freaks*, which is derived from ✱MARIVAUX's
The Double Inconstancy, Heggie sets his
protagonists against one another in the
context of global capitalism, as a reluctant
trainee with an international coffee-shop
company finds herself at the centre of
personal and political entanglements with her
activist boyfriend and the heir to the coffee-
shop business.

TRY THESE:
✱CARTWRIGHT's *Road* for a similarly dynamic use
of language; ✱BYRNE's *The Slab Boys Trilogy* for a
similarly volatile if more socialist view of Glasgow
working life; ✱MAMET's *Glengarry Glen Ross* for an
American equivalent of small-time capitalism;

Heggie has adapted *Don Juan* (1998) from
✷ MOLIÈRE and ✷ GOGOL's *Diary of a Madman* as
King of Scotland (2000).

HELLMAN, Lillian [1905 – 84]
American dramatist, screenwriter and journalist

PLAYS INCLUDE:

The Children's Hour (1934), *Days to Come*
(1936), *The Little Foxes* (1939), *Watch on the
Rhine* (1941), *The Searching Wind* (1944),
Another Part of the Forest (1946), *Montserrat*
(1949), *Regina* (1949), *The Autumn Garden*
(1951), *The Lark* (1955, from ✷ ANOUILH),
Candide (1956, musical), *Toys in the Attic*
(1960), *My Mother, My Father and Me* (1963,
adapted from Burt Blechman's novel *How
Much?*)

Playwright and long-time companion of
thriller writer Dashiell Hammett, Hellman's
wit is typical of the Dorothy Parker period
(she was a close personal friend). To
audiences now, however, Hellman is probably
less associated with the theatre than with the
writing of such classic films as *The Little
Foxes*, which starred Bette Davis. Her volumes
of autobiography, *Scoundrel Time*, *Pentimento*
and *An Unfinished Woman*, were the subject
of a huge literary controversy regarding their
historical reliability and truthfulness,
although her stand against the House Un-
American Activities Committee is legendary,
if still disputed.

Her plays are not much seen in Britain, By
modern standards, they are shamelessly melodramatic, though they do also have a moral
centre, ruthlessly exposing money as the most
corrosive of agents, particularly in the family.
Hellman's malign protagonists often have the
best of the fray (and afford golden opportunities for actresses to play a 'bitch'), but she uses
them to show human perversity and the
destructive power of evil on human relationships. Her world of decaying aristocrats and
the upwardly mobile middle classes is
frequently a world of moral bankruptcy.
Throughout her plays there is, too, a consistent concern to voice uncomfortable
emotional truths as well as socio-political
issues: in *Toys in the Attic*, her Southern
portrait of a man dominated by two sisters, it
is the injuries people inflict on each other in
the name of security and love; in *Watch on the
Rhine*, it is American non-interventionism,
the spectre of fascism and the Holocaust.
Several of her plays have women in central
roles, but by contemporary feminist standards they lack any radical reassessment –
rather, they reinforce certain female stereotypes.

Hellman is a character in the 1977 film
Julia, based on her memoirs, and *Lillian*,
William Luce's 1985 biographical play based
on her, proved that, posthumously, Hellman
remains as controversial as ever.

The Children's Hour

First produced in 1934, this is probably one of
her best-known and certainly most successful
plays. Audaciously, for its time, it tackles the
taboo subject of lesbianism, although the real
subject of the play is considered to be the
destructiveness of innuendo and rumour.
Predictably for the period, the tale is a tragic
one: one of the teachers is accused by a
revengeful pupil of having an 'unnatural' relationship with a colleague and commits
suicide. Hellman's achievement is to show the
consequences of the pupil's 'little lie' and,
perhaps inadvertently, the consequences of
society's intolerance towards lesbianism. The
National Theatre staged it in 1994.

TRY THESE:

✷ JONSON for characters as embodiments of moral
evil; ✷ TENNESSEE WILLIAMS for Southern settings; for
other female 'villains', ✷ EURIPIDES' *Medea*, ✷ IBSEN's
Hedda Gabler, ✷ RACINE's *Phèdre*; ✷ AYCKBOURN for
dramas of family life; ✷ MILLER's *The Crucible* for the
consequences of spiteful rumour; for a contrasting
contemporary treatment of plays on an anti-fascist
theme, Maxwell Anderson; ✷ CHEKHOV for family
sagas of tight narrative, leisurely discussion and
high moral intent: ✷ DANIELS' *Neaptide* for
lesbianism and teachers.

HENLEY, Beth [1952 –]
American dramatist

PLAYS INCLUDE:

Am I Blue (1973), *Crimes of the Heart* (1979),
The Miss Firecracker Contest (1980), *The
Wake of Jamey Foster* (1982), *The Debutante*

Ball (1985), *The Lucky Spot* (1986), *Abundance* (1989), *Control Freaks* (1992), *Signature* (1995), *L-Play* (1996), *Impossible Marriage* (1998), *Family Week* (2000)

Born in Jackson, Mississippi, Henley epitomises the Southern Gothic voice in American playwriting. *Crimes of the Heart*, her Pulitzer Prize-winning play, introduced Henley's cheerfully eccentric tone and lunatic domestic tangles. Set five years after Hurricane Camille, *Crimes of the Heart* generates a comic tempest of its own as the three McGrath sisters struggle to make their peace with a world that never quite matches their perceptions of it. Her later plays extended Henley's gallery of Southern eccentrics who counter the world's cruelties with daffy strategies for survival, though none has been as well received as *Crimes of the Heart*.

TRY THESE:
✴CHEKHOV's *Three Sisters* for another family of grown sisters clinging to a vision of a world elsewhere; ✴LARSON, ✴LEVI LEE, ✴NORMAN for playwrights with a similar Southern sensibility; ✴KAUFMAN and Hart for families bound by their own peculiar logic.

HEYWOOD, Thomas   [1574 – 1641]
English dramatist

PLAYS INCLUDE:
A Woman Killed with Kindness (1603), *The Fair Maid of the West* (pre-1610, published 1630), *The English Traveller* (published 1633)

Heywood was a prolific writer and sometime actor who claimed to have contributed to over 200 plays, of which some twenty survive. He wrote in just about every genre and style available to him. Trevor Nunn created 'a comical/tragical adventure entertainment celebrating the birth of a nation' out of the two parts of *The Fair Maid of the West* for the RSC in 1986. *A Woman Killed with Kindness*, a realistic treatment of domestic strife in a bourgeois context, is particularly interesting for its husband who forgives his adulterous wife and her lover rather than pursuing revenge. Northern Broadsides revived it in 2003.

TRY THESE:
Heywood's treatment of adultery in *A Woman Killed with Kindness* contrasts strikingly with ✴SHAKESPEARE's in *Othello*; *The Fair Maid of the West* is one of many Renaissance plays to use the so-called substitute bed mate trick which occurs most notably in ✴MIDDLETON's *The Changeling* as well as ✴SHAKESPEARE's *All's Well That Ends Well* and *Measure for Measure*; the anonymous *A Yorkshire Tragedy* for an interesting Renaissance parallel to *A Woman Killed with Kindness*.

HIGHWAY, Tomson   [1951 –   ]
Canadian dramatist

PLAYS INCLUDE:
The Rez Sisters (1987), *Dry Lips Ought to Move to Kapuskasing* (1989)

Highway is one of the major forces in Native People's theatre in Canada. For many years, the Native people or 'Indians' of North America have felt that their culture was something both used and abused by the white people. In Canada, in recent years, Native people have started to claim back theatre for themselves, producing work that is performed on reservations and in urban community centres for the indigenous population. Often the plays are written in indigenous languages as well as English and feature familiar 'spirits' from native culture. *The Rez Sisters*, reminiscent of ✴MICHEL TREMBLAY's *Les Belles Soeurs*, follows the adventures (and misadventures) of seven Native women who leave their reservation to go to Toronto in order to take part in The Biggest Bingo Game in the World. Both funny and tragic, it portrays their lives with affection and sympathy, showing both the spirituality and the difficulty of life for contemporary Native people. Both this play, and its companion piece *Dry Lips* (about seven Native men and hockey) won the Dora Mavor Moore Award for Best New Play of the Year, one of the most prestigious awards in Canada. Highway's work is virtually unknown on stage in Britain, despite some academic interest, but both the plays mentioned here have been published.

TRY THESE:

✱ SOYINKA for a Nigerian playwright combining African and Western cultures; Jatinder Verma for one who synthesises Asian with Western culture; ✱ HORSFIELD's *Red Devils Trilogy* for 'leaving the reservation'.

HILL, Errol   [1921 –   ]
Trinidadian dramatist and academic

PLAYS INCLUDE:

Brittle and the City Fathers (1948, later known as *Oily Portraits*), *Square Peg* (1949), *The Ping-Pong* (radio 1950; staged 1953), *Dilemma* (1953), *Broken Melody* (1954), *Wey-Wey* (1957), *Strictly Matrimony* (1959), *Man Better Man* (1960; originally 1957), *Dimanche Gras Carnival Show* (1963), *Whistling Charlie and the Monster* (1964), *Dance Bongo* (1965)

Hill is a major figure in the creation of a West Indian theatre through his work as writer, director, actor, editor of play anthologies, author of the standard work *The Trinidad Carnival* and academic (he has held posts in the West Indies, Nigeria and the USA). His aim, in his own words, has been 'to treat aspects of Caribbean folk life, drawing on speech idioms and rhythms, music and dance, and to evolve a form of drama and theatre most nearly representative of Caribbean life and art'. He draws on folklore associated with the calypso and carnival traditions in *Man Better Man*, which he selected to represent him in his own edition of three Caribbean plays (*Plays for Today*, Longman, 1985), with its obeah man brought in to help a young lover to win his bride in a duel with the village stick-fighting ('calinda') champion. The original version was written in prose and had no music, but in its current form it uses calypso verse and music in a comic style that celebrates aspects of folk culture that have survived despite colonial rule.

TRY THESE:

✱ MATURA is a Trinidadian-born dramatist who shares many of Hill's interests, particularly in carnival in *Play Mas* and in folk culture in *Meetings*; ✱ SYNGE's *Playboy of the Western World* (and Matura's reworking of it as *Playboy of the West Indies*) for one of the classic celebrations and interrogations of folk culture in drama; ✱ WALCOTT as the pre-eminent Caribbean dramatist who also shares Hill's concern for a rich theatrical language expressing Caribbean culture as fully as possible; ✱ BREUER's *The Warrior Ant* and John Constable's *Black Mas* for white writers' treatment of carnival; ✱ CROSS's *Blues for Railton* and *Mass Carib* also celebrate pre-colonial, pre-Christian Caribbean cultures in music.

HOCHHÜTH, Rolf   [1931 –   ]
German dramatist

PLAYS INCLUDE:

The Representative (1963, *The Deputy* in the USA), *Soldiers* (1967), *Guerrillas* (1970), *The Midwife* (1972)

Hochhuth spent some years as a reader with a publishing firm, potentially a useful training for writing 'documentary' dramas. His international success as a dramatist derived from the controversial nature of his best-known plays. *The Representative* showed Pope Pius XII as failing to do anything to prevent the Holocaust because he was more concerned about the spread of Communism and the state of the Church's finances. It was filmed by Constantin Costa-Gavras as *Amen* in 2002. *Soldiers* deals with Churchill's 1943 decision on saturation bombing of German cities, and he is also accused of conniving at the assassination of the Polish leader Sikorski. An attempt to put on *Soldiers* at the National Theatre in 1967 led to a burst of patriotic objection that did nothing for the positions of either Olivier or Kenneth Tynan. Hochhüth suffers from being unable to make up his mind whether the great moments of history are caused by individual decisions or by economic and social forces, though in *Guerrillas* he still seems to think that American society could be changed by disposing of a small number of industrialists.

TRY THESE:

Erwin Piscator for documentary theatre in the 1920s; Peter Brook's *US*, Heinar Kipphardt's *In the Matter of J. Robert Oppenheimer* (1964), ✱ WEISS's *The Investigation* (1965) for documentary theatre in the 1960s; ＊BRENTON's *The Churchill Play* for an equally controversial portrait of the statesman.

Ulrike Meinhof for an extraordinary portrait of woman as terrorist.

HOLBOROUGH, Jacqueline   [1949 –   ]
British dramatist

PLAYS INCLUDE:
A Question of Habit (1979), *Killers* (1980), *Fallacies* (1983), *Decade* (1984), *The Garden Girls* (1985), *The Sin Eaters* (1986), *Dreams of San Francisco* (1987), *The Way South* (1989)

Holborough was an actress before she started writing out of her own experience – a short stay in Durham high-security prison, the result of placing an ad in the paper and subsequently being charged for conspiracy. Her early plays were devised with Jenny Hicks and members of the women prisoners company Clean Break, which they co-founded. *A Question of Habit*, *Killers* and *The Sin Eaters* deal with such subjects as lesbianism, mother and daughter relationships, terrorism and maximum-security wings. Holborough has a very specific 'tone' – partly humorous, partly realistic, with a real capacity for creating recognisably sympathetic, three-dimensional characters. *The Garden Girls* showed the interrelationship between institution, class and peer group in creating conflict in prison. It also challenged the idea of women criminals as hysterics and neurotics, showing their imprisonment to be the penalty for retaliating against ill treatment from men or infringing some social code of the way women ought to behave. *Dreams of San Francisco* is a ferociously satiric comment on late 1980s feminism's capitulation to 'Thatcherite' market forces. Holborough has gone on to write extensively for British television.

TRY THESE:
＊BEHAN's *The Quare Fellow*, ＊TOM MCGRATH's *The Hard Man*, ＊PUIG's *Kiss of the Spider Woman* for penal life; for the relationship between women, mental illness and custodial treatments, ＊CRAZE's *Shona*, ＊EDGAR's *Mary Barnes*, ＊MURRAY's *Bodycell*; ＊CHURCHILL's *Top Girls* and *Serious Money* for other images of opportunism in the Thatcher decade; ＊GEMS' *Dusa, Fish, Stas and Vi* for women interacting; ＊FO and ＊RAME's

HOLMAN, David
British dramatist

PLAYS INCLUDE:
Drink the Mercury (1972), *Adventure in the Deep* (1973), *No Pasaran* (1976), *The Disappeared* (1979), *Big Cat, Big Coat* (1980), *Peacemaker* (1983), *Susummu's Story* (1983), *1983* (1983), *No Worries* (1984), *Small Poppies* (1986), *Solomon and the Big Cat* (1987), *Whale* (1989), *O. U. T. Spells Out* (1996), *The Tractor Girls* (2002)

Holman has been writing for stage, radio, film and opera for over thirty years. His work is usually performed for or by children of all ages. His sympathy with children goes back to his rather bleak childhood in Haringey, north London. Bullied at primary school, he says, as 'a weed in glasses', he drew his main consolation from books and awe-struck visits to museums. His plays are consequently perceptive about loners, such as the Australian country-girl, moved to a city life that renders her powerless in *No Worries*. But they are also wider-ranging, energetic pieces put over with a stinging outrage at incidences of injustice. Holman is not afraid to place moral issues before his young audiences and many of his plays explore environmental questions. These include *Drink the Mercury*, about the effects of heavy-metal pollution on fishermen in Japan; *Adventure in the Deep*, whose subject is the despoliation of the ocean; *Big Cat, Big Coat* and *Solomon and the Big Cat*, which concern endangered species in Africa, and *Whale*, based on the real-life race by Americans and Russians in 1988 to free whales trapped under the ice in the Arctic, interwoven with an ancient Inuit (Eskimo) myth.

Other widely performed plays include *No Pasaran*, about a Jewish boxer in Nazi Germany, *The Disappeared*, about victims of repression in Argentina, and three 'peace' plays, *Peacemaker*, *Susummu's Story* (about Hiroshima and the atom bomb) and *1983* (written for various age ranges and all presented by Theatre Centre) – which were attacked by certain members of the British Tory government for their pacifism. In *The Tractor Girls* he set two female Ipswich Town supporters loose in Moscow to face the realities of modern Russia.

TRY THESE:

✳HIGHWAY's *The Rez Sisters* follows the journey of some Native Canadians to the Big City; ✳AYCKBOURN has written extensively for children; ✳KESSELMAN's *Becca*, about a young girl who is shut up in a cupboard, uses fantasy and music to push the boundaries of children's theatre; ✳CASDAGLI, ✳SHEPPHARD and ✳DAVID WOOD are other British writers for children.

HOLMAN, Robert   [1952 –   ]
British dramatist

PLAYS INCLUDE:

Coal (1973), *The Natural Cause* (1974), *Outside the Whale* (1976), *German Skerries* (1977), *Mucking Out* (1978), *Other Worlds* (1983), *Today* (1984), *The Overgrown Path* (1985), *Making Noise Quietly* (1986), *Across Oka* (1988), *Rafts and Dreams* (1990), *Bad Weather* (1998), *Holes in the Skin* (2003)

Born in North Yorkshire, the son of a farm manager and a teacher, Holman moved to London at nineteen and spent two and a half years working in the newsagents on Paddington Station; perhaps his immersion in the world gives his plays their peculiar realism, but few writers chart human truths so perceptively, particularly the truths that accompany sudden intimacy. 'I always think you can hear silence', a character comments in his play *The Overgrown Path*, and that's what Holman does: he keeps time with the human dialogues that go unspoken but are, nonetheless, felt. *Outside the Whale* is a fictional biography of George Orwell in the 1930s and, *Today* is a probing treatment of English idealism in the same period. *Making Noise Quietly* is a trio of plays about relationships that flourish and flail under the strains of gender and class. Written in a temperate, considered mode, its title summed up what Holman had been doing: making noise quietly – and invaluably. *Rafts and Dreams* tackles the long-term damage of child abuse

through a surreal ecological fantasy, and *Across Oka* is concerned with global conservation, focusing on the plight of the Siberian Crane. *Bad Weather* concerns the arrival of a figure from the past and how it affects a man who escaped prison after a fracas at a Chinese restaurant. Holman remains an enigmatic writer whose work has never quite achieved the success it deserves.

TRY THESE:

✳FRAYN's *Benefactors* for English idealism; ✳PAGE (especially *Salonika*) for often elliptical domestic conflict; ✳DANIELS' *Beside Herself* also tackles the long-term effects of child abuse, ✳WARD's *Apart from George* confronts it indirectly; ✳BUTTERWORTH's *The Night Heron*, ✳TERRY JOHNSON for ecological and global worries.

HOME, William Douglas   [1912 –   ]
British actor and dramatist

PLAYS INCLUDE:

Now Barabbas . . . (1947), *The Chiltern Hundreds* (1947, *Yes M'Lord* in the USA), *The Thistle and the Rose* (1949), *The Reluctant Debutante* (1955), *Betzi* (1964), *The Queen's Highland Servant* (1967), *The Secretary Bird* (1967), *Lloyd George Knew My Father* (1972), *The Dame of Sark* (1974), *The Kingfisher* (1977), *After the Ball is Over* (1985), *Portraits* (1987), *Christmas Truce* (1989)

An actor who appeared in many of his own plays, and whose experience shows in their careful construction, Home was rejected by the 'angries' of the late 1950s as an irrelevant writer of upper-class and well-made plays. How many of them knew of his court martial for refusing to take part in what he thought was a senseless attack on Le Havre in World War II is open to conjecture. Although many of his plays are set in the world of lords and debutantes, the plots are often developed from real life. *The Chiltern Hundreds*, for example, was suggested by the political activities of his father's butler, *The Reluctant Peer* was linked to his Prime Minister brother's resignation of his title and *After the Ball is Over* juxtaposes a hunt ball with a bill to outlaw fox hunting. His subjects range from a chronicle play of events leading to the

Battle of Flodden Field (*The Thistle and the Rose*) to Napoleon's last love affair (*Betzi*), and marriage in *Lloyd George Knew My Father* and *The Secretary Bird*. His other biographical/historical works included *The Dame of Sark* (about the German occupation of the Channel Islands in World War II), *Portraits* (about the painter August John) and *The Queen's Highland Servant* (about Queen Victoria and John Brown). He also wrote about the *Christmas Truce* in World War I. His early play *Now Barabbas . . .* , a study of life in a prison, from the arrival of a condemned murderer to his execution, plumbed much greater depths than his later work, including what was then a very daring treatment of a homosexual friendship.

Home writes about the people he knows but he is not a Tory propagandist – their behaviour, prejudices and eccentricities are the butt of his humorous observation, which relies more upon elegant construction and skilful timing than dazzling wit.

TRY THESE:
✱ SHERIDAN for similar comedies of an earlier time; ✱ BEHAN's *The Quare Fellow*, ✱ GENET, John Herbert's *Fortune and Men's Eyes* for death-cell dramas; ✱ AYCKBOURN for acerbic treatment of the middle and lower-middle classes; ✱ COWARD for more bitter observation of the British 'country house' set; ✱ COONEY and ✱ TRAVERS for farce; ✱ PASCAL's *Theresa* for a less rosy view of the occupation of the Channel Islands.

HOOD, Kevin   [1949 –   ]
British dramatist

PLAYS INCLUDE:
Beached (1987), *The Astronomer's Garden* (1988), *Sugar Hill Blues* (1990), *Hammett's Apprentice* (1993), *So Special* (1998)

A chemistry graduate and sometime research biochemist, born and raised in Spennymoor, County Durham, Hood devised *The Fence* (about the experiences of the Greenham Common peace campaigners) with a teacher colleague and a group of pupils. It was performed at the Albany Empire and on the Edinburgh Fringe. In 1988, the Croydon Warehouse premiered the play that first brought Hood serious attention: *The Astronomer's Garden*. Charting rivalries both professional and sexual amongst the scientific community at the Greenwich Observatory in the eighteenth century, the play was likened to the film work of Peter Greenaway. Working as the Warehouse's writer-in-residence, Hood produced *Sugar Hill Blues*, an intricate tale, partly set on board ship, of two couples, divided by class and race and brought together by jazz in the 1950s. The experiences of prejudice and class among the four are explored with an ironic commentary from a fifth, chorus-like character, Norman. Although at times overflowing with ideas and themes, Hood's depiction of the power relations between his characters is fascinating and he displays a shrewd instinct for the use of music on stage. However, Ian Shuttleworth thought that *So Special* (Manchester Royal Exchange) 'never really escapes the furrow of what might be called "Royal Court by numbers": deprived youth, urban squalor, violence and the occasional bit of graphic grotesquerie'. Hood's television work includes episodes of *The Bill*, *Eastenders*, *Grange Hill* and *Silent Witness*, as well as the adaptation of Minette Walters' *The Echo*.

TRY THESE:
✱ AUGUST WILSON's *Ma Rainey's Black Bottom* for another play with jazz as a major component; ✱ STOPPARD for 'over-cleverness'; ✱ BALDWIN's *The Amen Corner* for religious obsession; ✱ DANIELS' *The Devil's Gateway* for Greenham; race and ships are treated rather differently in Heidi Thomas's *Indigo*; ✱ GOOCH's *Female Transport*, ✱ WERTENBAKER's *Our Country's Good* for ships, class and prejudice; ✱ BOND for deprived youth at the Royal Court.

HOPKINS, John   [1931 – 98]
British dramatist

PLAYS INCLUDE:
This Story of Yours (1968), *Find Your Way Home* (1970), *Economic Necessity* (1973), *Next of Kin* (1974), *Losing Time* (1979), *Absent Forever* (1987)

Hopkins is best known for the creation of BBC TV's *Z-Cars*, a police series that changed the way in which the force was presented. His stage plays have been as strong as his television work. In *This Story of Yours*, a self-loathing detective in a bad marriage, with a job that both repels and fascinates him, beats a suspected child rapist to death. *Find Your Way Home* shows the relationship between a young occasional male prostitute and a married man who leaves his wife to live with him. Hopkins paints a bleak picture of the homosexual scene and of the difficulties they face, uncompromising and unsentimental, but it is as much about the difficulties of making any relationship as about homosexuality. Hopkins' dramas are strong meat, firmly rooted in contemporary experience, and confronting both private and public problems. He died, almost unnoticed, in California and his stage work is in urgent need of professional revival.

TRY THESE:

✶ GILL (*Mean Tears*), ✶ SHERMAN (*Bent*), ✶ WHITEMORE's *Breaking the Code*, ✶ WILCOX (*Rents*) for other plays about the difficulty of homosexual relationships; G. F. Newman's *Operation Bad Apple* for 'bent' police; ✶ BRENTON's *Sore Throats* for a graphic portrait of domestic violence and the difficulty of heterosexual relationships.

HOROVITZ, Israel [1939 –]
American dramatist, screenwriter, actor and producer

PLAYS INCLUDE:

The Comeback (1957), *Rats* (1963), *Line* (1967), *The Indian Wants the Bronx* (1968), *It's Called the Sugar Plum* (1968), *Morning* (1969), *Spared* (1973), *The Primary English Class* (1976), *The Wakefield Plays* (1979), *The Good Parts* (1983), *Today I Am a Fountain Pen* (1985), *A Rosen by Any Other Name* (1986), *North Shore Fish* (1987), *The Chopin Playoffs* (1987), *Park Your Car in Harvard Yard* (1987), *Sunday Runners in the Rain* (1987), *Year of the Duck* (1989), *The Widow's Blind Date* (1989), *Lebensraum* (1996)

Ironically, since the incident that led to *The Indian Wants the Bronx* occurred when Horowitz was studying drama in England,

this prolific New England playwright, who has written more than fifty plays, is little known in Britain. The very long-running *Line* demonstrates the fiercely competitive nature of the human condition as people struggle for places in a queue. *The Indian Wants the Bronx* is a study in the evolution of terrorism as two streetwise toughs confront a passive Indian at a bus stop. A teacher becomes frustrated and hostile as she explains basic English skills to a class where no one speaks the same language in *The Primary English Class*. Just below the surface in these plays, there lurks a menace that erupts in psychic violence. In *The Widow's Blind Date*, a young widow returns to her home town with the sole purpose of exacting justice on two of her high-school classmates who gang-raped her twenty years earlier. This is Horovitz's Grand Guignol revenge play, where frustration, isolation and anger coalesce into a climax fraught with mental, verbal and physical violence. *Lebensraum* is a dark satire based on the idea of Germany offering to receive six million Jews as reparation for the Holocaust.

TRY THESE:

For psychological and physical violence, ✶ ALBEE's *Who's Afraid of Virginia Woolf?*, ✶ DURANG's *Sister Mary Ignatius Explains It All for You*, ✶ MEDOFF's *When Ya Comin' Back Red Ryder*, ✶ PINTER's *The Birthday Party*; for revenge plays, ✶ DÜRRENMATT's *The Visit* and ✶ MASTROSIMONE's *Extremities*; ✶ IONESCO's *The Lesson*, ✶ RATTIGAN's *French Without Tears*, ✶ TOWNSEND's *Groping for Words* for other versions of language classes; ✶ C. P. TAYLOR's *Good* for the Holocaust.

HORSFIELD, Debbie [1955 –]
British dramatist

PLAYS INCLUDE:

Out on the Floor (1981), *Away From It All* (1982), *All You Deserve* (1983), *Red Devils* (1983, trilogy comprising *Red Devils*, *True Dare Kiss* and *Command or Promise*), *Touch and Go* (1984, now known as *Revelations*)

Although Manchester-born Horsfield has written plays on computer dating (*Touch and Go*), northern discos (*Out on the Floor*) and more youthful dilemmas (*All You Deserve*), her theatrical reputation rests on *Red Devils*, the saga of four female Manchester United supporters. The three plays have a compulsive drive (like good soap opera) as they follow the progress of four friends through early adulthood, work and personal crises, often conflict-ridden but held together by loyalty and a shared obsession for Manchester United football team – Horsfield's own particular passion. Michael Billington has even dubbed her the funniest woman dramatist since ✱SHELAGH DELANEY. Certainly, there is the same youthful energy, gritty turn of phrase and spiky humour, but Horsfield also reflects a quarter of a century in which feminism, unemployment, the increasing north–south divide, television and the consumerist society have changed perceptions. Horsfield's television career includes the series *Making Out*, *Cutting It* and *Sex, Chips and Rock 'n' Roll*, which she converted into a stage musical for the Royal Exchange in 2002.

TRY THESE:
✱DANIELS and ✱RAIF as other writers to emerge in the early 1980s; Victoria Wood's humour springs from the same northern roots; ✱MACDONALD for female adolescent badinage; ✱RUSSELL's *Educating Rita* seems like a forerunner to *Touch and Go* and his *Stags and Hens* exploits a disco setting, as does ✱GODBER's *Putting on the Ritz*; ✱PAGE's *Golden Girls* is a different look at young women, individually and in a group, at the competitive end of sport; ✱GEMS' *Dusa, Fish, Stas and Vi* for another young quartet coming to terms with womanhood; ✱DYER's *Rattle of a Simple Man* deals with a soccer fan from the north hitting the Big City; ✱TERSON's *Zigger-Zagger* is the definitive football supporters play; for an equivalent male trilogy, ✱BYRNE's *The Slab Boys*.

HORVÁTH, Ödön
Joseph von   [1901 – 38]
German-language dramatist

PLAYS INCLUDE:
Italienische Nacht (1931, *Italian Night*), *Geschichten aus dem Wiener Wald* (1931, *Tales from the Vienna Woods*), *Kasimir und Karoline* (1932, *Casimir and Caroline*), *Figaro Lässt sich Schieden* (1937, *Figaro Gets a Divorce*), *Don Juan Kommt aus dem Krieg*

(produced 1952, *Don Juan Comes Back from the War*), *Zür schönen Aussicht* (written 1926, performed 1969, adapted by Kenneth McLeish as *The Belle Vue*, 1996)

Horváth, like ✱AESCHYLUS and ✱MOLIÈRE, tends to be remembered anecdotally for the way he died; he was killed in the Champs Elysées when a tree struck by lightning fell on him, leaving several plays, novels and film scenarios unfinished. His plays were banned when the Nazis came to power, then neglected in Germany until the 1950s. He has been increasingly recognised as an important dramatist in Britain and the USA since the 1970s. His peculiar mixture of disdainful criticism of bourgeois capitalist greed and hypocrisy, sharp ironic observation of lower-middle-class stupidity, and melancholy resignation may stem partly from his background. He was born in Fiume (now Rijeka, but then a part of the Austro-Hungarian Empire) of an aristocratic Hungarian-speaking family and spent much of his life on the move – first because his father was a diplomat, then in search of artistic success, and finally in exile from the Nazis. *Tales from the Vienna Woods* is a hard and cynical picture of the lower middle classes, with a strong storyline; *Figaro Gets a Divorce* is set some years after *The Marriage of Figaro* and gets its effects by unexpectedly putting ✱BEAUMARCHAIS's characters into a detailed social context; *Don Juan Comes Back from the War* is a very sardonic play, showing Don Juan as a modern disillusioned war veteran.

✱CHRISTOPHER HAMPTON, who translated *Tales from the Vienna Woods* and *Don Juan* for National Theatre productions in 1977 and 1978, also anachronistically included him in *Tales from Hollywood* (1983) as part of the German community in exile; Horváth did in fact mean to join them towards the end of his life.

TRY THESE:
✱KROETZ for further development of the 'Volksstück', or plays dealing with working-class life; ✱BRECHT for contemporary attacks on the capitalist system, though Horváth tends to despair rather than recommending positive action; ✱CHEKHOV's *Platonov*, reworked and

retitled *Wild Honey* in ✴FRAYN's adaptation, was also known as *Don Juan in the Russian Manner*.

HOUGHTON, Stanley   [1881 – 1913]
British dramatist

PLAYS INCLUDE:
The Dear Departed (1908), *Independent Means* (1909), *The Younger Generation* (1910), *Hindle Wakes* (1912)

Part of the 'Manchester School' of playwrights, Houghton wrote all his successful plays for the Gaiety Theatre in Manchester, before dying untimely young. *Hindle Wakes*, the most controversial at the time and the most frequently revived, is the story of the independent-minded mill-hand Fanny Hawthorn, who is unrepentant after spending a weekend in Llandudno with the mill-owner's son, and turns down his offer of marriage. It is an effective mixture of the comic and the serious, with strong feminist overtones and a *Doll's House*-type ending that nowadays leaves us asking a number of awkward questions about contraception and her possibilities of future employment.

TRY THESE:
✴BRIGHOUSE for another 'Manchester School' playwright; Elizabeth Baker's *Chains*, Cecily Hamilton's *Diana of Dobson's* and Githa Sowerby's *Rutherford and Son* for women dramatists of the period; Allan Monkhouse's *Mary Broome* for a contemporary treatment of a similar situation to that in *Hindle Wakes*.

HOWE, Tina   [1937 –   ]
American dramatist

PLAYS INCLUDE:
The Nest (1969), *Birth and Afterbirth* (1973), *Museum* (1976), *The Art of Dining* (1979), *Painting Churches* (1983), *Coastal Disturbances* (1986), *Approaching Zanzibar* (1987), *Pride's Crossing* (1997), *Rembrandt's Gift* (2002)

Howe deserves to be much better known in Britain, where her work has seldom been staged professionally. She once said 'God help me if I ever write a realistic play', instead 'I take a familiar reality and lift it about six feet off the ground.' *Birth and Afterbirth*, which enraged feminists even more than men and non-feminists, is a hallucinatory, absurdist look at the ways in which a new birth affects a family. *Museum* has an art exhibit as its set. Praised for its wit, humour and wry view of modern art, the play has been described both as a medieval *theatrum mundi* and a contemporary comedy of manners. It is concerned with the artist's hunger to make art, and the viewer's hunger to consume art: literally, here, for the museum-goers destroy the exhibit. *The Art of Dining* is a more classic comedy of manners, a hilarious send-up of *haute cuisine* and its concomitant rituals. *Painting Churches* concerns Mags, a painter with a deep need for her staid, intimidating parents to recognise her talent. The writing is distinguished for close attention to the small but telling character detail, and for its ✴CHEKHOV like sympathics. *Coastal Disturbances* is a valentine about three generations of lovers on a beach in Nantucket. According to Howe, *Approaching Zanzibar* is about death, love, birth and rebirth. In *Pride's Crossing* the ninety year old heroine, a record-breaking cross-Channel swimmer in her youth, looks back over her life, while in *Rembrandt's Gift* a contemporary elderly couple are about to be evicted from their home when Rembrandt pops by for a visit.

TRY THESE:
Absurdists like ✴IONESCO and ✴PIRANDELLO; ✴FUGARD (see his *Road to Mecca*, another play about the formation of an artist), ✴AUGUST WILSON, ✴LANFORD WILSON for their breadth of emotional generosity; ✴LEONARD for treatments of the formation of an artist; ✴PHILIP BARRY, ✴GURNEY for ruefully comic views of the American upper class; ✴HARE's *Wrecked Eggs* for an Englishman's view of East Coast sensibilities and its companion piece *The Bay at Nice* for the uses of art; ✴REZA's *Art*, ✴WERTENBAKER's *Three Birds Alighting in a Field* for contrasting views on art as commodity; ✴BARKER's *Scenes from an Execution*, ✴DEAR's *The Art of Success* for the nexus between art and politics; ✴BARNES' *Leonardo's Last Supper* for an unexpected encounter between an artist and a family; ✴BUFFINI, ✴CHURCHILL's *Top Girls*, ✴ISITT, ✴WHITEHEAD for variations on mealtime.

HUGHES, Declan   [1963 –   ]
Irish dramatist

PLAYS INCLUDE:
I Can't Get Started (1990), *Digging for Fire*
(1991), *Love and a Bottle* (1991, from
✻FARQUHAR), *New Morning* (1993),
Halloween Night (1997), *Twenty Grand*
(1998), *Boomtown* (1999, with Pom Boyd
and Arthur Riordan), *Tartuffe* (2000, after
✻MOLIÈRE), *Shiver* (2003)

Hughes co-founded the Rough Magic Theatre
Company with Lynne Parker and continues to
work with them as an associate artist. In *I
Can't Get Started* he explores the relationship
between Dashiell Hammett and ✻LILLIAN
HELLMAN, paralleling his narrative of their
lives with a noirish detective story, a theme
that he takes up again in *Twenty Grand*. He
also engages with other writers in his
reworkings of ✻FARQUHAR and ✻MOLIÈRE;
his *Tartuffe* is set in a 1970s Dublin trying to
come to terms with the repercussions of
Vatican II. Although the typically Irish theme
of exile still runs through his work, much of it
is concerned with a contemporary Ireland of
graduates who have worked abroad, the
dotcom revolution and globalisation rather
than just the Celtic twilight. Reunions loom
large in *Digging for Fire*, *New Morning* and
Halloween Night as characters take stock of
their lives in the light of new revelations about
the past, but both *New Morning* and
Halloween Night also create a typically Irish
sense of the uncanny. The countryside in *New
Morning* may have been reduced to a place to
go camping in but the stranger who 'appears
as if from nowhere' is from an older tradition,
as is the isolated old holiday house in
Halloween Night where the guests end up
facing an uncertain fate after a series of
possibly supernatural episodes that have
exposed and tested them like the survivors in
Théodore Géricault's painting *The Raft of the
Medusa*. In *Shiver* the trials of the contemporary characters faced with downsizing and
the failure of dotcom start-ups are ultimately
contextualised by a story of a misguided nineteenth-century gold rush, which eventually
failed, leaving the former miners to return to
quarrying out defences against the sea.

TRY THESE:
✻BOLGER, ✻CARR, ✻SEBASTIAN BARRY, ✻FANNIN,
✻FRIEL, ✻MURPHY, ✻REID, ✻WALSH for other
contemporary Irish writers; ✻CHRISTIE for strange
events in isolated houses.

HUGHES, Dusty   [1947 –   ]
British dramatist

PLAYS INCLUDE:
Commitments (1980), *Heaven and Hell*
(1981), *Molière* (1982, from ✻BULGAKOV),
Bad Language (1983), *Philistines* (1985, from
✻GORKY), *Futurists* (1986), *Jenkins' Ear*
(1987), *Metropolis* (1989, book of the musical, from Fritz Lang), *Life with Mr Gopal*
(1990), *The Angelic Avengers* (1990, from
Karen Blixen's novel), *A Slip of the Tongue*
(1991), *Helpless* (2000)

Born in Lincolnshire and educated at
Cambridge, Hughes was once the theatre
editor of the London listings magazine *Time
Out* and the artistic director of the Bush
Theatre. Hughes came to attention with his
play about English Trotskyites, *Commitments*,
and consolidated his somewhat wry, acidic
point of view with the bitterly funny *Bad
Language*, about university disaffection
amongst the Cambridge ranks. *Futurists*, set
in a Petrograd café in 1921, charts, with
exhilarating theatricality, a literary movement
whose fate was contrastingly bleak. In the
process, Hughes explores the paradox that a
century ushered in by ✻CHEKHOV and
✻GORKY gave way to the Cheka and Stalin.
Jenkins' Ear, set in a 'small central American
country north of Nicaragua', was prosaic and
jumbled, the best of political intentions
notwithstanding. *Metropolis*, the musical for
which he co-wrote the libretto and lyrics with
American songwriter Joseph Brooks, fared no
better. *A Slip of the Tongue* is an attempt to
deal with the Velvet Revolution in
Czechoslovakia through the life of a dissident
writer, and *Helpless*, described by the
Independent as belonging to the 'left-wing
menopausal male moan-in' genre, attempted
to evaluate the trajectories of a generation
focused through the night of the Labour election victory in 1997

TRY THESE:
✱SIMON GRAY, ✱LUCIE for *Bad Language*-like depictions of Oxbridge; ✱NELSON's *Principia Scriptoriae*, ✱POMERANCE's *Foco Novo*, ✱PUIG's *Kiss of the Spider Woman* for Latin America; ✱HAMPTON's *Philanthropist*, ✱MAMET's *Oleanna*, ✱C. P. TAYLOR's *Allergy* for universities; ✱BRENTON and Tariq Ali's *Moscow Gold* for Russian history and artistic movement: ✱EDGAR for dissidents and ✱HAVEL for the real thing; ✱MAYAKOVSKY for the period of *Futurists*; ✱TREVOR GRIFFITHS' *The Party* for socialist angsts.

HUGHES, Holly   [1956 –]
American dramatist/actor

PLAYS INCLUDE:
The Well of Horniness (1984), *The Lady Dick* (1986), *Dress Suits to Hire* (1987), *World Without End* (1989), *Preaching to the Perverted* (2000)

Hailing from Saginaw, Michigan, Hughes, a pre-eminent lesbian dramatist and performance artist, made headlines in 1990 along with three other controversial artists, when she was denied a National Endowment for the Arts grant. Eventually defeated in the Supreme Court, she produced her response in her monologue *Preaching to the Perverted*. She became a playwright by accident, writing her first campy and overtly sexual romp, *The Well of Horniness*, as a challenge. She found her voice in *Dress Suits to Hire*, commissioned by lesbian actors Peggy Shaw and Lois Weaver. The work is quintessential 'Dyke Noir', exploring the darker side of the gay women's movement, in a brash and overt portrayal of lesbian seduction. One sister locks herself in their costume shop following her sibling's murder, and relives their lives together in an orgiastic fantasy of past, present and future. Using the inventory of the shop they dress up, strip down and change identity to heighten and prolong foreplay, seduction and fulfilment.

Hughes sometimes antagonises other lesbians and feminists because she refuses to present lesbian fairy tales where women come out, get it on and live happily ever after. She makes her women brash, and sometimes trashy, lesbian sex objects, and glories in reclaiming words like 'pussy', 'slut' and 'whore' that were thrown out with women's liberation.

TRY THESE:
For homosexual erotic plays, ✱GENET's *The Maids* and ✱KESSELMAN's *My Sister in This House*; for plays on lesbian themes, ✱CHAMBERS' *Last Summer at Blue Fish Cove* and ✱MARCUS's *The Killing of Sister George*; for personal monologues, ✱SPALDING GRAY; ✱ENSLER's *Vagina Monologues* for a feminist reclamation of language.

HUGHES, Langston   [1902 – 67]
American dramatist, poet and novelist

PLAYS INCLUDE:
Mulatto (1928), *Mule Bone* (1930, with Zora Neale Hurston), *Scottsboro Limited* (1932), *Don't You Want to be Free* (1936), *The Sun Do Move* (1942), *Street Scene* (1947, lyrics for musical), *The Barrier* (1949, opera), *Simply Heavenly* (1957, musical), *Soul Gone Home* (1959), *Black Nativity: A Gospel Song-Play* (1961)

One of the guiding lights of the Harlem renaissance, Hughes was in the vanguard of modern black American literature. Known primarily for his poetry, he also worked with theatres throughout his career. Hughes himself credited Paul Laurence Dunbar, Walt Whitman and Carl Sandburg as his literary models, but his writing was also clearly influenced by black folklore, dialect and music. He treated contemporary subjects in a timeless way, and the language of both his poetry and his plays is bluesy and melodic. His strengths were in characterisation – both of individuals and of societies – and in his glorious use of language. Hughes' best-known play, *Mulatto*, tells of a mulatto son's rejection by his white father, a Georgia plantation owner. In a violent confrontation, the son kills the father and then commits suicide. While the racial subject is important to the play, Hughes concentrates on the more universal issue of a father's denial of love for his son. In the 1930s, Hughes became politically radicalised. He served for two years as a reporter in Moscow, and was the only black American correspondent in the Spanish Civil War. During this period he wrote political activist plays, *Scottsboro Limited*, exploring the racial issues surrounding the rape trial of the 'Scottsboro Boys', and the agitprop piece *Don't You Want to be Free*. The Young Vic gave *Simply Heaven* its European premier in 2003.

TRY THESE:
Hughes worked with Kurt Weill on a musical version of ✷RICE's *Street Scene*; for a white Southern perspective on interracial relations, ✷GREEN's *In Abraham's Bosom*; ✷BARAKA's *Dutchman* and *Slave Ship* for bitter plays by a jazz-influenced poet; for black women's perspectives, ✷HANSBERRY's *A Raisin in the Sun* and ✷SHANGE's *for colored girls who have considered suicide when the rainbow is enuf*; ✷BOUCICAULT's *The Octoroon* for an early treatment of race issues in the USA; ✷WOLFE's *Spunk* is an adaptation of three short stories by Zora Neale Hurston.

HUNTER, N. C.
(Norman Charles)   [1908 – 71]
British dramatist

PLAYS INCLUDE:
All Rights Reserved (1935), *A Party for Christmas* (1938), *Waters of the Moon* (1951), *A Day by the Sea* (1953), *A Touch of the Sun* (1958), *The Tulip Tree* (1962)

Beginning as a writer of light comedies, Hunter turned to plays of atmosphere and character, such as *Waters of the Moon* and *A Day by the Sea*, which the H. M. Tennent management presented with star casts at the Theatre Royal, Haymarket. Hailed by some critics of the time as 'English ✷CHEKHOV', they do not seem quite so impressive today, although *Waters of the Moon* makes very occasional appearances.

TRY THESE:
✷BAGNOLD for another dramatist of the period; ✷CHRISTIE's *Ten Little Indians*, ✷O'NEILL's *The Iceman Cometh* and *Long Day's Journey into Night* for plays in which isolated groups learn home truths as in *Waters of the Moon*.

HUTCHINSON, Ron   [1946 –   ]
Irish dramatist

PLAYS INCLUDE:
Says I, Says He (1978), *Eejits* (1978), *Anchorman* (1978), *Christmas of a Nobody* (1979), *The Irish Play* (1980), *Risky City*

(1981), *Into Europe* (1981), *The Dillen* (1983), *Rat in the Skull* (1984), *Babbit: A Marriage* (1987; musical from Sinclair Lewis's novel), *Burning Issues* (2000), *Lags* (2001), *The Beau* (2001)

Hutchinson is best known in the theatre as the author of two plays about Britain and Ireland (*The Irish Play* and *Rat in the Skull*) but he has also written for television and film. Although Hutchinson's work includes the highly successful Stratford-set promenade production *The Dillen*, which used The Other Place and locations within Stratford, *Rat in the Skull* is probably the best of his plays. It's a fine study of the convoluted, almost incestuous, relationship between a Protestant RUC police officer and a Catholic terrorist suspect played out in a London police station populated with English policemen who want to keep their noses clean. Deceptively simple in its style, with many virtual monologues to the audience, the play never settles for an easy answer in its analysis of the interplay of personal and political motives and perspectives that lead to the intractability of the situation. Hutchinson's recent theatre work includes *Burning Issues*, an exploration of the relationship between a writer's life and opinions and his status as a writer; *Lags*, a play about theatre in prisons; and a play about Beau Brummell.

TRY THESE:
✷DE ANGELIS for an analogue of *The Dillen*; Hector MacMillan's *The Sash* for Orangemen in Glasgow; ✷FINNEGAN, ✷FRIEL, ✷MARIE JONES, ✷MCGUINNESS, ✷MORRISON, ✷MORNIN, ✷PARKER, ✷REID for contemporary Irish views of Northern Ireland; ✷BEHAN and ✷O'CASEY for earlier periods; ✷BARKER, ✷BRENTON, ✷RUDKIN offer perspectives from the mainland; G. F. Newman's *Operation Bad Apple* and ✷NIGEL WILLIAMS' *WCPC* for the police; ✷BENNETT's *Kafka's Dick* for biography and the artist; ✷ELIOT for a writer whose biography has become an issue.

HWANG, David Henry   [1957 –   ]
Asian-American dramatist

PLAYS INCLUDE:

F.O.B. (1980), *Dance and the Railroad* (1981), *Family Devotions* (1981), *The House of Sleeping Beauties* (1983), *The Sound of a Voice* (1983), *Rich Relations* (1986), *M. Butterfly* (1987), *Bondage* (1992), *Face Value* (1993), *Trying to Find Chinatown* (1996), *Golden Child* (1997)

A first-generation Asian-American from a white, suburban California neighbourhood, Hwang is fascinated by the crosscutting of Asian and American stereotypes and the conflicts that arise from assimilation into the mainstream. *F.O.B.*, an abbreviation of 'Fresh Off the Boat', confronts the assimilation question head-on. It is set in a restaurant in Chinatown, where its characters, all Chinese college-age immigrants, must deal with the problems of being a minority in America. Hwang exposes a ruthless caste system within the Chinese-American subculture, where social climbing means abandoning one's roots.

M. Butterfly, Hwang's most powerful and moving play to date, is loosely based on a true story of a French diplomat who falls in love with a Chinese actress, only to discover she is really a man. Set against the backdrops of the Peking Opera and Puccini's *Madame Butterfly*, it explores and explodes culturally biased stereotypes and their use to justify political and sexual exploitation. He has done something similar with his 2002 reworking of *Flower Drum Song*.

TRY THESE:

For exploding and mocking sexual stereotypes, ✴CHURCHILL's *Cloud Nine* and ✴ORTON's *What the Butler Saw*, ✴GOTANDA's *Yankee Dawg You Die* for American stereotyping of Asians; for problems of different ethnic groups, ✴KUREISHI's *Borderline*, ✴SOBOL's *The Ghetto*, ✴AUGUST WILSON's *Ma Rainey's Black Bottom*, ✴WOLFE's *The Colored Museum*; Robert Lepage's *The Dragon's Trilogy* for Chinese Canadians.

IBSEN, Henrik [1828 – 1906]
Norwegian dramatist

PLAYS INCLUDE:
Cataline (1850), *Lady Inger of Ostraat*
(1854), *The Feast at Solhaug* (1856), *The
Vikings at Helgeland* (1858), *Love's Comedy*
(1862), *The Pretenders* (1863), *Brand* (1866),
Peer Gynt (1867), *Emperor and Galilean*
(1873), *Pillars of Society* (1877), *A Doll's
House* (1879), *Ghosts* (1881), *An Enemy of the
People* (1882), *The Wild Duck* (1884),
Rosmersholm (1886), *The Lady from the Sea*
(1888), *Hedda Gabler* (1890), *The Master
Builder* (1892), *Little Eyolf* (1894), *John
Gabriel Borkman* (1896), *When We Dead
Awaken* (1899)

Ibsen's influence on modern drama has been
enormous. Rebecca West (who took her name
from the heroine of *Rosmersholm*) expresses
the feelings of many who felt the impact of the
first productions of Ibsen in London: 'Ibsen
converted me to the belief that it is ideas which
make the world go round.' Most of his early
plays were traditional historical dramas, very
much influenced by the German theatre of
Hebbel and ✱SCHILLER. They were unsuccessfully produced at the theatre in Bergen, where
Ibsen worked as an assistant to the director,
Ole Bull. After the theatre went bankrupt,
Ibsen moved to Oslo where his satirical verse
drama *Love's Comedy* was produced successfully. He travelled to Italy and Germany, living
for two years in Rome where he wrote *Brand*.
Never really intended for production it is often
performed in an abridged version because of
staging problems. However, it established
Ibsen's reputation in Norway and across
Europe and led to the awarding of a state
pension, which left him free from financial
worry and able to devote himself to writing.
He spent most of the rest of his life in Italy and
Germany. *Peer Gynt*, the last of Ibsen's verse
dramas, challenged traditional dramatic

forms, with its use of fairy tale, fantasy and
dream to investigate motivation and will
through a young man's quest.

From this point on Ibsen's plays were
written in prose, and attempted, as Ibsen
wrote to his publisher, 'the very much more
difficult art of writing the genuine, plain
language spoken in real life'. The plays that
follow *Peer Gynt* are the beginnings of Ibsen's
development of a naturalist drama and a
refusal of traditional forms of theatre. *Pillars
of Society*, *A Doll's House* and *Ghosts* mark a
decision to write about contemporary life:
they are claustrophobic studies of small-town
parochial life, and of the conflicts, hypocrisies
and destruction that families and small
groups inflict on one another. They begin to
develop a form of characterisation and action
in which the emphasis is not on action, but on
psychological complexity. In Ibsen's later
plays these dramatic techniques move close to
symbolism. *The Wild Duck* and *Hedda Gabler*
extend the symbolic elements that are already
apparent in *A Doll's House* and *Ghosts*, and in
Rosmersholm he moved to a thoroughly
psychological drama.

While Ibsen is seen as the great Naturalist
dramatist, Ibsen himself was careful to distin-
guish his work from Zola's Naturalism, and
once said: 'Zola descends into the sewer to
bathe in it, I to cleanse it', a salutary warning
to anyone trying to tease out the complexities
and nuances of dramatic forms.

Productions of the plays before *Peer Gynt*
are rare but *A Doll's House* and *Hedda Gabler*
are regularly revived as star vehicles with
feminist overtones, *Ghosts* has taken on a new
life in the light of both AIDS and contemporary debates about euthanasia, and the other
late plays make fairly regular appearances.

A Doll's House
A Doll's House is the study of the marriage of
Nora and Torvald. In the first act, Nora is

Peer Gynt by Henrik Ibsen, in a version by Frank McGuinness, directed by Conall Morrison, National Theatre, 2000. Chiwetel Ejiofor, Patrick O'Kane, Joseph Marcell. (Colin Willoughby/ArenaPAL)

childlike, singing and taking pleasure in domesticity and her child. Her husband refers to her as a 'skylark', a 'squirrel', but the charm of their relationship takes on an uneasy edge as Nora has to beg for money from him, and her economic dependency becomes brutally clear. Nora attempts to enter into an economic transaction on her own, as she confides to her friend, the dying Dr Rank. But the moneylender blackmails her, and she comes to recognise her own dependence and gullibility. She dances an impassioned tarantella, an expression of her as yet unspoken rage and frustration. In the final scene of the play, Nora confronts Torvald with her own realisation that she has moved from her father's doll's house into yet another, and that she must leave both him and her child to find her own independence. The play ends with the door slamming behind her.

A Doll's House was greeted with shock on its first production: both its style and subject matter were seen as radical and subversive. The play's form was technically innovative, in its use of contemporary and simple language and dress, and it became a topic of international debate. Pamphlets and books were written about it, sermons given and public debates held about it, and the text sold out within a month of its first printing. Feminism was a central issue in Norway at the time, and for Ibsen himself; his wife, Susannah, was an outspoken feminist, and the Norwegian novelist Camilla Collett had taken him to task about the representation of women in his earlier plays. The play was based on an actual incident, but unlike Nora who boldly leaves the 'doll's house', the real woman ended her life in an asylum for the insane. In the notes for the play Ibsen writes: 'There are two kinds of moral laws, two kinds of conscience; one for men and one quite different for women. In practical life, woman is judged by masculine law, as though she weren't a woman but a man. A woman cannot be herself in modern society. It is an exclusively male society, with laws made by men.' According to one critic: 'With the slamming of the door behind Nora, the theatres of Europe woke up.' The play is still often revived since its themes still remain all too pertinent.

TRY THESE:
Ibsen powerfully influenced ✱SHAW, who wrote a defence of him in *The Quintessence of Ibsenism*; ✱STRINDBERG, although he would have denied it, was much influenced by Ibsen; ✱HAMPTON was inspired by Ibsen's studies of gender relations to write *Treats*; ✱OSBORNE's *Look Back in Anger* could be regarded as a reworking of *A Doll's House*; ✱DANIELS' *Ripen Our Darkness* is a modern-day version of the rebellious wife, striking out for independence; ✱RHONE's *Two Can Play* goes two-thirds of the way down the line only to cop out at the end; ✱FREISTADT's *Woman with a Shovel* and ✱RAME's *A Woman Alone* as studies of a woman pushed to extremes; images of women striving for independence run deep in much of women's writing, from ✱DELANEY to ✱DE ANGELIS; Elizabeth Robins' *Votes for Women*, a fine 'personal is political' play from 1907.

IKOLI, Tunde   [1955 –   ]
British dramatist

PLAYS INCLUDE:
Short Sleeves in Summer (1974), *On the Out* (1977), *Scrape Off the Black* (1977), *Sink or Swim* (1981), *Wall of Blue* (1982, part of *Breach of the Peace*), *Sleeping Policemen* (1983, with ✱HOWARD BRENTON), *Duckin'n'Divin'* (1984), *Week In Week Out* (1985), *Soul Night* (1985), *The Lower Depths* (1986, from ✱GORKY), *Please and Thank You* (1986; as a double bill with *Soul Night* under the title *Banged Up*)

One of Britain's leading black dramatists in the 1980s, Ikoli had a long and fruitful relationship with Foco Novo, whose artistic director Roland Rees directed many of his works. Ikoli, born in the East End to a Nigerian father and a Cornish mother, was encouraged to involve himself in drama by a social worker, wrote and co-directed *Tunde's Film* at the age of eighteen, and became a professional writer. His non-Caribbean background may help Ikoli to look beyond the stereotypes of black writing in Britain, to investigate the realities of survival in a world which is increasingly hostile to those who have been identified as losers, be they black or white. Perhaps this comes over most clearly in *Please and Thank You*, where a nervous, newly appointed, black, well-educated social worker finds his first client, a white, poorly educated woman, about to put her head in the oven, and in *The Lower Depths*, where his long admiration of *GORKY is put to use to show the persistence of the attitudes and situations of the original in the new/old world of Thatcherism. Ikoli's collaboration with *BRENTON on *Sleeping Policemen* was highly unusual since, after a workshop period, each wrote his own play and they were then intercut to form what Michael Billington called 'a radicalised, phantasmagoric *Under Milk Wood*'.

TRY THESE:
The brothers' reunion in *Scrape Off the Black* has been compared to *O'NEILL's *Long Day's Journey Into Night*; *MARCHANT's *Lazy Days Ltd* and *PHILLIPS' *Strange Fruit* also fiercely centre on two brothers; *MATURA is another black dramatist to rework the classics; *KAY, *PINNOCK, *RUDET are among a newer generation of black women dramatists; *CARTWRIGHT's *Road* was also seen as an *Under Milk Wood* for the 1980s.

INGE, William   [1913 – 73]
American dramatist

PLAYS INCLUDE:
Come Back Little Sheba (1950), *Picnic* (1953), *Bus Stop* (1955), *The Dark at the Top of the Stairs* (1957), *A Loss of Roses* (1959), *Natural Affection* (1962), *Where's Daddy?* (1966), *Summer Brave* (1973)

The son of a travelling salesman, Inge had his heyday in the 1950s when he wrote four Broadway hits back to back, several of which were made into well-known films, particularly *Bus Stop*, with Marilyn Monroe. Chronicles of small-town America, Inge's plays can seem dated today in their rather obvious symbolism and bald Freudian psychology, but he can paint a poignant image of desolation – as in *Come Back Little Sheba*, in which the lost dog Sheba functions as an image of the child the central couple, Doc and Lola Delaney, will never have. A homosexual, Inge wrote often about sexual magnetism, comically, in *Bus Stop*, between a Montana braggart and a nightclub singer,

and, more seriously, in *Picnic*, in which the sexually attractive drifter Hal galvanises a Kansas community. The film *Splendor in the Grass* (1961) features Inge in a bit part as a minister.

TRY THESE:
*TENNESSEE WILLIAMS, a friend of Inge's, for small-town despair and dashed hopes; *MEDOFF, *NEMETH for more recent plays set off the American beaten track; *ALBEE's *Who's Afraid of Virginia Woolf?* for childlessness.

INNAURATO, Albert   [1948 –   ]
American dramatist

PLAYS INCLUDE:
Urlicht (1971), *I Don't Generally Like Poetry But Have You Read 'Trees'* (1972, with *CHRISTOPHER DURANG), *The Transfiguration of Benno Blimpie* (1973), *The Mitzi Gaynor Story, or, Gyp* (1973, with *CHRISTOPHER DURANG), *The Idiots Karamazov* (1974, with *CHRISTOPHER DURANG), *Gemini* (1976), *Earth Worms* (1977), *Ulysses in Traction* (1977), *Passione* (1980), *Coming of Age in SoHo* (1985), *Magda and Callas* (1988), *Gus and Al* (1988), *Herself as Lust* (1991)

Is he a South Philadelphian *SHAW, as one New York critic once suggested, or a voyeur with a gleeful interest in the grotesque? Whatever one's individual slant, opinions on Innaurato are unlikely to be neutral, since his emotional, Italianate writing – Christopher Durang meets Lina Wertmuller – tends to elicit equally emotional responses. At his best, his plays, and their images, are frighteningly immediate and powerful, as in his early *The Transfiguration of Benno Blimpie*, in which the obese, unattractive Benno gorges himself to death. Food is also central to his greatest success, *Gemini*, which lasted four years on Broadway. Set on the twenty-first birthday of a sexually and socially confused Harvard undergraduate, the comedy is loud, rude and psychologically insightful, in Innaurato's typical blend. His follow-up Broadway show, *Passione*, was better on character than on overall concept (a circus fat lady's diatribe against the grapefruit diet still reverberates), a problem that also beset *Coming of Age in*

SoHo. *Magda and Callas* had much of the histrionic loopiness of *Gemini* (as would befit a play about a declining diva), but many critics found it paled in comparison with most of Innaurato's other work. Innaurato took on those same reviewers in *Gus and Al*. Al is Innaurato himself, pained by bad notices, who travels back to *fin-de-siècle* Vienna to meet and commiserate with another troubled artist, Gustav Mahler.

TRY THESE:

✽ KAUFMAN and Hart for great scenes of familial hurlyburly; ✽ Fierstein for gay dilemmas treated with an absence of hand-wringing; ✽ DE FILIPPO's *Saturday, Sunday, Monday* and ✽ HOWE's *The Art of Dining* for other scenes of gastronomic mayhem.

IONESCO, Eugène   [1912 – 90]
French dramatist, born in Rumania

PLAYS INCLUDE:

La cantatrice chauve (1950, *The Bald Prima Donna* or *The Bald Soprano*), *La Leçon* (1951, *The Lesson*), *Les Chaises* (1952, *The Chairs*), *Victimes du devoir* (1953, *Victims of Duty*), *Amédée ou comment s'en débarasser* (1954, *Amédée or How to Get Rid of It*), *L'Impromptu de l'Alma ou Le caméléon du berger* (1956, *Improvisation* or *The Shepherd's Chameleon*), *Le nouveau locataire* (1957, *The New Tenant*), *Tueur sans gages* (1959, *The Killer*), *Rhinocéros* (1960, *Rhinoceros*), *Le roi se meurt* (1962, *Exit the King*), *La soif et la faim* (1966, *Hunger and Thirst*), *Macbett* (1966), *Voyages chez les morts* (1982, *Journey Among the Dead*)

Ionesco was born in Rumania, spent his childhood in France and his student days in Bucharest, and then settled in Paris in his twenties; this may have led to some of his questioning of identity. His short (and probably best) plays, *The Bald Prima Donna*, *The Lesson* and *The Chairs*, became popular all over the world in the 1950s, but as he became more acceptable to the establishment his plays grew longer and lost some of their power to please and shock. *The Bald Prima Donna* epitomises the 'Theatre of the Absurd' in that it tries to reject all established theatrical conventions: it has no linear plot, proceeding instead by a series of disparate 'ten-minute takes'; its characters are interchangeable (indeed at the end of the play the Martins begin it again with the Smiths' dialogue) and the attempts at communication gradually disintegrate from cliché to reworded proverb to meaningless syllables. It is less nightmarish than *The Lesson* or *The Chairs*, but it has considerable staying power.

Ionesco wrote a certain amount of dramatic theory, besides two plays about the act of playwriting, and in 1958 he engaged in a lively controversy with Kenneth Tynan, about the necessity for plays to be rooted in reality and to engage with society. Ionesco declared himself against (and free from) any political ideology: 'No political system can deliver us from the pain of living, from our fear of death, our thirst for the absolute.'

Ionesco's combination of inexhaustible and often hilarious linguistic invention with brooding despair in the face of death and contingency still has a good deal of force. What remains in the memory is a number of highly theatrical images; the rhinoceros, typifying the thick-skinned man of immovable conviction; the vast dead body in the next room haunting the pair in *Amédée*, that may or may not symbolise their former love; the girl killed by the word 'knife' in *The Lesson*; the stage filled with expectant empty chairs, addressed in vain by a dumb orator, in *The Chairs*; and the man in a bare room in *The New Tenant*, gradually engulfed by furniture, and the final turning off of the light – a simple but nightmarish metaphor for life.

Although Théâtre de Complicité achieved a huge success with *The Chairs* in the late 1990s, Ionesco is now mainly produced by fringe and student groups in Britain rather than professional companies. Ionesco himself was last seen in London at Riverside Studios in 1983 in one of the strangest productions ever put on the London stage – Simone Benmussa's production (in French) of Virginia Woolf's *Freshwater*, a private but quite funny Bloomsbury joke, in which he played Alfred Lord Tennyson, his wife was the maid, Nathalie Sarraute the butler, and ✽ SNOO WILSON a porpoise.

TRY THESE:

✶STOPPARD, who borrowed the device of the clock that struck at random from *The Bald Prima Donna*, and used it in *Travesties*; ✶SIMPSON for verbal invention and logical paradoxes, though without ¨the desperation; ✶COCTEAU's film *Le Testament d'Orphée (The Testament of Orpheus)* for a similar retrospective to *Journey Among the Dead*; ✶JARRY and Boris Vian for further adventures into the 'Theatre of the Absurd'.

ISHERWOOD, Christopher

See AUDEN, W. H.

ISITT, Debbie   [1966 –]
British director/dramatist

PLAYS INCLUDE:

Gangsters (1988), *Punch and Judy: The Real Story* (1989), *Valentino* (1990), *Femme Fatale* (1990), *Matilda Liar!* (1994), *Nasty Neighbours* (1995), *The Woman Who Cooked Her Husband* (1991), *You Never Know Who's Out There* (1992)

Isitt founded the award-winning touring theatre company Snarling Beasties in 1986. Although she is establishing a significant reputation as a screenwriter, she is probably best known to theatregoers for *Nasty Neighbours* and *The Woman Who Cooked Her Husband*, which was revived in the West End in 2002. *Nasty Neighbours*, which is summed up quite well by its title, was staged simultaneously by many companies that belong to the Little Theatre Guild of Great Britain under the British Telecom BT Biennial scheme. *The Woman Who Cooked Her Husband* is also well summed up by its title but the interest is in how it all came to happen. The revival pleased audiences rather more than (male) critics who declared that feminism had moved on and it was all too caricatured and cartoon-like.

TRY THESE:

✶AYCKBOURN, ✶BUFFINI, ✶WHITEHEAD for dinner parties from hell; ✶GODBER as another BT Biennial dramatist; ✶CHURCHILL, ✶DANIELS, ✶WERTENBAKER for other versions of feminism.

JARRY, Alfred [1873 – 1907]
French dramatist

PLAYS INCLUDE:
Ubu Roi (1896, *King Ubu*), *Ubu Enchaîné* (1900, *Ubu in Chains*), *Ubu sur le Butte* (*Ubu on the Butte*, published 1906), *Ubu Cocu* (*Ubu the Cuckold*, published 1944)

For a play that ran for only two nights when it first appeared, and could barely be heard at the first of these performances, *King Ubu* has had a considerable after-life. Jarry's first version was written with other school friends as a puppet play when he was fifteen, satirising an unpopular physics master, who then became a caricature of the greedy and cowardly French bourgeoisie. It shows a schoolboy's cruelty, love of lavatory jokes, and parody of ✳SHAKESPEARE, French Romantic drama, and Rabelais, besides a joyous taste for inventing words. When staged at the Théâtre de l'Oeuvre in 1896, it almost caused a riot, and it has been popular ever since – the Surrealists loved it, Apollinaire and ✳IONESCO acknowledged its influence, and someone is always putting it on again, with varying emphases.

TRY THESE:
Apollinaire's Surrealist *Breasts of Tiresias*; for word-play and subversive invention, ✳CAMPBELL, ✳CHURCHILL, particularly *The Skriker*, ✳IONESCO, ✳KOPIT, ✳SIMPSON, ✳STOPPARD; Paul Zaloom for mime, clowning and puppetry.

JEFFREYS, Stephen [1950 –]
British dramatist

PLAYS INCLUDE:
Like Dolls or Angels (1977), *Mobile 4* (1978), *Year of the Open Fist* (1979), *The Vigilante Trail* (1979), *Jubilee Too* (1980), *Imagine* (1981), *Peer Gynt* (1981), *Clearing House* (1982), *Hard Times* (1982, from Dickens), *Carmen* (1984), *Futures* (1984), *Returning Fire* (1985), *Valued Friends* (1989), *The Clink* (1990), *A Going Concern* (1993), *The Libertine* (1995), *I Just Stopped By to See the Man* (2000)

Jeffreys' *Like Dolls or Angels* won the Best New Play award at the *Sunday Times* National Student Drama Festival in 1977. An apprenticeship with Pocket Theatre, Cumbria, and Paines Plough paid off with the Hampstead Theatre hit, *Valued Friends*, which won him the *Evening Standard's* Most Promising Playwright award. In this subtle comedy, set during the London property boom of the 1980s, four friends who have been renting a flat together since student days succumb to the temptation to buy it at a knockdown price, trading their caring 1970s values for Thatcherite greed, and their communal harmony for individualist division. Jeffreys does not, however, withdraw sympathy from his characters, who emerge regenerated from their collision with changing times. Jeffreys is never afraid to seek contemporary parallels in the past or in other cultures and the result is often both comic and instructive. *The Clink*, an ambitious political satire ostensibly set in the economic gloom of sixteenth-century Merrie England, follows the skulduggery in the corridors of power surrounding the succession to the Virgin Queen, while *A Going Concern* also tackles intergenerational rivalries for control of the family billiards table business. *The Libertine* dramatises the life of the Restoration Earl of Rochester and his love for the actress Elizabeth Barry and was first presented in tandem with ✳ETHEREGE's Man of Mode, whose hero Dorimant is supposed to be based on Rochester. *I Just Stopped By* is about the ways in which white singers have exploited the blues and the complex interactions when a white singer attempts to bring back a legendary black artist from an obscurity that partly reflects his desire to protect his daughter who has been a political activist.

TRY THESE:
Jeffreys adapted Richard Brome's *A Jovial Crew* for the RSC in 1992; ✱LUCIE's *Fashion*, ✱HARE's *Secret Rapture* for 1980s state-of-the-nation plays; ✱CRIMP's *Dealing with Clair* and Stephen Fagan's *The Hard Shoulder* for more property-related issues; ✱GREENBERG for an American equivalent. ✱DE ANGELIS (see also *Playhouse Creatures*) and ✱WERTENBAKER have written plays that were originally paired with Max Stafford-Clark productions of, respectively, ✱GOLDSMITH's *She Stoops to Conquer* and ✱FARQUHAR's *The Recruiting Officer*; ✱AYCKBOURN's *A Small Family Business* for similar themes to *A Going Concern*; ✱FAGON's *Four Hundred Pounds* involves a game of billiards.

JELLICOE, (Patricia) Ann   [1927 –   ]
British dramatist, director and teacher

PLAYS INCLUDE:
The Sport of My Mad Mother (1958), *The Knack* (1961), *Shelley; or, The Idealist* (1965), *The Rising Generation* (1967), *The Giveaway* (1968), *You'll Never Guess* (1973), *The Reckoning* (1978), *The Tide* (1980)

From 1979, Jellicoe became involved in putting on plays with the people of Lyme Regis, Dorset, and channelled her energies into community theatre with casts of up to 150 in promenade performances and many more in support activities. Jellicoe has been the catalyst for their development, often as director and dramatist, through the Colway Theatre Trust, which she helped found. Her style of working has been widely copied and she is now consulted internationally on such projects.

Before that she had been at the forefront of developments in theatre since her early involvement with the Royal Court Writers Group. *The Sport of My Mad Mother* is a fantasy about a group of teddy boys led by a sort of earth mother. Based on action, not text, and exploiting the medium of theatre as her work has continued to do, it baffled audiences who had recently found *Look Back in Anger* revolutionary. Perhaps the most extreme example of this tendency is *The*

Rising Generation, a commission for the Girl Guides, in which a great mother figure urges the girls to reject men, but the youngsters finally opt for cooperation and set off together to colonise outer space. Unsurprisingly, the Girl Guides did not put it on, although a truncated version was eventually staged in 1967. *The Knack*, about the relationships and shifting power balances between a woman and three men sharing a house, could seem flat and confusing on the page but sparkles in performance and was a major success. *Shelley*, a documentary of the poet's life from university to his death, showed a more conventional approach.

TRY THESE:
✱BARKER, ✱EDGAR, ✱CHARLES WOOD for dramatists commissioned by Jellicoe to write community plays; ✱ARDEN's *Serjeant Musgrave's Dance*, ✱OSBORNE's *Look Back in Anger*, ✱WESKER's *Trilogy* for contrasting contemporary treatments of women with men by male writers; ✱BECKETT, ✱PINTER for contemporary break-up of traditional forms.

JENKIN, Len   [1941 –   ]
American dramatist

PLAYS INCLUDE:
Limbo Tales (1980), *Dark Ride* (1981), *My Uncle Sam* (1983), *Five of Us* (1983), *A Country Doctor* (1986, from Kafka), *A Soldier's Tale* (1986, with Paul Magid), *American Notes* (1988), *Pilgrims of the Night* (1991), *Ramona Quimby* (1992, from Beverly Cleary), *Like I Say* (1998)

Virtually unknown in Britain, although *Like I Say* had a rehearsed reading at the Royal Court in 1998, Jenkin is not a playwright who caters to the interests of matinee audiences of senior citizens or those evening performances for tired businessmen. Consistency in plotting or character development has little interest for him, and his plays are frequently disorienting. Given to expressing his feelings and aspirations through nocturnal journeys into mythic environments, Jenkin has created a following that enjoys discovering the shrewd observations he implants in his abstract approach to theatre.

TRY THESE:
* GLASPELL's *Trifles* for piecing together a narrative; * PINTER for elliptical treatment of experience; * IONESCO for opacity and surprise.

JESURUN, John   [1951 –   ]
American artist, dramatist, director and screenwriter

PLAYS INCLUDE:
Chang in a Void Moon (1982), *Red House* (1984), *Number Minus One* (1984), *Dog's Eye View* (1984), *Changes in a Void* (1985), *Deep Sleep* (1986), *White Water* (1986), *Black Maria* (1987), *Sunspot* (1989), *Imperial Motel* (*Faust*) (1997), *The End of Cinematics* (2002)

A Hispanic-American playwright, Jesurun creates multimedia events, with non-linear plot structures, telescopic wordplay and rapidly kaleidoscoping images; his works always include film and video segments, and are designed to reach out to the 'television generation'. His multifocus performance style both seduces and disorients with its multiple moving arenas of simultaneous action. Knowing it is impossible to take in the whole theatre piece, Jesurun wants the audience members to participate in the play by selecting their own points of focus.

TRY THESE:
For the effect of film on our self-image, * SHEPARD's *Angel City*; for minimalist structure, * BECKETT's *Play* and *Not I*; for multifocused performance, Richard Schechner, * BOGART and Martha Clarke's *Endangered Species*; for the use of electronic images in live performance, Laurie Anderson and the Wooster Group; * BRENTON's *Hess is Dead* for onstage televisions; * PIRANDELLO's *Six Characters* for argument between 'actors' and 'characters'.

JOHN, Errol   [1924 – 88]
Trinidadian actor and dramatist

PLAYS INCLUDE:
Moon on a Rainbow Shawl (1956)

John's acting roles include Othello at the Old Vic in 1962, but he is best known for his play *Moon on a Rainbow Shawl*. Winner of the 1956 *Observer* Play Competition, it was produced at the Royal Court in 1958 and revived in 2003 by the Eclipse Company set up to tour middle-scale venues with work by black artists. The play shows a trolley-bus driver abandoning the girl he has made pregnant in his determination to escape from a realistically presented Caribbean backyard life surrounded by prostitution, petty thieving and poverty.

TRY THESE:
* DELANEY's *A Taste of Honey* for a play of the same period dealing with similar issues to *Moon on a Rainbow Shawl*; * WATERHOUSE and Willis Hall's *Billy Liar* for contemporary escapism; for a 1980s view of the East End, * ALRAWI's *A Colder Climate*; for other treatments of strain put onto personal relationships through poverty and racism, * ABBENSETTS, * IKOLI, * MATURA, * PHILLIPS, * RECKORD.

JOHNSON, Catherine   [1957 –   ]
British dramatist and screenwriter

PLAYS INCLUDE:
Boys Mean Business (1989), *Dead Sheep* (1991), *Shang-a-Lang* (1998), *Mamma Mia* (1999, book of the Abba musical), *Little Baby Nothing* (2003)

Johnson's reputation was established with her early work at London's Bush Theatre, culminating in *Shang-a-Lang* in which three women celebrate a fortieth birthday by going to Butlins for a Glam Rock tribute. The occasion inevitably creates an opportunity for stocktaking, truth-telling and reprising youthful fantasies. Presumably it was the link with tribute bands that meant Johnson was entrusted with the book of the Abba musical.

TRY THESE:
* RUSSELL's *Shirley Valentine* for midlife stocktaking; * ORTON's *The Erpingham Camp* for another view of a holiday camp.

JOHNSON, Terry   [1955–   ]
British dramatist and director

PLAYS INCLUDE:
Days Here So Dark (1981), *Insignificance* (1982), *Unsuitable for Adults* (1984), *Cries*

from the Mammal House (1984), *Tuesday's Child* (1986, with Kate Lock), *Imagine Drowning* (1991), *Hysteria* (1993), *Dead Funny* (1994), *The London Cuckolds* (1998, from Edward Ravenscroft), *Cleo, Camping, Emmanuelle and Dick* (1999), *The Graduate* (2000, from Charles Webb), *Hitchcock Blonde* (2003)

A John Whiting Award winner, Johnson has established himself as a major interpreter of the ways that we use culture to define ourselves, reflect ourselves and escape from ourselves. His early work includes the somewhat portentous Viking/Scottish *Days Here So Dark*, and *Tuesday's Child*, which deals with the complications that arise following the discovery of an Irish virgin's apparently immaculate pregnancy. *Cries from the Mammal House* is a dramatically powerful meditation on themes of conservation, religious and political enlightenment, family life and child abuse which deserves to be more widely staged. *Insignificance* is a heady mix of issues and characters as Marilyn Monroe and Einstein demonstrate the theory of relativity with interruptions from Joe DiMaggio and Senator McCarthy. The brave, tender, awkward *Imagine Drowning* found him making new-age and global warnings – and meditating again on personal violence, 'the dark nugget' within, and the challenge of disability. *Hysteria* confronts the dying Freud with questions about why he changed his theories about the origins of mental disorder in ways that resemble a sex farce mediated through an encounter with Salvador Dali who did actually visit him in the last months of his life. *Dead Funny* deals with a group of men devoted to the comedians Benny Hill and Frankie Howerd and failing to come to terms with their own human frailties. *Cleo, Camping Emmanuelle and Dick* pursues similar themes, this time through the relationships of some of the stars of the *Carry On* films.

Witty, imaginatively concerned with important questions about natural and personal power and responsibility, the creation of myth and the gap between public and private personas, Johnson's plays are impressively willing to address the big themes. His readiness to tackle the wider canvas makes his a refreshing talent in a climate increasingly dominated by miniaturists, and he combines the comic with astringent insight in ways that few can equal.

TRY THESE:
✱ BRECHT's *Galileo* and ✱ BRENTON's *The Genius* deal with the responsibilities of scientists; ✱ DÜRRENMATT's *The Physicists* takes a surreal look at scientists; ✱ CHURCHILL's *Top Girls* brings together a wide group of disparate characters out of historical time; ✱ STOPPARD's *Hapgood* juggles with theories of physics, espionage and the nature of responsibility; ✱ MILLER's *After the Fall* has echoes of Marilyn Monroe; ✱ LEVY's *Pax* and *Clam* also give global warnings; Anna Furse's *Augustine (Big Hysteria)*, ✱ PETER SHAFFER, ✱ WRIGHT for psychologists/psychiatrists; Johnson is also a skilled director (including the television adaptation of ✱ AYCKBOURN's *Way Upstream*) and adapter; compare his version of *The Graduate* with ✱ HARE's *The Blue Room* for excited comment on star actresses' nudity; John Fisher's *Jus' Like That* for another British comedy great, Tommy Cooper; Sean Foley and Hamish McColl's *The Play What I Wrote* for Morecambe and Wise.

JONES, Charlotte   [1968 –   ]
British dramatist

PLAYS INCLUDE:
Airswimming (1997), *Martha, Josie and the Chinese Elvis* (1998), *In Flame* (1999), *Humble Boy* (2001)

Jones' breakthrough came with the success of *Humble Boy* at the National Theatre and subsequently in the West End. In *Airswimming* she had dealt with the scandal of women who were incarcerated in lunatic asylums in the 1920s for having illegitimate babies and then forgotten about. *Martha, Josie and the Chinese Elvis* is set around a birthday party for which a Chinese Elvis impersonator has been hired, while *In Flame* also draws on two different historical periods to consider how far women's situation has actually changed since the early twentieth century. *Humble Boy* draws on the scientific quest for a unified field theory and on bee-keeping to suggest that families are a microcosm of the universe that need some kind of escape from

Humble Boy by Charlotte Jones, directed by John Caird, National Theatre, 2001. Diana Rigg as Flora, Simon Russell Beale as Felix. (Pete Jones/ArenaPAL)

chaos and that the hive needs to be properly organised. ✱MARK RAVENHILL has commented that, with its 'middle-class country garden . . . , fine blend of wit and pathos with a smattering of intellectual ideas and great parts for leading actors', *Humble Boy* has 'all the elements of a rather old-fashioned commercial play'.

TRY THESE:

Humble Boy has been seen as a rewrite of ✱SHAKESPEARE's *Hamlet* (Jones' husband was in a production of the play at the National and gave the script to Simon Russell Beale who eventually played the lead); ✱BAGNOLD, ✱HUNTER for the kind of plays Ravenhill was talking about; the use of science in *Humble Boy* drew comparisons with ✱FRAYN's *Copenhagen* and ✱STOPPARD's *Arcadia*, but see also ✱BRENTON's *The Genius*.

JONES, Marie   [1949 –   ]
Northern Irish dramatist

PLAYS INCLUDE:

Lay Up Your Ends (1983), *Oul Delf and False Teeth* (1984), *Now You're Talkin* (1985), *Gold on the Streets* (1986), *Girls in the Big Picture* (1986), *Somewhere Over the Balcony* (1987), *Weddings, Wee'ins and Wakes* (1989), *The Hamster Wheel* (1990), *The Blind Fiddler of Glendaugh* (1990), *A Night in November* (1994, as *A Night to Remember* 1998), *Women on the Verge of HRT* (1996), *Stones in His Pockets* (1996), *Ruby* (2000)

Belfast-born, Jones founded Charabanc, the Belfast touring company, with four other actresses to provide themselves with employment after months of being unemployed, and to give themselves more challenging and interesting work than they were being offered when jobs did come their way. Jones became the company's main writer and went on to establish a solo reputation. Charabanc shows, drawing on the history of the province, involved intensive research and hours of interviews that Jones then turned into scripts. Most productions were naturalistic in form, though *Somewhere Over the Balcony* experimented with a more surrealistic treatment. Subjects ranged from the 1911 Belfast mill girls' strike through the disillusionment with Labour politics since World War II, the complexities of reconciliation between Protestant and Catholic, emigration, rural social patterns and pressures, and the effects of the British Army presence and institutionalised violence on Catholic residents in a Belfast high-rise block. *The Hamster Wheel*, by contrast, took a look at the more general but no less tortuous problems involved in dealing with disability. *A Night to Remember* is a one-man show about football and sectarianism while *Women on the Verge of HRT* covers similar territory to ✱WILLY RUSSELL's *Shirley Valentine* from an Irish perspective. In *Ruby* Jones examines the career of the Belfast-born 1950s singing star Ruby Murray. Her biggest hit to date has been *Stones in His Pockets*, a two-hander that demands its cast change identities in a kaleidoscopic tale of the interaction between members of a rural community and a visiting film crew. It offers many comic opportunities for scrutinising both the sheer madness of filmmaking and the ways in which images of Ireland are crafted for the benefits of film, but it also explores the corrosive effects of immersion in celluloid fantasies and the role of the audience in validating the packaging of fantasy.

TRY THESE:

For other playwrights writing on the subject of Northern Ireland, ✱DEVLIN, ✱FINNEGAN, ✱HUTCHINSON, ✱KILROY, ✱MCGUINNESS, ✱MORNIN ✱REID, ✱MCCAFFERTY, ✱GARY MITCHELL; for the vernacular and exploration of a Catholic rural community, ✱FRIEL's *Translations* and *Dancing at Lughnasa*; ✱SYNGE's *Playboy of the Western World*; ✱GEMS for other female stars; for filmmaking, ✱DARKE's *The Oven Glove Murders*, ✱KAUFMAN and Hart, ✱ODETS, ✱RABE's *Hurlyburly*, ✱CHARLES WOOD.

Stones in His Pockets by Marie Jones, directed by Ian McElhinney, Lyric Theatre Belfast production at the Ambassadors Theatre, 2000. Conleth Hill as Charlie, Sean Campion as Jake. (Colin Willoughby/ArenaPAL)

JONSON, Ben   [1572–1637]

English dramatist, poet and actor

PLAYS INCLUDE:

Every Man in His Humour (1598), *Every Man Out of His Humour* (1599), *Poetaster* (1601), *Sejanus His Fall* (1601), *Eastward Ho* (1605, with * GEORGE CHAPMAN and * JOHN MARSTON), *Volpone* (1605), *Epicene or The Silent Woman* (1609), *The Alchemist* (1610), *Catiline* (1611), *Bartholomew Fair* (1614), *The Devil Is an Ass* (1616), *The Staple of News* (1625), *The New Inn* (1629), *The Magnetic Lady* (1633)

Jonson worked as a bricklayer, served as a soldier, became an actor, escaped hanging after killing another actor in a duel by virtue of his ability to read Latin (which meant he could claim what was called benefit of clergy), and became a highly successful dramatist in his own day, although his subsequent reputation has been eclipsed by that of his contemporary and fellow actor * WILLIAM SHAKESPEARE. As well as being a successful dramatist, Jonson wrote many of the court entertainments known as masques, working with architect and stage designer Inigo Jones until they quarrelled over the respective importance of their own contributions to the shows.

Jonson was an energetic and somewhat turbulent figure who engaged in the theatrical controversies of his time in *Poetaster*, which attacked * MARSTON and * DEKKER. He then collaborated with * MARSTON on *Eastward Ho*, which landed them and their co-author * CHAPMAN in prison for offending powerful Scots at the Court. His tragedies, *Sejanus* and *Catiline*, both on Roman subjects, are very seldom performed and his current theatrical fortunes tend to depend on *Volpone* and *The Alchemist*, with occasional forays to *Bartholomew Fair* (which takes place in and around the famous annual fair as a wide cross-section of society join in its pleasures and pitfalls). The RSC has staged a number of the other comedies over the years, including *Every Man in His Humour* (an imbroglio of jealous husband, braggart soldier, knowing servants and would-be gallants), *The New Inn* (a saturnalian feast of role reversals with a spice of clothes fetishism) and *The Devil is an Ass* (in which a trainee devil coming to London is mercilessly outplayed by the human devils). Their most recent revival is *Eastward Ho*, a city comedy that attracted favourable responses as part of the 2002–3 season of rarely revived plays. Perhaps surprisingly, *Epicene*, with its man who marries a woman who is supposed to be completely silent only to discover that she is not silent and eventually that she is not a woman, has still not attracted significant recent theatrical interest.

The Alchemist

Jonson's galaxy of would-be street-wise dupes, get-rich-quick speculators, religious hypocrites, sexual opportunists and over-reaching con men (and woman) remains a devastating and delightful critique of the unacceptable faces of capitalism. There is a kind of manic farcical drudgery in running this London dream factory, with the partners reacting increasingly frenetically as new markets open up for their corporate strategy of marketing and planning consultancy, brothel-keeping and speculation in human and other currencies of all kinds. The alchemical jargon can be a problem if you read the play, but treat it as the equivalent of someone trying to sell you insurance or convert you to the beauties of the latest model of computer (or car) and you won't go far wrong.

Volpone

Another satire on the acquisitive society, set in a Venice that reflects contemporary London, *Volpone* uses the beast fable to characterise its stereotypes: Volpone (the fox) and Mosca (the fly) prey on the carrion birds (Voltore, Corbaccio and Corvino, the vulture, the crow and the raven) who come to prey on the apparently dying Volpone. There is the same delight in trickery as in *The Alchemist* and we tend to admire the comic verve of the protagonists as they outsmart those who are trying to outsmart them. The whole play ends more sourly than most comedies, with Volpone and Mosca overreaching themselves and an outbreak of near poetic justice that leaves you questioning the right of the venal judges to administer justice.

TRY THESE:

✳MARLOWE's *Tamburlaine* and *Doctor Faustus* and
✳MASSINGER's *A New Way to Pay Old Debts* for
portrayals of characters overreaching themselves;
for satirical comedies about the acquisitive
society, ✳BEHN, ✳BRECHT's *The Threepenny Opera*,
✳CHURCHILL's *Serious Money* ✳CONGREVE,
✳GAY's *The Beggar's Opera*, ✳MIDDLETON,
✳WYCHERLEY; for Venetian capitalism,
✳CLIFFORD's *Losing Venice* and ✳SHAKESPEARE's
Merchant of Venice; ✳JONSON and
✳SHAKESPEARE are characters in ✳BOND's *Bingo*;
Michael Coveney described *The New Inn* as 'The
Winter's Tale meets *Nicholas Nickleby*'; ✳BARNES
adapted several of Jonson's comedies; his work
and ✳BRENTON and ✳HARE's *Brassneck* and
Pravda and ✳NICHOLS' *The National Health*
resemble *Bartholomew Fair* in taking the
temperature of a nation.

Volpone by Ben Jonson, directed by Matthew Warchus, National Theatre, 1995. Michael Gambon, Simon Russell Beale. (Michael Ward/ArenaPAL)

K

KANE, Sarah [1971 – 99]
British dramatist

PLAYS:
Blasted (1995), *Phaedra's Love* (1996), *Cleansed* (1998), *Crave* (1998), *4.48 Psychosis* (2000)

One of the most talented dramatists of the 1990s, Kane's debut with *Blasted* was firmly in the tradition of the great Royal Court scandals and her notoriety was sealed by her suicide in 1999. These two events should not be allowed to obscure the achievement of her five completed stage plays, which range across generic and linguistic expectations to comprise a significant body of work. *Blasted* starts off as an apparently realist play, set in a hotel room, about a decaying journalist and his (abusive) relationship with a young woman before modulating into an even more nightmarish scenario as war bursts into the room in the shape of a soldier who proceeds to commit atrocity after atrocity on the journalist before his own death. The play maps a territory of rape, violence and cannibalism that is redeemed to some extent by the woman's altruism. It was greeted with the howls of critical execration that traditionally herald innovative work, and the absence of any guidance within the play as to how the audience is meant to evaluate events may explain some of the discomfort. So too may the fact that the majority of the critics were male and Kane wasn't. *Phaedra's Love* tackles the familiar classical incest themes in ways that seemed more shocking to some critics because of Kane's updating of the setting, and *Cleansed*, with its penis transplant, rats carrying off dismembered feet and conversion of a university into a concentration camp, did little to win over her critics. With *Crave* things began to change, presumably because the spare writing and almost abstract relationships between 'characters' removed many of the elements that had outraged the critics. By the time that *4.48 Psychosis* (the title refers to the time when, allegedly, most suicides take place) was staged posthumously it seemed like a prophetic account of her death, but stylistically it follows the model of *Crave* rather than the earlier work. Kane had already developed a tough, minimalist poetic diction that allowed her to create great complexity and haunting theatrical images that can legitimately be compared to ✱BECKETT and ✱PINTER (who recognised her talent with a personal letter at the time of the critical furore over *Blasted*).

TRY THESE:
✱EURIPIDES, ✱RACINE, ✱SENECA for earlier versions of the Phaedra story; ✱BOND's *Saved* for a play that caused a similar furore to *Blasted* (and which shares with it a problematic lack of explicit evaluation of its material); ✱ELIOT's poems rather than his plays for parallels; ✱RAVENHILL for a controversial male contemporary of Kane's whose depiction of sexual violence was treated less hysterically; ✱WELSH's *Trainspotting* as another contemporary work that escaped the opprobrium heaped on Kane.

KANIN, Garson [1912 – 99]
American dramatist, director and actor

PLAYS INCLUDE:
Born Yesterday (1946), *The Smile of the World* (1949), *The Rat Race* (1949), *The Live Wire* (1950), *Do Re Mi* (1960, musical), *Peccadillo* (1985), *Happy Ending* (1989)

Kanin graduated from the American Academy of Dramatic Arts and began his career as an actor in *Little Ol' Boy* (1933), before becoming an assistant director to the legendary ✱GEORGE ABBOTT. Kanin's own directorial credits include *The Diary of Anne Frank* (1955) and *Funny Girl* (1964). With his wife, Ruth Gordon, he wrote the screenplays for *Woman of the Year* (1942), *Adam's Rib* (1949), *Pat and Mike* (1952), *The Girl Can't Help It* (1957) and many more. Thematically, his dramatic material deals with a witty battle of the sexes. In *Born Yesterday* Billie Dawn, a dumb blonde, accompanies tough Harry Brock, the scrap-iron millionaire, to Washington, DC. Harry is in the capital to buy Congressional support for favourable business legislation. Finding Billie a social liability, he engages reporter Paul Verrall to give her 'class'. Paul makes Billie into a socially responsible citizen and in the process the two fall in love. Together they outmanoeuvre and defeat Harry, relieving him of millions of dollars.

TRY THESE:
✱ SHAW's *Pygmalion* is the social engineering play; ✱ BARRY, ✱ GURNEY, ✱ HOWE, ✱ KAUFMAN and Hart, ✱ SIMON, ✱ WILDER for chronicles of class in the USA.

KAUFMAN, George S.   [1889 – 1961]
American dramatist

HART, MOSS   [1904 – 61]
American dramatist

JOINT PLAYS INCLUDE:
Once in a Lifetime (1930), *Merrily We Roll Along* (1934), *You Can't Take It With You* (1936), *I'd Rather Be Right* (1937, book for the Richard Rodgers musical), *The Fabulous Invalid* (1938), *The Man Who Came to Dinner* (1939), *The American Way* (1939), *George Washington Slept Here* (1940)

For period pieces of Americana in towns both small and large, told with affection and wit, few playwrights could match this duo who, although they had other collaborators throughout their careers, had their finest moments together. While their terrain shifted from Hollywood during the talkies (*Once in a Lifetime*, memorably revived by the RSC in 1980) to a remote Ohio town (*The Man Who Came to Dinner*), the two took pleasure in parody but remained sentimentalists at heart, particularly – as in *The Fabulous Invalid* –

when the subject involved was the stage. ('We mustn't let that die', the idealistic young director remarks stirringly of the theatre at the close of the play.) Even the potentially astringent *Merrily We Roll Along*, a story of lost ideals told in flashbacks, has gone on to exert an emotive pull that can be seen not only in Stephen Sondheim's ill-fated musical version, but in such similar-themed pieces as ✱ SIMON GRAY's *The Common Pursuit*. In their plays, emotional decency wins out over rules and regulations; they are foes of the reactionary, friends of the eccentric.

You Can't Take It With You
Set in New York in 1936, this three-act Pulitzer Prize-winner is one of the most cheerfully anarchic of American plays. A celebration of innocence and relaxation as well as personal eccentricity, it pitches the idiosyncratically zany Vanderhof clan against the boring money-minded conformists in the world around them. The part of Grandpa Vanderhof, a man who opted not to become rich 'because it took too much time', is one of the most delightful on the American stage. The play sets off small comic explosions of fireworks, much like those being lit on stage, and Kaufman and Hart aren't beyond bringing in a Russian countess, Olga, at the eleventh hour to raise spirits again.

TRY THESE:
✱ COWARD's *Hay Fever* for a more lethal hymn to family eccentrics; ✱ O'NEILL's *Ah, Wilderness!* and ✱ SAROYAN's *The Time of Your Life* for complementary comic Americana; ✱ BARRY for deflations of pomposity; ✱ DURANG, ✱ GURNEY, ✱ HENLEY, ✱ KONDOLEON for contemporary comic shenanigans; ✱ HAMPTON's *Tales from Hollywood* and ✱ CHARLES WOOD's *Veterans* for filmmaking; ✱ ABBOTT and John Cecil Holm's *Three Men on a Horse* for more warm-hearted live-and-let-live moralities.

KAY, Jackie   [1961 –   ]
British dramatist, poet and novelist

PLAYS INCLUDE:
Chiaroscuro (1986), *Twice Over* (1988), *Twilight Shift* (1993)

Kay is now best known for her adult poetry and fiction and her writing for children. Brought up in Scotland and a graduate of Stirling University, Kay's early theatre pieces are characterised by their experimental mix of forms. *Chiaroscuro*, commissioned by Theatre of Black Women, is a delicate but potentially powerful piece in which cultural histories, friendship, 'coming out' as a lesbian and the difficulties of communication in a largely white-dominated and heterosexual world are confronted and overcome. For each of the four women it is a journey, their reunion and acknowledgement at the end a measure of how far they have travelled and how far they still have to go. *Chiaroscuro*, as the word itself implies, is about light and shade, variation and change and requires a subtle balancing act in performance. *Twice Over* elaborates, with great good humour and not a little pathos, some of the issues introduced in *Chiaroscuro*: 'coming out' (this time the revelations turn on a recently deceased grandmother), race, class and an implied plea for honesty in all relationships, whatever their inclination. *Twilight Shift* is about the explosive impact of gay relationships in a Scottish mining community.

TRY THESE:
✱ SHANGE's *for colored girls who have considered suicide when the rainbow is enuf* for influence and transformatory theatre; ✱ RUDET's *Basin* for another treatment of black women's friendship, labelling and lesbianism; ✱ CORRIE for a different take on Scottish mining communities.

KEARSLEY, Julia   [1947 –   ]
British dramatist

PLAYS INCLUDE:
Wednesday (1979), *Baby* (1980), *Waiting* (1982), *Leaving Home* (1986), *Under the Web* (1987)

A northern dramatist, Kearsley is an observer in the naturalistic, 'slice of life' mould, who uses irony as a leavening counterweight to the darker schisms revealed in the modern nuclear family. *Wednesday*, first produced at London's Bush Theatre and later on Broadway, earned her the Susan Smith Blackburn Prize runner-up award for Best New Female Playwright. Whilst some critics have commented on her somewhat shaky plotting techniques, others find her work overly televisual. Nearly all, however, agree on the emotional authenticity of her characters and her capacity to reveal hidden tensions and truths beneath the surface of family life, in looking after a son with learning difficulties (*Wednesday*) or an aged mother (*Under the Web*), or coping with the consequences of a father leaving home (*Leaving Home*). *Waiting*, written in response to the Yorkshire Ripper murders, divided critics, some of whom saw it as an outright feminist tract. Kearsley's plays certainly reflect contemporary disharmonies – the self-delusional defences, the aggressions of women in the home – with faithful accuracy and affection.

TRY THESE:
✱ AYCKBOURN and ✱ LEIGH for other scenes from family life; ✱ BILL's *Curtains*, ✱ MACDONALD, ✱ RAIF's *Fail/Safe* for mother–daughter relationships under stress; ✱ MUNRO's *Bold Girls* for more female self-delusion; ✱ BLESSING's *Eleemosynary*, ✱ DE FILIPPO's *Ducking Out* for post-stroke gallows humour; ✱ NICHOLS' *A Day in The Death of Joe Egg* for a surreally bitter view of caring for a child with disabilities; ✱ GANNON's *Keeping Tom Nice* is on a similar theme; Graeae for alternative views of disabilities.

KEATLEY, Charlotte   [1960 –   ]
British dramatist

PLAYS INCLUDE:
Underneath the Arndale (1982), *Dressing for Dinner* (1983), *The Iron Serpent* (1984), *Waiting for Martin* (1987), *My Mother Said I Never Should* (1987), *Our Father* (1994), *The Dream of Reason Produces Monsters* (1999)

London-born Keatley has worked as a theatre critic, actress and radio and television scriptwriter, but her national reputation rests on her astonishing 1987 tour de force *My Mother Said I Never Should*, a brilliantly assured treatment of four generations of women as they struggle with the everyday traumas of domestic life. A complex and moving play, it shifts effortlessly across time and place using repeated motifs and properties to convey the textures of everyday life and to bring out the underlying significance of the apparently trivial and humdrum.

TRY THESE:

✱HAYES, ✱MACDONALD, ✱NORMAN, and ✱SIMON's *Lost in Yonkers* for mothers and daughters; ✱GRANVILLE-BARKER's *The Voysey Inheritance*, ✱MAUGHAM's *For Services Rendered*, ✱PRIESTLEY's *Time and the Conways* for families over time.

KEEFFE, Barrie   [1945 –   ]
British dramatist

PLAYS INCLUDE:

Only a Game (1973), *Scribes* (1975), *Gotcha* (1976), *Abide With Me* (1976), *Gimme Shelter* (1977), *A Mad World My Masters* (1977), *Barbarians* (1977), *Frozen Assets* (1978), *Sus* (1979), *Bastard Angel* (1980), *Black Lear* (1980, revised as *King of England*, 1988), *Chorus Girls* (1981), *Better Times* (1985), *My Girl* (1989), *Not Fade Away* (1990), *Wild Justice* (1990), *Shadows on the Sun* (2001)

An East Londoner who started out as an actor and journalist, Keeffe has established a career as a gritty, hard-driving writer whose affiliation with the East End was maintained via his sustained relationship with the Theatre Royal, Stratford East. A playwright with a vigorous sense both of comedy and of social responsibility, he is known for his topicality and the controversy it can cause. His television play *Gotcha*, for example, was the subject of a BBC ban, but nevertheless received premieres in San Francisco and Moscow. Keeffe paints an unromanticised portrait of contemporary England, occasionally using past events, as in *Better Times*, about the 1921 imprisonment of thirty East End Labour councillors who refuse to levy an unfair government rate, to illuminate local government problems over rate-capping in the mid-1980s. His *A Mad World My Masters*, written in 1977 and revised in 1984, placed a Margaret Thatcher lookalike amidst an updated response to ✱THOMAS MIDDLETON's similarly titled 1608 comedy. In *King of England*, a revision of his earlier *Black Lear* for Temba, a widower decides to return

to the West Indies after thirty-five years in England, only to find that one of his daughters doesn't share his feelings of gratitude towards the UK. *Sus*, written in the year of Thatcher's election, is a prophetic view of relations between young blacks and the police. *My Girl* is about a young East End couple struggling to retain their marriage in impoverished circumstances. *Shadows on the Sun* returns to historical material, examining the French Revolution through the relationship between Danton and Robespierre. Keeffe is best known for his debut film script in 1980 for John MacKenzie's gangster drama *The Long Good Friday*.

TRY THESE:

✱BARKER, ✱BRENTON, ✱EDGAR, ✱TREVOR GRIFFITHS, ✱KUREISHI for committed topical writing; ✱BABE's *Kid Champion*, ✱HARE's *Teeth 'n' Smiles*, ✱SHEPARD's *Tooth of Crime* for Bastard Angel-like rock stars on the skids; ✱BOND's *Lear* for another modern version of ✱SHAKESPEARE's *King Lear*.

KEMPINSKI, Tom   [1938 –   ]
British dramatist

PLAYS INCLUDE:

Duet for One (1980), *Self-Inflicted Wounds* (1985), *Separation* (1987), *Sex Please, We're Italian!* (1991), *When the Past is Still to Come* (1992), *What a Bleedin' Liberty* (1996), *Addicted to Love* (1996)

A sometime actor, London-born Kempinski is best known for his two studies of relationships between women with life-threatening illnesses and their male confidants. *Duet for One* traces the gradual unmasking by a paternal psychologist of the problems of the concert violinist who will never play again, and *Separation* tells a story of a mainly telephonic relationship between a London-based reclusive one-hit writer (widely if mistakenly regarded as a self-portrait) and a New York actress with a potentially fatal disease. Both plays offer very strong parts for their protagonists; both verge on the sentimental and the melodramatic (but don't cross the line). *Self-Inflicted Wounds* is about a Nazi hunter who finds himself unable to publish his findings, and Kempinski has also adapted Jean-Claude Grumberg's *The Workshop* (known in the USA as *The Workroom*) and *Dreyfus*.

TRY THESE:
✱ GURNEY's *Love Letters*, James Roose-Evans' adaptation of Helene Hanff's *84 Charing Cross Road*, Bernard Slade's *Same Time Next Year* and ✱ WATERHOUSE's *Bookends* for long-distance relationships; ✱ CLARK and ✱ YOUNG for people with disabilities; ✱ TERRY JOHNSON, ✱ PETER SHAFFER and ✱ WRIGHT for psychiatrists/psychologists; ✱ HAMPTON's *Portage to San Cristobal* and ✱ WEISS for Nazi hunters.

KENNEDY, Adrienne   [1931 –   ]
American dramatist

PLAYS INCLUDE:
Funnyhouse of a Negro (1964), *The Owl Answers* (1965), *A Rat's Mass* (1966), *In His Own Write* (1967, from John Lennon, with Victor Spinetti), *A Lancashire Lad* (1980), *The Alexander Plays* (1992, comprising *The Ohio State Murders, She Talks to Beethoven, The Film Club* and *The Dramatic Circle*), *Sleep Deprivation Chamber* (1996, with Adam P. Kennedy)

One of the most innovative American playwrights to appear during the 1960s, Kennedy blends symbols, historical figures, racial images and myths in highly surreal plays. Avoiding linear plots, Kennedy creates theatrical nightmares, fragmented mental states of characters who sometimes change costumes to show changing personalities or separating aspects of themselves. Conventional dramatic conflict and dialogue do not exist, as Kennedy's characters show themselves to be torn mentally and emotionally within that obsessive contrast between the imagined elegance of white European royalty and the vulgar existence of black Americans in the rural South or the Northern ghettos. Much of the dramatised confusion within her characters rests upon issues of prejudice, racial heritage and sexual identity.

Funnyhouse of a Negro
Typical of her best work in both style and concept, this play dramatises the last moments on earth of a mulatto woman, Sarah, about to commit suicide after being unable to reconcile herself to her racially mixed heritage. An English major at a city college in New York, Sarah has traditional female fears and fantasies, yet her education only intensifies her internal conflict. She attempts to deny it with her adoration of Queen Victoria, but she experiences the White prejudice, the feeling of Black as evil and the sexual oppression bound to both traditions. In carefully worded yet fragmented monologues, Sarah the Negro and She Who is Clara Passmore are created in Sarah. The only characters external to Sarah are her boyfriend, the funnyhouse man, and her landlady, the funnyhouse lady, who mock Sarah throughout the play with their insane laughter.

TRY THESE:
✱ CHURCHILL and ✱ WERTENBAKER for inventive, non-linear tendencies and fragmentation; ✱ POWNALL's *Motorcar* for confused states of mind and racism; ✱ AYCKBOURN's *Woman in Mind* and ✱ DANIELS' *Beside Herself* for sexual identity and mental turmoil; ✱ HANSBERRY, ✱ PINNOCK, ✱ SHANGE, ✱ WALCOTT, ✱ WOLFE for other views of black experience; ✱ SNOO WILSON for inventive dramaturgy.

KESSELMAN, Wendy   [1940 –   ]
American dramatist, adapter and translator

PLAYS INCLUDE:
Becca (1977), *My Sister in This House* (1981), *The Juniper Tree: A Tragic Household Tale* (1982), *Maggie Magalita* (1985), *Merry-Go-Round* (1987), *I Love You, I Love You Not* (1987), *The Griffin and the Minor Canon* (1988), *Olympe and the Executioner* (1990), *The Butcher's Daughter* (1992), *The Diary of Anne Frank* (1997, adapted from the play by Frances Goodrich and Albert Hackett), *The Last Bridge* (2003)

Originally a songwriter and author of children's books, New Yorker Kesselman is probably best known in Britain through Nancy Meckler's 1986 staging of *My Sister in This House*, which won the Susan Smith Blackburn Prize. The story of the play – two sisters who murdered their mistress in Le

Mans – is perhaps best known through ✳GENET's *The Maids*, but Kesselman's original source was Janet Flanner's account in *Paris Was Yesterday*. Kesselman's version, which places the sisters in a realistic social context – a claustrophobic female household, petty obsessions, oppressions and stifled emotions – is an indictment of French bourgeois values rife with piercing psychological insights. In style it contrasts with Genet's extravagant hallucinatory treatment, which has the two sisters played by male actors in drag.

Kesselman's work includes a strand of engagement with the Holocaust, stretching from *I Love You, I Love You Not*, which delicately traces the relationship between a Jewish grandmother and granddaughter against a backdrop of German wartime memories, through her adaptation of *The Diary of Anne Frank*, which restores some material deleted by Otto Frank from later versions of the *Diary*, to *The Last Bridge*, based on the story of Holocaust survivor Barbara Lederman.

TRY THESE:

✳SARTRE for a different kind of claustrophobic 'household' in *Huis Clos*; ✳CHURCHILL's *Top Girls* and *Fen*, ✳GEMS' *Dusa, Fish, Stas and Vi* and *Piaf* for other treatments of women and class; ✳HAYES' *Skirmishes* for a contrasting treatment of sisters; ✳SHAPIRO's *Winter in the Morning* for an extended image of the Holocaust in the Warsaw Ghetto; ✳SOBOL; ✳LEBOW's *A Shayna Maid* and ✳MANN's *Annulla Allen: An Autobiography* for further female perspectives on the Holocaust.

KESSLER, Lyle   [1940 –   ]
American dramatist and screenwriter

PLAYS INCLUDE:
Watering Place (1969), *Possessions* (1978), *Orphans* (1985), *Robbers* (1990)

Born in Philadelphia, Kessler and his wife co-founded Imagination Workshop, which uses drama to work with hospitalised schizophrenics. *Watering Place*, about a Vietnam vet's angst-ridden encounter with the family of a dead buddy, opened and closed on Broadway in a single night. It was not until 1985, with

Orphans, that Kessler achieved any success. *Orphans* is set in the trashy living room of a North Philadelphia home which two brothers share after the death of their parents. One has been mentally disabled since childhood, the other is a petty thief who has imprisoned his brother in their home. One night the thief brings home a drunk, whom he gags and ties in a chair. But the drunk, a natty Chicago mobster, soon frees himself and assumes a control through which the three men, in their various idiosyncratic manners, expose both literally and metaphorically, through role-reversals and power struggles, the horrors of their orphaned lives. The younger brother dramatises a life of staring through closed windows; the mobster becomes a crying and pitiable figure revealing his Chicago orphanage experiences. *Orphans* won the Drama League Award, was produced in the West End with Albert Finney, and was made into a movie with Kessler writing the screenplay.

Critics have found Kessler's plays derivative of ✳SAM SHEPARD and ✳HAROLD PINTER but have also noted the strength of his characters as acting vehicles, and the passion of their dialogue.

TRY THESE:
✳MANN's *Still Life*, ✳RABE's *Streamers* for Vietnam plays; ✳SHEPARD's *True West* for battling brothers.

KHAN-DIN, Ayub   [1961 –   ]
British actor and dramatist

PLAYS INCLUDE:
East is East (1996), *Last Dance at Dum Dum* (1999)

Khan-Din is an actor who originally wrote *East is East* while he was at drama school. It eventually became a stage success and he adapted it into an equally successful film. Drawing heavily on his own experiences, it is a story of growing up in a mixed-race household in Salford in the 1970s, negotiating tensions and even violence between the parents, racial prejudice outside the home, intergenerational conflicts and battling over sexual and other identities within the family. His second play, which fared less well with the critics, is set in India where a group of ageing

Anglo-Indians are facing (or not) the realities of being anachronisms in a changing country.

TRY THESE:

✳BAINS, ✳GUPTA, ✳KUREISHI for young people whose families are of Asian origin trying to forge an identity in Britain; ✳EDGAR's *Destiny* for some of the issues surrounding Indian immigration to England; ✳TOWNSEND's *The Great Celestial Cow* for another angle on the topic; ✳GOTANDA, ✳HWANG for American-Asian experience.

KILROY, Thomas   [1934 –   ]
Irish dramatist

PLAYS INCLUDE:
The Death and Resurrection of Mr Roche (1968), *The O'Neill* (1969), *Tea and Sex and Shakespeare* (1976), *Talbot's Box* (1977), *Double Cross* (1986), *The Madame Macadam Travelling Theatre* (1991), *The Secret Fall of Constance Wilde* (1997)

Born in Callan, County Kilkenny, in southeast Ireland, Kilroy has combined his work as a dramatist with an active university teaching career in the English department at University College, Dublin, and as Professor of English at University College, Galway. One of Ireland's leading playwrights, Kilroy draws on different theatrical genres and moments of history, and he unapologetically requires a commitment from his audience in an effort to elicit 'an intellectual response to what's happening on stage'. Like many of his colleagues, Kilroy casts a sceptical glance at his country, and *The Death and Resurrection of Mr Roche* takes place at a celebratory party for an Ireland described, somewhat ironically, as 'on the move . . . up and up'. In *Talbot's Box*, Kilroy uses the story of a real-life Dublin labourer, Matt Talbot, to address the nature of modern-day sainthood. *Double Cross*, written for the Derry-based touring company Field Day, applies the psychology of dissimulation to two Irishmen who were roughly contemporary: Brendan Bracken, Churchill's Minister of Information, and William Joyce (Lord Haw-Haw), the Nazi sympathiser and fascist who was hanged in 1946, to explore, with unfashionable non-partisanship, the nature of 'treason', national identity and

racism. *The Madame Macadam Travelling Theatre*, also for Field Day, is about a touring company inadvertently finding themselves over the border in the Republic during World War II. In *The Secret Fall of Constance Wilde* Kilroy explores the tangled relationship of ✳OSCAR WILDE, his wife and Lord Alfred Douglas.

TRY THESE:

✳STOPPARD for overtly intellectual theatre which often plays fictional games with fact (see *Travesties* and particularly *Hapgood* for dealing in, amongst other things, the philosophical similarities of 'double agents' and physics); ✳FRIEL, ✳LEONARD for Irish contemporaries, both of whom write in more immediately recognisable modes; ✳BRECHT, Ariane Mnouchkine's *Mephisto*, ✳PIRANDELLO (whose *Six Characters* Kilroy adapted), for plays that link theatrics with power; Terry Eagleton's *Saint Oscar* for Wilde; Kilroy has also adapted ✳CHEKHOV's *The Seagull* and ✳IBSEN's *Ghosts*.

KLEIST, Heinrich von   [1777 – 1811]
German dramatist

PLAYS INCLUDE:
Amphitryon (1807), *Der zerbrochene Krug* (1808, *The Broken Jug*), *Penthesilea* (1808, produced 1878), *Käthchen von Heilbronn* (1810), *Die Hermannschlacht* (1810, produced 1860, *The Battle of Arminius*), *Prinz Friedrich von Homburg* (1811, produced 1821, *The Prince of Homburg*)

Kleist never really recovered from leaving the Prussian army and taking up the study of Kantian metaphysics; he was given to asking his friends of both sexes to join him in a suicide pact, and eventually a faithful female friend agreed. Most of his plays (except *The Broken Jug*, which is a good broad comedy using the structure of ✳SOPHOCLES' *Oedipus Rex*), display a neurotic emotional power, with verse to match; several were not performed until well after his death. A fine attempt to stage the epic mythological *Penthesilea* at London's Gate at Latchmere in 1983 featured Susannah York as the Amazon queen sinking her teeth into Achilles' bleeding heart and then killing herself in a frenzy of erotic violence. (Kleist changed the story from the usual versions in which Achilles kills Penthesilea.) *The Battle of Arminius*, a patriotic play (aimed at Napoleon) dealing with the German defeat of the Roman army, includes a German maiden called Thusnelda who sets a bear on her faithless Roman lover. *The Prince of Homburg* is a play that has been variously described as both fascist and subversive, in which the hero is sentenced to death for disobeying an order, even though his action won the battle, and comes to agree with the verdict (and be pardoned). *NEIL BARTLETT made a brave attempt at staging it for the RSC in 2002 but did not convince everyone that it was a lost masterpiece.

TRY THESE:

*SCHILLER's *William Tell* for a historical play proclaiming national freedom; Franz Grillparzer for plays in German dealing with mythology and with strong parts for women; *DANIELS' *Byrthrite*, *JARRY's *King Ubu*, *SHAKESPEARE's *The Winter's Tale* for plays in which bears appear on stage; Henry Livings' *Jug* is a version of *Der Zerbrochene Krug*.

KONDOLEON, Harry   [1955 – 94]
American dramatist

PLAYS INCLUDE:

The Côte d'Azur Triangle (1980), *The Brides* (1980), *Rococo* (1981), *Andrea Rescued* (1982), *The Fairy Garden* (1982), *Self-Torture and Strenuous Exercise* (1982), *Christmas on Mars* (1983), *Slacks and Tops* (1983), *The Vampires* (1984), *Linda Her* (1984), *Anteroom* (1985), *Zero Positive* (1988), *Saved or Destroyed* (produced 2000)

Virtually unstaged in Britain, Kondoleon tackled many aspects of modern life and mocked both the life he presented and the theatrical forms that he felt obligated to use. He wrote well-paced dialogue, and had a tart tongue given to expressing tasteless jokes and one-sentence messages, and to boasting a strange set of sensibilities. In *Christmas on Mars*, seen at London's Finborough Theatre in 2003, Kondoleon collects a number of odd characters: a male model, a casting director who is pregnant with his child, a homosexual who is a former flight attendant, and a mother who has returned to try to make amends with the daughter she abandoned twenty years earlier. They all need help in their searches for contentment, and the play ends on Christmas Day with the approaching birth and an assumption of sainthood on the part of the homosexual who is overwhelmed with his apparent wisdom. *Zero Positive*, a play about AIDS (from which Kondoleon died), emphasises the nonsensical with fantasy sketches, and eschews coherent plotting or concept.

TRY THESE:

*FIERSTEIN and *KRAMER for AIDS plays; Kondoleon's approach to drama has been compared to *DURANG and *ORTON; *AYCKBOURN for bad Christmases.

KOPIT, Arthur   [1937 –   ]
American dramatist

PLAYS INCLUDE:

The Questioning of Nick (1957), *On the Runway of Life, You Never Know What's Coming Off Next* (1958), *Across the River and Into the Jungle* (1958), *Sing to Me Through Open Windows* (1959), *Aubade* (1959), *Oh Dad Poor Dad Mama's Hung You in the Closet and I'm Feelin' So Sad* (1960), *Asylum, or What the Gentlemen Are Up To, Not to Mention the Ladies* (1963), *The Conquest of Everest* (1964), *The Hero* (1964), *The Day the Whores Came Out to Play Tennis* (1965), *Indians* (1968), *Wings* (1978), *Nine* (1980, book of the musical), *End of the World (with Symposium to Follow)* (1984), *Road to Nirvana* (1991, formerly *Bone-the-Fish*), *Y2K* (1999), *The Discovery of America* (2002)

Born in New York the son of a jeweller, Kopit's career stretches from Ionesco-like comic Absurdism (the celebrated *Oh Dad Poor Dad*, written while Kopit was still a Harvard undergraduate) to the Swiftian sting of *Road to Nirvana* (a scathing indictment of Hollywood first produced at Kentucky's Actors' Theatre of Louisville under the title *Bone-the-Fish* – a deliberate send-up of *MAMET's *Speed-the-Plow*). In between are some lengthily titled black comedies and two acclaimed dramas diametrically opposed in style and scope: *Indians*, which had its world premiere at the RSC, a ✱PIRANDELLIAN piece about cultural imperialism, with Buffalo Bill Cody as an early white liberal confronted by the ghosts of Indians who resented being put on display at his Wild West show; and *Wings*, an intimate, impressionistic play about an aviatrix who suffers a stroke. Kopit's recent work includes *Y2K*, a Kafkaesque nightmare in which a couple find that their identities have been destroyed.

Oh Dad Poor Dad Mama's Hung You in the Closet and I'm Feelin' So Sad

The man-eating and violent matriarch Madame Rosepettle arrives in Cuba on holiday with a silver piranha and two belligerent flowers, as well as her stammering 26-year-old son, in this crazed and noisy comedy, a deliberate pastiche of ✱IONESCO and ✱TENNESSEE WILLIAMS that made Kopit's international name. The son begins to discover women, but his efforts at seduction are continually thwarted – ✱JOE ORTON-style – by the tumbling corpse of his embalmed father. In between, his mother is pinioning him under blankets in order to keep him under control, and the domestic comedy spirals into a kind of chaotic disorder that suggests ✱KAUFMAN and Hart on speed.

TRY THESE:

✱PIRANDELLO, ✱STOPPARD for theatrical self-consciousness; ✱GELBER and ✱SCHISGAL for 1960s iconoclasm, American-style; ✱POMERANCE for analogously liberal looks at American history; ✱CLARK's *The Petition*, ✱DANIELS' *The Devil's Gateway*, ✱DARKE's *The Body*, ✱EDGAR's *Maydays*, ✱LANFORD WILSON's *Angels Fall* for other contemporary plays about the Bomb along the lines of *End of the World*, ✱VAN ITALLIE's *The Traveller* for another stroke victim (namely Joseph Chaikin); ✱DE FILIPPO's *Ducking Out* for a play on a similar theme; ✱RABE's *Hurlyburly* for vituperative Hollywood satire.

KOPS, Bernard   [1926 –   ]
British poet, novelist and dramatist

PLAYS INCLUDE:
The Hamlet of Stepney Green (1957), *The Dream of Peter Mann* (1960), *Enter Solly Gold* (1962), *Ezra* (1981), *Simon at Midnight* (1985), *Playing Sinatra* (1991)

First produced at about the same time as ✱ARNOLD WESKER, and from the same East End Jewish background (the privations and vigour of which are both reflected in his work), Kops declared in 1962 that he and his contemporaries ✱JOHN ARDEN, Alun Owen, ✱ROBERT BOLT, ✱WILLIS HALL and ✱WESKER would ensure that theatre would never again be a 'precious inner-sanctum for the precious few'. He believed then that by tackling issues of immediate social concern they could change the way the world works. However, his issues are the rather broad ones of the poor quality of working-class life, the futility of riches and the need for love and joy rather than hard political polemic. In *The Hamlet of Stepney Green* his Hamlet seeks revenge, but not against an actual murderer, and he ends the play optimistically, the ghost satisfied by the reconciled characters' promise to always carry a little revolution in their heart All his work is not so optimistic, though the conman 'rabbi' in *Enter Solly Gold*, posing as the long-awaited Messiah, brings a sense of real values and a new joy to the materialistic family he cons. The title character of *The Dream of Peter Mann*, like his namesake ✱IBSEN's Peer Gynt, sets out on a quest for riches, while in the dream which forms the second part of the play he finds himself in a world preparing for nuclear war, waking when the bomb explodes, and ending reconciled to home. In *Playing Sinatra* the famous singer provides a focus for the characters' fantasies. Kops' plays are always lively, though sometimes dramatically overstated and given to over-sentimentality.

TRY THESE:

✱PINTER for a similar background; ✱BLESSING's *Fortinbras*, ✱STOPPARD's *Rosencrantz and Guildenstern Are Dead* for dramatic responses to ✱SHAKESPEARE's *Hamlet*; ✱AYCKBOURN, ✱DE FILIPPO, ✱LAN's *Flight*, ✱SIMON's *Brighton Beach Memoirs*, ✱STOREY for family drama;

*HARWOOD's *Another Time* for a South African version; Jean-Claude Grumberg and *SOBOL for more specifically Jewish-oriented theatre.

KORDER, Howard   [1958 –   ]
American dramatist

PLAYS INCLUDE:
Life on Earth (1985), *Episode 26* (1985), *Fun* (1987), *Nobody* (1987), *Boy's Life* (1988), *Lip Service* (1986, television 1989), *Search and Destroy* (1990), *Love's Diatribe* (1990), *The Lights* (1993), *The Hollow Lands* (2000)

Frank Rich has written that Korder has a 'pungent voice'. Perhaps so; perhaps even modelled on *DAVID MAMET, who might claim Korder as a protégé, but in his earlier work it is also a voice of youthful humour – good humour from a male point of view, and satiric humour throughout – as Korder perceptively toys with the real life situations of the persistently young. *Love's Diatribe* is a comedy about two adult children who return home to live with their parents. On the other hand, *Search and Destroy* (seen at the Royal Court in 1993) is a dark, comic fable about the moral bankruptcy of America as a businessman-cum-film producer deals drugs and commits murder in order to produce a film version of a questionable self-help book. *The Lights*, which in 1996 was the last Royal Court production before its refurbishment, continues this theme in another exploration of the daily desperation of life in the big city. *The Hollow Lands* marks a change of focus to the origins of contemporary ills in an epic account of immigration and the nineteenth-century expansion of the USA to the West.

Boy's Life
In a chain of related blackout sketches Korder follows his three young protagonists through their continuing search for easy women. Belligerently heterosexual, the three freely admit their cynical approach to their adventures. Insensitive, rude, thoroughly manipulative in their associations with women, the 'boys' candidly confess their pessimistic views of mankind while trying to find something admirable in their boyish fun. Perhaps in contrast to the potentially offensive atmosphere for the more staid members of an audience, Korder creates a lightness and a sense of self-amusement in which the women characters insist on presenting their views, and the evening's entertainment slides unevenly away from moral judgements toward a position of boyish misanthropy that reveals both charm and a cutting edge.

TRY THESE:
*MACDONALD, *MAMET's *Sexual Perversity in Chicago*, *O'MALLEY's *Once a Catholic*, *SIMON's *Brighton Beach Memoirs*, *WEDEKIND's *Spring Awakening* for other versions of adolescence; *AYCKBOURN's *A Small Family Business* for business and drugs; *NICHOLS' *Poppy* for empire (and drugs), *C. P. TAYLOR's *Withdrawal Symptoms* for the decline of empire (and drugs); *The Lights* has a demolition scene that seemed particularly appropriate at the Royal Court; *KROETZ and *STOREY for onstage work.

KRAMER, Larry   [1935 –   ]
American author and dramatist

PLAYS INCLUDE:
Sissies' Scrapbook (1972), *The Normal Heart* (1985), *Just Say No: A Play About a Farce* (1989), *The Destiny of Me* (1993)

A graduate of Yale, Kramer began his career in London in the 1960s working as a story editor for Columbia Pictures. As a playwright, he is best known for *The Normal Heart*, a semi-autobiographical drama that made such an impact that its author merits an entry for sociological and historical reasons as much as anything else. Set in Manhattan over a three-year period from 1981 to 1984, the play is a howl of rage from a writer incensed at his city's sluggish response to the alarms of AIDS. A founding member of Gay Men's Health Crisis, Kramer casts as his onstage alter ego one Ned Weeks, a consciousness-raising writer who refuses to rest until such disparate institutions as the *New York Times*, the Mayor's office and the national government have given the fatal disease the attention it deserves. Wildly polemical and issue-obsessed – Kramer claims he was emboldened to write the play after seeing *DAVID HARE's *A Map of *the World* at the National Theatre – the play is basically a harangue written at white heat, and it ends with a deathbed scene that recapitulates dozens of 1930s movies, this time from a gay vantage point. *The Destiny of Me* also takes Ned Weeks as its hero, looking at similar themes from a more personal angle.

TRY THESE:

✴ IBSEN's *An Enemy of the People* as a play of ideas centred on illness; ✴ ODETS for social arousal; ✴ SHERMAN's *Passing By* for a pre-AIDS treatment of illness; ✴ FIERSTEIN (*Safe Sex*), ✴ NOËL GREIG, William M. Hoffman (*As Is*), Andy Kirby (*Compromised Immunity*), ✴ KONDOLEON's *Zero Positive* and ✴ KUSHNER for further AIDS-related plays; ✴ ELYOT, ✴ RAVENHILL for later responses.

KROETZ, Franz Xaver   [1946 –   ]
German dramatist

PLAYS INCLUDE:
Wild Game Crossing (1969), *Homeworker* (1971), *Staller Farm* (1972, *Farmyard* in the USA) *Ghost Train* (1972), *Request Concert* (1972), *Upper Austria* (1972), *Maria Magdalena* (1973, from Friedrich Hebbel), *Wider Prospects* (1974), *The Nest* (1975), *Agnes Bernauer* (1976, from Friedrich Hebbel), *Through the Leaves* (1978), *Mensch Meier* (1979), *Neither Fish Nor Fowl* (1981), *Fear and Hope in the German Federal Republic* (1984, later *Fear and Hope in Germany*), *Dying Farmer* (1985), *Help Wanted* (1986), *Dead Soil* (1992), *Der Drang* (1996, *The Urge*)

Kroetz is a German dramatist rooted in the 'Volksstück' (folk play) tradition. His subject matter is the contemporary industrial lower class, who he sees as caged animals reacting with long-repressed violence. Owing much to the influence of ✴ ÖDÖN VON HORVÁTH, Kroetz stresses the terrible living conditions, moral repression and linguistic deprivation of the working classes. His naturalistic attention to detail and precise use of Bavarian dialect recall Gerhart Hauptmann, as his characters grope for words to describe their despair and outrage. Their inability to fully articulate their frustrations leads to passionate violence also reminiscent of ✴ GEORG BÜCHNER's *Woyzeck*.

Kroetz uses dialect to express the limitations thrust on the lower classes, 'dispossessed of their language, of their ability to articulate'. For him, 'dialect is connected with work, with nature and landscape, with money even. Dialect is man's dirty underpants.' He often goes into naturalistic detail in the plays' frequently shocking action: *Homeworker* includes an unsuccessful abortion and the murder of a deformed child; *Staller Farm* offers masturbation on a toilet. By the mid-1980s, Kroetz had lost his belief in the theatre's potential to correct society's wrongs, noting that 'the theatre doesn't make a very good fist; it's essentially a peaceable force, it's honeycomb, papier-mâché in the face of a society which is riddled with horrific violence'. Several of his plays were mounted successfully in Britain during the 1980s: *Staller Farm* (London's Bush Theatre 1984, Manchester Library Theatre 1986–7) presents us with a naive country girl, Beppi, doubly hindered by both her class's lack of linguistic skills and her own mental slowness, which lead to seduction, pregnancy and further isolation. Its successor, *Ghost Train* (seen at the Bush in 1976 and the Library in 1987), shows her taking her baby to the city and encountering the violence and repression of the urban lower classes.

There has been a recent mini-revival with *The Nest* (seen at the Orange Tree, Richmond, in 1981 and the Bush in 1985) being revived by the Dead Earnest Company in 1997 and by Living Pictures in 2003. The play shows in short simple scenes the clichéd conversation and domestic detail of the lives of a lorry-driver and his wife, including a long silent sequence in which he dumps barrels of industrial waste in a bathing pool; theatricality takes over when the baby is burned by the waste, and he is thus driven to join the union. *Through the Leaves* (seen at the Bush in 1985), which almost eschews plot in showing the relationship between a lonely middle-aged pair, a female offal-seller and a construction worker, finally destroyed by the conditioned inadequacies of their language and sexual assumptions, was revived at the Southwark Playhouse in 2003 with Simon Callow and Ann Mitchell prior to a West End run.

TRY THESE:

＊BOND's *Saved* influenced many German dramatists of the 1970s with its violence and inarticulacy in speaking out against oppression; for Kroetz's thematic contemporaries, Rainer Werner Fassbinder, ＊HANDKE, ＊MÜLLER.

KUREISHI, Hanif   [1954 –   ]
British dramatist, novelist and screenwriter

PLAYS INCLUDE:

Soaking the Heat (1976), *The King and Me* (1979), *The Mother Country* (1980), *Tomorrow-Today!* (1980), *Outskirts* (1981), *Borderline* (1981), *Cinders* (1981, adaptation, from Christina Paul's translation, of a play by ＊GLOWACKI), *Artists and Admirers* (1982, with David Leveaux, from ＊OSTROVSKY), *Birds of Passage* (1983), *Sleep With Me* (1999)

Kureishi is probably best known now for his novel *The Buddha of Suburbia* (and its television adaptation) and his scripts for Stephen Frears' films *My Beautiful Laundrette* and *Sammy and Rosie Get Laid*, rather than for his theatre work. But all his works share similar concerns with the difficulties of making and establishing meaningful personal contacts in the face of major cultural obstacles, particularly those deriving from prejudice. Kureishi evokes brilliantly the wastelands of the inner cities and the casualties of endemic poverty of vision and racism, both white and non-white. *The King and Me* is a study of a young couple on a housing estate who are at once sustained and trapped by adherence to the Elvis Presley cult, but who eventually make a new start; *Cinders*, incidentally, shares the same concern with the role of media mythologies in shaping people's lives and responses. In *Tomorrow-Today!* urban blight is given added poignancy and urgency by the young characters' inability to believe in the future because of the nuclear threat. In *Outskirts* scenes from the past and present of two south London white men who once joined in a violent racial attack are intercut in a landscape of despair from which one has escaped to become a liberal teacher, while the other has become involved with a fascist organisation. *Borderline*, which caused some controversy in the Asian community because

white actors doubled both white and Asian parts in the Joint Stock production, is a fine evocation of the strains of living on the borderlines of different cultures and different conventions which shows a complex picture of class, racial and gender expectations across Asian and white communities. *Birds of Passage*, a Sydenham *Cherry Orchard*, shows the erosion of old loyalties to neighbourhood, class and family in the face of socio-economic changes made concrete in the shape of the Pakistani former lodger who buys the house he once stayed in. Kureishi's return to the theatre in 1999 with *Sleep With Me*, described by Michael Billington in the *Guardian* as 'a country-weekend play about a group of old university friends who have mostly succumbed to the bitch-goddess success', was not a great success.

TRY THESE:

＊ALRAWI, ＊BAINS for issues of ethnicity, Farrukh Dhondy's *Vigilantes* explores cultural clashes in the British Bangladeshi community; ＊MATURA's *Playboy of the West Indies* and *Trinidad Sisters* are reworkings of classics to West Indian settings; ＊CARTWRIGHT, ＊FLANNERY's *Savage Amusement*, ＊TREVOR GRIFFITHS' *Oi for England*, ＊KEEFFE, ＊MARCHANT, ＊MOTTON, and ＊NIGEL WILLAMS' *Class Enemy* tackle themes of urban deprivation; ＊BLEASDALE's *Are You Lonesome Tonight?* for a musical portrait of the 'King'; Kureishi has adapted ＊BRECHT's *Mother Courage*.

KUSHNER, Tony   [1956 –   ]
American dramatist

PLAYS INCLUDE:

A Bright Room Called Day (1987), *Angels in America* (*Millennium Approaches*, 1991, and *Perestroika*, 1992), *Slavs!* (1996), *Homebody/Kabul* (2001)

Kushner's reputation has been made with truly epic plays that tackle some of the really big issues of our times. *A Bright Room Called Day*, which looks at the way that the Nazis triumphed because of the failure of the opposing parties to organise effectively, marks Kushner out as one of those rare American dramatists who is not unhappy to be seen as directly concerned with politics and how history might be relevant to the present. *Angels in America*'s two parts play for over seven hours and in that time his 'gay fantasia on national themes' takes off from the domestic situations of a gay couple, a Mormon trying to negotiate his sexual identity and the lawyer Roy Cohn to encompass the greater part of creation. In *Slavs!* he explores the impact of the break-up of the USSR and in *Homebody/Kabul* he tackles the interaction between the West and Afghanistan. The play was conceived before the attack on New York in September 2001 but has taken extra force from subsequent events. *Like Angels in America* it is very long (around four hours) and it uses non-traditional structure to make its points. The first part is a long monologue by the 'homebody', a middle-aged woman who creates an image of Kabul as a mystic release from her decaying marriage. The rest of the evening concerns her husband and daughter going to the real Kabul to try to find out what happened to her when she did actually go there. Kushner's political questioning and his willingness to demand that theatre should stand up to consider the big issues marks him out as a major figure in an age dominated (particularly in America) by a conservative agenda.

TRY THESE:
✳FIERSTEIN and ✳KRAMER for AIDS; ✳BRENTON and Tariq Ali for political engagement and the collapse of the Soviet Union; Ranjit Bolt for a successful British adaptation of ✳CORNEILLE's *L'Illusion Comique* to parallel Kushner's *The Illusion* (1988); Kushner has also adapted S. Ansty's *The Dybbuk* as well as ✳BRECHT and ✳GOETHE; ✳SHERMAN's *Bent* for parallels to *A Bright Room Called Day*; for a woman using fantasy to escape from a deathly marriage, ✳AYCKBOURN's *Woman in Mind*; for the 'exotic', ✳HARE's *A Map of the World*.

KYD, Thomas   [1558 – 94]
English dramatist

PLAYS INCLUDE:
The Spanish Tragedy (*c.* 1589)

Kyd's *The Spanish Tragedy* is, for all practical purposes, the play that started the vogue for revenge tragedy in the Elizabethan theatre, but unlike many trendsetters it still bears comparison with its successors. The details of Kyd's life and career are somewhat obscure: London born, he may well have followed his father's profession of scrivener, and he was working in the theatre by 1585. The main biographical information we have about him comes from 1593 when he was arrested and charged with blasphemy. After ✳MARLOWE's suspicious death, Kyd claimed that the 'blasphemous' material found in his home had belonged to Marlowe since they had shared a room at one point. Whatever the truth of the matter, Kyd's death just over a year after he was released may well have been related to his sufferings in prison. Kyd is thought to have been the author of an earlier version of *Hamlet* as well as other works, most of which have not survived. All the ingredients of the later revenge plays are to be found in *The Spanish Tragedy*, some derived from ✳SENECA, some indebted to the Elizabethan picture of ✳MACHIAVELLI: the search for justice thwarted by corruption, ingenious murders, the masque that converts pretend deaths into real ones, the ghost, the play within the play, madness, the dumb show, and the Machiavellian villain. But there is more to it than sensationalism: the theme of revenge serves as a way of dramatising and heightening everyday conflict, thus opening up revenge tragedy as a medium for presenting major issues in a dramatically effective way.

TRY THESE:
Most Renaissance tragic dramatists used revenge plots and malcontent figures: ✳SHAKESPEARE's *Hamlet* is the most famous example of both, and there are notable examples in ✳MARSTON, ✳MIDDLETON, ✳TOURNEUR and ✳WEBSTER; ✳KOPS' *The Hamlet of Stepney Green* for a modern Jewish variation.

LABICHE, Eugène   [1815 – 88]
French dramatist

PLAYS (MAINLY WRITTEN IN COLLABORATION) INCLUDE:

Un Chapeau de Paille d'Italie (1851, *An Italian Straw Hat*), *Le Voyage de M. Perrichon* (1860, *M. Perrichon Takes a Trip*), *La Poudre aux Yeux* (1861, *Dust in Your Eyes*), *Célimare le Bien-Aimé* (1863, *Beloved Célimare*), *La Cagnotte* (1864, *The Piggy-Bank*), *Le Plus Heureux des Trois* (1870, *The Threesome*)

The most successful writer of French farce, and certainly the most prolific, Labiche published fifty-seven plays, but had a hand in perhaps a hundred more. Given this vast output, it is not surprising that he is distinguished less for originality than for the professionalism with which he reworks all the oldest and most reliable jokes. Labiche had a sunny temperament, helped no doubt by the success that brought him the money for a chateau in Sologne and eventually a seat in the French Academy. His satire of the bourgeois is often sharp but his plays are more genial and less manic than ✱ FEYDEAU's, which may explain why they are staged less often in Britain. *An Italian Straw Hat* has an unequalled chase theme, as a hapless bridegroom, followed by his entire wedding party, rushes around Paris in search of a replica straw hat for one that has been eaten by his horse in circumstances of maximum embarrassment to the owner. Many of the plays would bear revival and ✱ NEIL BARTLETT, who adapted *The Threesome* for the Lyric, Hammersmith, in 2000, suggests that Labiche shared with ✱ MARIVAUX two essential comic gifts of 'great concision (characters are too busy dealing with situations to explain themselves or their feelings) and great cruelty'.

TRY THESE:
✱ AYCKBOURN, ✱ ORTON, ✱ PINERO, ✱ TRAVERS for English variations; ✱ FRAYN's *Noises Off* for the best theatrical exposure of the mechanisms of farce; ✱ SIMON.

LaBUTE, Neil   [1963 –   ]
American filmmaker and dramatist

PLAYS INCLUDE:

In the Company of Men (1992), *Bash* (1999, comprising *Medea Redux*, *Iphigenia in Orem*, *A Gaggle of Saints*), *The Shape of Things* (2001), *The Distance from Here* (2002), *The Mercy Seat* (2002)

LaBute studied at Brigham Young University and there is a strong Mormon element in his work, particularly the original versions of the plays in *Bash*. However, he also spent time at the Royal Court and the result is a heady mix of American and British influences. He has quickly established himself as a clinical observer of modern America from the anomie of the bored workers who abuse a deaf woman in *In the Company of Men* to the three killers of *Bash*. In *The Shape of Things* the debates about the nature of art and of relationships are concluded as Susannah Clapp put it with a 'distinctive lack of resolution: LaBute is never afraid of leaving an audience with a nasty taste in their mouths'. *The Distance from Here* presents a picture of a blighted American suburbia of alienation, lack of moral bearings and violence, and *The Mercy Seat* dares to suggest that the September 2001 attack on the World Trade Center did not lead to a universal increase in moral stature as a husband and father who has survived the attack contemplates pretending to have died so that he can begin a new life with his mistress.

LaBute has been compared to ∗BOND, ∗MAMET,
∗PINTER, ∗POLIAKOFF; the treatment of art in
The Shape of Things recalls ∗REZA and the trans-
formation of the man recalls ∗SHAW's *Pygmalion*.

LAN, David   [1952 –   ]
South African-born dramatist and director

PLAYS INCLUDE:
Painting a Wall (1974), *Bird Child* (1974),
Paradise (1975), *Homage to Bean Soup*
(1975), *Winter Dancers* (1977), *Red Earth*
(1978), *Sergeant Ola and His Followers*
(1979), *Flight* (1986), *A Mouthful of Birds*
(1986, with ∗CARYL CHURCHILL), *Desire*
(1990), *The Ends of the Earth* (1996)

Born in Cape Town, where he was a teenage
magician and puppeteer, Lan arrived in
Britain in 1972 to study social anthropology
and lived in Zimbabwe from 1980 to 1982. He
has combined his career as a dramatist with
working as a director and is currently the
Artistic Director of the Young Vic. Consider-
ations of racism and anthropology are central
to many of his own plays, which concern
themselves with the search for both political
and personal freedoms. *Paradise*, set during
the Peninsular War, lacks the basis of personal
experience or research which gives substance
to his other work, whether the Canadian
Indian culture of *The Winter Dancers*, the
cargo cult of *Sergeant Ola and His Followers* or
the African background of his other plays. *A
Mouthful of Birds*, developed with ∗CARYL
CHURCHILL for Joint Stock from the cast's
improvisations, is a collage of variations
growing from the Dionysus story. Exploring
sexism, racism and other forms of exploitation through ritual, dance and strong visual
theatre rather than any verbal dialectic, it is a
totally different experience to its predecessor
Flight, a Jewish family chronicle.

TRY THESE:
South African-born playwrights ∗FUGARD,
∗HARWOOD, ∗LEVY and ∗WRIGHT;
∗POLIAKOFF's *Breaking the Silence* for another
family chronicle of Jewish origins; and ∗SOBOL,
whose *Ghetto* Lan translated; Lan has also
adapted ∗CHEKHOV's *Uncle Vanya* and *The Cherry
Orchard*, ∗EURIPIDES' *Ion*, and Giovanni Verga's *La
Lupa*.

LAPINE, James Elliot   [1949 –   ]
American dramatist

PLAYS INCLUDE:
Photograph (1977, from Gertrude Stein),
Table Settings (1979), *Twelve Dreams* (1981),
Sunday in the Park with George (1984, book),
Into the Woods (1986, book), *Falsettoland*
(1990, book), *Passion* (1994, book)

Lapine was a photographer and graphic
designer before he became interested in the
theatre. His work has won him an OBIE, a
New York Drama Critics' Circle Award and a
Pulitzer Prize. He has worked successfully as a
director and has written the book for several
musicals. Lapine's interest in psychology is
apparent in *Twelve Dreams*, an exploration of
the theories of Freud and Jung as revealed in
the dreams of a 12-year-old girl. His serious
approach to life which surfaces throughout is
well illustrated in his retelling of some of
Grimm's fairy tales in *Into the Woods* (with
Sondheim), where he wants his audience to
avoid repeating the mistakes of history.
Sunday in the Park with George (with
Sondheim) concerns the conflict between an
artist who devoutly follows his principles and
the critics who fail to appreciate his creativity.
Act 1 shows the nineteenth-century French
painter Georges Seurat thinking about and
creating his best-known pointillist work, *A
Sunday Afternoon on the Island of La Grand
Jatte*. Act 2, set in 1980, dramatises the creative
struggle of a fictional American descendant of
Seurat, who practises his art with a laser beam
and photo projections. A number of critics
thought that Sondheim and Lapine trivialised
their subject matter; others found their vision
of love and art in a high-tech world sufficient
and lauded it as an ambitious innovation in
American musical theatre.

TRY THESE:
∗POWNALL's *An Audience Called Edouard* for a
Manet-based parallel with *Sunday in the Park*;
∗WRIGHT's *Mrs Klein* for psychiatrists; ∗REZA's *Art*
and ∗WERTENBAKER's *Three Birds Alighting in a
Field* for modern plays about art.

LARSON, Larry   [1948 –   ]
American dramatist and actor

PLAYS INCLUDE:

Far from the Peaceful Shores (1987), *Christmas at the Palace* (1987), *Tent Meeting* (1983, with ✳ REBECCA WACKLER and ✳ LEVI LEE), *The Blood Orgy Series* (1983–7, *Mirandolina Unchained*, *The Grubb Chronicles* and *Tales of Rat Alley*, with ✳ LEVI LEE), *Some Things You Need to Know Before the World Ends: A Final Evening with the Illuminati* (1986, with ✳ LEVI LEE), *Nicholas DeBeaubien's Hunchback of Notre Dame* (1997, with ✳ LEVI LEE, ✳ REBECCA WACKLER and John Kohler), *The Bench* (2002, with ✳ LEVI LEE)

Although Larson, ✳ REBECCA WACKLER and ✳ LEVI LEE (the Southern Theatre Conspiracy) act and work independently, their most successful work has been collaborative. Satire, fast paced humour and a mocking of thoughtlessly accepted conventions mark their plays. *Some Things You Need to Know Before the World Ends* has been quite widely performed in the USA. It has been described as a two-man knockabout, blackout comedy about sermons and sacrilege. In essence, the pair of actors ridicule every creed – political, economic, religious – that perverse minds can manipulate and sheep-like human beings can follow with stubborn and thoughtless persistence.

TRY THESE:

✳ CAMPBELL and ✳ SNOO WILSON for anarchic humour; for parallels to the play-within-play elements of *Nicholas DeBeaubien's Hunchback of Notre Dame*, ✳ FRAYN, ✳ MAMET, ✳ STOPPARD.

LAVERY, Bryony   [1947 –   ]
British dramatist

PLAYS INCLUDE:

I Was Too Young at the Time to Understand Why My Mother Was Crying (1976), *Sharing* (1976), *Grandmother's Footsteps* (1976), *The Catering Service* (1977), *Helen and Her Friends* (1978), *Bag* (1979), *The Wild Bunch* (1979), *Gentlemen Prefer Blondes* (1979, from Anita Loos), *Family Album* (1980), *Missing* (1981), *Zulu* (1981), *The Black Hole of Calcutta* (1982), *Götterdämmerung* (1982), *For Maggie, Betty and Ida* (1982), *Hot Time* (1984), *Calamity* (1984), *Origin of the Species* (1984), *Witchcraze* (1985), *The Mummy* (1987), *The Headless Body* (1987), *Kitchen Matters* (1990), *Her Aching Heart* (1991), *Peter Pan* (1991, with ✳ NONA SHEPPHARD), *Nothing Compares to You* (1995), *Goliath* (1997, from Beatrix Campbell), *Ophelia* (1997), *Frozen* (1998), *A Wedding Story* (2000), *The Magic Toyshop* (2001, from Angela Carter)

Lavery has been prodigious in her output: satire, sketches, plays for children, cabaret, television and radio. At one end, she is scriptwriter for the highly original National Theatre of Brent (anarchic interpreters of grand myths and legends, usually played by two or at most three performers); at the other, frequent provider of, in the *Guardian's* words, 'wistful satire, ingenious fantasy'. But behind the satire Lavery has also sought to question and challenge a whole range of assumptions. An open lesbian feminist writer – 'I am passionately dedicated to the rediscovery of women's strength through positive theatrical presentation' – her problem has been finding the right balance between content and style, a difficulty perhaps exacerbated by the collaborative process of many of the fringe companies she has worked with – Women's Theatre Group, Monstrous Regiment, Gay Sweatshop, Theatre Centre, Clean Break – which can leave a writer with a lot of demands to fulfil. *Calamity* (a spoof on the Wild West), *Witchcraze* (about connections between witches in the seventeenth century and the women protesting against cruise missiles at the Greenham Common airbase), *The Mummy* (about death, mothers and daughters) and *Origin of the Species* (Darwinism revisited) were all criticised for being 'ill-organised' – a flaw not detected in the earlier plays, *Helen and Her Friends*, *Bag*, *Family Album* and *The Catering Service* (an allegory on paramilitarism) produced by Les Oeufs Malades, the company Lavery set up with her friends Gerard Bell and Jessica Higgs. *Her Aching Heart* is a brilliantly shameless pastiche of romantic fiction given a lesbian twist. *Kitchen Matters*, loosely based on ✳ EURIPIDES' *The Bacchae*, is typical Lavery –

witty and wacky, ransacking a number of theatrical conventions with glee but with a serious intent – to attack homophobia and, in passing, to warn against allowing theatre to wither on the vine from lack of funds.

TRY THESE:

✶CHURCHILL and ✶DUFFY for versions of *The Bacchae*; ✶DANIELS' *Byrthrite* for witches, and *The Devil's Gateway* for Greenham scenes; ✶EDGAR's *May Days* also takes us to Greenham; for a lesbian version of the Wild West, Tasha Fairbanks; for the original Peter Pan, ✶BARRIE; for the original Ophelia, ✶SHAKESPEARE's *Hamlet*; for another Ophelia, ✶LEVY.

LAWRENCE, D. H. (David Herbert)   [1885 – 1930]
English novelist, poet and dramatist

PLAYS INCLUDE:

The Widowing of Mrs Holroyd (1914), *Touch and Go* (1920), *David* (1926), *A Collier's Friday Night* (staged 1965), *The Daughter in Law* (staged 1967), *The Fight for Barbara* (staged 1967)

Lawrence is widely recognised as one of the most important novelists of his period, but his dramatic work was virtually unknown until ✶PETER GILL's productions in the 1960s established his credentials as a naturalistic dramatist of the highest quality. *A Collier's Friday Night* dramatises much the same material from Lawrence's own life that figures in *Sons and Lovers*, with a marriage of opposites and a mother jealous of her son's girlfriend, while *The Widowing of Mrs Holroyd* is about another marriage in trouble that is terminated by the miner husband's death in a pit accident. In *The Daughter in Law* the territory is fairly familiar: we discover that a miner who recently married above himself has impregnated another woman, but the main battle, as the title suggests, is between the typically Lawrentian smothering mother and the new wife for the soul of the miner. The psychological battles are set against the background of a miners' strike that determines the outcome of the struggle between wife and mother.

TRY THESE:

✶GILL's own plays for points of comparison; ✶IBSEN and ✶STRINDBERG for naturalism and the battle of the sexes; ✶KEATLEY for mothers; ✶LOWE and ✶WHITTINGTON for Nottingham; ✶CORRIE for miners.

LEBOW, Barbara   [1936 –   ]
American dramatist

PLAYS INCLUDE:

I Can't Help It (1965), *Little Joe Monaghan* (1981), *A Shayna Maidel* (1984), *The Adventures of Homer McGundy* (1985), *Cyparis* (1987), *The Keepers* (1988), *Trains* (1991), *Tiny Tim Is Dead* (1992), *Lurleen* (1999)

Lebow is best known for her play *A Shayna Maidel*, Yiddish for 'A Pretty Girl', which continues to be performed in regional theatres throughout the United States. This haunting play about the reunion between a concentration-camp survivor and her sister who came to America before World War II explores the guilt of those who were spared the horror of the Holocaust. Lebow examines the personal emotional context rather than the historical or political issues surrounding the Holocaust. The play includes dream sequences and memory scenes, although the action takes place in the present. Lebow has also written and directed several plays with homeless people, addicts, prisoners and the elderly, including *Tiny Tim Is Dead*, a contemporary take on Dickens, and *Lurleen*, about Lurleen Wallace, the first female governor of Alabama.

TRY THESE:

✶HARE's *Plenty* for flashback scenes and the effect of war on the psyche; ✶RABE for the aftermath of another war, Vietnam; ✶MILLER's *Death of a Salesman* and ✶PETER SHAFFER's *Equus* for flashback technique; ✶FLANNERY's *Singer*, Jean Claude Grumberg and ✶SHERMAN's *Bent* for drama of the Holocaust.

LEE, Leslie [1935 –]
American dramatist

PLAYS INCLUDE:

Elegy to a Down Queen (1970), *First Breeze of Summer* (1975), *Colored People's Time* (1982), *Hannah Davis* (1987), *The Rabbit Foot* (1988), *Golden Boy* (1989, musical from *ODETS), *Ground People* (1990), *Black Eagles* (1991), *Spirit North* (1998?)

Lee grew up in a small town in eastern Pennsylvania. His plays depict black American middle-class life and family values. Lee contrasts the confused and restless younger generation with the stability of the older generation in *First Breeze of Summer*, his best-known work. In *Hannah Davis*, Lee explores the lives of a highly successful suburban black Philadelphia family. The founding patriarch recalls his affair with the play's title character, the town trollop, much to the amazement of his children, an opera singer, a TV celebrity and a mayor. *The Rabbit Foot* tells two stories about impoverished blacks in rural Mississippi just after World War I. The stories reflect conflicting drives – an urge to head north for better opportunities against a reluctance to leave cherished people, places and customs. In *Colored People's Time* Lee deals with the emergence of black pride during the Harlem Renaissance. In the musical *Golden Boy* (a black version of *CLIFFORD ODETS' 1930s drama), Lee chronicles the life of a Harlem boxer, Joe Wellington. *Black Eagles* explores the racism confronted by the USA's first squadron of black fighter pilots in World War II. *Spirit North* tackles issues of race, class and justice.

TRY THESE:

*BALDWIN, *HANSBERRY, *MAUGHAM's *For Services Rendered*, *O'NEILL's *Long Day's Journey into Night*, *PRIESTLEY's *Time and the Conways*, *AUGUST WILSON for contrasting family sagas; Zora Neale Hurston and *LANGSTON HUGHES for writers who were part of the Harlem Renaissance.

LEE, Levi [1940 –]
American dramatist

PLAYS INCLUDE:

Tent Meeting (1983, with *REBECCA WACKLER and *LARRY LARSON), *The Blood Orgy Series* (1983–7, *Mirandolina Unchained*, *The Grubb Chronicles* and *Tales of Rat Alley*, with *LARRY LARSON), *Some Things You Need to Know Before the World Ends: A Final Evening with the Illuminati* (1986, with *LARRY LARSON), *Nicholas DeBeaubien's Hunchback of Notre Dame* (1997, with *LARRY LARSON, *REBECCA WACKLER and John Kohler), *The Bench* (2002, with *LARRY LARSON)

Lee co-founded the Southern Theatre Conspiracy with *LARRY LARSON and *REBECCA WACKLER. Taking aim at religious fundamentalism in the South, Lee and his associates shattered conventions with their boisterous irreverence in *Tent Meeting*. Most of the play takes place in a trailer on the road, as the preacher, having kidnapped his daughter's deformed baby from a scientific laboratory, decides that he is Jesus in disguise and heads for a tent meeting in Canada.

TRY THESE:

*GANNON's *Keeping Tom Nice*, *POTTER's *Brimstone and Treacle* for God and disability; *BECKETT's *Waiting for Godot* for mysterious messages and divine non-intervention; *FRIEL's *The Faith Healer*.

LEIGH, Mike [1943 –]
British filmmaker, dramatist and director

PLAYS INCLUDE:

The Box Play (1966), *Bleak Moments* (1970), *Wholesome Glory* (1973), *The Jaws of Death* (1973), *Babies Grow Old* (1974), *The Silent Majority* (1974), *Abigail's Party* (1977), *Ecstasy* (1979), *Goose Pimples* (1981), *Smelling a Rat* (1988), *Greek Tragedy* (1989)

Salford-born Leigh trained as an actor at the Royal Academy of Dramatic Art, then moved to the Camberwell and Central Schools of Art and the London Film School before becoming associate director of the Midlands Arts Centre, Birmingham. His first original play, *The Box Play*, evolved from improvisation work in Birmingham.

Abigail's Party by Mike Leigh, directed by David Grindley, Hampstead Theatre, 2002. Steffan Rhodri as Tony, Elizabeth Berrington as Beverly, Jeremy Swift as Laurence. (Colin Willoughby/ArenaPAL)

Leigh developed a form of theatre based on structured improvisation; as he has said: 'It's necessary that the improvisations serve a particular theme or idea. I discover the substance of the play during rehearsals.' Working closely with actors, his plays develop out of a long process of workshops and improvisation from which Leigh devises a final script. Actors work in great detail with their characterisation, often beginning by developing their character alone with Leigh, and then moving towards meeting other characters gradually over the rehearsal period. For example, Anthony Sher has described his experience of preparing for his role as an Arab in *Goose Pimples* by dressing the part, exploring the West End of London in character and taking great pride in being treated in character by a London taxi driver. The process has the effect of constructing a very intense and stylised form of naturalistic theatre, which can border on caricature. Nonetheless it often works very well for television and film.

Abigail's Party

Abigail's Party is structured around a group of neighbours who meet for drinks while one couple's teenage daughter is holding a party. The play is set in the living room of the fearsome hostess, Beverley. The play charts the tensions of the relationships as they move over the course of the evening to a final dramatic conclusion. The experience of the play is something like spending an evening among a group who become increasingly embarrassing and painful to watch. A wickedly sharp satire on lower-middle-class social pretensions, it can be overplayed to the point of parody but the 2002 anniversary production suggested that it has transcended its original context and is likely to join the comedy of manners pantheon.

TRY THESE:

✴AYCKBOURN, ✴BENNETT, ✴LUCIE, ✴ORTON for satire on English middle-class pretensions; ✴ALBEE's *Who's Afraid of Virginia Woolf?*, ✴DE FILIPPO, ✴REDDIN, ✴SIMON for international comparisons; ✴BEHN, ✴CONGREVE, ✴GOLDSMITH, ✴SHERIDAN, ✴WILDE, ✴WYCHERLEY for historical comparisons; ✴BECKETT's *Waiting for Godot* and ✴ODETS' *Waiting for Lefty* for plays in which (like *Abigail's Party*) the title character never appears.

LEONARD, Hugh   [1926 –   ]
Irish dramatist

PLAYS INCLUDE:

The Big Birthday (1956), *A Leap in the Dark* (1957), *Madigan's Lock* (1958), *Walk on the Water* (1960), *The Poker Session* (1964), *The Family Way* (1964), *Mick and Mick* (1966), *The Au Pair Man* (1968), *The Patrick Pearse Motel* (1971), *Da* (1973), *Summer* (1974), *Irishmen* (1974), *Time Was* (1976), *A Life* (1978), *The Mask of Moriarty* (1986), *Pizzazz* (1986, comprising *Pizzazz*, *A View From the Obelisk* and *Roman Fever*)

Born John Keyes Byrne, Leonard is one of Ireland's most popular contemporary playwrights, and his success has led to the same sorts of misconceptions that plague ✴ALAN AYCKBOURN in England. Indeed, like Ayckbourn, Leonard frequently indicts the same moneyed bourgeois audience who flock to see his plays, and even his crowd-pleasers (such as *The Patrick Pearse Motel*, which uses the conventions of French farce to comment on the development of modern-day Ireland) have their moments of bile as well. Leonard repeatedly explores the link between the present and the past, and between people and their country. In *A Walk on the Water*, the exiled protagonist comes home to Ireland for his father's funeral, only to encounter his erstwhile companions from an era that now seems lost both to them and to their city. *Mick and Mick* refracts the same sentiment through the eyes of an Irishwoman working in Britain who returns to Ireland and who sees with the clarity of an outsider. The *Pizzazz* plays delve even further into questions of rootedness: each is about 'travellers apart from their natural environment', says Leonard, 'trying to retain their memories of a lost time and place while also enjoying the special challenges of their new homes'. (Leonard extends his examination of this balancing act in his two memoirs, *Out After Dark* and *Home Before Night*.)

Leonard has also written fiction and many adaptations (his *Stephen D.*, taken from Joyce, remains a model of its kind) and pastiche (*The Mask of Moriarty*, about Sherlock Holmes's sidekick), but he's best known for the quasi-autobiographical comedy-drama *Da* and *A Life*, two plays opposed both in tone and subject matter – the first finds life in death, the other death in life. In *Da* the middle-aged Charlie comes to terms with his dead foster father, the 'da' of the title. A gardener who has made a lifetime career out of exasperating his son, 'da' is a ghost who just won't lie down, and the play is a comic exorcism with darker shades as well. The man who gave Charlie his first job, the civil servant Desmond Drumm, has the floor in *A Life*, in which he is diagnosed as having cancer.

TRY THESE:
✳FRIEL, ✳KILROY, ✳MURPHY for Leonard's pre-eminent contemporaries, who examine the Irishman's relationship to his country; ✳BOLGER, ✳BARRIE's *Mary Rose*, ✳CARR, ✳MORTIMER's *A Voyage Round My Father* and ✳O'NEILL for familial ghosts, both literal and figurative; ✳HOWE's *Painting Churches* and ✳LANFORD WILSON's *Lemon Sky* for analogous contemporary American plays about adult children and their parents.

LESSING, Gotthold Ephraim   [1729 – 81]
German dramatist and critic

PLAYS INCLUDE:
Miss Sara Sampson (1755), *Minna von Barnhelm* (1767), *Emilia Galotti* (1772), *Nathan the Wise* (1779)

Lessing combined the theory and practice of drama in much the same way as ✳GRANVILLE-BARKER and ✳SHAW; his witty and influential theatre criticism, collected as the *Hamburgische Dramaturgie* (1769), includes both reviews of live performances at the National Theatre in Hamburg and general thoughts on the way German drama should develop. The direction he advocated was away from the previous influence of French classical tragedy and towards ✳SHAKESPEARE and Diderot as models for the writing of plays about everyday bourgeois life (though not with everyday incidents). He wrote several plays following his own precepts: *Miss Sara*

Sampson is a domestic tragedy owing much to Samuel Richardson's *Pamela*, but too sententious and violent in its end. *Emilia Galotti*, though equally emotional, works much better, as the story of the father killing his daughter (at her request) to save her from dishonour; the narrative line is strong, and the political protest at the princely abuse of power is striking, though it is carefully distanced by an Italian Renaissance setting. *Minna von Barnhelm* is an enjoyable romantic comedy of a penniless officer discharged under a cloud at the end of the Seven Years' War, and scrupulously refusing to marry his betrothed because she is an heiress. She gets him in the end, of course. Steven Pimlott staged *Nathan the Wise*, Lessing's great plea for religious tolerance, at Chichester in April 2003.

TRY THESE:
✳GOETHE and ✳SCHILLER for eighteenth-century German drama and the influence of ✳SHAKESPEARE; *Minna von Barnhelm* is not dissimilar in tone to ✳SHERIDAN and ✳GOLDSMITH; ✳CORNEILLE's *Le Cid* brings the issues of women's honour related to man-made social codes firmly to the fore.

LETTS, Tracy   [1965 –   ]
American actor and dramatist

PLAYS INCLUDE:
Killer Joe (1994), *Bug* (1996)

A former actor with the Steppenwolf company, Letts described *Killer Joe* as 'a return to the old Chicago school of rock 'n' roll, kick-ass theatre'. It is certainly a violent study of trailer-trash American life without the Jerry Springer bodyguards. Chris suggests to his divorced father that they should kill his mother to get her life insurance so that he can pay for the cocaine that she has stolen from him. Killer Joe is the hitman they hire, who demands Chris's sister as a down payment. And so it goes on. *Bug* occupies similar territory, this time a seedy motel room where an ageing waitress in a dead-end job encounters a young man with a past.

TRY THESE:
Letts's work has similarities to ✳BOND, ✳KANE, ✳LABUTE, ✳MAMET, ✳POLIAKOFF; ✳MILLER's *Death of a Salesman* for another use of insurance money.

LEVY, Deborah   [1959 –   ]
South African-born dramatist, poet and novelist

PLAYS INCLUDE:
Eva and Moses (1983), *Pax* (1984), *Dream Mama* (1985), *Clam* (1985), *Ophelia and the Great Idea* (1985, later *Pushing the Prince into Denmark*), *The Naked Cake* (1986), *Our Lady* (1986), *Heresies* (1986), *Silver Herrings* (1989), *Judith and Holofernes* (1990, with ✳HOWARD BARKER), *Swallowing Geography* (1991), *Nights at the Circus* (1991, from Angela Carter), *The B File* (1994), *Macbeth False Memories* (2000)

Levy has made a mark as a writer in several genres. *Pax*, for the Women's Theatre Group, is a complex, densely worded play so rich in allusion and ideas as to feel like a hallucinatory journey into the contemporary female psyche. This rummage through female archetypes, its exploration of mothers and daughters, philosophical meditations on death, patriarchy, the Holocaust and survival, and its confrontations with past, present and warnings of a precarious future in a nuclear age, remains a landmark in mid-1980s feminism. *Heresies*, commissioned for the short-lived RSC Women's Group and created through workshop improvisations, is a distillation of contemporary modes of sexual and other politics, seen through the eyes of different archetypes (Cholla the Displaced Person, Leah the Composer, etc.) that seemed unusually short on plausibility, but long on emotional power. Even when not sparking on all plugs, the power and intelligence of Levy's writing and the breadth of her vision about such recurrent themes as grief, displacement, the nuclear threat, resistance, the importance of female values, and survival make hers a singular and uncompromising talent.

TRY THESE:
✳YANKOWITZ's *Alarms* for a heightened Cassandra treatment of the nuclear future; ✳LAVERY for another Ophelia and her *Origin of the Species* for a feminist reassessment of history; ✳FREISTADT's *The Celebration of Kokura* and ✳LOWE's *Keeping Body and Soul Together* for peace themes; ✳DE ANGELIS and ✳KANE for similarly allusive use of language.

LINNEY, Romulus   [1930 –   ]
American dramatist

PLAYS INCLUDE:
The Sorrows of Frederick (1967), *Holy Ghosts* (1971), *The Love Suicide at Schofield Barracks* (1972), *Esther* (1973), *Autopsie* (1973), *Childe Byron* (1977), *Tennessee* (1979), *The Captivity of Pixie Shedman* (1981), *The Death of King Philip* (1984), *Why the Lord Came to Sand Mountain* (1984), *A Woman Without a Name* (1986), *Unchanging Love* (1989, from Chekhov), *2* (1990), *Mountain Memory* (1997)

Linney is seldom produced in Britain. Raised in Tennessee and North Carolina and educated at the elite Oberlin College and Yale Drama School, Linney is concerned with big themes – history, religion, and the meaning of art in the light of history and religion. Linney's plays, many of which are set in the rural American South, are often referred to as 'gothic'. Partly this is due to the subject matter, which often derives from folklore and myth: snake handlers (*Holy Ghosts*), illusion (*Tennessee*), ghosts (*Childe Byron*, *The Captivity of Pixie Shedman*). The gothic label stems also from Linney's language, in which characters' day-to-day speech may be heightened and lyrical. *The Sorrows of Frederick*, about Frederick II of Prussia, is, as Mel Gussow noted, 'not primarily an epic about wars and power plays, but an interior psychodrama about what goes on in the crumbling mind of a philosopher-king'. *The Love Suicide at Schofield Barracks* is presented as a court investigation into the death of an army general and his wife. Each witness adds his or her testimony until the completed mosaic reveals that the couple committed a ritual double suicide to protest against the Vietnam War. Hermann Goering, Hitler's second-in-command, is the subject of *2*.

TRY THESE:
✳ SHEPARD for an alternative mode of American Gothic; ✳ LANFORD WILSON's *Fifth of July* as an anti-Vietnam play with a domestic setting; ✳ PIRANDELLO's *Henry IV* for parallels and contrasts with *The Sorrows of Frederick*.

LITTLEWOOD, Joan   [1914 – 2002]
English actress and director

PRODUCTIONS INCLUDE:
Oh What a Lovely War (1963)

Littlewood overcame conditions of continuous financial crisis to create productions of great energy and power with Theatre Workshop from negligible resources. One of the first British directors to make extensive use of improvisation, she had remarkable skills in developing performances. Littlewood was trusted by ✳ BRECHT with the first British production of *Mother Courage* (Barnstable 1955), which she directed as well as playing the title role, and should be remembered as much for the anti-nuclear war *Uranium 235* (by Ewan McColl), a pro-peace *Lysistrata* and classic productions of *Volpone* and *Richard II* as for the plays by ✳ BEHAN, ✳ DELANEY and Lionel Bart which gained wide audiences when Theatre Workshop productions transferred to the West End from the Theatre Royal Stratford East.

In 1963 the company produced *Oh What a Lovely War*, a fiercely satirical, anti-war World War I documentary built around popular songs and presented as a pierrot show. This passionate account of the horrors of war gained some of its contemporary urgency from a sense that the world was once more on the brink of extinction in the wake of the Cuban missile crisis. The Theatre Workshop style, with its apparently improvisational quality, its intercutting of styles and scenes, its use of songs and its rediscovery of the value of montage, played an important part in creating a wider theatrical environment more suited to an emerging desire to break away from the narrowly deterministic qualities of Naturalism.

TRY THESE:
✳ LEIGH for a different kind of improvisation;
✳ JOHN MCGRATH, ✳ JELLICOE for 'community';
✳ MCGUINNESS, ✳ WHELAN for World War I.

LOCHHEAD, Liz   [1947 –   ]
Scottish poet, playwright and performer

PLAYS INCLUDE:
Blood and Ice (1982), *Shanghaied* (1983, revised as *Britannia Rules*), *Dracula* (1985), *Mary Queen of Scots Got Her Head Chopped Off* (1987), *The Big Picture* (1988), *Patter Merchants* (1989), *Jock Tamson's Bairns* (1990), *Quelques Fleurs* (1991), *Perfect Days* (1998), *Medea* (2000, from ✳ EURIPIDES), *Miseryguts* (2002, from ✳ MOLIÈRE's *Le Misanthrope*)

Lochhead has a painter's eye for local colour and situation, a wordsmith's ability to shape that perception into vital language, and underpinning all this a strong sense of how female sexuality influences actions and reactions within past history and modern society. *Blood and Ice* has undergone several changes since its first production, but the main thrust of the piece is unchanged: the nature of female creativity. The plot concerns the hectic, febrile relationship between Byron and the Shelleys and the circumstances that led to Mary Shelley's penning *Frankenstein*. Mary's 'natural' creations were, of course, her children, but they died. Enter that most unnatural of creations, the monster which Frankenstein, defying the laws of flesh and blood, brings to life and which Mary, so conscious of mortalities around her, makes immortal in print. Why? asks Lochhead. And supplies a fascinating, shrewd scenario of how an impressionable girl not only takes on womanhood and its periodic burdens but begins to question society's perception of womankind. *Blood and Ice* is a landmark play in Scottish women's writing.

'We bleed. Even when you don't prick us' could be the byword of many of Lochhead's women, whether they be out of history or off the Byres Road in Glasgow. Lochhead doesn't ignore or sanitise the human mess of sex, menstruation or birth any more than she avoids the mess and confusion of human relationships. She will poke marvellous, well-judged fun at pretension – female or male – but she has compassion and insight when it comes to analysing how and why men and women so often get it wrong about themselves and about each other. *Jock Tamson's*

Bairns, a performance piece Lochhead created with Communicado, revealed just how closely she scans the Scottish psyche as well as her fellow man and woman. Subtitled 'The Last Burnt Supper', the project took the patriotic and macho myths surrounding Scotland's national hero-bard, Robert Burns, and used them to point up the underlying sadness and inadequacy of a race that celebrates the poet's drunkenness and womanising as much as, if not more than, his poems and his politics. Here Lochhead was on some of her best territory, the Scotsman's apparent inability to express emotion, except when drunk, or at a football match, or when no one's looking.

She has translated ✱MOLIÈRE into nippy, colloquial Scots, penned monologues and adapted Bram Stoker's *Dracula* for the stage, a dramatisation that understands the bone-marrow issues of sex, possession, surrender and redemptive love which are the (almost subconscious) subtext of the novel. And, being Lochhead there are rich female resonances to Renfield's litany of 'The blood is the life' *Quelques Fleurs* interweaves two monologues by a couple whose marriage is disintegrating and *Perfect Days* is about the pressures on a woman who is nearing forty and beginning to worry about motherhood.

TRY THESE:
Other contemporary Scottish women dramatists include Marcella Evaristi, Anne-Marie de Mambro, ✱MUNRO; ✱MACDONALD's *When I Was a Girl I Used to Scream and Shout* is strong on love and conflict between mothers and daughters; ✱BRENTON's *Bloody Poetry* also grapples with sexism and the Shelleys; Lochhead also adapted ✱MOLIÈRE's *Tartuffe*.

LONERGAN, Kenneth   [1963 –]
American dramatist and screenwriter

PLAYS INCLUDE:
This Is Our Youth (1996), *The Waverly Gallery* (1999), *Lobby Hero* (2001)

Lonergan was one of the scriptwriters on *Gangs of New York* and on *Analyze This*. In *This Is Our Youth* he presents us with a group of rich New York young adults in the early 1980s who find themselves alienated from both their parents and the values of the world they live in. *The Waverly Gallery* is about an elderly woman with Alzheimer's disease who owns the gallery of the title and how her disease affects her family. In *Lobby Hero* Lonergan presents a set of shifting alliances and moral dilemmas about race, gender, justice and responsibility as a doorman battles with his conscience in the face of conflicting pressures from the police and his boss. In all three plays Lonergan creates character and sets scenes wittily and economically, creating an informal trilogy of New York life.

TRY THESE:
✱MAMET for similar economy of dialogue and scene setting, ✱CORTHRON for a different angle on contemporary American life; Lonergan has been compared favourably to ✱MILLER, and to ✱SHAW.

LORCA, Federico García   [1898 – 1935]
Spanish dramatist, poet and artist

PLAYS INCLUDE:
The Butterfly's Evil Spell (1920), *Mariana Pineda* (1927), *In Five Years' Time* (1930), *The Public* (1930), *Blood Wedding* (1932), *Yerma* (1934), *Dona Rosita la Soltera* (1935), *The House of Bernarda Alba* (1935)

As a student Lorca forged close friendships with Salvador Dalí and Luis Bunuel. Surrealism was something that sat easily with Lorca – *The Public* and *In Five Years' Time* are Surrealistic fantasies – but he was mistrustful of intellectual and literary elites, and his plays are rooted in Spanish folklore and traditions. His second play, *Mariana Pineda*, told the story of a heroine of the revolution of the 1830s. Lorca thought of himself as a playwright for the Spanish people; he became involved in 1931 with a travelling theatre group, La Baracca, which toured classic Spanish drama throughout the regions of Spain. Many of his texts employ farce, folk tale and poetry, popular and traditional forms, to make them accessible.

Lorca's most important works are those which bring together his passionate feeling for the history and traditions of Andalusia with his poetic power. The 'trilogy of the

Spanish Earth' – *Blood Wedding, Yerma* and *The House of Bernarda Alba* – is firmly rooted within Spanish communities, and concerned with marriage, sexuality and the constraints and commitments of the community. *Blood Wedding* is based on an actual story Lorca came across in a newspaper fragment that told of a family vendetta and a bride who ran away with the son of the enemy family. The first act is relatively naturalistic, but in the second, the moon and death appear in an extraordinarily powerful image to oversee the fleeing lovers. *The House of Bernarda Alba* is a play exclusively of women, in which the destructive power of the matriarch Bernarda Alba becomes a metaphor for sexual repression and constraints on liberty.

On 19 August 1936, in the early days of the Spanish Civil War, Lorca was shot by the fascist paramilitary Black Squad. His body lies in an unmarked grave, but he remains Spain's most celebrated playwright.

Yerma

Yerma means 'the barren one'. The play is a powerful study of a peasant woman, obsessed with the desire for a child. But childlessness in Lorca's hands becomes a metaphor for other kinds of barrenness: Yerma's marriage is not only sterile because it has not produced children; her racking pain is quite clearly a desire for another way of being. In a community of traditional wisdoms and attitudes to marriage, Yerma is offered the commandments of marriage: 'You must obey your husband who is your owner and master'; and while keeping to her own code of honour, recognises that she is alone in her integrity. In a final act of revenge she strangles her husband, recognising that he can never satisfy her and that she has been denied the one positive outcome of her marriage, a child. The play is a powerful study of sexual hypocrisies, of the constraints on women of traditional 'femininity', and of 'machismo' on men. *Yerma* was given a magnificent and legendary production by Victor Garcia (later revived by Nuria Espert) in which the play was performed on a huge trampoline and billowing drapes.

TRY THESE:
✷ ORTON writes with a bitter awareness of sexual hypocrisies; ✷ KESSELMAN's *My Sister in This House* is another claustrophobic household of sexual repression; ✷ LAVERY's *Mummy* naughtily satirises a typically claustrophobic household; Robert David Macdonald for translations of Lorca; Lindsay Kemp's *The Cruel Garden* is based on Lorca's life; Anna Furse's *Yerma's Eggs* for a modern take on *Yerma*.

LOWE, Stephen   [1947 –]
British dramatist

PLAYS INCLUDE:
Cards (1971), *Stars* (1976), *Touched* (1977), *Shooting Fishing and Riding* (1977), *Sally Ann Hallelujah Band* (1977), *The Ragged Trousered Philanthropists* (1978, from Robert Tressell), *Glasshouses* (1981; retitled as *Moving Pictures*), *Tibetan Inroads* (1981), *Strive* (1982), *Trial of Frankenstein* (1984), *Seachange* (1984), *Keeping Body and Soul Together* (1984), *Desire* (1986), *Demon Lovers* (1987), *The Storm* (1987, from ✷ OSTROVSKY), *Divine Gossip* (1988), *William Tell* (1989, from ✷ SCHILLER), *Paradise* (musical, 1990), *The Alchemical Wedding* (1998)

Lowe has tended to centre on socialist and feminist themes which he has tackled from a wide variety of angles: in *Cards* the idea is that Donald McGill-style seaside postcards are actually photographs of real people whom we see discussing their work as they wait for their photographs to be taken; *Stars* shows two couples acting out film fantasies during World War II; *Shooting Fishing and Riding* is a play about rape, based on Susan Brownmiller's *Act of Will*. Lowe has written about the Falklands in *Strive* and, allegorically, in *Seachange*, and about the Chinese annexation of Tibet in *Tibetan Inroads*. He is always a challenging playwright with a strong concern for human dignity and a firm commitment to the idea of 'a decent, equal, peaceful future', which comes over strongly in his two best-known works, *Touched* and *The Ragged Trousered Philanthropists*. *Touched*, set in Nottingham in the period between the end of Word War II in Europe and the surrender of Japan, explores the relationship between a group of working-class women as they hope and fear for the future, set against the background of the discovery of Belsen, the election of the Labour government and the dropping of the first atomic bombs. Lowe's version of the socialist classic *The Ragged Trousered Philanthropists*, first developed in workshops with Joint Stock, is a moving account of the struggle of working men to come to an understanding of their oppression and carry the fight back to the capitalists. *The Alchemical Wedding* takes the alchemist's search for a means of transmuting base metal into gold as a metaphor for an exploration of the nature of marriage.

TRY THESE:

✱ HARE's *Fanshen*, another Joint Stock play, shows the Chinese working classes reaching an understanding of the roots of their situation; Marc Blitzstein's *The Cradle Will Rock*, ✱ MILLER, and ✱ ODETS' *Waiting for Lefty* for comparable American examples; ✱ BRENTON and ✱ HARE, separately and together, have written plays which, like *Touched*, take Angus Calder's *The People's War* as their inspiration; others to take the Falklands War as their theme are ✱ MARCHANT in *Coming Home* and ✱ PAGE in *Falkland Sound/Voces de Malvinas*; Tony Roper's *The Steamie* for a Scottish working-class community of women; ✱ DUNN's *Steaming* for another English version: ✱ JONSON for *The Alchemist*.

LUCAS, Craig   [1951 –   ]
American dramatist

PLAYS INCLUDE:

Missing Persons (1980), *Marry Me a Little* (1980, with Norman Rene), *Reckless* (1983), *Blue Window* (1984), *Three Postcards* (1987, musical), *Prelude to a Kiss* (1990), *God's Heart* (1997), *The Dying Gaul* (1998), *Stranger* (2000), *This Thing of Darkness* (2002, with David Schulner)

In his address to the first American National Gay and Lesbian Theatre Conference in 1990 Lucas attributed his dramatic development and style to his homosexuality, his study with the poet Anne Sexton (who advised him to make his writing 'strange') and, later in his career, the AIDS epidemic. In *Reckless* a wife leaves home on Christmas Eve to escape her husband's plan to have her killed for an insurance settlement; an ironic and humorous convolution of American family ideology. He uses separate scenes presented simultaneously in *Blue Window* to highlight the coincidence and frailty of human relationships. In *Prelude to a Kiss*, the title of a tender ballad about one's yearning for another recorded by Ella Fitzgerald in 1938, Lucas takes two newlyweds who become spiritually separated and have their fidelity tested in an odd way. The young wife's body is overtaken by a dying man's soul, a strange and oblique reference to love and devotion in the era of AIDS. Specifically, can, or how will, the young husband remain faithful when his wife's soul has been overtaken by the spectre of death? His conundrum does not compromise the plot's romantic tone, it elevates the sense of the play to one of universality. *God's Heart* and *The Dying Gaul* both examine the ways in which the Internet impacts on modern relationships. *This Thing of Darkness* presents two young men graduating from high school and their later selves looking back on their aspirations from the compromises and failures of the future. Lucas has yet to make his mark in Britain.

TRY THESE:

✱ MILLER's *Death of a Salesman* for another version of dying to collect the insurance; S. Ansky's *The Dybbuk* for possession; ✱ ELYOT, ✱ FIERSTEIN, ✱ KONDOLEON, ✱ KRAMER, ✱ KUSHNER, ✱ RAVENHILL for AIDS; ✱ MARBER's *Closer* for the impact of the Internet; ✱ STOPPARD's *Arcadia* for time shifts.

LUCIE, Doug   [1953 –   ]
British dramatist

PLAYS INCLUDE:

John Clare's Mad Nuncle (1975), *Rough Trade* (1977), *We Love You* (1978), *Oh Well* (1978), *The New Garbo* (1978), *Heroes* (1979), *Poison* (1980), *Strangers in the Night* (1981), *Hard Feelings* (1982), *Progress* (1984), *Key to the World* (1984), *Force and Hypocrisy* (1986), *Fashion* (1987), *The Shallow End* (1997), *Love You, Too* (1998), *The Green Man* (2002)

Lucie made a reputation as the satirical chronicler of the underside of the bright new world of eighties style, be it that of the liberated new man in *Progress* or the marketing of politicians in *Fashion*, which, as the decade grew to a close, turned out to be ever more prescient. Lucie attacks those who use current trends for their own egocentric ends, but since that is almost everyone in his plays they achieve major heights of misanthropy in their depiction of a hard, uncaring, manipulative lifestyle. Lucie can be very funny in his presentation of the mannerisms and jargon of his characters, but there is no compensating warmth and little hope in a world in which cynicism is the norm and where the plots ensure that what little progress is made is ignored by the other characters. Lucie returned to the theatre at the end of the 1990s with *The Shallow End*, an attack on corporate takeovers in the newspaper business where staff are hired and fired at the magnate's daughter's wedding reception, *Love You, Too* (which tracks two couples from 1992 and 1997) and *The Green Man*, in which a group of men waiting in a pub express their varied discontents. Critical reactions to these new plays suggested that Luce had yet to find a distinctive voice for the new millennium.

Progress

Progress is an uncomfortably accurate presentation of right-on people attempting to grapple with all the hazards and pitfalls of negotiating the contradictions of patriarchy and capitalism while using a working-class battered wife as a medium for their own antagonisms. Many of the characters are homosexual or bisexual and there are important points about the manipulation of trendy ideas to give people sexual credibility, particularly the Men's Group's attempt to discuss pornography. Under the brilliantly vitriolic comedy of surface manners, there is a genuine sense of the waste of human potential as relationships collapse and sexual politics becomes sexual warfare.

TRY THESE:
✱BEHN, ✱CONGREVE, ✱COWARD, ✱JONSON, ✱ORTON, ✱REDDIN, ✱WYCHERLEY for manipulative societies where wit is at a premium;

✱DANIELS' *Masterpieces* for a contemporary feminist approach to the question of pornography; ✱CHURCHILL's *Cloud Nine* for polymorphous sexuality; ✱LEVY's *Heresies* for another view of sexual politics; ✱HAMPTON's adaptation of Laclos's *Les Liaisons Dangereuses* as the portrait of cunning and viperish manipulation; ✱CHURCHILL's *Serious Money*, ✱CRIMP, ✱JEFFREYS' *Valued Friends* for further brittle barometers of the age; ✱BRENTON and ✱HARE's *Brassneck* and *Pravda* for more successful approaches to some of the issues raised in *The Shallow End* and *Love You, Too*.

LUCKHAM, Claire   [1944 –   ]
British dramatist

PLAYS INCLUDE:
Scum (with Chris Bond, 1976), *Yatsy and the Whale* (1977), *Tuebrook Tanzi the Venus Fly Trap* (1978, later known as *Tugby Tanzi* and then *Trafford Tanzi*, 1980), *Aladdin* (1978), *Fish Riding Bikes* (1979), *Finishing School* (1982), *The Girls in the Pool* (1982, later known as *Gwen*), *Walking on Water* (1983), *Moll Flanders* (1986 from Defoe), *Imber* (1986), *Alice in Wartime* (1986), *Mary Stuart* (1988, from ✱SCHILLER), *Dogspot* (1994), *The Dramatic Attitudes of Miss Fanny Kemble* (1996)

Scum, an early exploration of sexual and socialist politics set in a laundry during the Paris Commune of 1871, was commissioned by Monstrous Regiment and co-written by Luckham and her husband, director Chris Bond. She was initially associated with Liverpool's Everyman and is best known for *Trafford Tanzi*, which has been performed all round the world (often with a different place name to reflect local geography) and translated into many languages. Her other plays have also explored female issues, particularly relationships between women, to each other and to work, with the series of monologues about women's friendship (*Fish Riding Bikes, Finishing School*), a typists' strike at Liverpool Council (*The Girls in the Pool*) and adaptations of Defoe's *Moll Flanders* and ✱SCHILLER's *Mary Stuart*. But there have also been a couple of community plays, including one about the whaling industry and the army occupation of Salisbury Plain (*Imber*). In *The Dramatic Attitudes of Miss Fanny Kemble*, Luckham explores the issues arising from the nineteenth-century actress's marriage to a slave-owner.

Trafford Tanzi

Trafford Tanzi, a storming visual and physical metaphor of female liberation (as it was then seen) enacted through an actual wrestling match between Tanzi and the various characters in her life, first started out doing the rounds of the pubs of Liverpool. Taken up and toured by various companies, it finally settled into a long and successful run at the Mermaid in London. *Trafford Tanzi*, with its direct appeal to audience participation, gives value for money as a theatrical experience as Tanzi changes from socially conditioned, feminine little girl to renegade and ultimate wrestler, meeting her husband on equal terms and literally throwing him. The play operates within both sporting and agit-prop conventions, eliciting gender-based responses from its audiences. Inevitably, given its genesis and the sport it uses, there isn't much room for subtlety in its sexual politics, but it is a robust reminder that actually sexism isn't always subtle and that ingrained attitudes are hard to dispel.

TRY THESE:

✶CHURCHILL, ✶DANIELS, ✶DUNN, ✶GEMS, ✶MACDONALD, ✶O'MALLEY, ✶PAGE for women writers of the period; for taking men on in their own sphere, ✶WERTENBAKER's *The Grace of Mary Traverse*; for an earlier counterpart, ✶MIDDLETON and ✶DEKKER's *The Roaring Girl*; ✶ROBERT DAVID McDonald adapted ✶SCHILLER's *Mary Stuart*; ✶BYRNE's *The Slab Boys Trilogy*, ✶LOWE's adaptation of Robert Tressell's *The Ragged Trousered Philanthropists* and ✶WESKER's *The Kitchen* for industrially based pieces; for other realistic sporting images, ✶GODBER's *Up 'n' Under*, ✶PAGE's *Golden Girls*, ✶SACKLER's *The Great White Hope*, ✶STOREY's *The Changing Room*; ✶CHURCHILL's *Top Girls* and *Serious Money* are two of the most successful variants of women making it on male terms; ✶BOUCICAULT for titles adapted to local situations.

LUDLAM, Charles   [1940 – 87]
American dramatist and performer

PLAYS INCLUDE:

Big Hotel (1966), *Conquest of the Universe or When Queens Collide* (1967), *Turds in Hell* (1969, with Bill Vehr), *The Grand Tarot* (1969), *Bluebeard* (1970), *Eunuchs of the Forbidden City* (1971), *Corn* (1972, music and lyrics by Virgil Young), *Camille* (1973), *Hot Ice* (1974), *Stage Blood* (1975), *Jack and the Beanstalk* (1975), *Isle of the Hermaphrodites or The Murdered Minion* (1976), *Caprice or Fashion Bound* (1976), *Der Ring Gott Farblonjet* (1977), *The Ventriloquist's Wife* (1978), *Utopia, Incorporated* (1978), *The Enchanted Pig* (1979), *A Christmas Carol* (1979), *Reverse Psychology* (1980), *Love's Tangled Web* (1981), *Secret Lives of the Sixties* (1982), *Exquisite Torture* (1982), *Le Bourgeois Avant-Garde* (1983), *Galas* (1983), *The Mystery of Irma Vep* (1984), *Medea* (1984), *How to Write a Play* (1984), *Salammbo* (1985), *The Artificial Jungle* (1986)

Playwright, actor, producer and director, Ludlam (who died from AIDS in 1987) is best known for his work with the Ridiculous Theatrical Company, which he founded in 1969. After graduating from Hofstra University in 1965, where he first developed his style of whimsical high camp and farce (though he felt the term 'camp' was homophobic), his work was sprinkled with puns, satire, reversals of logic and literary allusions. Bizarre alterations of classic plays, novels and films prevail in productions that alternate between homage and camp, a revisionist strategy to tear down the walls of the 'silent war waged against anyone who's different'.

If homosexual stereotypes are an issue in Ludlam's art, more so is liberation from preconceived notions of happiness and morality. Ludlam gave us an endearing, lovable and sometimes laughable portrait of the homosexual community without ever losing a biting satirical edge. *Hot Ice*, for example, is a mad anarchic comedy where dead bodies are put on ice for renewed life in some more peaceable era than the present. *Camille*, one of his most widely acclaimed works, starred Ludlam in the title role dressed as a beautiful woman, save for the exposed hair on his chest. The theme of forbidden love is ridiculed; the concept of undying love mocked. In *Bluebeard*, the plot hinges on Bluebeard's infatuation with creating a third gender by inventing a new genital. *The Mystery of Irma Vep* is a parody of just about every cliché of the gothic and the melodramatic from vampires (the title is a clue) to mummies.

TRY THESE:
✷ CHURCHILL's *Cloud Nine* and ✷ ORTON's *What the Butler Saw* for transvestism; ✷ DURANG for sexual spoofs; ✷ STOPPARD's *Rosencrantz and Guildenstern Are Dead* for new takes on the classics; ✷ JARRY's *Ubu Roi* for profaning theatrical traditions; ✷ BARTLETT for mould-breaking; Ludlam played Hedda in ✷ IBSEN's *Hedda Gabler*; *Stage Blood* is a version of ✷ SHAKESPEARE's *Hamlet*.

LUKE, Peter   [1919 –   ]
British dramatist

PLAYS INCLUDE:
Hadrian the Seventh (1967), *Bloomsbury* (1974), *Married Love* (1985)

Luke has written relatively few plays in the course of a varied career (wine trade, head of scripts for ABC Television, farming in Andalucia, director of the Abbey Theatre, etc.), but his version of Frederick Rolfe/Baron Corvo's novel *Hadrian VII* reproduced much of the neurotic fascination of that amazing piece of wish-fulfilment, and became an international hit. Hadrian VII, like Rolfe, was a failed priest but, unlike Rolfe, he was made Pope, forgave all his enemies at great and self-righteous length, and revolutionised the Church and the world before being assassinated by a crazed Irishman. Luke's play uses details from Rolfe's life and his other books as an effective frame for the story – at the end we see Rolfe standing on stage, clutching his manuscript, as he watches Hadrian's funeral. Later plays, such as *Bloomsbury*, about Virginia Woolf, and *Married Love*, about Marie Stopes, had only moderate success.

TRY THESE:
For other popes, ✷ BRECHT's *Galileo* and ✷ HOCHHÜTH's *The Representative*.

M

MacARTHUR, Charles
See HECHT, Ben

McCAFFERTY, Owen [1961 –]
Northern Irish dramatist

PLAYS INCLUDE:
Shoot the Crow (1997), *Mojo Mickybo* (1998), *No Place Like Home* (2001), *Closing Time* (2002), *Scenes from the Big Picture* (2003)

McCafferty has established himself as a poetic chronicler of the everyday hopes and fears of ordinary Belfast people in a series of inventive plays. In *Shoot the Crow* he presents four workmen aged from nineteen to sixty-five who are finishing off a tiling job. One is about to retire and needs money to buy a window-cleaning round to stave off death by boredom, one needs money to effect a reconciliation with the mother of his child, one wants to buy a motorbike and one wants to send his daughter on a school trip. They hatch plots to steal some excess tiles and form and re-form alliances before everything comes to nothing. The dialogue is sharp and the underlying issues emerge with an apparently effortless naturalism but the play is tightly constructed to reveal a texture of failed aspiration. *Mojo Mickybo* re-enacts a childhood friendship across the sectarian divide in which two actors play all the parts, populating a world with childlike simplicity as we gradually piece together the whispered evasions and concealed rifts that construct the adult worlds around them in a powerful presentation of the loss of innocence. *No Place Like Home*, a devised piece scripted by McCafferty, deals with issues of migration, while *Closing Time* is set in a run-down Belfast bar-cum-hotel in which the characters are the familiar losers of the genre, albeit with the added resonances of the Northern Irish political situation to contextualise their problems. The somewhat ironically titled *Scenes from the Big Picture* presents a day in the lives of Belfast folk as a funeral leads two brothers to the discovery of their father's allotment arms dump, businesses go under, raids on shops go wrong, the body of a missing son is discovered and people continue to mess up their lives without ever quite coming to understand their roles in the bigger picture.

TRY THESE:
✱ O'NEILL's *The Iceman Cometh* for bar-room desperation; ✱ KEATLEY's *My Mother Said* for childhood; ✱ CARTWRIGHT's *Road* for a panoramic picture of a day in the life; ✱ DEVLIN, ✱ MARIE JONES, ✱ REID for modern Belfast.

McDONAGH, Martin [1970 –]
British dramatist

PLAYS INCLUDE:
The Beauty Queen of Leenane (1996), *A Skull in Connemara* (1997), *The Lonesome West* (1997), *The Cripple of Inishmann* (1997), *The Lieutenant of Inishmore* (2000)

McDonagh writes about Ireland but he was born and brought up in London to Irish parents who later returned to Ireland, so his experience of the country derives mainly from childhood summer holidays. He wrote unsuccessfully for several years before the Druid Theatre in Galway decided to stage *The Beauty Queen of Leenane*, which initiated a flurry of productions in 1997, a flirtation with the film industry and a controversial return to the stage with *The Lieutenant of Inishmore*. In *The Beauty Queen of Leenane* the setting is rural Galway, where a domineering mother and her middle-aged daughter are locked in a dance of insult and abuse as the mother intervenes to destroy the daughter's hopes of romance. *A Skull in Connemara* literally involves digging up the past, as a gravedigger clearing old graves is confronted with suspicions about the death of his wife, and *The Lonesome West* has another pair locked in a dance of manic insult, this time brothers, one of whom has killed their father. These plays constitute a loose trilogy, linked thematically rather than by shared characters.

The Cripple of Inishmann tackles the familiar Irish questions of migration and how Irish identities are created in a sour account of the interaction between the Aran islanders and the famous documentary maker Robert Flaherty, in which an unloved islander is determined to escape to Hollywood but eventually cannot stomach the way the film industry creates its own version of the 'stage Irishman'. The second play in a projected Aran Islands trilogy, *The Lieutenant of Inishmore*, ran into serious difficulty with prospective producers before the RSC finally staged it in 2001 and the third play, *The Banshees of Inishmore*, still awaits production. *The Lieutenant of Inishmore* dared to attack conventional ways of treating 'The Troubles', showing Republican paramilitaries engaged in an extremely violent and macabre attempt to discover who was responsible for the death of a cat belonging to their leader 'Mad Padraig'.

McDonagh's plays negotiate a theatrically familiar Irish rural landscape with the eye of a dramatist who has been heavily influenced by the films of Martin Scorsese and Quentin Tarantino and the work of ✶DAVID MAMET. Like much of the work of the 1990s, the plays do not shrink from violent images and violent action, coupled with blackly comic wit, but they are the more unsettling for doing so within fairly traditional dramatic structures.

TRY THESE:
✶MCPHERSON for contrast; for different versions of rural Ireland, ✶CARR, ✶FRIEL, ✶SYNGE; ✶BOUCICAULT, ✶MARIE JONES, ✶SHAW for stage and film Irishmen; ✶TENNESSEE WILLIAMS' *The Glass Menagerie* for fragile mother–daughter relationships.

MacDONALD, Sharman [1951–]
British dramatist

PLAYS INCLUDE:
When I Was a Girl I Used to Scream and Shout (1984), *The Brave* (1988), *When We Were Women* (1988), *All Things Nice* (1991), *Shades* (1992), *The Winter Guest* (1993), *Borders of Paradise* (1995), *After Juliet* (1999)

With her wit and razor-sharp observation, Glasgow-born actress-turned-writer Macdonald has made a speciality out of revealing the growing pains of young Scottish girls' rites of passage to womanhood. She is particularly strong on the conflict of emotions inherent in burgeoning sexual awareness, but the huge success of her first play, *When I Was A Girl I Used to Scream and Shout* – a painful, bitterly funny study of a Scottish childhood and adolescence for which she won the *Evening Standard's* Most Promising Playwright award for 1984 – may have owed as much to its voyeuristic pleasures as to its intrinsic artistic merit. *When I Was A Girl* is a remarkably honest study in stunted womanhood – of compromised choices, mother–daughter warfare, the dead hand of Presbyterianism and the pull of the past in the present. Although Macdonald can be caustically humorous about adolescent sexual curiosity, she also has a remarkable skill in deciphering and uncovering the emotional terrain of young women, as subsequent plays have shown. In *All Things Nice*, the variations on some of those themes are wittily and delicately worked out in a young Scottish schoolgirl's ambivalent relationships with her immediate circle: her best friend, her mother (absent in the Middle East), her grandmother and her grandmother's 'friend', her boyfriend and an offstage 'flasher'. While the pains of adolescence remain a significant feature in her work she has also developed a fine eye for age and grief (*The Winter Guest*, later filmed by Alan Rickman with Emma Thompson and Phyllida Law) and extended her study of adolescence via *Borders of Paradise* to the aftermath of *Romeo and Juliet* as the surviving Capulets and Montagues attempt to adjust to the new situation.

TRY THESE:
✱DELANEY, ✱KEARSLEY, ✱KEAILEY, ✱PAGE for mother–daughter relationships; ✱O'MALLEY for a Catholic variation on sexual repression; ✱DUNN, ✱MCINTYRE, and ✱WASSERSTEIN's *The Heidi Chronicles* for comparisons; ✱BYRNE's *The Slab Boys Trilogy* (Scottish), ✱SIMON's *Brighton Beach Memoirs* (American) for male adolescence; ✱MORNIN's *Kate* and ✱REID for Irish adolescence; ✱SHAKESPEARE for *Romeo and Juliet*; ✱BARKER, ✱LEVY for alternative views of Shakespearian material.

McGRATH, John   [1935 – 2002]
British dramatist and director

PLAYS INCLUDE:
A Man Has Two Fathers (1958), *Events While Guarding the Bofors Gun* (1966), *Random Happenings in the Hebrides* (1970), *Trees in the Wind* (1971), *Soft or a Girl* (1971, revised as *My Pal and Me*), *Fish in the Sea* (1972), *The Cheviot, the Stag and the Black, Black Oil* (1973), *The Game's a Bogey* (1974), *Little Red Hen* (1975), *Yobbo Nowt* (1975, also known as *Mum's the Word* and *Left Out Lady*), *Joe's Drum* (1979), *Bitter Apples* (1979), *Swings and Roundabouts* (1980), *Blood Red Roses* (1980), *Nightclass* (1981), *Rejoice!* (1982), *The Women of the Dunes* (1983), *The Baby and the Bathwater* (1984), *Behold the Sun* (1985, opera libretto with Alexander Goehr), *All the Fun of the Fair* (1986, with others), *Mhàri Mhór* (1987), *Border Warfare* (1989), *John Brown's Body* (1990), *Watching for Dolphins* (1991), *The Wicked Old Man* (1992), *The Silver Darlings* (1994, after Neil Gunn), *Half the Picture* (1994, with Richard Norton Taylor), *The Last of the MacEachans* (1996), *Worksong* (1997), *HyperLynks* (2001, revised 2002)

McGrath was among the most inventive and prolific of contemporary socialist dramatists. He was a co-founder of *Z Cars* (an innovation in television police series), and directed arts shows, documentaries and new plays until 1965 when he left full-time television work to concentrate on writing his own plays. In 1971 he founded 7:84 Theatre Company. Much of his subsequent theatre work as a writer and director was for either the English or Scottish 7:84 companies (and subsequently Wildcat) but he continued to write, direct and produce for television and film, and remained an insistent and important voice in socialist debates around drama, theatre and cultural forms, both in his theory and in his practice.

Besides his own plays, much of McGrath's writing has been a reinterpretation of classic theatre texts. His version of *The Seagull* (1961) sets ✱CHEKHOV's play in the contemporary Scottish Highlands; *The Caucasian Chalk Circle* (1972) is set in a building site and McGrath has added a prologue spoken by Liverpool workers (a reworking which ✱BRECHT would surely have approved). His last work, *HyperLynks*, was a monologue on multinationals, suicide bombers and anti-globalisation protests.

The Cheviot, the Stag and the Black, Black Oil
The Cheviot, the Stag and the Black, Black Oil is a musical, which takes the form of a traditional Highland ceilidh, exemplifying the 7:84 principle of political theatre which is also a 'good night out'. It was developed with the 7:84 Scotland Company, who researched the text, and devised the music and performance in rehearsal with McGrath. The play is a chronicle of the economic exploitation of the Highlands, from the nineteenth-century 'clearances', which cleared land for profits from the Cheviot sheep, through the migration of Highlanders to Canada, to the appropriation of land for grouse-shooting, the development of North Sea oil and tourism. The play also celebrates working-class struggle, from the refusal to enlist for the Crimean War to organised resistance against landlords. The television version, filmed in performance to a Highlands audience in 1977, uses ✱BRECHTIAN alienation effects to demonstrate the mythologising of Scottish history.

TRY THESE:
Among the dramatists McGrath reworked are ✱ARDEN (*Serjeant Musgrave Dances On*, 1972), ✱ARISTOPHANES (*Women in Power; or Up the Acropolis*, 1983), ✱BRECHT (*The Caucasian Chalk Circle*; 1972), David Lindsay (*Ane Satire of the Four Estates*, 1996); ✱TERSON (*Prisoners of the War*,

1972); ✻BRECHT is a central influence; ✻ARDEN and D'Arcy, ✻BRENTON, ✻EDGAR and ✻GRIFFITHS are contemporary 'political' dramatists who have differing views of the most effective ways of reaching audiences; *Swings and Roundabouts* is a reworking of ✻COWARD's *Private Lives*.

McGRATH, Tom   [1940 –   ]
British dramatist

PLAYS INCLUDE:
The Great Northern Welly Boot Show (1972*), Laurel and Hardy (1976), The Hard Man* (1977*), The Android Circuit* (1978*), Sisters* (1978*), The Innocent* (1979*), Animal* (1979*), 123* (1981*), The Nuclear Family* (1982*), The Gambler* (1984*), End of the Line* (1984*), Pals* (1984*), Kora* (1986*), Thanksgiving* (1986*), Trivial Pursuits* (1988*), City* (1989*), The Dream Train* (1999)

Already known as a musician and the creator of *International Times*, McGrath joined with Billy Connolly to celebrate the Upper Clyde Shipbuilders' work-in with *The Great Northern Welly Boot Show*, and since then has built a solid reputation as a playwright. To date his work has taken most of its impetus from autobiographical incident or from real events: *Laurel and Hardy* (recently revived at the Oldham Coliseum) is about the careers of the two comedians; *The Hard Man* is closely based on the life of Jimmy Boyle, Scotland's best-known ex-convict; *The Innocent* stems from his own involvement with drugs and the 'alternative society' of the 1960s; *123* clearly drew on personal experience of attempts to shake off society's demands with the aid of Buddhism and mythology. *Animal* is probably his most exotic piece, presenting a colony of apes under scrutiny from zoologists, with delightful and frequently comically surreal visions of ape movement and relationships, before tragedy results from contact with the humans. In *The Dream Train* McGrath uses Bach's *Goldberg Variations* to counterpoint an allusive and elusive action that is in some senses an enactment of the music.

The Hard Man
Based on the life of Jimmy Boyle, this is a startling impressionistic account of a life of violence. A clever use of non-naturalistic devices and direct address to the audience establishes a terrifying underworld of unthinking brutality and exposes the conditions which breed it, only to uncover an equally appalling world in the violence of prison life as authority tries to contain and break the spirit of dangerous inmates. It is a measure of McGrath's honesty that he does not turn his central character into a stereotyped 'victim of society', but that having established him as a truly terrifying figure wedded to uncontrollable violence – telling his own version of the events depicted – he then finds in him a symbol for the enduring human spirit, at a point when he crouches naked in a cage smeared with excrement to protect himself from the attacks of prison officers. The play is a stimulating exercise in sustained anti-naturalism and theatricality in the service of serious thought.

TRY THESE:
✻BRYDEN, Donald Campbell, Stewart Conn, Hector MacMillan, Roddy McMillan as other Scottish dramatists of the 1970s; ✻TERRY JOHNSON's *Cries from the Mammal House*, ✻O'NEILL's *The Hairy Ape* are zoological allegories; for more prisoner portraits, various adaptations of *In the Belly of the Beast* by Jack Henry Abbott, ✻GENET's *Deathwatch*, John Herbert's *Fortune and Men's Eyes* and Miguel Pinero's *Short Eyes*; ✻DORFMAN's *Death and the Maiden*, ✻POWNALL, ✻C. P. TAYLOR's *Good* for the power of music.

McGUINNESS, Frank   [1953 –   ]
Irish playwright

PLAYS INCLUDE:
The Factory Girls (1982*), Baglady/Ladybag* (1985*), Observe the Sons of Ulster Marching Towards the Somme* (1985*), Innocence* (1986*), Carthaginians* (1988*), Mary and Lizzie* (1989*), The Bread Man* (1990*), Someone Who'll Watch Over Me* (1992*), The Bird Sanctuary* (1994*), Mutabilitie* (1997*), Dolly West's Kitchen* (1999)

McGuinness was born into a Catholic family in Buncrana, County Donegal, where his mother worked in a local shirt factory and his father was a breadman. He went to University

College Dublin and took a Masters degree in English and medieval studies, and has taught at the University of Ulster, University College Dublin and St Patrick's College Maynooth. He wrote his first play, *The Factory Girls*, during a spell of unemployment. It is a funny, racily written tale of a group of women in a Donegal shirt factory who, faced with cuts and closure and advised to accept redundancies, decide to occupy the building. Its form is conventional and its tone naturalistic, and although well received it did nothing to prepare public or critics for the towering poetic language and the expressionistic forms, the passion and compassion combined with high moral and intellectual seriousness of his later work. His inspiration seems to be the need to give a voice to those who are oppressed or ignored, whether that is a group of factory workers, Protestant soldiers killed at the Somme, a victim of incest (*Baglady*), or two Irish sisters who lived with and influenced Engels yet who have been written out of history (*Mary and Lizzie*). He has an enviable ability to understand the other person's point of view (many mistakenly took him for a Protestant after *Observe the Sons*), and this gives him the rare distinction of being able to write excellent parts for women. His preoccupations are classically Irish as he himself admits (oppressed people, mother figures, father figures, religion, Irishness), but although he is a political writer there are no easy answers to be found in his work. In *Someone Who'll Watch Over Me* (loosely based on the experiences of Brian Keenan) he tackled the issue of how hostages relate to one another and maintain their spirits; in *Mutabilitie* he explored the English in Ireland in the late sixteenth century through the poet Edmund Spenser and ✱SHAKESPEARE, while *Dolly West's Kitchen* takes place in neutral Ireland in 1944 where two American soldiers and a British captain spar with the natives and each other.

Observe the Sons of Ulster Marching Towards the Somme

Inspired by a visit to two war memorials, McGuinness had to 'confront my own bigotry' to write about the Protestant experience in World War I. An old man's reminiscences take tangible shape when the ghosts of his comrades in arms rise up to meet him. The play is both a criticism and a celebration of the Irish obsession with the dead – the past must be understood, but bitterness and regret must not prevent progress. We see Pyper, the old man, in his youth as a mercurial, provocative, cynical middle-class sculptor who claims to have joined up to die. We see eight men the night they join up, on leave after several months at the front, and finally on the eve of the Battle of the Somme. Pyper eventually earns the respect of the others and the love of one in particular, and he is the only one to survive the war. Unable to rebuild the world as he had hoped, he is left behind to speak for the dead. The play was first presented at the Abbey Theatre, directed by Patrick Mason and then at the Hampstead Theatre, London, directed by Michael Attenborough. It won almost every prize available: the London *Evening Standard's* Most Promising Playwright award, the Rooney Prize for Irish Literature, the 1985 Harvey's Best Play award, the Cheltenham Literary Prize, the *Plays and Players* Award and the London Fringe Award for Best Playwright and Best Play.

TRY THESE:
McGuinness has adapted ✱BRECHT, ✱CHEKHOV, ✱IBSEN, ✱LORCA's *Yerma*, ✱OSTROVSKY's *The Storm*, ✱SOPHOCLES' *Electra*, ✱STRINDBERG's *Miss Julie*, and Ramon del Valle-Inclan's *Barbaric Comedies*; ✱REID's *My Name, Shall I Tell You My Name* also confronts an Orangeman's memories of World War I; ✱FINNEGAN's *The Spanish Play* explores Irish Protestants and Catholics in Spain during the Civil War; other contemporary Irish playwrights include ✱FRIEL, ✱KILROY, ✱MCPHERSON; ✱DANIELS' *Beside Herself* also looks at the after-effects of incest; *Innocence* is about Caravaggio: for other plays about artists, ✱BARKER *Scenes from an Execution*, ✱POWNALL's *An Audience Called Edouard*.

MACHADO, Eduardo   [1953 –   ]
Cuban/American dramatist

PLAYS INCLUDE:
The Modern Ladies of Guanabacoa (1983), *Fabiola* (1984), *Broken Eggs* (1984), *Stevie*

Wants to Play the Blues (1990), *In the Eye of the Hurricane* (1991), *Havana Is Waiting* (2001)

Machado was born to a wealthy family that was forced to flee Castro's Cuba. He arrived in the United States when he was eight years old without being able to speak English. The Machado family settled in Los Angeles, where Eduardo was raised. These circumstances help to set the background for Machado's auto-biographical 'Floating Islands' plays: *The Modern Ladies, Fabiola* and *Broken Eggs. The Modern Ladies* takes up the family story in 1930s Cuba and explores the complex caste system. In *Broken Eggs* a wedding requires the attendance of the brides' divorced father, who insists on bringing his second wife to the party. Accepting the father's remarriage also means accepting the reality of lost dreams and exile in Los Angeles. In *Stevie Wants to Play the Blues*, Machado breaks away from Cuba and the family to explore the life of 'Stevie', based on the real-life story of a young woman who can only realise her desire to become a jazz pianist by becoming a man. *Havana Is Waiting* is about Machado's decision to visit Cuba and the emotions it stirs within him.

TRY THESE:

✳ DE FILIPPO for Italian family sagas; Manfred Karge's *Man to Man*, most of ✳ SHAKESPEARE's comedies, ✳ WERTENBAKER's *New Anatomies* for cross-dressing; ✳ TRIANA is another well-known Cuban dramatist; ✳ HARE's *Wrecked Eggs* for use of a similar metaphor to *Broken Eggs*.

MACHIAVELLI, Niccolo di Bernardo dei   [1469 – 1527]
Italian political theorist and occasional dramatist

PLAYS INCLUDE:
La Mandragola (1518), *Clizia* (1525)

Machiavelli was a civil servant in Florence under the republican government that succeeded the rule of Savonarola. He wrote his plays, and also *The Prince* (1513), in compulsory retirement in the country after the restoration of the Medici. *The Prince* was inspired by the expedient political methods of Cesare Borgia, rather than vice versa, but it

led to Machiavelli's reputation in England and elsewhere for advocating the ruthless and amoral pursuit of power. Although *La Mandragola* is one of the best of Italian Renaissance comedies, it is probably Machiavelli's reputation as a political Demon King that leads to its occasional appearance on the modern stage (as against plays by, say, Bembo or Ruzzante). It is a classical example of academic wish-fulfilment; the rich old lawyer Nicia is cuckolded by the dashing young scholar Callimaco, with the assistance of the parasite Ligurio and a pretended potion made from the mandrake root. Surprisingly, all live happily ever after.

TRY THESE:

✳ MARLOWE used 'Machiavel' as a prologue for *The Jew of Malta*; Shared Experience adapted *Comedy Without a Title* from Ruzzante; Giordano Bruno's *Il Candelaio* is another Italian Renaissance comedy that surfaces very occasionally in the modern repertory; ✳ JONSON and ✳ WYCHERLEY for intrigue comedies.

McINTYRE, Clare   [1953 –   ]
British dramatist

PLAYS INCLUDE:
I've Been Running (1986), *Low Level Panic* (1988), *My Heart's a Suitcase* (1990), *The Thickness of Skin* (1996), *The Changeling* (2001, from ✳ MIDDLETON and ✳ ROWLEY),*The Maths Tutor* (2003)

McIntyre turned to writing plays after spending some years acting on stage and in television and films. *I've Been Running*, her first play, a sharp two-hander, delved into the murky waters of contemporary sexual politics to take a look at the division between the young modern woman (a bit of a health freak, but questioning and curious about life) and her sluggish, complacent boyfriend who can't understand what she is on about at all. *Low Level Panic* has made the biggest splash. Opening with a bathroom scene, it is about three young women sharing a flat together, with some sharp and revealing writing (naturalistic dialogue and monologues of internalised thoughts) on images, commer-cialisation, female sexual fantasies, and the more frightening realities as women experience them on the street. The action seldom extends beyond the bathroom (except for a monologue scene recounting a street attack on one of the women and a fantasised revenge sequence to do with an advertising hoarding), and lacks overall development. Nonetheless, *Low Level Panic* accurately articulates the thoughts, fears and feelings of many young women. *My Heart's a Suitcase* deals with the emotional baggage with which we surround ourselves and, like *Low Level Panic*, succeeds in conveying the textures of quiet desperation in everyday life, rather than gripping you with a strong plot line. *The Thickness of Skin* deals with the question of how altruistic you can afford to be if other people are taking advantage of you. McIntyre adapted *The Changeling* for Graeae in 2001, removing the Isabella subplot and updating the period to the 1960s.

TRY THESE:
✱ PINNOCK draws attention to similar issues in *Picture Palace*; ✱ SHAPIRO's *Dead Romantic* looks into the sexual politics scrum; ✱ WHITEHEAD's *Alpha Beta* is an older, male, though equally pessimistic, view of coupledom; ✱ DUNN's *Steaming* is set in a larger, public, bath; ✱ TREMBLAY's *Albertine in Five Times* for an even more extended application of the monologue technique to express internal thoughts and feelings, ✱ ADSHEAD, ✱ MACDONALD, Julia Schofield for other actress-writers.

McINTYRE, Dennis   [1943 – 90]
American dramatist

PLAYS INCLUDE:
Modigliani (1978), *Split Second* (1986), *National Anthems* (1986), *Established Price* (1987)

McIntyre's *Modigliani*, following the painter's artistic achievement and commercial failure, was a poignant testament to his struggle as a playwright, since the play was written in 1966 but not produced until 1978, a predicament McIntyre faced repeatedly as he tried to have his plays presented in New York. *Split Second* is an uncompromising examination of personal integrity in a racially charged confrontation, while McIntyre's thinly disguised contempt for the acquisition and materialism of the 'me' generation of America serves as the thematic core of *National Anthems*. His last work, *Established Price*, was a timely scrutiny of corporate takeovers. His early death from cancer suspended hopes for additional plays that would demonstrate McIntyre's ability to address global issues through personalised situations.

TRY THESE:
✱ ALBEE's *Who's Afraid of Virginia Woolf?* ✱ LEIGH's *Abigail's Party*, ✱ PINTER's *The Birthday Party* for celebrations that go wrong; ✱ LUCIE for a British chronicler of the 'me' generation; ✱ CHURCHILL's *Serious Money* for takeovers; ✱ POWNALL for artists of various kinds.

McLAUGHLIN, Ellen   [1957–   ]
American dramatist and actress

PLAYS INCLUDE:
Days and Nights Within (1987), *A Narrow Bed* (1987), *Infinity's House* (1988), *Iphigenia and Other Daughters* (1995), *Tongue of a Bird* (1997), *Helen of Troy* (2002, from ✱ EURIPIDES)

McLaughlin has said her plays demonstrate an interest in the 'potency of thought in dramatic action'. *Days and Nights Within*, based upon the imprisonment of Erica Wallach, depicts one woman's struggle to maintain personal integrity while undergoing extreme physical and psychological strain. *Infinity's House*, the structural opposite of *Days and Nights Within*, includes thirty-seven characters and is set in the American West during three very different time periods. A sweeping work compared to its predecessor, *Infinity's House* remains rooted in the interpersonal relationships of people bound together by coincidence, as does *Tongue of a Bird*, which follows a woman rescue pilot as she searches for a missing girl. *Iphigenia and Other Daughters* is, in McLaughlin's own words, 'a meditation on feminism', which reworks ✱ EURIPIDES' *Iphigenia* plays and ✱ SOPHOCLES' *Electra*.

A Narrow Bed
A Narrow Bed was co-winner of the 1987 Susan Smith Blackburn Prize for women

playwrights. The plot moves between past and present circumstances stemming from the Vietnam War. It shows individuals pressured to change ideals that were shaped by whether they decided to fight or to protest against that conflict. The thread of the play lies in personal stories from members of a farm commune. One woman's husband remains missing in action, a tragic and unexplained reversal of his earlier activism against the war. Another woman's husband lies dying of alcoholism, the last man of the farm and another mockery of the ideals that founded the commune. The women's steadfast friendship serves as a challenge to the Vietnam generation, and others, about the solidity of their values.

TRY THESE:

✷ MURRAY's *Body-Cell* for a woman imprisoned; ✷ WESKER's *Caritas* for a more voluntary confinement; ✷ KOPIT's *Indians* for the American West; ✷ MANN, ✷ RABE for Vietnam plays; John Barton and Kenneth McLeish for reworkings of Greek plays and legends; Peter Arnott's *White Rose* for female pilots.

McLEAN, Linda
Scottish dramatist

PLAYS INCLUDE:
One Good Beating (1998), *Riddance* (1999), *Shimmer* (2002), *Word for Word* (2003)

McLean's *One Good Beating* and *Riddance* both deal with intimate family dramas, the secrets and lies of domestic violence. Her latest play, *Word for Word*, broadens the exploration of hidden secrets to examine how an ancient people that has dwindled into a tiny group eking out an existence in a desolate urban landscape encounter a war cameraman on assignment to record them before they become extinct.

TRY THESE:

✷ AESCHYLUS for the original dysfunctional family; ✷ DANIELS for more recent ones; Maclean has adapted *Olga* by Finland's Laura Ruohonen.

McLURE, James   [1951 –   ]
American dramatist

PLAY INCLUDE:
Lone Star (1979), *Pvt. Wars* (1979), *Laundry and Bourbon* (1980), *The Day They Shot John Lennon* (1983), *Thanksgiving* (1983), *Wild Oats* (1983, after John O'Keeffe), *Max and Maxie* (1984), *The Very Last Lover of the River Cane* (1985), *Lahr and Mercedes* (1985), *Fran and Brian* (1988), *Napoleon Nightdreams* (1987), *The Agent* (1989), *The Hair Cut* (1990), *Iago* (2000)

Born in Louisiana and educated in Texas, McLure first pursued a career as an actor. He made his mark as a playwright in New York with plays about Texas. His tough-talking bar-room brawlers spoke Texan, a hyperbolic language frequently punctuated with hilarious backwoods expressions. McLure then turned his attention to the urban romantic landscape, emerging as a sensitive and witty observer of the post-Woodstock generation, a generation suffering from loss of innocence and idealism while being overburdened by materialism. His version of *Wild Oats* is set in the Wild West; *Iago*, set in London in the 1950s, is a play about onstage affairs that parallel and contrast with real-life entanglements, deriving from Laurence Olivier and Vivien Leigh's tempestuous marriage.

Lone Star
Lone Star takes its name from the long-necked bottled beer made in Texas that is consumed in great quantities in this one-act play. Roy, the only 'Viet Nam Vet' in Maynard, Texas, is the play's hero. Although he has been home from the war for two years, he does nothing but drink and tell stories about his wartime prowess and his sexual conquests. Roy is both worshipped and feared by Ray, his kid brother, and Cletis, an appliance-store salesman. During the course of the play, Cletis steals Roy's 1959 pink Thunderbird and smashes it to pieces. Ray, who fears being thought of as Cletis's accomplice, decides to distract Roy by revealing that he slept with Roy's wife, Elizabeth, while Roy was away at war. Although the play contains the seeds of a violent and tragic confrontation, McLure converts the tension into an uproarious folk farce.

TRY THESE:
✱ MANN's *Still Life*, ✱ LINNEY's *Love Suicide at Schofield Barracks*, ✱ LOWE's *Touched* and ✱ RATTIGAN's *Flarepath* for British wartime domestic dramas; ✱ HARWOOD's *The Dresser* for backstage Shakespearian drama.

McNALLY, Terrence [1939 –]
American dramatist

PLAYS INCLUDE:
Things That Go Bump in the Night (1965), *Botticelli* (1968), *Noon* (1968), *Sweet Eros* (1968), *Next* (1969), *Where Has Tommy Flowers Gone?* (1971), *Whiskey* (1973), *Bad Habits* (1974), *The Ritz* (1975), *Broadway, Broadway* (1978), *It's Only a Play* (1982), *The Rink* (1984, musical), *Frankie and Johnny in the Clair de Lune* (1987), *The Lisbon Traviata* (1989), *Up in Saratoga* (1989), *Hope* (1989), *Kiss of the Spider Woman* (1990, musical), *Lips Together Teeth Apart* (1991), *Love! Valor! Compassion!* (1995), *Master Class* (1995), *A Perfect Ganesh* (1995), *Corpus Christi* (1998), *Ragtime* (1998, musical from E. L. Doctorow's novel), *The Full Monty* (2000, musical)

McNally began his career as a writer of black comedy and satire, developing his craft in the off-Broadway movement of the late 1960s and 1970s. A mordant social critic, his characters were eccentric, displaced victims of society desperately seeking refuge. In his early works, McNally's craft is rooted in finding contemporary situations and embellishing them with a prickling display of verbal humour. He has never been afraid to rewrite his plays two or three times even after openings. The results of McNally's persistence are now apparent. His plays continue to crackle wittily yet they have moved closer to reality, showing a compassionate understanding of character and relationships. His work has often explored aspects of being gay: *The Lisbon Traviata* reworks operatic elements and *Love! Valor! Compassion!* is about an artistic and personal crisis in the life of a gay choreographer. *Corpus Christi* has attracted hostility from both Christian and Muslim fundamentalists for reimagining Christ and his disciples as being gay.

Frankie and Johnny in the Clair de Lune
Frankie and Johnny chronicles the developing relationship between two ordinary middle-aged people who work at the same restaurant. Frankie is an embittered, self-protective waitress fearing commitment, while Johnny, a short-order cook, is ready to serve up heaping measures of marriage and family. We discover them after a passionate, get-acquainted session of lovemaking discussing all the reasons why their relationship can't succeed. Obviously, their level of physical intimacy belies deeper feelings of alienation and distrust. In this play McNally has managed to connect humour with character, allowing Frankie and Johnny to reveal themselves through repartee that is both funny and painful. The play moves from night towards a rosy dawn suggesting that intimacy is possible even in an age when everything seems to militate against it.

TRY THESE:
✱ COWARD's *Private Lives* for an oddly parallel view of human relationships; ✱ LUCIE, ✱ AYCKBOURN, ✱ SIMON for variations on comedy of manners; *Master Class* is about Maria Callas, ✱ POWNALL's is about Prokofiev and Shostakovich.

McPHERSON, Connor [1972 –]
Irish dramatist

PLAYS INCLUDE:
The Lime Tree Bower (1995), *St Nicholas* (1997), *The Weir* (1997), *Dublin Carol* (2000), *Port Authority* (2001)

Dublin-born McPherson achieved his major success so far with *The Weir*, which has been produced worldwide. Some critics have suggested that the play panders to traditional stage images of Ireland with its rural storytelling of ghostly encounters and uncanny events taking place in a moribund country pub. Others have suggested that McPherson's dramaturgy in general too often tends to the static interweaving of monologue. But the overwhelming response to *The Weir* has been one of admiration for its control of dramatic narrative and for a ✱ CHEKHOV-like grasp of how to use the telling detail to open up a world of meanings. In *Dublin Carol*

McPherson reworks some traditional Dickensian Christmas themes of revelation and emotional stocktaking in an undertaker's office on Christmas Eve. In *Port Authority* a young man, a middle-aged man and an old man deliver three monologues about love with no interaction between them. As McPherson has said, they could be the same person at different stages in his life or they could be separate individuals linked by the port building, but the result is an allusive meditation on issues of universal significance arising from particular experience.

TRY THESE:

McPherson has spoken of being influenced by ✻MAMET and by ✻BECKETT (he directed *Endgame* for the complete television Beckett project); ✻MCDONAGH for contrast; for different versions of rural Ireland, ✻CARR, ✻SYNGE; ✻FRIEL for intercutting Irish monologues.

MAHONEY, Mick   [1959 –]
British dramatist

PLAY INCLUDE:

Friday Nights (1981), *When Your Bottle's Gone in SE1* (1983), *Up for None* (1984), *Swaggers* (1996), *Sacred Heart* (1999), *Food Chain* (2003)

Despite winning the Verity Bargate Award for *Up for None* and the *Time Out* Best New Play award for *Swaggers*, Mahoney remains a relatively unsung dramatist. *Sacred Heart* at the Royal Court takes the familiar situation of two men who had been inseparable as children, fell out as adults and meet twenty years later and creates a well-structured chamber piece about dashed hopes, compromises and failure.

TRY THESE:

✻ELYOT's *The Day I Stood Still*, ✻IBSEN's *The Wild Duck*, ✻MCCAFFERTY, ✻NEILSON's *Penetrator* for contrasting meetings of old friends in new situations.

MAMET, David   [1947 –]
American dramatist and screenwriter

PLAYS INCLUDE:

American Buffalo (1975), *Sexual Perversity in Chicago* (1976), *Duck Variations* (1976), *Reunion* (1977), *The Woods* (1977), *The Water Engine* (1977), *A Life in the Theatre* (1978), *Lakeboat* (1981), *Edmond* (1982), *Glengarry Glen Ross* (1983), *Vermont Sketches* (1984), *Prairie du Chien* (1985), *The Shawl* (1985), *The Frog Prince* (1985), *Speed-the-Plow* (1988), *Sketches of War* (1988), *Bobby Gould in Hell* (1989), *Uncle Vanya* (1991, from ✻CHEKHOV), *Where Were You When It Went Down* (1991), *Oleanna* (1992), *The Cryptogram* (1995), *The Old Neighborhood* (1997, comprising *The Disappearance of the Jews*, 1982, *Jolly and D.*, 1989), *Boston Marriage* (1999)

Chicago-born Mamet is that unique American dramatist whose work seems simultaneously absolutely indigenous to the USA and peculiarly European. While his expletive-laden language and volatile situations seem part of an innately American idiom, his understanding of linguistic wordplay and of silence recalls such European forebears as ✻BECKETT and ✻PINTER. The co-founder of Chicago's St Nicholas Theatre Company, where he functioned as both playwright in residence and artistic director, he writes with that city's street-wise, colloquial rhythm, whether on subjects as dense as the underside of American capitalism (for example the real-estate salesman in *Glengarry Glen Ross*) or as relatively benign as the intertwined lives and careers of two actors (*A Life In the Theatre*). His plays rarely have more than two or three characters, and works like *Edmond* – an impressionistic tableau about one man's descent into Sodom and Gomorrah in New York – are unusual. More typical is a piece like *The Shawl*, a three-character play about a charlatan seer, which further dissects a topic – the psychology of the con game – that Mamet returns to time and again (it's the raison d'être of *House of Games*, the 1987 film with which he made his directorial debut). His plays, of course, speak of another kind of shawl: the cloak of language beneath which lies a multiplicity of human instincts too few playwrights address with Mamet's courage. *Oleanna* caused major controversies about political correctness on both sides of the Atlantic with its portrait of a male university teacher's dealings with a female student.

American Buffalo

Three small-time crooks bungle a coin robbery, and out of their comedy of frustration Mamet weaves an exhilaratingly telling and poignant account of avarice and ambition in which the promise of monetary gain makes everyone both victor and victim. (The title refers to an American coin, an old nickel that Bobby, the young addict, finds in Act 2.) At once edgy and elegiac in tone, the play is also a rending treatment of friendship under stress, and its three roles – the master-mind Teach, the older shopowner Donny, and his side-kick Bobby – are superbly written. 'Fuckin' business' reads the last line of Act 1, and few plays have summed up the price of the capitalist ethic with such terse and moving irony.

TRY THESE:

✳ MILLER (especially *Death of a Salesman*) and ✳ ODETS for socially conscious writing, often about the limits of American capitalism; for serio-comic satires on business, ✳ CHURCHILL's *Serious Money*, ✳ REDDIN's *Life During Wartime*; ✳ BÜCHNER's *Woyzeck* for *Edmond*-like descents into a psychological hell; ✳ BULGAKOV's *Black Snow*, ✳ KAUFMAN and Hart, ✳ MCNALLY's *It's Only a Play*, ✳ NELSON's *Two Shakespearean Actors* for works about the theatre; ✳ RABE for raw examination of male relationships; ✳ SHEPARD for American archetypes; ✳ MARCUS for a male treatment of lesbians to compare with *Boston Marriage*.

MANN, Emily   [1952 –   ]
American playwright and director

PLAYS INCLUDE:
Annulla Allen: Autobiography of a Survivor (1974), *Still Life* (1980), *Execution of Justice* (1983), *Nights and Days* (1985), *Betsey Brown* (1989, from ✳ SHANGE), *Having Our Say* (1995, from Sarah and Bessey Delaney), *Greensboro* (1996)

Mann is a director and dramatist whose 'Theatre of Testimony' harks back to the Federal Theatre's Living Newspapers in its dependence on factual material. *Annulla Allen* is about a concentration-camp survivor; *Execution of Justice*, which confronts the homophobia that led to the murder of San Francisco mayor George Moscone and city supervisor Harvey Milk, is based on trial transcripts; *Having Our Say* is based on the reminiscences of two black sisters about a hundred years of struggles; and *Greensboro* tackles the deaths of anti-Ku Klux Klan demonstrators in Greensboro in 1979.

Still Life, Mann's most famous work, won six OBIEs. Presented as a clever cross-cutting of three monologues, it is a Vietnam War play based on taped interviews with a veteran, his wife and his mistress, and shows how war can transform a gentle man into an eager and willing killer.

TRY THESE:
For the Vietnam War, ✳ RABE's *Streamers* and *The Basic Training of Pavlo Hummel*; for courtroom dramas about actual events, ✳ WEISS's *The Investigation* and Tom Topor's *Nuts*; for black struggles in the USA, ✳ BALDWIN, ✳ BARAKA, ✳ BULLINS, ✳ HANSBERRY, ✳ AUGUST WILSON, ✳ WOLFE's *The Colored Museum*.

MARBER, Patrick   [1964 –   ]
British comic, radio and television writer, director and dramatist

PLAYS INCLUDE:
Dealer's Choice (1995), *Closer* (1997), *Howard Katz* (2001), *After Miss Julie* (radio 1995, staged 2003)

Unlike many dramatists, Marber turned to the stage after a successful radio and television career working with Steve Coogan amongst others. His first play, *Dealer's Choice*, centres on addiction to gambling and *Howard Katz* is about a failing middle-aged theatrical agent, but *Closer* caught the mood of the 1990s in a defining way. The basic story is of four people meeting, forming relationships, failing in those relationships, changing partners and attempting to reconnect, but it is played out across a postmodern cityscape of lap-dancing and cybersex in a laconic, bleak, witty language whose very texture reinforces the atmosphere of anomie. The characters themselves are representative figures – a stripper, a journalist, a photographer and a doctor – who fail to achieve the fulfilment they are looking for. Some might argue that the doctor being a skin specialist and the journalist a writer of obituaries loads the play's metaphorical and thematic dice, but the enormous popularity of the play suggests that it struck chords with many of its audience as an accurate anatomy of its subject.

TRY THESE:

Closer is highly reminiscent in both its comedy and its pain of ✱COWARD's *Private Lives*; according to the *Sunday Times, Closer* was 'one of the best plays of sexual politics in the language', on a par with ✱ALBEE's *Who's Afraid of Virginia Woolf?*, ✱HARE's *Skylight*, ✱MAMET's *Oleanna*, ✱PINTER's *Old Times*, ✱TENNESSEE WILLIAMS' *A Streetcar Named Desire*; ✱SCHNITZLER's *La Ronde* and its many derivatives for other takes on sexual politics; ✱STRINDBERG for the original *Miss Julie*.

MARCHANT, Tony   [1959 –   ]
British dramatist and television writer

PLAYS INCLUDE:

Remember Me? (1980), *London Calling* (1981), *Thick as Thieves* (1981, comprising *London Calling* and *Dealt*), *Stiff* (1982), *Raspberry* (1982), *The Lucky Ones* (1982), *Welcome Home* (1983), *Lazy Days Ltd* (1984), *The Attractions* (1987), *The Speculators* (1987), *The Fund Raisers* (1997)

A grammar-school-educated, working-class East Ender of Catholic parents, Marchant's early plays showed a remarkable capacity to articulate the problems and feelings of East End youngsters with sensitivity and compassion. *Remember Me?* is a young, unemployed school-leaver's cry of outrage against the educational system. In *The Lucky Ones* (those who have jobs) a group of young East Enders battle for advancement in the bowels of a large stockbroking firm opposed by an emblematic working-class rebel anti-hero who refuses to bend the knee to the system. In contrast, *Raspberry* is a short study about the

social stigmas surrounding abortion and infertility, treated with great skill, shown through the growing friendship between two women who find themselves in hospital in adjoining beds. *The Attractions* is a fascinating study about violence, juxtaposing examples from the past (it is set in a museum of horrors on Britain's south coast) with present-day manifestations, and triggered once again by one of those not enjoying the fruits of Thatcherism. *The Speculators* concentrated on the foreign-exchange market where, said Marchant, the jumping pound was more synonymous with national identity. Marchant subsequently devoted himself to writing for television.

Welcome Home
Commissioned by Paine's Plough, this was one of the first plays to take a look at the Falklands War. Characteristically, Marchant spent time with an army unit before sitting down to write, and his beautifully constructed play constantly mirrors that authenticity. Centred round a group of paratroopers assembled to bury one of their number with full military honours, it refuses to present its soldiers as ciphers and demonstrates its understanding of the army mentality and its disadvantages (in the shape of an over-zealous corporal whose belligerence and neo-fascism are barely under control). In its awareness of the emotional and psychological price paid in that South Atlantic exercise, Marchant's play makes a tangible plea for a new kind of masculinity, based on an acknowledgement of weakness as much as forced machismo.

TRY THESE:

✱SHERRIFF's *Journey's End* makes similar points about the psychological traumas of war; ✱NOËL GREIG's *Poppies* for Gay Sweatshop explored a pacifist ethic; ✱ROBERT HOLMAN and ✱PAGE have dealt with aspects of the Falklands; for comparison with post-Vietnam responses see ✱MANN's *Still Life*, ✱RABE's *Streamers*; for a jaundiced study of go-getting comparable with *Speculators*, ✱CHURCHILL's *Serious Money*, ✱LUCIE's *Fashion*; ✱ELLIS's *Chameleon* looks at being on the make from a black perspective; ✱GLENDENNING's *Donny Boy*, ✱TERRY JOHNSON's

Imagine Drowning and Heinar Kipphardt's *Brother Eichmann* are other investigations into the roots of violence; ✶CRAZE's *Angelus* and ✶ROCHE's *A Handful of Stars* for contemporary protest expressed through anti-heroes; ✶CARTWRIGHT's *Road* is an outcry against unemployment; ✶KEEFFE for East End sensibilities; Che Walker's *Flesh Wound* for contemporary crimes.

MARCUS, Frank   [1928 – 96]
British dramatist and critic

PLAYS INCLUDE:
The Formation Dancers (1964), *The Killing of Sister George* (1966), *Notes on a Love Affair* (1972)

Born in Germany, but arriving in Britain in 1939, Marcus acted, directed and ran an antiques business as well as writing. With well over a score of plays produced, he is best known for *The Killing of Sister George*, a study of a disintegrating lesbian partnership in which the butch half is a radio soap lead about to be killed off in the programme. A serious study of caring, need and dominance, its sadness is heightened by its hilarity. Unfortunately, because of the paucity of mainstream plays with lesbian characters, *The Killing of Sister George* has become the stereotypical image of lesbians and their relationships, and despite many variants on the fringe to the contrary, *Sister George* maintains a fierce hold on the public imagination. Marcus's earlier success, *The Formation Dancers*, a much lighter four hander, presents feigned infidelity as a method of regaining an unfaithful husband, but the treatment of women and love is a recurrent theme in much of his later work.

TRY THESE:
Marcus adapted Hauptmann, Kaiser, ✶MOLNAR and ✶SCHNITZLER; ✶DYER's *Staircase* for a comparable treatment of male homosexuality; ✶DUFFY's *Rites*, ✶HELLMAN's *The Children's Hour* for earlier examples of lesbian themes; ✶DANIELS, ✶DAVIES' *Prin*, ✶LAVERY's *Her Aching Heart* for different treatments of lesbian love.

MARGULIES, Donald   [1954 –   ]
American dramatist

PLAYS INCLUDE:
Resting Place (1982), *Gifted Children* (1983), *Found a Peanut* (1984), *The Model Apartment* (1988), *The Loman Family Picnic* (1989), *What's Wrong with This Picture* (1990), *Sight Unseen* (1991), *Collected Stories: A Play* (1996), *Dinner with Friends* (1998)

Margulies' Jewish heritage is his dramatic foundation and is demonstrated by his ability to capture Jewish humour and values in believable characters and caricatures. *What's Wrong with This Picture* surrounds the death of a Brooklyn housewife with humour, and demonstrates Margulies' sensitive insight into how the woman's surviving husband and son reconcile their familial relationship. In *The Loman Family Picnic* a family reveals some of their less admirable traits prior to the eldest son's bar mitzvah. The mother relishes the social importance of the event and the father transforms into a green-eyed avaricious monster. The play's unusual dramatic effects include the ghostly appearance of an aunt who died in the Holocaust plus four separate endings. Primarily a dramatist, Margulies also has written screenplays and a number of television scripts. *Collected Stories* and *Dinner with Friends* were his first plays to be staged professionally in London. In *Collected Stories* the emphasis is on betrayal when a creative-writing teacher discovers that one of her students has cannibalised her experiences in a novel. *Dinner with Friends* is about how a couple breaking up affects their friends.

TRY THESE:
The Loman Family Picnic gets its title from the youngest son's efforts to write a musical version of ✶MILLER's *Death of A Salesman*; ✶SIMON, ✶WASSERSTEIN for American Jewish upbringings; ✶KOPS, ✶WESKER for British equivalents; ✶HOCHHÜTH, ✶C. P. TAYLOR's *Good* for Holocaust plays; ✶AYCKBOURN, ✶HAYES, ✶KEATLEY, ✶O'NEILL for families; ✶MAMET's *Oleanna* for difficult teacher–student relationships.

MARIVAUX, Pierre Carlet de Chamblain de   [1688 – 1763]
French dramatist and novelist

PLAYS INCLUDE:
Arlequin Poli par l'Amour (1720, *Harlequin Polished by Love*), *La Double Inconstance* (1723, *The Double Inconstancy*), *Le Jeu de l'Amour et du Hasard* (1723, *The Game of Love and Chance*), *L'Ile des Esclaves* (1725, *The Island of Slaves*), *Le Triomphe de l'Amour* (1732, *The Triumph of Love*), *L'Heureux Stratagème* (1733, *Successful Strategies*), *Les Fausses Confidences* (1737, *False Admissions*), *L'Épreuve* (1740, *The Test*), *La Dispute* (1744, *The Dispute*)

Marivaux was born of a nouveau riche family (his father started as Carlet and added the 'de Chamblain' and 'de Marivaux' as he moved up the pecking order), but lost his money in the Mississippi scheme (the French equivalent of Britain's South Sea Bubble), and so was forced to make his living by writing plays and novels, by journalism, and by relying on the generosity of various noble ladies who welcomed his wit in their salons. His long association with the Comédie Italienne and their lively acting helped to make his plays successful; indeed it was noticeable that those of his plays put on by the Comédie Française worked much less well. His best-known plays deal with the beginnings of love, often unrecognised and sometimes unwelcome, through subtle dialogue rather than complicated plots. This delicate dialogue was found affected by some of his contemporaries, who called it 'marivaudage', but in fact it wears (and acts) very well. Out of fashion in English for most of the twentieth century, he now seems to be doing rather better, particularly in translations by *NEIL BARTLETT and *TIMBERLAKE WERTENBAKER, which successfully bring out the complexity and ambiguity of these delightful plays. Clearly Marivaux is not as difficult to translate as people have long said.

TRY THESE:
*BEAUMARCHAIS for eighteenth-century French comedy, though with much broader brushstrokes and a larger canvas; *TURGENEV's *A Month in the Country* for a comparable game of love and chance, but without a happy ending; *COWARD's *Private Lives* for a set of mixed doubles like *The Double Inconstancy*.

MARLOWE, Christopher   [1564 – 93]
English dramatist

PLAYS INCLUDE:
Tamburlaine the Great, Parts I and II (1587), *Doctor Faustus* (*c.* 1588), *The Jew of Malta* (*c.* 1589), *Edward II* (*c.* 1592), *The Massacre at Paris* (*c.* 1592), *Dido, Queen of Carthage* (*c.* 1593)

Marlowe led a brief and turbulent life in which he was involved in espionage, accused of heretical opinions and killed in a pub brawl before the case was tried, in circumstances that suggest that he may have been eliminated to avoid political embarrassment. He also managed to write plays that gave a new impetus to Renaissance theatre writing. Unfortunately, some of them have only been preserved in mangled form but, with the exception of the two last plays, they are still staged fairly regularly. *Tamburlaine* is interesting because of Marlowe's use of what *JONSON called the 'mighty line' to display the superhuman characteristics of its hero, who starts off a shepherd in Part I, conquers the world, and then dies in Part II. The play presents a full circle of Fortune's Wheel but there is little dramatic conflict and no particular tension within the presentation of Tamburlaine himself – his tragedy arises simply from the fact that, in the end, he is not superhuman. *The Jew of Malta*, a savage farce, also has a larger-than-life protagonist, the comic villain Barabbas, who indulges in wholesale Machiavellian slaughter until he, literally, falls into one of his own traps. *Edward II* has a more developed set of conflicts between characters and. although the verse is less obviously memorable than in some of Marlowe's other works, there is a satisfying movement in the play as Edward's fortunes decline and Mortimer's rise only to fall again.

Doctor Faustus
Faustus sells his soul to Mephistopheles in return for twenty-four years of magic power

The Jew of Malta by Christopher Marlowe, directed by Michael Grandage, Almeida Theatre, 1999.
Ian McDiarmid as Barabas, David Yelland as Ferneze. (Henrietta Butler/ArenaPAL)

but those years are spent mainly in comic conjuring exercises and slapstick. Although there is powerful verse and a real tragic situation at the beginning and at the end, the play can tend to sag in the middle since many directors find it hard to reconcile the clowning with the sense of Faustus's tragic situation. The best productions are those which try to bring out the way in which these scenes show Faustus frittering away the possibilities open to him, thus emphasising the tragedy of his bargain.

TRY THESE:
Other plays which use the Faust legend are ✱GOETHE's *Faust*, ✱BRENTON and ✱HARE's *Pravda* and ✱HAVEL's *Temptation*; ✱SHAKESPEARE's *Merchant of Venice* offers an interesting comparison with Marlowe's treatment of the Jews; ✱BRECHT adapted *Edward II* and the English version of his play is sometimes staged; ✱KYD, ✱MIDDLETON, ✱WEBSTER for other English Renaissance dramatists.

MAROWITZ, Charles [1934 –]
American director, dramatist, editor and critic

PLAYS INCLUDE:
Artaud at Rodez (1975), *Hamlet* (1965, after ✱SHAKESPEARE), *A Macbeth* (1969, after ✱SHAKESPEARE), *An Othello* (1972, after ✱SHAKESPEARE), *The Shrew* (1973, after ✱SHAKESPEARE), *Measure for Measure* (1975, after ✱SHAKESPEARE), *Variations on The Merchant of Venice* (1977, after ✱SHAKESPEARE), *Hedda* (1981, after ✱IBSEN), *Sherlock's Last Case* (1987), *Wilde West* (1989)

Marowitz, born in New York, came to Britain in the 1950s to act and direct, playing a crucial part in many important theatrical developments over many years before eventually returning to the USA. With Thelma Holt at the Open Space Theatre from 1968 to 1979, he staged a wide range of plays, including work by ✱PETER BARNES, ✱HOWARD BARKER, ✱HOWARD BRENTON, ✱DAVID EDGAR, ✱TREVOR GRIFFITHS and ✱SAM SHEPARD. Marowitz's own 'collage' or cut-up versions of classics (particularly ✱SHAKESPEARE) used film-like techniques to switch rapidly from one image to another, dream or nightmare sequences, verbal and visual shock tactics, simple sets and aggressive lighting. His *Hamlet* is probably the most successful of these, perhaps because the play is so familiar to most audiences, but the Black Power *An Othello* and the feminist *Shrew* are also effective. *Sherlock's Last Case*, a Conan Doyle pastiche, did quite well on Broadway in 1987–8. In *Wilde West* Marowitz brings ✱OSCAR WILDE together with Jesse James.

TRY THESE:
Peter Brook, for collaboration on ✱ARTAUD-influenced work; ✱BLESSING's *Fortinbras* draws on *Hamlet*, as does ✱GILBERT's *Rosencrantz and Guildenstern* and ✱STOPPARD's *Rosencrantz and Guildenstern Are Dead*.

MARSTON, John [1576 – 1634]
English dramatist

PLAYS INCLUDE:
Antonio and Mellida (1599), *Antonio's Revenge* (1600), *The Dutch Courtesan* (1604), *The Malcontent* (1604), *The Fawn* (1605; also known as *Parasitaster*), *Eastward Ho* (1605, with ✱GEORGE CHAPMAN and ✱BEN JONSON)

Marston, like John Donne, eventually became an Anglican clergyman, but before that he had a fairly successful career as a satirical poet and dramatist, being heavily involved in the so-called 'War of the Theatres' in which a number of dramatists, including ✱JONSON, attacked one another in a succession of plays. He often wrote within the popular revenge conventions of his day but both *Antonio and Mellida* and *The Malcontent*, despite the sordidness and corruption of their court worlds and their apparently tragic dynamic, have 'happy' endings. *The Dutch Courtesan* also operates on the fringes of tragicomedy. *Antonio's Revenge*, the second part of *Antonio and Mellida*, is, however, a fully fledged revenge tragedy in the traditional Elizabethan mode. Although his tendency to dwell on excretion and sexuality is probably more acceptable than it might once have been, Marston tends to be an occasional rather than a regular feature of the contemporary repertory, perhaps because so many of his characters, situations and plots are to be found elsewhere in Renaissance drama, handled in ways that have proved more acceptable to modern audiences. *The Malcontent* and his collaborative work *Eastward Ho* both figured in the RSC's 2002 season of rarely staged Renaissance plays.

TRY THESE:

Most Renaissance dramatists used revenge plots and malcontent figures: ✱SHAKESPEARE's *Hamlet* is the most famous example of both, but ✱KYD's *The Spanish Tragedy* started the vogue for revenge and there are notable examples in ✱MIDDLETON, ✱TOURNEUR and ✱WEBSTER; there are disguised Dukes (like Malevole in *The Malcontent*) in many Renaissance plays, notably ✱SHAKESPEARE's *Measure for Measure* and *The Tempest*; Malevole has also been compared to the protagonist of ✱BRECHT's *The Good Person of Szechwan*.

MASSINGER, Philip   [1583 – 1640]
English dramatist

PLAYS INCLUDE:

A New Way to Pay Old Debts (1625), *The Roman Actor* (1626), *The City Madam* (1632)

Massinger eventually succeeded ✱FLETCHER as resident dramatist with the King's Men, writing jointly or singly some fifty-five plays. The manuscripts of eight of them were used to line pie dishes in the eighteenth century and others have also failed to survive. *A New Way to Pay Old Debts* is a satirical comedy of contemporary manners, which uses such stock elements as young lovers outwitting parental marriage plans, a young man reduced to poverty who is still a gentleman at heart, and a wily servant outwitting his master. The extravagant extortions and ultimate madness of its apparently larger-than-life protagonist Sir Giles Overreach have long been a favourite with actors and audiences. In fact, Overreach is based on the historical Sir Giles Mompesson, a particularly outrageous figure of the period who was eventually tried and convicted for his corrupt practices. *The City Madam* (also a citizen comedy, but its prodigal turns out to be corrupt when given a second chance) was revived in the 1960s and is probably due for

another production, and *The Roman Actor*, with its three plays within plays and a speech defending the profession of actor, figured in the RSC's 2002 season of rarely staged Renaissance plays.

TRY THESE:

✱MARLOWE's Tamburlaine and Faustus are probably the most famous Renaissance over-reachers, though ✱SHAKESPEARE's *Twelfth Night* contains another fine comic example in Malvolio; ✱DEKKER, ✱HEYWOOD, ✱MIDDLETON and ✱JONSON wrote comedies of contemporary London life; many Restoration comedies by writers such as ✱BEHN and ✱WYCHERLEY tackle similar themes, as does ✱CHURCHILL's *Serious Money*; ✱BRENTON and ✱HARE's *Pravda* offers a contemporary portrait of the megalomaniac businessman; for plays about the theatre, ✱FRAYN's *Noises Off*, ✱PIRANDELLO's *Six Characters in Search of an Author*, ✱BULGAKOV's *Molière*.

MASTROSIMONE, William   [1947 –   ]
American dramatist

PLAYS INCLUDE:

The Woolgatherer (1980), *Extremities* (1981), *A Tantalizing* (1982), *Shivaree* (1983), *The Undoing* (1984), *Nanawatai* (1985), *Cat's Paw* (1986), *Tamer of Horses* (1986), *The Understanding* (1987), *A Stone Carver* (1988), *Sunshine* (1989), *Like Totally Weird* (1998), *Bang, Bang, You're Dead* (1999)

Acclaimed for his play and film versions of *Extremities*, Mastrosimone has fearlessly taken on the tough themes of our day: rape, pornography, vengeance, power and guilt, shooting sprees (*Bang, Bang, You're Dead*). His plays present unbalanced characters thrown into intense and dangerous situations that threaten their survival. In *Extremities*, a woman fights off an attempted rape and traps her attacker. In her rage, her dilemma is whether to destroy him or let him go – a choice that she cannot make. Controversial because of its difficult subject matter, the play was lauded by some and criticised by others for its overly happy conclusion that we are all bound by a common humanity.

This idea was examined earlier in *The Woolgatherer*, where a disturbed girl obsessed with images of death and violence and collecting men's sweaters projects her fears onto a mythical friend and brings home a trucker looking for a sexual encounter. Mastrosimone shows us the pain and humour involved in two desperate people's struggle to reach out and trust.

TRY THESE:
✴ SHAKESPEARE's *Titus Andronicus* for treatment of rape; ✴ BARAKA's *The Dutchman* and ✴ NORMAN's *Getting Out* for women committing violence; ✴ PINTER's *The Birthday Party* and ✴ SHEPARD's *True West* for power struggle in relationships; ✴ DORFMAN's *Death and the Maiden* for the ethics of revenge after rape and torture.

MATURA, Mustapha   [1939 –   ]
Trinidadian-born dramatist

PLAYS INCLUDE:
Black Pieces (1970), *As Time Goes By* (1971), *Bakerloo Line* (1972), *Nice* (1973), *Play Mas* (1974), *Black Slaves, White Chains* (1975), *Rum an' Coca Cola* (1976), *Bread* (1976), *Another Tuesday* (1978), *More More* (1978), *Independence* (1979), *Welcome Home Jacko* (1979), *A Dying Business* (1980), *One Rule* (1981), *Meetings* (1981), *The Playboy of the West Indies* (1984, after ✴ O'CASEY), *Trinidad Sisters* (1988, after ✴ CHEKHOV), *The Coup: A Play of Revolutionary Dreams* (1991)

Trinidad-born Matura settled in England in the 1960s; he eventually established himself as one of Britain's major black dramatists and co-founded the Black Theatre Cooperative with Charlie Hanson. His work has concentrated on the black experience in Britain and on Trinidadian issues, and he has also developed versions of classics adapted to his own interests. The common thread is Matura's interest in the contradictions that arise when people drawn from different social and racial groups interact. This stems partly from Trinidad's rich mixture of people of African, East Indian, Chinese, Spanish, British, Portuguese and French descent, as a result of its colonial past. Like many contemporary writers Matura is particularly interested in colonialism as a state of mind as well as a physical institution. Thus in *Play Mas* people

of Indian and African descent work out power relations against the background of Carnival and of independence; in *Independence* different versions of independence are mobilised in contradiction. In *Meetings* we see the tensions between old and new focused in a wealthy couple, one nostalgic for traditional cooking (and, by extension, a life rooted in the old values), the other enslaved to the values of American economic colonialism. Matura has a great gift for witty and revealing dialogue which he puts to particularly good use in his adaptations of the classics; *The Playboy of the West Indies* is an adaptation of ✴ SYNGE's *Playboy of the Western World*. *Trinidad Sisters* is a particularly poignant relocation of ✴ CHEKHOV's *Three Sisters*, as a statement of 'mother country' and its mental stranglehold.

TRY THESE:
✴ IKOLI, another black dramatist whose early career was also fostered by the director Roland Rees, successfully adapted ✴ GORKY's *The Lower Depths* for a mainly black cast; ✴ CHURCHILL's *Cloud Nine* looks at the relationship between the patriarchal and the colonial impulses; ✴ FRIEL's *Translations* offers an Irish dimension; ✴ KEEFFE is a white writer who has used a theme drawn from the classics to underpin his portrayal of black British experience, in *Black Lear* (revised as *King of England*); ✴ ABBENSETTS, ✴ HILL, ✴ JOHN, ✴ PHILLIPS, ✴ PINNOCK, ✴ RECKORD, ✴ RHONE, ✴ RUDET, ✴ WALCOTT, ✴ WHITE for variations on black experience.

MAUGHAM, William
Somerset   [1874 – 1965]
English novelist and dramatist

PLAYS INCLUDE:
A Man of Honour (1903), *Penelope* (1909), *Our Betters* (1917), *Caesar's Wife* (1919), *Home and Beauty* (1919), *The Circle* (1921), *East of Suez* (1922), *The Constant Wife* (1926), *The Letter* (1927), *The Sacred Flame* (1928), *The Bread Winner* (1930), *For Services Rendered* (1932), *Sheppey* (1933)

Maugham's twenty-two plays, mainly neatly constructed comedies, are entertaining and witty and still often revived. The plays may tend to moralise, but, though they are set in the fashionable middle class to whom he was seeking to appeal, Maugham by no means toes the establishment line. Although his closet homosexuality does not figure in his plays, his unsatisfactory marriage may have influenced the criticism of the divorce laws found in *Home and Beauty* and the debate on economic and social sexism in *The Constant Wife*. In *For Services Rendered* his cynical wit is put aside to show the caustic effect of war on family life and in *Sheppey* he shows hostile public reaction to a barber who, on winning a lottery, attempts to use his winnings according to Christ's teaching. *The Sacred Flame*, probably the best of his serious dramas, shows his greatest depth of feeling in a study of unrequited love, part of a murder story that offers a defence of euthanasia.

The Circle

Maugham's finest comedy, *The Circle* was booed at its premiere. An MP and his wife await the arrival of his mother, whom he has not seen since childhood, when she ran away with a married man. When she and her lover arrive, no longer a romantic couple but she a middle-aged, over made-up scatterbrain and he an elderly balding man, who was forced out of a brilliant political career, they bicker over the 'sacrifices' each made to be with the other. When the young wife then falls for a house guest the parallels between wife and mother become clear. Though others try to dissuade her from throwing away her marriage, she is eventually won by her lover's realistic, if romantic, declaration: 'I don't offer you peace and quietness. I offer you unrest and anxiety. I don't offer you happiness. I'm offering you love.'

TRY THESE:

✱ SYNGE's *In the Shadow of the Glen* for a lover offering unrest and anxiety; ✱ COWARD for similar cynical wit with flashes of social comment; ✱ SHAW's *The Marriage* for discussion of the institution; ✱ RATTIGAN for comparable neat construction and subversive tackling of socially unacceptable themes; ✱ LUCIE, ✱ REDDIN for modern equivalents; ✱ WILDE for the 'woman with a past'.

MAYAKOVSKY, Vladimir Vladimirovich   [1893 – 1930]
Russian poet and dramatist

PLAYS INCLUDE:

Vladimir Mayakovsky (1913), *Mystery-Bouffe* (1918), *A Comedy of Murder* (1927), *The Bedbug* (1929), *The Bathhouse* (1930)

Born in Georgia, Mayakovsky espoused the Bolshevik cause at an early stage, and became a champion of Futurism. After the 1917 Revolution he was a leading activist in the new art forms, but with the rise of Stalinism he was subjected to increasingly severe criticism from the Communist Party bureaucracy for individualism and Formalism. In the early 1920s he was a great experimenter with form, writing many fragments and one-act pieces, drawing on a great variety of sources, but he is best known for his two last plays – brilliantly inventive satires on the Soviet bureaucracy of the late 1920s. These attacks hardly endeared him to his opponents, and he committed suicide in a fit of depression, convinced that the Revolution had been subverted.

The Bathhouse

A deeply corrupt official, Pobedonosikov, is informed that a man called Kranov has invented a time-machine, with the intention of employing it in the service of the Peoples' Revolution. Pobedonosikov refuses to listen to the inventor, finding the present power he wields entirely satisfactory and unwilling to risk any change, initiative or responsibility. However, when a miraculous Woman from the Future appears from 2030 AD to assist the Soviet people, Pobedonosikov claims the time-machine as his own. He is left behind when the Woman transports the ordinary people off to the glorious future, leaving only his fellow bureaucrats to console him.

TRY THESE:

✱ DUSTY HUGHES' *The Futurists* is a political satire featuring Mayakovsky as a character; ✱ BRENTON and Tariq Ali's *Moscow Gold* for Russian art and politics; ✱ POWNALL's *Master Class* is a vivid evocation of Stalinist pressure on artists; ✱ STOPPARD's *Every Good Boy Deserves Favour* for satire on the Soviet way of dealing with dissidents; ✳HAVEL and ✳MROZEK are modern east European dramatists who have clashed with their states; ✳GOGOL's *The Government Inspector* is the classic Russian bureaucracy play.

MEDOFF, Mark   [1940 –   ]
American dramatist

PLAYS INCLUDE:

The Kramer (1973), *The Wager* (1973), *When You Comin' Back Red Ryder?* (1974), *Doing a Good One for the Red Man* (1974), *The War on Tatem* (1974), *The Conversion of Aaron Weiss* (1977), *Children of a Lesser God* (1979), *The Hands of Its Enemy* (1986), *The Heart Outright* (1986), *The Majestic Kid* (1986), *The Homage that Follows* (1987), *Gunfighter: A Gulf War Chronicle* (1991), *Road to a Revolution* (2002, with Phyllis Frelich)

The Illinois-born son of a doctor and a psychologist, Medoff's reputation still rests on *Children of a Lesser God*, a love story between a hearing therapist for the deaf, James Leeds, and his stubborn and proud non-hearing student, Sarah Norman. The role of Sarah has given long-overdue exposure to several deaf actresses, including Phyllis Frelich, Jean St Clair, Marlee Matlin and Elizabeth Quinn. The play's substantial success on Broadway, in London and as a film prompted the predictable backlash that Medoff was simply milking the tear-jerking potential inherent in any disability drama, but Medoff has continued to work with Frelich and their most recent work, *Road to a Revolution*, was commissioned by the Deaf West Theater of Los Angeles, which tends to refute any suggestion that he was some kind of disability tourist.

TRY THESE:

✳CLARK's *Whose Life Is It Anyway?*, ✳POMERANCE's *The Elephant Man*, ✳YOUNG's *Crystal Clear* for comparative treatments of disability; Graeae for a British company of disabled performers whose approach to disability is decidedly upbeat.

MERCER, David   [1928 – 80]
British dramatist

PLAYS INCLUDE:

The Buried Man (1962), *The Governor's Lady* (1965), *Ride a Cock Horse* (1965), *Belcher's Luck* (1966), *After Haggerty* (1970), *Flint* (1970), *White Poem* (1970), *Duck Song* (1974), *Cousin Vladimir* (1978), *Then and Now* (1979), *No Limits to Love* (1980)

The son of an engine driver in a working-class northern family, Mercer trained at art school. Heavily influenced at certain periods in his life by R.D. Laing (he had a mental break-down in 1957) and Marxism, his work reflects a disturbingly penetrating analysis of the individual in relation to society, with a critical judgement that left him politically unaligned and increasingly subject to attacks by left-wing critics. As such he brought a variety of perspectives to bear on situations ranging from the ✳ORTONESQUE comedy of *Flint* (about an agnostic vicar and a suicidal young girl) to the examination of infantilism in *Ride a Cock Horse* (in which a writer finds himself regressing emotionally following three unfortunate encounters with women). In *After Haggerty*, the title character – Godot-like – never arrives; instead a drama critic and, at times, an American woman occupy the stage. His fondness for disorienting monologues is echoed in *Duck Song*, a philosophical pastiche set in the home of a wealthy artist. *Cousin Vladimir* is a 'whither England?' piece, pitting a morally neutral Russian dissident against an acute and incisive Englishman. *Then and Now* examines the mounting despair felt by two people seen at two points in their lives – aged twenty and fifty. Mercer's stage success was surpassed by his acclaim on television and film, and his screenplay for Karel Reisz's film *Morgan!*, about an eccentric artist hovering on the brink of insanity, is a classic of the 1960s. His work is overdue for revival.

TRY THESE:

✳PETER SHAFFER (especially *Equus*) for exaltations of passion over reason; ✳BRENTON (especially *Weapons of Happiness*), ✳FRAYN's *Benefactors*, ✳HARE (especially *Plenty*) for left-wing disillusion-ment and lapsed idealism; ✳EDGAR's *Maydays* for another encounter between a dissident and the English; ✱STOPPARD and ✱POWNALL's *Master Class* for artistic freedom of the individual against political dogma; ✱TREVOR GRIFFITHS' *The Party* for a Mercer-like character.

MERRIAM, Eve   [1916 – 92]
American poet, dramatist and writer

PLAYS INCLUDE:
Inner City (1972, later version as *Sweet Dreams*), *Lady Macbeth of Westport* (1972), *Out of Our Father's Houses* (1975), *The Club* (1977), *Viva Reviva* (1977), *At Her Age* (1979), *Dialogue for Lovers* (1980, from ✱SHAKESPEARE's sonnets)

Merriam first came to public attention in the USA as a dramatist in 1972, with the musical *Inner City*, an adaptation of her book *The Inner City Mother Goose*. Set in a private men's club in 1903, *The Club* is notable for its use of female actors to portray male roles. As staged by Tommy Tune, this 'chamber musical' featured provocative, androgynous costumes lampooning male patriarchal stereotypes. *Viva Reviva*, a 'musical awakening', consists of four sections, which use the characters of Eve, Penelope, Ophelia and Joan of Arc to illustrate the oppression of women. This time, Merriam adds male counterparts – Adam, Ulysses and Hamlet – using male performers to make her feminist point. *At Her Age*, commissioned by the Theatre for Older People, addresses the problems of ageing.

TRY THESE:
✱CHURCHILL's *Cloud Nine*, which shows how stereotypical social forces determine the roles women play, and *Top Girls* and *Fen* for their portrayal of women trying to assert themselves in a man's world; ✱DANIELS' *Beside Herself* for female archetypes.

MEYER, Marlane   [1953 –   ]
American dramatist and television writer

PLAYS INCLUDE:
Etta Jenks (1987), *Kingfish* (1988), *Geography of Luck* (1989, *Moe's Lucky Seven* (1994), *The Chemistry of Change* (1998), *The Mystery of Attraction* (2002)

Meyer developed a distinctive playwriting style that has been recognised in various competitions (the Susan Smith Blackburn Prize in New York and the South Coast Repertory Playwriting Competition in California), and has received critical acclaim on both coasts of the United States and, for *Etta Jenks*, in Britain. Meyer's writing might seem best suited to cinema's naturalism but productions have eschewed the realistic and gritty nature suggested by her characters (pornographic film actresses and drugged-out male prostitutes) for a representational style that evokes a sense of fable. Meyer is less interested in specific issues like pornography and prostitution and more interested in the moral, social and ethical questions that the existence of these societal extremities represents. Meyer is disarming because she does not offer judgement about the situations or characters but allows the audience to draw their own conclusions.

Etta Jenks
Etta Jenks is the story of a young dream-filled woman who buys into the rags-to-riches American myth and believes she can become a Hollywood star if she can produce a good audition tape. For her the prize is worth any cost, including becoming a pornographic film actress in order to pay for the tape. The play is a parable about life being manipulated for business purposes. *Etta Jenks* symbolises a culture in which identity has become a commodity and individuality so devalued that prostitution, at least for Meyer, is an apt symbol for contemporary life. The play extends that idea to a chilling conclusion as Etta Jenks is co-opted by the pornographic business, exploiting it to buy the murder of her former producer. She ends the domination that ruled her not with compassion and true self-assertion, but by being ruthless.

TRY THESE:
✱DANIELS' *Masterpieces* for another treatment of pornography; ✱ADSHEAD's *Thatcher's Women*, ✱TERSON's *Strippers* for the economics of the sex industry; ✱DORFMAN's *Death and the Maiden* shows the female protagonist wreaking an awful revenge on a possible one-time oppressor; for more female turning of the tables, ✱EURIPIDES'

The Bacchae and ✱LAVERY's *Kitchen Matters,*
which gives it a homophobic twist.

MIDDLETON, Thomas   [1580 – 1627]
English dramatist

PLAYS INCLUDE:
A Mad World, My Masters (1606), *A Chaste
Maid in Cheapside* (1611), *The Roaring Girl*
(1611, with ✱THOMAS DEKKER), *A Fair
Quarrel* (1617, with ✱WILLIAM ROWLEY),
Women Beware Women (1621), *The
Changeling* (1622, with ✱WILLIAM ROWLEY)

The current interest in themes of gender, class
and power has made Middleton a more
widely staged dramatist than ever before,
since his plays are particularly concerned with
female psychology and preoccupied with the
relationship between love, duty and money.
His Citizen Comedy, *A Chaste Maid in
Cheapside*, has been seen as one of the
theatre's richest investigations of the topics of
money, sex and society but his best-known
works are the two tragedies *Women Beware
Women* and *The Changeling*, in which he
again treats the relationship between money,
sex and power. An RSC production of *The
Roaring Girl* showed the continued relevance
of this fictionalised account of the life of Moll
Cutpurse, based on a real woman who
scandalised early seventeenth-century society
by her non-conformist ways (see ✱DEKKER
for more on *The Roaring Girl*). Middleton is
now often credited with writing *The
Revenger's Tragedy* (1607), previously ascribed
to ✱CYRIL TOURNEUR, under whose name it is
discussed in this book.

The Changeling
There are no great affairs of state at stake in
The Changeling, no kingdoms fall, no royal
houses die out. It is far more of a domestic
tragedy than many of the great Renaissance
tragedies and it is very much a play about lack
of perception and failure, sometimes deliberate, to understand the probable results of
actions. In particular the heroine, Beatrice-
Joanna, fails to see that playing on the
malcontent De Flores' passion for her in order
to get him to rid her of her unwanted
betrothed in favour of another man is

unlikely to be without consequences for her
own future freedom of action, and she
becomes sucked into the vortex of passion
which brings them both to their deaths. There
is the usual Renaissance pattern of dumb
shows, dropped handkerchiefs, severed
fingers, dances of madmen, and so on, but it
is almost all still credible in modern terms
(with the exception of the virginity test
potions) and the result is a powerful unmasking not only of individual psychology but
also, particularly in the subplot, of the
constraints which determine the subordinate
status of women within society.

TRY THESE:
The modernity of Middleton's interests has
encouraged contemporary dramatists to adapt
his work, notably ✱KEEFFE with his modern
version of the comedy *A Mad World, My Masters*
and ✱BARKER with his rewriting of the later parts
of *Women Beware Women*; most Renaissance
dramatists used revenge plots and malcontent
figures: ✱SHAKESPEARE's *Hamlet* is the most
famous example of both, and there are notable
examples in ✱TOURNEUR and ✱WEBSTER; for
modem equivalents of *The Roaring Girl*,
✱WERTENBAKER's *New Anatomies* and *The Grace
of Mary Traverse*; ✱BEHN for a late seventeenth-
century female view of similar themes.

MILLER, Arthur   [1915 –   ]
American dramatist

PLAYS INCLUDE:
The Man Who Had All the Luck (1944), *All
My Sons* (1947), *Death of a Salesman* (1949),
The Crucible (1953), *A View from the Bridge*
(1955), *A Memory of Two Mondays* (1955),
After the Fall (1964), *Incident at Vichy* (1964),
The Price (1968), *Fame* (1970), *The Creation
of the World and Other Business* (1972), *Up
from Paradise* (1974), *The Archbishop's Ceiling*
(1977), *The American Clock* (1980), *Two-Way
Mirror* (1984), *Danger: Memory!* (1987), *The
Ride Down Mt. Morgan* (1990), *The Last
Yankee* (1991), *Broken Glass* (1994), *Mr Peter's
Connection* (1998)

The son of a clothing manufacturer hard hit
by the Depression, Miller, a native New
Yorker, established his reputation as a social

The Changeling by Thomas Middleton and William Rowley, directed by Dawn Walton, Southwark Playhouse, 2002. Naomi Taylor as Beatrice-Joanna. (Pete Jones/ArenaPAL)

The Crucible by Arthur Miller, directed by Kenny Ireland, The Touring Consortium, 1998. (Mark Douet/ArenaPAL)

dramatist in the tradition of *IBSEN with *All My Sons*, a surprisingly timely tale of World War II venality that up-ends the cosy world of small-town America in which it is set. *Death of a Salesman*, his Pulitzer Prize-winning parable about the failure of the American dream, remains his most popular play. *The Crucible* – an exposure of McCarthyism in 1950s America filtered through the witch trials of seventeenth-century Salem, Massachusetts – is perhaps his most politically charged play. *A View from the Bridge* contrasts private morality and public pressure in the story of a Brooklyn longshoreman, Eddie Carbone. *After the Fall* attracted attention for gossip-related reasons: to what extent could the suicidal Maggie in Miller's play be read as the writer's portrait of his late wife, Marilyn Monroe? The prices people pay for choices they have made is an obsessive Miller theme, made explicit in *The Price* and also in *Danger: Memory!*, in which efforts to forget pain cost people their memories.

Miller's reputation in the United States has not held up as well as it has in Britain. His self-conscious use of language (sometimes compared to *O'NEILL's in its linguistic shortcomings) has been compared unfavourably to *TENNESSEE WILLIAMS' lyricism (as though there wasn't room for both) and he has been criticised for cumbersome metaphors and pontifical tendencies, although this may reflect a general American unease with consciously 'political' writing. Still, Miller's unceasing attention to questions of public and private integrity have distinguished his career and rightly earned him the respect of theatregoers on both sides of the Atlantic.

Death of a Salesman

Despite its portentous subtitle, 'Certain Private Conversations in Two Acts and Requiem', Miller's play is still capable of packing a wallop – its regular revivals attest to its undiminished emotional power. Willy Loman, a pathetic and potentially tragic American Everyman, loses his job at age 63 and kills himself in a last-ditch effort to raise the money his family needs. At once particular and general, lean and overripe, linear and abstract in its cross-cutting in time, Miller's play is one of the profoundest examinations yet of the American dream. As the major American drama of the 1940s *Death of a Salesman* engendered several major critical appraisals, mostly centring on whether the play ranks as a modern tragedy. Many critics have taken exception to the designation of tragedy, finding the play morally clichéd and Loman's character lacking the insight generally expected of a tragic hero. Nonetheless, Miller's interweaving of the realistic and poetic in the play, and his rich characterisations still have wide appeal. A production of the play in China prompted Miller's 1984 memoir, *Salesman in Beijing*.

TRY THESE:

*HELLMAN, *IBSEN, *ODETS and *SHAW as dramatic moralists; *MARGULIES' *The Loman Family Picnic* for a black comedy about a Jewish salesman's family; *MAMET (especially *Glengarry Glen Ross*), *MEYER, *NEMETH for soured visions of the American dream.

MILNER, Ron(ald)   [1938 –]
American dramatist

PLAYS INCLUDE:

Life Agony (1965), *Who's Got His Own* (1966), *The Warning: A Theme for Linda* (1969), *Jazz Set* (1974), *What the Wine-Sellers Buy* (1974), *Going Away Party* (1974), *Seasons Reasons* (1980), *Crack Steppin'* (1982), *Don't Get God Started* (1987), *Checkmates* (1987), *Roads of the Mountaintop* (1988)

Since the 1960s, Milner has been an articulate spokesperson for the black theatre movement in America, seeking to reveal the historic and current problems faced by blacks in the United States, although his work is not staged in Britain. Milner encourages the work of playwrights and co-founded the Spirit of Shango Theatre in his birthplace, Detroit, Michigan, to give substance to his belief that black artists should work with their roots in their own communities. *Who's Got His Own* concerns a black family that is all but destroyed by the anger and grief they experience at the hands of an uncaring white world. *What the Wine-Sellers Buy* evokes some feminist controversy, as it suggests that black women, though defined by the men in their lives, often exert negative influence on the black male community. The play, nevertheless, also embodies the writer's most enduring theme that moral choices are not only possible, but positive. *Seasons Reasons* concerns a man imprisoned in the 1960s and released in the 1980s, only to find that his once-radical friends are now members of the 'establishment'.

Milner often draws upon jazz, gospel and blues, feeling that music can express everything inherent in black culture. In *Jazz Set*, using music written and performed by Max Roach, each musician becomes a character who becomes one with his or her instrument. 'I try to find a way to blend music with drama – otherwise, the drama is European. Black culture is ritualistic.' Milner's musical *Crack Steppin'* is subtitled 'a comic book operetta in Rhythm and Blues'. *Don't Get God Started*, a gospel musical centring on a group of born-again Christians, relies even more heavily on music. In *Checkmates*, Milner probes issues beyond black/white conflict such as the 'generation gap' and 'yuppie values' through the perspective of black America. Milner's two married couples show the changing importance of jobs, women and material gain in the lives of everyday citizens; they exemplify the issue of competitiveness in modern marriage and how deeply it contrasts with the marriages of generations past.

TRY THESE:

✱ SHANGE, especially for *colored girls who have considered suicide when the rainbow is enuf* and *Spell No. 7* for their oppositional view of male–female relationships in the black community; ✱ HANSBERRY's *Raisin in the Sun*, which Milner himself claims to have been a strong influence; ✱ ALBEE's *Who's Afraid of Virginia Woolf?* for married couples across the generation gap; ✱ CROSS for black British concern with ritual.

MINGHELLA, Anthony   [1954 –]
British dramatist and film-maker

PLAYS INCLUDE:
Child's Play (1978), *Whale Music* (1981), *A Little Like Drowning* (1984), *Love Bites* (1984), *Two Planks and a Passion* (1984), *Made in Bangkok* (1986)

Of Italian parentage, brought up on the Isle of Wight, Minghella established himself as a dramatist capable of an impressive breadth of themes and periods before moving into other media, with the success of the film *Truly Madly Deeply* leading to other films such as *The English Patient* and *Iris*. In *A Little Like Drowning*, an episodic flashback drama about an Italian family uprooted to England, a conversation between the elderly Nonna and her granddaughter Anastasia gives way to a series of pained recollections about her now-dead husband, Alfredo, who left her for an English mistress. Domestic discord continues in *Love Bites*, about a family reunion that disintegrates into recriminations. *Two Planks and a Passion* shifts the scene to 1392 and to preparations in York for a Passion play at the Feast of Corpus Christi, a religious event turned all too secular by the greed and avarice of a community suddenly visited by Richard II. *Made in Bangkok*, his best-known play, continues Minghella's interest in issues of ethical and moral compromise. Commissioned by Michael Codron for a commercial engagement, *Made in Bangkok* was a risky venture about sexual exploitation that must have surprised tourists who thought it would be a spicy follow-up to *No Sex Please, We're British*. Five Britons arrive on an 'Eastern Promise' holiday in Asia – one woman, Frances, and four sex-starved men – only to find that geographical displacement leads to its own emotional truth-telling as the men are revealed to be rapacious wolves and Frances becomes an all too obvious authorial stand-in. An extended essay about exploitation, the play is too smart to be prurient itself, but it never quite packs the punch Minghella seems to assume it will.

TRY THESE:

✱ CHURCHILL, ✱ DUSTY HUGHES and ✱ LOWE for a similar kind of peculiarly English staccato rhythm; ✱ ADSHEAD's *Thatcher's Women*, ✱ MEYER's *Etta Jenks*, Julia Schofield's *Love On the Plastic* and ✱ TERSON's *Strippers* as plays about the sexual exploitation of women; ✱ NICHOLS' *Poppy*, ✱ C. P. TAYLOR's *Withdrawal Symptoms*, ✱ WALL's *Amongst Barbarians* for other views of British excursions in the Far East; ✱ GILL's *The York Realist* for a modern engagement with the medieval *Mysteries* and ✱ HARRISON for a modern adaptation of them.

MITCHELL, Adrian   [1932 –   ]
British poet, dramatist and novelist

PLAYS INCLUDE:
Tyger (1971, after William Blake), *The Pied Piper* (1986, after Robert Browning), *The Snow Queen* (1990, after Hans Christian Andersen), *The Lion, the Witch and the Wardrobe* (1998, after C. S. Lewis), *Alice in Wonderland* and *Through the Looking Glass* (2001, after Lewis Carroll), *Peter Rabbit and His Friends* (2002, after Beatrix Potter)

Mitchell's distinguished career as an author of plays for children and a campaigner for children's theatre is only one facet of his many contributions to the development of the modern British theatrical scene. In the 1960s he worked with Peter Brook on two key events in modern British theatre, adapting ✻PETER WEISS's *Marat/Sade* and contributing to *US*. Subsequently he worked with the 7:84 company and Welfare State. He adapted John Berger's *A Seventh Man* for the Foco Novo company (1976) and has had long relationships with both national companies. He has also adapted plays by ✻CALDERÓN, ✻GOGOL, ✻GOLDONI, ✻IBSEN, ✻JOSÉ TRIANA and ✻LOPE DE VEGA.

TRY THESE:
For dramatists writing for children, ✻CASDAGLI, ✻DAVID HOLMAN, ✻SHEPPHARD, ✻DAVID WOOD.

MITCHELL, Gary   [1965 –   ]
Northern Irish dramatist

PLAYS INCLUDE:
That Driving Ambition (1995), *Sinking* (1997), *In a Little World of Our Own* (1997), *Tearing the Loom* (1998), *As the Beast Sleeps* (1998), *Trust* (1999), *Energy* (1999), *Marching On* (2000), *The Force of Change* (2000)

Mitchell writes from within the Northern Irish Protestant context, offering important insights into the loyalist tradition, often using a thriller format. *Tearing the Loom* examines the 1798 rebellion; *As the Beast Sleeps* is about how the lives of loyalist paramilitaries changed when the ceasefire took away their high-status roles as protectors of the population against the threat from nationalist paramilitaries and left them unemployed and emasculated. *Trust* tackles the ways in which the unnatural situation distorts everyday values and situations as a UDA hardman debates whether to organise a punishment beating as a response to his son being bullied at school. In *The Force of Change* Mitchell shows us the complexities of the situation as RUC police officers interrogate UDA suspects while negotiating their own prejudices and preferences. It is particularly acute in showing the ways in which age and youth, cynicism and idealism, male and female interact in ways that defy stereotype. *Tearing the Loom* is unusual amongst Mitchell's plays in tackling a historical topic, the 1798 rebellion, but it is still concerned with the interaction between the personal and the political contexts.

TRY THESE:
✻HUTCHINSON's *Rat in the Skull* for another RUC interrogation; ✻HOPKINS for naturalistic and ✻IONESCO for non-naturalistic interrogations; ✻FO and ✻MCDONAGH for terrorists; ✻DEVLIN, ✻MORRISON, ✻MUNRO, ✻REID for modern Belfast.

MITCHELL, Julian   [1935 –   ]
British novelist, dramatist and writer

PLAYS INCLUDE:
Half-Life (1977), *The Enemy Within* (1980), *Another Country* (1981), *Francis* (1983), *After Aida* (originally *Verdi's Messiah*, 1986), *Falling Over England* (1994), *August* (1994, from ✻CHEKHOV's *Uncle Vanya*)

Mitchell is best known as a dramatist for *Another Country* (filmed with Rupert Everett as the iconic gay/rebel), which explored the link between sexual identity and political awareness in a British public-school setting, echoing the background of the MI5 spy Guy Burgess. Critics were less kind to his bio-piece on St Francis of Assisi, *Francis*, which smacked somewhat of unimaginative schools radio, unable to match his sharp political edge in religious ideology.

TRY THESE:
✱BENNETT's *Single Spies* and ✱STOPPARD's *Hapgood* for secret agents; St Joan is the most popular theatrical saint: ✱ANOUILH, ✱BRECHT, ✱SHAW, ✱SHAKESPEARE's *Henry VI Part I* and ✱TERSON for good examples; ✱HARE's *Plenty*, like *Falling Over England*, concerns itself with Suez; ✱FRIEL for Irish relocations of ✱CHEKHOV to compare to the Welsh setting of *August*.

MOFFATT, Nigel   [1954 –   ]
Jamaican-born dramatist

PLAYS INCLUDE:
Mamma Decemba (1985), *Lifetime* (1985), *Celebration* (1986), *Walsall Boxed In* (1987), *Musical Youth* (2001)

Mamma Decemba, written for Temba, won the Samuel Beckett Award for 1986. Moffatt's play centres on the disillusionment of Caribbean immigrants with 'the home country', seen through the eyes of two older women, Mamma Decemba and her friend. But in *Mamma Decemba*, written in patois though the play is set in 'inner-city England', Moffatt has created a unique character whose shifts of mood and impenetrable grief as she mourns her recently deceased husband are handled with a sensitivity that goes beyond the individual and gives the play a universal appeal. Moffatt has written for television and radio and worked with young playwrights in the West Midlands. *Musical Youth* is about the trials and tribulations of the Birmingham Boy Band of the same name.

TRY THESE:
✱MATURA, ✱PHILLIPS, ✱WHITE for other plays on the theme of disillusionment with the mother country; ✱PINNOCK for a female perspective; ✱HARE's *Teeth 'n' Smiles* and ✱KEEFFE's *Bastard Angel* for rock bands.

MOLIÈRE (Jean-Baptiste Poquelin)   [1622 – 73]
French dramatist and actor-manager

PLAYS INCLUDE:
Les Précieuses Ridicules (1658, *The Affected Ladies*), *L'École des Femmes* (1662, *The School for Wives*), *Don Juan* (1665), *Le Misanthrope*

(1666, *The Misanthrope*), *Le Tartuffe* (*Tartuffe*, written 1664, produced 1667), *Georges Dandin* (1668), *Le Bourgeois Gentilhomme* (1671, *The Would-be Gentleman* or *The Bourgeois Gentleman*), *Les Fourberies de Scapin* (1671, *The Tricks of Scapin* or *Scapino*), *Les Femmes Savantes* (1672, *The Learned Ladies*), *Le Malade Imaginaire* (1673, *The Hypochondriac* or *The Imaginary Invalid*)

Molière was the eldest son of a wealthy Paris tapestry merchant in the king's service, and was well educated with a view to following his father's occupation. Instead, however, he went off with a troupe of actors, and toured in the provinces for fifteen years before making any success in Paris. This apprenticeship, and having to share the Palais-Royal theatre for half the week with an Italian *commedia dell'arte* troupe, gave him a very thorough theatrical grounding. He became France's most complete man of the theatre; he was as good a comic actor as he was a comic dramatist. He produced his own plays and managed his company against strong attacks from the respectable (though he enjoyed the firm support of Louis XIV), and he died with his make-up on. His output ranges from knockabout farce to conversation pieces, to political satire, to court spectacles with elaborate machinery, to subtle comedies of character, all happily still holding the stage. His only failure was a heroic drama, *Don Garcie de Navarre*; being disinclined to waste, he salvaged some of the text and used it for Alceste's more lofty sentiments in *The Misanthrope*.

The Misanthrope
Q: Will the noble, uncompromising, universally admired Alceste win his lawsuit despite his refusal to butter up the judges and his inability not to tell the truth about the awful verses of the powerful Oronte? A: No. Q: Will he marry the brilliant, beautiful, bitchy Célimène or the quiet, devoted Eliante? A: Neither. Célimène cannot face the thought of all that rustic high thinking, and Eliante very sensibly decides that she will be happier with Alceste's more worldly and less demanding friend Philinte. The rest is just brilliant conversation. The world divides into those

who think Alceste is Molière's funniest creation, and those (like Rousseau) who are shocked that Molière should have held up to ridicule this virtuous and Rousseau-like man.

TRY THESE:
Ranjit Bolt and Jatinder Verma for adaptations of Molière; ✶RACINE for seventeenth-century French tragedy, though they were on bad terms; English Restoration comedy (e.g. ✶ETHEREGE, ✶WYCHERLEY) has much in common with Molière; ✶HAMPTON's *The Philanthropist* is an 'answer' to *The Misanthrope*; ✶BULGAKOV's *Molière*; David Hirson's *La Bête*, a contemporary verse comedy about a Molière-like troop of actors.

MOLNAR, Ferenc   [1878 – 1952]
Hungarian dramatist

PLAYS INCLUDE:
Liliom (1909), *The Guardsman* (1910), *The Swan* (1914), *The Play in the Castle* (1924, *The Play's the Thing* in the USA), *Olimpia* (1927), *The Good Fairy* (1931)

Beginning as a writer of farces and light-hearted satirical comedies of Hungarian city life but later gaining international success, Molnar is known less by name than by his work. *The Devil* (1907), a reworking of the Faust theme, was an early success; *The Wolf* (1912) surfaced in the West End in 1973 and *The Guardsman* at the National Theatre in 1978, as a musical at the Donmar Warehouse in 1997 and at the Albery in 2000; *The Swan* is best known through a Grace Kelly/Alec Guinness film version and *Liliom* in its hugely successful musical adaptation *Carousel*. ✶TOM STOPPARD reworked *The Play in the Castle* as *Rough Crossing* (National Theatre, 1984) with initially disastrous results – changing the setting to a transatlantic liner, adding a parody musical (with a score by André Previn), complicating the plot and turning an elegant trifle into a heavy-handed wreck. Although the P. G. Wodehouse version for Broadway is much closer to the spirit of the original, Stoppard's version became popular in the USA. In the original version a young composer overhears his fiancée in a passionate exchange with another man; to save the situation a playwright dashes off a short play (a pastiche of one by Sardou) to convince the composer that all he heard was a snatch of a rehearsal. Molnar's touch is almost always light and his work often has elements of fantasy, as in the father's return to earth in *Liliom* and the usherette's dream adventures in *The Good Fairy*.

TRY THESE:
Molnar's work has been adapted by ✶MARCUS; Nicolle Freni's *Brooklyn E5* for a lesbian variation on *Liliom*, involving the return of a ghostly (and benevolent) father; ✶BARRIE's *Mary Rose* for returning ghosts; ✶ANOUILH, ✶GIRAUDOUX for elements of fantasy; ✶FRAYN, ✶STOPPARD for plays-within-plays.

MORGAN, Abi
British dramatist

PLAYS INCLUDE:
Skinned (1998), *Sleeping Around* (1998, with ✶HILARY FANNIN, Stephen Greenhorn and ✶MARK RAVENHILL), *Splendour* (2000), *Tender* (2001), *Tiny Dynamite* (2001)

Morgan's range is already considerable, from fairly conventional scripts to *Tiny Dynamite*, a Paines Plough/Frantic Assembly collaboration that used a wide range of theatrical devices. *Splendour* takes the basic situation of a group of people waiting for another to arrive, but invests it with great resonance: we are waiting for the General in a mansion on the outskirts of some east European city, the military are rumbling in the background, revenge is in the air. *Tender* deals with a modern urban landscape peopled with characters whose random (and not so random) interactions stand for a whole society trying to cope with the pressures of contemporary life. In *Tiny Dynamite* two old friends linked by a traumatic childhood incident meet a young woman who acts as a catalyst for a series of revelations and resolutions.

TRY THESE:
✶CHURCHILL, ✶EDGAR for reactions to the collapse of communism in eastern Europe; ✶BECKETT and ✶PINTER for waiting;

*SCHNITZLER's *La Ronde* for parallels with *Sleeping Around* and *Tender;* *MARBER's *Closer* for parallels with the landscape of *Tender.*

MORNIN, Daniel   [1956 –   ]
Northern Irish dramatist

PLAYS INCLUDE:
Mum and Son (1981), *The Resting Time* (1981), *Kate* (1983), *Short of Mutiny* (1983), *Comrade Ogilvy* (1985), *The Murderers* (1985), *Built on Sand* (1987), *Weights and Measures* (1988), *At Our Table* (1991)

Belfast-born Mornin spent three years in the navy and travelled extensively in Asia and North Africa before coming to rest in London. *Short of Mutiny* was admired for its authenticity of crew life, social dynamics and observation about class and the wretchedness of life aboard for those at the wrong end of command. Although it was his first play it was not produced until 1983, when it was viewed in a post-Falklands War context. *Built on Sand*, a non-naturalistic piece that uses flashbacks, is as much a study in political cynicism as it is about the young Belfast journalist Andrew's obsession with finding answers to the murder of his girlfriend. *Kate*, which shows the daily pressures of living in Belfast, is as harrowing in its depiction of the young, sullen son, already 'lost' and committed to violence and the loyalist paramilitaries, as it tries to be optimistic in its portrait of Kate, determined to get a typing qualification despite life falling apart all around her. *The Murderers* is the violent, inevitable end of the conundrum, going behind the scenes of a bloody sectarian killing, to reveal the same bigotry that both IRA and loyalist leaders in *Built on Sand* feed off, and which leads to the killings being seen as part of some atavistic male initiation rite. Mornin's novel *All Our Fault, Nothing Personal*, also on paramilitary themes, was filmed as *Nothing Personal* in 1996.

TRY THESE:
*DEVLIN, *MARIE JONES, *MUNRO's *Bold Girls,* *REID for more plays on Belfast and its effect on women; *FINNEGAN for historical and social explorations of Northern Ireland conflicts;

*LOWE's *Seachange* for flashback style; *ROBERT HOLMAN's *Lost in Making Noise Quietly,* *PAGE, for more post-Falklands reprises, both army and navy; Tom McClenaghan's *Submariners* for navy crews under pressure; *WILLIS HALL's *The Long and the Short and the Tall* for inter-ranks service strife; *TERRY JOHNSON's *Imagine Drowning,* *MARCHANT for further modern explorations of the roots of violence.

MORRISON, Bill   [1940 –   ]
Northern Irish dramatist, actor and director

PLAYS INCLUDE:
Please Don't Shoot Me When I'm Down (1969), *Tess of the D'Urbervilles* (1971, from Thomas Hardy), *Patrick's Day* (1972), *Conn and the Conquerors of Space* (1972), *Sam Slade is Missing* (1972), *The Love of Lady Margaret* (1973), *The Irish Immigrant's Tale* (1976), *The Emperor of Ice Cream* (1977, from Brian Moore), *Flying Blind* (1977), *Ellen Cassidy* (1978), *Dr Jekyll of Rodney Street* (1979), *Scrap!* (1982), *Cavern of Dreams* (1984, musical with Carol Ann Duffy), *Be Bop a Lula* (1988), *Love Song for Ulster* (1993)

Morrison's greatest success is *Flying Blind*, one of a number of plays produced during a fruitful association with the Liverpool Everyman. Set in contemporary Belfast, it uses broadly farcical mechanisms and devices – overheard conversations, inopportune exits and entrances, frustrated seductions, robings and disrobings – to present a portrait of a society impotent to solve its problems (the fact that none of the men can achieve an erection is metaphorically as well as farcically appropriate). The old certainties and convictions have given way to male withdrawal into the safer world represented by the music of Charlie Parker or to the fanaticism of the paramilitaries. Everyone is 'flying blind' without navigational aids, including the Protestant paramilitary who has to keep taking off his hood because he can't see without his glasses and the female babysitter who wants to borrow *Fear of Flying*. This powerful, disturbing and funny play ends in a welter of gunfire, urine, death and reconciliation which defies conventional theatrical expectations, just as the characters' lives have been forced out of conventional moulds by the political situation.

TRY THESE:
The issues raised have counterparts in plays by ✱FRIEL and ✱O'CASEY; ✱ORTON provides an example of the extension and subversion of the boundaries of farce in *Loot* and *What the Butler Saw*; Hector MacMillan's *The Sash* offers a Scottish angle on the Irish situation; ✱MARIE JONES' *Somewhere Over the Balcony* also takes a farcical, surreal approach to present day Belfast; for other Belfast-touched subjects, ✱DEVLIN, ✱FINNEGAN, ✱MORNIN, ✱REID.

MORTIMER, John   [1923 –   ]
British dramatist, journalist, novelist and barrister

PLAYS INCLUDE:
The Dock Brief (1957), *What Shall We Tell Caroline* (1958), *Lunch Hour* (1960), *The Wrong Side of the Park* (1960), *The Judge* (1967), *Come As You Are* (1970, comprising *Mill Hill*, *Bermondsey*, *Gloucester Road*, *Marble Arch*), *A Voyage Round My Father* (1970), *Collaborators* (1973), *Heaven and Hell* (1976, comprising *The Fear of Heaven*, *The Prince of Darkness*, later retitled *The Bells of Hell*), *The Lady from Maxim's* (1977, from ✱FEYDEAU), *A Little Hotel on the Side* (1984, from ✱FEYDEAU)

Despite a very Establishment and traditional background, Mortimer has consistently espoused liberal positions in his writing and involvement in theatre. An enormously prolific writer, whose television series include the tremendously popular *Rumpole of the Bailey*, Mortimer was a key figure in anti-censorship debates, giving testimony which was active in abolishing the censorship power of the Lord Chamberlain and speaking out against the attacks on ✱HOWARD BRENTON's *The Romans in Britain*.

However, his own writing is, for the most part, very gentle and often nostalgic. *The Dock Brief*, the play that really made his name, went through the process that has been true of many of Mortimer's plays: first written for radio, it was then staged, and finally televised. *Voyage Round My Father* is an autobio-graphical account of Mortimer's father, a lawyer who resolutely denied his own blind-ness. It is a powerful and moving study of a man who is clearly monstrous in some aspects but who is, nonetheless, drawn with enormous affection. The play is almost an elegy for him, and for Mortimer's stalwart mother who bore his father's eccentricities with enormous patience. First produced as a radio play, it was then staged, and later televised with Laurence Olivier as the father.

TRY THESE:
✱OSBORNE, whom Mortimer acknowledges as an influence; ✱DE FILIPPO's *Ducking Out* and ✱WHITE's *The Nine Night* both have central *monstres sacrés* father figures, as does ✱O'NEILL's *Long Day's Journey Into Night*.

MOTTON, Gregory   [1962 –   ]
British dramatist

PLAYS INCLUDE:
Rain (1984), *Chicken* (1987), *Ambulance* (1987), *Downfall* (1988), *Looking at You (Revived) Again* (1989), *The Life of St Fanny* (1990), *A Message for the Broken Hearted* (1993), *The Terrible Voice of Satan* (1993), *Cat and Mouse (Sheep)* (1995), *A Little Satire* (1997), *A Monologue* (1998), *Praise Be to Progress* (1999), *God's Island* (2000)

Motton's work is primarily concerned with the harsh world of those living on the edges of society – the homeless, the destitute and the handicapped, both physically and emotion-ally. He is a poetic writer, sometimes compared to ✱SAMUEL BECKETT in their common lack of naturalism and easy intelligibility. He depicts a brutal world where dreams and aspirations are already a thing of the past and his plays have been described as 'bafflingly opaque'. His grotesque satirical vision and tendencies to abstraction mean that his own work is currently more popular on mainland Europe than it is in Britain, and much of his recent work has premiered in France.

His world is peopled with lost souls, frequently crippled physically – as with the wife in *Looking at You* – or emotionally, as with Pedro in *Ambulance*. In *Ambulance* his characters are the homeless of any city for whom an ambulance light is not a bringer of safety and warmth but something that terrifies and probably brings trouble. The story centres on Ellis, an alcoholic tramp who finds a dead baby and believes it is the one she herself lost twenty years earlier. The baby takes her on a journey into the past. *Looking at You* follows the journey of an Irish vagrant, returning to his native country, and his relationships both with a young girl, whom he meets on the road and who hopes he will fall in love with her, and his wheelchair-bound, embittered wife who presides over his old home. *A Little Satire* is about the British general election of 1997 and *Cat and Mouse* (*Sheep*) is a more abstract satire of the nature of modern capitalism and democracy. *Praise Be to Progress* presents a decaying bourgeoisie moving from racist murder to self-cannibalism and grave robbing, while *God's Island* began as a commission to adapt *The Tempest* but became more of a theological parable encompassing both Old and New Testament.

TRY THESE:

American publicity for *Cat and Mouse* (*Sheep*) compares it to ✱BRECHT, ✱IONESCO, ✱JARRY and George Orwell; ✱BARNES for some parallels in the grotesque; Motton has adapted ✱BÜCHNER, ✱FOSSE and ✱STRINDBERG; ✱GORKY for similar visions of social outcasts and yearning; ✱IKOLI's *The Lower Depths* for a multiracial East End version; ✱CARTWRIGHT's *Road* for another version of contemporary disenchantment; ✱PINTER for characters as menacing symbols of external reality; ✱TENNESSEE WILLIAMS for a contrasting American treatment of the loss of dreams; ✱BOLGER for a contemporary Irish native returning to Dublin.

MROZEK, Slawomir   [1930 –   ]
Polish dramatist and cartoonist

PLAYS INCLUDE:

Police (1958), *Charlie* (1961), *Out at Sea* (1961, also known as *The Ship-Wrecked Ones*), *The Party* (1962), *The Enchanted Night* (1963, also known as *What a Lovely Dream*), *Tango* (1964), *Emigrés* (1975), *The Hunchback* (1976), *A Summer's Day* (1983), *Love in the Crimea* (1993), *The Reverends* (1996), *The Beautiful Sight* (1998), *The History of the People's Republic of Poland* (1998)

Mrozek was probably one of the best-known eastern European playwrights in the West, if only because he found himself there after protesting about Poland's role in the occupation of Czechoslovakia; his passport was withdrawn, but he managed to escape to Paris. He returned to Poland in the 1990s. His plays are often absurdist in style, but the background is not so much a meaningless universe as an irrational and arbitrary totalitarian state, and his tone is satirical and sardonic rather than despairing. Jan Kott, the eminent Polish critic, wrote brilliantly on Mrozek, elucidating what might seem, to the uninitiated, an alien universe.

The first Mrozek work done in English was Martin Esslin's adaptation of a short story, *Siesta*, for radio in 1963. *Emigrés* is a two-hander between AA the Intellectual and XX the Worker, both exiles in a sordid basement somewhere in the free world, fantasising and bickering on New Year's Eve. *A Summer's Day* is another two-handed philosophical tug-of-war between Sux, an overachiever, and Unsux, an underachiever, both of whom wish to commit suicide; there is an intervening lady (who goes off with Sux, of course). *Tango*, in ✱TOM STOPPARD's adaptation, is probably Mrozek's most familiar work. In this play, questions of freedom and authority in the modern state are raised through the metaphor of an anarchic family with an intellectual but authoritarian son who is trying to reform it. He fails to maintain control, and brute force takes over in the form of Eddie the butler. The play, besides being full of logical paradoxes and knotty arguments of the Stoppard kind, is also very funny. His later work, which looks at contemporary issues such as the collapse of the Soviet Union, the break up of Yugoslavia and the recent history of Poland, has not yet been seen in Britain.

TRY THESE:

✱HAVEL for another eastern European playwright with kindred themes and techniques; ✱STOPPARD for *Professional Foul, Every Good Boy Deserves*

Favour and *Squaring the Circle*, which treat similar themes; ✶BRECHT's *Conversations in Exile* has similarities to *Emigrés*; for other Polish writers: Witold Gombrowicz; Czeslaw Milosz; ✶GLOWACKI's *Cinders* was co-adapted by ✶KUREISHI; ✶GEMS adapted Stanislawa Przybyszewska's *The Danton Affair*; ✶EDGAR for parallel interests to the later works.

MÜLLER, Heiner   [1929 – 95]
German dramatist and director

PLAYS INCLUDE:
The Scab (1956), *The Construction Site* (1957), *The Correction* (1958), *Herakles 5* (1966), *Philoctetes* (1966), *Oedipus Tyrant* (1966), *The Horatian* (1968), *Mauser* (1970), *Germania Death in Berlin* (1971), *Macbeth* (1972), *The Battle* (1974), *Hamletmachine* (1977), *Quartet* (1981), *Despoiled Shore/Medeamaterial/Landscape with Argonauts* (1984), *Civil WarS Act IV* (1984), *Germania 3* (1996)

Müller's unique political theatre transcended even the Berlin Wall. His family chose to move to the West but Müller stayed in the East, where his plays (many of which explore the problems of a failed socialist utopia) were banned from 1961 to 1973. His life, politics and art reflect the divided German nation that existed for most of his life. Heir to ✶BERTOLT BRECHT's position as premier German playwright, Müller served as dramaturg at the Berliner Ensemble from 1970 to 1975 and he was appointed as its director shortly before his death.

His early works are Brechtian Lehrstücke (teaching plays), and his poetic drama, like Brecht's, finds its roots in Expressionism; but he goes far beyond Brecht's parable formula as a means of expressing the political and historical contradictions of the world. His mature plays abandon conventional plot, dialogue and characterisation; instead, they are collages that he called 'synthetic fragments' in which disparate scenes and metaphoric visions are juxtaposed non-sequentially to create meaning through clashes of image and text. Müller suggested that the director should actively confront the script and add elements that compound the

levels of meaning. This disjuncture between words and actions has attracted the collaboration of Robert Wilson, who created several mise-en-scènes, including *Civil WarS Act IV*, around Müller texts.

Many of Müller's plays are deconstructions of classical texts or historical dramas, with *Hamletmachine*, his kaleidoscopic response to ✶SHAKESPEARE's play, probably being the most familiar in Britain. *Germania Death in Berlin* presents violent images and themes from Prussian history and mythology. In this kaleidoscope of German history, Müller chronicles the brutalisation of the German people, in which Nazism is seen as the natural culmination of Prussian militarism. Here, Goebbels gives birth to Hitler's child, which turns out to be a thalidomide wolf. Although Müller has been hailed as the most important playwright since ✶SAMUEL BECKETT and he has a high academic reputation, his work has not been widely seen in Britain.

TRY THESE:
Robert Wilson and Peter Sellars for postmodern direction; ✶BÜCHNER for influences on style; Erwin Piscator for early Lehrstücke; Pina Bausch and Martha Clarke for powerful stage imagery; ✶SHAKESPEARE for *Hamlet*; ✶LEVY, ✶MAROWITZ, ✶STOPPARD for other responses to *Hamlet*.

MUNRO, Rona   [1959 –   ]
Scottish dramatist

PLAYS INCLUDE:
The Bang and Whimper (1982), *The Salesman* (1982), *Fugue* (1983), *The Bus* (1984), *Watching Waiters* (1984), *Piper's Cave* (1985), *The Way to Go Home* (1987), *Off the Road* (1988), *Saturday at the Commodore* (1989) *Bold Girls* (1990), *Your Turn to Clean the Stair* (1992), *The Maiden Stone* (1994), *Iron* (2002)

Munro was born in Aberdeen and much of her work has been Scottish-based – besides her stage plays, she has contributed to various Scottish radio and television series, as well as young people's theatre. She still writes for 'The MsFits', a feminist double act she formed with Fiona Knowles, although she no longer performs. As a playwright, however, her plays show an arresting and penetrating line of psychological enquiry and an interesting willingness to experiment with forms.

Fugue, her first full-length play, revealed preoccupations that she has continued to explore and develop with deepening intensity. It is about a young girl's retreat into herself and her past and has strong poetic and pastoral overtones. *Watching Waiters*, commissioned by BBC Radio Scotland, is a tense, powerful journey into the female psyche – a woman, possibly on the verge of a breakdown, confronts her inner state of being (strong images of being trapped behind glass) and makes connections between vulnerability, self-image and the sensuality of food and sex. Part nightmare, part investigation, like the best of therapies (it even has an alter ego interrogator), it confronts past ghosts in order to move forward to self-affirmation.

Intimations of ghosts are also present in *Bold Girls*, which won the 1990 Susan Blackburn Award for best women's play. Ostensibly it is a heart-warming, albeit familiar, tale of Belfast women struggling against the odds to keep house and home together when menfolk are taken away to prison or killed, but Munro's treatment endows the play with something more than mere melodrama. Subtly, she builds a complex pattern of relationships which ultimately reveal the ghosts as being the illusions and self-deceptions that women employ to sustain the reality about their relationships with men, which otherwise might not be tenable. Women's solidarity is also shown to be highly vulnerable under such strains and far from straightforward. *The Maiden Stone* divided critics with its presentation of an actress and her travelling company in the north-east of Scotland early in the nineteenth century but *Iron* was praised for its exploration of the conflicting emotions and reactions of a mother and daughter when the daughter visits the mother in prison, fifteen years after the daughter, then only ten, had discovered her father murdered by her mother.

TRY THESE:

✶DANIELS' *Beside Herself* and ✶NORMAN's *Getting Out* for plays that employ an alter ego to investigate areas of the female psyche; ✶MACDONALD for more Scottish scrutiny of mother–daughter relationships at close quarters; ✶MARIE JONES' *Beyond the Balcony* and ✶REID's *Joyriders* for other plays which, like *Bold Girls*, use Belfast's Divis Flats for their central location; ✶REID's *Tea in a China Cup* for more pictures of generations of women and attitudes to community; ✶DUNN and ✶GEMS for earlier examples of women struggling to find solidarity; Tony Roper's *The Steamie* is another Scottish writer's portrait of women together in Glasgow's bath-houses; ✶LOCHHEAD, as another Scottish dramatist/performer; ✶DE ANGELIS for other actresses.

MURPHY, Tom   [1935 –   ]
Irish dramatist

PLAYS INCLUDE:
On the Outside (1961, with Noel O'Donoghue), *A Whistle in the Dark* (1961), *Famine* (1966), *A Crucial Week in the Life of a Grocer's Assistant* (televised 1967, staged as *The Fooleen*, 1969), *The Morning After Optimism* (1971), *On the Inside* (1974), *The Vicar of Wakefield* (1974, from ✶GOLDSMITH's novel), *The Sanctuary Lamp* (1975), *She Stoops to Conquer* (1982 from ✶GOLDSMITH), *The Gigli Concert* (1983), *Bailegangáire* (1985), *A Thief of a Christmas* (1985), *Too Late for Logic* (1989), *The Patriot Game* (1991), *She Stoops to Folly* (1995, from ✶GOLDSMITH's novel *The Vicar of Wakefield*), *The Wake* (1996), *The House* (2000)

One of Ireland's leading dramatists, Murphy was born in Tuam, County Galway. Kenneth Tynan applauded *A Whistle in the Dark*, which deals with an Irish family in Coventry, but Murphy has never received as much recognition in Britain as his contemporary ✶BRIAN FRIEL or as the Irish writers of the 1990s. His concern with Irish history in, for example, *Famine* (about the great famine of the 1840s) and *The Patriot Game* (the 1916 Easter Rising) is far from parochial, nor is his sustained engagement with the work of ✶OLIVER GOLDSMITH. Themes of emigration and return, engagement with and disaffection from the church and the community values associated with it are common features of his work throughout his career, but he uses a variety of approaches that enrich the texture of his plays, drawing not only on Irish myths and stereotypes but on those of the wider European tradition. *The Morning After Optimism* creates a Jungian fairytale forest, while in *The Gigli Concert* he draws on the Faust myth, as a failed alternative spiritual therapist gets drawn into a scheme to help a disturbed millionaire sing like the opera singer Beniamino Gigli. In *Bailegangáire* an uncompleted but often-repeated story has to be concluded if three women are to be able to proceed with their lives. *The Wake* and *The House* continue to explore the theme of return from exile to an Ireland which no longer matches the imagined world left behind and which therefore calls into question the very existence of that world.

TRY THESE:
✱BOLGER, ✱CARR, ✱FRIEL, ✱DECLAN HUGHES, ✱MCCAFFERTY for other aspects of Irish life.

MURRAY, Melissa   [1954 –   ]
British dramatist and poet

PLAYS INCLUDE:
Bouncing Back with Benyon (1977, with Eileen Fairweather), *Hot Spot* (1978), *Belisha Beacon* (1978, with Eileen Fairweather), *Hormone Imbalance* (1979), *Ophelia* (1979), *The Admission* (1980), *The Execution* (1982), *The Crooked Scythe* (1982–3), *Coming Apart* (1985), *Body-cell* (1986)

Murray's output in the 1970s and 1980s reflected the diversity of styles women playwrights adopted in the search for ways of expressing the female experience: revue (*Hormone Imbalance*, a surreal gay cabaret), agitprop (*Bouncing Back with Benyon*, a pro-abortion piece), blank verse (*Ophelia*, a parody of ✱SHAKESPEARE seen from a lesbian feminist perspective), rhyming verse (*The Crooked Scythe*) and historical epic (*The Execution*). *Coming Apart*, which won the Verity Bargate Award, showed the best and the worst of Murray's style: a certain untidiness in the overall plot – the interaction of four characters, trapped in memories of the past in a Berlin boarding house – but a haunting,

elusive quality capable of evoking a disturbing sense of paranoia, fear and disorientation, and a considerable sympathy for the vulnerable and isolated. Murray touched on this theme in a different way in *The Admission*, an angry forty-minute piece about society's approach to treating women and mental illness. *Body-cell* combines these themes of isolation and society's controlling techniques in the portrait of a female political prisoner in Durham prison, confined to solitary for disruptive behaviour, and her increasing withdrawal from human contact as a result of it. Murray published a volume of short stories (*Changelings*) in 1996 and her radio play *Peacemakers* (2001) focused on Alfred Nobel's decision to institute a peace prize.

TRY THESE:
For states of isolation, ✱COLLINS' *Judgement*, ✱RAIF's *Another Woman*, ✱STRAUSS's *Great and Small*; for women and mental illness, ✱AYCKBOURN's *A Woman in Mind*, ✱CRAZE's *Shona*, ✱EDGAR's *Mary Barnes*, ✱MERCER's *In Two Minds*; for women in prison, ✱HOLBOROUGH; ✱NORMAN's *Getting Out* for an American comparison; ✱NICHOLS' *Privates on Parade* for a concert party.

NAGY, Phyllis [1962–]

American dramatist domiciled in Britain

PLAYS INCLUDE:
Weldon Rising (1992), *Entering Queens* (1992), *Butterfly Kiss* (1994), *The Scarlet Letter* (1994, after Nathaniel Hawthorne), *Trip's Cinch* (1994), *Disappeared* (1992), *The Strip* (1995), *Never Land* (1998), *The Talented Mr Ripley* (1998, after Patricia Highsmith)

Nagy settled in London after an exchange took her to the Royal Court, and much of her subsequent work has premiered in Britain, although it still mainly deals in American life. *Weldon Rising* deals with reactions from New York gays and lesbians to a homophobic murder, while in *Butterfly Kiss* the murder is of a woman by her daughter and the story retraces the factors that led up to the murder as the daughter's lover also tries to make sense of events. The usual criticism of lesbian scenes in both plays was matched by some unease from the gay press about the gay characters not being positively presented. *Disappeared* is another urban horror story about a woman who leaves a bar and is never seen again, and Michael Coveney accurately describes *The Strip* as 'a rich transatlantic tapestry of coming and going'. One exception to Nagy's American themes is *Never Land*, set in France, which presents a disintegrating anglophile French family, and is scheduled for a West End production in 2003.

Clearly Nagy writes from a postmodern viewpoint in which traditional dramatic forms and notions of causality and closure are not necessarily appropriate criteria for judgement, but she divides critical opinion between those like Michael Coveney who see her as top-class writer and those like Dominic Dromgoole to whom she 'sounds like someone being a writer, rather than someone writing about being'.

TRY THESE:
✴GLASPELL for trying to make sense of women's lives; ✴WALLACE for another American in England; ✴KANE, ✴NEILSON, ✴RAVENHILL for contemporaries; ✴MILLER for presentations of the downside of the American dream; Nagy has adapted ✴CHEKHOV's *The Seagull*.

NEILSON, Anthony

Scottish dramatist

PLAYS INCLUDE:
Welfare My Lovely (1990), *Normal* (1991), *Penetrator* (1993), *Year of the Family* (1994), *Heredity* (1995), *The Censor* (1997), *The Night Before Christmas* (1999), *Edward Gant's Amazing Feats of Loneliness* (2002), *Stitching* (2002), *The Lying Kind* (2002)

A controversial writer whose stage images and robust language are not for the faint-hearted or conventional, Neilson established himself with a series of sexually explicit and graphically violent plays that challenged audiences in the early 1990s. *Normal* is based on the true story of a German serial killer of the early 1930s and poses the question of how his behaviour, which the play goes into in some detail, could possibly be described as normal. Although the period of the play would allow a simplistic equation of serial-killer normality with Nazi atrocity, Neilson avoids this and also makes the audience engage in questioning their own motivations for watching the play: at one point a potential murder victim tries to escape via the auditorium and is hauled back on stage and the audience becomes complicit in the murderous process. *Penetrator* is a deceptively simple story of two flatmates being disturbed by the unexpected arrival of an old friend, who is clearly mentally disturbed. By the end of the play one flatmate has been displaced by the returnee after a ferocious mental and physical battering, although it ends with images of childhood happiness that pick up on the presentation of friendship throughout the violence. Although pornography figures in *Penetrator*, it become central in *The Censor*, in which a female pornographic filmmaker tries to convince a censor of the artistic merit of her film and in doing so cures him of his impotence by acting out his most secret sexual fantasy. The play is extremely explicit and yet the relationship comes over as tender and the play was less controversial than might have been expected. However, *Stitching*, with its references to the Moors murders, managed to upset not just the usual suspects but some members of the audience.

Neilson's work has always had comic elements within the violence and he attempted a formal farce in *The Lying Kind*, in which two policemen, come to deliver bad news on Christmas Eve, find it hard to get to the point, while outside a vigilante group is attempting to kill a suspected paedophile. Although the farce machinery worked well, critics were divided about how far Neilson succeeded in melding it with his serious points about the use and misuse of information.

TRY THESE:

✸ PINTER for the unexpected arrival and subsequent violence; ✸ ORTON for black farce; ✸ KANE and ✸ RAVENHILL for contemporaries: compare *Penetrator* with ✸ BRENTON's *Skinny Spew* for violence to stuffed toys and ✸ OSBORNE's *Look Back in Anger* for stuffed animals and homoerotic tensions between flatmates.

NELSON, Richard   [1950 –   ]
American dramatist

PLAYS INCLUDE:

The Killing of Yablonski (1975), *Conjuring an Event* (1976), *Jungle Coup* (1978), *The Vienna Notes* (1978), *Bal* (1979), *Rip Van Winkle or The Works* (1981), *The Return of Pinocchio* (1983), *An American Comedy* (1983), *Between East and West* (1984), *Principia Scriptoriae* (1986), *Some Americans Abroad* (1989), *Sensibility and Sense* (1989), *Two Shakespearean Actors* (1990), *Columbus and the Discovery of Japan* (1992), *Misha's Party* (1993, with Alexander Gelman), *New England* (1994), *The General from America* (1996), *Goodnight Children Everywhere* (1997), *Madame Melville* (2000), *James Joyce's The Dead* (2000)

Chicago-born Nelson is one of the few American playwrights to address political issues in the manner of British writers like ✸ DAVID HARE or ✸ HOWARD BRENTON. Indeed, he says his interest in 'primarily social' themes can be 'lonely' for an American writer, and in recent years his work has generally found more of an audience in Britain than in the United States. Nelson has written both large sweeping works (his four-hour *Rip Van Winkle* plays like a parody of *Faust* crossed with *Peer Gynt*) and more focused two-character dramas such as *Between East and West* (about a Czech director and his wife experiencing culture shock in New York). *The Vienna Notes* is a comedy about the contradictions between the glamorous public image of an American senator and the corrupt man within. The varied ways we manipulate language and obstruct communication are at the centre of *Conjuring an Event* (about journalism), *Principia Scriptoriae* (featuring writers caught in a right-wing Latin American police state), and *Sensibility and Sense*, with its many heated debates about the alleged distortions in one character's memoirs.

Culture shock, specifically the Anglo-American variety, has become a cornerstone of his work, although *Misha's Party* deals with a failure to understand the significance of the 1991 Moscow coup and *Columbus and the Discovery of Japan* tackles the first big misunderstanding about America. The tensions between appearance and reality figure in *Some Americans Abroad*, about tweedy American literature professors infatuated with an England that doesn't exist. *Two Shakespearean Actors* takes Anglo-American misunderstanding back into the nineteenth century when the rivalry between two actors playing Macbeth – the Briton William Charles Macready and the American star Edwin Forrest – led to riots in New York. *The General from America* takes the issue back to the revolution and the case of Benedict Arnold, and *Goodnight Children Everywhere* addresses another moment of cultural dislocation when a young evacuee returns from Canada in 1945. *Madame Melville* combines the traditional theme of the cultural and social confrontation between America and Europe with another familiar topic, the sexual initiation of an adolescent, played in the London production by former child star Macaulay Culkin.

Nelson's embrace of private and public concerns no doubt prompted the producers of *Chess* to call on him when they needed someone to revise their troubled musical's book, but he was unable to save it.

TRY THESE:
Tamsin Oglesby's *Us and Them* for contemporary failures of Anglo-American communication; ✳MILLER and ✳ODETS as earlier American writers with an overt social conscience; ✳HARE's *A Map of the World* and ✳DUSTY HUGHES' *Jenkins' Ear* for contrasting treatments of contemporary realpolitik; ✳BECKETT's *Catastrophe*, ✳TREVOR GRIFFITHS' *The Party*, ✳HARE's *Fanshen*, ✳PINTER's *One for the Road*, ✳PUIG's *Kiss of the Spider Woman* as contemporary treatments of similar themes; ✳BULGAKOV's *Black Snow*, ✳FRAYN's *Noises Off* for other treatments of the nature of theatre; Nelson has adapted plays by ✳BEAUMARCHAIS, ✳BRECHT, ✳CHEKHOV, ✳FO, ✳GOLDONI, ✳MOLIÈRE and ✳STRINDBERG.

NEMETH, Sally [1960 –]
American dramatist

PLAYS INCLUDE:
Modem Lit (1982), *Pagan Day* (1985), *Holy Days* (1983), *Mill Fire* (1990), *Spinning into the Blue* (1990)

Although Chicago-born Nemeth made something of a reputation in Britain in the 1980s, her work has not been seen here recently. *Holy Days* is a taut, slice-of-life saga set in the US southern dust bowl in the early part of the last century. Brian Stirner's immaculate and atmospheric 1988 production won three London Fringe Awards. *Mill Fire* is another journey into the dark hinterland of grief, loss, anger and the patterns of marital need. It is realistically structured yet unconventional in its use of flashbacks and a Greek-like chorus of

mill wives to reflect and comment. *Spinning into the Blue* is a play with abortion at its core, in which the process of healing through anger and 'giving it up' is a central theme.

TRY THESE:
✳MEYER's *Etta Jenks* for a similarly unsentimental view of the options available to women; ✳FUGARD; ✳O'CASEY for similar views of women's lot.

NESTROY, Johann Nepomuk [1801 – 62]
Austrian actor, singer and dramatist

PLAYS INCLUDE:
Einen Jux will er sich machen (1842, *He's Out for a Fling*)

Nestroy's range of talents was even wider than ✳MOLIÈRE's (his first professional appearance was as Sarastro in *The Magic Flute*) and his seventy-seven surviving plays (most of them satirical comedies) still hold the stage in Vienna, but little of his work has so far been translated into English. However, *Einen Jux Will Er Sich Machen* (itself based on two English farces) forms the basis both of ✳THORNTON WILDER's successive versions, *The Merchant of Yonkers* (1938) and *The Matchmaker* (1954) (which became the musical *Hello, Dolly!* in 1963), and of ✳STOPPARD's *On the Razzle* (National Theatre, 1981). Stoppard dealt with the problem of translating the rich Viennese dialect by ignoring it altogether, omitting subplot, comic songs and local references, and letting his own line in outrageous wordplay enliven a good basic farce plot about two shop assistants having a stolen day out on the town (Vienna, of course).

TRY THESE:
✳HORVÁTH, for adding a political element to Nestroy's folk-play tradition; ✳LABICHE's *La Cagnotte* for the theme of country folk having a day out on the town (Paris, of course).

NICHOLS, Peter [1927 –]
British dramatist

PLAYS INCLUDE:
A Day in the Death of Joe Egg (1967), *The National Health* (1969), *Forget-Me-Not-Lane*

(1971), *Chez Nous* (1974), *The Freeway* (1974), *Harding's Luck* (1974), *Privates on Parade* (1977), *Born in the Gardens* (1979), *Passion Play* (1981, *Passion* in the USA), *Poppy* (1982), *A Piece of My Mind* (1986), *So Long Life* (1995), *Blue Murder* (1996)

Nichols was born in Bristol, trained as an actor with the Bristol Old Vic and worked there until he was called up to National Service in the RAF and went to India and Malaya, a crucial experience for *Privates on Parade*, which is set in a song and dance unit in Malaya. According to Nichols: 'To make an audience cry or laugh is easy – they want to . . . this is only worth doing if one thereby catches a whiff of life, a true tang of the bitter mixture we all have to drink.'

A Day in the Death of Joe Egg, Nichols' first stage play, is probably still the one with which he is most associated. It is openly autobiographical, drawn from the experience of his own disabled daughter. The play employs bitterly funny backchat between the father and mother, and brings in jazz and tap dance, in its exploration of the strains on a relationship of living with what the father calls a 'human parsnip'. Nichols writes very unsettling comedies; even the tragic subject of *A Day in the Death of Joe Egg* is handled with a bitter wit, and he has taken a delight in experimenting with popular forms, often using an improbable form to make a satirical point. *The National Health* deals with a hospital ward full of patients who are in pain or dying, and puts them together with a hospital romance. *Privates on Parade* uses the form of the revue show to explore army life and the British presence in Malaya, while *Poppy* uses pantomime and music hall to chart the British involvement in the Chinese opium wars, and has a wonderful alienation effect: the pantomime horse gets shot. *Poppy* also employs a pantomime singsong, in which a character uses all the pantomime devices to encourage the audience to sing along, only to confront them with the awareness of the racist and imperialistic implications of what they are singing. *Passion Play* is an elegant and witty dissection of middle-class adultery that gains extra resonance through the device of representing the characters' normally unspoken thoughts by other actors. *A Piece of My Mind* is a bitter comedy about Nichols' own difficulties with writing, and his resentment that his challenging and uncomfortable comedy was not more successful. Unsurprisingly it was badly reviewed, but it contains some bravura writing and effects. *So Long Life* presents an eighty-fifth birthday party at which hidden tensions emerge as the family manoeuvre and jostle for position, and *Blue Murder* is a typical Nichols combination of generic frustrations: in the first part a would-be dramatist finds himself with a ready-made murder plot and in the second his attempts to gain the Lord Chamberlain's approval (for this is before the abolition of censorship in 1968) become a Whitehall farce.

TRY THESE:
✶BENNETT, ✶JOHN MCGRATH, ✶WESKER, ✶WHELAN are among the dramatists for whom National Service was a significant experience; ✶STOPPARD appears thinly disguised as Miles Whittier (a pun) in *A Piece of My Mind*; Graeae for a sustained engagement with issues of disability; ✶BARNES and ✶ORTON share something of Nichols' sense of the macabre in humour; ✶AYCKBOURN, ✶CHEKHOV, ✶IBSEN, ✶PINTER's *The Birthday Party* and ✶ELIOT's *Family Reunion* for domestic revelations at social events.

NORMAN, Marsha   [1947 –   ]
American dramatist

PLAYS INCLUDE:
Getting Out (1977), *Third and Oak* (1978, comprising *The Laundromat* and *The Pool Hall*), *Circus Valentine* (1979), *'Night Mother* (1982), *The Holdup* (1983), *Traveler in the Dark* (1984), *Sarah and Abraham* (1988), *The Secret Garden* (1991, musical), *Loving Daniel Boone* (1992), *Trudy Blue* (1994)

The Kentucky-born daughter of an estate agent, Norman made her reputation on the basis of *Getting Out* and *'Night Mother*. The former is a terse and aggressive, if schematic, account of a woman's reassimilation into society after an eight-year prison term, with two actresses representing the central character at different phases of her life: the incarcerated, wilder Arlie and her maturer self, Arlene. *'Night Mother* won the 1983 Pulitzer Prize. Its harrowing portrait of the suicidal but pragmatic Jessie Cates and her panic-stricken mother ruthlessly up-ends the American family-in-crisis play. In telling its story to the onstage ticking of six clocks, *'Night Mother* is an unusual instance of a play whose stage time equals real time. *Traveler in the Dark* fared less well with the critics and *Trudy Blue* has been seen in several versions in the USA. The RSC staged Norman's musical version of Frances Hodgson Burnett's *The Secret Garden* at Stratford in 2000.

TRY THESE:
✷ PAGE's *Real Estate*, ✷ TENNESSEE WILLIAMS' *The Glass Menagerie*, ✷ ZINDEL's *The Effect of Gamma Rays* are some of the many plays showing mothers and daughters locked in combat; ✷ BABE, ✷ MAMET, ✷ SHAWN for the willed aggression of the writing; ✷ LANFORD WILSON's *Talley's Folly* for a comparable sense of the weight of silence, and the use of real time; ✷ O'NEILL's *Strange Interlude* for an earlier example of an expressionistic treatment of the protagonist's inner life;
✷ MILLER's *Death of a Salesman* is a previous generation's look at a suicide in the making.

O

OAKES, Meredith [1946 –]

Australian-born, British resident dramatist, librettist and translator

PLAYS INCLUDE:

The Neighbour (1993), *The Editing Process* (1994), *Faith* (1997), *Man for Hire* (2002)

There is no typical Oakes play. Her first major success was *The Editing Process*, in which an academic journal becomes the victim of a corporate takeover and ends up sharing a building with a rock magazine. Corporate politics and modern management practices are at the heart of a comedy of bad faith. In *Faith* the routine deceptions of realpolitik necessitate the death of an American mercenary captured fighting for the Argentinians in the Falklands War. In both plays there is a process of editing, smoothing out anything that gets in the way of the desired official reality. *Man for Hire* shows an apparently ineffectual man seeking employment as a security guard and turning into the glue that holds a community together. Oakes has translated Thomas Bernhard, ✴HORVÁTH, Jakob Lenz, ✴STRINDBERG and the contemporary Austrian Werner Schwab and German Moritz Rinke, as well as creating the librettos for Gerald Barry's Handel-based *The Triumph of Beauty and Deceit* and the forthcoming adaptation of *The Tempest* by Thomas Adès.

TRY THESE:

✴BRENTON and ✴HARE's *Pravda* for newspaper publishing takeovers; ✴SCHIMMELPFENNIG and ✴VINAVER for office politics, ✴LONERGAN's *Lobby Hero* for another security guard.

O'BRIEN, Richard [1942 –]

British actor, composer, lyricist, director and dramatist

PLAYS INCLUDE:

The Rocky Horror Show (1973), *Top People* (1984)

O'Brien was responsible for one of the great cult successes of the 1970s and one of the great cult failures of the 1980s. *The Rocky Horror Show*, a camp combination of transvestism, the Frankenstein story and music, began at the Royal Court Theatre Upstairs and has now achieved a kind of independent existence of its own, virtually impervious to criticism, as much a cultural monument in its own way as ✴AGATHA CHRISTIE's *The Mousetrap*. Its initial success owed much to the energy and commitment of its first cast, who included Tim Curry, Julie Covington and O'Brien himself, but it has now become equally its audience's property with people regularly dressing up as their favourite characters, joining in the songs and dialogue, throwing confetti at the wedding, and so on. There are, particularly in the USA, conventions and fan clubs and the whole camp cult has become a phenomenon that transcends the bounds of theatre or of cinema (the film version, made in 1975 with many of the original cast, has much the same effect as the stage version). *Top People* was an unmitigated disaster that deservedly lasted less than a week in London.

TRY THESE:

For Frankenstein variations, ✴DE ANGELIS's *Breathless*, ✴LOCHHEAD; for aspects of camp, ✴ORTON, ✴EICHELBERGER; the physicality and energy of *The Rocky Horror Show* can also be found in the work of ✴BERKOFF.

O'CASEY, Sean   [1880 – 1964]
Irish dramatist

PLAYS INCLUDE:

The Shadow of a Gunman (1923), *Juno and the Paycock* (1924), *The Plough and the Stars* (1926), *The Silver Tassie* (1928), *Within the Gates* (1933), *The Star Turns Red* (1940), *Purple Dust* (1940), *Red Roses for Me* (1942), *Cock-a-Doodle Dandy* (1949), *Bedtime Story* (1951), *The Bishop's Bonfire* (1955), *The Drums of Father Ned* (1960)

One of the great dramatists of the twentieth century, O'Casey is best remembered for the early Dublin plays but his later exuberant, equally politically conscious, tragicomic epics deserve as wide an audience as the so-called Dublin Trilogy (*The Shadow of a Gunman, Juno and the Paycock, The Plough and the Stars*). O'Casey, largely self-taught, and politically active, was initially fostered by the Abbey Theatre but ✱YEATS' rejection of *The Silver Tassie*, which now seems astonishingly misguided, led to O'Casey's departure from Ireland and a career marked by further controversy and misunderstanding. *The Silver Tassie* is an anti-war play that extends O'Casey's dramaturgy into a highly stylised quasi-liturgical second act; the mixture of styles suggests the difference between the normal world and the world of the war. O'Casey's socialism, his hatred of priestly influence in Ireland and his ceaseless experimentation with form all contributed to his relative eclipse in the professional theatre and it is surprising that, in an era more receptive to large-scale non-linear political work, some of the later plays have yet to be given major productions. *Cock-a-Doodle Dandy* in particular deserves a wider audience, with its lifesize dionysiac Cock struggling against capitalism and the church, the forces of repression that attempt to quell the human spirit. Not that the earlier plays have outlived their welcome: O'Casey's presentation of the heady contradictions of the struggle for Irish independence is still horribly relevant to the present, not only in terms of an understanding of the intractability of that situation, but also in more general terms of an analysis of the sheer messiness and mixture of impulses and dynamics in any political situation.

Juno and the Paycock

A brilliant mixture of the comic and tragic that takes in the abduction and murder of Juno's son (Johnny) who has informed on a Diehard colleague, her unmarried daughter Mary's pregnancy and attitudes to it, the posturings of her feckless husband (the Paycock of the title), the apparent rise in the social status of the family as the result of a supposed inheritance, and its collapse when the will turns out to have been badly drafted. There are major issues here about the poisoned inheritance of Ireland, the importance of received attitudes in determining people's responses to both political and personal issues, the role of women in both sustaining and fracturing male vanities, but they emerge for us in truly epic style as we are faced with a necessity for practising complex seeing and thinking above the flow of the action as well as with it. The final scene, with the room stripped of furniture, Juno and Mary departed to Juno's sister's, Johnny dead, and the drunk and oblivious Paycock telling his pal Joxer that the whole world is 'in a terr . . . ible state o' . . . chassis', is a fine example of O'Casey's ability to present contradictions simultaneously and in memorable theatrical form.

The Plough and the Stars

Set during the Easter Rising of 1916, *The Plough and the Stars* is more directly concerned with great political events than *Juno and the Paycock*, but the focus is still largely on ordinary people and their reactions to events; although some of Padraic Pearse's speeches are spoken by the Voice in Act 2, he is not identified by name. Again we have a tenement setting, an assortment of representative characters and the mixture of the comic and the tragic, but here the mood is darker and the dispossession of the Irish is clearer. The play ends in another fine dramatisation of contradiction, with Dublin burning as two English soldiers sit drinking tea and singing 'Keep the Home Fires Burning' in the room from which the Irish inhabitants have been expelled; the hope embodied in the women and the pregnancy in *Juno* has been snuffed out in this play by death and by madness, and the men are generally as ineffectual as before.

TRY THESE:

O'Casey declared that he was influenced by ✱BOUCICAULT and ✱SHAKESPEARE; ✱CORRIE and ✱BRECHT have much in common with O'Casey; ✱MCGUINNESS's *Observe the Sons of Ulster Marching Towards the Somme* also deals with the Irish and World War I; ✱BEHAN had much of the energy, if less of the discipline, of O'Casey; ✱SHERRIFF's *Journey's End*, ✱WILLIS HALL's *The Long and the Short and the Tall* and Theatre Workshop's *Oh What a Lovely War* offer different accounts of war; ✱BRENTON and ✱EDGAR have something of the same energy and willingness to experiment in order to make political points; of the many writers now writing about Northern Ireland, ✱DEVLIN's *Ourselves Alone*, ✱FINNEGAN's *North* and ✱MARIE JONES's *Gold in the Streets* attempt to show the intractable contradictions of the situation in all their socio-politico-religious complexity; ✱MCDONAGH, ✱MORRISON, ✱MUNRO, ✱REID for contrast; Elizabeth Robins' *Votes for Women* for a second act to compare with *The Plough and the Stars*.

ODETS, Clifford   [1906 – 63]
American dramatist

PLAYS INCLUDE:

Awake and Sing (1935), *Waiting for Lefty* (1935), *Till the Day I Die* (1935), *Paradise Lost* (1935), *Golden Boy* (1937), *Rocket to the Moon* (1938), *Night Music* (1940), *Clash by Night* (1941), *The Big Knife* (1949), *The Country Girl* (1950), *The Flowering Peach* (1954), *The Silent Partner* (written in 1937, produced posthumously in 1972)

'I would say that I have shown as much of the seamy side of life as any other playwright of the twentieth century, if not more', the Philadelphia-born Odets once commented. And as a chronicler of moral malaise, Odets is hard to beat, even when his chosen milieus (as in the Beverley Hills playroom of *The Big Knife*) deceptively evoke a ✱NOËL COWARD comedy, not a scabrous indictment of the 'noisy, grabbing world' of Hollywood. Odets was the star dramatist of the Group Theatre and his early plays *Waiting for Lefty* and *Awake and Sing* were both premiered there. *Golden Boy* is a play about a violinist-turned-boxer that makes genuine individuals out of archetypes. Although his plays can seem melodramatic and ponderous, at their best their moral vigour is stirring, and they provide notable acting opportunities, particularly of a dry, hard-boiled sort. The 1964 musical version of *Golden Boy* was revived in London in 2003.

Waiting for Lefty

A taxi union votes to go on strike in Odets' landmark 1935 drama, as important for its radical socialist form as for its message. Produced by the Group Theatre and directed by its co-founder, Harold Clurman, the staging planted actual cabbies in the audience, which gave a charge to the final rallying cry, 'Strike!' The Lefty of the title, one of the union leaders, never arrives, but Odets uses the action to launch an assault on capitalism in the kind of denunciation of avarice that few American playwrights have fielded since. The play is didactic agitprop, but also testimony to an era in American playwriting when plays were seen to make a difference – not marginalised escapist 'entertainments' as they are all too often viewed now, despite genuine inheritors of Odets' vision like ✱ARTHUR MILLER and ✱DAVID MAMET.

TRY THESE:

The early plays of ✱O'NEILL (especially *The Hairy Ape*) and Marc Blitzstein's folk opera *The Cradle Will Rock* for both subject matter and experimental form; ✱BECKETT's *Waiting for Godot*, ✱MERCER's *After Haggerty* for other plays where the title character never appears; ✱RABE's *Hurlyburly* for later, equally bitter writing about Hollywood.

OLIVE, John   [1949 –   ]
American dramatist

PLAYS INCLUDE:

Minnesota Moon (1979), *Clara's Play* (1981), *Standing on My Knees* (1981), *The Voice of the Prairie* (1987), *Killers* (1988), *Evelyn and the Polka King* (1992), *The Ecstasy of St Theresa* (2001), *The Summer Moon* (2002, previously as *I Clap My Hands*)

Olive's life has been a blend of Midwestern American values and cultural urbanity. Born in Japan, Olive has spent most of his life in

Minnesota, where many of his plays are set. *Minnesota Moon* presents two young men as they share an evening near an old farmhouse drinking beer, reminiscing and dreaming; one is off to college and the other to stay in the small town. *Clara's Play* brings together an ageing woman, attached to a crumbling Minnesota farm, and a young Norwegian handyman bound for a life in the West. *Voice of the Prairie* crosses ideals in time rather than personalities, as radio players recollect travels of an earlier generation, intersecting people and values from past and present. Olive has expanded his dramaturgy with plays that are solid entertainment (*Killers*), provocative psychological inquiries centred on schizophrenia (*Standing on My Knees*) American–Japanese relations (*The Summer Moon*) and ventures into film, television, radio and opera libretti.

TRY THESE:

✳TENNESSEE WILLIAMS' *Glass Menagerie* for a delicate psychological balance; ✳KEMPINKSI's *Duet for One*, ✳WRIGHT's *Mrs Klein* for mental anguish; ✳CRAZE's *Shona* and ✳EDGAR's *Mary Barnes* for outright portrayals of schizophrenia; ✳BARKER's *Scenes from an Execution*, ✳GLASPELL's *Alison's House*, ✳WHITEMORE's *Stevie* for female creative artists; ✳GOTANDA, ✳HWANG for Japanese-Americans.

O'MALLEY, Mary   [1941 –   ]
British dramatist

PLAYS INCLUDE:

Superscum (1972), *A 'Nevolent Society* (1974), *Oh If Ever a Man Suffered* (1975), *Once a Catholic* (1977), *Look Out . . . Here Comes Trouble* (1978), *Talk of the Devil* (1986)

London-born chronicler of north London and the London Irish, O'Malley saw an article in the *Stage* about a school chum who was writing plays for the RSC and she felt she could do as well. *Superscum*, about a man living well on social security, *A 'Nevolent Society*, about three Jewish boys in Stoke Newington, and *If Ever a Man Suffered*, about incest in an Irish family in Cricklewood, all followed quickly. But the big break came with *Once a Catholic*,

which brought her a year's writer-in-residency at the Royal Court. Semi-autobiographical and set in a north London convent school, our Lady of Fatima, her hysterically funny dig at Catholicism, damnation and the sexual stirrings of adolescent girls, won her both the *Evening Standard* and *Plays and Players* Most Promising Playwright awards. Cathartically, *Once a Catholic* seems to have been one way of O'Malley releasing herself from the oppression of school life, which felt 'like a big black cloud hanging overhead' and where she was told 'Mary O'Malley, you'll never be any good' (she was told to leave school at sixteen because she was always playing truant). 'Really it was an epitaph to the Irish living in England as I remember them in my youth and Catholicism as taught before the 2nd Vatican Council.' She continued in the same vein, to some extent, in *Talk of the Devil*, a family saga with ✳ORTONESQUE echoes with its mixture of sex, religion and death (including visitations from an imaginary Devil got up in black leather). Her early experiences as a young wife and mother, married to a Jew, and contemplating Judaic conversion, also ended up as a television comedy, *Oy Vey Maria*. *Once a Catholic*, with its emblematic Marys (all the girls are called Mary), however, remains a rare and hilarious female expression of adolescent retaliation against Catholic dogma and the authoritarianism and hypocrisy of school that should be compulsory viewing for every generation.

TRY THESE:

For scenes from school life, Denise Deegan's Angela Brazil spoof *Daisy Pulls It Off*, Muriel Spark's classic Presbyterian variation *The Prime of Miss Jean Brodie*; for adolescent female yearnings, ✳MACDONALD, ✳WEDEKIND's *Spring Awakening*; for a male Irish view, ✳LEONARD's adaptation of James Joyce's *Portrait of the Artist as a Young Man*, or for an English view, ✳BENNETT's *Forty Years On* and John Dighton's *The Happiest Days of Our Lives*; for a complete contrast, ✳KENNEDY's *A Lesson in Dead Language*, which uses visual imagery bordering on the grotesque to make its point about the education of young women; ✳NIGEL WILLIAMS' *Class Enemy* and Bill Cain's *Stand Up* tragedy are contemporary versions of waste of potential in schools.

O'NEILL, Eugene   [1888 – 1953]
American dramatist

PLAYS INCLUDE:

Beyond the Horizon (1920), *The Emperor Jones* (1920), *Anna Christie* (1921), *The Hairy Ape* (1922), *Welded* (1924), *All God's Chillun Got Wings* (1924), *Desire Under the Elms* (1924), *The Great God Brown* (1926), *Marco Millions* (1928), *Strange Interlude* (1928), *Lazarus Laughed* (1928), *Mourning Becomes Electra* (1931), *Ah! Wilderness* (1933), *More Stately Mansions* (1938), *The Iceman Cometh* (1939; performed 1946), *Long Day's Journey Into Night* (1940; performed 1956), *A Touch of the Poet* (1940), *A Moon for the Misbegotten* (1943)

One of the leading American playwrights of all time, O'Neill was born in New York, the son of the actor James O'Neill. His own tortured and often sorrowful upbringing prompted several of the greatest family dramas ever written – works that take a scalpel to the blood ties that bind, finding the inextricable link between pain and passion where affections hover precariously over the abyss. O'Neill came of age as a playwright with the Provincetown Players, contributing most of their significant works. Greatly influenced by the Greeks (his *Mourning Becomes Electra* is a New England reworking of *The Oresteia*) and by ✶STRINDBERG (in his expressionist period), his plays can seem cumbersome and pedantic, and his aspirations occasionally exceed his achievement. The plays themselves avoid easy classification, whether tending towards the modernist (*Strange Interlude*, with its Faulknerian stream of consciousness) or the opaque (*The Great God Brown*), the surprisingly comic (*Ah! Wilderness*) or the ineffably sad (*Long Day's Journey Into Night*). A four-time recipient of the Pulitzer Prize, O'Neill also became, in 1936, the first (and only) American playwright to win the Nobel Prize for Literature.

The Iceman Cometh

Written in 1939 but not performed until seven years later, *The Iceman Cometh* shows O'Neill at both his most ponderous and, for many, his most profound, as his lumbering symbolism and sometimes archaic language (the biblical 'cometh' of the title) yield before the cumulative majesty of a text which does not let the audience out of its grip until both they and the characters have been brought up short by the death of their collective illusions. Set in Harry Hope's saloon in 1912, the play is a devastating evening of pipe dreams gone sour, with Hickey as the Virgil of the occasion leading us through this bar-room Inferno. With a large cast (nineteen) and a long running time (about five hours), the play has both marvellous vignettes and rending monologues; and it highlights the emphasis on personal truth-telling that would obsess O'Neill through all his late plays.

Long Day's Journey Into Night

O'Neill's patterning of family pathology – a lifelong interest spanning the Oedipal tensions of *Desire Under the Elms* and the father–daughter relationship of *A Touch of the Poet* – reaches its most lacerating pitch in this play written 'in blood and tears', but not performed until 1956, three years after the author's death. The most directly auto-biographical of O'Neill's plays, it plunges directly to the heart of familial darkness in its account of a single day amongst the tormented Tyrone clan: the Irish-born father James, the miserly paterfamilias feeding on his memories as a stereotyped matinee idol; his morphine-addicted wife Mary; and their two sons, the ruthlessly honest drinker Jamie and his younger brother Edmund, O'Neill's unsparing vision of himself as a young, tubercular artist. The roles are as challenging as any in the English-language theatre, and actors as diverse as Laurence Olivier, Charles Dance, Robert Ryan, Jack Lemmon and Earle Hymen have taken on the part of the father, while Jessica Lange, Florence Eldridge and Constance Cummings were notable Marys.

TRY THESE:
✶SHAKESPEARE (especially *King Lear*), ✶IBSEN (especially *Ghosts*) for distilled family tragedies; ✶ALBEE's *Who's Afraid of Virginia Woolf?*, ✶WHITEHEAD's *Alpha Beta*, for more recent domestic plays which have a cathartic effect; ✶FUGARD for one of the best of a large battalion of plays portraying a portrait of the artist-as-a-

Long Day's Journey into Night by Eugene O'Neill, directed by Robin Phillips, Lyric Theatre, 2000. Charles Dance as James Tyrone, Jessica Lange as Mary Tyrone. (Colin Willoughby/ArenaPAL)

young-man ('*Master Harold*'... *and the Boys*);
✱HELLMAN's *Little Foxes* and ✱TENNESSEE
WILLIAMS' *Cat on a Hot Tin Roof* for probing
treatments of 'mendacity'; ✱GORKY's *The Lower
Depths* for earlier images of barflies; ✱IBSEN's *The
Wild Duck* for another (blessedly shorter)
treatment of the saving lie.

ORTON, Joe   [1933 – 67]
British dramatist

PLAYS INCLUDE:
The Ruffian on the Stair (broadcast 1964,
staged 1966), *Entertaining Mr Sloane* (1964),
Loot (1965), *The Erpingham Camp* (televised
1966, staged 1967), *The Good and Faithful
Servant* (televised 1967, staged 1971), *Funeral
Games* (televised 1968, staged 1970), *What
the Butler Saw* (1969)

Orton shocked delighted audiences by offering taboo subjects discussed in dialogue of the
greatest propriety by characters moving
through plots of sometimes Byzantine
contrivance. He claimed to draw incident and
dialogue straight from life, making full use of
the phraseology and platitudes of official
jargon, the contrived headlines of the tabloid
press and the euphemisms of pretentious
respectability. His characters adopt the moral
values of the world as he observed it – a police
inspector is by nature corrupt, a man is
expected to have an affair with his secretary, a
psychiatrist is himself habitually deranged,
exceptional genital endowment is a natural
feature of a heroic statue (even of Winston
Churchill). Though the audiences that gave
Orton West End success probably dismissed
this as a world of high-camp fantasy, its
parallels can be found in the pages of the daily
and Sunday papers. Orton is not setting out a
critique of society, he is simply holding a
mirror up to it. Nevertheless, the humour of
his plays does come largely from this apparent
dislocation, in which the socially unacceptable is treated as the commonplace, authority
figures are stripped of their disguises and all is
orchestrated with the physical and coincidental mechanisms of farce. Orton is unlikely
really to shock you – most audiences will lap
up his apparently outrageous naughtiness –
but take him seriously and you will find that

today's world is even nearer to the world he
created.

It is now almost impossible to view
Orton's work without remembering his own
life, so graphically described in John Lahr's
Prick Up Your Ears and the film based on it,
and recorded in Orton's own diaries, but his
promiscuous cottaging and murder by his
male lover affected his work only in bringing
it so suddenly to an end. Perhaps his most
accomplished play is *Entertaining Mr Sloane*,
in which an attractive young murderer thinks
he has captivated a woman and her brother
into giving him a cushy life but finds the
tables turned and himself trapped as their
sexual toy. *The Good and Faithful Servant*
shows a compassion not evident in his other
work and a more conscious criticism of the
way in which society treats its non-achievers.

Loot
Basically a parody of a stock detective play,
Loot presents a pair of young male lovers who
have robbed a bank and hidden the loot in the
coffin of one boy's mother – who had been
murdered by her nurse who plans to marry
the father before disposing of him in turn. A
bent detective, posing as a water board
official, completes the main cast. Contrasts
between the manner of the dialogue (often
quite formally stylised) and the substance of
the situation, opportunities for hilarious
business with the body to prevent discovery,
and other farce devices keep the laughs
coming. In the end everyone gets a piece of
the share-out except the murdered woman's
husband, the only truly innocent, who is
hauled off to jail to take the rap. Or is he
actually the most culpable for his blindness to
the corruption of the world around him and
his complicity in preserving the facades of
respectability?

TRY THESE:
✱AYCKBOURN's *Absurd Person Singular* and
Bedroom Farce for more abrasive comedies of
suburbia; ✱COONEY, ✱TRAVERS for farce;
✱BENNETT's *Habeas Corpus* and *Enjoy* for darker
shades of grey along Orton lines; ✱PINTER for
that strange mixture of menace amid the
mundane; ✱KONDOLEON and ✱LUDLAM for
American farcical plays.

What the Butler Saw by Joe Orton, directed by Phyllidà Lloyd, National Theatre, 1995. (Mark Douet/ArenaPAL)

OSBORNE, John   [1929 – 94]
British dramatist and screenwriter

PLAYS INCLUDE:
The Devil Inside Him (with Sheila Linden, 1950), *Personal Enemy* (with Anthony Creighton, 1955), *Look Back in Anger* (1956), *The Entertainer* (1957), *Epitaph for George Dillon* (with Anthony Creighton, 1958), *The World of Paul Slicky* (1959), *A Subject of Scandal and Concern* (1961), *Luther* (1961), *Plays for England* (*The Blood of the Bambergs, Under Plain Cover*) (1963), *Inadmissible Evidence* (1964), *A Patriot for Me* (1966), *The Hotel in Amsterdam* (1968), *Time Present* (1968), *West of Suez* (1971), *A Sense of Detachment* (1972), *The End of Me Old Cigar* (1975), *Watch It Come Down* (1975), *Déjàvu* (1991)

Born in London of what he described as 'impoverished middle-class' parents, Osborne worked as journalist for a number of trade magazines before he became an assistant stage manager and acted in repertory companies (an experience he draws on in *The Entertainer*).

Osborne's *Look Back in Anger* seemed to mark a watershed between the theatre of the 1930s and 1940s, and the new 'contemporary style' of the 1950s and 1960s which developed at the Royal Court and at the Theatre Royal, Stratford East. In a contemporary review Kenneth Tynan described it as 'the best young play of its decade' and journalists christened a whole group of new writers 'Angry Young Men'. Osborne, previously unknown, was hailed by one critic as 'the voice of our generation', and became the first of the many 'discoveries' of the Royal Court's policy of Writer's Theatre.

His next play, *The Entertainer*, explored the 'state of England' through the music-hall act of a shabby song and dance man, intercutting extracts from his failing act with his increasingly desperate home life. In *Luther* he adopted a quasi-Brechtian style to explore the origins of the Reformation, and in *Inadmissible Evidence* his tendency to write plays with a protagonist surrounded by ciphers found an ideal form in its virtual monodrama of a solicitor cracking up surrounded by emanations from his life all unable to penetrate his psychic shields. *A Patriot for Me*, a tale of skulduggery in the Hapsburg court in the period before World War I, caused one of the Royal Court's battles with the censors because of the drag ball in its second act and its general presentation of homosexuality. *Déjàvu*, a sequel to *Look Back in Anger*, revisits some of the scenes and themes of the original but unfortunately the 'Angry Young Man' of the 1950s soured in middle age, as the titles of Osborne's autobiographies *A Better Class of Person* and *Almost a Gentleman* suggest, and his splenetic misogynistic and homophobic outbursts threatened to obscure his historical significance. *Look Back in Anger* remains the play most likely to be revived but *The Entertainer* and *Luther* also appear quite regularly. The RSC staged *A Patriot for Me* in 1995 and *The Hotel in Amsterdam* was at the Donmar Warehouse in the autumn of 2003.

Look Back in Anger
Although it may not be the best of Osborne's plays, nor the best play of his generation of writers, it has come to stand as a key text for modern British drama. It came to express a widespread disillusion with post-war England, and contains a central statement of frustration from its anti-hero Jimmy Porter, which became a cry for a whole generation: 'there aren't any good brave causes left'. Jimmy Porter became the epitome of the Angry Young Man in his harangue on contemporary values. Jimmy is the single figure who dominates the stage, his bitterness the point of identification for the audience. His wife, the middle-class Alison, takes the brunt of his onslaughts, spending much of the play ironing, and taking abuse from Jimmy before finally leaving. The play ends with Alison's return, and the two cling together, addressing each other in child's language in an attempt to forge some kind of intimacy. Jimmy's treatment of Alison is now far harder to endorse than it appears to have been in the 1950s, and the play has lost some of its power. The play's setting and form is very social realist; the dingy bedsit where Jimmy and Alison live gave rise to the term 'kitchen sink' drama. Osborne himself has described *Look Back in Anger* as 'a formal, rather old-fashioned play' and, in retrospect, it is.

Osborne 'couldn't abide' ✱IONESCO's plays;
✱ARDEN, ✱WILLIS HALL and ✱WESKER were
categorised with Osborne as 'Angry Young Men';
✱MILLER saw Look Back in Anger as the play which
launched a new realism in a British theatre that
had been 'hermetically sealed from reality';
✱CRAZE's male protagonist in Angelus is a Jimmy
Porter for the 1980s; Osborne's misogyny has
✱STRINDBERGIAN elements; ✱TREVOR GRIFFITHS'
Comedians is a very different treatment of stand-
up comedy from The Entertainer; Osborne adapted
✱IBSEN's Hedda Gabler, ✱DE VEGA's La Fianza
Satisfecha as A Bond Honoured, ✱SHAKESPEARE's
Coriolanus as A Place Calling Itself Rome, and
✱WILDE's The Picture of Dorian Gray.

OSMENT, Philip
British actor, director and dramatist

PLAYS INCLUDE:
Telling Tales (1982), This Island's Mine
(1988), Who's Breaking? (1989), Listen
(1990), Sleeping Dogs (1993), The Dearly
Beloved (1993), What I Did in the Holidays
(1995), The Undertaking (1996), Flesh and
Blood (1996), Wise Guys (1998), Buried Alive
(2001), Little Violet and the Angel (2001),
Leaving (2002)

Former artistic director of Gay Sweatshop,
Osment has worked with many of Britain's
leading fringe companies as an actor, writer or
director. Although he has written extensively
for young audiences with such groups as
Theatre Centre and M6, his work transcends
narrow curriculum-based issues to explore
wider contexts of how people relate to each
other in traumatic situations and how they
can negotiate viable ways of living in the face
of everyday horrors. Who's Breaking? explores
reactions to HIV among young people, Listen
deals with cancer and deafness, Sleeping Dogs
is a modern Balkan Romeo and Juliet, Wise
Guys tackles the familiar question of how
alienated young men drawn to drugs and
petty crime can break out of the cycle of
neglect and abuse, while Leaving tackles the
increase in young men killing themselves in
rural Ireland.

There is no typical Osment play, even if
certain themes recur. This Island's Mine is a
close-textured presentation of life in the early
1980s, deftly touching on a whole raft of
issues including varieties of racism, homophobia and contemporary anomie, but The
Dearly Beloved centres on a church choir and
The Undertaking is about friends travelling to
Ireland to scatter the ashes of a friend who
died of AIDS. Osment often presents
dysfunctional families such as the non-
Archers farming folk of his Devon trilogy
(The Dearly Beloved, What I Did in the
Holidays and Flesh and Blood), and he often
uses time shifts to lay bare questions of
inheritance (both literal and metaphorical),
the relationships between past events and
current crises and the relationship between
political and personal issues. Buried Alive
again explores past and present via a tabloid
investigation of the private life of a famous
photojournalist, while Little Violet and the
Angel, which won the Peggy Ramsay Award, is
a children's play about the importance of
making the right choices.

TRY THESE:
Osment has been compared to ✱AYCKBOURN,
✱CAMERON, ✱CHEKHOV, ✱LEIGH, ✱ROCHE and
✱O'NEILL; for disaffected youth, ✱CORTHRON,
✱PRICHARD; for the incest theme in Holidays
compare ✱POLIAKOFF.

OSTROVSKY, Alexander
Nikolayevich   [1823 – 86]
Russian dramatist

PLAYS INCLUDE:
The Bankrupt (later It's All in the Family, or A
Family Affair, 1848), Stick to Your Own Sleigh
(1853), The Storm (1859), The Scoundrel (or
Diary of a Scoundrel, 1868), The Forest
(1871), Artists and Admirers (1881)

Ostrovsky was the virtual founder of the
Russian theatre. He wrote forty-seven plays,
many more than ✱GOGOL or ✱TURGENEV,
and unlike them was a professional man of
the theatre. He studied at Moscow University
but failed Roman Law, and then worked as a
clerk in the commercial courts until he was
forced to resign in 1851 after the publication
of A Family Affair. Although the play was
banned, Ostrovsky's readings of it were a wild

success in intellectual high society in Moscow, and this made his name. It, and his liaison with a charming but plebeian actress, also got him cut off without a penny, and he spent the next few years as a well-respected but very poor literary hack in Moscow. The first of his plays to be performed was *Stick to Your Own Sleigh* (i.e. 'know your place') in 1853, and from then until his death in 1868 he was Russia's most important playwright. His plays range from broad comedies to the nightmare tragedy *The Storm* (which is the source for Janacek's *Katya Kabanova*). They are all set in more or less contemporary Russia, sometimes backdated to appease the censor, and are all vigorously critical of the society they depict, actors being the only group shown in a consistently favourable light. He is now staged fairly frequently in Britain, although the range is restricted as yet to a small number of plays.

A Family Affair

The censor said it all: 'A rich Moscow merchant deliberately declares himself bankrupt. He transfers all his property to his clerk, whose interests he hopes to identify with his own by marrying him to his daughter. Being as great a rogue as himself, the clerk accepts daughter, property and money and then allows his father-in-law to be thrown into a debtors' prison. All the characters in the play – the merchant, his daughter, the lawyer, the clerk and the matchmaker – are first-rate villains. The dialogue is filthy. The entire play is an insult to the Russian merchant class.'

TRY THESE:

✶GOGOL's *The Government Inspector*, for an earlier satire on corruption in provincial Russian society; Isaac Babel's *Marya*, for a later one. ✶JONSON's *Volpone* for satire on greed and over-reaching plotters, ✶AYCKBOURN (who adapted *The Forest*) and ✶DE FILIPPO for modern critical social comedies; ✶DEAR and✶ELYOT for other Ostrovsky adaptations.

OTWAY, Thomas   [1652 – 85]
English dramatist

PLAYS INCLUDE:

Alcibiades (1675), *Don Carlos* (1676), *Titus and Berenice* (1676, after ✶RACINE), *The Cheats of Scapin* (1676, after ✶MOLIÈRE), *Friendship in Fashion* (1678), *The History and Fall of Caius Marius* (1679), *The Orphan; or, The Unhappy Marriage* (1680), *The Soldier's Fortune* (1680), *Venice Preserv'd; or, A Plot Discovered* (1682), *The Atheist; or, The Second Part of The Soldier's Fortune* (1683)

Otway began his theatrical career as an actor but suffered from such stage fright at his undistinguished debut that he switched to playwriting. *Don Carlos* is written in rhyming couplets, other plays in blank verse. Otway became known as 'the tragedian of love' but although his work was popular he died in penury. From its premiere until the mid-nineteenth century his most successful play, *Venice Preserv'd*, was probably revived more frequently than any other play not by Shakespeare, and it still has considerable theatrical power. A bleak blank-verse tragedy about the family and the state, loyalty and personal honour, and sexual politics, it includes a scene of grotesque comic sexuality and self-abasement by a masochistic nobleman, echoing the corruption of the Venetian state against which the protagonists Pierre and Jaffeir plan revolt. *The Orphan*, once almost as popular as *Venice Preserv'd*, is seldom revived today, but *The Soldier's Fortune*, a typical example of Restoration comedy, is occasionally staged.

TRY THESE:

Caius Marius is an adaptation of ✶SHAKESPEARE's *Romeo and Juliet*; for other post-Restoration writers of verse tragedy whose work is still (occasionally) staged, ✶DRYDEN and ✶SHELLEY; other Restoration comic dramatists are ✶BEHN, ✶CONGREVE, ✶ETHEREGE, ✶WYCHERLEY; for more satire on sexual abasement, *Nana*, in ✶OLWEN WYMARK's adaptation and, for a high-camp lesbian variety, Split Britches' stylish *Dress Suits to Hire*.

OVERMYER, Eric   [1951 –   ]
American dramatist and screenwriter

PLAYS INCLUDE:
Native Speech (1984), *On the Verge, or The Geography of Yearning* (1985), *In Perpetuity Throughout the Universe* (1988), *In a Pig's Valise* (1989), *Mi Vida Loca* (1990), *Heliotrope Bouquet by Scott Joplin and Louis Chauvin* (1991), *Dark Rapture* (1992)

Overmyer's plays display his 'lifelong obsession with the American language'. Although critics have compared him to *TOM STOPPARD, he feels that his playing with words and visual images, although based on intuitive and subjective thought processes, has as its aim serious social and cultural commentary. *Native Speech* is a post-apocalyptic vision mainly told through the hip renegade radio broadcasts of a character called Hungry Mother. In *On the Verge* three intrepid Victorian lady explorers on a beach become caught up in an erudite and unconventional play on words. As their imaginative flight begins to take wing, they find themselves hurled through time and space only to arrive on the banal shores of 1950s America. Their startling journey makes it possible for them to find the uncommon in the commonplace. *In Perpetuity* deals with the resurgence of anti-Asian and anti-Semitic prejudices in the USA. However, *In a Pig's Valise* is a film noir spoof with music and *Heliotrope Bouquet* is a lyrical memory play about the jazz great of the title. Overmyer has written extensively for television but his stage work has not been seen recently in Britain.

TRY THESE:
*PRIESTLEY's *Time and the Conways* for time shifts; *CHURCHILL and *WERTENBAKER for inventive use of time and language; for prejudice *ABBENSETTS, *FLANNERY's *Singer*, *FULLER, *KUREISHI's *Borderline*, *WALCOTT.

OWEN, Gary]
Welsh dramatist

PLAYS INCLUDE:
Crazy Gary's Mobile Disco (2001), *Fags* (2001), *After Life* (2002), *Heavenly* (2002), *The Shadow of a Boy* (2002), *The Drowned World* (2002), *Amser Canser* (2003), *Here Comes Everybody* (2003), *The Low Hundreds* (2003)

Owen's meteoric rise began with *Crazy Gary's Mobile Disco*, a co-production between Paines Plough and Sgript Cymru (a new writing company for Wales). It uses linked monologues to paint a picture of how three young working-class men cope with life in a small Welsh town. The overall atmosphere is of an anti *Under Milk Wood* mediated through *CARTWRIGHT's *Road*. Owen's National Theatre debut, *The Shadow of a Boy*, a story of childhood fears and fantasies with sci-fi elements, was less well received, but *The Drowned World*, a Graeae/Paines Plough collaboration, used to considerable effect the idea of a society where today's conventional overvaluing of physical appearance has been reversed, and managed to focus the nuclear annihilation fears better than in *Shadow*, by equating the beautiful people's charismatic radiance with the dangers of radiation.

TRY THESE:
*CHURCHILL's *Far Away* for contemporary apocalypse; *BOND for disaffected youth; Dic Edwards for another contemporary Welsh dramatist.

OWENS, Rochelle   [1936 –   ]
American dramatist and poet

PLAYS INCLUDE:
The String Game (1965), *Istanboul* (1965), *Homo* (1966), *Beclch* (1966), *Futz* (1968), *Kontraption* (1971), *He Wants Shih* (1971), *The Karl Marx Play* (1973), *K. O. Certaldo* (1975), *Emma Instigated Me* (1976), *The Widow and the Colonel* (1977), *Mountain Rites* (1978), *The Writer's Opera* (1979), *Chucky's Hunch* (1981), *Who Do You Want Peire Vidal* (1982), *The Mandrake* (1983)

Brooklyn-born Owens belongs to the school of formally innovative and iconoclastic playwrights associated with the rise of off-Broadway in the 1960s – people who had a highly emotive, deeply contradictory attitude to the theatre, a medium whose form they tended to admire even as they distrusted or alienated the audience. (Owens has said that she sees theatre as a 'life-sustaining force' for a public that 'wishes to be summoned from its sleep'.) Her best-known work, *Futz*, made into a controversial 1969 film, is, in the words of New York critic Michael Feingold, 'the keystone play of the decade'. It's a violent piece about a man, Cyrus Futz, in love with a pig, Amanda, and the ménage-à-trois between the two of them and a woman, Marjorie Satz. Images of excess and shock often figure in her work: *Beclch*, a play about four white adventurers in Africa, includes a lethal cockfight; in *The String Game* a priest chokes to death on spaghetti among a community of Eskimos he has just chided for thinking erotic thoughts. *The Karl Marx Play* is, in many ways, her freest and funniest work – a surrealist pastiche in which the black jazz musician, Leadbelly, Friedrich Engels and his wife wait for Marx to write *Das Kapital*.

TRY THESE:

✦ VAN ITALLIE's *America Hurrah* for benchmark avant-garde American plays of the 1960s, *Futz*-style; ✱ DREXLER, ✱ FORNES, ✱ GELBER and early ✱ KOPIT for hallucinogenic, surreal drama; ✱ CHURCHILL and ✱ LAN's *A Mouthful of Birds* for another disturbing pig image; adaptations of Orwell's *Animal Farm* for a political parable of porcine dimensions; ✱ DARKE's *The Monkey* for a less successful handling of the animalistic ménage-à-trois; ✱ KENNEDY's *A Rat's Mass* and ✱ YANKOWITZ's *Slaughterhouse Play* offer further theatrical images of the grotesque.

OYAMO (Charles F. Gordon) [1943 –]
American playwright

PLAYS INCLUDE
Breakout (1972), *The Juice Problem* (1974), *The Resurrection of Lady Lester* (1981), *Mary Goldstein and the Author* (1981), *A Hopeful Interview with Satan* (1989), *The Return of the Been-To* (1989), *In Living Color* (1989, with music by Olu Dara), *The Stalwarts* (1990), *Let Me Live* (1991, with music by Olu Dara), *I Am a Man* (1994), *Mundele Ndombe* (2001)

OyamO's work has not been staged professionally in Britain. Originally a writer of poetry, short stores and a children's book, OyamO began in the 1970s to work with the Lafayette Theatre and the Negro Ensemble Company. He sees Afro-Americans struggling for a sense of their own destiny amidst cultural, political and economic oppression.

In *Breakout*, two young black convicts challenge the repressiveness of society; the 'breakout' of the title is as much an escape from the urban slums as it is from the penal system. OyamO's interest in Black African identity compelled him to travel extensively in Africa during the early 1970s, where he discovered that, as an Afro-American, 'he's a child who's been taken away from home and made into a completely different kind of person. He goes back home, and no one recognizes him.' In *The Return of the Been-To*, a dramatic odyssey chronicling such a trip, OyamO explores the differences and similarities between African and American Black identities. With *The Resurrection of Lady Lester*, based on the legend of noted jazz musician Lester Young, OyamO uses music, transformations, time elisions and multiple casting to provide a kaleidoscopic view of the impact of racism on black musicians. *Let Me Live* portrays the wrongful imprisonment of black union leader Angelo P. Herndon in 1932: the protagonist's fellow inmates have been imprisoned on exaggerated charges, and Herndon himself is subjected to a kangaroo court, stressing the oppressive and unfair plight of the black at the hands of white society.

TRY THESE:

✱ SHANGE's *for colored girls who have considered suicide when the rainbow is enuff* influenced OyamO's *Mary Goldstein*; ✱ MILNER, ✱ WOLFE for other black Americans using jazz music in a variety of ways; ✱ FO and ✱ RAME's *One Woman Plays*, ✱ RUSSELL's *Shirley Valentine*, for women trapped in roles with some resemblance to *Mary Goldstein*.

PAGE, Louise [1955 –]

British dramatist

PLAYS INCLUDE:

Want-Ad (1976), *Lucy* (1977), *Tissue* (1978), *Hearing* (1979), *Housewives* (1981), *Salonika* (1982), *Falkland Sound/Voces de Malvinas;* (1983), *Real Estate* (1984), *Golden Girls* (1984), *Beauty and the Beast* (1985), *Goat* (1986), *Diplomatic Wives* (1989), *The Statue of Liberty* (1997), *The Big Adventure* (2002)

Page was a leading light of the 'second wave' of young women playwrights of the early 1980s. Something of a minimalist and a writer of spare dialogue, her plays reflect a generation of women where feminism is assumed, if not overt. Her plays have ranged from the unpredictable and surreal time-warp of *Salonika* to the hermetic domesticity of *Real Estate*, and the large-scale and ambitious reworking of the old fairy tale *Beauty and the Beast*. An early play, *Tissue*, touches sensitively on the trauma of a young woman facing breast cancer, whilst the later *Golden Girls*, about women and sport, takes a leaf out of ✳CARYL CHURCHILL's book in tackling women and ambition. This issue is also touched on in the earlier *Real Estate*, an unflattering picture of post-feminist woman and the selfishness of daughters, in which the mother definitely has the last and better word – mother–daughter relationships are a recurring theme in Page's work. Much of her reputation, however, rests on *Salonika*, with which she won the 1982 George Devine Award. *Salonika* is a surrealistic account of the effect of World War I on a widow returning to the Greek beach where her husband had died sixty-five years earlier (he reappears during the course of the play), and on her elderly spinster daughter. Critics hailed it as 'haunting' and a remarkably mature piece of work on the themes of futility and the frictions of mother–daughter relationships.

TRY THESE:

For 'ghosts' of other generations brought on stage, see ✳BARRIE's *Mary Rose*, ✳BOND's *Summer*, ✳ELIOT's *The Family Reunion*, ✳IBSEN's *Ghosts*, ✳LOWE's *Seachange*; for the friction of mother–daughter relationships, ✳KEARSLEY, ✳MACDONALD, ✳RAIF; for images of the post-feminist woman ✳HOLBOROUGH's *Dreams of San Francisco*, ✳LEVY's *Heresies*; *The Statue of Liberty* is a short modern variant on ✳STRINDBERG's *Miss Julie*.

PARKER, Stewart [1941 – 88]

Northern Irish dramatist

PLAYS INCLUDE:

Spokesong (1975), *Catchpenny Twist* (1977), *Kingdom Come* (1977), *I'm a Dreamer, Montreal* (1979), *The Kamikaze Ground Staff Reunion Dinner* (1979), *Nightshade* (1980), *Iris in the Traffic Ruby in the Rain* (1981), *Blue Money* (1984), *Heavenly Bodies* (1984), *Northern Star* (1984), *Pentecost* (1987), *Lost Belongings* (1987)

With a skilful grasp of the surreal effects of everyday speech, and an obvious delight in wordplay, Parker's plays are fast-moving, openly surreal and very entertaining, although they frequently deal with the serious issues of the Troubles and their consequences for the lives of individuals. He repeatedly asserts that there is a force for life and independence that transcends political slogans and allegiances. In *Catchpenny Twist* the main characters are forced out of Ireland by violence and killed by a terrorist bomb in a foreign airport, but in the end their dreams of songwriting fame seem vastly superior to those of the politically 'enlightened' who condemn them for the irrelevance of their lives to the historic cause. In *Northern Star* Parker studies Irish history through the lives of its greatest playwrights from ✳SHERIDAN to ✱BECKETT, a breathtaking exercise in skill and imagination with an operatic use of theatrical styles to present the response of each dramatist to his particular period.

Spokesong

Spokesong charts a family history through twentieth-century Ulster, in which a tenuous survival of individual eccentricity over political violence and faceless bureaucracy finally blossoms, despite the dehumanising forces ranged against it. Frank struggles to maintain the family bicycle shop against threats of redevelopment, the car culture, and the bombs of terrorists while battling with his hostile brother Julian for the hand of the beautiful Daisy. Interwoven with Frank's story is that of his grandparents. The bicycle and its adherents take on symbolic value as the preservers of humanity, hope and simplicity, and Daisy finally rescues Frank from defeat and despair. The play is effectively allied to music hall and the 'good night out' philosophy, with songs, illustrative episodes and emphatic good nature underlining its central theme.

TRY THESE:

✱O'CASEY for his sagas of Irish family life;
✱DEVLIN, ✱GARY MITCHELL, ✱MORRISON,
✤MUNRO, ✱REID for modern Belfast;
✱FINNEGAN, ✱MORNIN for varying views of the Troubles; ✱WOLFE's *The Colored Museum* for a parallel to *Northern Star*.

PASCAL, Julia   [1949 –   ]
British director and dramatist

PLAYS INCLUDE:

Far Above Rubies (1984), *Theresa* (1990), *A Dead Woman on Holiday* (1991), *The Dybbuk* (1992), *Heroine* (1996), *St Joan* (1997), *The Yiddish Queen Lear* (1999), *Woman on the Moon* (2001), *The Golem* (2002), *Crossing Jerusalem* (2003)

A Manchester-born actor and director who founded her own company in 1985, Pascal has established her reputation as a dramatist with a loose trilogy of plays exploring issues associated with the Holocaust. In *Theresa* the eponymous heroine escapes Vienna for London to find work as a nanny with an employer who decides they will be safer in the Channel Islands, and is forced by bureaucracy to stay behind because she is a German citizen, a move which leads inevitably to her deportation and to a death camp. The nightmarish narrative is told through a range of theatrical techniques that both mirror the European cultural heritage and express its breakdown. *A Dead Woman on Holiday* approaches the issue though the post-war trials at Nuremberg, and *The Dybbuk* takes S. Anski's Jewish classic of ghostly possession as the basis for an invocation of the spirits of the Holocaust dead and the resilience of their cultural aspirations. Pascal's other work is also often characterised by engagement with big cultural icons, such as St Joan, or ✱SHAKESPEARE in *The Yiddish Queen Lear*. In *Woman on the Moon* she deals with the uncomfortable political ironies that ensured that Werner von Braun escaped close scrutiny about any involvement with the Holocaust because the Americans wanted the technical expertise that would allow them to create their own guided missiles (and eventually to land on the moon). Her latest play, *Crossing Jerusalem*, deals with the contemporary conflicts between Palestinians and Israelis as an Israeli family beset by domestic squabbles tries to celebrate a birthday in an Arab restaurant in Jerusalem. Pascal skilfully weaves together family tensions, the grievances of a Palestinian whose father has been dismissed from his job by the Jewish matriarch and the realities of politics in a divided city to show the complex strands that create intractable situations.

TRY THESE:

✱HOME's *The Dame of Sark* for the occupation of the Channel Islands; Pascal directed ✱ALRAWI and ✱FINNEGAN's *Soldiers*; ✱ANOUILH and ✱SHAW for other St Joans; ✱C. P. TAYLOR's *Good for the Holocaust*; ✱MARLOWE's *The Jew of Malta* and ✱SHAKESPEARE's *The Merchant of Venice* for anti-Semitism; ✱BLOCK and ✱HARE for other approaches to the contemporary Palestinian situation.

PATERSON, Stuart   [1954 –   ]
Scottish playwright

PLAYS INCLUDE:
Apetalk (1981), *Secret Voice* (1982), *Beowulf* (1982), *Merlin the Magnificent* (1982), *Fighting Talk* (1983), *Confessions of a Justified Sinner* (1983, from James Hogg), *The Snow Queen* (1983), *Clean Sweeps* (1984), *Germinal* (1984), *In Traction* (1985), *Mr Government* (1986), *Beauty and the Beast* (1987), *The Cherry Orchard* (1989), *Cinderella* (1989), *George's Marvellous Medicine* (1990), *King of the Fields* (1999), *Puss in Boots* (2001)

Paterson's reputation rests mainly on his plays for children. He has a flair for making huge and complex questions of moral good and evil not just accessible to a young audience but positively entertaining for them. The value of family ties is a recurring theme in Paterson's work. Putting material gain, or one's ego, before keeping faith with those who are kind and caring results in comeuppance – usually of a risible, slapstick nature – while forgiveness of those who have 'erred and recanted' is mandatory. The tenor of the magical adventure plays, like *Merlin the Magnificent* and *The Snow Queen*, is that other people *matter* and that true happiness is not bought or got by vicious means. In *Cinderella* the romantic Cinders does not marry her Prince; she discovers that he saw her only as another beautiful acquisition and so she goes off with the kitchen boy who had fallen in love with her when she was dressed in rags and covered in grime!

The importance of family is also significant in Paterson's plays for adults. *Mr Government* has a returning brother opening up old family wounds, and in *King of the Fields* the emphasis is once again on brothers as they struggle for control of the family business.

TRY THESE:
For other British playwrights writing for children, ✱AYCKBOURN, ✱CASDAGLI, ✱DAVID HOLMAN, ✱JULIAN MITCHELL, ✱SHEPPHARD, ✱DAVID WOOD; ✱KESSELMAN's *Becca* for malevolent sprites in cupboards similar to that in *Secret Voice*; for adult rearrangements of *Cinderella*, try ✱GLOWACKI's *Cinders* and ✱DREW GRIFFITHS' and Cheryl Moch's *The Real True Story of Cinderella*; for returning family members disrupting settled lives, ✱IBSEN.

PENHALL, Joe   [1967 –   ]
British dramatist

PLAYS INCLUDE:
Some Voices (1994), *Pale Horse* (1995), *Love and Understanding* (1997), *The Bullet* (1998), *Blue/Orange* (2000)

One of the ways that critics earn their living is by creating order out of chaos and movements out of disparate voices, so Penhall has earned the reputation as the most 'warm-hearted' (Michael Billington) of the batch of new writers whose work emerged in the mid-1990s. Like many of his contemporaries, Penhall writes about a community that is supposed to care for its less privileged members but actually finds it difficult enough to care for itself. Although he finds the world just as alienating and alienated as his contemporaries, in an interview with Brian Logan he attacked the idea that 'desperation is some sort of spiritual release which strikes a chord in all of us'. In fact he can deal with subjects that are just as difficult as those of his contemporaries, particularly mental illness (in *Some Voices* and *Blue/Orange*) but also the depression that follows the death of a wife (*Pale Horse*), the destructive impact of a friend on a relationship (*Love and Understanding*) or the brutalities of losing your job (*The Bullet*).

TRY THESE:
✱KANE, ✱RAVENHILL, ✱UPTON for contemporaries; for schizophrenia ✱CRAZE, ✱EDGAR, ✱MERCER, ✱STOPPARD, ✱HEATHCOTE WILLIAMS; for NHS bureaucracy to compare with *Blue/Orange*, ✱NICHOLS, ✱TOWNSEND.

PHILLIPS, Caryl   [1958 –   ]
St Kitts-born writer

PLAYS INCLUDE:
Strange Fruit (1980), *Where There Is Darkness* (1982), *The Shelter* (1983)

Phillips was born in St Kitts but was brought up in Leeds and Birmingham, before going to Oxford University to study English literature. Apart from his stage output, Phillips has been prolific in every other writing medium with films, novels, television documentaries, radio plays, and interviews and extensive lecturing.

His plays express the generational conflicts and bitter reproaches of that generation of young blacks brought up in Britain but with deep roots in Caribbean culture, the most powerful statement of which is *Strange Fruit*, a tragic tale of disillusionment and lives blighted by race. Centred around a school-teacher, Vivien Marshall, and her two sons, it is a graphic, painful account of a family caught between two cultures, tearing each other apart as they fight out their destinies; the mother still upholding white values, one son opting for Rastafarianism, the other ultimately rejecting everything the mother (i. e. 'mother country') has stood for. *Where There Is Darkness* is another passionate treatment of a similar theme: a West Indian father, success-fully settled in Britain as a social worker, is on the point of returning to the Caribbean. The conflict between him chauvinistic, aggres-sive and clearly intended by Phillips as symbolic of racism's brutalising effect – and his quieter son who is about to thwart his father's ambitions, reflects wider social ills and is drawn with great persuasion and subtlety. *Shelter*, on the other hand, a more schematic treatment of colonialism and its repercussions, contrasts eighteenth- and twentieth-century relations between the sexes (the first half has a white woman–black man/master–slave Robinson Crusoe type twist to it) but is less successful in creating credible human beings.

TRY THESE:
Many black Caribbean writers have dealt with the theme of disillusionment with the old country, including ✱CROSS, ✱MATURA, ✱MOFFATT, ✱PINNOCK, ✱RECKORD and ✱WHITE; ✱IKOLI's *Scrape Off the Black* focuses on two brothers; ✱WALCOTT's *Pantomime* is another twist on the Robinson Crusoe theme; ✱MILLER's *A View from the Bridge* has the father protagonist as a complex victim/aggressor; ✱KUREISHI's *Borderline* examines living on the borderlines of cultures

from an Asian perspective; ✱ALRAWI's *A Child in the Heart* is equally concerned about mixing cultures; see also ✱SHANGE, ✱WOLFE's *The Colored Museum* for a satirical account of how white society has created 'the black image'.

PINERO, (Sir) Arthur Wing   [1855 – 1934]
British dramatist

PLAYS INCLUDE:
The Magistrate (1885), *The Schoolmistress* (1886), *Dandy Dick* (1887), *The Second Mrs Tanqueray* (1893), *The Benefit of the Doubt* (1895), *Trelawney of the 'Wells'* (1898), *The Gay Lord Quex* (1899), *His House in Order* (1906)

During his lifetime, Pinero was most renowned for his 'problem plays', above all *The Second Mrs Tanqueray*. These, despite the skill of their construction, have virtually died with the problems they dealt with. However, *Trelawney of the 'Wells'* remains a charming if sentimental picture of the mid-Victorian theatre, in which the passage of time has made the realistic characters seem stagy and the theatrical characters seem drawn from life; and his excellent farces are still regularly revived. *The Magistrate* has elements in common with ✱FEYDEAU's *A Little Hotel on the Side* – the visit to the dubious hotel in Act 1 by most of the characters, unknown to each other, the police raid, the desperate attempts to avoid discovery – but the taboos that are transgressed, this being nineteenth-century England, are not sexually oriented. Mr Poskett, a metropolitan magistrate, is merely trying to conceal the fact that he has been taken for a night out by his stepson, and Mrs Poskett is trying to hide the fact that this stepson, who is thought to be a precocious fourteen, is actually nineteen, she having lied about her age. Similarly, in *Dandy Dick*, the dreadful secret that involves the Dean of St Marvell's in a night in prison is merely that he has placed a bet on a horse to save his tottering spire (and he doesn't even win the bet), but the nimble plotting and the lively dialogue can still effortlessly keep our attention.

TRY THESE:

✴DUMAS and ✴SHAW for plays about the 'woman with a past' – *Mrs Warren's Profession* is partly an attack on the glamorising of that attractive figure; ✴GOLDSMITH's *She Stoops to Conquer* for another comedy that partly hinges on the age of a stepson.

PINNOCK, Winsome   [1961 –   ]
British dramatist

PLAYS INCLUDE:

A Hero's Welcome (1986, revised version 1989), *The Wind of Change* (1987), *Leave Taking* (1987), *Picture Palace* (1988), *A Rock in Water* (1989), *Talking in Tongues* (1991), *Mules* (1996), *Can You Keep a Secret?* (1999), *Water* (2000)

London-born Pinnock is a black playwright who is now teaching creative writing at London Metropolitan University. *Leave Taking* is an account of conflicts between a Jamaican mother who settled in Britain and the two daughters she raised here. It is as much a search for identity as a study in the generation gulf and sibling rivalries. Pinnock again mixed contemporary feelings with older, ritual beliefs in the person of the obeah woman, a symbol of continuity and tracing of roots which many recent black playwrights, from ✴EDGAR WHITE to ✴DEREK WALCOTT, have reclaimed. *Picture Palace*, commissioned by the Women's Theatre Group, was an entertaining if slightly untidy attempt to look at the difference between celluloid fantasy and real-life experiences in the lives of four young cinema usherettes – a structure that enabled her to explore a theme that was much in vogue amongst young women writers in the late 1980s: male violence. *A Rock in Water*, about civil-rights leader Claudia Jones, was worthy but more of a docudrama. Far more theatrically accomplished was *A Hero's Welcome*, produced by the Women's Playhouse Trust, which was runner-up in the 1990 Susan Smith Blackburn Awards. A rites of passage piece set in Jamaica in 1947, it tackled the familiar territory of emigration to the 'mother country' through the aspirations of young Jamaicans setting off for England, and the return to Jamaica of a young black soldier at the end of World War II.

Its unsentimental but sensitive characterisation of both men and women, young and old, showed Pinnock's growing maturity and sensitivity to personal interiors. *Can You Keep a Secret?* (written for the BT National Connections project) explores what happens when a fight leaves a black boy dead, while *Mules*, written for Clean Break, looks at black women drug couriers.

TRY THESE:

✴MOFFATT's *Mamma Decemba*, ✴PHILLIPS' *Strange Fruit*, for more first-generation immigrant mother figures; ✴CROSS for ritual; ✴KAY for emotionally transforming journeys; ✴NOËL GREIG, and ✴SHERMAN's *Bent* for gay examples; ✴DANIELS' *Masterpieces*, ✴CLARE MCINTYRE's *Low Level Panic* for further essays into male violence and the female image; Tasha Fairbanks' *PULP* for Siren, a Marlowesque lesbian thriller treatment of images, choices, compromises and survival; ✴MOTTON, a contemporary male voice, treats dreams and fantasies very differently; ✴HAYES for mothers and daughters and sibling rivalries; *Water* is a response to ✴CHILDRESS's *Wine in the Wilderness*.

PINTER, Harold   [1930 –   ]
British dramatist, actor and director

PLAYS INCLUDE:

The Room (1957), *The Birthday Party* (1958), *The Hothouse* (written 1958, staged 1980), *A Slight Ache* (1959), *The Dwarfs* (1960), *The Dumb Waiter* (1960), *The Caretaker* (1960), *A Night Out* (1960), *The Collection* (1961), *The Lover* (1963), *Tea Party* (1965), *The Homecoming* (1965), *The Examination* (1966), *The Basement* (1967), *Landscape* (1968), *Silence* (1969), *Night* (1969), *Old Times* (1971), *Monologue* (1973), *No Man's Land* (1975), *Betrayal* (1978), *Family Voices* (1981), *Other Places* (1982, made up of *Family Voices*, *Victoria Station*, *A Kind of Alaska*), *One for the Road* (1984), *Mountain Language* (1988), *The New World Order* (1991), *Party Time* (1991), *Moonlight* (1993), *Ashes to Ashes* (1996), *Celebration* (1999), *Remembrance of Things Past* (2000, with Di Trevis, from Pinter's *The Proust Screenplay*), *Press Conference* (2002)

The Caretaker by Harold Pinter, directed by Patrick Marber, Comedy Theatre, 2000. Michael Gambon as Davies, Rupert Graves as Mick. (Colin Willoughby/ArenaPAL)

Born in the East End, the son of a Jewish tailor, Pinter, like *JOHN OSBORNE, was an actor, and where Osborne always seems to be writing leading parts for himself, Pinter offers a vision of life as it might seem to an attendant lord with a minor part, always at the periphery of half-understood events. His earlier writing in particular seems like the quasi-naturalism of the thriller without its characteristic closure and disclosure. Pinter's series of what became called 'comedies of menace' (Irving Wardle), in which mysterious characters and unexplained events combine to unsettle the spectator with a sense of a half-grasped reality which remains elusively inscrutable, were initially greeted with almost complete critical incomprehension. *The Birthday Party* was variously described in the national papers as 'half-gibberish', 'puzzling', a 'baffling mixture'. As Pinter himself put it in a 1962 speech, 'below the word spoken is the thing known and unspoken'. Gradually audiences learned to understand and to enjoy the lack of precise explanation of plot and motivation and Pinter was recognised as a major writer.

He has been claimed as a British exponent of the Theatre of the Absurd, although his plays often begin from an ostensibly naturalistic context, which breaks down into a threatening and sometimes surreal world. The plays are often structured around the intrusion of a menacing stranger into an apparently safe world, who then becomes a catalyst for the return of the repressed. Although Pinter was initially seen as the least political of his immediate contemporaries, his interest in the structures of power and of patriarchy was fundamentally political and it was no real surprise when he began to explore more narrowly political issues in his later writings and to speak out publicly on controversial issues. His distinctive theatrical voice remains a major force in the contemporary repertory, both in revivals and in new work.

Pinter is also a major film writer, whose credits include *The Servant* (1963), *The Quiller Memorandum* (1966), *The Go-Between* (1971), *The French Lieutenant's Woman* (1981) and *The Handmaid's Tale* (1990).

The Birthday Party

Initially greeted with critical incomprehension, *The Birthday Party* has become a classic account of the menacing potential of everyday life. Stanley is the only guest of a seaside boarding house, fussed over by an Oedipally smothering landlady and a would-be girlfriend. His cosy retreat from the demands of the world is threatened by two menacing strangers who have come to take him away. His attempts at resistance are futile and he is eventually removed. Explanations of the action abound, with Stanley seen as everything from a baby being born to a member of a criminal organisation being tracked down by his former colleagues, but the strength of the play is that it draws on what seems like a basic fear that 'they' know your guilty secret and can track you down in the end.

TRY THESE:

*RATTIGAN, who interpreted *The Caretaker* as an Old Testament allegory; *IONESCO for similarities to *The Birthday Party*; *BECKETT shared Pinter's refusal to analyse his plays and his paradoxical precision of language but ambiguity of meaning; *ORTON for an extension of the mundane into the surreal; *STOPPARD for his interest in the fraudulence of memory; *PUIG's *Mystery of the Rose Bouquet* as a multifaceted exercise in memory; *TREMBLAY's *Albertine in Five Times* for a Proustian play; *SIMPSON, a Pinter contemporary and exponent of the British vein of Absurdism; *ARDEN, *OSBORNE, *WESKER as Pinter's contemporaries; Peter Hall linked productions of *Betrayal* and *COWARD's *Design for Living*.

PIRANDELLO, Luigi   [1867 – 1936]
Italian dramatist

PLAYS INCLUDE:

The Vice (1898), *Scamander* (1909), *Sicilian Limes* (1910), *The Doctor's Duty* (1913), *Liola* (1916), *Right You Are – If You Think So* (1917), *Cap and Bells* (1917), *The Pleasure of Honesty* (1917), *Man, Beast, and Virtue* (1919), *Mrs Morli, One and Two* (1920), *Six Characters in Search of an Author* (1921), *Henry IV* (1922), *Naked* (1922), *Each in His Own Way* (1924), *Diana and Tuda* (1926), *The New Colony* (1928), *Lazarus* (1929), *Tonight We Improvise* (1930), *To Find Oneself*

(1932), *When Someone is Somebody* (1933), *No One Knows How* (1934), *The Mountain Giants* (1937)

Born into a wealthy Sicilian family with a history of liberal and revolutionary beliefs, Pirandello attended the Universities of Rome and Bonn. His wife, suffering from mental disorder, was obsessed with the notion that Pirandello was unfaithful. He continued to live a miserable and withdrawn life until his wife was consigned to a mental institution in 1919. During this period of withdrawal he began writing plays, and in the early 1920s he achieved considerable fame, winning the support of Mussolini and worldwide acclaim. He won the Nobel Prize in 1934.

Pirandello's influence is particularly powerful on the Theatre of the Absurd. His plays are about a deeply perplexing, frequently hostile universe populated by characters who are themselves inconstant. He is fascinated by the masks people adopt in altering social circumstances, by the possibilities of multiple personality and the relativity of truth. Again and again his plays return to themes of deception and self-deception, entangling the audience in nets of paradox. The surface naturalism of his style of writing serves to heighten the contradictions that beset his characters, who are generally speaking unspectacular minor bourgeois figures rather than Promethean heroes. The plays have an obvious intellectual appeal. Pirandello's great achievement is to make them also highly theatrical.

Six Characters in Search of an Author

A rehearsal in the theatre is disrupted by the unexpected intrusion of a strange family group, who claim to be characters from an incomplete play. In the hope that the actors can finish the work, the family act out scenes from their life, but these prove full of contradiction and contention. The Father has become estranged from the Wife early in their marriage; he has brought up their son in isolation, while she has lived with the man she loved and had three children by him. The Father interprets this as proof of his benevolence; the Wife accuses him of ruthless self-interest, cruelty and lechery. The Father

confesses that he encountered the Stepdaughter in a brothel. The Stepdaughter blames the Father for her life of shame. The Son turns his back both on the Father and the rest of the family. Then the Little Girl is discovered drowned, and the Younger Boy kills himself. In the horrified confusion that follows in the theatre, the family insist that the events witnessed have been real, while the actors insist that they must be illusion.

TRY THESE:
✱KILROY and ✱STOPPARD for similar interest in role-playing; ✱ANOUILH's *The Rehearsal* has Pirandellian influences; ✱NOËL GREIG's *Angels Descend on Paris* deals in gay sexual role-playing; ✱GRASS's *The Plebeians Rehearse the Uprising* plays with the notion of the play-within-the-play from a political perspective; for plays about theatrical illusion, and identity, ✱SHAKESPEARE's *Hamlet* (the 1987 National Theatre production of *Six Characters* made *Hamlet* the play the actors were rehearsing) and *A Midsummer Night's Dream*; ✱SHERMAN adapted *Right You Are* as *Absolutely Perhaps*.

PLATER, Alan   [1935 –   ]
British dramatist and writer

PLAYS INCLUDE:
Close the Coalhouse Door (1968, with music by Alex Glasgow), *And a Little Love Besides* (1970), *Trinity Tales* (1975, with music by Alex Glasgow), *The Fosdyke Saga* (1977, from Bill Tidy, with music by Bill Wrigley), *On Your Way, Riley!* (1982), *Prez* (1984, with music arranged by Bernie Cash), *Going Home* (1990), *I Thought I Heard a Rustling* (1991), *Sweet Sorrow* (1990), *Peggy For You* (1999), *Tales from the Backyard* (2001)

Plater trained as an architect before he became a professional writer in 1961. He has written many plays for radio and television, novels and film scripts as well as plays for the theatre. Much of his work reflects his northern roots, his sympathy for the working classes and his belief in comedy as a medium for making important points. *Close the Coalhouse Door*, probably still his best-known play, is a musical celebration of coal miners from a strong socialist angle, *Trinity Tales* relocates some of the *Canterbury Tales* to a contemporary secular pilgrimage to the Rugby League Cup Final at Wembley. He has a lifelong interest in jazz (which inspired *Prez*, about Lester Young) and in popular forms of theatre, which inspired *On Your Way, Riley!*, a study of the strange relationship between the female impersonator Arthur Lucan (Old Mother Reilly) and his wife Kitty McShane, as well as his dramatisation of Bill Tidy's *The Fosdyke Saga*, a parody comic strip about a family of tripe merchants. *Peggy For You* is a tribute to Peggy Ramsay, the play agent whose clients included a very significant percentage of the most important British dramatists from the 1950s until her death.

TRY THESE:

✱CORRIE and ✱EDGAR's *That Summer*, ✱GODBER, ✱STOREY for miners; ✱GODBER for general parallels and contrasts; Ramsay's clients included ✱ARDEN, ✱AYCKBOURN, ✱BOLT, ✱BOND, ✱BRENTON, ✱CHURCHILL, ✱HAMPTON, ✱HARE, ✱ORTON; other plays inspired by music hall/ variety include Sean Foley and Hamish McColl's *The Play What I Wrote* (Morecambe and Wise) and John Fisher's *Jus' Like That* (Tommy Cooper).

POLIAKOFF, Stephen   [1952 –   ]
British dramatist

PLAYS INCLUDE:

A Day with My Sister (1971), *Lay-By* (1971, with ✱HOWARD BRENTON, ✱BRIAN CLARK, ✱TREVOR GRIFFITHS, ✱DAVID HARE, Hugh Stoddart and ✱SNOO WILSON), *Berlin Days* (1973), *The Carnation Gang* (1974), *Clever Soldiers* (1974), *Heroes* (1975), *Hitting Town* (1975), *City Sugar* (1975), *Strawberry Fields* (1977), *Stronger Than the Sun* (1977), *Shout Across the River* (1978), *American Days* (1979), *The Summer Party* (1980), *Breaking the Silence* (1984), *Coming in to Land* (1987), *Playing with Trains* (1989), *Sienna Red* (1991), *Blinded by the Sun* (1996), *Sweet Panic* (1996), *Talk of the City* (1998), *Remember This* (1999)

Although he began writing plays in 1969 Poliakoff first came to prominence with *Hitting Town* and *City Sugar* for the understated precision with which he evoked the sham comforts of anonymous shopping malls, fast-food outlets and motorway service areas, while exploring readily identifiable, unlikeable and deeply alienated characters. He is particularly effective in capturing the curious absence of real passion in people smothering in webs of superficiality, and the sense of conscious distress behind even the most glibly desperate – exemplified by the radio DJ in *City Sugar*. The plays are notable for a strong sense of isolation and of communication replaced by half-hearted buzzwords and slogans. He conveys – rather surprisingly given his settings – an accurate sense of particular physical spaces, underlined by their actual emptiness: public spaces deserted at night; the enclosed but lonely world of the late-night radio phone-in; surveillance cameras and unseen observers rendering even his most aggressive characters exposed and vulnerable. In *Strawberry Fields* a brother and sister romanticise themselves as renegades and guerrillas, but they seem to be in flight from nothing more tangible than their own imagined fears of pursuit.

Later plays moved away from urban blight. In *Breaking the Silence* a scientist-inventor (based on Poliakoff's own grandfather) on the run from the Russian Revolution is holed up with his family in a railway carriage. In *Coming in to Land* another political refugee, a Polish woman seeking asylum in Britain, is the focus for a study on the nature of oppositional attraction, bureaucracy, immigration and East and West. Poliakoff's concerns have also transferred very effectively to television, particularly in *Caught on a Train*, which starred Peggy Ashcroft. Poliakoff takes up the theme of the neglect of inventors in modern Britain in *Playing with Trains* and returns to an earlier theme – incest between siblings – first mooted in *Hitting Town*, for his 1991 film, *Close My Eyes*. He has subsequently written for both stage and screen, with the stage play *Talk of the City* bridging both media in a fictional tale of the fledgling BBC television service in the late 1930s. Although he has continued to explore the relationship between emerging technologies and how we view our lives in both media, his television series *Perfect Strangers* and *The Lost Prince* engaged more convincingly with issues of memory and the construction of realities than *Remember This*, which was widely regarded an underwritten.

TRY THESE:
Jonathan Gems, ✱JENKIN and ✱MOTTON are contemporary writers whose characters are equally in flight; ✱OVERMYER's *Native Speech* for desperate DJs; ✱STOPPARD for political dissidents; ✱BOLT's *Flowering Cherry* for a grandiose dreamer sacrificing his family, as in *Breaking the Silence*; Alexander Gelman's *We the Undersigned* also takes piece in a Russian railway carriage.

POLLOCK, Sharon   [1936 –   ]
Canadian dramatist

PLAYS INCLUDE:
Compulsory Option (1971), *Walsh* (1973), *And Out Goes You* (1975), *The Komogata Maru Incident* (1976), *Blood Relations* (1980), *Doc* (1985), *Getting It Straight* (1989), *Fair Liberty's Call* (1993), *Moving Pictures* (1999), *End Dream* (2000), *Angel's Trumpet* (2001)

Pollock is best known in Britain for *Blood Relations*, inspired by the true story of Lizzie Borden who, according to popular rhyme, 'took an axe/And gave her mother forty whacks' and then gave her father forty-one (she was actually acquitted of murdering them but it makes for a less interesting rhyme!). In Pollock's version who dunnit is less important than why it was done: the claustrophobic tensions, repressions and slow violences of family life, are refracted through the device of having her story acted out ten years after the historical events by her actress friend while the 'real' Lizzie plays the role of the family maid. Women have come to the fore in Pollock's later plays but she has always been interested in the borderlines between normal and abnormal behaviour, the central and the marginal in a culture, as in the histor-ically based *Walsh*, in which the Mountie Major of the title is torn between the values of his government and those of Sitting Bull, and *The Komagata Maru Incident*, in which a government agent who is himself of mixed race is sent aboard a ship full of Asian refugees who are being refused entry into Canada. Her work deserves to be more widely seen outside her native country.

TRY THESE:
✱TREMBLAY and ✱WALKER, for other Canadian dramatists; ✱GENET's *The Maids* and ✱KESSELMAN's *My Sister in This House*, both based on the same actual case, are also concerned with role-playing and family tensions leading to murder; parent killing is a staple of drama from Orestes in ✱AESCHYLUS' *Oresteia*, Oedipus in ✱SOPHOCLES' *Oedipus Rex*, Hamlet in ✱SHAKESPEARE's *Hamlet* to ✱BILL's *Curtains*; ✱KOPIT's *Buffalo Bill and the Indians* is another meditation on the native American/white culture clash; see ✱HIGHWAY for views from the other side; Stephen Mallatratt's very successful adaptation of Susan Hill's *Woman in Black* also uses the re-enactment device.

POMERANCE, Bernard   [1940 –   ]
American dramatist

PLAYS INCLUDE:
Foco Novo (1972), *Someone Else Is Still Someone* (1974), *The Elephant Man* (1977), *Quantrill in Lawrence* (1980), *Melons* (1985)

A Brooklyn-born long-time London resident, Pomerance seems – on the basis of his few widely seen plays – to be drawn to dialectics often at the expense of powerful writing. In *Foco Novo*, which gave its name to the theatre troupe Pomerance helped to found, an unnamed Latin American military dictator-ship pits its citizens against the state, the guerrilla outsiders against the technologically obsessed Americans. *The Elephant Man*, his best-known play, is based on a true-life story in which a Victorian doctor, an anatomist named Treves, finds his definition of normality challenged by the Elephant Man of the title, a physically deformed, dream-obsessed visionary. *Quantrill in Lawrence* explores a bloody episode of the American Civil War involving the James brothers, while *Melons*, set in a New Mexico melon patch in 1906, has its own would-be Treves, Carlos Montezuma, an Indian rights activist torn between the new world of the American colonialist and the ageless rituals of the native Indians. Pomerance's moral and ethical concerns are laudable, but he remains a playwright who may, perhaps, be creatively hamstrung by the burden of a monster hit.

The Elephant Man

In twenty-two short scenes with titles, Pomerance has written a major play that goes beyond prurient interest in its hunched, malformed central figure to touch on matters of faith, romance, and theatricality itself. To the left of the stage stands a strapping, well-built actor, who, as the description of his character is heard, assumes the stooped posture and slurred diction of the grotesquely misshapen John Merrick, labelled 'the elephant man' by nineteenth-century circus owners who used him as a freak attraction. A compassionate but career-minded physician, Treves, takes Merrick under his wing, undergoing a painful self-analysis that strips bare Victorian preconceptions about normality and the parameters of faith. The play features a superb part for a woman – the actress Mrs Kendal, who offers Merrick his one brief moment of eros. A raging success both in Britain and on Broadway, the play sparked interest in its subject, and a 1980 film was made with the same title, bypassing Pomerance's text.

TRY THESE:

✱ PETER SHAFFER's *Equus* for doctor–patient conflict as metaphor; ✱ KOPIT's *Indians* for stage treatment of an often ignored area; ✱ NELSON for his spare, enunciatory style and a shared interest in history and politics; ✱ FORNES' *The Conduct of Life* for another treatment of Latin American brutality; other writers staged by Foco Novo include ✱ BRECHT, ✱ BRENTON, ✱ DURAS, ✱ IKOLI.

POWNALL, David   [1938 –   ]
British dramatist, radio dramatist and novelist

PLAYS INCLUDE:
Crates on Barrels (1975), *Ladybird, Ladybird . . .* (1975), *Music to Murder By* (1976), *Richard III Part Two* (1977), *Barricade* (1977), *Motocar* (1977), *An Audience Called Edouard* (1978), *Livingstone and Sechele* (1978), *Beef* (1981), *Master Class* (1983), *The Viewing* (1987), *King John's Jewel* (1987), *Black Star* (1987), *My Father's House*

(1991), *Nijinsky: Death of a Faun* (1991), *Rousseau's Tale* (1991), *Elgar's Rondo* (1993), *Getting the Picture* (1998)

Pownall, co-founder of the touring company Paine's Plough, is an inventive dramatist who characteristically yokes together apparently disparate material to create plays in which the audience is invited to enjoy itself by engaging with complex issues and the deconstruction of received patterns of thinking. His main interests so far have been in politics, history, the arts, music and Africa. *Music to Murder By* combines both music and history in its study of the composer Peter Warlock reincarnating himself as the sixteenth-century composer Gesualdo in order to, literally, kill his writing block; *Motocar*, set in a mental hospital in Zimbabwe just before independence, is a powerful evocation of history and the relationship between personal and public madness; *Richard III Part Two*, a meditation on the construction and uses of history, begins with George Orwell telling us about 1984 and switches to an Orwellian present in which the Ministry of Sport is about to market its new game, 'Betrayal', about Richard III and the Princes in the Tower. *An Audience Called Edouard* starts with the actors on stage in the attitudes of Manet's painting *Déjeuner sur l'herbe* with Manet supposed to be out front in the audience painting the scene; add to this the arrival of an incognito Karl Marx and we have a potent brew.

After the success of *Master Class*, Pownall's touch seems to have deserted him, at least as far as the critics were concerned. *The Viewing*, in which a mysterious potential house-buyer turns out to be God come to stop a blind scientist from destroying the world, was generally thought to be emptily portentous, and *King John's Jewel*, in which we see a different John to the normal version, seemed to be too static for many tastes. *Black Star* is about the nineteenth-century black actor Ira Aldridge, and Pownall tackles some similar issues in *Getting the Picture*, where Irish nationalism, early photography and race all collide as the photographer Matthew Brady takes a photograph of former president Andrew Jackson, who is being importuned by a woman who wants to enlist his help in the cause of Daniel O'Connell and by his own black housekeeper who wants him to free their children from slavery. *My Father's House* is about the Chamberlain family, whose contributions to political life included two prime ministers, while *Nijinsky: Death of a Faun* and *Elgar's Rondo* each deal with episodes in the lives of their eponymous protagonists. With Pownall there is always the chance that the material brought together will fail to gel, but when it does he can be one of the most exciting and entertaining dramatists around.

Master Class

In an imagined encounter in 1948 Stalin, Prokofiev, Shostakovich and Zhdanov engage in debate about the right formula for socialist music, but the terms of the debate are skewed by the composers' knowledge that Stalin can simply have them killed if they don't fall into line. Stalin equates artistic freedom, atonality and lack of melody with political irresponsibility: the people need uplifting with simple music they can understand to get them through the aftermath of war and the composers have a duty to provide it. The whole relationship between the state and the individual is brought into play in a way that is both entertaining and chilling, particularly at the end of the first act when Prokofiev is asked to choose his favourite record and Stalin proceeds systematically to destroy the record collection so that the second act is played on a visual and aural carpet of broken music.

TRY THESE:

✱SNOO WILSON is like Pownall with the brakes off; ✱TERRY JOHNSON's *Insignificance* brings together mythic figures in a similar way to much of Pownall's work, but without the time shifts; Peter Parnell's *Romance Language* uses historical figures in a very different way; ✱STOPPARD's *Every Good Boy Deserves Favour* and ✱WILCOX's *78 Revolutions* tackle the theme of music in Russia; ✱C. P. TAYLOR's *Good* does the same for Nazi Germany; ✱SHAKESPEARE's *Richard III* is the effective starting point for modern popular attitudes to Richard; ✱PRIESTLEY's *An Inspector Calls* for another mysterious visitor come to set the world to rights; Nigel Gearing's *Snap* for photographic pioneer Edward Muybridge.

PRICHARD, Rebecca   [1971 –   ]
British dramatist

PLAYS INCLUDE:
Essex Girls (1994), *Fair Game* (1997, from Edna Mazya's *Games in the Backyard*), *Yard Gal* (1998)

Prichard is a chronicler of contemporary teenage life at the harsher end of the spectrum. Her debut play, *Essex Girls*, sketches in a landscape of deprivation – smoking in the girls' toilets of the comprehensive, visiting the teenager lone mother in the high-rise block – that was followed up with gang rape in her adaptation from Edna Mazya. *Yard Gal*, a commission for Clean Break, deals with the life of girl gangs.

TRY THESE:
✱CORTHRON for an American equivalent to *Yard Gal*; ✱GEMS, ✱HORSFIELD, ✱MACDONALD, ✱UPTON for adolescent girls.

PRIESTLEY, J. B.
(John Boynton)   [1894 – 1984]
British dramatist, novelist, commentator and essayist

PLAYS INCLUDE:
The Good Companions (1931, with Edward Knoblock, from his own novel), *Dangerous Corner* (1932), *Eden End* (1934), *Time and the Conways* (1937), *I Have Been Here Before* (1937), *When We Are Married* (1938), *Music at Night* (1938), *Johnson Over Jordan* (1939), *Desert Highway* (1943), *They Came to a City* (1943), *An Inspector Calls* (1945), *The Linden Tree* (1947), *Summer Day's Dream* (1950), *The Scandalous Affair of Mr Kettle and Mrs Moon* (1955)

Priestley wrote forty-seven plays (including one for Pollock's toy theatres), an opera libretto, screenplays, television and radio plays and twenty-eight novels – quite apart from a much greater number of books of travel, political comment, literary biography, etc. Most of his plays are carefully plotted and mainly conventional in form, even allowing for the split, serial and circular theories of time which shape the three 'time plays': *Dangerous Corner*, *Time and the Conways* and

An Inspector Calls, by J. B. Priestley, directed by Stephen Daldry, Playhouse Theatre 2001. (Pete Jones/ArenaPAL)

I Have Been Here Before. More unconventional in breaking out of the domestic box set are: *Johnson Over Jordan*, which follows its protagonist through the fourth dimension of immediate after-death; *Music at Night*, which explores the thoughts and lives of the audience at a concert; *They Came to a City*, which pictures a socialist utopia; and *Desert Highway*, written for army actors, which shows a tank crew marooned in the desert with a flashback to their prototypes in ancient times. Priestley was much more adventurous than most dramatists being performed on Shaftesbury Avenue at the time, but he quite consciously sought to work within the limits acceptable to contemporary audiences. While experimenting in one direction he felt 'it is dangerous to try and advance on all fronts at once'. Nevertheless, although the demands he makes of audiences may be slight compared to those some dramatists make, even his lightest comedies embody a critique of society and behaviour and a presentation of ideas beyond the humour and narration of their surface. Their optimism may now date his more overtly political pieces, but *Time and the Conways*, the comedy *When We Are Married* and *An Inspector Calls* are frequently revived.

An Inspector Calls

A detective who is investigating the death of a young woman visits a middle-class Yorkshire household. As the background to the tragedy is revealed, the circles of responsibility and guilt spread to affect almost everyone. At the end of the play, the announcement of the visit of a detective inspector questions the detective's real identity and reveals the play as a metaphor for our own failure to accept our responsibility to others.

The play, written at the end of World War II, is heavily ironised by being set before the outbreak of World War I, which invests the confident pronouncements of the unthinking paterfamilias with an aura of ignorant complacency. The desperate attempts by most of the family to wriggle out of their social responsibility indict them, their class and their generation, and Priestley's otherworldly auditor demands that we learn from their example. The play was given a legendarily successful production by Stephen Daldry in 1992 that was widely hailed as rescuing the play from cosy rep interpretations. Some felt it was a case of a directorial concept overwhelming a play that didn't actually need rescuing but the production played for many years, outliving the Thatcher government, if not the Thatcherite attitudes that it was widely taken to attack.

TRY THESE:
✳BRIGHOUSE, ✳RUSSELL, ✳WATERHOUSE and Willis Hall for other plays rooted in the north of England; ✳MAUGHAM's *For Services Rendered* for a critique of conventional values within a traditional form; ✳TREVOR GRIFFITHS and ✳WESKER as socialist dramatists who tend to work with available forms; ✳BOND and ✳BRENTON as socialist dramatists who use more radical approaches; ✳BRECHT for communal responsibility; ✳BAGNOLD for domestic revelations; ✳HARWOOD's *The Dresser* and ✳MAMET's *A Life in the Theatre* for other views of theatre life

PUIG, Manuel   [1932 – 90]
Argentine novelist, dramatist and film director

PLAYS INCLUDE:
Kiss of the Spider Woman (1981), *Mystery of the Rose Bouquet* (1981), *Under the Mantle of Stars* (1982)

Puig studied at film school in Rome and became a successful novelist before having his first play produced. *Kiss of the Spider Woman*, based on his own novel, is widely known from the film version, which he also directed. Both this and *Mystery of the Rose Bouquet* are two-handers for contrasting characters, offering marvellous opportunities for actors, and exploring stormy and intricate relationships. Puig uses these small-scale pieces to reflect the culture in which they are set and perhaps suggests – in the transformation that the interaction works on each character – a possibility of social change. Both are set in enclosed worlds, *Mystery of the Rose Bouquet* in an expensive health clinic where a rich and mischievous old woman, who has already sacked four nurses, and the poor, apparently unqualified, nurse who is now looking after her, begin to find a pattern of similarity in their lives. As they relive their memories of sadness, failure and sometimes of roses, they both torment and rehabilitate each other. As in his novels, such as *Betrayed by Rita Hayworth*, the characters' imagination and fantasies are explored, thus lifting his plays out of strictly naturalistic forms.

Kiss of the Spider Woman

Kiss of the Spider Woman is set in an Argentinian prison cell where a camp window-dresser, found guilty of fooling around with a fifteen-year-old, is shut up with a macho Marxist revolutionary and promised release if he can pry secrets from him. As affection and dependence develop between the men, climaxing in physical consummation, the fey-gay who escapes from reality in reliving B-picture romances (oblivious to their fascist background and ideology) learns that caring for individuals is not enough, accepts social responsibility and recognises his own integrity, while the revolutionary learns reciprocal respect and the value of the individual. This is a homosexual love story, a study of power – not only of authority over the individual but between the prisoners themselves – and an argument for the innocence of love that demolishes conventional bourgeois values while skilfully embroiling the audience in the conflicts of loyalty and betrayal.

TRY THESE:
For other imprisoned homosexuals, ✱GENET's *Deathwatch*, John Herbert's *Fortune and Men's Eyes*, ✱SHERMAN's *Bent*; for studies of power relationships, ✱BECKETT's *Endgame* and *Catastrophe*, ✱PINTER's *One for the Road* and *No Man's Land*; for contrasting two-handed female relationships, ✱HAYES' *Skirmishes*.

R

RABE, David [1940 –]
American dramatist

PLAYS INCLUDE:
The Basic Training of Pavlo Hummel (1971), *Sticks and Bones* (1971), *The Orphan* (1973), *In the Boom Boom Room* (1973), *Streamers* (1976), *Goose and Tom-Tom* (1980), *Hurlyburly* (1984), *Those the River Keeps* (1991), *A Question of Mercy* (1997), *The Dog Problem* (2001)

A tough, gritty, often abrasive writer, Rabe is distinguished by his trilogy about the Vietnam War. This begins with the untidy *The Basic Training of Pavlo Hummel*, continues on to the stark, ironic *Sticks and Bones* and climaxes with the altogether startling *Streamers*, one of the great American plays of the 1970s. Set in 1965 in a Virginia army barracks, the play makes the scabrous point that war is an internal condition that occasionally finds an external release. The play takes its title from the word for a parachute that fails to open, but the play itself floats on a bloody and pained compassion for all of society's victims. This natural state of aggression finds its peacetime equivalent amongst the Hollywood sharks who populate *Hurlyburly*, a sour and rancid end-of-the-world play which is as flowery and overwritten as *Streamers* is swift and sharp. In *Those the River Keeps*, Phil, a character from *Hurlyburly*, an emerging actor in Los Angeles, is trying desperately to break with his gangster past. His newfound stability and young marriage, however, are dramatically threatened by the arrival of Sal, a hit-man and former friend. The play, which features long conversations about the past, is concerned with the dangerous magnetism of one's personal history, and with the difficulties of starting anew. *A Question of Mercy* tackles issues of AIDS and euthanasia in the days before the availability of combination therapies.

TRY THESE:
✴GENET's *Deathwatch*, Miguel Pinero's *Short Eyes* for similar dramas of enclosure; ✴BABE for often jagged, sometimes over-literary language; ✴C. P. TAYLOR's *Lies About Vietnam* links the public problem with the personal; ✴MANN's *Still Life* provides haunting documentary-like responses; ✴DARKE's *The Dead Monkey* for the LA malaise; ✴KRAMER for AIDS.

RACINE, Jean [1639 – 99]
French dramatist and historiographer-royal

PLAYS INCLUDE:
Le Thébaïde (1664, *The Theban*), *Alexandre le Grand* (1665, *Alexander the Great*), *Andromaque* (1667, *Andromache*), *Les Plaideurs* (1668, *The Litigants*), *Britannicus* (1669), *Bérénice* (1670), *Bajazet* (1672), *Mithridate* (1673, *Mithridates*), *Iphigénie* (1674, *Iphigenia*), *Phèdre* (1677, *Phaedra*), *Esther* (1689), *Athalie* (1691, *Athalia*)

Racine was orphaned at the age of four, and brought up at Port-Royal by the Jansenists, he escaped them for most of his adult life, but they got him in the end. A good scholar and an admirer of the Greek tragic dramatists (*Les Plaideurs* is his only comedy), he took naturally to the neo-Aristotelian rules that ✴CORNEILLE found so constricting; his relentless dramas run their course in twenty-four hours or less, in one location, with no subplots to lessen the intensity. His characters manage to combine uncontrollable passion, self-interest and a merciless lucidity; the restrictions of the rhymed Alexandrine couplets and the limited vocabulary help to channel the force of the events. After the comparative failure of *Phèdre*, Racine was reconciled with Port-Royal and wrote no more secular plays; the last two, on Biblical subjects, were written for Madame de Maintenon's school for young ladies at St Cyr, but the subjects are from the Old Testament, and the doom is just as inevitable. It used to be the received wisdom that Racine's plays were not successful in English because they were impossible to translate, but recent productions have disproved this.

Phèdre

Phèdre is based on ✶EURIPIDES' *Hippolytus*, but with concessions to the seventeenth-century French taste for *vraisemblance*; Hippolyte spurns his stepmother's forbidden love because he is in love with Aricie rather than because he is vowed to Diana, and the gods are obsessionally present in the characters' minds rather than appearing on the stage. The tension rises inexorably and logically from scene to scene; as often in Racine, if you pray to the gods your prayer is always answered (such as Thésée's prayer to Neptune to kill his son), but by then it is not what you want at all.

TRY THESE:
✶EURIPIDES, from whom Racine borrowed the plots of *Phèdre* and *Iphigénie*; ✶MOLIÈRE for a seventeenth-century French comic dramatist; Robert David Macdonald, ✶HARRISON, Ted Hughes, Edwin Morgan for recent Racine translations; Craig Raine's *1953* (1992) updates *Andromaque* to an Italy where the allies have lost World War II.

RAIF, Ayshe   [1952 –   ]
British dramatist

PLAYS INCLUDE:
Cafe Society (1981), *Another Woman* (1983), *A Party for Bonzo* (1985), *Fail/Safe* (1986), *Caving In* (1989), *I'm No Angel* (1993)

Of Turkish-Cypriot parentage, Raif is a superb observer of emotional currents, with an ear for dialogue that is angry, and painful in its accuracy. *I'm No Angel*, about Mae West, is an exception to the rule that her plays are naturalistic domestic drama about life at the sharp end of urban existence: single women in lonely bedsits (*Another Woman*), marriage torn apart by the effects of unemployment (*A Party for Bonzo*), and the repressive bonds that can tie mother–daughter relationships in

knots (*Fail/Safe*). Though the plays are bleak, there is often a mordant humour at work. Some critics have found her work to be closer to television drama, which she has also written.

TRY THESE:
For female monologue about isolation/alienation, ✶SHAPIRO and Meera Syal's *One of Us*; for comparative states of isolation, ✶COLLINS' *Judgement*, ✶KROETZ's *Request Programme*, ✶MURRAY's *Bodycell*, ✶STRAUSS's *Great and Small*; for relationships between mothers and daughters, ✶KEARSLEY, ✶MACDONALD; for marriage under stress, ✶ALBEE's *Who's Afraid of Virginia Woolf?*, ✶SPENCER, ✶STRINDBERG, ✶WHITEHEAD's *Alpha Beta*; for frustrated daughters, ✶HAYES' *Skirmishes*; Raif adapted ✶TREMBLAY's *Les Belles Soeurs* (*The Sisters-in-Law*).

RAME, Franca   [c. 1930 –   ]
Italian actress, dramatist, and collaborator with ✶DARIO FO

PLAYS INCLUDE:
It's All Bed, Board & Church (1977, also known as *All House, Bed and Church* or *Female Parts* or *One Woman Plays*, comprising *Waking Up, Same Old Story, A Woman Alone* and *Medea*, with others in other performances), *The Mother* (1982), *Tomorrow's News* (1982), *Ulrike Meinhof* (1982), *I Don't Move, I Don't Scream, My Voice Is Gone* (1983, also known as *The Rape*), *The Open Couple* (1983)

This remarkable actress-cum-playwright, daughter of one of the last of Italy's companies of strolling players, has worked with her husband, Italy's premier political free-thinking socialist and satirist ✶DARIO FO, for many years, collaborating on many plays and productions and running their own companies. A physical performer of enormous energy and dynamism, Rame's monologues reflect equally that emotional intensity and her political commitments. Her plays have focused on a variety of women's issues, often as a result of her own experiences, and are testaments to the various forms of women's oppression in Italian society – from the state, the church and men. *The Mother, Ulrike*

Meinhof and *Tomorrow's News* arose directly out of her activism on behalf of political prisoners. In *The Mother*, the mother's account of a young terrorist's trial and sentence recreates not only the intensity of maternal feelings and their chilling climax, but instils a growing sense of society's collective responsibility towards the young man and his fate. *The Rape* is an account, all the more chilling for its economy and understatement, of an attack on Rame herself, motivated, she believes, by political opponents. Its simple step-by-horrific-step description of a young woman being gang-raped and tortured (with a cigarette) is as powerful a statement about male violence – *SARAH DANIELS notwithstanding – as you are likely to see. *Female Parts*, a series of monologues (co-written with *FO), based on conversations with a range of Italian women, reflects their problems in a subversive mix of styles from the bitterly ironic and farcically anarchic to feminist reappropriation of fairy tales and the Medea myth. *The Open Couple*, again co-written with *FO, is yet a further example of the comic grotesque as a couple come to grips with the painful truths and double standards of extra-marital relationships.

TRY THESE:

*RAIF's *Another Woman* for a British equivalent of the solo woman; for a surreal account of rape, Eve Lewis's *Ficky Stingers* (which with *PAGE's *Tissue* is an equivalent double bill of fear, anger and pain); *BRECHT's *The Mother* for contrast; *RUSSELL's *Shirley Valentine* for more watered-down feminism performed solo; *DORFMAN's *Death and the Maiden* examines the emotional repercussions and feelings of revenge in the aftermath of rape and torture, as does *MASTROSIMONE's *Extremities*.

RATTIGAN, Terence (Mervyn)   [1911 – 77]
British dramatist

PLAYS INCLUDE:
French Without Tears (1936), *After the Dance* (1939), *Flare Path* (1942), *While the Sun Shines* (1943), *Love in Idleness* (1944), *The Winslow Boy* (1946), *Playbill* (1948, comprising *The Browning Version* and *Harlequinade*), *Adventure Story* (1949), *Who is Sylvia* (1951), *The Deep Blue Sea* (1952), *The Sleeping Prince* (1953), *Separate Tables* (1954), *Variation on a Theme* (1958), *Ross: A Dramatic Portrait* (1960), *In Praise of Love* (1974, comprising *Before Dawn* and *After Lydia*), *Cause Célèbre* (1977)

A master craftsman in plot construction and writing telling dialogue, Rattigan first gained fame with *French Without Tears*, a bright comedy about would-be candidates for the Civil Service learning French at a French resort. He maintained his light touch through plays such as *The Sleeping Prince*, a Laurence Olivier/Vivien Leigh vehicle about a middle-aged prince falling in love with a chorus girl, which Olivier filmed with Marilyn Monroe as *The Prince and the Showgirl*. In the late 1950s Rattigan's obvious commercial appeal led enthusiasts for the work of *JOHN OSBORNE and the new generation of more politically motivated dramatists to dismiss his work as irrelevant. Nevertheless, Rattigan, working within the format of the well-made play, tackled issues far deeper than those of conventional Shaftesbury Avenue entertainment, though he presented them with a skill that avoided alienating the respectable, middle-class, middle-aged theatregoer whom he personified as 'Aunt Edna'.

He is now recognised once again as a sensitive anatomist of repressions and inhibition. In *Flare Path* he explored the strains on Battle of Britain flyers and their civilian friends and families. In the factually based *The Winslow Boy* his subject was the wrongful dismissal from a military academy of a boy accused of stealing a postal order, and in *The Browning Version* he examined the pressure on a teacher being forced into retirement with his wife unfaithful and even the pupil who seems to share his ideals abandoning him. *In Praise of Love* tackled incurable illness and *Cause Célèbre* is based on a famous case of a woman and her lover, who murdered her husband. *The Deep Blue Sea*, originally written as a story of male homosexuals following a tragedy concerning an actor with whom Rattigan was in love, touches tragic heights in its presentation of a woman leaving her husband for a man who does not return her love. Rattigan's understanding of the pain of relationships transcends sexual orientation, although *Adventure Story*, a psychological study of Alexander the Great, makes no attempt to explore the Alexander–Hephaiston relationship. Presumed homosexual rape is a central element in *Ross*, a presentation of T. E. Lawrence after Arabia, but the removal of censorship did not bring any overt exploration of his own sexuality to Rattigan's work.

Separate Tables

Both plays in this double bill offering contrasting roles for the leading lady and leading man are set in the same Bournemouth private hotel with the same subsidiary characters. In the first a drunken Labour ex-junior minister is unexpectedly confronted with the ex-wife who divorced him for cruelty but for whom he still feels passionately. The second shows reactions to the exposure of a bogus major, bound over on a charge of insulting behaviour in a cinema, especially those of a repressed spinster with a bullying mother whom he has befriended. As in much of Rattigan's work, a comparatively slight idea is enriched by a deep understanding of the needs and inadequacies of human relationships. Kenneth Tynan regretted 'that the major's crime was not something more cathartic than mere cinema flirtation', but supposed 'the play is as good a handling of sexual abnormality as English playgoers will tolerate'. This was in the days of the Lord Chamberlain's censorship, and in fact Rattigan is said to have originally intended the charge to be a homosexual one.

TRY THESE:

✴MAUGHAM and ✴TENNESSEE WILLIAMS for similar treatments of homosexual themes; ✴LESLIE LEE's *Black Eagles* for another perspective on World War II flyers; ✴CLARK's *Whose Life Is It Anyway?* for a play about incurable illness; many British comedies for jokes at the expense of funny foreigners, from ✴SHAKESPEARE's *The Merry Wives of Windsor* onwards (✴SHUE's *The Foreigner* provides a twist on this genre).

RAVENHILL, Mark [1966–]
British dramatist

PLAYS INCLUDE:
Shopping and Fucking (1996), *Faust Is Dead* (1997), *Handbag* (1998), *Sleeping Around* (1998, with ✴HILARY FANNIN, Stephen Greenhorn and ✴ABI MORGAN), *Some Explicit Polaroids* (1999), *Mother Clapp's Molly House* (2001)

One of the key members of the 'In Yer Face' generation of the mid-1990s, Ravenhill became notorious because of both the explicit title and the explicit action of *Shopping and Fucking*, but the tabloid headlines and government outrage failed to recognise the true value of a play that explored rather than recommended the emptiness of a type of modern living. For some of the characters the only way to feel anything is to feel pain, and they all live in a world of commodification in which dinners for one and phone sex replace human contact, and intimacy is both desirable and something to be feared. The bleakness of the picture is redeemed to some extent by the final image of the young woman Lulu insisting on sharing her food with her male friends. As well as tapping into this modern alienated world, which he also does in *Some Explicit Polaroids* (a sensitive study of personal and political interaction, AIDS and love), Ravenhill has addressed the antecedents of some contemporary attitudes and some contemporary theoretical explanations of the modern world in his other plays. In *Faust Is Dead* he takes a famous French philosopher who expresses some postmodern views about reality that come into sharp collision with reality, all mediated through the Faust story and equipped with a chorus. *Handbag* plays with ✴WILDEAN issues of nature and nurture, intercutting nineteenth-century scenes with contemporary difficulties about fertility and parenting, while *Mother Clapp's Molly House* uses operatic pastiche and eighteenth-century and contemporary settings to ask questions about the need to belong, the importance of nurturing and the problems of establishing a stable identity.

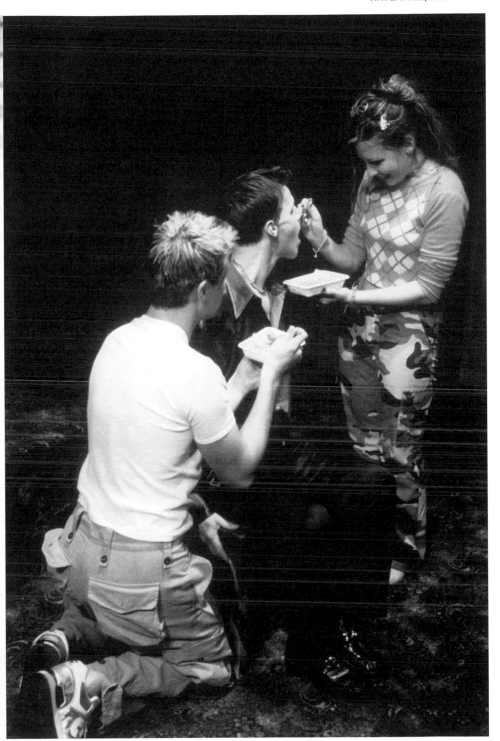

Shopping and Fucking by Mark Ravenhill, directed by Max Stafford-Clark, Royal Court production at the Ambassadors Theatre, 1996. Andrew Clover, Kate Ashfield, Anthony Rhyding. (Fritz Curzon/ArenaPAL)

TRY THESE:
✱BOND's *Saved* and ✱KANE's *Blasted* for similar controversy and for similar small gestures of hope; ✱GOETHE and ✱MARLOWE for Faust; ✱WILDE's *The Importance of Being Earnest* for *Handbag*; ✱WANDOR's *AID Thy Neighbour* for fertility issues: ✱ELYOT and ✱HARVEY for contrasting approaches to gay life; ✱CARTWRIGHT for urban desolation.

RECKORD, Barry
Jamaican dramatist

PLAYS INCLUDE:
Adella (1954; revised version, *Flesh to a Tiger*; 1958), *You in Your Small Corner* (1960), *Skyvers* (1963), *Don't Gas the Blacks* (1969), *A Liberated Woman* (1970), *Give the Gaffers Time to Love You* (1971), *X* (1972), *Streetwise* (1984)

A black Jamaican, educated at Oxford, which he left in 1952, Reckord's first play centres on a woman in a Jamaican slum trying to choose between white medicine and local magic to save her dying baby. She is insulted by the white doctor with whom she has begun to fall in love and the play ends melodramatically with her killing both her baby and the black 'shepherd' doctor in a parallel of her people's struggle to throw off both superstition and white domination. Reckord's other work for the stage, however, has been more concerned with class than colour. *You in Your Small Corner* shows a black bourgeois Brixton family in which the successful mother looks down on the local poor whites; and in his best-known play, *Skyvers*, set in a London comprehensive school, the pupils react violently against the social inadequacy of their parents and teachers and the suppression of talent and lack of opportunity. Although his next two plays present, in *Don't Gas the Blacks*, a black couple in which the wife has a black lover, and, in *A Liberated Woman*, a black couple in which the wife has a white lover, he is concerned less with racism as such than with personal freedom and sexual politics. Produced by Joint Stock, *X* is a two-hander in which an Oxford don is visited in his college rooms by his daughter, a believer in the ideas of Wilhelm Reich. She

strips preparatory to taking a shower and then settles down to an increasingly outspoken conversation with her father, in which they both describe their sexual disappointments and she reveals the 'X' of the title: a suppressed sexual longing for her father.

TRY THESE:
✱JOHN, ✱RHONE, ✱WALCOTT, ✱WHITE, for Caribbean-located plays; ✱ABBENSETTS, ✱MATURA, ✱PHILLIPS for plays about British blacks with roots in the Caribbean; Judith Johnson's *Exclude Me*, ✱KEEFFE and ✱TERSON for failures in the educational/social system; ✱DURANG and ✱O'MALLEY for contrasting comic swipes at the Catholic educational system, and ✱WEDEKIND's *Spring Awakening* for a study of school children; ✱TREVOR GRIFFITHS for a writer influenced by Wilhelm Reich; ✱FORD's *'Tis Pity She's a Whore*, ✱SHELLEY's *The Cenci*, ✱SOPHOCLES' *Oedipus*, ✱TREMBLAY's *Bonjour, Bonjour* for quite different treatments of incest.

REDDIN, Keith   [1956 –]
American dramatist and actor

PLAYS INCLUDE:
Throwing Smoke (1980), *Life and Limb* (1984), *Desperadoes* (1985), *Rum and Coke* (1985), *Highest Standard of Living* (1986), *Big Time* (1987), *Plain Brown Wrapper* (1987), *Nebraska* (1989), *Life During Wartime* (1990), *Innocents' Crusade* (1991), *Maybe* (1993, from Alexander Shatrov) *Brutality of Fact* (1997), *Synergy* (2002), *Frame 312* (2002)

Merging historic settings and actual events with contemporary social and political issues, Reddin writes classic idea plays with an ever-present layer of comedy. His first full-length play, *Life and Limb*, follows a disabled Korean War veteran as he returns to alcoholism and marital separation in his suburban New Jersey home; Reddin mingles such serious issues with a spoof of 1950s family life, mirroring scenes from television's *I Love Lucy* and imitating the pace of *The Honeymooners*. He sees this blend as an effective medium, saying 'I want to take a tough look at the society of the '50s, but at the same time I never want to bore anyone.'

In *Rum and Coke*, Reddin uses the Bay of Pigs incident to reflect on current US foreign policy in Latin America, following a young Yale graduate who encounters conflict between his ethics and his duty to the Central Intelligence Agency. *Highest Standard of Living* follows the studies and travels of a Columbia doctoral student in Moscow and after his return to New York, echoing the style of Russian theatre that proceeded Stalin's crackdown on artistic freedom, and combining political issues with humorous culture-clash jokes and an Act 2 tone reminiscent of Hollywood spy thrillers. Echoing the stark savage atmosphere of ✴DAVID MAMET's *Edmond*, *Big Time* illustrates the deterioration of personal relationships in the world of big business. The play is a sad look at the spoiled, self-centred American generation of the 1980s, where success and money claim priority.

The New Jersey veteran in *Life and Limb*, the Yale graduate in *Rum and Coke* and the travelling doctoral student in *Highest Standard of Living* all seem to reflect Reddin's own upbringing, experiences and idealistic search for hope in a cruel world. Paul in *Big Time* is caught up in the pace-money-drug fever of the business world, but he's also an idealist, a man who loves his work, fights for his girl, and believes in hard work.

The Donmar Warehouse staged the world premiere of *Frame 312*, a revisiting of the Kennedy assassination that intercuts scenes from the 1960s with the 1990s, as a woman reveals that she has frames from Abraham Zapruder's original film of Kennedy's assassination that show that there was a second assassin. The play opened in Britain because Reddin believes British theatre is more open to political drama, whereas, 'most of our drama is just domestic . . . the kid comes home, says, "I'm gay"; the mother says, "I have cancer", and they all hug. American drama is all about closure and reconciliation . . . I'm interested in stories that are more ambiguous'.

TRY THESE:

✴BARKER's *Alpha Alpha* and *That Good Between Us*, ✴BRENTON's *The Churchill Play* and *The Romans in Britain*, for their juxtaposition of historic events with current politics; Reddin himself acknowledges the influences of ✴HARE and ✴FO; ✴LUCIE's *Progress* and *Fashion* are less hopeful but criticise society even more harshly; ✴CRIMP and ✴JEFFREYS for more puncturing of 'yuppie' moves; *Synergy* is a Faustian satire about Hollywood comparable to ✴BRENTON and ✴HARE's *Pravda*; Reddin has adapted ✴BULGAKOV's *Black Snow*.

REID, Christina   [1942 –   ]
Northern Irish dramatist

PLAYS INCLUDE:
Did You Hear the One About the Irishman? (1982), *Tea in a China Cup* (1983), *Dissenting Adults* (1985), *Joyriders* (1986), *My Name, Shall I Tell You My Name* (1987), *The Belle of Belfast City* (1989), *Clowns* (1996), *I'm the King of the Castle* (1999)

Reid is an unsentimental, sardonic chronicler of the domestic minutiae by which communities pass on attitudes. Reid does not use the Belfast troubles as the centrepiece of her plays, but their existence is never very far away, controlling and determining destinies. *Tea in a China Cup*, for example, takes an irreverently humorous if painful look at matriarchal influences in the daily, domestic rituals of one working-class Protestant family over a fifty year span. *My Name, Shall I Tell You My Name*, a delicate two-hander about a grandfather, a survivor of the Somme and member of the Orange Order, and his granddaughter, also highlights the way views become entrenched through history and family. A fiercely pacifist play, it is equally a beautifully crafted study in human relationships, and a cry of anguished despair. *Joyriders*, by contrast, takes a tougher, almost surreal tone to show the effect of the Troubles on four young no-hopers from Belfast's notorious Divis Flats, paralleling their lives with those in ✴O'CASEY's *Shadow of a Gunman*. Reid returned to the characters in *Clowns*. In her BT National Theatre Connections play *I'm the King of the Castle* Reid explores the aftermath of World War II in Belfast.

TRY THESE:
For other images of Belfast, ✱DEVLIN's *Ourselves Alone*, like *Tea in a China Cup*, focuses on women-centred responses to their environment; ✱FINNEGAN, ✱MARIE JONES's *From the Balcony*, also set in the Divis Flats, for another, even wackier view of confronting everyday madness with madness; ✱GARY MITCHELL, ✱MORNIN, ✱MUNRO's *Bold Girls* also examine the effects on women of living in Belfast.

REZA, Yasmina   [1959 –   ]
French actress, dramatist and novelist

PLAYS INCLUDE:
Conversations après un enterrement (1987, *Conversations after a Burial*), *La Traversée de l'hiver* (1990, *Winter Crossing*), *Art* (1994), *L'homme du hazard* (1995, *The Unexpected Man*), *Trois versions de la vie* (2000, *Life × 3*)

Reza became an international figure with the phenomenal success of *Art*, which has won awards across Europe and America. *Art* deals with the reactions of a man's friends to his purchase of an expensive white-on-white painting. Essentially it's a reworking of the theme of the emperor's new clothes that raises the question of how to negotiate the value of friendship, of art and of social status. Although the play's phenomenal success may in part reflect the public perception that much modern art is too self-referential and self-absorbed and that monetary values are subverting aesthetic ones, it also explores the limits of friendship and how far we live in a world of surfaces (Serge, the painting's buyer, is a dermatologist). *The Unexpected Man* has also been an international hit. Again the premise is straightforward: an author travelling by train from Paris to Frankfurt shares a compartment with one of his fans and Reza explores the relationships between their perceptions of each other and actual reality, using monologue to contrast their different views. In *Life × 3* Reza takes an unfortunate social solecism – the dinner guests turning up a day early – and plays it through three times with minor changes leading to huge consequences.

TRY THESE:
✱WERTENBAKER's *Three Birds Alighting on a Field* for art, friendship and value; ✱AYCKBOURN for ingenious formal adventures with bourgeois rituals; ✱HAMPTON has translated Reza' plays into English and she has translated ✱BERKOFF's *Metamorphosis* into French.

RHONE, Trevor   [1940 –   ]
Jamaican dramatist

PLAYS INCLUDE:
Not My Fault, Baby (1965), *The Gadget* (1969), *Smile Orange* (1970), *Comic Strip* (1973), *Sleeper* (1974), *School's Out* (1975), *Old Story Time* (1979), *Two Can Play* (1980), *Everyman* (1981), *The Game* (1982), *One Stop Driver* (1992), *Dear Counselor* (1997), *Bellas Gate Boy* (2002)

Born in Kingston, Jamaica, Rhone went to Britain in the 1960s (where he studied at the Rose Bruford College) but returned to Jamaica disappointed with the roles offered to him as a black actor, which he later said didn't begin to express black lives. Out of this frustration eventually came the impetus to write plays that did, and a desire to set up a theatre in Jamaica. In 1965, with some colleagues, (including director Yvonne Brewster), he set up the Barn Theatre (initially in the garage of a friend's home) with a mix of both Caribbean and non-Caribbean plays.

He is best known outside his own country for comedies like *Smile Orange, Two Can Play* and *School's Out*. Rhone specialises in broad situation comedy (one of his role models is ✱ALAN AYCKBOURN) written with great verve and energy, inside which often lurk shrewd observations about Jamaican life. *Smile Orange*, a farcical treatment of tourists getting taken for a ride, has something serious to say about Third World economics and methods of survival; *School's Out*, for all its playful characterisation, is also a fairly pessimistic, highly critical portrait of the inadequacies of the Jamaican educational system, and reactionary attitudes that inhibit its change. *Two Can Play*, his most popular play, has been performed all over the world. It is an enjoyable if sentimental two-hander on the old theme of marriage, given a new twist to do with female enlightenment. Gloria and Jim are undergoing a crisis in their marriage; Gloria is the downtrodden family organiser, Jim the usual male chauvinist. Gloria goes north to the USA to make a marriage of convenience (the two are planning on emigration to escape the Jamaican political unrest of the 1970s) and her return triggers a reassessment and process of rediscovery for them both.

TRY THESE:

For more sparring couples, and resurgent wives, ✳DANIELS' *Ripen Our Darkness* and *The Devil's Gateway*; for more acid marital conflicts, ✳WHITEHEAD's *Alpha Beta*; for other Caribbean writers, ✳HILL, ✳WALCOTT, ✳WHITE.

RIBMAN, Ronald   [1932 –   ]
American dramatist

PLAYS INCLUDE:

Harry, Noon and Night (1965), *The Journey of the Fifth Horse* (1966), *The Ceremony of Innocence* (1967), *Passing Through from Exotic Places* (1969), *Fingernails Blue As Flowers* (1971), *The Poison Tree* (1973), *Cold Storage* (1976), *Buck* (1983), *Sweet Table at the Richelieu* (1987), *A Serpent's Egg* (1987), *The Rug Merchants of Chaos* (1991)

Ribman's characters are verbal and articulate, and his plays pose serious moral dilemmas that frequently end with unanswered questions. One could say Ribman expresses the theme of man's inhumanity to man, but this kind of simplistic reduction is unworthy of the material and fails to take into consideration his consistent presentation of victims who are often self-victimised. *Cold Storage*, Ribman's most successful play, is a black comedy about a pair of wheelchair-bound patients contemplating death. Armenian Joseph Parmigian and Jewish Richard Landau are cancer patients. The older Parmigian diabolically needles his younger companion. Landau becomes irritated and professes that his youth spent in a Nazi death camp has made him indifferent to life. Parmigian helps Landau to discover that what he takes for indifference is guilt – a guilt that has robbed Landau of life. The revelation provides the opportunity for Landau and Parmigian to share stories and come together. Their laughter begs the question whether the two men can sustain their courage. During the play, we see Landau's indifference begin to crumble and wonder whether Parmigian's wit is as centred as it seems.

TRY THESE:

✳FLANNERY's *Singer*, ✳LEBOW's *A Shayna Maiden* for the aftermath of the Holocaust; ✳DANIELS' *Masterpieces* and ✳MEYER's *Etta Jenks* for the pornography industry, which Ribman examines in *Buck*; ✳C. P. TAYLOR's *Good* for moral dilemmas presented wittily.

RICE, Elmer   [1892 – 1967]
American dramatist, director and producer

PLAYS INCLUDE:

On Trial (1914), *The House in Blind Alley* (1916), *The Iron Cross* (1917, with Frank Harris), *A Diadem of Snow* (1918), *For the Defense* (1919), *It Is the Law* (1922), *Wake Up, Jonathan!* (1921, with Hatcher Hughes), *The Adding Machine* (1923), *Close Harmony* (1924, with Dorothy Parker), *Cock Robin* (1928, with Peter Barry), *Street Scene* (1929), *The Left Bank* (1931), *Counsellor-at-Law* (1931), *We, the People* (1932), *Flight to the West* (1940), *A New Life* (1943), *Dream Girl* (1945), *The Winner* (1954), *Cue for Passion* (1958)

In Rice's career, passion and pragmatism reached an uneasy balance. The passion is that of a democratic leftist working for social causes; the utility is that of a theatre professional eager to make a good living.

Born Elmer Leopold Reizenstein, the son of a poor New York bookkeeper, Rice showed an early talent for language, logic and theatre. After working his way through law school, he quit his first legal job to write *On Trial*. This thriller murder melodrama, the hit of the 1914 season, is the first American play to use the technical device of the flashback.

Rice's next few plays show the influence of ✳IBSEN and ✳SHAW: they deal with progressive causes, including child labour reform, women's rights and the Russian Revolution. Unable to find producers, he returned to writing courtroom melodramas and other popular entertainments. For the rest of his career, he would alternate serious, experimental work with crowd-pleasing melodramas and comedies: he never succeeded in uniting the two.

The 1920s gave Rice his greatest artistic successes. *The Adding Machine*, a dark, expressionistic work, presents the universe as a heartless corporate enterprise in which human beings are mere raw material. *Street Scene* depicted life in New York's slums by revolving a number of subplots around a melodrama of love and murder. (A 1947 musical version of *Street Scene*, with lyrics by ✱LANGSTON HUGHES and music by Kurt Weill, is still occasionally performed.) *Street Scene* was the first of the many plays which Rice was to produce and direct. In the late 1930s, he organised the New York office of the Federal Theatre Project, the Roosevelt Administration's programme to employ out-of-work theatre people. There he played a central role in the development of the Federal Theatre's 'living newspapers', agitprop presentations of contemporary social problems. For the remainder of his career he continued alternating between commercial and experimental work.

TRY THESE:
For a nineteenth-century image of New York's slums, ✱BOUCICAULT's *The Poor of New York*; for urban criminals, ✱BRECHT's and Weill's *Threepenny Opera*, ✱GAY's *The Beggar's Opera*, ✱KAUFMAN and Hart; for American Expressionism, ✱O'NEILL's *The Emperor Jones*; for another expressionistic look at an automated society, Sophie Treadwell's *Machinal*.

RIDLEY, Philip   [1964 –   ]
British novelist and dramatist

PLAYS INCLUDE:
The Pitchfork Disney (1990), *The Fastest Clock in the Universe* (1992), *Ghost from a Perfect Place* (1994), *Fairytaleheart* (1998), *Apocalyptica* (1998), *Sparkleshark* (1999), *Vincent River* (2000)

Ridley still lives in the East End of London where he was born. He has written plays and novels for both children and adults. A common thread across his theatre work is the importance of storytelling, which is often seen in an almost psychoanalytical sense as having a therapeutic value in encouraging people to come to terms with their situations and to find ways through them (*Apocalyptica, Sparkleshark*). However, he trained at St Martin's School of Art and sees links between his theatre work and that of the artists who were represented in the 1997 Sensation exhibition. Certainly his stage images can be extremely lurid, and he was at the forefront of the nineties tendency towards explicit language and action. *The Pitchfork Disney* involves vomiting and cockroach eating, *The Fastest Clock in the Universe* has paedophilia and a pregnant woman being beaten up, and *Ghost from a Perfect Place* has an explicit torture scene. Since the torture victim is himself a Kray-like gangster (Ridley wrote the script of the film *The Krays*), our sympathies are not entirely with him, though the girl gang who are enlisted to do the torturing may not evoke much pity either. The violence in Ridley's work can be unsettling and it raises questions about the extent to which the portrayal of violence can itself consume an audience's capacity to react to what else is going on in the plays, but Ridley does raise many important issues about our society and how we respond to each other.

TRY THESE:
Ridley has been compared to the ancient Greek dramatists, (✱AESCHYLUS, ✱EURIPDES, ✱SOPHOCLES) both for his structure and for his use of violence; ✱BARKER, ✱BOND, ✱KANE, ✱ORTON, ✱PINTER, ✱SHEPARD, ✱TENNESSEE WILLIAMS for parallels and influences.

ROCHE, Billy   [1949 –   ]
Irish dramatist, singer and novelist

PLAYS INCLUDE:
A Handful of Stars (1988), *Poor Beast in the Rain* (1989), *Belfry* (1991), *Amphibians* (1992), *The Cavalcaders* (1993), *Haberdashery* (1998), *On Such As We* (2001)

Roche hails from Wexford, in the Irish Republic, which provides the location for his much-acclaimed Wexford trilogy, *A Handful of Stars* (which won the John Whiting Award), *Poor Beast in the Rain* and *Belfry*. Roche's Ireland is the traditional pastoral landscape familiar from stage and filmic tradition but it also reflects the growth of a modern world of creeping urban values replacing a moribund rural life (in *Amphibians* all except one of the herring fishermen have given up to work in the mussel-packing factory). Roche's characters have been sidelined from their dreams and tend to live in the mist of memory. But he treats each one with amused affection – nowhere more so than in *A Handful of Stars*, a funny, playful tale of initiation into manhood, a Wexford *Rebel Without a Cause*. The familiar dilemmas of whether to stay or leave for a possibly better life elsewhere are reflected in *Poor Beast in the Rain*, which is set in a Wexford betting shop. Danger Doyle coincidentally chooses the weekend of the All-Ireland hurling finals to return home to attempt to convince the adolescent daughter of the woman he ran away with ten years before to go to live with them in London. It finally doesn't seem to matter much whether or not the girl leaves the safety of a small town for the uncertainty of the metropolis. But Roche produces two hours of sparkling dialogue in the mouths of the six beautifully rounded characters. The plays tend to be driven by character rather than plot and his settings reflect the inconsequentially mundane lives of his characters: the billiard hall in *A Handful of Stars*, the betting shop in *Poor Beast in the Rain*, the shoe-repairers in *Cavalcaders* and the barber's shop in *On Such As We* all operate to underpin a precise observation of life that transcend the accidental to offer more universal insights.

TRY THESE:

✶SYNGE's *Playboy of the Western World* for another young Irish anti-hero; ✶FRIEL, ✶MCPHERSON, ✶MURPHY for parallels, ✶MCDONAGH for contrast.

ROWLEY, William   [c. 1585 – 1626]
English dramatist

PLAYS INCLUDE:
A Fair Quarrel (c. 1615 with ✶THOMAS MIDDLETON), *A Shoemaker, A Gentleman* (c. 1617), *The Witch of Edmonton* (1621, with ✶JOHN FORD and ✶THOMAS DEKKER), *The Changeling* (1622, with ✶THOMAS MIDDLETON)

Rowley, who was a comic actor, is noted for his collaborative works with others and probably had a hand in the writing of some fifty plays. *The Changeling* and *A Fair Quarrel* (both with ✶MIDDLETON) and *The Witch of Edmonton* (with ✶FORD and ✶DEKKER) are still performed. His own works are not revived, but the Globe gave a rehearsed reading of *A Shoemaker, A Gentleman* in 2000.

RUDET, Jacqueline   [1962 –   ]
British dramatist

PLAYS INCLUDE:
Money to Live (1984), *God's Second in Command* (1985), *Basin* (1985), *Take Back What's Yours* (1989)

Born in London's East End but brought up in Dominica, Rudet started out as an actress before forming her own group, Imani-Faith, to provide theatre for and about black women. A naturalistic writer with a television sense and lively line in dialogue, she made a dazzling debut with the hard-hitting *Money to Live* (presented by the Black Theatre Co-op), a domestic drama about stripping that tackled its subject with a rare lack of cant and undisguised anger at men who see women only as sexual objects. *Basin* is a conversation piece about the love and communality between black women, with Rudet's sparky dialogue providing some easy humour amongst the sometimes tense encounters as three women work out the meaning of friendship.

TRY THESE:

✶TERSON's *Strippers* for a rather more complex, treatment of the subject; ✶GEMS' *Treats* is set in a strip club; ✶ADSHEAD's *Thatcher's Women* and Julia Schofield's *Love on the Plastic* also look at the economic pressures and moral hypocrisies around prostitution; ✱KAY's *Chiaroscuro* for another play about black women exploring friendship, lesbianism and labels; ✱PINNOCK is another contemporary black playwright.

RUDKIN, (James) David   [1936 –   ]
British dramatist

PLAYS INCLUDE:
Afore Night Come (1960), *Burglars* (1970), *The Filth Hut* (1972), *Cries from Casement As His Bones Are Brought to Dublin* (1973), *Ashes* (1973), *No Title* (1974), *The Sons of Light* (1976), *Sovereignty Under Elizabeth* (1977), *Hansel and Gretel* (1980), *The Triumph of Death* (1981), *Space Invaders* (1984), *Will's Way* (1985), *The Saxon Shore* (1986)

Rudkin was hailed as a major playwright when *Afore Night Come*, already produced while he was an Oxford student, was taken up for production by the RSC in 1962. The play touches on themes which are developed in his later work, such as concern for the countryside, abhorrence of atomic weapons, chemical and other pollution, the idea of homosexuality as a natural and innocent manifestation of love, and an awareness of English–Irish confrontation, while his dialogue is both richly poetic and steeped in the rural, Anglo-Saxon dialects of his own area around the Black Country and Worcestershire. Its revival in 2001 was greeted with respect rather than acclamation, with recognition of its historical importance rather than its continued vitality. In *Afore Night Come* the continuity with the past seems ominous and evil but in other work, such as the television play *Penda's Fen* (1974), the past (in the persons of King Penda and Sir Edward Elgar) seems to be in guardianship, though *White Lady* (1987) showed nature overwhelmed by deadly petrochemicals.

Afore Night Come remains the most accessible of Rudkin's major stage works. More complicated structures appear in *Ashes*, a searingly painful account of an infertile couple's attempts to have a child (a fairly blatant – and equally anguished – metaphor for the violence and sterility of the Northern Ireland situation) that also offers political, anthropological and psychological viewpoints. *The Triumph of Death*, partly about Martin Luther, is concerned with the way that organised Christianity seeks power through association with established forces. Rudkin comes from a revivalist background but his plays question the ideology of sectarian religion and seek a closer communion with the natural world. They can be bafflingly dense, with allusions to Christian and pre-Christian mythologies as in *The Sons of Light*, a complex science-fantasy fable worked on over eleven years (1965–76) resulting in an eight to nine-hour play which was reshaped to about three hours' playing time and then further cut for the published text as performed by the RSC in 1977. Dedicated to the late Dr Robert Ollendorf, a Reichian therapist of whom the character Nebewohl is a portrait in reverse, it is divided into three main sections linked to the stages of the Christian mythology of the 'Harrowing of Hell'. It is set on a Scottish island ruled by a 'Benefactor' operating a religion of vengeance. Beneath the earth is a factory colony of workers kept from rebellion by a promise of heaven. A new pastor and his sons arrive, one of whom eventually descends among the workers, reawakens their self-awareness and destroys the subterranean complex to reclaim the island for its inhabitants. This is paralleled by the reclamation of a young girl from schizophrenia – a resurrection of both the individual and the culture from spiritual and religious repressions.

TRY THESE:
✱TREVOR GRIFFITHS and ✱RECKORD for Reichian influences; ✱CRAZE's *Shona*, ✱EDGAR's *Mary Barnes* for contemporary treatment of schizophrenia; for Caribbean exploration of pre-Christianity; ✱CROSS's *Mass Carib* and *Blues for Railton*; for writers of dialect, ✱CHURCHILL's *Fen*, ✱WARD's *Apart from George*; ✱ARDEN and D'Arcy for similar antipathies to the British establishment; for another image of infertility, ✱LORCA's *Yerma*; for Irish anguish, ✱MCDONAGH, ✱O'CASEY; for illness on stage, ✱GANNON, ✱NICHOLS' *A Day in the Death of Joe Egg*, ✱SOPHOCLES' *Philoctetes*; for moral disgust, ✱ANOUILH, ✱BECKETT; for equally gory physical detail, ✱KANE's *Blasted*,

✱ SHAKESPEARE's *Titus Andronicus*; Rudkin's adaptations include ✱ EURIPIDES' *Hippolytus*, ✱ GENET's *Deathwatch* and *The Maids*, ✱ IBSEN's *Peer Gynt* and *When We Dead Awaken*.

RUSSELL, Willy   [1947 –   ]
British dramatist, songwriter and singer

PLAYS INCLUDE

Keep Your Eyes Down (1971), *Sam O'Shanker* (1972, musical version 1973), *When the Reds* (1972), *Tam Lin* (1972), *John, Paul, George, Ringo and . . . Bert* (1974), *Breezeblock Park* (1975), *One for the Road* (1976, originally *Painted Veg and Parkinson*), *Stags and Hens* (1978), *Educating Rita* (1979), *Blood Brothers* (1981, musical version 1983), *Our Day Out* (1983, from 1977 TV play), *Shirley Valentine* (1986)

One of the most often produced contemporary dramatists, Russell's work is closely linked with Liverpool (he was born in nearby Whiston) and the Everyman Theatre, which mounted his first professional production and commissioned other plays from him, including *John, Paul, George, Ringo and . . . Bert*. This musical about the Beatles brought him national success and was called 'a powerful statement about innocence and corruption that is also an hilariously funny evening out'. Such a balance between comment and exhilarating entertainment can be found right through Russell's work. *Educating Rita*, a two-hander about a middle-aged lecturer and a 'raw-diamond' working-class woman student – especially in its film version – put Russell on the international map. Russell himself left school at fifteen, returning to college years later because he had decided to become a teacher and a playwright, although the play probably owes as much to his regional background and time spent as a ladies' hairdresser. Many regard him as totally unpatronising about the working class, and his female characters are particularly vivid. In both *Educating Rita* and *Shirley Valentine* – a Liverpudlian monologue with marvellous jokes (but little feminist consciousness) – he makes use of minimal resources, but he is equally adept at handling large groups of characters. A good example is *Stags and Hens*

(filmed as *Dancing Thru' the Dark*), in which bride and groom, each with their own friends on a last, prenuptial night out, both choose the same club for their celebration. In this shrieking, puking world, with major sections set in the toilets, Russell is no outsider and audiences can share both the fun and pain of his characters at grass-roots level.

Blood Brothers

Loosely based on the old 'Corsican Brothers' story of twins brought up in different classes, *Blood Brothers* has a superb creation in the character of the working-class mother. It is a deeply felt picture of different social backgrounds, although its middle-class characters are perhaps less convincing than the working-class ones, despite the parable-like nature of its overall construction. The songs are able to succeed outside the show, but they are an integral and necessary part, adding to our understanding of the characters. A very long running smash hit that offered a social document disguised as melodrama, although some regard it as the opposite.

TRY THESE:

✱ BOUCICAULT for *The Corsican Brothers*; for the north, ✱ BLEASDALE, ✱ BRIGHOUSE, ✱ DELANEY, ✱ DUNBAR, ✱ HORSFIELD, ✱ HOUGHTON, ✱ PLATER, ✱ WATERHOUSE and Willis Hall's *Billy Liar*; ✱ GODBER's *Bouncers* for a graphic, funny, but essentially damning portrait of British yobbism at play.

S

SACKLER, Howard [1929 – 82]
American dramatist

PLAYS INCLUDE:
Uriel Acosta (1954), *The Yellow Loves* (1959), *A Few Inquiries* (1964), *The Pastime of Monsieur Robert* (1966), *The Great White Hope* (1967), *Goodbye, Fidel* (1980), *Semmelweiss* (1981)

Born in New York, Sackler started out as a poet and worked on films throughout his life, but he remains best known for his 1967 play *The Great White Hope*, a thinly fictionalised account of the celebrated African-American boxer Jack Johnson, who became the world heavyweight champion in 1908. A sprawling epic, the play is socially and ethically exemplary; as drama, however, it has dated. Sackler was writing from the viewpoint of late 1960s white liberal guilt, and too many of the play's would-be challenges to the audience have more to do with assuaging Sackler's own uneasy conscience than with any genuine assault on the fourth wall. His follow-up plays were equally episodic, but nowhere near as successful, particularly *Goodbye, Fidel*, a rambling saga about a patrician Cuban widow about to be exiled from a country in tumult.

TRY THESE:
✱MILLER for social conscience; ✱BALDWIN and ✱HANSBERRY for other representations of black experience from before the Black Power era; ✱FULLER, ✱AUGUST WILSON, ✱WOLFE for later black treatments of racism; ✱PAGE's *Golden Girls* for a rare account of women and sport and racism; ✱FUGARD for a contrasting white playwright tackling large issues of racism and social awareness.

SAMUELS, Diane [1960 –]
British dramatist

PLAYS INCLUDE:
Kindertransport (1993), *100 Million Footsteps* (1997), *The True Life Fiction of Mata Hari* (2002)

Samuels explores characters trapped between possible realities in both *Kindertransport* and *The True Life Fiction of Mata Hari*. Eva, who escapes from Nazi Germany on one of the trains that brought out Jewish children (the Kindertransport of the title), builds a new life but is forced to confront the reality of her origins when her daughter accidentally discovers some forgotten letters. In *The True Life Fiction of Mata Hari*, the eponymous World War I spy is being questioned about giving information to the Germans but the truth is concealed beneath layers of misinformation.

TRY THESE:
✱SHERMAN's *Bent*, ✱PASCAL, ✱SOBOL for the Holocaust; ✱STOPPARD's *Hapgood*, ✱WHITEMORE's *Pack of Lies* for other spies.

SAROYAN, William [1908 – 81]
American dramatist

PLAYS INCLUDE:
My Heart's in the Highlands (1939), *The Time of Your Life* (1939), *Love's Old Sweet Song* (1940), *The Beautiful People* (1941), *Across the Board on Tomorrow Morning* (1942), *Talking to You* (1942), *Hello, Out There* (1942), *Get Away Old Man* (1943), *The Cave Dwellers* (1957), *Sam the Highest Jumper of Them All* (1960)

After the successes of his first two plays Saroyan's career appeared to be as bright and positive as the characters in them (*The Time of Your Life* won both the New York Drama

Critics' Circle Award and the Pulitzer Prize). However, his lack of discipline as a playwright and erratic behaviour as a collaborator made it impossible for him to develop his talents. Critics became tired and suspicious of his easy optimism during World War II, and later his impressionistic characters seemed out of place with the revelations of Nazi atrocities. Not until twelve years after the war did another Saroyan play, *The Cave Dwellers*, win a Broadway mounting. *The Cave Dwellers*, depicting a collection of misfits occupying a theatre slated for demolition, seemed to fit in with the Theatre of the Absurd vogue. However, Saroyan's sentimental ending betrayed the play's anachronistic point of view.

The Time of Your Life

The habitués of Nick's Saloon on the San Francisco waterfront are a fascinating lot of exuberant misfits: Joe, a young loafer with money and a good heart; Tom, his disciple and errand boy; Kitty, the whore with the heart of gold; Kit Carson, an old Indian fighter; Willy, the pinball maniac; Harry, a natural-born hoofer; an Arab harmonica player; and a Negro, a boogie-woogie pianist. Into this company comes a group of society slummers and later Blick, heel and head of the Vice Squad. Blick intends to arrest Kitty, but first he intends to force her to strip. In the ensuing action, Carson shoots Blick and the pinball machine spouts coins and flashes forth 'American Destiny'. The Arab says, 'No foundation. All the way down the line': an apt description of Saroyan's comedy. Still, the play has been frequently revived with success on both sides of the Atlantic. Produced as a period piece, it continues to please audiences.

TRY THESE:

✹ O'NEILL's *The Iceman Cometh* is *the* saloon-bar tragedy; Robert Patrick's *Kennedy's Children* uses a bar-room setting; ✹ OSBORNE's *The Entertainer* for decay in the theatre; ✹ KAUFMAN and Hart for commercially successful warm-hearted plays.

SARTRE, Jean-Paul   [1905 – 80]
French philosopher, novelist and dramatist

PLAYS INCLUDE:

Les Mouches (1943, *The Flies*), *Huis Clos* (1944, *No Exit, Vicious Circle* or *In Camera*), *Les Mains Sales* (1948, *Crime Passionnel, The Assassin* or *Dirty Hands*), *Le Diable et le Bon Dieu* (1951, *The Devil and the Good Lord* or *Lucifer and the Lord*), *Kean* (1953, after Dumas père), *Les Séquestrés d'Altona* (1959, *Altona* or *Loser Wins*)

Playwriting was never Sartre's main occupation, but he had a high degree of success with it, and his plays and his philosophy interact in an interesting manner. His first known play is *Bariona*, a nativity play he wrote in a prisoner-of-war camp in 1940, and staged there with the help of priests; it was a semi-disguised anti-colonialist play about the occupation of Judea. He subsequently favoured a 'theatre of situations' rather than a psychological theatre, with characters defined by their actions rather than their intentions, the better to explore his ideas about existentialism and the possibility of individual freedom. *The Flies* shows Orestes accepting full responsibility for the killing of Aegisthus, rather than being a prey to fate, as in the Greek versions. It also has overtones of French attitudes, including Sartre's own, to the Nazi occupation. *In Camera*, with its gradual revelation that the scene is hell, and its three characters who have lived in 'bad faith' must stay there for eternity, is perhaps his best bit of construction. In *The Devil and the Good Lord* the hero manages to achieve 'authenticity' in his actions (of which Sartre approved) by rejecting in turn attempts to be thoroughly evil or thoroughly good. By the time he reached *Altona*, however, Sartre had given up hope about man's ability to choose how to act, and adopted a Marxist perspective towards what seems to be the development of post-war Germany but is in fact a metaphor for the French war in Algeria.

Sartre's plays were important in opening post-war French drama to serious subjects, and in persuading playwrights to engage with politics and philosophy, but they were not experimental in form. For Sartre, anti-capitalism implied no break with Aristotelian models of theatre; unlike *BRECHT, he used fairly conventional and illusionistic forms of playmaking, though his characters do now seem to talk a lot. *IONESCO called his plays political melodramas, but this underestimates their complexity and ambiguity. Satre was awarded, but declined, the 1964 Nobel Prize for Literature.

Kean

Kean is a reworking of Dumas père's Romantic drama, with substantial additions, and it is the play that displays most clearly Sartre's idea of theatre. Kean's ontological insecurities impel him to assume identities not his own (for he has none); at the same time, his free access to both princes and people gives him and others the illusion that it is easy for genius to move up in a class-ridden world. Kean's constant awareness of his own psychological and social paradoxes allowed Sartre to turn theatre against itself without using Brechtian techniques of disjunction. Kean is also a marvellous part for a bravura actor.

TRY THESE:
Albert Camus for French plays with philosophical content; *ARDEN and D'Arcy for *The Business of Good Government*, another Nativity play with a political message; *PIRANDELLO for the questioning of the distinction between acting and life; *BRECHT for anti-capitalist plays with non-Aristotelian forms; *AESCHYLUS, *EURIPIDES, *SOPHOCLES for Greek tragedy; *ELIOT for a dramatist who consciously tried to refute Sartre's ideas.

SAUNDERS, James   [1925 –   ]
British dramatist

PLAYS INCLUDE:
Alas, Poor Fred: A Duologue in the Style of Ionesco (1959), *Next Time I'll Sing to You* (1962), *A Scent of Flowers* (1964), *The Italian Girl* (1967, with Iris Murdoch, from her novel), *The Borage Pigeon Affair* (1969), *Bodies* (1977), *The Girl in Melanie Klein* (1980, from *RONALD HARWOOD), *Fall* (1981), *Making It Better* (radio 1991, staged 1992)

Saunders has written in many styles with considerable success but his best-known works are probably *Next Time I'll Sing to You* and *Bodies*. In the early 1960s, there was considerable interest in the life of a hermit, Jimmy Mason, who died in 1942 (*EDWARD BOND's *The Pope's Wedding* is partly a response to his story), but in *Next Time I'll Sing to You* Saunders devotes most of the dramatic action to a desultory attempt by a group of actors trying to stage a play about Mason. The apparently disorganised inconsequential presentation leaves a space through which we gradually come to question not only the reasons for his particular mode of existence but also our own. *Bodies* takes a familiar theme of two couples who had committed adultery with each other meeting many years later. Each couple has, apparently, tackled their problems differently but, as Tish Dace suggests, Saunders has dramatised 'alternative routes to wasting one's personal emotional riches'.

TRY THESE:
*BECKETT, *IONESCO for Saunders' absurdist elements; *AYCKBOURN generally for theatrical games playing, and *Absent Friends* for a comparison with *A Scent of Flowers*; *PRIESTLEY for another dramatist who collaborated with Iris Murdoch.

SCHILLER, Johann Christoph Friedrich von   [1759 – 1805]
German dramatist and poet

PLAYS INCLUDE:
Die Räuber (1782, *The Robbers* or *The Highwaymen*), *Fiesco* (1782), *Kabale und Liebe* (1784, *Intrigue and Love*), *Don Carlos* (1787), the *Wallenstein* trilogy (1798–9), *Maria Stuart* (1800, *Mary Stuart*), *Wilhelm Tell* (1804, *William Tell*)

Schiller, the son of an army surgeon, was a young military doctor himself when his first play, *Die Räuber*, appeared – though safely set in the sixteenth century, it was an instant success for its contemporary revolutionary appeal, its *Sturm und Drang* claims for the rights of the individual, and its doubling of the parts of the good and bad brothers.

Schiller went on to become one of the major German verse playwrights, a professor of history at the University of Jena, and a close friend of *GOETHE, but he never had quite enough money to live on, and never quite achieved respectability. *Maria Stuart* has the characteristics of all Schiller's 'historical' plays: powerful language, long aria-like speeches, dramatic confrontations, and a somewhat cavalier attitude to historical fact. The 'big scene' is a meeting between Mary Stuart and Elizabeth Tudor that never actually happened, and both queens are courted by a vacillating Lord Leicester. It makes a splendid, somewhat operatic play (and indeed a fine opera by Donizetti), but its success in southern Britain is perhaps inhibited by the national difficulty in taking seriously a play which casts Elizabeth I as the villain.

TRY THESE:
*GOETHE for eighteenth century German verse tragedy; *FO for a similar failure to understand Elizabeth I, *CORNEILLE and *RACINE for French classical tragedy; *SHAKESPEARE's history plays also take liberties with historical fact for dramatic effect; *LOCHHEAD's *Mary Queen of Scots* for a contemporary Scottish perspective; *BOLT's *Vivat! Vivat! Regina* for another attempt to deal with Elizabeth and Mary.

SCHIMMELPFENNIG, Roland   [1967 –]
German dramatist

PLAYS INCLUDE:
Die ewige Maria (1996, *The Eternal Maria*), *Keine Arbeit für die junge Frau im Frühlingskleid* (1996, *No Work for the Young Woman in the Spring Dress*), *Die Zwiefachen* (1997, *The Duplicates*), *Aus den Städten in die Wälder, aus den Wäldern in die Städte* (1998, *From the Cities into the Woods, From the Woods into the Cities*), *Fisch um Fisch* (1999, *Fish for Fish*), *Vor langer Zeit im Mai* (2000, *A Long Time Ago in May*), *MEZ* (2000), *Die arabische Nacht* (2001, *Arabian Night*), *Push Up 1–3* (2001, *Push Up*)

Still relatively little known in Britain, Schimmelpfennig has been widely staged in Germany where he was a dramaturg at the Schaubühne in Berlin. *Push Up*, seen at the Royal Court in 2002, is about office politics and the failure of a female boss to help the career of another woman in the office. Interestingly, the author intercuts the present scenes with monologues from the protagonists that explore the reasons for their positions in the main encounters. In *Arabian Night* (toured by the Actors Touring Company, also in 2002) the setting is a decaying tower block in which the lives and fantasies of the inhabitants intersect on a hot summer evening.

TRY THESE:
*CHURCHILL's *Top Girls*, *VINAVER for office politics; *NICHOLS' *Passion Play* for revelations of underlying thoughts; *THOMPSON, *TREMBLAY's *Solemn Mass* for urban landscapes to compare with *Arabian Night*; *STRAUSS for an older contemporary.

SCHISGAL, Murray   [1926 –]
American dramatist

PLAYS INCLUDE:
The Typists (1960), *The Tiger* (1960), *Luv* (1964), *Fragments* (1967), *The Basement* (1967), *Jimmy Shine* (1968), *A Way of Life* (1969), *An American Millionaire* (1974), *All Over Town* (1974), *Twice Around the Park* (1982), *The Rabbi and the Toyota Dealer* (1985), *Road Show* (1987)

Since he launched his playwriting career in London in 1960 with a series of one-act plays at the British Drama League, New York-born Schisgal has written fifty plays – many of them little-known one-acts – and a variety of television shows and films, pre-eminently the Oscar-winning smash *Tootsie* (1982). His first New York success, *Luv*, is a three-character absurdist farce in which the suicidal Harry Berlin meets former schoolmate Milt Manville, who decides to unload his wife Ellen on the hapless Harry. The play once thought to make Schisgal 'a household word', it prompted critic Walter Kerr's dubious encomium that Luv was better than *Waiting for Godot*. In *Jimmy Shine*, a comic vaudeville about despair, a failed abstract painter looks back on a life of frustration and fantasy. *All*

Over Town, a ✱FEYDEAUESQUE farce set amidst Manhattan neurotics, is a mixed-identity comedy in which a canny black delivery boy called Lewis is mistaken for an unemployed, lusty white youth called Louie Lucas. *Road Show* is a comedy about midlife crisis centring on two high-school lovers who meet twenty years on.

TRY THESE:
✱SIMON (especially *The Prisoner of Second Avenue*), ✱FEIFFER, ✱GARDNER's *I'm Not Rappaport* for New York neuroticism and urban misadventures; ✱KOPIT's *Oh Dad, Poor Dad* for ✱IONESCO-influenced high jinks comparable to *Luv*; ✱BECKETT for the real thing.

SCHNITZLER, Arthur   [1862 – 1931]
Austrian dramatist

PLAYS INCLUDE
Anatol (1893), *Liebelei* (1895, *Dalliance*), *Das Weite Land* (1911, *Undiscovered Country*), *Reigen* (1902, *La Ronde*), *Der Einsame Weg* (1904, *The Lonely Road*)

Schnitzler, the son of a rich Jewish doctor, studied medicine and psychoanalysis in late nineteenth-century Vienna, and his plays about the Viennese permissive society combine light comedy, satire, voyeurism and apparent disapproval in an uneasy but appealing mixture. The plays are predictably popular today: ✱TOM STOPPARD's free translations *Undiscovered Country* and *Dalliance* appeared at the National Theatre in 1979 and 1985 respectively. In 1982, as soon as *La Ronde* came out of copyright, there were three staged versions and one televised version of it within three months *La Ronde* is a series of ten episodes (the Prostitute picks up the Soldier, the Soldier seduces the Chambermaid, the Chambermaid seduces the Young Gentleman . . . the Count picks up the Prostitute). Its first performance in Berlin in 1920 was greeted with shock-horror and prosecutions of all concerned. It had a similar reception in Vienna in 1921, as did Max Ophuls' film version in 1950, though the film is far less sour and realistic than Schnitzler's original.

TRY THESE:
Robert David Macdonald has translated Schnitzler; ✱WEDEKIND's *Lulu* for erotic cynicism, ✱MOLNAR for Austro-Hungarian comedy, but with quite a different tone; ✱NESTROY for another Viennese dramatist translated by ✱STOPPARD; ✱NOËL GREIG's *Angels Descend on Paris* for more sexual role-playing; ✱GENET's *The Maids* and *The Balcony* for role-playing taken to a high art; the broad structure of *La Ronde* has been the inspiration for a number of contemporary works, some specifically inspired by the play, others utilising the idea of a chain of writers or scenes, including ✱HARE's *The Blue Room*, Sarah Phelps' *Modern Dance for Beginners*, Carlo Gebler's *Ten Rounds*, ✱FANNIN, Stephen Greenhorn, ✱MORGAN and ✱RAVENHILL's *Sleeping Around*, the *NT 25 Chain Play* (by ✱SEBASTIAN BARRY, ✱BENT, ✱BLOCK, ✱BUFFINI, ✱BURKE, ✱DANIELS, ✱DEAR, Anthony Drewe, ✱ELYOT, ✱GUPTA, ✱ZINNIE HARRIS, ✱TERRY JOHNSON, ✱CHARLOTTE JONES, ✱LEE HALL, ✱HARVEY, ✱LAN, ✱MCGUINNESS, Angus MacKechnie, ✱MARBER, ✱RIDLEY, Bella Rodrigues, ✱SHERMAN, Stephen Sondheim, ✱STAFFORD, ✱STEPHENSON, George Stiles, ✱TEEVAN), Oleg and Vladimir Presnayakov's *Terrorism*, Bonnie Greer's *Jitterbug*.

SENECA, Lucius Annaeus   [c. 4 BC – 65 AD]
Roman philosopher and dramatist

PLAYS INCLUDE:
Medea, Phaedra, Agamemnon, Oedipus, Thyestes

Seneca's verse plays were almost certainly not intended for the public stage, but scholars disagree as to how (if at all) they were performed at Nero's court – the view that they were intended for dramatic recitation seems to owe something to their long rhetorical speeches, and something to so-called 'unstageable' scenes such as the reassembling of Hippolytus' dismembered body by his father. However, their static action and bloodthirsty plots were a major influence on the Elizabethan playwrights (e.g. ✱SHAKESPEARE's *Titus Andronicus* and ✱KYD's *The Spanish Tragedy*). ✱ARTAUD, who regarded Seneca as the greatest classical dramatist and the nearest in approach to his projected Theatre of

Cruelty, planned to stage his own adaptation of *Thyestes* in 1934. The most important major production of a play by Seneca remains Peter Brook's *Oedipus*, in a version by Ted Hughes, at the Old Vic in 1968. The production combined a powerful and direct text, filled with violent images of bloodshed and horror, delivered in a distanced monotone by largely static actors; complex choral work broken up into separate sounds and rhythms, wails and hums and hisses, accompanied by electronic music; and a light political dusting of possible references to Vietnam. It was an interesting mixture of the *ARTAUDIAN and the *BRECHTIAN, and was received with respect (though it was said of Brook that he had 'gradually become the purveyor of avant-garde clichés to the mass audience').

TRY THESE:

*SHAKESPEARE for *Titus Andronicus*; *EURIPIDES, *RACINE for versions of the Hippolytus/Phaedra story; *ARTAUD for the Theatre of Cruelty; Robert Wilson, whose *Civil Wars* includes a section based on Seneca's Hercules plays.

SHAFFER, Anthony (Joshua) [1926 – 2001]
British dramatist and novelist

PLAYS INCLUDE:

This Savage Parade (1963), *Sleuth* (1970), *Murderer* (1975), *Widow's Weeds* (1977), *The Case of the Oily Levantine* (1979, also known as *Whodunnit*)

Shaffer was a barrister before moving into film and television production and then becoming a full-time writer in 1969. *This Savage Parade*, originally given only a Sunday-night performance but revived later, concerns the secret trial of a Nazi war criminal in Israel. Only *Sleuth* has gained both critical and popular acclaim. It is both a clever and intricate thriller and a parody of the genre. The protagonist is even a thriller writer, who plans to avenge himself on his wife's lover. With a construction like a series of Chinese boxes it demonstrates great technical skill. Though the characterisations never attempt to rise above those of the conventional thriller, they offer the opportunity for bravura perform-

ances. It was successfully revived in 1999 and 2002, on both occasions with Peter Bowles.

Shaffer wrote the screenplay for *Sleuth*, *The Wicker Man* and *Frenzy* as well as collaborating on a number of novels with his twin brother, *PETER SHAFFER.

TRY THESE:

Robert Shaw's *The Man in the Glass Booth* for another play about the trial of a war criminal; *STOPPARD's *The Real Inspector Hound* for thriller parody; Ira Levin's *Deathtrap* for a similar kind of plot; *HAMPTON's *The Portage to San Cristobal of A.H.* for a play about the Israelis and war criminals; Joseph Kesselring's *Arsenic and Old Lace* for a comedy thriller; *CHRISTIE (Shaffer wrote the screenplays for three films with Peter Ustinov as Hercule Poirot), Wilkie Collins' *The Woman in White* and Stephen Mallatratt's very successful adaptation of Susan Hill's *The Woman in Black* for thrillers.

SHAFFER, Peter [1926 –   ]
British dramatist

PLAYS INCLUDE:

Five Finger Exercise (1958), *The Private Ear* (1962), *The Public Eye* (1962), *The Royal Hunt of the Sun* (1964), *Black Comedy* (1965), *White Lies* (1967, revised as *White Liars*, 1968), *The Battle of Shrivings* (1970, revised as *Shrivings*, 1975), *Equus* (1973), *Amadeus* (1979), *Yonadab* (1985), *Lettice and Lovage* (1987), *Whom Do I Have the Honour of Addressing?* (radio 1989, staged 1996), *The Gift of the Gorgon* (1992)

Born in Liverpool and educated at Cambridge, Shaffer perpetuates infinite variations on a theme: the conflicts between reason and faith/mediocrity and genius/man and God, as examined from a variety of historical viewpoints. In *The Royal Hunt of the Sun* the debate occurs between Atahualpa and Pizarro, the Inca and the atheistic Spanish conqueror of Peru. In *Equus*, it is a clash between a psychoanalyst and his charge – a self-tormenting doctor devoid of passion and the patient who has committed an extraordinary act of passion and violence. *Amadeus*, which became an acclaimed Oscar-winning film in 1984, shifts the argument to the creative arena, as it pits the aberrant

Amadeus by Peter Shaffer, directed by Peter Hall, Old Vic Theatre, 1998. David Suchet as Salieri. (Nigel Norrington/ArenaPAL)

genius Wolfgang Amadeus Mozart against the decent but uninspired court composer Antonio Salieri, who may or may not have poisoned him. The play has been very successful, partly because of the opportunities to present Mozart's musical genius, partly because of the opportunity to present his scatological mindset. In all three plays, Shaffer weds his argument to a strong sense of the theatrical, not to mention an underlying repressed homoeroticism. The former, if not the latter, forsook him in the biblical *Yonadab*, an *Amadeus*-like tale of envy drawn from the Old Testament's Second Book of Samuel.

Shaffer has written comedy, as well, including four plays for Maggie Smith: *The Private Ear, The Public Eye, Black Comedy* (in which the stage is lit when the characters think it is dark and vice versa), and *Lettice and Lovage*, in which the two heroines enact their own variant on Shaffer's obsessive opposition of the eccentric outsider (Lettice) and the social conformist (Lotte). In *The Gift of the Gorgon* the conflict is between a recently dead dramatist and his wife, as re-enacted for his obsessed unacknowledged son. Set on a Greek island and drawing on the myth of Perseus and Medusa, it once again pits intellect against emotion, passion against the rational.

Shaffer is a committed reviser of his own work, and as well as the named variants mentioned in the play list the majority of his plays have been reworked for major revivals. Is Shaffer a great playwright or merely a clever manipulator of the middlebrow? The jury is out on that, but one thing is clear: Shaffer has a highly developed sense of the market second to none.

Equus

A stable boy blinds six horses after a frustrated sexual liaison in Shaffer's award-winning play, which was a huge hit both in London (with Alec McCowen) and on Broadway (with Anthony Hopkins and – among others – Richard Burton, later in the run) in John Dexter's mightily theatrical, swift production. Burton starred in Sidney Lumet's ill-fated 1977 film, where the realism of the genre mitigated the thesis of the play. How could one put any faith in Dr Dysart's envy for the tormented Alan, when we had just seen, in full blood-drenched realism, the climactic episode that was supposed to have triggered such thoughts? The film has the odd effect of rendering hollow and emptily rhetorical what on stage is a verbal thrill: the agony between the self-laceratingly literate Dysart and his semi-articulate, disturbed young patient – a tension between the realms of intellect and passion that is a thematic constant for this playwright.

TRY THESE:

✱MERCER for celebrations of the rebel; John Peielmeier's *Agnes of God*, ✱POMERANCE's *The Elephant Man* for plays that pit doctors against patients, and definitions of normality against an unhingement that may be preferable; for historical sweep, ✱BOLT's *A Man for All Seasons*, ✱WHITING's *The Devils* and, by contrast, ✱DEAR's debunking *The Art of Success* for a similar and shocking reassessment of an artist; ✱POWNALL for composers; ✱TERRY JOHNSON and ✱WRIGHT for psychologists/psychiatrists; *Black Comedy* was paired with ✱STOPPARD's *The Real Inspector Hound* for a revival in 1999; John Peter compared *The Gift of the Gorgon* to ✱EURIPIDES' *Bacchae*.

SHAKESPEARE, William   [1564 – 1616]
English dramatist

PLAYS (MANY DATES APPROXIMATE) INCLUDE: *Henry VI, Parts II* and *III* (1591), *The Comedy of Errors* (1592), *Henry VI, Part I* (1592), *Richard III* (1593), *The Two Gentlemen of Verona* (1593), *The Taming of the Shrew* (1594), *Titus Andronicus* (1594), *Love's Labour's Lost* (1595), *Richard II* (1595), *Romeo and Juliet* (1595), *A Midsummer Night's Dream* (1595), *King John* (1596), *The Merchant of Venice* (1596), *Henry IV, Parts I* and *II* (1597), *Much Ado About Nothing* (1598), *As You Like It* (1599), *Henry V* (1599), *Julius Caesar* (1599), *The Merry Wives of Windsor* (1600), *Twelfth Night* (1600), *Hamlet* (1601), *All's Well That Ends Well* (1602), *Troilus and Cressida* (1602), *Measure for Measure* (1604), *Othello* (1604), *King Lear* (1605), *Macbeth* (1606), *Antony and Cleopatra* (1607), *Timon of Athens* (1607), *Coriolanus* (1608), *Pericles* (1608), *Cymbeline* (1609), *The Winter's Tale* (1610), *The Tempest* (1611), *Henry VIII* (1613, with

✱JOHN FLETCHER), *The Two Noble Kinsmen* (1613, with ✱JOHN FLETCHER)

Shakespeare was a dramatist, actor, poet, land and theatre owner. He wrote most of his plays for the company of which he was part owner, and worked in all the popular genres of his time. He also wrote *Cardenio* with ✱FLETCHER (now lost) and probably part of *Sir Thomas More*. Many other Renaissance plays have been attributed to him, often on scanty or non-existent evidence. The strongest recent claims have been made for *Edmund Ironside* and for *Edward III* (*c.* 1594), which is increasingly accepted as being Shakespearian and was given the imprimatur of a Royal Shakespeare Company production in 2002.

Shakespeare's plays based on English history cover the period from *King John* to *Henry VIII* and include two tetralogies (*Richard II, Henry IV, Parts I* and *II*, and *Henry V* form one, and *Henry VI, Parts I, II* and *III* and *Richard III* the other), which are extremely effective when performed as a group (as done by the RSC in John Barton's adaptations under the title of *The Wars of the Roses* in the 1960s and readapted in 1988 by ✱CHARLES WOOD as *The Plantagenets*), even though they are perfectly viable as individual plays. The English Shakespeare Company went one further than the RSC in staging both tetralogies in tandem with considerable success. *Richard III* and *Henry V* have always attracted bravura interpretations, as has Falstaff in *Henry IV*. Shakespeare also wrote four plays drawn from Roman history (*Titus Andronicus, Julius Caesar, Antony and Cleopatra, Coriolanus*). *Julius Caesar* and *Antony and Cleopatra* form a linked pair, although the politics of *Julius Caesar* is exclusively social whereas that of *Antony and Cleopatra* is also sexual. *Titus Andronicus* is a fine example of revenge tragedy, considered unstageable until Peter Brook showed the way with Laurence Olivier in 1955, but now a fairly regular sighting. *Coriolanus* is sometimes seen as a political vehicle (though there is dispute about whether its sympathies lean right or left), sometimes as a psychological study of mother–son relations and of repressed homosexual attraction between Aufidius and Coriolanus.

Shakespeare's comedies are almost exclusively of the romantic kind with 'boy meets girl/loses girl/finds girl' plots in which the young women (played in Shakespeare's time by highly trained young male actors), who are generally presented as intelligent, witty, down-to-earth, practical, resourceful and highly desirable, navigate their way through many complications (often associated with the fact that they are disguised as men) in order to arrive at marriages to men whose claim to our approval is that the women love them. Even in the most romantic plays there is a subplot to distance us from the romantic goings on. Bottom and his fellow amateur actors in *A Midsummer Night's Dream* provide incidental satire on the whole business of putting on a play and on the idea of romantic tragedy. In *Twelfth Night*, Malvolio's comic humiliation can easily turn into something that sours the whole romantic impulse of the play. Jacques compares the stream of couples about to get married at the end of *As You Like It* to the animals entering the Ark and, of course, Shylock in *The Merchant of Venice*, sometimes seen as a tragic hero, is always likely to cast a disturbing shadow over the romantic comic mood of the play's final act. In *All's Well That Ends Well* and *Measure for Measure* there are similar tensions between the dynamics and conventions of comedy, the events portrayed, and the means of characterisation, which lead them to be dubbed 'problem plays'. Similarly, *Troilus and Cressida* is a resolutely unheroic look at the Trojan War, which plays off its presentation of the sordid against the implied heroic image of a mythical period.

The tragedies *Othello, Hamlet, Macbeth*, and *King Lear* have traditionally been regarded as the peak of Shakespeare's achievement and their heroes as amongst the greatest challenges for actors. Interpretations of the plays, and the parts, have differed greatly but there generally has been more interest recently in giving full weight to other characters, rather than concentrating simply on the hero. The group of tragicomedies or romances Shakespeare wrote at the end of his career (*Pericles, Cymbeline, The Winter's Tale* and *The Tempest*) are noteworthy for their epic dramaturgy and refusal to be bound by

The Tempest by William Shakespeare, directed by Jonathan Kent, Almeida Theatre, 2000. Aidan Gillen as Ariel. (Colin Willoughby/ArenaPAL)

naturalistic probability. With the return of non-naturalistic approaches to theatre making since the middle of the twentieth century, their stock has risen appreciably. *The Winter's Tale* is now seen as a bold piece of dramaturgy that encompassed a whole cycle of existence from tragedy to an informed renewal of life and *The Tempest* has been mined interestingly for its colonial subtexts as much as it was once for intimations of Shakespeare's supposed farewell to his arts.

Shakespeare is one of the greatest challenges for directors, designers and actors, who adopt a wide variety of approaches, from the reverent to the iconoclastic. There is one tradition that attempts to give the full texts in an approximation of Renaissance stage conditions, and this tends to mean elaborate costumes, few lighting changes and an emphasis on verse speaking, all of which can quite easily become funereal. At the other extreme there is the jazzy update in which the text is heavily cut and altered, the period and setting are anywhere and nowhere and the whole thing becomes a vehicle for an imposed directorial concept. Most modern productions avoid the worst excesses of either approach but use the full resources of the modern theatre and attempt to bring out themes and issues that are at least latently present in the plays. Certain plays are particularly open to interpretation, such as *The Taming of the Shrew*, which is a battleground – crudely – between those who believe that Shakespeare supported Petruchio in violence against women and those who see it as a play in which the only two lively characters deserve one another.

Declan Donnellan's productions for England's Cheek by Jowl seem, on the whole, to have been able to tread a fine balance between a modernist and popular approach while still retaining respect for the text. Kenneth Branagh's Renaissance Company, set up to move away from the director dictatorship that actors such as Simon Callow and Branagh felt had dominated the British theatre for too long, saw productions by the likes of Judi Dench and Geraldine McEwan. The company perhaps erred on the side of taking too many liberties but Branagh's film of *Henry V* (which he directed and starred in) has proved to be one of the most successful of cinematic Shakespeares, supplanting the Olivier version in the hearts of many and contributing to a major revival of film interest in Shakespeare. Michael Bogdanov and Michael Pennington's English Shakespeare Company's history cycles, too, found a way of escaping from the hidebound, although this could degenerate into irrelevance rather than irreverence while Anthony Quayle's Compass touring company steered a fairly traditional line.

Despite the director-dominated atmosphere of the RSC, at its best its work is hard to beat and its record bears witness to a solid stream of productions that have acquired a legendary stamp – from the early 1960s Peter Hall/John Barton history plays, Brook's landmark *King Lear* and *A Midsummer Night's Dream*, through productions by John Barton (whose versions of *Love's Labour's Lost* did much to reclaim it for the stage), Howard Davies, Trevor Nunn, Terry Hands, Adrian Noble and Bill Alexander (who has continued with some very interesting multicultural productions at Birmingham Rep). With the exception, however, of the late Buzz Goodbody, and Deborah Warner, women as directors of Shakespeare at Stratford remain conspicuous by their absence. The National Theatre has a patchier record with Shakespeare, even though Peter Hall and Trevor Nunn had both headed the RSC, but Nunn ended his NT reign in 2003 with a *Love's Labours Lost* that relocated it to a pre-World War I setting that seemed apposite to the period just before the beginning of another Gulf war.

Although newspaper critics can still find casting black actors in Shakespearian parts other than Othello problematic, fine productions by Alby James and Yvonne Brewster with black casts, and black actors from Rudolph Walker, Cathy Tyson and Alton Kumalo to Josette Simons, David Oyelo and Adrian Lester have shown that Shakespeare must not be seen as a white preserve. Traditional gender roles have been subverted too, with all-male productions being joined by productions of *King Lear* with Kathryn Hunter in the lead role, Fiona Shaw as Richard II, Vanessa Redgrave as Prospero and Jane Lapotaire as Hamlet.

Twelfth Night by William Shakespeare, directed by Tim Carroll, Globe Theatre, 2002. Mark Rylance as Olivia. (Colin Willoughby/ArenaPAL)

The arrival of the Sam Wanamaker-inspired reconstruction of the Globe on London's South Bank under the artistic direction of Mark Rylance has thankfully not been solely an antiquarian or Disneyland version of Shakespeare, but has seen a determination to engage with the challenges of the space as though it was a just a theatre as well as an approximation of the original theatrical conditions. The 2003 season had three companies: one male, one female (responsible for the production of *The Taming of the Shrew*) and one mixed. Another innovation that could have been an academic exercise came from the Northern Broadsides troupe under Barrie Rutter. Committed to playing the classics in northern voices, they have produced a memorable Shakespeare uncluttered by the accretions of psychological realism or received pronunciation. British theatre has also benefited from productions from other countries, particularly the Ninagawa Company from Japan, and British regulars under the auspices of Thelma Holt. With Shakespeare's plays appearing in the West End, being guyed affectionately in the long-running Reduced Shakespeare Company's *The Complete Works of William Shakespeare* (*Abridged*), forming the mainstay of many summer open-air festivals and providing the rationale for the existence of both the Globe and the RSC, there seems little doubt, to adapt Jan Kott, that Shakespeare is still our contemporary.

TRY THESE:

For other Renaissance dramatists, ✷BEAUMONT, ✷CHAPMAN, ✷FLETCHER, ✷FORD, ✷HEYWOOD, ✷JONSON, ✷KYD, ✷MARLOWE, ✷MARSTON, ✷MASSINGER, ✷MIDDLETON, ✷TOURNEUR, ✷WEBSTER; for adaptations/reworkings of Shakespeare, ✷DRYDEN and Davenant's *The Tempest*, ✷MAROWITZ's collage versions of several plays; Peter Ustinov's *Romanoff and Juliet*; the musical *West Side Story* as an updating of *Romeo and Juliet* to New York; *Kiss Me Kate* is a reworking of *The Taming of the Shrew* into a clever showbiz musical in which the offstage lives of the stars parallel the story of their musical adaptation of *The Shrew*; ✷WESKER's *The Merchant* is a counter-argument to *The Merchant of Venice*; ✷BLESSING's *Fortinbras*, ✷MURRAY's *Ophelia*, ✷STOPPARD's

Rosencrantz and Guildenstern Are Dead and ✷C. P. TAYLOR's *Ophelia* are each rather more than *Hamlet* through the eyes of the supporting cast, as, in its way, is ✷GILBERT's *Rosencrantz and Guildenstern*; ✷BECKETT's *Endgame* for *Hamlet* reverberations; ✷BRENTON's *Thirteenth Night* reworks *Macbeth* and his *Pravda* (with ✷HARE) draws on *Richard III*; Barbara Garson's *MacBird* was a 1960s reinterpretation featuring President Lyndon Johnson as the title character; ✷BOND's *Lear* reassesses Shakespeare's, and his *Bingo* reassesses Shakespeare himself; ✷BARKER's own response to *King Lear* is *Seven Lears*; ✷KEEFFE's *King of England* is an Afro-Caribbean/East End transposition; ✷RATTIGAN's *Harlequinade* is set during rehearsal of *Romeo and Juliet*; ✷SHAW disliked *Cymbeline* so much he produced an 'improved' final act in *Cymbeline Refinished*; ✷JARRY's *Ubu Roi* contains elements of *Macbeth* and several other Shakespeare plays; ✷KLEIST's *The Schroffenstein Family* is a version of the *Romeo and Juliet* story; Aimé Césaire's *A Tempest* turns the Shakespeare original into a biting commentary on colonialism; ✷MÜLLER's *Hamletmachine* was especially compelling in Robert Wilson's 1986 staging; ✷NELSON's *Two Shakespearean Actors* for a portrait of Edwin Forrest and William Charles Macready, rival nineteenth-century stars; ✷BRECHT (Shakespeare's world had a major influence on his dramaturgy, and one of Brecht's last plays was a reworking of *Coriolanus*); Edward (son of Peter) Hall's *Rose Rage* for a recent adaptation of the *Henry VI* plays; Anne Marie Di Mambro's *Tally's Blood* for an Italian/Scottish *Romeo and Juliet* set around the time of World War II; the RSC staged *The Tamer Tamed*, ✷FLETCHER's sequel to *The Taming of the Shrew*, in 2003; *Bomb-itty of Errors* for a hiphop version of *The Comedy of Errors*.

SHANGE, Ntozake   [1948 –   ]
American dramatist

PLAYS INCLUDE:

for colored girls who have considered suicide when the rainbow is enuf (1974), *where the mississippi meets the amazon* (1977), *Spell No. 7* (1978), *A Photograph: Lovers-in Motion* (1979), *Black and White Two Dimensional Planes* (1979), *Boogie Woogie Landscapes* (1980), *It Hasn't Always Been This Way* (1981), *Savannahland* (1981), *Bocas* (1982),

Betsey Brown (reading, 1982 and, with ✱EMILY MANN, full production, 1986), *The Jazz Life* (1984), *Take Off from a Forced Landing* (1984), *from okra to greens* (1985), *Ridin' the Moon in Texas* (1986), *Betsy Brown* (musical, 1991), *The Love Space Demands* (1991), *Nomathemba* (1996, with Ladysmith Black Mambazo)

Creator of the long-running Broadway show *for colored girls who have considered suicide when the rainbow is enuf*, Shange (born Paulette Williams) is a South Carolina-born poet, professor and performer, author of novels and books of poetry, who rejects the term 'playwright' as irrelevant to the way she thinks and works. Some have found her dialogue too rhetorical, her anger too insistent, and the structure of her pieces too loose, but her contribution to the creation of a black feminist theatrical aesthetic has been groundbreaking.

Shange is a poetic/political writer in the best sense of the 'personal is political' school of feminist writing, and her 'choreopoems', as she calls some of her performance pieces, combine words, music and dance as integral components in expressing the realities of black life on stage. Greatly influenced by the women's movement and California's radical women's presses, Shange's best-known works contain shattering accounts of racial humiliations and pain but balance the anger and images of victimisation with communal celebration and pride. *for colored girls* started out as a handful of Shange's poems in a Berkeley bar before developing into the innovative music-theatre piece which moved to Broadway following a highly successful stint at the Public Theatre in New York. It is a consciousness-raising account of the trials, tribulations and, importantly, endurance of black American womanhood. The highly acclaimed production was subject to some criticism of its images of black males. *Spell No. 7* is a more bitter, ironic comment on the images, internalised self-hatred and stereotyping of black entertainers. Productions of Shange's works in Britain have not fared particularly well, partly perhaps because of the difficulties of transplanting cultural references and colloquialisms to another clime.

TRY THESE:
✱GEMS' *Piaf* for a play whose colloquial language had similar problems of understanding when it made the transatlantic crossing; ✱WOLFE's *The Colored Museum* for bitter satires on the theme of black stereotypes (including Shange); ✱KENNEDY's *A Lesson in Dead Language* deals with young women's education through a vivid, almost grotesque visual image; ✱BARAKA, ✱CHILDRESS, ✱HANSBERRY, ✱LANGSTON HUGHES, Zora Neale Hurston as contrasting and influential black writers; ✱RUDET's *Basin* for a British expression of black women's shared history; ✱KAY's *Chiaroscuro* for a similar British black theatre practice.

SHANLEY, John Patrick   [1950 –]
American dramatist, screenwriter and director

PLAYS INCLUDE:
Saturday Night at the War (1978), *Welcome to the Moon* (1982, six short plays), *Danny and the Deep Blue Sea* (1983), *Savage in Limbo* (1985), *The Dreamer Examines His Pillow* (1986), *Women of Manhattan* (1986), *All for Charity* (1987), *Italian American Reconciliation* (1988), *The Big Funk* (1990), *Beggars in the House of Plenty* (1991), *Four Dogs and a Bone* (1993), *Missing/Kissing* (1996, comprising *Missing Marisa* and *Kissing Christine*), *Psychopathia Sexualis* (1996), *Cellini* (1998), *Where's My Money* (2001)

This Bronx-born writer first earned notice with the Circle in the Square production of *Danny and the Deep Blue Sea*. Here, confused and troubled working-class characters, programmed to self-destruct after years of emotional deprivation, struggle to find wisdom and salvation through love. This was the first of four autobiographical plays (*The Dreamer Examines His Pillow, Savage in Limbo* and *Italian American Reconciliation* were the others) that explore how a man learns emotional responsibility and confronts the demands of a loving relationship. His plays are often romantic melodramas, and Shanley openly admits targeting 'the big, big emotions', as well as using his writing as pragmatic personal therapy. Shanley captures New York speech rhythms and ethnic local colour. He admits his personal longing for the Italian's connection to the body, and creates Italian-American characters possessed of the Irish gift of the gab. His later plays push the limits of realism, and *The Big Funk* is openly absurdist in style. Although he won an Academy Award for his screenplay for *Moonstruck*, his experiences, on the evidence of *Four Dogs and a Bone*, which is about making a film, were as traumatic as those of many other dramatists. In *Psychopathia Sexualis* the plot concerns a struggle for the soul of an artist between his fiancée and his psychiatrist who, unable to cure the artist of his fetish for his father's socks, has stolen them. Shanley's work has been staged in Britain but he has yet to achieve a major success.

TRY THESE:

✷ MCNALLY's *Frankie and Johnny in the Clair de Lune* for another play featuring two down-and-out New Yorkers battling through their emotions; ✷ MAMET for aggressive male characters and for the traumas of filmmaking; ✷ FEIFFER and ✷ OSBORNE for struggling relationships; ✷ KEMPINSKI for autobiographical angst; ✷ MARIE JONES and ✷ CHARLES WOOD for the joys of cinema; *Cellini* is about the Renaissance artist Benvenuto Cellini: for a contrast see ✷ BARKER's *Scenes from an Execution*; for therapists, ✷ HAMPTON's *The Talking Cure*, ✷ ORTON's *What the Butler Saw* and ✷ WRIGHT's *Mrs Klein*.

SHAPIRO, Jacqui   [1961 –   ]
British dramatist

PLAYS INCLUDE:
Family Entertainment (1981), *Thicker Than Water* (1981), *I'm Not a Bloody Automaton You Know!* (1982), *Sharon's Journey* (1981), *One of Us* (1983, with Meera Syal), *Up the Garden Path* (1983), *Trade Secrets* (1984), *Dead Romantic* (1984), *Three's a Crowd* (1985), *Dance Gazer* (1985), *How Odd of God* (1986), *Winter in the Morning* (1988)

Though Shapiro once confessed she had been writing ever since she could remember, and had several one-act plays and monologues performed whilst at Manchester University, it was her first major play, *One of Us*, that brought her to public prominence. Winner of a Yorkshire Television award in the 1983 National Student Drama Festival, this one-woman monologue that took on racism as seen through the eyes of a Birmingham Asian girl was performed with great panache by Meera Syal (who also co-wrote it) and is notable for its sharp social observation about prejudices and the pressures imposed on a young Asian girl battling for independence – spry, funny and tragic all at the same time.

Trade Secrets, for the Women's Theatre Group, tackled pornography and violence and an imagined world without men, but its fragmentary structure and characterisations left something to be desired; *Dead Romantic* (a Soho Poly commission) was, however, a snappy comedy of recognisable 'ideological' angsts getting in the way of physiological lust. *Winter in the Morning*, taken from Janina Bauman's horrific account of life for Polish Jews under the Nazis in the Warsaw Ghetto, succeeded best in the way it translates its adolescents' yearnings to the stage and as a reminder of the distortion of human values under extreme conditions. The cabaret-within-a-play, caricaturing Hitler and money-grabbing Ghetto Jews alike, was more problematical.

TRY THESE:

✷ BAINS' *The Fighting Kite* gives another image of the young Asian woman's bid for independence; ✷ TOWNSEND's *The Great Celestial Cow* looks at cross-cultural pressures on Asian women in Britain; ✷ MACDONALD and Lynda Barry's *The Good Times Are Killing Me* for more female adolescent growing pains; ✷ DANIELS' *Masterpieces* is *the* rad fem play on pornography and violence; ✷ MCINTYRE's *Low Level Panic* and ✷ PINNOCK's *Picture Palace* contrast romantic dreams and marketed images with more frightening day-to-day realities; ✷ GEMS' *Loving Women*, ✷ TERRY JOHNSON's *Unsuitable for Adults* deal with the difficulties of feminism and heterosexual tangles; ✷ COLLINS' *Judgement* looks at the corruption of human values under extreme pressures; Jean-Claude Grumberg, ✷ KESSELMAN's *I Love You, I Love You Not*, ✷ JULIA PASCAL's *Theresa*, ✷ SAMUELS, ✷ SOBOL's *Ghetto* for aspects of World War II and the Holocaust.

SHAW, George Bernard   [1856 – 1950]
Irish dramatist and critic

PLAYS INCLUDE:

Widower's Houses (1892), *Arms and the Man* (1894), *Candida* (1897), *The Devil's Disciple* (1897), *The Man of Destiny* (1897), *You Never Can Tell* (1899), *Captain Brassbound's Conversion* (1900), *Mrs Warren's Profession* (1902), *John Bull's Other Island* (1904), *The Philanderer* (1905), *Man and Superman* (1905), *Major Barbara* (1905), *The Doctor's Dilemma* (1906), *Caesar and Cleopatra* (1907), *Getting Married* (1908), *The Shewing Up of Blanco Posnet* (1909), *Press Cuttings* (1909), *Misalliance* (1910), *The Dark Lady of the Sonnets* (1910), *Fanny's First Play* (1911), *Overruled* (1912), *Androcles and the Lion* (1913), *Pygmalion* (1913), *Great Catherine* (1913), *The Music Cure* (1914), *O'Flaherty VC* (1917), *Heartbreak House* (1920), *Back to Methuselah* (1922), *Saint Joan* (1923), *The Fascinating Foundling* (1928), *The Apple Cart* (1929), *Too True to Be Good* (1932), *On the Rocks* (1933), *Village Wooing* (1934), *The Simpleton of the Unexpected Isles* (1935) *The Millionairess* (1936), *Cymbeline Refinished* (1937), *Geneva* (1938), *In Good King Charles's Golden Days* (1939), *Buoyant Billions* (1948), *Far Fetched Fables* (1950), *Why She Would Not* (1957)

Shaw, among the most widely produced of playwrights, and prolific man-of-letters (he published major essays on ✱IBSEN and Wagner as well as many on political and artistic issues of the day), won the Nobel Prize for Literature in 1925, and refused a peerage on principle. An active socialist for most of his life, he was a leading member of the Fabian Society, a co-founder with Sidney and Beatrice Webb of the *New Statesman*, helped to establish the London School of Economics, and was a leading figure in the campaign for a National Theatre.

It is often claimed that Shavian theatre sacrifices dramatic effect and characterisation for the sake of ideas, but with the hindsight of post-Brechtian theatre, Shaw can be seen as an innovator in bringing a challenging theatre of ideas to the West End and to theatres all over the world. The skill that Shaw always demonstrates with paradox becomes dialectical drama in his most successful plays.

Born in Dublin of Anglo-Irish parents, Shaw worked briefly in an estate agent's office before moving to London in 1876. He became a music critic and also reviewed books and the visual arts, before moving into drama criticism for the *Saturday Review*, producing some of the wittiest and wisest reviews ever of theatre. Through his reviewing Shaw gained a thorough awareness of the forms of contemporary theatre which informs his own writings: *Heartbreak House* and *Major Barbara* play with the conventions of dramatic form, while *The Fascinating Foundling* is a pastiche of contemporary commercial West End theatre writing. His first critical and commercial success came with *Arms and the Man*, a comedy with a moral; a contemporary reviewer described Shaw as 'the most humorously extravagant paradoxer in London' (no mean praise, since ✱OSCAR WILDE was a contemporary contender for the title). Besides their inventiveness and wit, Shaw's plays consistently dealt with controversial and often taboo subjects; in 1893 *Mrs Warren's Profession* (her profession of brothel keeper is not respectable) was banned by the Lord Chamberlain, and was not produced until 1925 (the year in which Shaw's Nobel Prize had unequivocally established him as a Grand Old Man of the British theatre). *Candida* was written as a response to ✱IBSEN's *A Doll's House*, and Ibsen's philosophy of naturalistic theatre became an informing influence on Shaw's work. Ibsen's exploration of non-realist forms in *Peer Gynt* was also influential: *Back to Methuselah* demonstrates the mix of fantasy, allegory and historical breadth that is an important aspect of Shaw's later (and less often produced) writings.

Man and Superman established Shaw as one of the most important of contemporary dramatists, and initiated a period of Shaw's most popular (both then and now) plays: *Major Barbara*, *Pygmalion*, *Saint Joan* and *Heartbreak House*. Shaw was very much involved with the staging of his plays; his stage directions are thorough and copious, and each play has a substantial preface and sometimes, as in *Pygmalion*, continues beyond the actual ending of the play. Shaw is probably most widely known through the musical version of *Pygmalion*, which with the libretto of Alan Jay Lerner became *My Fair Lady*.

Major Barbara

Major Barbara is a play that explores the nature of charity and wealth. Subtitled a 'discussion in three acts', the play puts contemporary debates about poverty on stage, and subjects them to dramatic investigation. The first act appears to be a standard 'drawing-room comedy', as Lady Britomart and her son Stephen display conventional wit and discuss the marriages of the family daughters; the appearance of a long-lost father completes the apparent conventional melodrama. However, Barbara, one of the daughters, is a Major in the Salvation Army, committed to the battle against poverty, while her father, Undershaft, is an arms manufacturer and a staunch defender of capitalism. In the next act, the curtain rises on a Salvation Army housing shelter (a real challenge to contemporary West End theatre audiences used to drawing-room comedy), and the play confronts Barbara with the fact that her concept of 'charity' rests on a capitalist system. Undershaft demonstrates that he financially supports the shelter, and that it is funded from the profits of breweries, a paradox that overturns the Salvation Army principle of teetotalism. In the final act Barbara and her academic lover Cusins confront Undershaft in a debate about the nature of poverty. Their debate is not a simple one; each employs unexpected arguments, and Undershaft effectively wins. Barbara finally comes to the realisation that her philosophy of faith, hope and charity depends upon the capitalism espoused by Undershaft, and accepts his patronage. The questions raised by the play remain unanswered, however: while Barbara may accept Undershaft, the audience is reminded that his philosophy of a charity made possible by wealth and profit is based on his manufacture of lethal weaponry. *Major Barbara* demonstrates that concepts of 'morality', 'liberty' and 'redemption' can only be abstractions in the face of poverty, and that what is necessary is an economic system based on the principle, as Shaw says, 'to each according to their needs, from each according to their means'. While the play was very much written in response to contemporary topical debates about poverty, its arguments remain potent.

TRY THESE:

✷ WILDE, for an Irish background and a very different approach to theatre; ✷ STRINDBERG was a major figure for Shaw, in championing a theatre of ideas; Shaw appears as a character in ✷ WHITEMORE's play *The Best of Friends*; ✷ JOHN MCGRATH shared Shaw's commitment to using dramatic form for socialist ideas; ✷ BRECHT, whose *The Good Person of Szechwan*, like *Major Barbara*, explores the interdependence of charity and capitalism; ✷ TREVOR GRIFFITHS is another dramatist who extends contemporary dramatic forms to socialist ends; ✷ BARKER, ✷ BOND ✷ BRENTON tend to be more formally innovative; ✷ ALRAWI's *A Child in the Heart* and Jonathan Falla's *Topokana Martyr's Day* as plays that confront the paradoxes of charity in relation to the Third World.

SHAWN, Wallace   [1943 –   ]
American dramatist, screenwriter and actor

PLAYS INCLUDE:
Our Late Night (1975), *A Thought in Three Parts* (1977), *Marie and Bruce* (1979), *The Hotel Play* (1981), *My Dinner with Andre* (1981, with Andre Gregory), *Aunt Dan and Lemon* (1985), *The Fever* (1990), *The Designated Mourner* (1996)

Although celebrity-spotters may recognise him through his appearances in *Deep Space Nine*, Shawn is also one of America's most unpredictable and subversive dramatists, whose plays made a significant impact in British theatre in the 1980s and who is still revived today. Whether epic (*The Hotel Play*) or intimate (*My Dinner with Andre*), seemingly straightforward or sinuously ironic, Shawn's plays get under the skin in a way audiences may not even realise until several days after the event. His targets are the nightmarishness of domesticity – the couple who can't stop firing invective at one another in his one-act *Marie and Bruce* – as well as hypocrisy disguised as doing-good, and the ceaseless quest for meaning in a society hell bent on its own extinction. *The Fever*, a monologue delivered by Shawn on a bare stage, perhaps best distils the anxiety and guilt suppressed by most well-to-do American liberals when confronted by Third World poverty. It was revived at the Glasgow Citizens Theatre in 2003.

Aunt Dan and Lemon

Overlong yet underwritten, at once wordy and evasive, *Aunt Dan* is a fascinating jumble of a drama about the relationship between a charismatic American don at Oxford, Aunt Dan, and the sickly young Leonora (Lemon) whom she befriends. A lifelong voyeur whose seemingly calm exterior belies a moral blankness inside, Lemon invites the audience into her sickroom only to lead us into a disquieting diatribe against the cult of compassion, in which the Nazis' extermination of the Jews is seen as a mere extension of our annihilation of cockroaches. The tone of the play is its most elusive aspect, and Shawn gives his actors and his director wide room to manoeuvre. Still, the writing itself remains maddeningly opaque; this is a dark treatise on moral pathology that can't quite illuminate the troubled and troubling people at its core.

TRY THESE:
✱ FEIFFER, ✱ MAMET for cut-throat dissections of the American psyche; ✱ ALBEE (especially *Who's Afraid of Virginia Woolf?*), ✱ STRINDBERG for images of marital malaise; ✱ FRAYN's *Benefactors* for the underside of idealism; ✱ SPALDING GRAY for powerful monologues that catch the jangling, frayed nerve ends of our societies.

SHELLEY, Percy Bysshe   [1792 – 1822]
English radical and poet

PLAYS INCLUDE:
The Cenci (1819)

The Romantic poet cast several of his works in dramatic form but only *The Cenci* seems ever to have been performed and that long after his death. A five-act drama in sub-Shakespearian style, it retells a true story Shelley had heard in Rome: Beatrice Cenci is raped by her father, an establishment figure protected by Church and society, and eventu-

ally murders him. Its theme of incest was probably a reason why it was not staged for so long. Although it is not a great play it is much better than Byron's or Tennyson's attempts at writing for the stage, and occasional revivals, such as the Bristol Old Vic production seen at London's Almeida Theatre in 1985, demonstrate its theatrical vitality.

TRY THESE:
For modern verse plays, ✱ ELIOT and ✱ FRY; ✱ BRENTON's *Bloody Poetry* and ✱ JELLICOE's *Shelley* for plays about Shelley; Jack Shepherd's *In Lambeth* for a play about William Blake meeting Tom Paine; ✱ ARTAUD's is the most famous production of a version of *The Cenci*; Shelley's dramaturgy was much influenced by the Renaissance dramatists: ✱ FORD's *'Tis Pity She's a Whore* is probably the most famous Renaissance treatment of incest; for contemporary approaches to incest, ✱ RECKORD's *X* and ✱ TREMBLAY's *Bonjour, Bonjour*, for a black American feminist version, ✱ KENNEDY's surreal account, *A Rat's Mass*.

SHEPARD, Sam   [1943 –   ]
American dramatist and actor

PLAYS INCLUDE:
Cowboys (1964), *The Rock Garden* (1964), *La Turista* (1967), *The Tooth of Crime* (1972), *Curse of the Starving Class* (1977), *Buried Child* (1978), *Suicide in B-Flat* (1976), *Seduced* (1978), *True West* (1980), *Fool for Love* (1983), *A Lie of the Mind* (1979), *Savage/Love* (1979, with Joe Chaikin), *States of Shock* (1991), *Simpatico* (1994), *When the World Was Green* (1996, with Joe Chaikin), *Eyes for Consuela* (1998, from Octavio Paz)

Is Shepard the pre-eminent dramatic observer of the American myth, or the greatest exemplar of it? Whatever one's stance, the Illinois-born playwright has achieved a near-legendary status through a combination of his commanding laconicism and decades of plays which defy classification as they move from the overtly fantastical (some of his early one-act plays) to long, piercing reveries about families rent asunder (*A Lie of the Mind*). Shepard eschews the tidy dramatics and often pat psychology that make Broadway hits, and his plays tend to take place in the American equivalent of the outback, far from the East Coast swells. Shepard is the poet par excellence of the American mythic imagination and its debased frontier mentality. Drawing from such diverse (and generally non-literary) sources as popular music (rock 'n' roll, jazz, country and western), sci-fi, Hollywood Westerns and the beat poets, his early plays offer intensely theatrical pastiches of legend and actuality. When *Suicide in B-Flat* first opened at Yale Repertory Theatre, one critic characterised it as 'a free-form jazz opus by Ornette Coleman to a text by Wittgenstein translated by Abbott and Costello'. His track record off-Broadway and in London, though, has been exemplary; indeed, his *Tooth of Crime*, an intriguing 'style war' between two rock musicians, Hoss and Crow, was written during Shepard's London residency (at the Bush) in the early 1970s.

Many of his middle-period plays mix comic Absurdism with Pinter-style game-playing; his Pulitzer Prize-winning *Buried Child* takes the form of a homecoming, as a man and his girlfriend return to the family farm in Illinois. In *True West*, two brothers in a southern California suburb squabble and swap identities, while taking potshots at American mythmaking, both Hollywood-style and otherwise. *A Lie of the Mind* posits two families, one in California, the other in Montana, separated by a mileage that is spiritual not spatial. 'I don't think it's worth doing anything unless it's personal', Shepard says, and despite his increasing fame as a film star and matinee idol, his work shows no signs of accommodating itself to the mob he has never courted. This was reaffirmed by his first stage play in years, *States of Shock*, that had a limited off-Broadway run at the American Place. It featured a pair of crazed Vietnam veterans (portrayed by John Malkovich and Michael Wincott) who do their best to bring the insanity of war home to a roadside restaurant occupied by an all-American middle-aged couple. The man's response to the war is masturbation while his wife remains demure and distant. The play's images resonated loudly as the USA was in the midst of its first Gulf War.

Fool for Love

'You're gonna erase me', May tells her former lover Eddie when they re-encounter one another in a motel room on the edge of the Mojave Desert, and Shepard's play is about exactly that – the threat of emotional erasure generated by a love so combustible that it doesn't know its own limits. A long-running success off-Broadway and a West End transfer from the National Theatre, the four-character drama set in Shepard's favoured terrain, the American south-west, epitomises this play-wright's method: at once violent and oblique, highly charged and digressive. The play has been described both as a *Phaedra* on amphetamines and a visceral but ultimately empty vehicle for actors. Whatever one's response, there's no denying Shepard's ability to elicit a charge from his re-examination of the ethos of the American cowboy, as the romantically ravaged Eddie lassoes bedposts instead of the woman with whom he should have never become entangled.

TRY THESE:

✶KESSLER's *Orphans*, ✶MAMET, ✶PINTER for their juxtaposition of violent spoken encounters with equally violent and abrupt silences; ✶STRAUSS's *The Tourist Guide*, ✶STRINDBERG's *Miss Julie* for studies of explosive sexual attraction; ✶FORNES, ✶TERRY, ✶VAN ITALLIE for other American experimentalists of the 1960s; ✶AESCHYLUS, ✶EURIPIDES, ✶SOPHOCLES for the ultimate family curse plays; ✶O'NEILL for archetypal 'family as battlefield' plays; ✶WELLMAN for improvisational approach to language and disposable culture.

SHEPPHARD, Nona   [1950 –   ]
British dramatist and director

PLAYS INCLUDE:
Off the Rails (1979), *The Last Tiger* (1984), *Getting Through* (1985), *Beulah's Box* (1986), *Robyn Hood* (1988), *The Snow Queen* (1989), *Peter Pan* (1991, with ✶BRYONY LAVERY), *Sleeping Beauty* (1992, with ✶BRYONY LAVERY), *The Lady Dragon's Lament* (1995), *Crazy Lady* (2000), *In the Parlour with the Ladies* (2002)

A prolific author, director and adapter, Shepphard has a warmth of perception and a robustness of style that make her work both a popular and a sustaining experience for young audiences. Her plays span the age ranges. *Beulah's Box*, for instance, one of several plays for the Quicksilver Theatre Company, was targeted at eight to ten year olds. It tells the story of a sad, wordless creature, put upon by a mean employer, who crawls through a mysterious box and finds a world of contrasts, colour, individuality and a wealth of languages. Reinforced by quirky and flexible set designs, it uses multilingualism as evidence of strength rather than as a perfunctory duty.

Getting Through, written for Theatre Centre, provided girls about to move on, at the age of twelve, to senior school with useful bolstering. Caz's greatest ambition is to build a radio transmitter – not a project for a girl, so she's told. Despite feeling alone and vulnerable in a new environment, she sticks to her guns. Interestingly, *Getting Through* had its mirror counterpart in *Over and Out*, written by Shepphard with ✱BRYONY LAVERY, and produced in tandem. In this, another Caz, in a science-fiction world, escapes from the drab and unsympathetic world of the Norms and makes contact, via a transmitter, with Caz of the first play. These plays, in their short-story versions, are the only works by Shepphard currently available in print

Shepphard's pantomimes have been high spots of the Christmas season at the Drill Hall, exuding a wicked humour and subverting gender roles with a robustness which is clearly as appealing to adult audiences as her children's plays are to younger audiences.

TRY THESE:

✱CASDAGLI, ✱DAVID HOLMAN, ✱KESSELMAN, ✱ADRIAN MITCHELL, ✱DAVID WOOD are other dramatists writing for children; Cheryl Moch's *Cinderella* for a subversion of traditional pantomime gender roles.

SHERIDAN, Richard Brinsley [1751 – 1815]
Irish dramatist, theatre manager and politician

PLAYS INCLUDE:
The Rivals (1775), *St Patrick's Day; or, the Scheming Lieutenant* (1775), *The Duenna* (1775), *A Trip to Scarborough* (1777), *The School for Scandal* (1777), *The Critic, or, a Tragedy Rehearsed* (1779), *Pizarro* (1799)

Son of a Dublin actor-manager and lexicographer and a playwright-novelist, Sheridan was intended for a career at the Bar, but his elopement and marriage to Elizabeth Linley brought him need of money and led to him writing *The Rivals*, based on his observation of society at Bath and his own experiences.

Sheridan bought ✱DAVID GARRICK's share of Drury Lane in 1776 and managed the theatre for over twenty years, though after becoming a Member of Parliament in 1780 he devoted most of his writing skills to speeches in the House. Sheridan watched Drury Lane burn down in 1809 from an inn opposite, remarking: 'Cannot a man take a glass of wine by his own fireside?' He became more and more beset by money troubles, and when he died in Savile Row in 1815 there were bailiffs at the door. His plots are fast moving and his dialogue witty, and though without the sexual explicitness of Restoration dramatists his plays have much in common with their comedy of manners. Although his characters often have identifying names in the tradition of ✱JONSON – Snake, or Lady Sneerwell (in *The School for Scandal*), for instance – they are nevertheless rounded creations rather than mere caricatures. They include the famous Mrs Malaprop (in *The Rivals*). *The Critic* is a burlesque of the contemporary stage that has not lost its point and is occasionally revived, while *The Rivals* and *The School for Scandal* have won a permanent place in the repertoire. Undoubtedly his finest work, *The School for Scandal* presents the arrival from the country of Lady Teazle, a naive young wife, and her exposure to, and education in, London Society, against a background of intrigue and a parallel plot concerning an inheritance involving virtuous and corrupt brothers. The 'screen scene', in which her much older husband, Sir Peter, discovers Lady Teazle in hiding, must rank with the Malvolio letter scene as amongst the finest in English comedy. Sheridan's most popular work in his own times was *Pizarro*, a spectacular reworking of a German play.

TRY THESE:

✱SHAW's *Pygmalion* offers some parallels between Professor Higgins and Sir Peter learning to accept a lively young woman; ✱FARQUHAR shows society, earlier in the century, visiting the provinces; ✱BEHN's *The Lucky Chance* and ✱WYCHERLEY's *The Country Wife* for earlier and more robust treatment of town/country conflicts; ✱GOLDSMITH's *She Stoops to Conquer* for a contemporary version; ✱STOPPARD's *The Real Inspector Hound* is a modern play about critics.

SHERMAN, Martin   [1938 –   ]
American dramatist

PLAYS INCLUDE:

Passing By (1972), *Cracks* (1973), *Bent* (1977), *Messiah* (1981), *When She Danced* (1984), *A Madhouse in Goa* (1987), *Some Sunny Day* (1996), *Rose* (1999), *A Passage to India* (2002, from E. M. Forster)

Born in Philadelphia, and educated at Boston University, Sherman was resident playwright at Playwrights' Horizons in New York before going to England, where his *Passing By* was one of half a dozen plays in the 1975 lunchtime season of gay plays put on by Ed Berman at the Almost Free. Sherman is probably best known, however, for *Bent*, a play about the Nazi persecution of homosexuals, one of the plays that arose out of Gay Sweatshop's production of *As Time Goes By* which looked at homosexual persecution in three different periods.

Bent subsequently turned up at the Royal Court and on Broadway with some star names – Ian McKellen and Tom Bell in Britain, Richard Gere and briefly Michael York on Broadway – and scored considerable success. It has gone on to be performed all over the world.

His follow-up play, *Messiah*, a parable of redemption set in 1665 Poland in the period following the Cossacks' massacre, was less well received. However, both *When She*

Danced, the story of dancer Isadora Duncan's marriage to the Russian Sergei Esenin in 1923 Paris, and *A Madhouse in Goa* had better luck (Vanessa Redgrave appeared in both in the West End). *Some Sunny Day* is a wartime spy thriller set in Cairo, while *Rose* uses the life of an elderly Russian Jewish refugee as a focus for a meditation on the events of the last century.

Bent

One of the early plays to show gays in a sympathetic and unsensationalistic light, *Bent* used two quite distinct styles: a first half of a *Boys in the Band* type bitchery and a second act set in Dachau with a ✱BECKETTIAN-type duologue between the central character, the tormented Max, and his lover, Horst. This may be partly due to the fact that though ostensibly set in the 1940s, the play is informed by and exudes a 1970s Gay Liberation consciousness and is therefore as much concerned with issues of changing personal politics as it is with historical perspective. Two exchanges also stand out: Max's scene with his elderly, discreet Uncle Freddie and, later, the verbally arrived-at orgasm between the two incarcerated men.

TRY THESE:

✱DREW GRIFFITHS; ✱NOEL GREIG for *As Time Goes By* and his *Angels Descend on Paris* for a different treatment of homosexuals under Nazi repression; ✱PUIG's *Kiss of the Spider Woman* for its exploration of homosexuality in a South American political and prison setting; ✱FIERSTEIN, ✱KRAMER, ✱LANFORD WILSON as other American playwrights who write unabashedly gay plays; ✱WHITEMORE's *Breaking the Code* for homosexuality British-style during World War II; *Cabaret* for glimpses of pre-war gay politics in Germany; ✱GENET's *Deathwatch* for another treatment of prison and homosexuality; *Midnight's Children* in the stage version by Salman Rushdie, Tim Supple and Simon Reade for a comparison to *A Passage to India*; Sherman has adapted ✱PIRANDELLO's *Right You Are* as *Absolutely Perhaps*.

SHERRIFF, R. C.
(Robert Cedric)   [1896 – 1975]
British dramatist and novelist

PLAYS INCLUDE:
Journey's End (1928), *Badger's Green* (1930), *St Helena* (1935), *Miss Mabel* (1948), *Home at Seven* (1950)

Sherriff is virtually a one-play author, though he had a long career as a dramatist and wrote some notable screenplays (*The Dam Busters*, *Mrs Miniver*, *Goodbye Mr Chips*). *Journey's End* was first put on as a Sunday-night production with the little-known Laurence Olivier playing Captain Dennis Stanhope, and in spite of doubts about the commercial prospects of a realistic play about World War I, it ran and ran (though without Olivier, who had gone into *Beau Geste* instead). The tension between the public-school ethos (which the play accepts) and the grinding horror of trench warfare at its worst, produces one of the 'strongest' plays ever written, and it works surprisingly well whenever revived. It is frequently put on by amateur groups in Britain, in spite of the problems inherent in making a dug-out collapse at the end (see Michael Green, *The Art of Coarse Acting*).

TRY THESE:
*O'CASEY's *The Silver Tassie* for a very different expressionist treatment of the war zone; *WILLIS HALL's *The Long and the Short and the Tall*, *LESLIE LEE's *Black Eagles* and *RATTIGAN's *Flare Path* deal with World War II; *NOEL GREIG's *Poppies* is a fiercely pacifist play, seen from a gay perspective; the crop of post-Falklands plays by Greg Cullen, *ROBERT HOLMAN, *MARCHANT and *PAGE all make their anti-war points in various ways; *LITTLEWOOD and Theatre Workshop's *Oh What a Lovely War* remains the World War I testament; for Vietnam, *LINNEY, *MCNALLY, *MANN, *RABE, *TERRY.

SHINN, Christopher   [1975 –   ]
American dramatist

PLAYS INCLUDE:
Four (1998), *What Didn't Happen* (1998), *Other People* (2000), *The Coming World* (2001), *The Sleepers* (2002), *Where Do We Live* (2002)

Born in Hartford, Connecticut, Shinn is a witty anatomist of contemporary American urban anomie. Influenced by seeing *MARK RAVENHILL's *Shopping and Fucking*, he sent off a play to the Royal Court, where he made his debut with *Four* in 1998. In *Four* his subject is the lives of four residents of his home town on the 4th of July, Independence Day. The four people cross-connect in various ways: adolescent boy out to explore his (homo)sexuality with a much older man who is the father of a young woman who is making up her mind whether to go out with a rather average boy. The landscape is the familiar modern dehumanised world of meaningless public spaces that we find in many contemporary plays, in which isolated people make fleeting disturbing connections with one another and try to find or create their identities in a world without signposts. Even *The Coming World*, which is set on the coast, charts the consequences of urban follies.

TRY THESE:
*MARBER's *Closer*, *POLIAKOFF's *Hitting Town* and *City Sugar* for British anomie; *CORTHRON, *GILMAN for American contrasts.

SHIRLEY, James   [1596 – 1666]
English dramatist

PLAYS INCLUDE:
The Traitor (1631), *Hyde Park* (1632), *The Gamester* (1633), *The Cardinal* (1641)

Like *HEYWOOD, Shirley owes his current (albeit very limited) theatrical standing to the RSC's policy of producing forgotten but lively plays by *SHAKESPEARE's near contemporaries, in his case *Hyde Park*, which appears not to have been staged for some 300 years before the 1987 revival. In his own time, after leaving the Anglican priesthood on his conversion to Catholicism, Shirley was a popular and prolific dramatist, but his work has suffered in the general theatrical neglect of the plays of this period. *The Traitor* and *The Cardinal* are very much in the revenge-tragedy tradition with plots reminiscent of *KYD, *MIDDLETON, *SHAKESPEARE, *TOURNEUR and *WEBSTER. The comedies are concerned with contemporary manners and London life, using locations, characters and themes that are more familiar to us in their post-Restoration forms. *Hyde Park* proved to be stageworthy and *The Gamester* has a double bed-trick in which a man pays off gambling debts by allowing the winner to take his place in bed with the woman he was about to commit adultery with; his wife later informs him that she has taken the other woman's place, but it all turns out not to have happened and decorum of a kind is maintained.

TRY THESE:
For the comedies ✱BEHN, ✱ETHEREGE, ✱JONSON, ✱MIDDLETON, ✱WYCHERLEY as immediate predecessors and successors; other largely forgotten dramatists of the pre-Civil War period are Richard Brome and William Davenant; ✱SHAKESPEARE uses the bed-trick in both *Measure for Measure* and *All's Well that Ends Well* and ✱MIDDLETON and ✱ROWLEY use the same device in their tragedy *The Changeling*.

SHUE, Larry   [1946 – 85]
American dramatist and actor

PLAYS INCLUDE:
The Nerd (1981), *The Foreigner* (1985), *Wenceslas Square* (1988)

Shue's untimely death (in a plane crash as he was about to join the New York cast of the musical *The Mystery of Edwin Drood*) ended his developing careers in playwriting and acting. Both *The Nerd* and *The Foreigner* demonstrate Shue's reliance on situation- and character-based humour. Neither play broke new ground and whether Shue would have grown as a playwright is conjecture, but *The Nerd* is popular with amateur groups and was revived at the Belgrade, Coventry, in 1999. *Wenceslas Square* dramatises an incident from Shue's life. It follows a college theatre professor and his protégé on their trip to Czechoslovakia. The professor has visited the country as a college student during the Dubcek regime. His return serves as research for a book about the effects of the Soviet repression upon the arts. Both the professor and the student are shocked by the lack of free speech and thought that had marked the

professor's earlier visit. The contrast is punctuated by the professor's flashbacks and by the apparent self-reflection that the professor sees in his young student. Shue incorporates humorous devices used in his other plays – mistaken identify and communication problems, for example – and he includes a melancholy tone that makes the audience aware of the consequences of artistic repression.

TRY THESE:
✱HAVEL for the real thing; ✱STOPPARD for similar themes; ✱EDGAR's *The Shape of the Table* for the end of the Cold War; ✱FRIEL's *Translations* and ✱NELSON's *Some Americans Abroad* for cultural dissonances.

SIMON, Neil   [1927 –   ]
American dramatist

PLAYS INCLUDE:
Come Blow Your Horn (1961, with Danny Simon), *Little Me* (1962, musical), *Barefoot in the Park* (1963), *The Odd Couple* (1965, revised 1985), *Sweet Charity* (1966, musical), *The Star-Spangled Girl* (1966), *Plaza Suite* (1968), *Promises, Promises* (1968, musical), *The Last of the Red Hot Lovers* (1969), *The Gingerbread Lady* (1970), *The Prisoner of Second Avenue* (1971), *The Sunshine Boys* (1972), *The Good Doctor* (1973), *God's Favorite* (1974), *California Suite* (1976), *Chapter Two* (1977), *They're Playing Our Song* (1979), *I Ought to Be in Pictures* (1979), *Fools* (1981), *Brighton Beach Memoirs* (1983), *Biloxi Blues* (1985), *Broadway Bound* (1986), *Jake's Women* (1988), *Rumors* (1988), *Lost in Yonkers* (1991), *Laughter on the 23rd Floor* (1993), *London Suite* (1994), *Proposals* (1997) *The Dinner Party* (2000), *45 Seconds from Broadway* (2001)

The New York-born Simon is the most successful living American playwright. After beginning as a television sketch writer for Phil Silvers and, briefly, Tallulah Bankhead, Simon has written roughly one play or musical libretto a year since the early 1960s, and almost all have been commercial – if not critical – successes. (*The Good Doctor*, adapted from eleven ✱CHEKHOV tales, was the rare example of the opposite.) He is a screenwriter of distinction, with both original scripts and adaptations of his own plays. Steeped in snappy repartee and one-liners Simon has been criticised for sacrificing psychological truth to the convenient punch line and glossing over difficult situations (alcoholism in *The Gingerbread Lady*, a widower's bereavement in *Chapter Two*) in time for a tidy final curtain. His autobiographical trilogy, *Brighton Beach Memoirs*, *Biloxi Blues* and *Broadway Bound* attempted to rectify that, but each has its soft and sentimental patches as well as its charms. Critics hailed *Lost in Yonkers* as Simon's deepest work, and it won the Pulitzer Prize for drama as well as that year's Tony Award for best play. His three *Suite* plays show Simon economically recycling and developing an idea across two coasts of America and two continents.

Brighton Beach Memoirs

'The world doesn't survive without families', announces Kate, the mother in the play, and Simon gives us an extended family of seven eking out a living in the Brighton Beach section of Brooklyn on the eve of World War II. Fifteen-year-old Eugene, a chirpy adolescent discovering baseball, girls and writing, is clearly Simon's alter ego, but more interesting are the adults – his mother, father and spinsterish Aunt Blanche, all of whom are written in warm, rich hues. The play is undoubtedly cosy – Simon is not ✳EUGENE O'NEILL – but at its best it's an evocative memory play, as pleasing as a faded family snapshot you've had for years.

TRY THESE:
✳MILLER's *Death of a Salesman* for the prototype of the father in *Brighton Beach*; ✳TENNESSEE WILLIAMS for earlier, harder-edged views of families; ✳MARGULIES and ✳WASSERSTEIN as younger American Jewish humorists; ✳AYCKBOURN for comparison and contrast as another dramatist whose use of comic forms led to a serious undervaluing of his work; ✳MACDONALD for adolescents growing up; ✳DURAS for plays about memory of a more elliptical kind; ✳FUGARD for the formation of the artist as a young man.

SIMPSON, N. F. (Norman Frederick)   [1919 –   ]
British dramatist

PLAYS INCLUDE:
A Resounding Tinkle (1957), *The Hole* (1958), *One Way Pendulum* (1959), *The Cresta Run* (1965), *Was He Anyone?* (1972)

Simpson was first a bank clerk and then an English teacher in adult education; in 1957 he won third prize in the *Observer* playwriting competition with *A Resounding Tinkle*. He has perhaps suffered from being overanalysed as an Absurd dramatist and classed as less 'serious' than ✳IONESCO. His logical paradoxes and flow of verbal invention are ultimately more like ✳GILBERT and Lewis Carroll than Ionesco. It is difficult to forget Arthur Groomkirby in *One Way Pendulum*, expounding his utterly convincing reasons for having to train these weighing machines to sing the Hallelujah Chorus so that he could take them to the North Pole and melt the ice around it, but it is probably a mistake to go through Simpson's work for profound thoughts about the desperation of the Human Condition.

TRY THESE:
✳JARRY and (more politically inclined) ✳SNOO WILSON for similar approaches to theatre; Simpson has adapted ✳DE FILIPPO.

SMITH, Dodie   [1895 – 1990]
British dramatist and novelist

PLAYS INCLUDE:
Autumn Crocus (1931), *Service* (1932), *Bonnet over the Windmill* (1937), *Dear Octopus* (1938), *I Capture the Castle* (1954)

Smith is best remembered for her children's novels *A Hundred and One Dalmatians* (in its various film manifestations) and *I Capture the Castle*, which was to become a play and film. Though now rarely performed (*Dear Octopus* does sometimes surface), Smith's work typifies the notion of the 'well-made play' for the West End. Her plays are domestic, if sophisticated, comedies in three acts, delivered with a certain wit and charm. Her first professionally produced play was

Autumn Crocus, a Tyrolean romance, and her most successful was *Dear Octopus*. Described by Smith in her autobiography as 'a play of lamplight, candlelight, firelight, sunset deepening into twilight . . . a play of youth and age', the Octopus of the title is the family, brought together for a golden wedding celebration. As the drama of the 1930s comes up for reassessment her work may well be due for a revival at any moment.

TRY THESE:

For other 'well-made plays', ✴GALSWORTHY, ✴HELLMAN, ✴RATTIGAN; Smith's contemporaries include ✴BAGNOLD, ✴HUNTER, ✴PRIESTLEY; Heidi Thomas scripted the 2003 film of *I Capture the Castle*.

SOBOL, Joshua (Yehoshua)   [1939 –   ]
Israeli dramatist

PLAYS INCLUDE:

The Days to Come (1971), *Status Quo Vadis* (1973), *Soul of a Jew* (1982, also known as *Weininger's Night*), *Ghetto* (1984), *Palestinian Girl* (1985), *Adam* (1988), *The Jerusalem Syndrome* (1988), *Underground* (1991) *The Father* (1995, with Niklas Frank), *Village* (1995), *Crocodiles* (2001), *Homeless Ben Gurion* (2002), *Eye Witness* (2002), *Real Time* (2002)

Born in Israel, Sobol was educated in Paris at the Sorbonne and began writing short stories before turning to the stage and television. He has been a playwright-in-residence and co-artistic director of the Haifa Municipal Theatre and writes passionately and expansively on issues facing Israelis as Jews, reflecting the dilemma of the Israeli personality torn between the residual fears induced by the Holocaust and a macho belief in their own supremacy and power. *Soul of a Jew* deals with the final hours of Jewish philosopher Otto Weininger and his struggles with Zionism, anti-Semitism, and his Jewish identity. The title itself can be found in 'Hatikva', the Israeli national anthem. Weininger ultimately commits suicide at twenty-three, unable to find a resolution to this conflict. As a result, *Soul of a Jew* was extremely controversial.

Sobol's most frequently-produced work is *Ghetto*, a drama about the theatre run by a company of actors in the Jewish ghetto in Vilna (now Vilnius, Lithuania) from January 1942 until its liquidation by the Germans in September 1943. Using diaries, historical evidence and survivors' accounts, Sobol combines cabaret-style songs and satire to create a play-within-a-play depicting the daily struggle of the Jewish company to endure and survive in the ghetto. *Ghetto*, the first play in Sobol's 'Ghetto Triptych', has received critical acclaim worldwide, in productions in Berlin, London, Chicago, Washington, Los Angeles, New York and even Vilna.

Sobol's 1988 play *The Jerusalem Syndrome* is perhaps better known for the political stir it caused than as a dramatic work. Sobol clearly means to parallel the historic plight of Palestinians and Jews by juxtaposing a ragged group of actors dramatising the Jewish revolt against the Romans in 66 AD with today's Palestinians in the Occupied Territory. Disturbing to Israelis, it engendered a heated debate in the Knesset. The play was allowed to open, but its shocking scenes (including a Jewish soldier shooting a refugee woman) caused demonstrations, interrupted performances, and police arrests of nearly 150 people in the theatre. In Haifa, many of the theatre's subscribers walked out. Under the pressure of censorship, both Sobol and artistic director Gedaha Besser were forced to resign.

Sobol has since completed his ' Ghetto Triptych' with the plays *Adam* and *Underground*. The latter, focusing on the problems of a medical ward in the Vilna ghetto, was given its first European productions in Oslo, Bonn and Wuperthal in 1989 and its first American production at the Yale Repertory Theatre in 1991 under the direction of Adrian Hall. Having progressed from a documentary-like style in his earlier plays, Sobol now feels his work to be best described as 'expressionist'. As his international reputation has grown he has worked extensively in German-speaking countries. His *The Father*, staged in Vienna and co-written with Niklas Frank, was about Niklas's father, the Nazi Hans Frank, who was hanged as a war criminal in 1946. Subsequently they collaborated on *Alma* (1996), about the life of Alma Mahler.

TRY THESE:
For socially-concerned drama set in a backdrop of war or violence, see Sidney Kingsley's *Dead End* and *The Patriots*, Robert Sherwood's *Abe Lincoln in Illinois* and *There Shall Be No Night*, and Maxwell Anderson's *Winterset*; ✶LITTLEWOOD's *Oh What a Lovely War*, ✶O'CASEY's *The Silver Tassie*, ✶C. P. TAYLOR's *Good* for disturbing visions of war; ✶BOND, ✶GOGOL, ✶O'CASEY, ✶SYNGE for trouble with censors; Sobol had written one of the pieces in *Consequences*, a Foco Novo commission unstaged because of the company's demise, together with ✶BRENTON, ✶DUNN, ✶TREVOR GRIFFITHS, ✶IKOLI, ✶NIGEL WILLIAMS, ✶SNOO WILSON and ✶WYMARK; ✶LAN translated the National Theatre's version of *Ghetto*; Jean-Claude Grumberg for another Jewish trilogy; ✶PASCAL for plays about the Holocaust and about the current Palestinian situation.

SOPHOCLES   [496 – 406 BC]
Greek dramatist

SURVIVING PLAYS INCLUDE:
Ajax (c. 442), *Antigone* (c. 441), *Oedipus the King* (c. 429), *Philoctetes* (c. 409), *Oedipus at Colonus* (406), *Women of Trachis* (date unknown), *Electra* (date unknown)

Sophocles is credited with the introduction of a third actor to Greek drama, thus widening the possibilities of the dramatic conflict; also with introducing those mysterious revolving scenic devices, the *periaktoi*. He is said to have won eighteen prizes at the Festival of Dionysus, and to have written over a hundred plays altogether. Aristotle based his account of tragedy in *The Poetics* on Sophocles, thus influencing his successors for centuries. The British crime novelist Dorothy L. Sayers claimed him as the originator of the detective story, and Freud's reading of the Oedipus story is central to the development of psycho-analysis.

Oedipus the King
The story of the stranger who becomes ruler of Thebes by solving the riddle of the Sphinx and marrying the widow of the late king, only to find, after relentlessly interrogating one man after another, that the sins which have brought the plague to Thebes are his own, and

that he has killed his own father and married his mother, has one of the most tightly knit and relentless plots in the history of drama. The power of the dialogue may be lost in translation, but the impeccable construction means that the play is effective in any language.

TRY THESE:
✶AESCHYLUS, ✶ARISTOPHANES, ✶EURIPIDES and Menander for surviving Greek plays; ✶BERKOFF and ✶HARRISON for modern British versions of Greek subjects; ✶ANOUILH for updating *Antigone* to deal with the theme of collaboration in wartime France, ✶GIRAUDOUX for a version of *Electra*, ✶COCTEAU for a version of the Oedipus story; the Living Theatre for an idiosyncratic use of the Antigone story; ✶BREUER's *Gospel at Colonus* for a modern reworking of *Oedipus at Colonus*; Seamus Heaney's *The Cure at Troy*, his plangent and moving plea for reconciliation (on the far side of revenge) in Northern Ireland is based on *Philoctetes*.

SOYINKA, Wole (Arkinwande Oluwole)   [1934 –   ]
Nigerian dramatist, novelist and poet

PLAYS INCLUDE:
The Swamp Dwellers (1958), *The Lion and the Jewel* (1959), *The Invention* (1959), *A Dance of the Forests* (1960), *The Trials of Brother Jero* (1960), *Camwood on the Leaves* (1960, radio), *The Strong Breed* (1964), *Kongi's Harvest* (1964), *The Road* (1965), *Madmen and Specialists* (1970), *Jero's Metamorphosis* (1973), *The Bacchae: A Communion Rite* (1973, from ✶EURIPIDES), *Death and the King's Horseman* (1975), *Opera Wonyosi* (1977, from ✶BRECHT's *The Threepenny Opera*), *Requiem for a Futurologist* (1983), *A Play of Giants* (1985), *Mandela's Earth* (1988), *Ibadan* (1994), *The Beatification of Area Boy* (1995), *The Open Sore of a Continent* (1997), *The Burden of Memory* (1999), *King Baabu* (2001, after ✶JARRY's *Ubu Roi*), *Samarkand* (2002)

Soyinka was born in western Nigeria and studied at the Universities of Ibadan and Leeds. He spent several years after graduation in London, a period when he was closely associated with the Royal Court. Soyinka became a member of the Writer's Group led by William Gaskill and Keith Johnstone, and the Court staged *The Invention* as a Sunday Night performance, directed by Soyinka himself.

Soyinka returned to Ibadan as a Research Fellow in Drama in 1960 and went on to become a powerful and influential figure in African theatre, developing a dramatic voice which reflected Nigeria's recent political history in a manner influenced by both African culture and Western literary traditions; as such, he was the founder of the 1960 Masks Theatre. But in 1967 he was arrested for alleged activities in support of Biafra by the federal government, and held as a political prisoner for two years. On his release, Soyinka became Director of the Drama School at the University of Ibadan, and later Research Professor. He then continued to work in Nigeria at the University of Ife, although he has travelled internationally with his writing. *Madmen and Specialists* was first staged at the National Playwrights Conference at the Eugene O'Neill Theatre Center in the USA. In 1973 Soyinka was an Overseas Fellow at Churchill College, Cambridge, and in that year he wrote *Death and the King's Horseman*, probably his best-known play. He was awarded the Nobel Prize for Literature in 1986. He fell foul of the Nigerian regime again in the 1990s because of his opposition to its policies and escaped from the county on the back of a motorbike, although he now mainly divides his time between the USA and Nigeria.

Death and the King's Horseman
A powerful fable aimed at British colonialism, *Death and the King's Horseman* is based on an actual event that took place at Oyo in Nigeria in 1945 involving the interrupted ritual suicide of the King's Horseman. Nigerian custom dictated that a favoured servant should follow his master after his death. A British colonial officer, however, orders Jinadu, the Horseman, to be arrested and Jinadu's son, in the end, takes his own life. Employing dance, mime, music and folklore, it is a rich expression of Yoruban culture engaging with ideas of honour, leadership and

colonial ignorance. Interestingly, the play was coolly received in Nigeria, respectfully in the UK (in the Royal Exchange's 1990 production) and with some enthusiasm in the US.

TRY THESE:
✱BOND, ✱ JELLICOE, ✱ WESKER were also members of George Devine's Writer's Group, set up at the Royal Court in 1958; Yemi Ajibade another Nigerian playwright, whose *Fingers Only* is set in a small Nigerian town; ✱DUFFY also draws on ✱EURIPIDES' *The Bacchae* for her *Rites*; as does ✱LAVERY for *Kitchen Matters*; Ola Rolimi's *The Gods Are Not to Blame* is a reworking of *Oedipus* in Yoruban terms.

SPENCER, David   [1958 –   ]
British dramatist

PLAYS INCLUDE:
Releevo (1987), *Space* (1987), *Blue Hearts* (1989), *Killing Cat* (1990), *Glass Hearts* (2001)

Spencer trained as a scientist but became disillusioned with science's inability to explain things emotionally. To all intents and purposes, he is a graduate of adult education writing courses (at the City Lit in London, where he took classes in poetry, short story, and modern fiction), turning to plays because, he said, he liked to write in the first person but had problems with characters' interior thoughts. His scientific training has left him with a reductionist mind – 'Life's an expression of fundamental forces' – and a deeply deterministic – some might say pessimistic – outlook on human behaviour.

Releevo, Spencer's first play, won the 1986 Verity Bargate award and almost universal acclaim. A bleak and blistering account of a young working-class couple's marital break-up, it was one of a long line of wide-eyed, baleful chronicles of the nuclear family and its fall-out in the late 1980s. His second play, *Space*, dealt with domestic violence and battered wives, the roots of violence and its impact on individuals, whilst *Killing the Cat* (another Verity Bargate winner) touched on alcoholism and incest (between father and daughter and brother and sister). Written in a sparse but pungent Yorkshire dialect, the emotional violence his characters endure inspires a sense of sadness. Described thus baldly, Spencer's plays may sound harrowing. Painful they certainly are but the plays are also shot through with compassion and a poetic realism that borders on despair and that has carried forward to his latest play, *Glass Hearts*, premiered at the Southwark theatre in 2001.

TRY THESE:

✱DUNBAR, ✱KEARSLEY, ✱RAIF for domestic working-class ruptures; ✱STOREY for an older generation of northern family dramas; ✱TERRY JOHNSON's *Imagine Drowning* and ✱MARCHANT's *The Attraction* for other treatments of the roots of violence; ✱TREMBLAY's *Bonjour, Bonjour* and ✱WARD's *Apart from George* for hints of incest; for plays within a play (like *Killing the Cat*), see ✱ANOUILH's *The Rehearsal*, ✱PIRANDELLO's *Six Characters in Search of an Author* and *Henry IV*, and ✱TREMBLAY's *The Real World*; for onstage present-ation of a younger self, ✱DANIELS' *Beside Herself* and ✱NORMAN's *Getting Out* offer parallels with *Killing the Cat*.

STAFFORD, Nick   [1959 –   ]
British dramatist

PLAYS INCLUDE:

Bad City (1987), *Extraordinary Behaviour* (1988), *Easy Prey* (1989), *Moll Cutpurse* (1989), *The Devil's Only Sleeping* (1990), *The Canal Ghost* (1990), *Back of the Bus* (1991), *The Go-Between* (1995), *Grab the Dog* (1995), *The Whisper of Angels' Wings* (1997), *Battle Royal* (1999), *Luminosity* (2001)

A dramatist who has served a typical apprenticeship in community and small-scale touring companies, Stafford's *Moll Cutpurse* offers an interesting take on ✱MIDDLETON and ✱DEKKER's *The Roaring Girl* with parallels to the situation of Margaret Thatcher's Britain. Unfortunately the general critical view of the National Theatre produc-tion of *Battle Royal*, which deals with the stormy relationship between the Prince Regent and his wife Caroline, both in the immediate aftermath of the French Revolution and later when he is about to be crowned king, was that it was overlong and underwritten. Although Stafford's play finds

some interesting parallels between royal life at the ends of the eighteenth and twentieth centuries, ✱ALAN BENNETT's *The Madness of George III* had effectively cornered that royal market. *Luminosity* tackles big themes of social responsibility, hypocrisy, race and gender in the context of one family trying to come to terms with its history in South African diamond mining, but most critics thought that its use of three different time periods led to a long evening that seemed to generate more light than heat.

TRY THESE:

✱FUGARD, ✱HARWOOD, ✱WRIGHT for South African issues; ✱SHAW's *Major Barbara* for morality, industry and compassion.

STEPHENS, Simon   [1971 –   ]
British dramatist

PLAYS INCLUDE:

Bluebird (1998), *Herons* (2001), *Port* (2002)

Stephens swiftly established himself as a significant voice after the usual round of 'writing bad plays that nobody wanted to buy, staging them in various dire fringe theatres [and] working in horrible jobs' ended when the Royal Court Young Writers Programme staged *Bluebird*. In this play a former novelist who has left his wife after accidentally killing their baby draws a kind of strength from his encounters with the random clients who use his cab. *Herons* tackles a familiar topic, teenage bullying, but in ways that transcend the usual clichés of the genre. Similarly *Port*, set in the author's home town, Stockport (which he has described as 'one of the most hopelessly boring places in the north of England), deals with another potentially clichaic situation, that of the young woman abandoned to bring up her younger brother and then abused by her partner, but finding a strength to confront her situation. Perhaps the element that comes over most strongly from Stephens is his sense that it is possible to confront the demons of modern life, not simply depict them.

TRY THESE:
∗BUTTERWORTH's *The Night Heron,* ∗CHEKHOV's *The Seagull* for other symbolic birds to compare with *Herons*; ∗DUNBAR for northern life.

STEPHENSON, Shelagh   [1955 –   ]
British dramatist

PLAYS INCLUDE:
The Memory of Water (1996), *An Experiment with an Air Pump* (1998), *Ancient Lights* (2000), *Five Kinds of Silence* (stage version 2000), *Mappa Mundi* (2002)

Stephenson was born in Northumberland. After reading drama at Manchester she established herself with a number of radio plays (including the award-winning *Five Kinds of Silence*) before turning to the stage with *The Memory of Water*, a hugely successful study of three sisters who have returned to the family home on the eve of their mother's funeral. The play traces them as they renegotiate their relationships with one another, retrace old battles and fight new ones. In *An Experiment with an Air Pump* she contrasted the world evoked by Joseph Wright's painting *An Experiment on a Bird in the Air Pump* with our contemporary world, doubling the characters from 1799 with those from 1999 and intercutting plots to establish parallels and contrasts between the ethical dilemmas of both periods, the role of science and the mechanics of love. After the success of her first two stage plays there was something of a critical backlash against her next two, with some critics arguing that *Ancient Lights* had too many of the trappings of contemporary comedy of manners in its tale of a group of ill-assorted characters spending Christmas in an isolated house in Northumberland, without fully using the comedy to explore the way public personas may hide underlying insecurities and to confront the ways in which we create our identities. Similarly the underpinning maps of different kinds of worlds in *Mappa Mundi* did not convince all critics and the references to miscegenation and to physics didn't please everyone, but it is already clear that Stephenson has a witty and imaginative approach to dramaturgy and that she is prepared to look beyond the quasi-documen-tary exploration of modern urban anomie that characterises many of her contemporaries.

TRY THESE:
∗BILL for funeral gatherings; ∗CHEKHOV for *Three Sisters*; ∗STOPPARD's *Arcadia* for an interest in science and a split time scheme; ∗CHURCHILL for adventurous doubling; ∗HARE for a different kind of *A Map of the World*; ∗AYCKBOURN for bad Christmases; ∗CHRISTIE for a classic isolated country house in *The Mousetrap*, ∗DECLAN HUGHES for a contemporary one.

STOPPARD, Tom   [1937 –   ]
Czech-born English dramatist

PLAYS INCLUDE:
A Walk on the Water (television 1963, staged 1964; revised as *The Preservation of George Riley*, 1964, and as *Enter a Free Man*, 1968), *'M' is for Moon Among Other Things* (1964), *The Dissolution of Dominic Boot* (1964, radio), *The Gamblers* (1965), *Rosencrantz and Guildenstern Are Dead* (1966), *Albert's Bridge* (1967, radio), *The Real Inspector Hound* (1968), *If You're Glad I'll be Frank* (1969), *After Magritte* (1970), *Where Are They Now?* (1970, radio), *Dogg's Our Pet* (1971), *Jumpers* (1972), *Artist Descending a Staircase* (1973, radio), *Travesties* (1974), *Dirty Linen* (1976), *Newfoundland* (1976), *Every Good Boy Deserves Favour* (1977), *Night and Day* (1978), *Dogg's Hamlet, Cahoot's Macbeth* (1979), *The Real Thing* (1982), *Hapgood* (1988), *Arcadia* (1993), *Indian Ink* (1995, as *In the Native State*, radio 1991), *The Invention of Love* (1997), *The Coast of Utopia* (2002, comprising *Voyage, Shipwreck, Salvage*)

Born in Czechoslovakia, Stoppard was brought up in Singapore, and moved to England in 1946. He began writing as a journalist in Bristol, and became involved in drama through his theatre reviewing. Very much influenced by ∗JOHN OSBORNE's *Look Back in Anger*, and recognising that in the late 1950s 'The theatre was suddenly the place to be', he resigned his job and moved to London, in a period when the new influences of European and absurdist theatre were hitting the London stage. His first plays were written for radio and television, but *Rosencrantz and Guildenstern Are Dead* established his reputation. The play, a sideways look at *Hamlet* from the perspective of two minor characters, intercuts their discussions while offstage in *Hamlet* with scenes and events from *SHAKESPEARE's play. First produced at the Edinburgh Festival, it was taken up by the National Theatre and staged in London to wide acclaim.

In the 1970s, Stoppard was involved with Ed Berman and the Interaction Group, with whom he developed *Dogg's Our Pet* and the West End success *Dirty Linen*.

Stoppard is among the most fashionable of contemporary playwrights; 'Stoppardian' is now used as a term for the display of verbal wit and intellectual games. His work is always full of verbal fireworks, intellectual references and literary jokes. Most of his plays are constructed around elaborate conceits: *Jumpers* puts a philosophical discussion of logic together with a troupe of acrobats; *Every Good Boy Deserves Favour* has a full-scale orchestra on stage in a play about Soviet dissidents; *Hapgood* relates the complexities of spying and double agents to nuclear physics. This method of highly improbable juxtaposition owes a lot to Surrealism, and, in *After Magritte*, Stoppard wrote a play around the elements of a Magritte painting (umbrellas, bowler hats, skies, etc.) located in a suburban household.

Stoppard's characteristic method of colliding two apparently discrete discourses continues to underpin his more recent work. *Arcadia* deals amongst other things with the clash between classical and romantic, past and present, literature and science. The contrasting worlds in *Indian Ink* are those of 1930s India and the 1980s, viewed through an Anglo-Indian relationship and its consequences. In *The Invention of Love* Stoppard returns to *WILDE, paralleling and contrasting his career with that of the poet A. E. Housman, with Wilde as the flamboyant romantic whose infatuation ended his career and Housman as the repressed scholar looking back newly dead on his younger self. A familiar Stoppardian figure, the academic trying to make sense of the past, looms large in each of these plays. *The Coast of Utopia* is an epic account of the revolutionary political and artistic movements of the mid-nineteenth century featuring, amongst others, Bakunin and *TURGENEV. Although Stoppard's ambition was applauded, on this occasion the general view was that he had been somewhat overwhelmed by his research and had failed to mould it into a fully viable work.

His television plays *Squaring the Circle* (1984, about Solidarity and Lech Walesa) and *Professional Foul* (1977) are both set in eastern Europe, and take up the questions of political dissidence under Communism that he raised in *Every Good Boy Deserves Favour*. He is an accomplished adapter of *CHEKHOV, *HAVEL, *MOLNAR, *MROZEK, *NESTROY and *SCHNITZLER and he won an Oscar for his contribution to the screenplay of *Shakespeare in Love*.

Travesties

Travesties is based on the actual historical oddity that Lenin, the Dadaist poet Tristan Tzara, and James Joyce must have been in Geneva in the same period. The events of the play and imagined meeting of the three are recounted by a minor British consular official whose major memory of the time is that he played a minor part in an amateur production of *The Importance of Being Earnest*. The three historical figures are thus cast into characters from *The Importance of Being Earnest*, and their work and influence is intercut with scenes from *WILDE's play. The comedy of *Travesties* does very much depend on the recognition of the literary references – audiences for the play tend to have an air of self-congratulation for getting the jokes – but it is (unlike some of Stoppard's other work) more than an exercise in displays of intellectual wit. It is also a poignant study of the self-aggrandisement of the consul, and a suggestive exploration of memory and of versions of historical events.

TRY THESE:

*IONESCO for logic games; *Rosencrantz and Guildenstern Are Dead* draws heavily on *BECKETT's *Waiting for Godot*; *AYCKBOURN and *PIRANDELLO for theatrical games; *POWNALL's *Master Class* for another look at Russian musical totalitarianism; *OVERMYER for another dramatist

Rosencrantz and Guildenstern Are Dead by Tom Stoppard, directed by Matthew Francis, National Theatre, 1995. Adrian Scarborough as Rosencrantz, Alan Howard as the Player King, Simon Russell Beale as Guildenstern. (Henrietta Butler/ArenaPAL)

in love with language; ✱HARE's *A Map of Utopia* for arguments about the Third World, using a film within the play device and a title taken from ✱WILDE.

STOREY, David   [1933 –   ]
British dramatist and novelist

PLAYS INCLUDE:
The Restoration of Arnold Middleton (1966), *In Celebration* (1969), *The Contractor* (1969), *Home* (1970), *The Changing Room* (1971), *Cromwell* (1973), *The Farm* (1973), *Life Class* (1974), *Mother's Day* (1976), *Sisters* (1978), *Early Days* (1980), *Phoenix* (1984), *The March on Russia* (1989)

Storey, the son of a Wakefield miner, was trained at Wakefield School of Art, and later at the Slade (an experience he draws on in his play *Life Class*). He then worked at a number of jobs, including a stint as a professional rugby-league player (an experience reflected in his novel *This Sporting Life* and *The Changing Room*). Storey is perhaps best known as an exponent of a form of slice-of-life drama. Several of his plays are concerned with men at work, and a recurrent device is the progression of work in real time over the course of the play: the building of a tent in *The Contractor*, or a rugby match (with complete team) in *The Changing Room*.

Storey's first play, *The Restoration of Arnold Middleton*, written in 1958, was disinterred for production by Lindsay Anderson during the filming of *This Sporting Life* in 1960. Anderson went on to direct *In Celebration*, *The Contractor*, *Home* and *The Changing Room* at the Royal Court, and all transferred to the West End.

Home is an atypical Storey play in that its setting is far from concrete – merely four chairs and a table and an encounter between four elderly people. Neither this nor the dialogue gives many clues as to the context; according to John Gielgud the text intrigued 'but somewhat mystified me'. Storey has said 'Halfway through the writing I discovered it was taking place in a lunatic asylum.' More in keeping with the usual Storey style is *In Celebration*, a searching essay on traditional family relationships, set in a northern mining

family, and following the return home of three sons for their parents' fortieth wedding anniversary. A grim exercise in fraternal truth-telling, more skeletons ooze from the cupboard in Storey's later sequel, *The March on Russia*, in which the same couple, the Pasmores, are once more the focus, this time on their sixtieth anniversary. This elegy for the post-World War II British working class, one that seems to speak of their displacement and spiritual vacuum despite material benefits, is proof, for some, of Storey at his vintage best. For others, it seemed like a voice from another age, now gone.

TRY THESE:
✱MERCER, whose career followed a similar trajectory and who also trained at the Wakefield Art School; ✱GODBER's *Up 'n' Under*, ✱PAGE's *Golden Girls* and ✱WILLIAMSON's *The Club* for the sporting life; ✱PINTER's *No Man's Land*; ✱DURRENMATT's *The Physicists*, ✱WEISS's *Marat/Sade*, ✱WHITE's *The Bootdance* for mental hospitals; Richard Bean's *Under the Whaleback* for trawlermen at work; Stephen Clark's *Making Waves* for lifeboatmen.

STRAUGHAN, Peter   [1968 –   ]
British dramatist

PLAYS INCLUDE:
Rat (1996), *The Ghost of Federico García Lorca Which Can Also Be Used As a Table* (1998), *Bones* (1999), *Fetish* (2000), *Cold* (2001), *Noir* (2002)

Straughan, a former musician, has written for theatre, radio, television and film. His territory is mainly the underworld of low-level criminality and feckless dreamers. *Bones* is a comedy thriller set in the 1960s, about two minor pornographers who kidnap Reggie Kray. *Cold*, set in a secure hospital, tackles the issues of whether those who commit evil acts can be treated or should be punished. In *Noir* the security guard who wants to be a private eye tails the wrong woman but achieves a kind of apotheosis in his degradation of a shoplifter. Rhoda Koenig has described the ✱LORCA play as a surrealist ferocious comedy.

TRY THESE:

✷BUTTERWORTH's *Mojo* for similar re-creation of an earlier criminal milieu; ✷PETER SHAFFER's *Equus* for the debate about madness and badness; ✷STOPPARD's *Every Good Boy Deserves Favour* for another take on the subject.

STRAUSS, Botho   [1945 –   ]
German dramatist, poet, novelist, translator and drama critic

PLAYS INCLUDE:

Die Hypochonder (1971, *The Hypochondriacs*), *Gross und klein* (1978, *Great and Small or Big and Little*), *Der Park* (1983, *The Park*), *Die Fremdenführerin* (1986, *Tourist Guide*), *Die Zeit und das Zimmer* (1988, *Time and the Room*), *Ithaka* (1996), *Die Ähnlichen* (1998, *Lookalikes*), *Der Narr und seine Frau heute abend in Pancomedia* (2001, *The Fool and His Wife Tonight in Pancomedia*), *Unerwartete Rückkehr* (2002, *Unexpected Return*)

Strauss is one of Germany's most prodigiously talented men-of-letters. A contemporary of filmmaker Rainer Werner Fassbinder and Austrian playwright ✷PETER HANDKE, his disenchantment with modern society and anti-naturalistic style seem to have frequently been misunderstood in Britain (though in Germany he is hailed as a considerable talent, not least for the work he has done as adapter/translator with the Schaubühne's director Peter Stein). In Britain, *Great and Small*, the story of Lotte, the rejected wife turned baglady who embarks on an epic and losing battle for love and affection, *Tourist Guide*, a reworking of timeless themes about intellect versus feeling, and the destructive power of erotic love, *The Park*, a misanthropic update of Shakespeare's *A Midsummer Night's Dream*, and *Time and the Room*, a study in urban angst, were greeted with less than general enthusiasm. The 1998 Edinburgh Festival staging of *Lookalikes* by Peter Stein continued to divide the critics. Perhaps the German sensibility does not travel well, or something has been lost in translation. Either way, Strauss remains an elusive, potent European voice railing against contemporary urban society and its selfish materialism.

TRY THESE:

For another image of the female encountering society, ✷WERTENBAKER's *The Grace of Mary Traverse*; ✷STRINDBERG's *Miss Julie* and ✷SHEPARD's *Fool for Love* for other themes of erotic love; ✷RUSSELL's *Educating Rita* for passion and intellect; for bleakness, ✷BECKETT, and for urban bleakness, ✷MOTTON; ✷HANDKE for a contemporary German language dramatist.

STRINDBERG, August   [1849 – 1912]
Swedish dramatist, novelist, poet and essayist

PLAYS INCLUDE:

Hermione (1869), *The Travels of Lucky Per* (1882), *The Father* (1887), *Miss Julie* (1888), *Creditors* (1888), *To The Stronger* (1890), *Playing with Fire* (1892), *Advent* (1898), *Damascus* (1898–1901, trilogy), *Gustaf Vasa* (1899), *Erik XIV* (1899), *Easter* (1900), *The Dance of Death* (1900), *A Dream Play* (1902), *Swan White* (1902), *The Ghost Sonata* (1907), *The Storm* (1907), *The Burnt Lot* (1907)

Strindberg's dramatic imagination is immensely powerful. Although his plays variously comprise historical drama, fairy tale, fantasy and symbolism he is most associated with a claustrophobic world of embittered relationships, repressions and embattled psyches. His plays' preoccupations with sexuality, irrationality and with the family as a site of struggle can make them seem like dramatisations of Freud's case studies.

Born in Stockholm, Strindberg studied medicine and worked as an actor, a journalist and a librarian. His three marriages all ended in divorce, and he held a great bitterness towards women, which he explores over and over again in his plays. Throughout his life Strindberg was beset by periods of insanity (he would probably now have been diagnosed a manic depressive), an experience he wrote about in his painful autobiography, *A Madman's Defence*.

His first plays were historical dramas and rural fairy tales, both preoccupations he explored throughout his writing life. His historical plays, however, take their events as dramatic frames from which to draw metaphors that explore issues of power. In

1882 the fairy play *The Travels of Lucky Per* moved him towards an exploration of fantasy.

Strindberg was much influenced by Zola's espousal of 'naturalism' in art. *The Father, Miss Julie, Creditors* and *The Stronger*, all plays which explore sexuality and power through a struggle of wills, are a significant part of the naturalist enterprise, although Strindberg has his own particular version of naturalism, which edges very close to symbolism: the plays are full of symbolic images and props, their situations fraught with symbolic resonance.

In *The Stronger* two women confront one another, but only one speaks, with the growing realisation that the woman she is addressing is the source of her own husband's infidelity. The 'psycho-dramas' of this period developed into full-scale fantasy plays in Strindberg's late work. *A Dream Play* and *The Road to Damascus* eschew any attempt at realism, in order to explore a form in which, in Strindberg's words, 'imagination spins and weaves new patterns: a mixture of memories, experiences, unfettered fancies, absurdities and improvisation'.

Although Strindberg has often been cast as a virulent misogynist (and his writings are indeed full of scathing accounts of women), he is so obsessed with questions of power and gender that his plays are very open to feminist readings.

Miss Julie

Miss Julie is an extraordinary play about power, sex and class set on Midsummer's Eve in the kitchen of a nobleman's house. According to Strindberg, in its pattern of 'three art-forms' the play conformed to his development of new forms: 'the monologue, the mime and the ballet'. The manservant Jean's fiancée, the servant Kristin, opens the play with a mime of her domestic duties, in which the class difference with Miss Julie, the nobleman's daughter, is established. As the evening winds on, Julie seduces Jean, and they resolve to run away together. The ballet occurs at the moment of the consummation: a group of peasants sing a Midsummer's Eve drinking song, and point up the class positions that are being negotiated in the offstage bedroom. The play charts the shifts in Jean and Julie's power relations. Julie begins with all the cards

because of her social position, but once she has given herself sexually, she is lost and her class power means nothing in the face of Jean's sexual power. She appeals to Jean, who urges her to kill herself, and the play ends with Julie leaving the stage, with the clear intent of suicide. Jean is left to face the class power of Julie's father.

TRY THESE:

The Wanderings of Lucky Per echoes ✱IBSEN's *Peer Gynt*; ✱SHAW was much affected by Strindberg's new 'theatre of ideas', cross-class sexual attraction is a mainspring of *Arms and the Man*; ✱GENET is among the writers to have exploited the form of dream and fantasy drama that Strindberg forged, and both Expressionism (e.g. Georg Kaiser and Ernst Toller) and Theatre of the Absurd can be seen as owing a great deal to Strindberg; ✱SHAKESPEARE's *A Midsummer Night's Dream* also deals with Midsummer sexual attraction; ✱STRAUSS's *The Tourist Guide* is a bleak modern meditation on the destructiveness of obsessive sexual attraction; Fassbinder's *The Bitter Tears of Petra von Kant* is in the tradition of Strindberg's obsession with power games in sexual attraction; ✱MARBER's *After Miss Julie* for a modern response to Strindberg.

SYNGE, J. M. (John Millington) [1871 – 1909]
Irish dramatist

PLAYS INCLUDE:

In the Shadow of the Glen (1903), *Riders to the Sea* (1904), *The Well of the Saints* (1905), *The Playboy of the Western World* (1907), *The Tinker's Wedding* (1909), *Deirdre of the Sorrows* (1910)

Synge played a significant part in the creation of the Abbey Theatre with ✱YEATS and ✱LADY GREGORY, both as manager and as dramatist. His plays are centred on the life and beliefs of Irish peasant communities in the west and in the Aran Islands, which he visited on Yeats' advice, but there is also a strong underpinning from Christian and classical sources. Synge's most famous play is *The Playboy of the Western World*, partly because of the riots associated with its first production, but mainly because of its assured handling of its tragicomic theme. The contrast between 'a gallous story and a dirty deed' lies at the heart of the different reactions to Christy's two apparent parricides, one safely performed far away and glamorised in the telling, the other done in full view of the community, both on stage and in the audience. With the loss of Christy, Pegeen Mike is left to the humdrum spirit-sapping of her previous existence and our responses are divided: Christy and his father are reconciled and Christy has matured, which suggests comedy. Pegeen Mike is left trapped and aware of her loss, which suggest self-knowledge purchased at almost tragic cost.

TRY THESE:
✱ MATURA's *Playboy of the West Indies* is a sparkling adaptation of the play to the Caribbean; ✱ O'CASEY's dramatisation of the urban Irish in *The Plough and the Stars* also caused a riot at the Abbey Theatre; *Playboy* is a comic reworking of the Oedipus story, as is ✱ BOND's *Saved*; the Orcadian George Mackay Brown's *The Stormwatchers* is reminiscent in tone and subject matter of *Riders to the Sea*; ✱ CHURCHILL's *Fen* includes a version of the story that provides the plot of *The Shadow of the Glen*; ✱ REID's *Joyriders* opens with the joyriders watching a scene from *The Shadow of the Glen* and then develops the parallels further.

TALLY, Ted [1952 –]
American dramatist and screenwriter

PLAYS INCLUDE:

Terra Nova (1977), *Night Mail and Other Sketches* (1977), *Word of Mouth* (1978), *Hooters* (1978), *Coming Attractions* (1980), *Little Footsteps* (1986), *The Gettysburg Soundbite* (1989)

Tally made his reputation early on with *Terra Nova*, a fascinating historically based drama that seems to bear little thematic or stylistic relation to his subsequent works. Set in 1911–12, the play tells the true story of Englishman Robert Scott's race to the Antarctic against Roald Amundsen, the Norwegian. But the play charts more a metaphysical than a physical contest, as Tally displays an unusual historical and temporal breadth. Few people would associate that play with the author of *Hooters*, a four-character comedy about sexual competition on a Cape Cod beach, distinguished by repeated use of the defamatory 'jerkwad!' Tally's satire on contemporary society in the deftly written *Coming Attractions* (media manipulation) and *Little Footsteps* (family) seemed a bit *easy*. He is now probably best known for his Oscar-winning script for *Silence of the Lambs*.

TRY THESE:

✶FEIFFER as an elder statesman satirist, and ✶DURANG, ✶LAPINE, Jonathan Reynolds as a newer breed working in the same bright, deliberately comic-book-like style; ✶RATTIGAN's *Ross* (about T. E. Lawrence) and *Bequest to the Nation* (Nelson and Lady Hamilton) and ✶BRENTON's *Scott of the Antarctic* are other plays about 'heroes'; ✶COLLINS' *The Ice Chimney* for its climbing anti-hero, Maurice Wilson.

TAYLOR, C. P. (Cecil) [1929 – 81]
British dramatist

PLAYS INCLUDE:

Allergy (1966), *Bread and Butter* (1966), *Lies About Vietnam* (1969), *The Black and White Minstrels* (1972), *You Are My Heart's Delight* (1973), *Gynt* (1973), *Schippel* (1974, from Carl Sternheim; later known as *The Plumber's Progress*), *Bandits* (1976), *Walter* (1977), *Ophelia* (1977), *Some Enchanted Evening* (1977), *Peter Pan and Emily* (1977), *And a Nightingale Sang* (1978), *Withdrawal Symptoms* (1978), *Peter Pan Man* (1979; originally as *Cleverness of Us*, 1971), *Bring Me Sunshine, Bring Me Smiles*, (1980, as *The Saints Go Marching In*), *Good* (1981)

Taylor's premature death only months after the initial success of the RSC production of *Good* robbed the British theatre of an extraordinarily versatile and talented dramatist who had been grossly undervalued in his lifetime. Born in Glasgow, but long time resident in the North-east, Taylor wrote some fifty plays for virtually every type of theatre – from the local village to the West End, via community theatre and television. Much of his work, from his first play to his last, included music, and his wry imagination and capacity for what ✶BRECHT called 'complex seeing' is exemplified in *Ophelia*, which is *Hamlet* from Ophelia's viewpoint, or *Withdrawal Symptoms*, which parallels its heroine's drug-withdrawal treatment with the pangs of withdrawal from empire. ✶J. M. BARRIE was the inspiration for *Peter Pan Man* and *Peter Pan and Emily*, in which Peter Pan becomes involved with a Newcastle working-class family. It is typical of the paradoxical nature of Taylor's career, and of the split in theatre-going audiences, that the majority of those who went to see Harry Secombe in the retitled *The Plumber's Progress* and the majority of those who went to see *Good* would have been extremely unlikely to recognise him as the author of both plays.

Good

Taylor's last play was notable for its willingness to confront the banality of evil in its study of its protagonist's gradual drift into Nazism through all the daily minor compromises, adjustments and accommodations which take him from being an emotional advocate of euthanasia in his fiction to advising on giving the Final Solution a caring façade. We can see the terrible seductive power of Nazism as something that offers the protagonist the possibility of a fixed position in a sea of moral uncertainties and doubts. The idea that public postures have the configuration of private derangements achieves a memorable form: throughout the play he is haunted by snatches of music, so that the discovery that the prisoners' band which greets him at Auschwitz is real represents his complete surrender to the inverted logic of the Third Reich.

TRY THESE:

✷ NICHOLS' *Poppy* covers similar imperial ground to *Withdrawal Symptoms*, but more noisily and with less certainty of tone; ✷ POWNALL's *Master Class* and ✷ STOPPARD's *Every Good Boy Deserves Favour* also examine the relationship between totalitarianism and music; ✷ BARNES' *Laughter* is another Auschwitz 'comedy'; *And a Nightingale Sang* covers similar wartime working-class territory to ✷ LOWE's *Touched*; ✷ EDGAR's *Destiny* is another study of fascism, British style.

TAYLOR, Tom   [1817 – 80]
British dramatist

PLAYS INCLUDE:

Masks and Faces (1852, with Charles Reade), *To Oblige Benson* (1854), *Still Waters Run Deep* (1855), *Our American Cousin* (1858), *The Overland Route* (1860), *The Ticket-of-Leave Man* (1863), *New Men and Old Acres* (1869)

Taylor was a professor of English at London University, a civil servant and, in later years, editor of *Punch*. He wrote over seventy plays, of which only *The Ticket-of-Leave Man* is now performed. *Our American Cousin*, with its star part, Lord Dundreary, might be worth reviving, but the unfortunate connection with Lincoln's assassination probably still militates against it. Although *The Ticket-of-Leave Man* is by no means the best of Victorian melodramas, it is revived occasionally. This is possibly because of its apparent social message about the problems of the rehabilitation of a man with a prison record, although the issue is completely fudged because our hero did not commit the crime in the first place. There is some unusual interest in the fact that the villain has the same problem, but the real attraction is Hawkshaw, the detective, and his mastery of disguise.

TRY THESE:

✷ BOUCICAULT, for nineteenth-century melodrama; ✷ GALSWORTHY's *Justice*, for a more realistic picture of the effects of prison.

TEEVAN, Colin
Irish dramatist

PLAYS INCLUDE:

The Big Sea (1990), *Here Come Cowboys* (1992), *Buffalo Bill Has Gone to Alaska* (1993), *Vinegar and Brown Paper* (1995), *The Crack and the Whip* (1997), *Iph . . .* (1999), *Svejk* (1999, from Jaroslav Hasek), *Marathon* (1999, from Edoardo Erba), *Cuckoos* (2000, from Guiseppe Manfridi), *The Walls* (2001), *Monkey* (2001), *Bacchai* (2002, from ✷ EURIPIDES)

Teevan has carved out a distinguished career as a translator/adapter, although his work on Peter Hall's production of John Barton's *Tantalus* was controversial. His own work reflects a strong awareness of theatrical tradition. *The Big Sea* (with a pun on cancer as 'The Big C'), set in a cancer ward as the patients play games to pass the time, derives from a medieval French Mardi Gras play, whereas both *Vinegar and Brown Paper* and *The Walls* use the familiar devices of a return home as a catalyst for revelation and confrontation. In *The Walls* it is Christmas Eve, the returning son is called Joseph and his wife is Mary, but the family's disintegration is matched by the actual removal of the house walls, a device that struck critics as too obvious.

TRY THESE:

✳AESCHYLUS, ✳EURIPIDES, ✳SOPHOCLES for Greek tragedy; ✳BRECHT for another approach to Schweik; *The Walls* was compared (unfavourably) to ✳IONESCO; ✳AYCKBOURN for Christmas revelations; ✳PINTER for *The Homecoming*.

TERRY, Megan   [1932 –   ]
American, writer, director and teacher

PLAYS INCLUDE:

Ex-Miss Copper Queen on a Set of Pills (1963), *Hothouse* (1964, produced 1974), *Calm Down Mother* (1965), *Comings and Goings* (1966), *Viet Rock* (1966), *The Gloaming, Oh My Darling* (1966), *Approaching Simone* (1970), *Nightwalk* (1973, with ✳SAM SHEPARD and ✳JEAN-CLAUDE VAN ITALLIE), *Hothouse* (1974), *Babes in the Bighouse* (1974), *Brazil Fado* (1977), *American King's English for Queens* (1978), *Attempted Rescue on Avenue B* (1979), *X-rayed Late* (1984, with Jo Ann Schmidman), *Sea of Forms* (1986, with Jo Ann Schmidman), *Walking Through Walls* (1987, with Jo Ann Schmidman), *Amtrack* (1988), *Body Leaks* (1990, with Sora Kimberlain and Jo Ann Schmidman), *Breakfast Serial* (1991), *Sound Fields: Are We Hear* (1992)

Hailed by Helene Keyssar as the 'mother of American feminist drama', Terry, who has written over sixty plays, deserves greater recognition in Britain. One of the major contributors to Joe Chaikin's Open Theatre in the late 1960s and early 1970s, she made her name with the American public with the now famous anti-war *Viet Rock* (the first rock musical), in a double bill with Open Theatre colleague ✳JEAN CLAUDE VAN ITALLIE's *America Hurrah*. The production made history, partly because of its anti-war stance, but also for the style of its presentation, which built on Chaikin's improvisational group work and Terry's favoured 'transformation' techniques – a way of looking at women's lives and theatre technique that informs much of her work. Her concerns have ranged over a wide spectrum of issues covering sexism,

violence, the materialism of American society, and political confusion, but the excitement of her work has been both in her gestural use of language and in the physical and theatrical immediacy of her *mise-en-scène*: sudden ✳BRECHTIAN changes of tempo; visual metaphors; satiric parodies culled from popular culture; lots of music (again often satirising familiar cultural references); gender swapping (in *Babes in the Bighouse* and in *Viet Rock* Terry used male actors to interpret females roles, and vice versa).

As writer-in-residence at the Omaha Magic Theatre in Nebraska she has worked extensively with Jo Ann Schmidman, the company's founder, on musicals and on works with specific relevance to the local community.

A British revival of the challenging *Approaching Simone* (about the remarkable life of French philosopher Simone Weil, who committed suicide by starving herself to death), is well overdue.

TRY THESE:

✳CHURCHILL's *Cloud Nine*, ✳YANKOWITZ's *Slaughterhouse* for gender-bending; ✳GEMS' *Dusa, Fish, Stas and Vi*, ✳DUFFY's *Rites* for women together; for American anti-war images, ✳MANN's *Still Life*, the Vietnam Vets Ensemble's *Tracers*; for searing poetic language, feminist politics and inventive production concepts, Karen Malpede and ✳SHANGE.

TERSON, Peter   [1932 –   ]
British dramatist

PLAYS INCLUDE:

A Night to Make the Angels Weep (1964), *The Mighty Reservoy* (1964), *Zigger Zagger* (1967), *Mooney and His Caravans* (1968, TV version 1966), *The Apprentices* (1968), *Spring-heeled Jack* (1970), *The 1861 Whitby Lifeboat Disaster* (1971), *But Fred, Freud is Dead* (1972), *Cul de Sac* (1978), *Strippers* (1984)

A working-class Geordie, Terson trained as a teacher after National Service and taught games for ten years, while collecting rejection slips for his early plays. In 1964 *A Night to Make the Angels Weep* began a close association with Peter Cheeseman and his Stoke Victoria Theatre-in-the-round. Since then Terson's output has been prolific (sixteen plays for Stoke alone in the following ten years) for both theatre and television. Equally at home with a two-hander, such as *The Mighty Reservoy* or *Mooney and His Caravans*, and the large casts of the National Youth Theatre, for whom he has written extensively, his plays often show an allegorical opposition of traditional or rural life and 'progress', but his greatest characteristic is the fluency of his dialogue and his ear for working-class speech. In his plays for the National Youth Theatre Terson has shown the ability to respond to ideas and individual talents coming from the company to rapidly create new material. His earliest plays, set in the Vale of Evesham, where he then lived, all have an air of menace. *The Mighty Reservoy* charts the relationship of the keeper of a new reservoir and a more educated, town-bred visitor who is drowned in Act 3 but whose spirit apparently returns to warn the drunken keeper of a crack in the reservoir. The reservoir becomes a dark obsession for the characters, and several critics have described their relationship with it as 'Lawrencian'. Many later plays reflect the style developed at Stoke for local documentary drama, including narration and rapid changes of locale. *Strippers*, a provocative examination of the downside of Thatcherism which shows working-class women taking to stripping as a response to the economic collapse of the north-east, raises as many questions about the way to present female exploitation as it answers about sexism and male double standards.

Zigger Zagger

His first play for the National Youth Theatre, *Zigger Zagger* brought both Terson and the NYT to public notice and is still his best-known work. A football crowd on the terraces surrounds the action played out before it of the dead-end prospects of a football-mad teenager. Songs and interjections from the terraces frame naturalistic scenes but these reinforce the overall content rather than providing ✱BRECHTIAN alienation. The criticism of a society that presents such no-hope prospects is implicit. Full of vitality, the play eschews any false sentiment and is as objectively critical of working-class parents and soccer stars as it is of probation officers and the Establishment.

TRY THESE:

✱RUDKIN, especially in *Afore Night Come*, has also recorded the brooding menace behind the tranquillity of rural Worcestershire; ✱BYRNE's *The Slab Boys* follows the problems of the developing adolescent in a tale about apprentices; ✱RECKORD's *Skyvers* for educational critique; ✱ADSHEAD, in *Thatcher's Women*, and Julia Schofield, in *Love On the Plastic*, also investigate the relationship between Thatcherism, unemployment in the north, and the sexual exploitation of women; ✱HORSFIELD for a football trilogy based around four female football fans; ✱ARDREY for aquatic ghosts.

TESICH, Steve   [1942 – 96]
American dramatist and screenwriter

PLAYS INCLUDE:
The Carpenters (1970*)*, *One on One* (1971), *Lake of the Woods* (1971), *Baba Goya* (1973, later revised and staged as *Nourish the Beast*), *Gorky* (1975), *The Passing Game* (1977), *King of Hearts* (1977, book for musical), *Touching Bottom* (1978, comprising *The Road, A Life, Baptismal*), *Division Street* (1980), *The Speed of Darkness* (1988), *Square One* (1990), *Commencement Exercises* (1991), *On the Open Road* (1992)

Although Tesich is best known as a screenwriter, his roots were in the theatre. Born Stoyan Tesich in Yugoslavia, the playwright arrived in America at the age of fourteen with little English and an immigrant's objectivity. In his plays and films, Tesich captures with life-size characters the hopes and disappointments of the American dream. *The Carpenters* concerns a radical son whose plan to kill his working-class father receives a twist of fate when his father unexpectedly kills him. In plays like *One on One*, which focuses on racial tension, Tesich uses music, black humour and purposeful exaggeration; in both *The Carpenters* and *Lake of the Woods*, the dramatic action is built on conflict, whereas his later plays evolve from character.

In these later plays, like *Baba Goya*, Tesich uses the family as a special symbol of America, a warm and convincing portrait of hope filled with humour and compassion. An idealistic streak runs throughout these works, which seem to remind people that they are better 'deep down' than they seem. *The Speed of Darkness* focuses on family of a different sort: two Vietnam veterans who share a dark secret as they meet again in South Dakota twenty years after their service. Tesich's first play in almost a decade, it is a stylistic departure, one that probes more realistically in the style of ✷ARTHUR MILLER or Robert Anderson. The play's two antagonists are direct opposites as characters, one a seemingly successful businessman, the other a menacing drifter. Tesich strongly criticises America's involvement in Vietnam. His disillusion is continued in *Square One*, which presents almost-soulless characters who meet, marry, breed and part. These cold characters exhibit Tesich's mourning for 'a time when people cared and felt'.

TRY THESE:

✷TREVOR GRIFFITHS' *Sam Sam*, ✷MILLER's *All My Sons* and *American Clock* for their use of family to make a political statement; ✷GALATI's 1989 adaptation of John Steinbeck's *The Grapes of Wrath* for a similar sense of a strong, core family and its personal battles fought against a backdrop of troubled American landscape; ✷MANN's *Still Life* for another Vietnam play.

THOMAS, Dylan   [1914 – 53]
Welsh poet

PLAYS INCLUDE:

A Child's Christmas in Wales (1950), *Under Milk Wood* (1954)

Anglo-Welsh poet Thomas was born in Swansea, and wrote his poetry while living precariously, earning money from articles, broadcasts and film scripts, and eventually from lecture tours in the USA, on one of which he died.

Under Milk Wood is probably the most famous radio play in English (well, Anglo-Welsh), but it has very little plot and very little conflict. It is more of a descriptive piece, opulently written and often very funny, about the inhabitants of Llareggub, that Platonic ideal of a Welsh coastal village, read by two narrators and a series of actors, mostly in monologue. It is more often staged in the USA than in Britain, where it is generally thought of as better heard than seen.

TRY THESE:

Brian Abbott's *Milk Wood Blues* featured Thomas losing the original manuscript of *Under Milk Wood* on a Soho pub crawl; ✷ARTAUD, whose life has also become mythical and a matter for plays; ✷EMLYN WILLIAMS' *The Druid's Rest* for another relentlessly picturesque view of the Welsh; ✷WILDER's *Our Town* does something similar for middle America; ✷CARTWRIGHT's *Road* has been called a 'radicalised *Under Milk Wood* for the 1980s'; for other ways of using monologues, ✷TREMBLAY; ✷OWEN and ✷EDWARD THOMAS for contemporary Welsh writing.

THOMAS, Edward
Welsh dramatist

PLAYS INCLUDE:

House of America (1989), *Adar Heb Aderydd* (1989), *The Myth of Michael Roderick* (1990), *Flowers of the Dead Red Sea* (1991), *East from the Gantry* (1992), *Envy* (1993), *Songs from a Forgotten City* (1995), *Gas Station Angel* (1998)

Thomas is a leading figure in the current explosion of Welsh theatrical activity through his company Fiction Factory and his own explorations of Welsh identity. Carole Woddis's description of *Gas Station Angel* is a fair summary of his work: 'part cartoon cut out, part grand guignol, part latter day soap beaten into bizarre shapes, it is Wales, and its mythological fairy-lands turned upside'. Some English reviewers argued that his work stereotypes the Welsh but the view from Wales seems to be that he interrogates the ways in which Welsh identities have been constructed rather than promulgating them.

TRY THESE:

✷OWEN for another contemporary Welsh writer; ✷DYLAN THOMAS and ✷EMLYN WILLIAMS for Welsh myth-making; ✷CHURCHILL's *The Skriker* for other contemporary fairies.

THOMPSON, Judith   [1954 –   ]
Canadian dramatist

PLAYS INCLUDE:
The Crackwalker (1980), *White Biting Dog*
(1984), *Pink* (1986), *I Am Yours* (1987), *Lion
in the Streets* (1990), *Perfect Pie* (2000),
Habitat (2001)

One of Canada's leading dramatists,
Thompson teaches drama at Guelph
University. Her work is becoming better
known in Britain, with stagings by Shared
Experience, and at the Gate, Hampstead
Theatre, Manchester and Glasgow. Her first
play, *Crackwalker*, sets the tone for much of
her work with its presentation of a Canadian
urban underclass. Lyn Gardner has described
I Am Yours as an 'eerie play about possessive
love'. *Lion in the Streets* uses the structure of
✱SCHNITZLER's *La Ronde* to present a cycle of
urban misery. *Habitat* tackles a familiar
problem of the local residents who do not
want a centre for problem teenagers in their
backyard.

TRY THESE:
✱HIGHWAY and ✱TREMBLAY as other inter-
nationally known Canadian dramatists; ✱BOND,
✱CARTWRIGHT for British urban underclasses;
Thompson has adapted ✱IBSEN's *Hedda Gabler*;
Morris Panych's *Auntie and Me* for another
Canadian success in Britain.

TOURNEUR, Cyril   [*c.* 1575 – 1626]
English dramatist

PLAYS INCLUDE:
The Revenger's Tragedy (1606, attributed to
Tourneur 1656), *The Atheist's Tragedy* (1610)

There is now very great scholarly doubt about
the 1656 attribution of *The Revenger's Tragedy*
to Tourneur, with ✱MIDDLETON being the
favoured alternative author, in which case
Tourneur becomes even more of a shadowy
figure. He was in the service of the Cecil
family and died after being put ashore from a
returning naval expedition to Cadiz. To add
posthumous insult to injury, the manuscript
of another play was lost in the eighteenth
century, when it was used by a cook,
apparently to line a pie dish, a fate it shared

with a number of other unique manuscripts.
The Atheist's Tragedy has been described as
'hilarious', particularly in view of the fact that
the protagonist D'Amville has to accidentally
brain himself as he attempts to execute the
hero; it is not likely to become a staple of the
contemporary theatre, although its stylistic
diversity and changes of mood offer interesting challenges to an adventurous company.
The Revenger's Tragedy, authorship controversy notwithstanding, has had several
productions since 1965, when it was revived
professionally at the Pitlochry Festival. The
most memorable production was Trevor
Nunn's 1966 RSC revival, which made Alan
Howard a star and gave full weight to the
play's satirical theatricality. Most of the
conventional elements of revenge tragedy are
here: the long delayed revenge, rape, the skull
of a dead woman used to poison the man
responsible for her death, incest and the
culminating masque which leads to multiple
deaths. But there is also a strong sense both of
the corruption of the world of realpolitik and
of the corruption of the revenger who has to
move in that world to achieve revenge.

TRY THESE:
Most Renaissance dramatists used revenge plots
and malcontent figures: ✱SHAKESPEARE's *Hamlet*
is the most famous example of both, but ✱KYD's
The Spanish Tragedy started the vogue for revenge
and there are notable examples in ✱CHAPMAN,
✱FORD, ✱MARSTON, ✱MIDDLETON,
✱SHAKESPEARE (*Titus Andronicus*) and
✱WEBSTER; amongst contemporary dramatists
✱BARNES has a gift for the wittily macabre.

TOWNSEND, Sue   [1946 –   ]
British dramatist and novelist

PLAYS INCLUDE:
Womberang (1979), *The Ghost of Daniel
Lambert* (1981), *Dayroom* (1981), *Bazaar
and Rummage* (1982), *Captain Christmas
and the Evil Adults* (1982), *Groping for Words*
(1983, revised as *Are You Sitting
Comfortably*), *The Great Celestial Cow*
(1984), *The Secret Diary of Adrian Mole aged
13¾* (1984), *Disneyland It Ain't* (1989), *The
Queen and I* (1994, from her novel)

The phenomenal success of her best-known creation, Adrian Mole, has tended to overshadow the fact that Townsend, suburban lower-middle-class mother of four, ex-hotdog stall and garage forecourt manager, youth-club worker and one-time Thames Television writer-in-residence at Leicester's Phoenix Theatre, has more than schoolboy strings to her bow.

Townsend's droll, down-to-earth kind of humour now and again takes on a surreal and surprisingly angry edge – as in *Womberang*, a comic-vitriolic swipe at the bureaucratic inadequacies of the National Health Service set in the normally stock situation of a hospital waiting-room, with a wonderfully vituperative working-class rebel, Rita Onions. *Groping for Words* also sets up the unprepossessing sitcom of an evening class in adult literacy, but turns it with warmth and humanity into quite a grim political warning about the link between illiteracy, frustration and the pent-up anger of society's underclass. *The Great Celestial Cow*, a fantasy-carnival for Joint Stock based on Townsend's observations of the Asian community in her home town of Leicester, intended to break down the stereotype of the 'passive' Asian woman, was unfortunately too broad for some, and arguably ended up inadvertently reinforcing the images it was supposed to be cracking. *The Secret Diary of Adrian Mole aged 13¾* (which started out life as an unsolicited radio script, then became a best-selling book before becoming a musical and a television series) and its sequel *The Growing Pains of Adrian Mole* will probably remain Townsend's enduring legacy. Of Mole, her spotty adolescent who turns his consistently cool eye on the antics of adult passion, Townsend wrote, somewhat prophetically: 'I wanted to put down what it was like for a certain type of person in 1981 – a class of person that's now deserting the Labour Party – and get it all down in detail because things are changing.' In *The Queen and I* she imagines a republican takeover that leaves the House of Windsor rehoused on a Leicester council estate. Out of Joint paired it wickedly with ✱JIM CARTWRIGHT's *Road*.

TRY THESE:

For school-oriented views of adolescence, Denise Deegan's *Daisy Pulls It Off* and ✱O'MALLEY's *Once a Catholic*; ✱BAINS' *The Fighting Kite* explores a young man's dual identity as a British Asian; few plays have advanced the disjunction of the Asian woman from her roots, but ✱KUREISHI's *Borderline* covers some of the ground and ✱SHAPIRO's monologue *One of Us* comes even closer; for contrasting hospital images, ✱MARCHANT's *Raspberry*, ✱NICHOLS' *The National Health*, ✱PAGE's *Tissue*; ✱DUNBAR for estate life.

TRAVERS, Ben   [1886 – 1980]
British novelist and dramatist

PLAYS INCLUDE:

The Dippers (1922), *The Three Graces* (1924), *A Cuckoo in the Nest* (1925), *Rookery Nook* (1926), *Thark* (1927), *Mischief* (1928), *Plunder* (1928), *A Cup of Kindness* (1929), *A Night Like This* (1930), *Turkey Time* (1931), *Dirty Work* (1932), *A Bit of a Test* (1933), *Chastity, My Brother* (1936), *O Mistress Mine* (1936), *Banana Ridge* (1938), *Spotted Dick* (1940), *She Follows Me About* (1945), *Outrageous Fortune* (1947), *Runaway Victory* (1949), *Wild Horses* (1952), *Corkers End* (1968), *The Bed Before Yesterday* (1975)

Travers' first plays were adaptations of his own novels but from 1925 to 1933 he became the 'house dramatist' for the Aldwych Theatre, London, with a succession of meticulously constructed farces written to exploit the talents of actor-manager Tom Walls (hero), Ralph Lynn (hero's friend), Robertson Hare (hen-pecked husband), Winifred Shotter (heroine) and Mary Brough (Amazonian female). Creating vehicles for the same team does make his characters somewhat predictable, but his plots are inventive, within the basic requirements of farce. Travers himself considered ✱FEYDEAU's type of farce far too mechanical and that everything should be absolutely true to life – though today it now seems a rather stylised 1930s kind of reality. His farces preserve the proprieties and restore the status quo – though, as in *Plunder* for instance, that may include an acceptance of corruption and duplicity. Their tension comes from fear of scandal and the conflict between the outbreak of sexuality and its suppression. On the page they present numerous appalling bad jokes, puns and non-sequiturs that can only be hilarious if played with conviction and precise timing.

In his last play, *The Bed Before Yesterday*, liberated from the Lord Chamberlain's censoring hand, he made explicit what had previously had to be conveyed implicitly. A prude, put off sex by her first bridal night and having survived two marriages without it, finds herself an impoverished widower to marry for company. Intrigued by hearing other women describe sexual passion she then demands it – and gets totally turned on! Though a relatively slight piece, it encapsulates a whole cycle of sexual experience from puritan rejection, through intrigue, experiment, awakening and infidelity, to final conjugal conviviality – and presents it from the woman's point of view.

TRY THESE:

✳LABICHE as the other acknowledged master of French farce; English farce is itself the subject of ✳FRAYN's *Noises Off*; ✳ORTON's *Loot* and *What the Butler Saw* owe much to Travers; ✳COONEY is the contemporary master of English farce.

TREMBLAY, Michel   [1942 –   ]
French Canadian dramatist

PLAYS INCLUDE:
Le Train (1964, *The Train*), *Les Belles-soeurs* (1965, *The Sisters-in-law* or *The Guid Sisters*), *La Duchesse de Langeais* (1969, *The Duchess of Langeais*), *A toi pour toujours, ta Marie-Lou* (1971, *Forever Yours, Marie-Lou*), *Hosanna* (1973), *Hello, là, bonjour*, or *Bonjour, Bonjour* (1974, *Hello, There, Hello*), *Sainte Carmen de la Main* (1976, *Carmen of the Boulevards*), *Damnée Manon, Sacrée Sandra* (1977, *Manon/Sandra*), *L'Impromptu d'Outremont* (1980, *The Impromptu of Outremont*), *Les anciennes odeurs* (1981, *Remember Me*), *Albertine in Five Times* (1984), *Le Vrai Monde?* (1986, *The Real World?*), *La Maison Suspendue* (1990), *Messe solennelle pour une pleine lune d'été* (1995, *Solemn Mass for a Full Summer Moon* or *Solemn Mass for a Full Moon in Summer*),

Encore une fois, si vous permettez (1998, *For the Pleasure of Seeing Her Again*)

Tremblay, a prolific novelist as well as playwright, was brought up in a working-class family in Montreal's impoverished East End, a fact that reflects itself over and over again in his plays. Reminiscent of ✳TENNESSEE WILLIAMS in his domestic and female obsessions (not surprisingly Tremblay has translated several of Williams' plays), Tremblay's heightened, voluptuous prose style, absorption with guilt, sexual fantasy and homosexuality also recalls ✳JEAN GENET and at his best he is as exciting, though without the misogyny. *Manon/Sandra*, a taut two-hander about ecstasy, sacred and profane, is the last in a cycle of plays developed from *The Sisters-in-law*, dealing with three sisters: Marie Lou in *Forever Yours, Marie-Lou* (considered Tremblay's masterpiece); her older sister Carmen in *Saint Carmen of the Boulevards*, and finally the younger sister Manon.

Albertine in Five Times continues Tremblay's exploration of women and their lives, being a lyrical, multifaceted view of a mother, ageing from thirty to seventy (and played, at least in the British version, by five different actresses). Somewhat deterministic in its never-ending cycle of woes, it is nonetheless a sensitive representation of the lives of Montreal working-class women, even if its static monologue structure seems more appropriate to radio than stage – a fault that could certainly not be laid at the door of *Manon/Sandra*, which, adventurously, plays with notions of gender and fantasy to thrilling effect. *The Real World?*, a fairly self-conscious 'making-of-the-artist-as-a-young-man' play, with its seething resentments and claustrophobic family discord, strikes a more naturalistic note even whilst seeming to experiment with notions of reality and fantasy by repeating scenes through the eyes of different members of the family. *Solemn Mass* uses the form of the Catholic mass to present a series of portraits of representative contemporary couples, including a lesbian pair, a gay duo, one of whom has AIDS, a father and daughter, a mother and son, a widow, and a heterosexual pair in the first pangs of romance.

TRY THESE:
Monologues have become a popular technique in modern drama: ✱CARTWRIGHT's *Road* (which bears comparison with *Solemn Mass*, ✱MCINTYRE's *Low Level Panic*, Robert Patrick's *Kennedy's Children*, ✱WARD's *Apart from George* all use monologues in a multifaceted way; ✱SHAKESPEARE got there sooner, of course, and his soliloquies in such plays as *Richard III*, *Hamlet*, and *Macbeth* are the perfect vehicle for contrasting the levels of action – the inner thoughts of the protagonist and what is going on onstage; for three sisters, ✱SHAKESPEARE's *King Lear* and ✱CHEKHOV's *Three Sisters*; for an alternative feminist version, *Lear's Daughters* by Elaine Feinstein; ✱LEONARD, ✱SIMON for other artists-in-the making; for claustrophobic households, ✱HELLMAN, ✱KESSELMAN's *My Sister in this House*, Robert Lepage for a contemporary Canadian theatrical auteur.

TRIANA, José   [1933 –]
Cuban dramatist

PLAYS INCLUDE.
El Major General (1956, *The Major General*), *Medea en el Espuio* (1960, *Medea in the Mirror*), *El Parque de la Fraternidad* (1961, *Fraternity Park*), *La Casa Ariendo* (1962, *The Burning House*), *La Muerte del Neque* (1963, *The Death of Neque*), *La Noche de los Asesinos* (*The Night of the Assassins, or, as The Criminals*, London, 1967), *Worlds Apart* (1986)

Triana is best known in Britain for two plays, *The Criminals* and *Worlds Apart*. An impressionistic drama about three children who may or may not have murdered their parents, *The Criminals* was the first Cuban play to be seen in Britain, and its raw, violent mix of reality and fantasy shocked some observers; others took its ✱GENET-like theatrics metaphorically, drawing an implicit analogy between familial oppression and that of the state. In *Worlds Apart*, set in Cuba between 1894 and 1913, a sprawling family saga unfolds against the background of political upheaval. With his interest in incident-filled family yarns told in a discursive, dreamlike fashion, Triana recalls great Latin American novelists like Márquez and Borges more than his play-

writing peers, although the sagas can get bogged down in Dallas-style soap operatics at the expense of dramatic finesse. Talawa staged *Medea in the Mirror* in 1996.

TRY THESE:
✱LORCA, and (more recently) ✱KESSELMAN's *My Sister in This House* for often violent enactments of social ritual, both in and outside the family; ✱MACHADO and ✱FORNES for Cuban-born playwrights with dream-like lyricism; ✱GELBER's *The Cuban Thing* and ✱SACKLER's *Goodbye, Fidel* for American treatments of a country in tumult.

TURGENEV, Ivan Sergeivich   [1818 – 83]
Russian anarchist and dramatist

PLAYS INCLUDE:
The Bachelor (1849), *A Poor Gentleman* (1851), *A Month in the Country* (written 1850, performed 1872)

Born the son of an impoverished nobleman in Orel, central Russia, Turgenev is one of the great nineteenth-century masters of psychological realism, on a par with Flaubert and George Eliot, and the pre-eminent forebear of ✱CHEKHOV, who would further refine Turgenev's incisive sense of character. Turgenev's own stage reputation rests on *A Month in the Country*, a romantic drama about an idle provincial wife who fails in love with her son's tutor. George F. Walker's adaptation of his novel *Fathers and Sons* has had many productions in the USA. ✱BRIAN FRIEL's adaptation of the same novel has been less successful in Britain.

A Month in the Country
One of the most frequently revived Russian plays after the work of ✱CHEKHOV, this play bears many similarities to that other master playwright. The story of the indolent Natalya's infatuation with her son's tutor, the play is also – like *The Cherry Orchard* – a portrait of a shifting society, emblematised both in the Trofimov-like tutor, Belyaev (a spiritual cousin to the celebrated nihilist Bazarov in *Fathers and Sons*), and in Natalya's Lopakhin-like husband, Islayev, with his triple interest in the forces of progress, mechanis-

ation, and the psychology of the workers. A languid witness to romantic evasions in which she participates and a world in flux in which she does not, Natalya herself recalls Yelena from *Uncle Vanya*.

TRY THESE:

✳GORKY for another Russian playwright who offers both acute insights into character and varying degrees of political comment on Russian society on the eve of change; ✳GOLDONI, ✳PETER SHAFFER's *Five Finger Exercise* and Stephen Sondheim's *A Little Night Music* for comparable depictions of romantic goings-on in a country setting; ✳MILLER for fathers and sons.

UHRY, Alfred [1937 –]
American lyricist and dramatist

PLAYS INCLUDE:
Here's Where I Belong (1968, musical), *The Robber Bridegroom* (1978, musical), *Swing* (1980, musical), *America's Sweetheart* (1985, musical), *Driving Miss Daisy* (1987), *The Last Night of Ballyhoo* (1997), *Parade* (1998, musical)

Born in Atlanta, Uhry began his theatrical career as a lyricist. The off-Broadway theatre Playwrights Horizons produced *Driving Miss Daisy* in 1987, and the play made such an impact that it quickly spawned touring companies to Chicago and London. After winning the Pulitzer Prize in 1988 it became one of the most-produced plays of the American regional theatre.

A small play, acutely observed and restrained, *Driving Miss Daisy* spans twenty-five years in the life of a widowed Jewish woman in Atlanta, starting in the year she acquiesces to her son's demand that she hire a chauffeur. The new employee, a black man named Hoke, at first finds himself unwelcome and uncomfortable around the brittle Daisy: she won't have anyone pointing out to her that she's no longer as able and independent as she once was. Before long, however, Daisy finds herself cherishing Hoke's offhand wit and warm attentiveness, and they stay together as car models change, their eyesight deteriorates, and racial politics starts to intrude upon their idyll.

Some have faulted Uhry for predictability and gratuitous references to the civil rights movement, but (remarkably, given its premise) this is not a sentimental play. Uhry is sure about what to put in and leave out in the pair's conversations, where to end scenes before they start to cloy, how long to make his play. And it doesn't seem so mechanical in performance, where fine actors can bring spontaneity and add to its charms. That seemed to be the consensus, at least, of the movie industry, which heaped praise (and Oscars) on Uhry's film version (after initially keeping their distance when it was proposed) and especially on its two stars, Jessica Tandy (who won an Oscar) and Morgan Freeman.

TRY THESE:
✶HENLEY and ✶TENNESSEE WILLIAMS for plays infused with the atmosphere of the American South that share some of Uhry's lyricism;
✶FUGARD, who dramatises the friction between blacks and whites in a contrasting way;
✶DURANG, ✶GURNEY, ✶TALLY, other writers associated with Playwrights Horizons, for a sense of the range of the theatre that first produced *Driving Miss Daisy*.

UPTON, Judy [1966 –]
British dramatist

PLAYS INCLUDE:
Everlasting Rose (1992), *Ashes and Sand* (1994), *Temple* (1995), *The Shorewatchers' House* (1995), *Bruises* (1995), *Stealing Souls* (1996), *Sunspots* (1996), *People on the River* (1997), *To Blusher with Love* (1997), *Pig in the Middle* (1998), *The Girlz* (1998), *Know Your Rights* (1998), *Confidence* (1998), *The Ballad of a Thin Man* (2000, after Chaucer's *The Pardoner's Tale*), *Sliding with Suzanne* (2001), *Team Spirit* (2002)

Upton comes from Shoreham-by-Sea and several of her plays draw on the peculiar liminal atmosphere of the seaside town that has seen better days, as experienced by its inhabitants, from the rampaging girl gang of *Ashes and Sand* and the domestic violence of *Bruises* to the start of the summer season in *Confidence*. Although much of her territory is the familiar stuff of contemporary urban decay and disaffection, she has sometimes focused this through aspects of the music business (*People on the River, To Blusher with Love*) and even the music industry and Chaucer in *The Ballad of a Thin Man*. In *Pig in the Middle* she wrote about the issues involved in medical advances such as pig organs being used in human transplants, and was rewarded with a staging at the House of Commons. *Team Spirit* tackles another topical issue with its exploration of the contradiction between being a single-handed yachtswoman and the need to obtain funding for the project by sharing the loneliness with an intrusive media in order to get the sponsorship to continue the voyaging.

TRY THESE:

✴CORTHRON, ✴ PRICHARD for girl gangs; ✴BOND's *Saved* for an earlier Royal Court version of disaffected youth; ✴PAGE's *Golden Girls* for sponsorship and sport; ✴PINTER's *The Birthday Party* for a seaside boarding house to compare to the one in *Bruises*; ✴MCLEAN for domestic violence.

VANBRUGH, John [1664 – 1726]
English dramatist, soldier and architect

PLAYS INCLUDE:
The Relapse (1696), *The Provoked Wife* (1697)

Vanbrugh's adventurous life included several spells as a soldier, a stay in the Bastille after being arrested in France as a spy, an attempt at theatrical management, and designing Blenheim Palace. He also found time to adapt plays from the French (including several by ✷MOLIÈRE) and finished two of his own. *The Relapse* takes over the characters from Colley Cibber's *Love's Last Shift* and deploys them in a complicated intrigue plot involving town/country contrasts, secret marriages, impersonation and mistaken identity. Although the continued success of both plays probably owes as much to their farcical elements (the humiliation of and satire at the expense of the aptly named Lord Foppington in *The Relapse* and the transvestite antics of Sir John Brute in *The Provoked Wife*), perhaps their most interesting feature is the presentation of unhappily married couples in which the faithful wife resists the temptations of a potential lover. In a period when divorce was practically non-existent Vanbrugh's refusal to adopt the mix-and-match 'happy' ending solution favoured by some of his contemporaries leaves his comedies curiously unresolved. There is an open-ended realism about his endings that suggests that they are resting points rather than conclusions. In the first version of *The Provoked Wife* Sir John wore a clerical costume rather than women's clothing for his drunken frolics; the scenes were probably altered in response to complaints about their disrespect to religion, but they are more thematically appropriate in their revised form.

TRY THESE:
Vanbrugh's comedies can be compared instructively with those of the other writers of Restoration comedy, ✷BEHN, ✷CONGREVE, ✷ETHEREGE, ✷FARQUHAR, ✷OTWAY, ✷WYCHERLEY, and with later exponents of comedy of manners such as ✷GOLDSMITH, ✷SHERIDAN, ✷WILDE, ✷COWARD, ✷SIMON, ✷LUCIE; ✷AYCKBOURN's pictures of marriage are reminiscent in some ways of Vanbrugh; ✷PINERO's *The Magistrate* offers another pillar of society in court as a result of drunken misdeeds.

VAN ITALLIE, Jean-Claude [1936 –]
Belgian-born American dramatist

PLAYS INCLUDE:
War (1963), *Almost Like Being* (1964), *I'm Really Here* (1964), *The Hunter and the Bird* (1964), *Where Is De Queen* (1965), *Motel* (1965), *Interview* (1966), *America Hurrah* (1966), *The Girl and the Soldier* (1967), *The Serpent: A Ceremony* (1968), *Take a Deep Breath* (1969), *Photographs: Mary and Howard* (1969), *Eat Cake* (1971), *The King of the United States* (1973), *Nightwalk* (1973, with ✷MEGAN TERRY and ✷SAM SHEPARD), *A Fable* (1975), *Bag Lady* (1979), *The Tibetan Book of the Dead* (1983), *The Traveller* (1987) *Ancient Boys* (1990)

Van Itallie was a central figure in the off-Broadway explosion of the 1960s. As a writer for the Open Theatre in New York City he structured his plays around the company's actor-centred improvisational work while infusing them with social and political awareness. His 1966 trilogy of social alienation, *America Hurrah*, is still considered one of the key works of the decade. Elsewhere, van Itallie has experimented with breaking down the expected form and structure of drama, eschewing conventions of plot in favour of archetypal situations (the story of the Garden of Eden and temptation in *The Serpent*) or anarchic satire (*Eat Cake*, a brief but telling assault on American consumerism). His later original works were more pedestrian. His forty-five-minute monologue *Bag Lady* never gets inside its peripatetic character's head, and *The Traveller*, based on the stroke and aphasia of his friend and former colleague Joseph Chaikin, too often sacrifices hoped-for lyricism to obvious dramaturgy. In *Ancient Boys*, a theatre designer discovers he has AIDS, prompting an exploration of individual and planetary disease, and the hope of salvation through art.

TRY THESE:

Van Itallie is better known of late for his ✴CHEKHOV translations; ✴SHEPARD and ✴TERRY for dramatists influenced by Chaikin's Open Theatre; ✴YANKOWITZ, another Chaikin devotee, wrote *Night Sky*, also inspired by her mentor's aphasia; ✴LORCA and ✴SOYINKA for emphasis on theatre as ritual; ✴OWENS' *Futz* for a seminal American play of the 1960s along the lines of *America Hurrah*; ✴DE FILIPPO's *Ducking Out*, ✴KEARSLEY's *Under the Web* and ✴KOPIT's *Wings* for plays featuring stroke victims; William Hoffman's *As Is*, ✴KONDOLEON's *Zero Positive*, ✴KRAMER's *Normal Heart*, for plays about AIDS.

VINAVER, Michel   [1927 –   ]
French dramatist and novelist

PLAYS INCLUDE:
Aujourd'hui ou Les Coreéns (1956, *The Koreans*), *Iphigénie Hotel* (1960), *Par-dessus bord* (1972, *Overboard*), *Chamber Theatre* (1978, consists of *Dissident, Il va sans dire, Nina, c'est autre chose* – *Dissident, Goes Without Saying, Nina, That's Something Else*), *Les Travaux et les Jours* (1979, *A Smile on the End of the Line*), *L'Ordinaire* (1983, *High Places*), *Les Voisins* (1984, *The Neighbours*), *Portrait d'une femme* (1984, *Portrait of a Woman*), *L'Émission de television* (1988, *The Television Programme*)

Vinaver (whose real name is Michel Grinberg) is one of the most important contemporary French dramatists. He began as a novelist, but has concentrated on plays since 1955, except for a long gap in the 1960s when his work for the Gillette company came first (they never seem to have found out about his second life, and their reactions to his unflattering pictures of international companies are not recorded). His first play, *The Koreans*, was put on by Roger Planchon in 1956, and shows alternately a group of French soldiers and some Korean villagers, with the events of the war reported and distanced. *Iphigénie Hotel* similarly shows de Gaulle's coming to power unreliably transmitted by radio to a group of tourists cut off in a hotel in Mycenae. Planchon also put on *Overboard*, Vinaver's first play after the twelve-year gap, an epic treatment of the fortunes of a toilet-roll company, shown from multiple viewpoints, with various styles of discourse hilariously juxtaposed. His later plays, like *A Smile on the End of the Line*, set in the Customer Service Department of a small, traditional firm whose staff are about to be replaced by computer technology, tend to show the lives and work of ordinary people, often employed in a big company, with the main events that affect them happening offstage. His plays are neither didactic nor naturalistic. The seemingly banal snatches of dialogue overlap and fragment, and the complex interweaving becomes clearer in performance than on the page. He says he regards theatre as 'a way of making the familiar very strange'. Sam Waters staged *The Television Programme* and *Portrait of a Woma*n at the Orange Tree, Richmond, in 1992 and 1995 respectively.

TRY THESE:

✴KROETZ for the 'théâtre du quotidien' (theatre of everyday life), but his political commitment is more overt; ✴HAVEL's Vanek plays and Alexander Gellman's *We the Undersigned* and *A Man with Connections* also focus on working lives, though with different emphases; Jerry Sterner's financial comedy, *Other People's Money*, concerns a traditional firm on the brink of takeover.

W

WACKLER, Rebecca [1949 –]
American dramatist and actress

PLAYS INCLUDE:
Tent Meeting (1983, with ✱LEVI LEE and ✱LARRY LARSON), *Nicholas De Beaubien's The Hunchback of Notre Dame* (1984, with ✱LEVI LEE); *Wild Streak* (1986), *The Gospel of Mary* (1989, with Ron Short), *Nicholas De Beaubien's Hunchback of Notre Dame* (1997, with ✱LARRY LARSON, ✱LEVI LEE and John Kohler, earlier version 1984)

Wackler co-founded the Southern Theatre Conspiracy with ✱LARRY LARSON and ✱LEVI LEE in 1979. Although she acts in films and commercials for a living, Wackler considers her playwriting the artistic thread that gives her life direction. The three authors toured their mockingly humorous satire *Tent Meeting* internationally. It is a kind of surreal mystery farce in which a self-proclaimed preacher drags his beleaguered son, daughter and deformed grandchild – who might be the new Christ – from Arkansas to Saskatchewan. Humour, even painful humour, has been one means through which she has tried to discover and dramatise truth in her plays. Myths and legends attract her imagination, and in *The Gospel of Mary* she uses the discovery of the gnostic gospels in Egypt in 1945 to develop the idea that Mary Magdalene has her own gospel and that she was also a disciple of Christ.

TRY THESE:
✱WERTENBAKER's *The Love of the Nightingale* for reworking legends; for women written out of history, ✱CHURCHILL's *Top Girls*, Helen Cooper's *Mrs Vershinin*, Elaine Feinstein's *Lear's Daughters*, ✱MURRAY's *Ophelia*, ✱C. P. TAYLOR's *Ophelia*.

WALCOTT, Derek [1930 –]
St Lucian-born dramatist

PLAYS INCLUDE:
Ti-Jean and His Brothers (1957), *Dream on Monkey Mountain* (1967), *The Joker of Seville* (1974, with Galt McDermot, from Tirso de Molina), *O Babylon!* (1976), *Remembrance* (1977), *Pantomime* (1978), *Beef, No Chicken* (1981), *The Isle Is Full of Noises* (1982), *The Last Carnival* (1982), *A Branch of the Blue Nile* (1983), *To Die for Grenada* (1986), *Steel* (1991, with Galt MacDermot), *The Odyssey* (1992, from Homer), *The Capeman* (1998, with Paul Simon)

Winner of the 1992 Nobel Prize for Literature, Walcott is one of the Caribbean's most important dramatists and men of letters. However, relatively few of his plays are known in the UK, despite the efforts of the director Yvonne Brewster.

Walcott's plays, as with those of many other Caribbean writers, are an attempt to find ways and means of expressing the richness of their cultural legacies. Rhythms of speech are important; so too is the use of music, ritual, myth and drumming. *Dream on Monkey Mountain* is regarded as a West Indian classic, an allegory about myth and history. *Remembrance* is a smaller-scale study of the legacies of colonialism, focused on the character of Albert Perez Jordan, teacher and fantasist. It is an affectionate, almost sentimental portrait of a far from sympathetic character irrevocably influenced by British rule (especially literature and wartime experiences) but left behind by time – a sort of epitaph to a dying breed. *O Babylon!*, by contrast, is a hymn to Rastafarianism that takes a hefty, ironical swipe at cracking capitalism, Kingston style, with additional music by Galt MacDermot of *Hair* fame. *The Last Carnival* portrays the crisis of a French Creole colonial family as it comes to terms with the rising Black Power movement. An uncertain future also preoccupies the small town in *Beef, No Chicken*, a strong portrait of the corruption that often comes with progress. Like *Pantomime*, *A Branch of the Blue Nile* has a theatrical setting: a Port-of-Spain troupe nearly falls apart from internal conflict.

Pantomime

This is probably Walcott's most accessible play and certainly one of his most popular. A neat twist on the Robinson Crusoe theme, Walcott's white master and black servant prepare a play to greet the tourists coming to visit the island of Tobago, but with the white hotel owner and one-time actor playing Man Friday. The device reaps a rich comic harvest in its own right, as well as gleefully giving vent to some painful historical taboos for the black community about race, gait and language. Indeed, one of its most enthusiastic receptions has been in Cardiff, where the implications about holding on to language were hugely appreciated by Welsh-language supporters in the audience.

TRY THESE:

✱FRIEL's *Translations* for another play about language as an instrument of invasion; ✱SHANGE also sees language as a symbol of oppression; ✱PHILLIPS' *The Shelter* is another, less successful version of the Robinson Crusoe theme; ✱MATURA's *Trinidad Sisters*, a transplanted *Three Sisters*, is a poignant portrayal of British imperial legacies; see also his *Playboy of the West Indies*; Rastafarianism is the consciousness behind ✱WHITE's *Lament for Rastafari*; ✱HASTINGS' *The Emperor* sees Haile Selassie in a rather different light; ✱WHITE's *The Nine Night*, ✱CROSS's *Mass Carib* and Dennis Scott's *Echo in the Bone* all use ritual to greater or lesser effect, Scott and Cross also with graphic references to slavery; Earl Lovelace's Trinidad-set *The New Hardware Store* is an implicit attack on capitalism (the oppressed reproducing oppressive lifestyles) though social comedy.

WALKER, George F.   [1947 –   ]
Canadian dramatist

PLAYS INCLUDE:
The Prince of Naples (1972), *Ambush at Tether's End* (1972), *Sacktown Rag* (1972), *Baghdad Saloon* (1973), *Beyond Mozambique* (1975), *Zastrozzi* (1977), *Gossip* (1977), *Ramona and the White Slaves* (1978), *Filthy Rich* (1979), *Rumours of Our Death* (1980), *Theatre of the Film Noir* (1981), *Science and Madness* (1982), *The Art of War* (1983), *Criminals in Love* (1984), *Better Living* (1986), *Beautiful City* (1987), *Nothing Sacred* (1988), *Love and Anger* (1988), *Escape from Happiness* (1991), *Tough* (1992), *Problem Child* (1997) *The End of Civilization* (1999), *Heaven* (2000)

One of Canada's most prolific dramatists, Walker was instrumental in the alternative theatre movement of the 1970s. His first works derived from the European absurd tradition, a point of departure that became less and less obvious as he developed as a writer. Walker is fascinated by pop culture and makes no attempt to draw a line of demarcation between it and so-called 'high culture': stage presences in *Beyond Mozambique* include Rita Hayworth, ✱CHEKHOV, Nelson Eddy and Victor Hugo. Walker also likes to mix different places and historical epochs within a work: *Ramona and the White Slaves*, set in an opium den in Hong Kong after World War I, is a prime example.

Zastrozzi, based on an encyclopaedia description of Shelley's novelette, did much to establish Walker as a dramatist of note outside Canada. Like earlier work, *Zastrozzi* comprises elements that may at first seem strange bedfellows: male–female sword-fights, gothic melodrama, B-movies, Grand Guignol, moral concerns and silly stage business. *Criminals in Love*, which won the Governor's Award in 1984, returns to Toronto's East End, the terrain of Walker's first plays. A continuation of the nature/nurture, destiny/free-will debates, the play is a farce that breaks the generic mould.

Walker tends to write clusters of plays on a particular theme or devoted to a particular character. The 'Power Plays' (*Gossip*, *Filthy Rich* and *The Art of War*) hinge on Tyrone

Power, a novelist manqué, obsessed with politics. *Criminals in Love*, *Better Living* and *Beautiful City*, all set in Toronto's East End, could also be considered a trilogy. *Problem Child* is the first of the six-play *Suburban Motel* cycle.

TRY THESE:
Nothing Sacred is Walker's adaptation of ✱TURGENEV's *Fathers and Sons*: as described by the author, the work is 'a Canadian comedy, not a Russian tragedy'; ✱TREMBLAY, a prolific Quebecois dramatist who shares some of Walker's thematic concerns and rootedness in a particular urban environment; ✱BRECHT, for theatrical techniques, especially as regards *The Art of War*.

WALL, Michael   [1951 – 91]
British dramatist

PLAYS INCLUDE.
Japanese Style (1984), *Blue Days* (1987), *Imaginary Wars in England* (1987), *Amongst Barbarians* (1989)

Wall's career followed a near-classic pattern of fringe work, radio plays, the odd one-off television drama and contributions to long-running series. Having studied English at university he worked at a variety of jobs including being a gravedigger and a sales assistant at Harrods. His extensive travel experience provides the material for much of his work. *Amongst Barbarians* won the Mobil Play Competition in 1988 and received productions both at the Royal Exchange Theatre, Manchester, and at the Hampstead Theatre, London. It concentrates on the reactions of two families who arrive in an Asian country in an attempt to save their sons who are about to be executed for drug running. The behaviour of the Westerners is infinitely more barbaric and uncivilised than that of the Asians whom they so self-righteously brand as savage. The questions raised are those of culture, civilisation and who is really a 'barbarian'.

TRY THESE:
✱GORKY's *Barbarians* asked a similar question; ✱MINGHELLA's *Made in Bangkok* followed Westerners as they travel to the Orient with an

equally jaundiced eye; ✱GLENDINNING and ✱HEGGIE are other Mobil Play winners.

WALLACE, Naomi   [1960 –   ]
American dramatist

PLAYS INCLUDE:
The War Boys (1993), *In the Heart of America* (1994), *The Girl Who Fell Through a Hole in Her Jumper* (1994, with Bruce McLeod), *One Flea Spare* (1995), *Birdy* (1996, from William Wharton), *Slaughter City* (1996), *The Trestle at Pope Lick Creek* (1998), *The Inland Sea* (2002), *The Retreating World* (2002), *Things of Dry Hours* (2002)

Wallace is from Kentucky but made her reputation through her work in Britain. She is 'unashamed' to be seen as a political writer, but prefers to see herself as 'engaged with questions of power and its myriad forms'. In *The War Boys* the vigilantes who patrol the US border with Mexico hunting down illegal immigrants tell each other stories about what brought them there, thus offering an audience a whole series of takes on the construction of masculinity (also a strong element in *Birdy*) and American xenophobia, a theme continued in *In the Heart of America* with reference to the first Gulf War. *One Flea Spare*, set in London at the time of the Great Plague, deals with how a group of people quarantined together survive and adapt to each other. It was taken up by the Human Festival and eventually won an OBIE. In *Slaughter City* Wallace turned to the turbulent history of the American meat-packing industry, whereas *The Inland Sea* tackles the reconstruction of the English countryside in the eighteenth century and how the great landscaping projects actually impacted on the people who designed and built them or were displaced by them. *The Retreating World* is a monologue inspired by a John Pilger article about the repercussions of the first Gulf War.

TRY THESE:
✱NAGY, ✱SHINN, ✱WERTENBAKER as American writers with very strong British connections; ✱DE ANGELIS, ✱JEFFREYS for Restoration England; ✱TREVOR GRIFFITHS for the first Gulf War; ✱ARDEN, ✱MANN, ✱MARCHANT for the effects of

war; *BRECHT's *St Joan of the Stockyards* for meat-packing; *STOPPARD's *Arcadia* for landscaping.

WALSH, Enda
Irish dramatist

PLAYS INCLUDE:
Disco Pigs (1996), *Sucking Dublin* (1997), *Misterman* (1999), *Bedbound* (2001)

Walsh made an astonishing debut with *Disco Pigs*, a surreal story of two teenagers who find their shared experience of the world fractured when Pig (the boy) attacks another boy that Runt (the girl) has dared to dance with. The play is a two-hander and gains much of its power from the linguistic exuberance of the extraordinary invented language shared between the two protagonists (which was jettisoned for the film version). *Sucking Dublin*, about the effects of a rape, mixes naturalistic dialogue with monologues and choric interventions, while the action of *Bedbound* takes place in a *BECKETTIAN space where a crippled daughter and her father talk to hold the demons at bay.

TRY THESE:
*BECKETT for influence; *FO, *SPALDING GRAY, *MCPHERSON for versions of monologue; *CARTWRIGHT for another bed; *CHURCHILL's *The Skriker* for a powerful invention of language.

WANDOR, Michelene   [1940 –   ]
British dramatist, poet, fiction writer and theoretician

PLAYS INCLUDE:
The Day After Yesterday (1972), *Spilt Milk* (1972), *To Die Among Friends* (1974), *Penthesilea* (1977, from *KLEIST), *The Old Wives' Tale* (1977), *Care and Control* (1977, scripted for Gay Sweatshop*)*, *Floorshow* (1977, with David Bradford, *CARYL CHURCHILL and *BRYONY LAVERY), *Whores D'Oeuvres* (1978), *Scissors* (1978), *AID Thy Neighbour* (1978), *Correspondence* (radio 1978, staged 1979*)*, *Aurora Leigh* (1979, from Elizabeth Barrett Browning), *The Blind Goddess* (1981, from Ernst Toller), *The Wandering Jew* (1987, with Mike Alfreds, from Eugene Sue)

Wandor's unique position is well summed up by Helene Keyssar: 'More than any single figure, Wandor is responsible for articulating and supporting the interaction of feminism, theatre, socialism and gay liberation in Britain'. Active in the reborn women's movement from its earliest days – *The Day After Yesterday* attacks the sexism of the Miss World contest, *Care and Control* is about the issue of lesbian mothers having custody of their children – Wandor has made significant contributions at both the theoretical and the practical level, as one of the few theatre practitioners with a strong academic background. As editor of the first four volumes of the Methuen anthologies of *Plays by Women*, she has made a significant body of women's dramatic writing available to those who were unable to see the plays in their first productions, and as author of *Understudies, Carry on Understudies* and *Look Back in Gender*, she has documented and analysed the undervalued contribution of women to the contemporary theatre, and the representation of women in the theatre.

A prolific radio dramatist, she has never achieved comparable critical success in the theatre: the National Theatre production of *The Wandering Jew* lasted for over five hours and, despite Mike Alfreds' acknowledged gifts with novel adaptations and Wandor's successful radio adaptations of Dostoevsky, Jane Austen and H. G. Wells, the general view was that the novel simply was not up to it. *Aurora Leigh* is a fine adaptation of Elizabeth Barrett Browning's verse novel that deserves a wider audience, and some of the earlier work, such as *Whores D'Oeuvres*, a fantasy about two prostitutes stranded on a makeshift raft on the Thames after a freak storm, is well worth reviving as more than a historical curiosity. It is probably worth pointing out that *AID Thy Neighbour* is a comedy about contemporary attitudes to the family focused on the question of Artificial Insemination by Donor, not a play about AIDS.

TRY THESE:
*DANIELS' *Neaptide* for another lesbian custody case; *ADSHEAD's *Thatcher's Women* for prostitution; *RAVENHILL's *Handbag* for babies and custody.

WARD, Nick [1962 –]
British dramatist and director

PLAYS INCLUDE:
Splendid Isolation (1986), *Apart from George* (1987), *The Strangeness of Others* (1988), *The Present* (1995)

Born in Geelong, Australia, but brought up in East Anglia, Ward had already won the George Devine Award (for *Apart from George* and *The Strangeness of Others*), by the age of 25. Interviewed around the time of *Apart from George*, Ward is reported to have said that he very quickly discovered how few words were needed to make a point. *Apart from George* and *The Strangeness of Others* seem to bear out both the strengths and weaknesses of that. There is no one like Ward for evoking a particular time and place. In *Apart from George*, it was the bleak and dour East Anglian Fens; in *Strangeness*, the 'faceless, heartless' belly of the beast that is contemporary London. In *Apart from George*, the economy of words, subtle accentuation of physical gesture and nuances and plangent violin accompaniment created an unforgettable picture. Comparisons with ✷CARYL CHURCHILL's *Fen* were obvious, and certainly the same sense of claustrophobic intensity and domestic misery brought on by geographical isolation were present. But Ward's central figure of George, the farm labourer made redundant, his dumb inability to communicate his despair and the repercussions on his wife and daughter (intimations of incest) were distinctively his own. The formula seemed to work less well in Ward's essay on the bitter, love-lorn metropolis. While Lyn Gardner, in *City Limits*, called it 'a brilliant impressionistic portrait', and the *Guardian*'s Michael Billington, 'a poet's vision of urban life', the tenor and framework of his dialogue seemed this time to draw only irritation. Whether it was the desperation expressed by his collection of oddballs and down-and-outers or, as another reviewer noted, 'the banality of their thoughts', it is hard to say. Discretion, it's said, can sometimes be the better part of valour. So brevity, it's true, can also be its soul. However, the current fad for ellipsis in new British writing betokens a more confused state: on the one hand, rich distillation; on the other, obfuscation and sterility.

TRY THESE:
Elizabeth Bond's *Farrowland* for rural gloom; ✷NEMETH's *Holy Days* for a superb evocation of time and place – the American Dust Bowl in the Depression – and more domestic rural tragedies; ✷DANIELS, ✷GODFREY, ✷HOLBOROUGH, ✷HORSFIELD, ✷MACDONALD, ✷MAHONEY, ✷SPENCER for other young writers who have passed through the National's studio wing under ✷PETER GILL and John Burgess; ✷CRIMP and ✷GILL himself, for British contemporaries economical with their words; *Heaven* by American Sarah Aicher (a victim of the Lockerbie disaster), ✷FIRTH's *Cardboard City*, ✷MOTTON's *Chicken* for more contemporary scenes of London's urban angst; George Tabori's *Mein Kampf Farce* for German and Jewish tramps; ✷GORKY's *The Lower Depths* for the definitive 'tramp' play; Ward has translated ✷STRINDBERG's *Ghost Sonata*.

WASSERSTEIN, Wendy [1950 –]
American dramatist

PLAYS INCLUDE:
Any Woman Can't (1973), *When Dinah Shore Ruled the Earth* (1975, with ✷CHRISTOPHER DURANG), *Montpelier Pizzazz* (1975), *Uncommon Women and Others* (1977), *Isn't It Romantic?* (1981, revised 1983), *Tender Offer* (1983), *Miami* (1986), *The Heidi Chronicles* (1988), *The Sisters Rosenweig* (1992), *An American Daughter* (1997), *Old Money* (2000)

One of the most commercially successful contemporary woman dramatists in the USA, Wasserstein has an ear for the hilarities of everyday dialogue and an ability to tap into the emotional insecurities facing many women of her generation. Detractors have found her humour too flashy and insubstantial, and feminist critics have generally eschewed her self-deprecating heroines. Wasserstein first came to prominence with *Uncommon Women and Others*, originally begun as a one-act play for her graduate thesis at the Yale School of Drama and later expanded to full length for its 1977 New York premiere. *Uncommon Women*, in which a group of women friends reminisce about their college years and the directions their lives have taken since, was quickly established as a favourite on the regional theatre circuit. The play was followed up by *Isn't It Romantic?*, the story of the friendship between a 28-year-old Jewish homebody and an elegant WASP. In *The Heidi Chronicles*, her 1988 Pulitzer Prize-winning Broadway hit, Wasserstein returned to the issues of women's choices as she followed the progress of Heidi Holland from high school to approaching middle age, with detours for college, consciousness-raising, career moves and childbearing questions.

TRY THESE:

✻ SIMON as a commercial comic dramatist drawing from Jewish family experiences; ✻ GURNEY, ✻ INNAURATO as other Dramatists' Horizons authors who write often about family pressures; Clare Booth Luce's *The Women*, ✻ CHURCHILL's *Top Girls*, ✻ DUNN's *Steaming*, ✻ FORNES' *Fefu and Her Friends*, ✻ GEMS' *Dusa, Fish, Stas and Vi* for contrasting gatherings of women; ✻ HENLEY's small-town Southern sensibility contrasts with Wasserstein's urban Northern one; ✻ SIMON GRAY's *Common Pursuit* for an Oxbridge contrast to *Uncommon Women*; ✻ KESSELMAN for another American Jewish dramatist of somewhat different sensibility.

WATERHOUSE, Keith   [1929 –   ]
British dramatist

PLAYS INCLUDE:
Jeffrey Bernard Is Unwell (1989), *Bookends* (1990), *Good Grief* (1998)

HALL, Willis   [1929 –   ]
British dramatist

PLAYS INCLUDE:
The Long and the Short and the Tall (1958)

JOINT PLAYS INCLUDE:
Billy Liar (1960), *Celebration: The Wedding and the Funeral* (1961), *England, Our England* (1962, revue), *All Things Bright and Beautiful* (1962), *Squat Betty* (1962), *Say Who You Are* (1965), *The Card* (1973, musical from Arnold Bennett)

Yorkshiremen from Leeds, these dramatists have worked both independently and together and are best known for their well-constructed, accurately observed studies of north-country life, frequently showing their characters' attempts to escape – actually or in fantasy – from their surroundings. However, one of their biggest commercial successes, *Say Who You Are*, is a farce set in Knightsbridge and other major successes have been *Saturday, Sunday, Monday* and *Filumena*, both adaptations of Neopolitan plays by ✻ DE FILIPPO.

Hall had already had productions – especially *The Long and the Short and the Tall* (1958), a moving play about a trapped group of soldiers and their Japanese prisoner in Malaya – and Waterhouse had published novels before their collaboration on the stage version of his *Billy Liar*. Both separately and together they have produced a number of screenplays (including *The Long and the Short and the Tall* (1961), *Whistle down the Wind* (1961), *A Kind of Loving* (1963), *Billy Liar* (1963)), radio and television plays and series, and revue material.

There is no typical Hall and Waterhouse play as far as subject matter is concerned. What you can expect is assured handling of naturalistic details, fresh and original writing in a sound structure and at least one role that is a gift to the actor. Waterhouse's *Jeffrey Bernard Is Unwell* (1989), is just such a gift. Based on the writings of its eponymous hero, a journalist with the *Spectator*, well known for his alcoholic adventures, it was a great success for Peter O'Toole. *Bookends* was less completely successful in its presentation of a friendship maintained by letters.

TRY THESE:

✻ BECKETT and ✻ IONESCO for the Theatre of the Absurd parodied in *Squat Betty*; ✻ PRIESTLEY (whose *Lost Empires* Waterhouse and Hall adapted as a musical in 1985 with Dennis King) for earlier and middle-class Yorkshire comedies; ✻ BENNETT for similar accurate, though often less naturalistic in structure, depictions of Yorkshire life (especially *Worm's Eye View*); ✻ STOREY for similar naturalistic portrayals of northern working-class life in the 1960s and early 1970s; ✻ RATTIGAN's *Flarepath*, ✻ SHERRIFF's *Journey's End* and ✻ WESKER's *Chips* with *Everything* for some different views of military life; ✱OSBORNE's *Inadmissible Evidence* for phantasmagoric self-destruction; ✱KEMPINSKI's *Separation* for a long-distance relationship.

WEBSTER, John   [c. 1580 – c. 1632]
English dramatist

PLAYS INCLUDE:
The White Devil (1612), *The Duchess of Malfi* (1613)

Webster, the son of a London coachmaker, had a legal training (which may explain the number of trial scenes in his plays) and probably wasn't a full-time professional dramatist. Although he did write plays about London life, his reputation rests on the two revenge tragedies set in Italy which bear out ✱T. S. ELIOT's remark that he 'was much possessed by death/And saw the skull beneath the skin'. This emphasis on corruption and death – in *The Duchess of Malfi* the Cardinal's mistress dies after kissing a poisoned bible – still encourages some people to side with ✱GEORGE BERNARD SHAW, who described Webster as the 'Tussaud laureate'. *The White Devil* and *The Duchess of Malfi*, both based on Italian history, are characterised by lavish use of violent and macabre deaths, adultery, dumb shows and apparitions; but they bring a new emphasis to the presentation of the tragic female protagonist since their central figures are victims of events rather than initiators of them, sacrifices to the power of patriarchy who pay the price for stepping out of line.

The Duchess of Malfi
The bare bones of the plot might seem to support the charge that Webster was simply out to give his audience a quick thrill through gruesome effects and sensational plotting. After all, the widowed Duchess makes a secret second marriage to her steward Antonio, thus incurring the wrath of her two corrupt brothers, Ferdinand and the Cardinal, who engineer plots to torment her and destroy the marriage, with the result being a final body count of ten. Not only is the number of deaths high, even by the generous standards of the Renaissance, but there is a heady mix of mistaken murders, dances of madmen,

tableaux of wax dummies, apparently severed hands and lycanthropy to go with it. But throughout the play there is a sense of the Duchess and Antonio as 'ordinary' people attempting to make sense of and to live 'normal' lives in a world that has no fixed positions or moral absolutes, in which good intentions are no salvation, and from whose absurdity there is no escape. Even in a bad production the play has the virtues of good melodrama, but in a brilliant one, such as Adrian Noble's 1980 production for the Manchester Royal Exchange with Helen Mirren as the Duchess, Pete Postlethwaite as Antonio, Mike Gwilym as Ferdinand, Julian Curry as the Cardinal and Bob Hoskins as the malcontent Bosola who does most of the dirty work, the play's resolute refusal to succumb to corruption and pervasive evil emerges very clearly.

TRY THESE:
Plays by ✱BECKETT and ✱BOND for that curious sense of an optimism that refuses to be bowed by the harshness of life; plays by other Renaissance dramatists, particularly ✱CHAPMAN, ✱FORD, ✱MARLOWE, ✱MARSTON, ✱MIDDLETON and ✱SHAKESPEARE (especially *Measure for Measure*, where Isabella is confronted by a similar atmosphere of changing moral absolutes) for the use of Machiavellian villains, revenge plots and malcontents; ✱BRECHT's *Galileo* and ✱HOCHHÜTH's *The Representative* for question-able cardinals; Robert David Macdonald's *Webster* takes a supposed look backstage at the Webster ménage; the young Webster is a character in the film *Shakespeare in Love*.

WEDEKIND, Frank   [1864 – 1918]
German dramatist

PLAYS INCLUDE:
Spring Awakening (1891) *The Earth Spirit* (1895), *The Marquis of Keith* (1900), *Pandora's Box* (1903)

Wedekind had a profound effect on the development of twentieth-century German drama. It is fair to regard him as an originator of Expressionism: his deliberate use of non-naturalistic and symbolic devices, his exaggerated and caricatured characterisation, and his deployment of music-hall and cabaret technique clearly influencing Toller, Kaiser and ✳BRECHT.

Wedekind's first play, *Spring Awakening*, was immediately controversial, both in its theme – adolescent sexuality and adult repression – and its anti-naturalistic style. His later plays continued to concern themselves with sex and society, and Wedekind was widely regarded as a scandalous libertine and anarchist. In fact, his work is very much concerned with morality, and his later work has a strongly religious flavour.

His plays display a major preoccupation with the clash between the irresistible force of Life – most strongly experienced as sex – and the immovable object of bourgeois hypocrisy and 'respectability'. In *Spring Awakening* the adults prefer the destruction of their children to a public admission of the facts of life; in the so-called 'Lulu' plays – *The Earth Spirit* and *Pandora's Box* – Lulu destroys a series of representative bourgeois males through her uninhibited but essentially innocent enjoyment of sex before her death at the hands of a madman. The power of Wedekind's writing is such that his plays continue to disturb and shock. They were still being refused a performing licence in Britain in the 1960s.

Spring Awakening

Stiefel, a fourteen-year-old boy, commits suicide rather than face his parents after failure at school. His diaries are found to contain a graphic account of sex written by another boy, Gabor. Horrified respectability expels Gabor from school for possessing this knowledge, and then sends him to a reformatory when his innocent and childishly ignorant girlfriend is found to be pregnant. The girl's mother forces her to have an abortion, and she dies as a result. Escaping from the reformatory, Gabor grieves over her grave and is confronted with Stiefel's ghost, exhorting him to join the other children in death. A strangely positive conclusion is reached, however, by the intervention of a mysterious figure who convinces Gabor that he must not abandon life.

TRY THESE:
Wedekind's personal quarrel with Gerhart Hauptmann played a part in his reaction against

Naturalism; ✳STRINDBERG was another major precursor of Expressionism; Georg Kaiser and Ernst Toller for Expressionism; Wedekind's controversial frankness about sex parallels ✳IBSEN's; ✳BARNES' *The Ruling Class* has parallels with the 'Lulu' plays; ✳BRENTON's *Romans in Britain* scandalised the moral majority with its naked buggery, intended as a metaphor for imperialism; ✳BOND's *Saved* still shocks with its baby-battering violence, a device used by the dramatist to show the dehumanising effects of capitalism; ✳KANE, ✳RAVENHILL for contemporary parallels and contrasts.

WEISS, Peter Ulrich [1916 – 82]
Czechoslovakian-born Swedish painter, novelist, director and dramatist

PLAYS INCLUDE:
The Persecution and Assassination of Jean-Paul Marat as Performed by the Inmates of the Asylum of Charenton under the Direction of the Marquis de Sade (1964), *The Investigation* (1965), *The Tower* (1967), *Discourse on the War in Vietnam* (1968), *Song of the Lusitanian Bogey* (1968), *How Mr Mockingpott was Relieved of His Sufferings* (1968), *The Insurance* (1969), *Trotsky in Exile* (1971), *Holderlin* (1971)

Born in Czechoslovakia of German parents and resident in Sweden from 1939, Weiss was an intensely political writer with a considerable range. *The Investigation* is a documentary based on the 1964 War Crimes Trial at Frankfurt, *The Insurance* a surrealist allegory, *Song of the Lusitanian Bogey* a record of an uprising in Angola and its suppression by the Portuguese. Weiss's work often attracted controversy – attempts to suppress *Discourse on the War in Vietnam* in Berlin, outrage at *Marat/Sade* in London – but no one could deny that his plays have a strong theatrical power as well as a forceful message.

Marat/Sade, which brought him an international reputation through the historic ✳ARTAUD-influenced 1964 RSC production by Peter Brook, is exactly what the full title describes. In an introduction Brook says: 'Everything about [the play] is designed to crack the spectator on the jaw, then douse him with ice-cold water, then force him intelligently to assess what has happened to him, then give him a kick in the balls, then bring him to his senses again.' The play includes a variety of arguments about revolutionary violence and an ironic picture of the revolution tamed by the new Empire but very likely to re-emerge.

TRY THESE:

✳ BÜCHNER's *Danton's Death*, ✳ GEMS' *The Danton Affair*, Ariane Mnouchkine's *1789* are all treatments of the French Revolution; ✳ HOCHHÜTH is concerned with similar issues, especially in *The Representative*.

WELLER, Michael   [1942 –   ]
American dramatist

PLAYS INCLUDE:

Moonchildren (1970), *Fishing* (1975), *Loose Ends* (1979), *The Ballad of Soapy Smith* (1983), *Ghost on Fire* (1985), *Spoils of War* (1988), *Lake No Bottom* (1990), *The Heart of the Art* (1999), *What the Night Is For* (2002)

Weller, the leading chronicler of the generation of Americans who came of age in the 1960s, populates his plays with writers, photographers, literary critics, filmmakers and cartoonists, who share his interest in reflective commentary. His knack for bright, outrageous dialogue and his ability to draw sympathetic, three-dimensional characters can be found in all of his works for the theatre. Although he has departed from his depiction of the socially committed, college-educated (Klondike goldrush hucksters in *The Ballad of Soapy Smith*), he is most at home dealing with these characters. In *Moonchildren* Weller drew a sympathetic picture of the Vietnam-era youth counter-culture. In *Loose Ends*, which culminates in the 1970s, Weller focuses on Paul and Susan, who meet in the Peace Corps and later become affluent. They pay a high price for their success and lose touch with their ideals and each other. *Spoils of War*, the last play of this loose trilogy, deals with the 1950s. This is Weller's most autobiographical work. The central character is a teenager who tries to reunite his divorced parents. The plays share the themes of a loss of continuity in relationships and the inability to express genuine feelings within a relationship. *Lake No Bottom*, a three-character drama, tells the story of an author who turns on his mentor and critic by writing a successful trashy novel. He is also having an affair with the critic's wife. The play explores the layers of subterfuge and deception that Weller believes are a part of the interdependent relationship between artist and critic. In *The Heart of the Art* he creates a black comedy out of the relationship between a would-be dramatist and a thinly disguised version of Joe Papp, while *What the Night Is For*, which marked the West End debut of Gillian Anderson, is a two-hander about two former lovers meeting again and trying to decide how to proceed with their lives.

TRY THESE:

Critics have compared Weller to ✳ CHEKHOV; ✳ LEVY's *Heresies*, ✳ LUCIE's *Progress*, Robert Patrick's *Kennedy's Children* for contemporary societies and their roots, ✳ BARKER's *Scenes from an Execution*, ✳ POWNALL's *Master Class*, ✳ STOPPARD's *The Real Inspector Hound* for artists and critics; ✳ CRIMP, ✳ SIMON GRAY as further contemporary chroniclers with a bitter taste; ✳ COWARD's *Private Lives* for a comparison with *What the Night Is For*.

WELLMAN, Mac John   [1945 –   ]
American dramatist

PLAYS INCLUDE:

Fama Combinatoria (1975), *The Memory Theatre of Giordano Bruno* (1977, radio), *Dog in the Manger* (1982, adaptation from ✳ DE VEGA), *Phantomnation* (1983), *The Professional Frenchman* (1984), *Harm's Way* (1984, radio play), *Energymen* (1985), *The Bad Infinity* (1985), *'1951'* (1986), *Cleveland* (1986), *Dracula* (1987), *Albanian Softshoe* (1989), *Sincerity Forever* (1990), *Crowbar* (1990), *Terminal Hip* (1990), *Seven Blow Jobs* (1991), *Antigone* (2002, after ✳ SOPHOCLES)

Wellman, one of America's most prolific and eclectic writers, has written radio plays, edited anthologies and taught playwriting. Most importantly, he has worked with particular theatres or artists to develop scripts. Wellman's work often features unusual wordplay and construction. His untraditional style

What the Night Is For by Michael Weller, directed by John Caird, Comedy Theatre, 2002. Gillian Anderson as Melinda Metz, Roger Allam as Adam Penzius. (Rowena Chowdrey/ArenaPAL)

has brought the accusation of sacrilege, as in the presentation of Christ in *Sincerity Forever*, a play that drew the ire of ultra-conservative Donald Wildmon and Senator Jesse Helms during their crusade to abolish National Endowment for the Arts funding for controversial artists. *Crowbar* was conceived for and then performed in New York's Victory Theatre just a month before its demolition. A man searches for his daughter during the intermission and links the physical exploration of the Victory Theatre with historical anecdotes. *Antigone* deconstructs the original in line with a post-September 11 sensibility, presided over by a narrator who, according to *The Village Voice*, was a cross between Santa Claus and Dionysus.

TRY THESE:

✱ JONSON's *Bartholomew Fair*, ✱ PIRANDELLO's *Six Characters in Search of an Author*, ✱ SHERIDAN's *The Critic*, ✱ STOPPARD's *The Real Inspector Hound*, for metatheatrical plays; ✱ BOND, ✱ BRENTON, ✱ KANE for British controversies

WELSH, Irvine   [1961 –   ]
Scottish novelist and dramatist

PLAYS INCLUDE:

Trainspotting (1994, adapted by Harry Gibson from Welsh's novel), *Headstate* (1994), *You'll Have Had Your Hole* (1998)

Welsh's hugely successful novel *Trainspotting* (1993) was also a major theatrical success. Part of a whole generation of works open about drug culture, the material has been given different inflection in its various versions (novel, play, film) but the play centres on the stories of the individual addicts. Questions have been asked about the extent to which the lifestyle is simply presented or praised or condemned, and Gibson reworked the stage version for New York to stress 'that people turn to drugs as an anaesthetic'. *Headstate* was a multimedia presentation of the state of the nation after fifteen years of right-wing government, and *You'll Have Had Your Hole*, which is set in a recording studio, also draws heavily on contemporary music, but both works continue to express ideas about what Gibson

described as 'the culture of poverty, boredom and violence' and the fact that 'there's always some drug around that's cheaper than food' (quoted by Aleks Sierz in *In-Yer-Face Theatre*).

TRY THESE:

✱ KANE, ✱ RAVENHILL for contemporary examples of controversial drama; ✱ GELBER, ✱ HEATHCOTE WILLIAMS for earlier drug dramas.

WERTENBAKER, Timberlake   [1951 –   ]
Anglo-French-American dramatist, now resident in Britain

PLAYS INCLUDE:

The Third (1980), *Case to Answer* (1980), *Breaking Through* (1980), *New Anatomies* (1981), *Inside Out* (1982), *Home Leave* (1982), *Abel's Sister* (1984, with Yvonne Bourcier), *The Grace of Mary Traverse* (1985), *The Love of a Nightingale* (1988), *Our Country's Good* (1988, from Thomas Kencally's *The Playmaker*), *Three Birds Alighting on a Field* (1991), *The Break of Day* (1995), *After Darwin* (1998), *Credible Witness* (2001)

Although Wertenbaker is American by birth, and French educated, her work has all been created within the British theatre. Her most successful plays, *The Love of the Nightingale* and *Our Country's Good*, offer an exhilarating contrast in their treatment of theatrical techniques. Like ✱ CARYL CHURCHILL she has shown a persistent interest in how notions of normality and self are constructed, and many of her plays contain a Faustian bargain in which knowledge is purchased at the expense of innocence. *Abel's Sister* (co-written with the disabled Yvonne Bourcier) is quite remarkable for its insights into both physical disability and, through its attendant characters of Vietnam veteran and young jaundiced radicals, emotional and spiritual disability. *The Grace of Mary Traverse*, on the other hand, is a picaresque eighteenth-century gallop with Faustian undertones – what price knowledge? – but also, and primarily, an exploration of the possibilities for women when they step outside their own environment. Wertenbaker had already engaged with this topic in *New Anatomies*, a sprawling, ambitious account of two rebellious women who broke the conventions of gender by dressing in male attire: the nineteenth-century explorer Isabelle Eberhardt and the music-hall performer Vesta Tilley.

Our Country's Good owed its success to its reaffirmation of the power of theatre to change lives and influence people for the better. The play shows convicts from the First Fleet staging the first theatrical production in Australia, ✶FARQUHAR's *The Recruiting Officer*. The play uses familiar backstage situations to debate the aesthetics and politics of the theatre and the philosophy of punishment, and the original production used devices such as cross-casting, multiple doubling and onstage changes of identity to further the debate about the relationship between environmental and genetic influences on character and behaviour. *The Love of the Nightingale* is a powerful and spare reworking of the myth of Philomel and Procne, which includes a staging within the play of the Phaedra story and an enactment of Bacchic rituals. Its use of the theatre within its design relates dialectically to that in *Our Country's Good*, where the theatre is regarded in terms of its power to transform the performers, rather than its audience. *Nightingale* is much more concerned with the making of myths, the power of language, gender roles, and the role of fantasy in more negative terms. Here the power of theatre is questioned alongside a powerful exploration of the construction of male and female roles.

With these two plays Wertenbaker established herself as one of Britain's most challenging and intellectually stimulating dramatists. *Our Country's Good*, certainly the cheerier of the two plays, has endeared itself to examiners and audiences alike. Wertenbaker has continued to explore important issues: *Three Birds Alighting on a Field* is a complex investigation of art that anticipates some of the issues of ✶REZA's *Art* by several years; *The Break of Day*, like *Our Country's Good*, was intended by Max Stafford-Clark to pair with a classic, in this case ✶CHEKHOV's *Three Sisters*, with which it shared a fin-de-siècle anatomising of its characters. In *After*

Darwin Wertenbaker again uses play-within-a-play elements, this time to consider the lessons of the voyage of *The Beagle* in a modern social context. *Credible Witness* might be seen as an asylum seekers play but in typical Wertenbaker fashion it moves beyond the immediate manifestation of the issue to consider the whole question of exile and cultural identity

TRY THESE:

For women in male clothes, ✶MIDDLETON and ✶DEKKER's *The Roaring Girl*, ✶SHAKESPEARE's *As You Like It*, *Twelfth Night* and *The Merchant of Venice*; for 'history' plays with contemporary parallels, ✶BARKER's *Victory* and *The Castle*, ✶DEAR's *The Art of Success*; ✶GOETHE's *Faust* for the philosophical knot; for images of disability, Graeae, ✶MEDOFF's *Children of a Lesser God*, ✶NICHOLS' *Day in the Death of Joe Egg* and ✶YOUNG's *Crystal Clear*; Wertenbaker has very successfully translated ✶MARIVAUX and Ariane Mnouchkine's *Mephisto*, and also three plays by Sophocles, *Oedipus the King*, *Oedipus at Colonus* and *Antigone*, under the title of *The Thebans* for the RSC; ✶EURIPIDES for *The Bacchae*; ✶RACINE for *Phèdre*; ✶TREVOR GRIFFITHS' *Comedians* for backstage debates about the function of art.

WESKER, Arnold   [1932 –   ]
British dramatist

PLAYS INCLUDE:

Chicken Soup with Barley (1958), *Roots* (1959), *I'm Talking About Jerusalem* (1960) (these three plays forming *The Wesker Trilogy*), *The Kitchen* (1959), *Chips with Everything* (1962), *The Nottingham Captain* (1962), *Menace* (1963), *Their Very Own and Golden City* (1965), *The Four Seasons* (1965), *The Friends* (1970), *The Old Ones* (1972), *The Wedding Feast* (1974, from Dostoevsky) *The Journalists* (1975), *Love Letters on Blue Paper* (1976), *The Merchant* (1977), *Caritas* (1981), *One More Ride on the Merry Go Round* (1981, produced 1985), *Sullied Hands* (1981, produced 1984), *Mothers* (1982), *Annie Wobbler* (1983), *Whatever Happened to Betty Lemon* (1986), *When God Wanted a Son* (1986, produced 1997), *The Mistress* (1991), *Blood Libel* (1991, produced 1996), *Three Women Talking* (1992), *Letter to a Daughter*

(1992), *Wild Spring* (1992, produced 1994), *Circles of Perception* (1996), *Denial* (written 1997, produced 2000)

Born in Stepney, the son of Jewish émigrés, Wesker worked as a furniture maker's apprentice, carpenter's mate, plumber's mate, farm labourer and bookseller's assistant and, after National Service in the Royal Air Force, as a pastry cook, an experience he draws on in *Chicken Soup with Barley* and *The Kitchen*. In 1956 he took a film course and began writing film scripts and for the theatre.

Much of his early writing is autobiographical; ✳JOHN ARDEN has termed it 'autobiography in documentary style'. *The Wesker Trilogy* uses a form of social realism to depict working-class life. *Chicken Soup with Barley* charts the experience of the Kahns, a Jewish family in the East End, over twenty years, from Mosley's Blackshirts in 1936 to the 1956 Soviet invasion of Hungary. These events are experienced from within a domestic world. The play traces the decline of the family, a group of people who come to stand for the disillusion of the post-war generations, as their hopes for the future turn to a loss of faith. *Roots* traces the intellectual and emotional growth of Beattie Bryant, whose emancipation from the offstage tutelage of Ronnie Kahn culminates in a thrilling declaration of independence. The play was enormously influential. In the last play of the trilogy, *I'm Talking about Jerusalem*, Wesker returns to the Kahn family; the Jerusalem of the title represents the hopes of the future in the face of the failure of socialist idealism (a reference to the call 'Next Year in Jerusalem!' of the Passover ritual). In *Chips with Everything* Wesker began to move away from a strictly naturalist form, and employed folk and popular song, a device he was to pursue in his later plays.

Wesker's more recent work has tended to move away from the broad chronology and canvases of his earlier work. In *Caritas* he explores the phenomenon of a fourteenth-century woman anchorite (a religious mystic and recluse) who literally walls herself up in a cathedral wall. *Annie Wobbler* and *Mothers* take the form of dramatic monologue. *The Merchant* is an intelligent reworking of ✳SHAKESPEARE's *The Merchant of Venice* from a Jewish viewpoint. Although the British theatre still revives his early plays, there has been a marked reluctance to stage his newer work, which is often premiered in other countries.

TRY THESE:

✳OSBORNE as the first of the generation of 'Angry Young Men'; ✳JOHN MCGRATH also forged alliances with the labour and trade union movements and generated labour support for the arts; ✳PINTER and Wesker share an East End Jewish background; ✳BOLT was imprisoned with Wesker for their anti-nuclear protest; ✳HORSFIELD for a contemporary writer who has written a trilogy – on young women and football; ✳TREMBLAY uses monologue techniques in *Albertine in Five Times*; ✳DELANEY's *A Taste of Honey* and ✳STOREY for other examples of social realism; ✳ALRAWI, ✳CARTWRIGHT, ✳DUNBAR and ✳MARCHANT for modern parallels.

WESLEY, Richard   [1945 –   ]
American dramatist

PLAYS INCLUDE:

The Black Terror (1971), *Gettin' It Together* (1972), *Strike Heaven on the Face* (1973), *Goin' Thru Changes* (1973), *The Past Is the Past* (1973), *The Sirens* (1974), *The Mighty Gents* (1974, originally called *The Last Street Play*), *Cotillion* (1975 musical), *On the Road to Babylon: A Musical Journey* (1979, musical), *The Dream Team* (1985, musical), *The Talented Tenth* (1989)

Born in Newark, New Jersey, and witness to its history of radical turmoil in the 1960s, Wesley became one of the most politically controversial dramatists of his generation. Influenced, as a young writer, by ✳AMIRI BARAKA and ✳RON MILNER, Wesley writes unsentimental realism, often fiercely philosophical and moral, and concerned with the ways in which social conditions and history affect identity. From 1968 to 1973 Wesley was a member of the New Lafayette Theatre, the prominent Harlem company, where he worked with ✳ED BULLINS, helped edit the theatre's magazine, and served as dramatist-in-residence. He came to the attention of Joe Papp in 1971, and the New York Shakespeare Festival produced Wesley's first full-length play, *The Black Terror*. A meditation on revolution, the play presents a black terrorist who has begun to question the usefulness of violence, and yet can't quite propose satisfactory alternatives. The play won Wesley the Drama Desk Award for most promising dramatist.

Wesley's second major play, originally called *The Last Street Play* when it opened at the Manhattan Theatre Club, became *The Mighty Gents* when it moved to Broadway. It could be a companion piece to *The Black Terror*, for in it Wesley again asks what happens after the revolutionary fire has gone out. Here, members of a black gang confront the unhappy truth that they're no longer powerful and vital players in Newark's streets. Anxious to recapture their youthful glory, but also to break out of the suffocating conditions of their past and become adults, the men are eloquent spokesmen for the diverse frustrations of the disenfranchised. The play also allowed Wesley to display his gift for imagining a broad range of characters, each finely observed, distinct, yet closely engaged with one another.

The Talented Tenth portrayed a group of 'buppies' (Wesley's term for black yuppies). Wesley says he grew exhausted with writing about the street and wanted to focus on those who escaped its dangers: the title refers to W. E .B. DuBois' term for the ten per cent of black Americans able to save the others from 'contamination and death'. Wesley's talented tenth – Harvard graduates, business executives and Republicans among them – are guilty about their privilege, their detachment from most of their fellow African-Americans, yet unsure about how to bring the much-needed change to their lives. The play marked a considerable shift for Wesley and, for audiences used to ✶AUGUST WILSON, made him difficult to classify. Part of the uncertainty about Wesley's artistic identity comes from his own desire to constantly redefine the nature of so-called black writing: 'Black playwriting is stagnating', Wesley wrote in 1972, at the start of a career spent jostling it back to life. And in 1989 he said to an interviewer who asked about the origin of *The Talented Tenth*, 'we'd written about drugs, about prostitution, about alienated youth. There had to be some new territory to be limned.' In 2003 Wesley was working on *Big Ideas*, described as a play about 'the black middle class in the post-Civil Rights era'.

TRY THESE:
✶BARAKA, ✶ BULLINS, ✶ FULLER for writers with similarly uncompromising social consciences; ✶KENNEDY, ✶ SHANGE for plays treating issues of black identity in a less naturalistic way; ✶NELSON, ✶ RABE for other kinds of politically informed writing; ✶CROSS, ✶ FAGON, ✶ IKOLI, ✶ MATURA for British parallels.

WHELAN, Peter   [1931 –   ]
British dramatist

PLAYS INCLUDE:
Captain Swing (1978), *The Accrington Pals* (1981), *Clay* (1982), *The Bright and Bold Design* (1991), *The School of Night* (1992), *Shakespeare Country* (1993), *Divine Right* (1996), *The Herbal Bed* (1998), *Nativity* (1999, with Bill Alexander), *A Russian in the Woods* (2001)

Whelan has a long and distinguished history of writing challenging plays, often making memorable theatre out of the bits of history that traditionally get left out, including nineteenth-century agricultural unrest (*Captain Swing*), the impact of the wholesale enlistment of the so-called Pals battalions in World War I on the men and women of Accrington (*The Accrington Pals*) and what it was like to serve in Berlin immediately after World War II (*A Russian in the Woods*). He has also tackled Renaissance themes in *The School of Night* (✶THOMAS KYD, Walter Ralegh and the mysterious death, or not, of ✶CHRISTOPHER MARLOWE) and *The Herbal Bed* (a dramatisation of the case of Susanna Hall, ✶SHAKESPEARE's daughter, who was accused of adultery) and Shakespeare himself in *Shakespeare Country* (a modern version of *A Midsummer Night's Dream*). *Divine Right* is a state-of-the-nation play set in 2000 in which, following the heir apparent renouncing his right to the throne, his son travels the country in disguise to try to understand his divided nation.

TRY THESE:
✱ MCGUINESS's *Observe the Sons of Ulster* for a World War I experience comparable to *The Accrington Pals*; ✱ LITTLEWOOD's *Oh What a Lovely War* for another view of World War I; ✱ JOHN MCGRATH, ✱ NICHOLS, ✱ WESKER for plays that grew out of their National Service experiences as *A Russian in the Woods* did out of Whelan's; ✱ TOWNSEND for a republican fantasy about the House of Windsor; ✱ STRAUSS for an updating of ✱ SHAKESPEARE's *A Midsummer Night's Dream*.

WHITE, Edgar   [1947 –   ]
Monserrat-born dramatist

PLAYS INCLUDE:
The Mummer's Play (1970), *The Wonderfule Yeare* (1970), *Seigsmundo's Tricycle* (1971), *Little Orfeo's Lay* (1972), *La Gente* (1973), *The Black Women* (1977), *Masada* (1978), *Lament for Rastafari* (1979), *Trinity* (1981), *The Nine Night* (1983), *Redemption Song* (1984), *The Boot Dance* (1984), *Moon Dance Night* (1987), *I Marcus Garvey* (1992), *Live From Galilee* (1992)

White studied at City College in New York and has had many plays produced there, including five by Joe Papp's Shakespeare Festival Theatre. In the 1960s he was involved with the seminal gathering of black actors, musicians and directors at the Keskidee Centre in north London. White writes particularly of disillusionment and of the quest for roots back in the Caribbean with a mixture of dry humour, sorrow and sometimes dreamy romanticism; his plays invariably introduce elements of mysticism and ritual into realistic settings as well as frequent references to Rastafarianism. Two of White's most popular plays, *The Nine Night* and *Redemption Song*, deal with the return and disillusionment of the exile. The Nine Night (the phrase refers to a Jamaican funeral ritual used to help a troubled soul pass to paradise) opens and closes the domestic comedy of the same name that highlights the disillusionment of those who went to Britain regarding themselves as British and Britain as 'the mother country' until they started to live there. In the central figure of Hamon, the troubled spirit on the eve of returning to the Caribbean with his son, White has created a character rich in comic pretensions as well as pathos (loss of illusions is also mirrored in loss of power in the home). His fanatical love of cricket – there is a wonderful scene where Hamon and his old friend drunkenly recreate the first West Indies Test victory over England – symbolises a whole generation's cast of mind and old 'adopted' values in conflict with the harsher ones of contemporary England. His son, brought up in England, prefers football to cricket. In *Redemption Song*, a richly ironic title in itself, Legion, a young dreamer and poet, returns home to claim his inheritance after his father's death, only to find he is as much of an outcast as he was in Britain. Legion is in limbo-land and, as White has written, stands for a generation of young immigrants, brought to Britain when small, but lost and rejected by both cultures as adults. White tends to concentrate, though by no means exclusively, on the experiences of males; *Moon Dance Night*, which focused on a smart urbanised black woman from London returning to the Caribbean for a holiday, seemed more like caricature.

TRY THESE:
✱ WALCOTT's *Oh Babylon* is a rock hymn to Rastafarianism; ✱ CROSS and David Simon's *Blues for Railton* is a highly successful marrying of the Caribbean past and British present – Dennis Scott's impressively wide-ranging exploration of black history and oppression *An Echo in the Bone* also uses the ritual of the Nine Night; ✱ MATURA, ✱ MOFFATT, ✱ PHILLIPS for plays dealing with diaspora disillusionment; ✱ RHONE for caricature; for cultural contrast, ✱ AYCKBOURN; for more images of patriarchy in retreat, ✱ DE FILIPPO's *Ducking Out*.

WHITEHEAD, Ted (Edward Anthony)   [1933 –   ]
British dramatist

PLAYS INCLUDE:
The Foursome (1971), *Alpha Beta* (1972), *The Sea Anchor* (1974), *Old Flames* (1975), *Mecca* (1977), *The Man Who Fell in Love with His Wife* (1984)

Whitehead worked in various manual jobs, in advertising and as a teacher, before becoming a full-time writer in 1971, when he was resident dramatist at the Royal Court. His television adaptations of Fay Weldon's *The Life and Loves of a She-Devil* (1987) and ✱STRINDBERG's *Dance of Death* (1984) and his work on the television series *Cracker* are indicative of his dominant interest in sexual politics, particularly of the obsessive kind. His theatre work is always closely observed and often comic, but there is an edge of uneasiness to the comedy as his characters engage in mating rituals and other games. In *The Foursome* he charts a brief sexual relationship between two couples and in *The Sea Anchor* the emphasis is on promiscuity and the nature of marriage. *Alpha Beta* is a raw battle of the sexes and a misogynistic tirade against marriage. *The Man Who Fell in Love with His Wife* is a revised version of his 1980 television play *Sweet Nothings*, in which a man becomes obsessed with what his wife is doing when she goes to work outside the home after twenty years of childcare and domesticity; the result is that she rediscovers herself and he crumbles into pathological jealousy.

Old Flames

Most of Whitehead's stage work is naturalistic in tone and texture, and he puts this to good use in *Old Flames*, which develops from a comedy-of-manners opening, with a man being put out to find that the woman who has invited him to dinner has also invited his ex-wives and his mother, into a kind of gothic farce as he discovers he is the menu. After the interval, and the dinner, the women sit around talking freely about their lives to one another in a way that is still rare in drama. Inevitably, the static nature and almost monologue quality of the second act has given rise to cries of lack of dramatic interaction, but the value placed on women's discourse is more than adequate compensation.

TRY THESE:
✱BUFFINI's *Dinner*, CHURCHILL's *Top Girls*, ✱EURIPIDES' *The Bacchae*, ✱ISITT's *The Woman Who Cooked Her Husband*, ✱SENECA's *Thyestes* and ✱SHAKESPEARE's *Titus Andronicus* for interesting eating habits; ✱IBSEN's *A Doll's House*

for a strained marriage; ✱RUSSELL's *Stags and Hens* for contemporary mating rituals; ✱SHAPIRO's *Dead Romantic* for sexual politics.

WHITEMORE, Hugh   [1936 –   ]
British dramatist

PLAYS INCLUDE:
Stevie (1977), *Pack of Lies* (1983), *Breaking the Code* (1986), *The Best of Friends* (1988), *God Only Knows* (2001)

A list of Whitemore's stage plays gives little indication of his versatility or distinguished career as a television and film writer – with such credits as the screenplay for *84 Charing Cross Road*, a Writers' Guild award for a television adaptation of *Cider with Rosie* (1971) and *Country Matters* (1972), as well as a clutch of television drama series. His stage plays, not surprisingly, show an equal craftsmanship, like an old Chippendale, with the same attention to detail. His portrayal of the Palmers Green poet Stevie Smith (*Stevie*) was as much a pinpointing of the minutiae of suburban claustrophobia as of the makings of a poet. In *Breaking the Code*, about Enigma code-breaker and homosexual Alan Turing, ideas of loyalty and national expediency are explored alongside homosexuality. *The Best of Friends*, an elegant celebration of friendship, dramatises the correspondence between ✱SHAW, Sir Sydney Cockerell and the Abbess of Stanbrook in Worcester. In *God Only Knows* a mysterious stranger disrupts four holidaymakers in Tuscany with a story about how the Romans manufactured the story of Christ's resurrection for political ends. He claims he revealed the truth and was put in a mental hospital from which he has just escaped. Is he mad, or is he telling the truth?

Pack of Lies

In *Pack of Lies*, suburbia sets the scene for a microscopic examination of emotional destruction. Set in 1961 with the Portland Spy case as its background, Whitemore chose to focus not so much on the spies (the Krogers) as on the way the Jacksons, the suburban couple who befriended and then betrayed them, were drawn into a web of deceit by MI6, and the effect on them. A subtle study in the pain of betrayal, of conflicting loyalties between friends and country, and of how the lives of ordinary people can be ruthlessly destroyed, it breathed new life into the old soap-opera form and became a compelling drama, particularly in the hands of Judi Dench and Michael Williams. *Pack of Lies* started out as a British television play and was also turned into an American television film (1986) (with Ellen Burstyn, Alan Bates and Teri Garr).

TRY THESE:
✷ SIMON GRAY, ✷ JULIAN MITCHELL also specialise in the 'well made' play and deal in loyalties and things British; ✷ BENNETT's *The Old Country* for betrayal and homosexuality; for images of ageing mothers, ✷ KEARSLEY's *Under the Web*, ✷ RAIF's *Fail/Safe*; Laclos' *Les Liaisons Dangereuses* (adapted by ✷ CHRISTOPHER HAMPTON) is entirely based on letters, but dramatised letters have been less frequent than anthologies, which over the years have formed the basis of solo performances about specific poets and writers (e.g. ✷ OSCAR WILDE in Michael McLiammoir's *The Importance of Being Oscar*, Michael Pennington's *Anton Chekhov*.

WHITING, John   [1917 – 63]
British dramatist

PLAYS INCLUDE:
Conditions of Agreement (1948), *A Penny for a Song* (1951, revised 1962), *Saint's Day* (1953), *Marching Song* (1954), *The Gates of Summer* (1956), *The Devils* (1961), *Conditions of Agreement* (1965), *No More A-Roving* (1975)

His death from cancer at forty-five cut tragically short one of the most intriguing playwriting careers of the post-war period, as Whiting, who began his career as a RADA-trained actor, showed a facility for both gentle comedies of character (*A Penny for a Song*) and large-scale and brutal tragedy (*The Devils*). In between came *Saint's Day*, about an 83-year-old poet, Paul Southman, at odds with the literary society that has scorned him (revived at the Orange Tree, Richmond, in 2002), and *Marching Song*, a story of political disaffection filtered through the individual tale of one Rupert Foster, a war criminal

invited to commit suicide by the chancellor of a newly powerless country (Britain?). None of Whiting's plays, except for *The Devils*, was particularly well reviewed during his life, and the intriguing characters of *A Penny for a Song* – in which an English coastal community awaits a Napoleonic invasion – only began to be appreciated following a 1962 revival, one year before his death. The Arts Council gave his name to one of the most prestigious awards for new writing.

The Devils
The Devils, commissioned by Peter Hall for the RSC, established Whiting as a major dramatist capable of a Jacobean richness of language, epic scope and bold, often shocking stage imagery. Based on Aldous Huxley's *The Devils of Loudun*, the play tells of the supposed 'possession' of a group of nuns in a seventeenth-century French priory. Sister Jeanne, a hunchback abbess, succumbs to an infectious hysteria, and leads the accusations that the lecherous priest, Grandier, is in league with the devil. A 1971 film adaptation by Ken Russell, starring Vanessa Redgrave and Oliver Reed, was expectedly over the top.

TRY THESE:
✷ BOLT's *A Man for All Seasons*, ✷ MILLER's *The Crucible* for historical contrast; ✷ BARKER and ✷ BOND (especially *Lear* and *The War Plays*) for the hair-raising intensity of the images and the elevated prose; ✷ ANOUILH, ✷ HOCHHÜTH's *Soldiers* for studies in disillusionment akin to *Marching Song*.

WHITTINGTON, Amanda   [1968 –   ]
British dramatist

PLAYS INCLUDE:
Player's Angels (1999), *Be My Baby* (2000), *Short Fuse* (2002, with Tim Etchells and Steve Waters), *The Wills's Girls* (2002), *Bollywood Jane* (2003)

Nottingham-born Whittington worked as a freelance journalist after leaving school and her early plays were staged in pubs in Nottingham. Her most successful play to date has been *Be My Baby*, set in the 1960s in one of those 'homes' where unmarried pregnant women are forced to give up their babies for adoption. She examined the women workers at the John Player cigarette factories in *Player's Angels*, which was followed by a similar exploration of W. D. and H. O. Wills in *The Wills's Girls*. East Midlands Arts describes the as yet unseen *Satin 'n' Steel* as being about a failed cabaret act and a failed marriage, while *Bollywood Jane* (Leicester Haymarket, May 2003) is advertised as 'bursting with life, song and dance' as 'local girl Jane escapes life into the fantasy world of Bollywood'.

TRY THESE:

✱ LAWRENCE and ✱ LOWE for other Nottingham dramatists; ✱ TREVOR GRIFFITHS' *Comedians* and ✱ HAYES' *Not Waving* for comedy acts and marital failures.

WILCOX, Michael   [1943 –   ]
British dramatist

PLAYS INCLUDE:

The Atom Bomb Project (1975), *Grimm Tales* (1975), *Roar Like Spears* (1975), *Phantom of the Fells* (1977), *The Blacketts of Bright Street* (1977), *Pioneers* (1977), *Dekka and Dava* (1978), *Rents* (1979), *Accounts* (1981), *Lent* (1983), *78 Revolutions* (1984), *Massage* (1986), *Green Fingers* (1990), *Mrs Steinberg and the Byker Boy* (2000)

Wilcox is probably best known for his plays about the gay community, although he has also tackled nuclear (in both the atomic and family senses) themes in *The Atom Bomb Project*, and reassessed folk tales in *Grimm Tales* and *Dekka and Dava*, which is a Newcastle version of *Hansel and Gretel*. His initial breakthrough came with *Rents*, a study of Edinburgh rent boys in which the staccato, episodic presentation represents the fragmented nature of their lives. He followed this with *Accounts*, in which the homosexual theme is only one element in an altogether gentler account of both literal and figurative balancing the books in an English hill farming family in the Scottish Borders. *Lent* is similarly gentle on the surface, with its picture of a boy spending his Easter holiday virtually alone in his prep school, although under the surface Michael Billington detected a lament

for the Peter Pan-like inability of British men to mature fully. In *78 Revolutions* Wilcox used two Americans attempting to record singers in the Russian Imperial Opera in the early days of recording as a means of investigating various kinds of cultural clash, but the enterprise turned into something more like an illustrated recital and lecture on the technicalities of recording. More controversial is *Massage*, in which Wilcox tackles questions of paedophilia. *Green Fingers* deals with hypocrisy and homophobia in Newcastle with a story of a young gardener accused of burglary, while *Mrs Steinberg and the Byker Boy* is ostensibly about a socialist charity shop (the Red Flag) being relaunched as the New Red Flag while a new arrival seduces one of the existing staff. Unsurprisingly, some critics detected topical allusions to wider political themes.

TRY THESE:

Wilcox acknowledges ✱ C. P. TAYLOR's influence and there are similarities between their interests in, for example, Peter Pan and retelling old stories; ✱ PARKER's *Spokesong* shares *Massage*'s bicycle-shop setting; ✱ POWNALL's *Master Class* and ✱ STOPPARD's *Every Good Boy Deserves Favour* also deal with the theme of music in Russia; ✱ C. P. TAYLOR's *Good* uses music in its investigation of Nazism; Wilcox's *Phantom of the Fells* is a reworking of ✱ SYNGE's *In the Shadow of the Glen*; for rather different versions of schooldays, ✱ JULIAN MITCHELL's *Another Country* and Denise Deegan's *Daisy Pulls It Off*; ✱ RUDKIN for another version of *Hansel and Gretel*.

WILDE, Oscar Fingal O'Flahertie Wills   [1854 – 1900]
Irish dramatist, poet, essayist and novelist

PLAYS INCLUDE:

Vera (1882), *The Duchess of Padua* (1891), *Lady Windermere's Fan* (1892), *A Woman of No Importance* (1893), *An Ideal Husband* (1895), *The Importance of Being Earnest* (1895), *Salomé* (1896)

Wilde's father was an ear surgeon, his mother an Irish nationalist who wrote political pamphlets and poetry. A graduate of Trinity College Dublin and later Oxford University

The Importance of Being Earnest by Oscar Wilde, directed by Christopher Morahan, Savoy Theatre, 2001. Patricia Routledge as Lady Bracknell. (Pete Jones/ArenaPAL)

he emerged from both as a brilliant scholar and had his first book of poetry published in 1881. With Walter Pater, Wilde became a focal point for the Aesthetic movement, popularising Pater's gospel of 'the ecstasy of beauty'. ✶GILBERT and Sullivan parodied his style in *Patience* with their portrayal of Bunthorne, a 'very, very sensitive young man', waving a lily. *Vera* and *The Duchess of Padua*, a verse drama, were both produced in New York, unsuccessfully, but *Lady Windermere's Fan* established Wilde as the darling of *fin de siècle* London. *A Woman of No Importance* and *An Ideal Husband* confirmed Wilde's position; but his reputation was precarious. Although he was celebrated for his social dramas and comedies, *The Picture of Dorian Gray* was branded as 'immoral', *Salomé* was banned by the Lord Chamberlain and the first night of his most successful play, *The Importance of Being Earnest*, was when the Marquess of Queensberry, father of his lover Lord Alfred Douglas, accused Wilde of homosexuality. After failing in a libel case against the Marquess, Wilde was tried for homosexuality and sentenced to the maximum penalty of two years' hard labour. While in prison he wrote *De Profundis* and his major poem, *The Ballad of Reading Gaol*. Released in 1897, a declared bankrupt, he moved to France where he lived until his death in Paris from meningitis.

The Importance of Being Earnest
Subtitled 'A Trivial Comedy for Serious People', Wilde's last major play has been described as 'the wittiest comedy in the English language'. Structurally, the play is a brilliant inversion and extension of theatrical conventions, with the elements of farce and melodrama thrown together to the point of absurdity. The plot of mistaken identity, long-lost brothers, frustrated romance and foundlings, is couched in the sophisticated and urbane wit of contemporary London society. According to Max Beerbohm: 'the fun depends on what the characters say, rather than on what they do; they speak a kind of beautiful nonsense, the language of high comedy, twisted into fantasy'. For ✶SHAW, however, 'three acts of studied triviality, however brilliant, are too much'.

TRY THESE:
✶BENNETT, ✶COWARD and ✶ORTON share with Wilde a camp wit and a sardonic awareness of the hypocrisies of conventional society manners; the elegant wit of Wilde's comedy owes a great deal to the eighteenth-century comedy of manners (writers such as ✶CONGREVE, ✶GOLDSMITH and ✶SHERIDAN); ✶STOPPARD plays with *The Importance of Being Earnest* in *Travesties*, as does ✶RAVENHILL in altogether darker fashion, in *Handbag*; Lindsay Kemp for a version of *Salomé*.

WILDER, Thornton   [1897 – 1975]
American dramatist

PLAYS INCLUDE:
The Trumpet Shall Sound (1927), *The Long Christmas Dinner* (1931), *Pulman Car Hiawatha* (1931), *The Happy Journey to Trenton and Camden* (1931), *Our Town* (1938), *The Merchant of Yonkers* (1938), *The Skin of Our Teeth* (1942), *The Matchmaker* (1954, revised version of *The Merchant of Yonkers*), *A Life in the Sun* (1955), *Three Plays for Bleecker Street* (1962)

A three-time Pulitzer Prize-winner, Wilder paints an often affectionate but astute picture of small-town American life, finding in the minutiae of experience the electrically charged matter of drama. Often mistaken as bland and cosy, Wilder can be surprisingly subversive both in form and content, and pain never lies far outside the borders of any of his scenes. In *The Long Christmas Dinner*, for example, a family gathering slowly reveals its darker shades until the would-be festivity has an air of melancholy more akin to James Joyce's *Dead* than, even, comparable scenes in ✶NEIL SIMON's *Brighton Beach Memoirs*. Catastrophe defines the human experience in *The Skin of Our Teeth*, a play that sees the history of mankind as a litany of encounters with chaos. Even the celebrated *Our Town* finds some sadness in its pastoral landscape. Wilder was, however, capable of a great laugh and in *The Matchmaker*, which inspired the legendary musical *Hello, Dolly!*, he wrote a classic farce about a woman who becomes engaged to the same penny-pinching man she has been trying to match up with somebody else.

Our Town

Beginning in Grover's Corners, New Hampshire, on a determinedly ordinary day in 1901, Wilder's Pulitzer Prize-winning play is one of the most often produced – and, perhaps, misunderstood – American plays in America, where it is seen as the theatrical equivalent of apple pie by people who overlook its depth. Embracing fourteen years over its prologue and three acts, the play is an exalted chronicle of the everyday – Wilder's attempt, as he puts it, 'to find a value above all price for the smallest events of our daily life'. Those events may be small, but they are significant, and Wilder takes a scalpel to human psychology in a way that restores an often-lacking immediacy to matters of love and loss. Innovative in form, the play is both abstract and utterly realistic, with its use of a Stage Manager to act as narrator and chorus, and the inexorable progression of its three acts, entitled 'anti illusionary', 'love and marriage' and 'death'. The story is about two families, the Webbs and the Gibbses, but it's Everyfamily, of course, as well – this is *our* town – Wilder makes clear, and his incisive and loving play is both the quintessential comment on Americana and the perfect by-product of it.

TRY THESE:

The Wooster Group appropriated portions of *Our Town* in *Route 1 & 9*; ✷ CHEKHOV, ✷ DYLAN THOMAS's *Under Milk Wood* and ✷ LANFORD WILSON (especially *The Rimers of Eldritch* and his narrative use of Matt in *Tally's Folley*) for ensemble pieces strongly allied to a sense of place and a similarly gentle yet tough-minded tone; ✷ SHAW's *Back to Methuselah* for the sweep of history; ✷ MEDOFF and ✷ SHEPARD for modern, often absurdist variants on Wilder's small-town reveries; ✷ GURNEY's *The Dining Room* as a 1970s WASP update of *The Long Christmas Dinner*; ✷ CARTWRIGHT's *Road* for a lethal British parallel to *Our Town*; ✷ AYCKBOURN's *The Norman Conquests* trilogy for another cataclysmic Christmas dinner; *The Matchmaker* and ✷ STOPPARD's *On the Razzle* are ultimately derived from John Oxenford's *A Day Well Spent* via ✷ NESTROY's *Einen Jux will er sich machen*.

WILLIAMS, (George) Emlyn   [1905 – 87]

Welsh dramatist, actor and director

PLAYS INCLUDE:

A Murder Has Been Arranged (1930), *The Late Christopher Bean* (1933, from Sidney Howard's play of the same name, itself a version of René Fauchois's *Prenez Garde à la Peinture*), *Spring 1600* (1934), *Night Must Fall* (1935), *The Corn Is Green* (1938), *The Light of Heart* (1940), *The Druid's Rest* (1944), *The Wind of Heaven* (1945)

Williams' plays epitomise the era of weekly rep and the well-made play. *Night Must Fall*, a 'psychological thriller' about the cheerful pageboy with a head in his hatbox, and the old lady in the wheelchair whom he doesn't quite murder, still has a good deal of theatrical force, and is the only play by Williams that is likely to wear well – except perhaps his genial comedy of Welsh public-house life *The Druid's Rest*, which is full of affectionately drawn characters of the kind he was brought up with. His other plays, including the more famous autobiographical *The Corn Is Green*, are marred by being too 'well made' and too sentimental. His two volumes of autobiography, *George* (1961) and *Emlyn* (1970), give as vivid a picture of life in north Wales, Oxford and the London theatre of the 1920s and 1930s as one is likely to find, and could be effectively dramatised, perhaps as a one-person show of the kind that he himself did so well.

TRY THESE:

✷ RATTIGAN for well-crafted plays partly based on autobiographical material; ✷ CHRISTIE for thrillers, Joseph Kesselring's 1941 *Arsenic and Old Lace* for a recently revived product of the same period.

WILLIAMS, Heathcote   [1941 –   ]

British dramatist

PLAYS INCLUDE:

The Local Stigmatic (1965), *AC/DC* (1970), *Hancock's Last Half-Hour* (1977), *The Immortalist* (1977), *At It* (1982; part of *Breach of the Peace*), *Whales* (1986), *Autogeddon* (1991)

Williams is one of the key figures of the counter-cultural landscape as the founding editor of *Suck* and the author of *AC/DC*, which was greeted as 'seminal to the seventies'. Williams' work is generally concerned with individuals at the margins of existence in a world that is hostile to the individual and to non-conformism in any form. Much of *AC/DC* now seems trapped in a kind of period aspic with its two schizophrenics and three hippies, its relentless energy and its linguistic violence, though it is itself critical of the ways in which hippiedom had become another form of conventional behaviour. The attack on 'psychic capitalism', the way in which the media set a conformist and coercive mindscape, is still as relevant as ever but the contemporary theatre has moved on to more detailed analyses of the ways agendas are set. *Hancock's Last Half-Hour* is likely to be revived more frequently, not only because it offers a fine part for an actor but because its meditation on the nature of the self, the relationship between performers and their audiences, the role of the media in creating and destroying individuals, and the meaning of comedy and of fame is more readily accessible. Williams' 1964 book *The Speakers*, about Speakers' Corner in Hyde Park where individuals put forward often bizarre socio-politico-religious theories to whoever will listen, was successfully dramatised by Joint Stock.

TRY THESE:
∗SNOO WILSON for works not entirely dissimilar to *AC/DC*; ∗ARTAUD for a highly physical idea of theatre; Bill Gaskill compared Williams to ∗CONGREVE on the strength of *AC/DC*; *Hancock's Last Half Hour* is one of many theatrical meditations on the role of the performer and of comedy, including Colin Bennett's *Hancock's Finest Hour*, ∗TREVOR GRIFFITHS' *Comedians* and ∗OSBORNE's *The Entertainer*; *The Local Stigmatic* is reminiscent of early ∗PINTER and ∗ALBEE's *The Zoo Story*.

WILLIAMS, Nigel   [1948 –   ]
British dramatist, novelist and screenwriter

PLAYS INCLUDE:
Double Talk (1976), *Class Enemy* (1978), *Easy Street* (1979), *Sugar and Spice* (1980), *Line 'Em* (1980), *Trial Run* (1980), *WCPC* (1982), *The Adventures of Jasper Ridley* (1982), *My Brother's Keeper* (1985), *Country Dancing* (1986), *Nativity* (1989), *Lord of the Flies* (1995, from Golding), *Harry and Me* (1996)

A versatile writer who has won awards for his fiction, translated ∗GENET and worked for the BBC, Williams made his initial impact as a gritty presenter of claustrophobic urban tensions in the classroom drama *Class Enemy* but branched out into political farce (*WCPC*) and analysis of myth-making and the co-option of the past in *Country Dancing*. Society has already given up on Williams' group of streetwise teenagers in *Class Enemy* as they mark time at school but he reveals the mixture of individual needs and aspirations beneath their surface of malcontent bravado. The bleakness of this world is continued into the sexual politics of *Sugar and Spice*, the racial politics of *Trial Run*, and the confrontation between pickets and the army in *Line 'Em*. There is more comedy in *WCPC* and *The Adventures of Jasper Ridley* but it remains based on a firm sense of the absurd waste and endemic corruption of society, even if the use of cartoon techniques and caricature sometimes gives rise to accusations of being patronising: in *WCPC* a straight policeman's mission to arrest cottaging gays spirals into farce, as first he discovers his sergeant in highly suspicious circumstances and is then frustrated in his attempts to bring him to 'justice' by the discovery that virtually everyone else in the force is involved in a gay conspiracy; Jasper Ridley is a picaresque hero in the Candide mould whose adventures include being sponsored by Prince Charles as Unemployed Young Person of the Year. In *My Brother's Keeper* we have family tensions at a dying old actor's bedside and in *Country Dancing* Williams examines the folk-song collector Cecil Sharp as he gathers songs from an old man just before World War I, using Sharp's antiquarian interests to make points about the function of song and the need to reclaim the past from myths which reduce its contradictions and sentimentalise its hardships. *Harry and Me* is about a television chat show in ratings free-fall.

TRY THESE:
✱HORSFIELD, ✱KEEFFE, ✱KUREISHI, ✱MAHONEY for images of contemporary urban life; ✱POWNALL's *Master Class*; ✱STOPPARD's *Every Good Boy Deserves Favour*, C. P. Taylor's *Good* for other variations on the musical theme; ✱HAYES' *Skirmishes* ✱IKOLI's *Scrape Off the Black*, ✱O'NEILL's *Long Day's Journey Into Night* for combative siblings; ✱WERTENBAKER's *The Grace of Mary Traverse* for contemporary female picaresque; ✱FLANNERY's *Our Friends in the North* and G. F. Newman's *Operation Bad Apple* for peculiar police procedures; for pickets and the army, ✱ARDEN's *Serjeant Musgrave's Dance*; ✱ORTON's *Loot* for realism spiralling off into farce.

WILLIAMS, Roy
British dramatist

The No Boys Cricket Club (1996), *Starstruck* (1998), *Lift Off* (1999), *The Gift* (2000), *Souls* (2000), *Clubland* (2001), *Sing Yer Heart Out for the Lads* (2002), *Fallout* (2003)

A former actor, Williams has written about the interaction between London and the West Indies, particularly for the older generation who left for a better life in England. In *The No Boys Cricket Club*, remembering her cricketing prowess in Jamaica helps a woman to transcend the mundane difficulties of her current life on a London council estate; in *Starstruck* the arrival of Stewart Granger in Kingston to make a film acts as a catalyst for the characters' financial and amatory aspirations. *The Gift* links Jamaica and Britain through two half-sisters, Bernice, the one who stayed, and Heather, the one who went to England, who returns after her son's murder. The Gift of the title is Bernice's supposed power to raise the dead and also the deeds of the family house that Heather will give to Bernice if she can exercise that power.

Williams' English-set plays prove him to be an acute observer of contemporary multicultural life. In *Lift Off* the subject is the complexity of interracial relationships on a London estate, while in *Clubland* the usual tale of boys refusing to be men as they try to pull is complicated by interracial tensions. In *Sing Yer Heart Out for the Lads* a pub team that has just won an important football match settles down to watch England play Germany. The black striker abuses the Germans but other people in the pub are equally hostile to him, even if their racism comes in different forms.

TRY THESE:
✱KEEFFE, ✱MATURA for the West Indies and Britain; ✱RECKORD for an earlier version of the difficulties of multiculturalism; ✱MARIE JONES for the impact of the film industry on a community; ✱GODBER, ✱RUSSELL for bad behaviour in clubs; ✱RICHARD HARRIS for cricket and ✱BRENTON and ✱IKOLI's *Sleeping Policemen* for the cricket World Cup.

WILLIAMS, Samm-Art   [1946 –   ]
American dramatist, screenwriter, producer and actor

PLAYS INCLUDE:
Welcome Back to Black River (1975), *The Coming* (1976), *Do Unto Others* (1976), *A Love Play* (1976), *The Last Caravan* (1977), *Birds Don't Sing* (1977), *Friends Sing* (1977), *Home* (1979), *The Sixteenth Round* (1980), *Friends* (1983), *Bojangles* (1985, musical), *Eyes of the American* (1985), *Eve of the Trial* (after ✱CHEKHOV) in *Orchards* (1986), *Cork* (1986), *Woman from the Town* (1990), *The Waiting Room* (2001), *The Dance on Widows' Row* (2002), *Conversations on a Dirt Road* (2002)

Born in Burgaw, North Carolina, Williams is best known for *Home*, which concerns a young black man who leaves his native South and goes North. He has said the idea for *Home* came to him while on a Greyhound Bus heading South one Christmas. In an interview with the *New York Times*, after the play moved to Broadway, Williams said he considered himself part of 'the pioneer generation that is going to have to start the new things rolling. The old, angry young black man is now the hungry young black man. Not that he is not angry, not that you do not want things to change. But there are so many things we wrote about in the past that are just old hat. Now we've got to show a different side of black life style. You know, all black characters don't have to be heroes. All black men do not have to be black macho, strong leaders of the household, knocking everybody down on stage. You can have very sensitive, very kind, very gentle, kinds of black men.'

Cork, which takes its title from the burnt substance used by nineteenth-century minstrels to darken their faces, is at once an exploration of negative black stereotypes and a homage to the entertainers who, for complex reasons, helped to perpetuate some of them. *Cork* is set in a contemporary West End theatre where Randy Madison, a black dramatist and actor, has won his first critical acclaim and substantial financial compensation. He is visited in his dressing room by the ghost of a legendary black minstrel, who asks him to cancel one performance in honour of American minstrels. 'You don't have to use cork', the ghost tells Madison, 'I wore it for you.' Williams spent many years in television, acting as executive producer on *The Fresh Prince of Bel-Air*; his plays would repay attention in the British theatre.

TRY THESE:

✱BARAKA, ✱BULLINS, ✱ELDER, ✱HANSBERRY, ✱WESLEY for contrasting techniques, settings and viewpoints of black life; ✱YOUNG's *Crystal Clear* for blind lovers; ✱SHANGE's *Spell No. 7* for more allusions to black minstrels and ✱WOLFE for the challenging of black stereotypes; ✱TOWNSEND for a different view of hospital waiting rooms to compare with *The Waiting Room*; Joseph Kesselring's *Arsenic and Old Lace* for a comparison to *The Dance on Widows' Row*; ✱FIRTH's *The Safari Party* for a view of heritage to contrast with *Conversations on a Dirt Road*.

WILLIAMS, Tennessee (Thomas Lanier)   [1911 – 83]
American dramatist

PLAYS INCLUDE:
Battle of Angels (1940), *The Glass Menagerie* (1944), *A Streetcar Named Desire* (1947), *Summer and Smoke* (1948), *The Rose Tattoo* (1951), *Camino Real* (1953), *Cat on a Hot*

Tin Roof (1955), *27 Wagons Full of Cotton* (1955), *Orpheus Descending* (1957), *Suddenly Last Summer* (1958), *Sweet Bird of Youth* (1959), *Period of Adjustment* (1960), *Night of the Iguana* (1961), *The Milk Train Doesn't Stop Here Anymore* (1962), *The Gnädiges Fräulein* (1966), *Kingdom of Earth* (1968, also called *The Seven Descents of Myrtle*), *Small Craft Warnings* (1972), *Outcry* (1973), *The Red Devil Battery Sign* (1975), *Vieux Carré* (1977), *A Lovely Sunday for Crève Coeur* (1979), *Clothes for a Summer Hotel* (1980), *Something Cloudy Something Clear* (1981)

The Mississippi-born son of a travelling salesman who, to quote from *The Glass Menagerie*, 'fell in love with long distance', Williams turned his own poignant life into the material for some of the most rending and luminous plays of our time. His father was cool, remote and given to calling him 'Miss Nancy' (Williams was gay); his mother, a rector's daughter, was unstable and his sister Rose was the victim of a lobotomy in 1937. After his own nervous collapse when he was twenty-three, Williams spent much of his life in various stages of ill health, and he frequently wrote about people (often women) on the brink of a breakdown – most memorably Blanche DuBois, in *A Streetcar Named Desire*, but also Zelda Fitzgerald in his late play *Clothes for a Summer Hotel*. His key themes are the physical ravages of time and the emotional ravages of deceit, and his plays often pit the sexes against one another on a continuum of regret in which both ravages take their toll: Blanche and Stanley in *Streetcar*, the alcoholic Brick and his wife Maggie the Cat in *Cat on a Hot Tin Roof*, the fading actress Princess Kosmonopolis and her young gigolo Chance Wayne in *Sweet Bird of Youth*. He is famous for his emotional honesty, but some of his most interesting plays are tinged with the grotesque, filled with foreboding, and often darkly comic. *Suddenly Last Summer* and *The Gnädiges Fräulein* are dazzling, weird examples.

After repeated critical success on Broadway for over two decades, often in the company of his frequent collaborator, the director Elia Kazan, Williams' fortunes turned sour in the late 1970s and 1980s, as play after

A Streetcar Named Desire by Tennessee Williams, directed by Trevor Nunn, National Theatre, 2002. Glenn Close as Blanche DuBois, Iain Glen as Stanley Kowalski. (Pete Jones/ArenaPAL)

play met poor receptions only to turn up (often) to better notices in London's West End. Critics often complained that his later plays were pale shadows of his earlier ones, leaving Williams the ironic embodiment of his own theme – a man victimised by memories of an earlier, more productive time.

The Glass Menagerie

A four-character work set in St Louis, this early memory play is an almost perfect miniature, which distils Williams' gift for transmuting autobiography into art. A talkative, domineering mother, Amanda Wingfield, runs roughshod over her shy daughter, Laura, and her rebellious son, Tom. In an effort to kindle a romance for Laura, she invites to dinner one of Tom's workmates, Jim, The Gentleman Caller, only to watch her well-intentioned plans fall to pieces as cruelly as the glass figurines in the menagerie of the title. Written with a fragile delicacy, the play offers not only a haunting portrait of the dramatist as a young man – the would-be poet Tom, who seeks solace in the cinema and bursts with dreams of 'the moon' – but also a quartet of superb parts that have been cornerstones of many actors' careers.

A Streetcar Named Desire

The play that brought Williams his first Pulitzer Prize (the second was for *Cat on a Hot Tin Roof* eight years later), *Streetcar* shows the dramatist at his sweatiest and most fevered best. The neurasthenic Blanche arrives in the 'Belle Reve' quarter of New Orleans to stay with her sister Stella, only to enter into a fraught battle of attraction and repulsion with Stella's bestial husband Stanley. A woman in need of constant pampering, Blanche has her illusions shaken by Stanley, who in turn feels his domestic territory to be at risk. A lyrical plunge into emotional territory that wipes out both the characters and the audience, the play ends as a showdown between two wounded, deceptively strong-willed souls, who find that the promised Elysian Fields where Stella lives hid a landmine of sorrow and pain.

TRY THESE:
✷GLASPELL, ✷TREMBLAY for hothouse atmospheres; ✷AUGUST WILSON and ✷LANFORD WILSON for their compassionate, graceful looks at often blighted lives; ✷SHEPARD for his dissections of the peculiar landscape of the American family; ✷FUGARD for his similarly sustained use of metaphor – he uses images of flames and candles in *Road to Mecca* the way Williams does in *The Glass Menagerie*.

WILLIAMSON, David   [1942 –   ]
Australian dramatist

PLAYS INCLUDE:
The Coming of Stork (1970), *The Removalists* (1971), *Don's Party* (1971), *Jugglers Three* (1972, as *Third World Blues*, 1997), *What If You Died Tomorrow?* (1973), *The Department* (1974), *A Handful of Friends* (1976), *The Club* (1977, also known as *Players* and *The Team*), *Travelling North* (1979), *Celluloid Heroes* (1980), *The Perfectionist* (1982), *Sons of Cain* (1985), *Emerald City* (1987), *Top Silk* (1989), *Siren* (1990), *Money and Friends* (1991), *Brilliant Lies* (1993), *Sanctuary* (1994), *Dead White Males* (1995), *Heretic* (1996), *After the Ball* (1997), *Corporate Vibes* (1999), *Face to Face* (1999), *The Great Man* (2000), *Up for Grabs* (2001), *A Conversation* (2001), *Charitable Intent* (2001), *Soulmates* (2002), *Birthrights* (2003)

For many years Williamson has been virtually the only Australian dramatist to receive any recognition in Britain. His plays are mainly dissections of Australian society that cast a sceptical eye on what he has described as its 'conformist philistine, sexist, and aggressive' aspects. For non-Australian audiences the danger is to assume that Williamson's studies are purely naturalistic, thus fuelling anti-Australian prejudice; for Australian audiences there is the danger that the delight of recognition may obscure the social criticism. In both cases, these are the classic dangers of a socially aware comic drama. Williamson has tackled many significant topics, from the roots of violence in *The Removalists*, through the fading dreams of youth in *Don's Party* to role-swapping in an 'open' marriage in *The Perfectionist*. The British reception of *Sons of*

Cain was perhaps typical: there was virtually unanimous praise for Max Cullen as a crusading newspaper editor, coupled with the usual journalists' refusal to admit any similarity between their own newspapers and the stage presentation of journalism and, more significantly, a rather dismissive attitude to a major Australian political scandal that formed the basis of the play on the grounds that it was parochial. *Emerald City* is an examination of the vexed relationship between popular appeal and artistic integrity. Although Williamson appears to come down on the side of integrity at the expense of popularity, the popular success of his own high-quality screenplays for *Gallipoli* (1981) and *The Year of Living Dangerously* (1983) suggests that another view is not untenable. Williamson was subjected to some criticism for Americanising *Up for Grabs* for Madonna's West End debut in 2002, but this story of skulduggery in the world for Fine Arts works well enough in any postmodern marketplace.

TRY THESE:
✶ LUCIE for modern dissections of British manners, ✶REDDIN for an American version; ✶ STOREY's *The Changing Room* for a view of rugby league comparable to *The Club*'s view of Australian Rules football; ✶ HUTCHINSON's *Rat in the Skull* for an analysis of police behaviour offering interesting parallels with *The Removalists*; ✶ BABE's *Buried Inside Extra* for American journalism, ✶BRENTON and ✶HARE's *Pravda* for British thoughts on the subject; ✶FO and ✶RAME's *The Open Couple* for a different treatment of an 'open' marriage; ✶BARKER's *Scenes from an Execution*, ✶REZA's *Art*, ✶WERTENBAKER's *Three Birds Alighting on a Field* for different takes on the power of art; Ray Lawler for an earlier and Joanna Murray-Smith for a later generation of Australian dramatists to be staged in London.

WILSON, August   [1945 –   ]
American dramatist

PLAYS INCLUDE:
Jitney (1982), *Ma Rainey's Black Bottom* (1984), *Fences* (1985), *Joe Turner's Come and Gone* (1986), *The Piano Lesson* (1987), *Two Trains Running* (1990), *Seven Guitars* (1995), *King Hedley II* (1999)

A black dramatist born in Pittsburgh, Wilson rapidly established himself in a short time as a key American dramatist capable of the sustained lyricism of ✶TENNESSEE WILLIAMS. Having begun his career as a poet, Wilson writes distinctively eloquent and passionate waves of speech that subordinate conventional exposition to a sheer pleasure in the richness of language; and he's at his most interesting when he subverts one's expectations of naturalism, as in *Joe Turner's Come and Gone*. He is currently in the middle of a cycle of plays about black life in the twentieth century, one play about each decade. His early play *Jitney*, set in a cab office in Pittsburgh in 1977, seen at the National Theatre in 2001, has been compared to both ✶CHEKHOV and ✶O'CASEY for the ways in which it creates a sense of actual life being lived. *Fences*, a family drama set in the Pittsburgh inner city in 1957 in the period just before America's simmering racial tensions came to the boil, won Wilson the Pulitzer Prize. In *Joe Turner's Come and Gone*, perhaps Wilson's most mysterious and dark play, and influenced, he says, by the paintings of Romare Bearden, the experiences of black Africans are painfully set against those of their American descendants in a Pittsburgh boarding house. Wilson won his second Pulitzer for *The Piano Lesson*, which also confronts the past. It focuses on a family's attempt to understand the history of slavery and exorcise its pain. In *Two Trains Running*, which takes place in Pittsburgh a month after the assassination of Martin Luther King Jr, the denizens of a greasy spoon debate the efficacy of the civil rights movement. *Seven Guitars* retells in flashback the story of the last week in the life of a blues guitarist trying to get to Chicago to make a record, and *King Hedley II*, seen at the Tricycle Theatre, Kilburn, in 2002, is another atmospheric portrait of neighbourhood life that gradually reveals the casual acceptance of an endemic pattern of low-level criminality that corrodes the lives of the characters.

Ma Rainey's Black Bottom
Set in a Chicago recording studio in 1927, *Ma Rainey* is a piercing look at American racism and bigotry – not just white against black but,

significantly, black against black – coupled with snatches of American blues music that reflect on and recapitulate the drama. Despite having her name in the title, the legendary Ma Rainey herself is a secondary figure in the play; central to it are the four musicians in her band – Slow Drag, Levee, Toledo and Cutler – who weave a tale of beauty and pain perfectly in keeping with the power of the music they perform.

TRY THESE:

✴LANFORD WILSON for dramatic lyricism; ✴BALDWIN, ✴HANSBERRY for earlier comparable treatments of black domestic life; ✴MILLER for examinations of the American dream gone sour; ✴KUREISHI, ✴MATURA for social acclimatisation; Heidi Thomas's *Indigo* for slavery; ✴MILNER, ✴WOLFE for integration of jazz into drama.

WILSON, Lanford   [1937 –   ]
American dramatist

PLAYS INCLUDE:

So Long at the Fair (1963), *Balm in Gilead* (1964), *Home Free* (1964), *The Madness of Lady Bright* (1965), *The Rimers of Eldritch* (1965), *Lemon Sky* (1970), *Serenading Louie* (1970), *The Great Nebula in Orion* (1970), *The Family Continues* (1972), *The Hot L Baltimore* (1973), *The Mound Builders* (1975), *Brontosaurus* (1977), *Fifth of July* (1978), *Talley's Folly* (1979), *Thymus Vulgaris* (1981), *Angels Fall* (1982), *Talley and Son* (1981, revised 1985), *A Betrothal* (1986), *Burn This* (1987), *A Poster of the Cosmos* (1988), *Sympathetic Magic* (1991), *Redwood Curtain* (1992), *Book of Days* (2001)

A writer with a ✴CHEKHOVIAN sense of human fallibility and compassion, Wilson is best known for his works spanning the generations of the Talley family in Lebanon, Missouri: *Talley's Folly*, is a sharp, clever two-hander about Matt Friedman's courtship of young Sally Talley in 1944. It won Wilson the 1980 Pulitzer Prize, but the first play of the trilogy, *Fifth of July*, is the most resonant. The third, the deliberately old-fashioned *A Tale Told*, has been revised to the newly titled *Talley and Son*. Wilson has also written well on topics beyond the Talley's Midwest farm:

his underrated *Angels Fall*, set on a New Mexico mission, is one of the most piercing, yet unpolemical, plays to date on the subject of nuclear fall-out. His 1987 *Burn This* is an affecting, if overwritten, piece about the relationship between a grief-stricken dancer and the volatile brother of her deceased lover.

Fifth of July

A homosexual who lost his legs in Vietnam might seem an unlikely figure to put at the centre of a comedy, but Wilson accomplishes the unexpected in *Fifth of July*, set on the day after American Independence Day in 1977. Ken Talley, the paraplegic schoolteacher who may or may not sell the Talley farmhouse, dominates this often rending, humane comedy about loss, acceptance and maturation – a *Cherry Orchard* rewritten for the post-1960s generation, with a casual acceptance of gay life that is gratifyingly free of cliché. The play has robust supporting roles (the singer Gwen is so strongly written that she can unbalance poorly directed productions), all put to the service of its author's keen-eyed sense of grace. Life may be painful or sad, but our best hope – this play tells us – is to make our own individual peaces and move on.

TRY THESE:

✴CHEKHOV for comic rue tempered with wisdom; ✴FUGARD for particular emphasis on human charity and redemption; ✴AUGUST WILSON for another American dramatist who uses storytelling to good advantage in his plays; ✴BRENTON's *The Genius*, ✴DARKE's *The Body*, ✴ROBERT HOLMAN's *The Overgrown Path* for British plays on the nuclear issue; ✴MANN's *Still Life* for the effects of Vietnam on life at home, ✴NOËL GREIG's *Poppies* and ✴OSMENT's *This Island's Mine* for British counterparts where the gay issue is a part of the general action; for incest, to compare with *Home Free*, ✴FORD, ✴POLIAKOFF.

WILSON, Snoo (Andrew)   [1948 –   ]
British dramatist and director

PLAYS INCLUDE:

Pericles (1970), *Pignight* (1971), *Blow Job* (1971), *Lay By* (1971, with ✴HOWARD

BRENTON, ✱BRIAN CLARK, ✱TREVOR GRIFFITHS, ✱DAVID HARE, ✱STEPHEN POLIAKOFF, Hugh Stoddart), *Boswell and Johnson on the Shores of the Eternal Sea* (1972), *England's Ireland* (1972, with ✱HOWARD BRENTON, Tony Bicât, ✱BRIAN CLARK, ✱DAVID EDGAR, Francis Fuchs, ✱DAVID HARE), *The Pleasure Principle* (1973), *Vampire* (1973), *The Beast* (1974, revised version as *The Number of the Beast*, 1982), *The Everest Hotel* (1975), *Soul of the White Ant* (1976), *England-England* (1977), *The Glad Hand* (1978), *A Greenish Man* (1978), *Flaming Bodies* (1979), *Spaceache* (1980), *Our Lord of Lynchville* (1983, revised as *Lynchville*, 1990), *Loving Reno* (1983), *The Grass Widow* (1983), *More Light* (1987), *Callas* (1990), *Darwin's Flood* (1994), *Sabina* (1998), *Moonshine* (1999)

After writing and directing with Portable Theatre, Wilson worked as a script editor for the BBC and as a resident dramatist with the RSC but, unlike his Portable contemporaries ✱DAVID HARE and ✱HOWARD BRENTON, he has never developed a sustained relationship with one of the major institutions. This probably relates to his eclectic and anarchic approach which, at its best, can juxtapose apparently discrete material and produce a theatrically exciting and spectacular event but can also lead to turgid self-absorption and a lack of disciplined writing. Wilson's interest in the occult, magic, politics, fantasy, and all the paraphernalia of the counter-culture leads to, for example, Jung, Freud, Enoch Powell and a talking ox in *Vampire*; gorillas emerging from 'a huge eyeball in the corner of the theatre' to enact a character's subconscious impulses in *The Pleasure Principle*; a fascist sailing an oil tanker to the Bermuda Triangle in the hope of entering a time warp to encounter the Antichrist in a previous manifestation during the Wyoming cowboy strike of 1886 (*The Glad Hand*); and ectoplasm, karma, piranha fish and marijuana in *The Grass Widow*. The occultist Aleister Crowley inevitably attracted Wilson's attention in *The Beast*, three girls sing from the top of Mount Everest to save the world from communism in *The Everest Hotel*; a magician has an incestuous relationship with his daughter in *Loving Reno*; Jerry Falwell

attempts to convert the Jews in *Our Lord of Lynchville*; a car crashes through a window in *Flaming Bodies*; and a pope dreams that Giordano Bruno asked ✱SHAKESPEARE to revise *Il Candelaio* in *More Light* (presumably this may not be unrelated to Wilson's own aborted version of *Il Candelaio* for the RSC). Maria Callas in *Callas*, and Sherlock Holmes, Conan Doyle and the Cottingley fairies in *Moonshine*, are all given the Wilson treatment. Some of this may work well, some of it may leave you cold, and it can be a close run thing between the two depending on the production and your own personal taste.

TRY THESE:
✱HEATHCOTE WILLIAMS' *AC/DC* is another example of early 1970s counter-cultural play making; ✱RECKORD's *X* is another modern treatment of incest; the extravagant imaginative quality of Wilson's work is generally reminiscent of ✱BARNES, and *The Everest Hotel* of ✱N. F. SIMPSON's *One Way Pendulum*; Wilson has been described as a political absurdist – the link would be with ✱GENET, ✱JARRY and ✱IONESCO rather than ✱BECKETT.

WOLFE, George C.   [1954 –   ]
American dramatist and director

PLAYS INCLUDE:
Up for Grabs (1975), *Block Party* (1976), *Back Alley Tales* (1979), *Paradise* (1985, book and lyrics), *Queenie Pie* (1986, libretto), *The Colored Museum* (1986), *Spunk* (1990, from Zora Neale Hurston), *Blackout* (1991) *Jelly's Last Jam* (1991)

While his early plays explore what it means to grow up black and male in America, Wolfe's most acclaimed work is *The Colored Museum*, which moved his writing into the area of social satire. On this larger canvas, Wolfe examines the entire African-American experience. *The Colored Museum* takes the audience through twelve museum exhibits that come to life, debunking the myths and stereotypes of the African-American experience. Among the topics satirised are 'afro' wigs and *Ebony Magazine*, as well as ✱LORRAINE HANSBERRY's *A Raisin in the Sun*, called *The Last Mama on the Couch Play*. In the 'museum', Wolfe lampoons sensitive targets such as black aspirations to white middle-class life. Confident in his identity and style, Wolfe daringly mocks the racist images that define and constrain African-Americans. Satire is not Wolfe's only interest. *Queenie Pie*, for which he wrote the libretto, is a musical eulogy to Duke Ellington, while *Jelly's Last Jam* does the same for Jelly Roll Morton. When asked why his production was not more political, Wolfe responded that being black and alive in America was already a political statement, and his work reflects this. He became the director of the New York Shakespeare Festival in 1993.

TRY THESE:
✱ OYAMO, especially *The Stalwarts*, which satirises black middle-class families; ✱ AUGUST WILSON's *Joe Turner's Come and Gone* and *Ma Rainey's Black Bottom* for how the music industry has treated black performers; Wolfe directed ✱ KUSHNER's *Angels in America*.

WOOD, Charles   [1932 –   ]
British dramatist

PLAYS INCLUDE:
Cockade (1963), *Don't Make Me Laugh* (1965), *Meals on Wheels* (1965), *Fill the Stage with Happy Hours* (1966), *Dingo* (1967), *H: or Monologues at Front of Burning Cities* (1969), *Welfare* (1970), *Veterans* (1972), *Jingo* (1975), *Has 'Washington' Legs?* (1978), *Red Star* (1984), *Across from the Garden of Allah* (1986)

Blackly comic views of the military and of filmmaking dominate the plays of Wood, who began his career as a stage manager and designer, largely for ✱ JOAN LITTLEWOOD. Wood spent five years in the army in the 1950s, and the experience doubtless facilitated the writing of plays like *Dingo*, a satirical piece set in a German prisoner-of-war camp and focusing on two World War II heroes, and *Jingo*, set amongst the British army in Singapore in 1941. Survivors of film sets are heroes of a sort, too, and Wood has often written about the art form where he made most of his money. *Veterans*, which starred two great theatrical Sirs, John Gielgud

and John Mills, focuses on two seasoned actors on the Turkey location shoot of a film. *Has 'Washington' Legs?* is a satire about a film being made of the American Revolution. The Russian-set *Red Star*, seen at the RSC, and the West End comedy *Across from the Garden of Allah*, a piece of anti-Hollywood bile, were poorly received. The 1988 BBC television screening of *Tumbledown* excited a political controversy over the treatment of a young officer badly wounded in the Falklands.

TRY THESE:
✱ BECKETT for the speech rhythms of plays like *Dingo*; ✱ DARKE's *The Oven Glove Murders*, ✱ KAUFMAN and ✱ HART, ✱ MARIE JONES, ✱ ODETS, and ✱ RABE's *Hurlyburly* for comic and/or bilious treatments of Hollywood and the film industry; ✱ MINGHELLA's *Made in Bangkok* for the Englishman abroad; ✱ WILLIS HALL's *The Long and the Short and the Tall* and ✱ NICHOLS' *Privates on Parade* for contrasting accounts of the British army; ✱ PAGE's *Falkland Sound/Voces de Malvinas* for another view of the Falklands War.

WOOD, David   [1944 –   ]
British dramatist

PLAYS INCLUDE:
The Owl and the Pussycat Went to Sea . . . (1968), *The Plotters of Cabbage Patch Corner* (1970), *The Gingerbread Man* (1976), *Nutcracker Sweet* (1977), *The Ideal Gnome Expedition* (1980), *Selfish Shellfish* (1983), *The See-Saw Tree* (1986)

Irving Wardle dubbed Wood 'the national children's dramatist'. A prolific and widely produced dramatist, Wood has also written copiously for films (the screenplay of *Swallows and Amazons*) and television. His touring children's theatre company, Whirligig, formed with John Gould in 1979, has toured Wood's plays to over a million children, and Wood has adapted work by virtually every writer for children from Enid Blyton and Roald Dahl to Dick King-Smith.

They are notably well-crafted plays with strongly drawn characters (frequently, like the testy Pepper-pot in *The Gingerbread Man*, high in idiosyncrasy), a keen sense of dramatic tension, and a striking feel for the visual magnificence possible in theatre. *The Gingerbread Man*, for instance, takes place on the vastly magnified surface of a kitchen dresser, while the insect plotters of Cabbage Patch Corner fight their fight against insecticide (green before their time) in a garden that acquires a magical life of its own. If at times the suspicion of a formula play exists, it is outbalanced by Wood's colour, humour and sheer professionalism.

TRY THESE:

✶CASDAGLI, ✶ DAVID HOLMAN, ADRIAN MITCHELL, ✶ SHEPPHARD for other dramatists writing for children.

WRIGHT, Nicholas   [1940 –   ]
South Africa-born British dramatist

PLAYS INCLUDE:

Changing Lines (1968), *Treetops* (1978), *The Gorky Brigade* (1979), *One Fine Day* (1980), *The Crimes of Vautrin* (1983), *The Custom of the Country* (1983), *The Desert Air* (1984), *Mrs Klein* (1988), *Cressida* (2000), *Vincent in Brixton* (2002)

Wright began his career as an actor and director before turning to playwriting in 1968 with *Changing Lines* at the Royal Court, where he worked as a casting director and – in 1976–7 – as joint artistic director. He has continued to work as a director and was an associate director at the National Theatre from 1994 to 1998. His own plays show an impressive range and a command of history and period. *Treetops*, set in Cape Town, draws upon his childhood as the youngest of three boys to emigrate from South Africa, and the African continent figures as well in *One Fine Day* (set on an East African coffee plantation), *The Custom of the Country* (racial acculturation in Johannesburg in the 1890s) and *The Desert Air* (a wartime satire set mostly in Cairo in 1942). *The Gorky Brigade* shifts the scene to Russia following the 1917 Revolution, and *The Crimes of Vautrin* – adapted from Balzac's *Splendeurs et Misères des Courtesans* – uses Paris in the 1830s to strike an anti-Thatcherite critique of a society worshipful of money and power. *Cressida* is a backstage drama set in the 1630s and *Vincent*

in Brixton does something similar in taking a relatively unknown set of circumstances (in this case the fact that Van Gogh spent some time living in Brixton) and using them to illuminate issues of art, illusion and love

Mrs Klein

In *Mrs Klein* Wright found a subject and a style that brought him major critical and popular success. A three-hander between female psychiatrists, including Melanie Klein and her daughter Melitta, it combines mother–daughter tensions, sibling rivalry, psychiatric case histories, soul baring, and a 'did he fall or did he push himself?' mystery. Klein's own important theoretical positions are subjected to destruction testing in Wright's subtle dramatisation of the contradictions of family life, as manifested in a family with a talent for the closest possible scrutiny of every nuance of speech or gesture.

TRY THESE:

Plays by expatriate South Africans include ✶HARWOOD's *Tramway Road* and Michael Picardie's adaptation of ✶CHEKHOV, *The Cape Orchard*; ✶FUGARD for South African life; ✶HARE's *Plenty* for the vagaries of British imperialism; ✶WYMARK's *Nana* as an adapted nineteenth-century French novel used to lash out at Britain today; ✶DARKE's *Ting Tang Mine*, ✶EDGAR's *Entertaining Strangers* for use of nineteenth-century contexts to comment on Thatcherite Britain; Peter Brook's *The Man Who*, Anna Furse's *Augustine (Big Hysteria)*, ✶JOHNSON, ✶KEMPINSKI for psychoanalysis/psychology; ✶DE ANGELIS for backstage life; ✶STRINDBERG for family life; Wright has adapted ✶IBSEN, ✶PIRANDELLO, ✶WEDEKIND; ✶WERTENBAKER's *Three Birds Alighting on a Field* for artistic inspiration.

WYCHERLEY, William   [1640 – 1716]
English dramatist

PLAYS INCLUDE:

Love in a Wood (1671), *The Gentleman Dancing Master* (1672), *The Country Wife* (1675), *The Plain Dealer* (1676)

Wycherley trained in the law but never practised, inherited one of Charles II's mistresses, married the Countess of Drogheda

The Country Wife by William Wycherley, directed by Max Stafford-Clark, Pit Theatre, 1994. Robin Northam, Debra Gillett, Robin Soans. (Henrietta Butler/ArenaPAL)

for her money and ended up in prison for her debts before settling down to burnish his literary reputation, which, however, rests on his plays and not on the verse to which he devoted the last thirty years of his life. The plays, robust, sexually explicit and satirical, are fine examples of what the term 'Restoration comedy' has come to mean, with their emphasis on the interrelationship of money, sex and power. But the really interesting point about Wycherley is that there is no obvious fixed authorial position for the audience to adopt. Wycherley used to be condemned, as many satirists are, for recommending the behaviour he presents in his plays; then he was praised for his celebratory presentation of a society in which the streetwise achieved their ends at the expense of those who failed to match their pretensions; now he seems to be a writer aware of the glitter and attractions of the life he presents but also aware of the void beneath. This comes over very clearly in *The Country Wife*, where the central character, Horner, is both hero and victim of the strategy which allows him unlimited sexual access to allegedly modest women but also condemns him to exhaustion as a provider of production-line orgasms, particularly in the scene where a number of women exhaust Horner's supply of what is euphemistically called china.

TRY THESE:

*MOLIÈRE's *Le Misanthrope* is a distant source for *The Plain Dealer*; there are similarities between Wycherley and the comedies of *JONSON as well as other Restoration comic writers such as *BEHN, *CONGREVE and *ETHERFGE; other writers of comedy of manners, such as *COWARD, *GOLDSMITH, *LUCIE, *REDDIN, *SHERIDAN, *WILDE; Wycherley's analysis of sex, class and power is reminiscent of *ORTON, and later *AYCKBOURN; *BOND's *Restoration* uses conventions and themes derived from the practice of Restoration writers to make modern points.

WYMARK, Olwen [1929 –]
American-born dramatist

PLAYS INCLUDE:
The Technicians (1967); *Speak Now* (1971), *Find Me* (1977), *Loved* (1978), *Please Shine Down on Me* (1980), *Best Friends* (1981), *Buried Treasure* (1984), *Lessons and Lovers* (1985), *Strike Up the Banns* (1988), *Brezhnev's Children* (1991, from Julia Vozneskaya)

Wymark's early plays (1967–70) were experimental in form, favourably compared to *BECKETT and described by Harold Hobson as 'atonal'. Born in America, Wymark came to Britain in the 1950s and married the actor Patrick Wymark, with whom she had four children. When she was widowed, she worked as a typist until Chattie Salaman of Common Stock Theatre Company encouraged her to write plays. In 1977 she became Gulbenkian Writer in Residence at Kingston Polytechnic and wrote *Find Me*, about a disturbed young girl who ended up in Broadmoor. Based on a true story it was written as a result of extensive discussions with the real parents and improvisations with students, and used a cast of eight (including *SHARMAN MACDONALD before she started writing) switching roles constantly to elucidate and 'find' the personality of the central character.

Since then her plays have become more naturalistic. ('What's the point of writing Absurd theatre when nobody's surprised by it any more? Monty Python killed all that', she says.) Usually they involve a central female character hitting out against the comfortable expectations of suburban family and friends. Cross-dressing, disguise and impersonation are subversive and liberating acts, often providing a catalyst for change and new insight. In *Loved*, two semi-real characters assume roles and engineer situations to provoke a reaction from an unresponsive husband and sister, while in her *Strike Up the Banns* (a later version of *Speak Now*), a bamboozled wife and mother dresses up as her husband's imaginary brother Rollo when her daughter's right-wing, moral crusading future father-in-law comes to dinner. Her husband retaliates by dressing up as Rollo's highly-strung wife Lillian.

Best known in recent years for adaptations of novels following the West End transfer of Zola's *Nana* by Shared Experience (1987), Wymark has been inundated with requests for adaptations, has worked extensively for television and radio and taught on creative writing course at Birmingham and Sheffield universities.

TRY THESE:
✴CHURCHILL and ✴ORTON for cross-dressing, ✴EDGAR's *Mary Barnes* and ✴MURRAY's *Body-cell* for young women in trouble; ✴AYCKBOURN for put-upon wives; Wymark has adapted work by ✴FO and ✴RAME, and Alexander Pushkin.

WYNNE, Michael
British dramatist

PLAYS INCLUDE:
The Knocky (1994), *Sell Out* (1998), *The Boy Who Left Home* (2000), *The People Are Friendly* (2002)

A native of Birkenhead, Wynne made his debut with *The Knocky* in the Royal Court's Coming On Strong young playwrights festival in 1994. It is a lively depiction of a family celebrating a birthday on a typical Royal Court estate. In *The Boy Who Left Home*, an adult fairy tale for ATC, a boy's attempt to find his way home involves him in tackling a series of traps laid by the forest demons. Wynne's latest play, *The People Are Friendly*, involves a Birkenhead native returning home after many years and discovering that the north–south divide is personal as well as political when her family fail to welcome her with open arms.

TRY THESE:
✴IBSEN for unhappy returns; ✴LEIGH, ✴PINTER for misfiring celebrations; ✴MURPHY's *The Morning After Optimism* for a fairytale forest; ✴DUNBAR for a Royal Court estate.

Y

YANKOWITZ, Susan [1941–]
American dramatist

PLAYS INCLUDE:
Terminal (1969), *Transplant* (1971), *Sideshow* (1971), *Slaughterhouse Play* (1971), *Boxes* (1972), *Acts of Love* (1973), *Wooden Nickels* (1973), *American Piece* (1974), *Still Life* (1977), *True Romances* (1978), *Qui est Anna Marx?* (1978), *Baby* (1983), *A Knife in the Heart* (1983), *Taking Liberties* (1986), *Alarms* (1987), *Monk's Revenge* (1988), *Utterances* (1991), *Night Sky* (1991), *Phaedra in Delirium* (1998)

New Jersey-born Yankowitz was an original member of Joe Chaikin's Open Theatre, one of the most influential groups in America's breakaway avant-garde theatre movement of the 1960s and 1970s, where company-created, physically intense, performer-centred styles of theatre held sway. Yankowitz collaborated on several texts with Chaikin, of which *Terminal* is the best known. An extraordinary and clinical exploration of death and morality, John Lahr said it sent 'audiences away thirsting for life'. The confrontational and highly controversial *Slaughterhouse Play*, written for Jo Papp's Public Theatre, had as its central metaphor butchered meat and a slaughterhouse where the genitals of black men were sold to white men as prize meat. British audiences were introduced to Yankowitz with *Alarms*, written in response to the Chernobyl disaster. Part surreal thriller, part passionate anti-nuclear polemic, it caught the agony of a contemporary Cassandra in the character of a crusading obstetrician.

TRY THESE:
✱LOWE's *Keeping Body and Soul Together*; Vladimir Gubaryev's extraordinary post-Chernobyl play, *Sarcophagus*; ✱LEVY's *Clam* is another anti-nuclear/sexual politics play; for other feminist images of grotesquery, ✱KENNEDY's *A Rat's Mass*, *A Lesson in Dead Language* and *Funnyhouse of a Negro*; ✱CHURCHILL's *Owners* and Myrna Lamb's *The Butcher's Shop* for other slaughterhouse images; *Night Sky* is one of a number of responses to Chaikin's post-stroke aphasia, ✱SHEPARD and ✱VAN ITALLIE for others; ✱EURIPIDES' *Hippolytus* for Phaedra.

YEATS, W. B. (William Butler) [1865 – 1939]
Irish poet, dramatist, theatre manager and politician

PLAYS INCLUDE:
The Countess Kathleen (1892), *The Land of Heart's Desire* (1894), *The Shadowy Waters* (1900), *Diarmuid and Grania* (1901, with George Moore), *Cathleen ni Houlihan* (1902), *The Pot of Broth* (1902), *Where There Is Nothing* (1902, revised with ✱LADY GREGORY as *The Unicorn from the Stars*, 1907), *The Hour Glass* (1903), *The King's Threshold* (1903), *On Baile's Strand* (1904), *Deirdre* (1906), *The Golden Helmet* (1908, revised as *The Green Helmet*, 1910), *At the Hawk's Well* (1916), *The Dreaming of the Bones* (1919), *The Only Jealousy of Emer* (1919), *The Player Queen* (1919), *Calvary* (1921), *King Oedipus* (1926), *Oedipus at Colonus* (1927), *The Resurrection* (1927), *Fighting the Waves* (1929), *The Words upon the Window Pane* (1934), *The Herne's Egg* (1938), *A Full Moon in March* (1938), *The King of the Great Clock Tower* (1938), *Purgatory* (1938), *The Death of Cuchulain* (1939)

As well as being one of the great poets of the twentieth century (he won the 1923 Nobel Prize for Literature), Yeats played a major part in establishing the modern Irish professional theatre through his managerial work at the Abbey Theatre and wrote throughout his life a series of mainly short plays, usually in verse, which are stylistically innovative, blending symbolist, oriental and Irish elements to create an art which, in his own words, does its work 'by suggestion, not by direct statement, a complexity of rhythm, colour, gesture, not space-pervading like the intellect but a memory and a prophecy'. Irish legend provides the material for most of the plays, from the early personifications of Ireland in the figure of Cathleen ni Houlihan to his final play, *The Death of Cuchulain*, which is the culmination of a lifelong interest in the Red Branch cycle of folk tales. His concern for the supernatural also finds an outlet in the séance of *The Words upon the Window Pane*, his play about Jonathan Swift. In many ways Yeats' interest in non-naturalistic use of sound, music, masks and colours anticipates much of the Performance Art of the present but outside Ireland he is seldom produced professionally.

TRY THESE:
✱SYNGE and ✱O'CASEY were originally staged at the Abbey when Yeats was part of the management; ✱ELIOT wrote the other most successful twentieth-century verse dramas – *Sweeney Agonistes* is particularly interesting to compare with Yeats; ✱MURRAY's *The Crooked Scythe* is a verse drama about the Black Death.

YOSHIMURA, James   [1950 –   ]
American dramatist

PLAYS INCLUDE:
Lion Dancers (1976), *Stunts* (1977), *Mercenaries* (1982), *Ohio Tip-Off* (1983), *Union Boys* (1985), *In Transit* (1989)

Yoshimura was born in Chicago and graduated from the Yale School of Drama, where *Stunts* was his award-winning graduate thesis. *Mercenaries*, Yoshimura's professional debut, is an incisive and uncompromising portrait of 'unofficial' political policy-making at its basest level; the play concerns three white American soldiers of fortune, Vietnam veterans, who are being held prisoner on a Caribbean island following an abortive coup. The boorish and jingoistic grunts come off as cogs in an even uglier machine when an American envoy sent to monitor the situation

agrees to their execution as part of face-saving deal. In later plays, Yoshimura returned to the themes of allegiances and divided loyalties within traditional male (though multiracial) enclaves: *Ohio Tip-Off* explores the lives of a group of minor-league basketball players; *Union Boys*, set in the reel room of a Chicago newspaper office, details the tensions between lifelong buddies being sold out by the paper and by their own union. Yoshimura has worked extensively in television, particularly on *Homicide: Life in the Street*, but his plays are virtually unknown in Britain.

TRY THESE:
✱NELSON's *Principia Scriptoriae* and ✱PINTER's *One for the Road* for plays with similar realpolitik themes; ✱HAVIS's *Hospitality* and *Haut Gout* for more surreal treatment of political game-playing and cultural displacement; ✱GOTANDA, ✱HWANG, for other contemporary Asian-American dramatists.

YOUNG, Phil   [1949 –   ]
British director and dramatist

PLAYS INCLUDE:
Crystal Clear (1983), *Kissing God* (1985), *Torpedoes in the Jacuzzi* (1987), *Total Orgasm* (1995)

After winning the award for Best Director at the National Student Drama Festival in 1976, Young went on to a career as a director in a variety of theatres including Leeds Playhouse, Leicester Haymarket and Croydon Warehouse. In 1983 he devised *Crystal Clear* through improvisation and workshops with a small group of actors. The play uses a naturalistic form to convey an intense and, at times, distressingly intimate sense of pressure, as Richard, an art dealer with diabetes, falls victim to the abrupt onset of blindness. Ironically, he is having a love affair with Thomasina, who is blind. Their gentle and genuinely touching relationship is highlighted by visits from Richard's ex-lover Jane, who, after trying unsuccessfully to maintain her previous place in his life, attempts to help him after his blindness. He drives her away, only to discover that Thomasina now rejects him, despite her feelings for him. In this way the defensive layers of politeness and passive acceptance that conceal the awful realities of life for the blind are stripped away to reveal the agony and desperation that lies beneath. This play won an *Evening Standard* Most Promising Playwright award. Since then Young has mainly worked as a director, latterly with the English theatre of Frankfurt.

TRY THESE:
✱ MEDOFF's *Children of a Lesser God* for deafness and its effects on personal relationships; ✱ CLARK's *Whose Life Is It Anyway* comically raises painful questions, on terminal illness, responsibility and dignity; ✱ VAN ITALLIE's *The Traveller* deals with aphasia (inability to make sense of words) with equal passion as well as beauty; the Graeae company for other, more upbeat, images of disability.

ZAJDLIC, Richard
British dramatist

PLAYS INCLUDE:
Infidelities (1990), *Rage* (1994), *Dogs Barking* (1999)

A Southampton University graduate, Zajdlic is probably best known for his major contributions to the television series *This Life* but he has also written extensively for the stage, often along similar lines. *Infidelities* is about the complications of young married life and *Dogs Barking* is a fierce account of the difficulties in negotiating the end of a relationship when property ownership is involved.

TRY THESE:
✱AYCKBOURN, ✱DECLAN HUGHES ✱LEIGH, ✱LUCIE for problems of contemporary life.

ZEPHANIAH, Benjamin   [1958 –]
British poet, novelist and dramatist

PLAYS INCLUDE:
Playing the Right Tune (1984), *Job Rocking* (1986), *Hurricane Dub* (1988, radio), *Streetwise* (1990), *Delirium* (1990), *Listen to Your Parents* (radio 2000, staged 2002)

Born in Birmingham, brought up in Jamaica, educated in a number of reform schools and by a short spell in prison, Rastafarian Zephaniah first came to prominence as a uniquely talented performance poet, chanting unaccompanied indictments of the Handsworth riots and police brutality to brisk Afro-Caribbean rhythms in the early 1980s.

Initially reluctant to accept the label of poet ('I'm not white and I'm not dead'), his popularity and his interest in the rhythm and power of words quickly grew, and he has diversified into broadcasting, journalism, music and theatre writing. In the late 1980s, the prospect of his appointment to a poetry chair at Cambridge caused a storm in the tabloid press. Although he has published several books of poetry, he rightly insists that his verse works best when spoken or listened to live; it therefore seemed natural he should turn to the theatre. His theatre work is characterised by a high political awareness and a wish to get away from the sex comedies that constitute a large part of the theatrical fare served up for black audiences. Although his popularity has brought acceptance from the cultural establishment, Zephaniah maintains that he is still angry and still wishes to change things. He sees his continuing work in theatre as just another part of his vocation 'to discover the poetry in everyday life'. He remains at the forefront of black writing, and is one of the few writers today who can successfully write verse plays.

Streetwise
Zephaniah's verse play explores the different reactions of four black Londoners to an attempt made by white councillors to sanitise and bureaucratise the Notting Hill Carnival. The violent attitudes of posse-leader Angel are contrasted to the peaceful, celebratory stance of Val and the pessimism of Bingy, who just wants to walk away. The question of response takes on a new urgency when the cool-headed local hero Streetwise enters, badly beaten after a racist attack. The play frustrated many since it offered alternatives with no conclusions, and Zephaniah's words lost some of their power in the actors' delivery. Nevertheless, his achievement remains in bringing both verse and black theatre to large, racially and socially mixed audiences.

TRY THESE:
Other contemporary black playwrights in Britain include ✱COOKE, ✱ELLIS, ✱MOFFATT, ✱PINNOCK; ✱RHONE's comedies are perhaps some of the work Zephaniah is reacting against; ✱CHURCHILL's *Serious Money* for modern use of verse.

ZINDEL, Paul   [1936 – 2003]
American dramatist, screenwriter and novelist

PLAYS INCLUDE:
Dimensions of Peacocks (1959), *Euthanasia and the Endless Heart* (1960), *A Dream of Swallows* (1962), *The Effect of Gamma Rays on Man-in-the-Moon Marigolds* (1966), *And Miss Reardon Drinks a Little* (1971), *The Ladies Should Be in Bed* (1973), *The Secret Affairs of Mildred Wild* (1973), *Ladies at the Alamo* (1977), *A Destiny on Half Moon Street* (1981), *Ladies on the Midnight Planet* (1982), *Amulets Against the Dragon Forces* (1989)

Zindel began his writing career with novels for and about teenagers. He went on to study playwriting with ✳EDWARD ALBEE, who directed Zindel's first play off-Broadway. The central theme of sensitive children dominated by demented parents, particularly the mother figure, runs through Zindel's plays. In *The Effect of Gamma Rays on Man in-the-Moon Marigolds*, his best-known work, we meet a dysfunctional family headed by an idiosyncratic, hateful widow living with her two daughters. The older daughter has passed the point of sanity while the younger one turns to a pet rabbit for love and comfort. The younger daughter's high-school science project, studying the effect of gamma rays on withering marigolds, yields the metaphor for the decay of the family, as well as of the self. Some of the marigolds do blossom, offering a symbolic ray of hope. Critics called the play touching, honest and compassionate and it won the Pulitzer Prize for drama, the New York Critics' Award and the Drama Desk Award in 1971. Zindel has often been criticised for an overly harsh view of women, but he stood by his work as an exorcism of personal experience, and maintained that for him, the view was valid.

TRY THESE:
✳TENNESSEE WILLIAMS' *The Glass Menagerie* and ✳MILLER's *Death of a Salesman* for dysfunctional American families; ✳DÜRRENMATT's *The Physicists*, ✳PIRANDELLO's *Henry IV*, Witkewicz's *The Madman and the Nun* for explorations of sanity and madness; ✳FREISTADT's *Chicken Licken* for more grotesque parents; ✳STEPHENSON for science; Susan Zeder for American children's plays.

 # Index

P